DENIALISM AND HUMAN RIGHTS

AF790503

DENIALISM AND HUMAN RIGHTS

Edited by
Roland Moerland
Hans Nelen
Jan Willems

intersentia
Cambridge – Antwerp – Portland

Intersentia Ltd
Sheraton House | Castle Park
Cambridge | CB3 0AX | United Kingdom
Tel.: +44 1223 370 170 | Fax: +44 1223 370 169
Email: mail@intersentia.co.uk
www.intersentia.com | www.intersentia.co.uk

Distribution for the UK and Ireland:
NBN International
Airport Business Centre, 10 Thornbury Road
Plymouth, PL6 7 PP
United Kingdom
Tel.: +44 1752 202 301 | Fax: +44 1752 202 331
Email: orders@nbninternational.com

Distribution for Europe and all other countries:
Intersentia Publishing nv
Groenstraat 31
2640 Mortsel
Belgium
Tel.: +32 3 680 15 50 | Fax: +32 3 658 71 21
Email: mail@intersentia.be

Distribution for the USA and Canada:
International Specialized Book Services
920 NE 58th Ave. Suite 300
Portland, OR 97213
USA
Tel.: +1 800 944 6190 (toll free) | Fax: +1 503 280 8832
Email: info@isbs.com

Denialism and Human Rights
© The editors and contributors severally 2016

The editors and contributors have asserted the right under the Copyright, Designs and Patents Act 1988, to be identified as authors of this work.

No part of this book may be reproduced, stored in a retrieval system, or transmitted, in any form, or by any means, without prior written permission from Intersentia, or as expressly permitted by law or under the terms agreed with the appropriate reprographic rights organisation. Enquiries concerning reproduction which may not be covered by the above should be addressed to Intersentia at the address above.

Cover photo © Nmaneer – Shutterstock

ISBN 978-1-78068-369-0
D/2016/7849/79
NUR 828

British Library Cataloguing in Publication Data. A catalogue record for this book is available from the British Library.

ACKNOWLEDGEMENTS

This book contains a selection of papers that were presented during the multidisciplinary conference 'Denialism and Human Rights'. This conference was organised by the Maastricht Centre for Human Rights on 22 and 23 January 2015. All the participants we spoke to afterwards emphasised that they had enjoyed the pleasant academic atmosphere, the debates, and the high quality of the presentations. Their enthusiasm reinforced our intention to bring the most interesting papers together in a book.

The conference could not have been organised without the financial support of a number of institutions. We are indebted to the Maastricht Centre for Human Rights, the Research Fund of the Maastricht Faculty of Law, the Limburg University Fund/SWOL, the Netherlands Organisation for Scientific Research (NWO), and Studium Generale for their donations.

The organisational support of Chantal Kuypers and Khalidah Ahmadi during the conference was invaluable. Khalidah was also a great help to us throughout the whole preparation period. We also want to thank Julie Peeters for her assistance in providing the layout for this book.

What we hoped to achieve with the conference was a reflection on denialism and human rights from a variety of angles and disciplines, and, additionally, to stress the relevance of the concept of denial to the contemporary debate on human rights issues. Without doubt, thanks to the contributions of the speakers and participants the conference served these purposes. This book elaborates on the central theme of the conference, and, hopefully, will further enhance the debate on denialism and human rights.

June 2016

Roland Moerland
Hans Nelen
Jan Willems

CONTENTS

PART I.
CHILDREN'S RIGHTS

CHAPTER I
INTRODUCTION

Roland MOERLAND, Hans NELEN and Jan WILLEMS

'After having rejected the scientific wisdom about AIDS, former South African president Thabo Mbeki and his government were directly responsible for many avoidable deaths according to research by Harvard University'. (*The Guardian*, 2008)[1]

'A discussion paper on Rwanda, prepared by an official in the Office of the Secretary of Defense stated: "Be Careful. Legal at State was worried about this yesterday – Genocide finding could commit [the US government] to actually 'do something'."' (Power, 2001)[2]

'In 2001, the House of Representatives passed a bill that would have required United States importers and manufacturers to certify and label their products "slave free." The defendants and others in the chocolate industry rallied against the bill, urging instead the adoption of a private, voluntary enforcement mechanism. A voluntary enforcement system was eventually adopted, a result that, according to the plaintiffs, "in effect guarantee[d] the continued use of the cheapest labour available to produce [cocoa] – that of child slaves."' (Doe v. Nestlé USA, Inc. 2014)[3]

'"The majority of civilians in Syria continues to bear the brunt of the ongoing conflict," the head of a United Nations-appointed human rights panel said today, noting that violence has escalated to an unprecedented level, humanitarian aid is arbitrarily denied and perpetrators of crimes have no fear of consequence.' (UN News Centre 2014)[4]

---

1 S. BOSELEY, 'Mbeki Aids denial "caused 300,000 deaths"' 2008 *The Guardian* <www.theguardian.com/world/2008/nov/26/aids-south-africa>.

2 S. POWER, *A problem from hell: America and the age of genocide*, Flamingo, London 2002.

3 United States Court of Appeals for the Ninth Circuit, John Doe I; John Doe II; John Doe III, individually and on behalf of proposed class members; *Global Plaintiffs-Appellants, v. Nestlé USA, Inc.*; Archer Daniels Midland Company; Cargill Incorporated Company; Cargill Cocoa, Defendants-Appellants. Appeal from the United States District Court for the Central District of California, *Stephen v. Wilson*, District Judge, Presiding Argued and Submitted December 2, 2013 – Pasadena, California Filed September 4, 2014 Before: Dorothy W. Nelson, Kim McLane Wardlaw, and Johnnie B. Rawlinson, Circuit Judges. No. 10-56739 D.C. No. 2:05-CV-05133- SVW-JTL.

4 UN News Centre, 'Impunity, unprecedented violence, denial of aid hallmarks of Syria conflict – UN rights panel' 2014 <www.un.org/apps/news/story.asp?NewsID=48070#.Vl1mSP6FPcs>.

1. RATIONALE OF THIS BOOK

The cases above illustrate that the safeguarding of human rights remains problematic, despite the proliferation of human rights instruments and the many actions taken by a variety of actors, such as governmental and non-governmental organisations, (individual) states and the international community in recent decades. Human rights violations do still occur and injustice remains rampant. Central to this problem appears to be that social, economic, cultural and political structures in societies provide for denialist defence mechanisms. Such deeply embedded denialism causes and/or facilitates human rights violations, because the true nature of the problems involved remains fully or partly unacknowledged and as a result appropriate action is not taken. In order to safeguard the effectuation of human rights, it is thus pertinent to acknowledge and address this problem of denialism and develop strategies to move beyond it.

To address the above-mentioned problem, an international conference was organised on the theme of Denialism and Human Rights by the Maastricht Centre for Human Rights. The conference took place on 22 and 23 January 2015 at the Faculty of Law of Maastricht University in the Netherlands. The organisers of the conference challenged scholars, practitioners and students from various disciplines and fields to unearth and address denialism in the context of their own particular areas of research. We invited them in particular to consider and deal with the following issues.

Firstly, a clear conception and definition of denialism should be developed. What exactly does denialism entail? On what social, economic, cultural and political structures and mechanisms in societies does it operate, and how? What ideologies and prejudices are involved?

Secondly, denialism operating in practice should be investigated and its relation to, and particular relevance for, human rights issues should be clarified. In which concrete cases do we see denialism 'at work'? What are the implications in terms of human rights? How is the effectuation of these rights blocked or obstructed? Is denialism only destructive or can it also be constructive? Can human rights discourse itself be in denial?

Thirdly, how should we deal with denialism and move to a situation of human rights consistent behaviour and change? Is it always possible to move from denial to compliance? What are suitable strategies or policies? Is legislation required? Which factors obstruct human rights change in denialist situations?

We welcomed abstracts and suggestions for panels related to the questions raised above and the conference theme more generally. To this end we encouraged scholars, practitioners, field workers, and students from various academic disciplines (such as law, psychology, political science, international relations, criminology, anthropology, sociology, etc.) and other relevant practice-based fields to apply.

The conference call triggered great international response from various actors working in different fields and this resulted in a conference format consisting of a mixture of small interdisciplinary workshop panels with plenary sessions. In total there were six plenary keynote sessions and 18 workshop panels.

2. THE PRESENT VOLUME

2.1. INTRODUCTION

Taking into account the particular theme of the conference it was important that the content of the conference was made available to a broader audience. Clearly, raising awareness is one of the most important ways of dealing with denial. Therefore we firstly asked the participants to provide us with their outlines and (PowerPoint) presentations and we made these available on the conference website together with the abstracts of their presentations.[5] Secondly, we asked participants to send us their conference papers because we also wanted to publish an edited volume containing a selection of the papers presented during the conference. This last idea has finally materialised itself in the volume at hand.

Apart from this introduction, the current volume contains 22 contributions. Although all papers engage with the conference theme, the contributions are eclectic not only in terms of the specific topics covered, but also with regard to the approaches taken by the authors. As to the last issue, readers will observe that while certain papers maintain a certain 'distance' from the object under study and try to stay more objective and neutral in how they deal with the subject matter, other authors are more engaging in their approach and identify themselves more closely with the issues being addressed.

From the overview of contributions presented below it will become clear that the concept of denial is utilised in various different ways depending on the specific topic, case or context. It is for this reason that the editors of this volume have decided to use the term 'denialism' for the title of the book, instead of simply 'denial'. The term 'denialism' does not denominate one specific form or variety of denial, but it refers to an overarching concept elaborated or explored from a human rights perspective.

---

5 See <maastrichtuniversity.nl/web/Faculties/FL/Theme/research_law/conferences_research_law/Past2015/DenialismAndHumanRights.htm>.

2.2. THEMES AND CONTRIBUTIONS

Due to the eclectic nature of the conference it was challenging to cluster the conference papers under sensible headings, but we managed to structure the volume as follows.

The first part concerns a more general introduction to the theme of denialism and human rights and it includes the keynote speeches of Willem de Haan (Professor emeritus of Criminology, VU University Amsterdam) and Irene Bruna Seu (Reader in Psychosocial Studies, University of London, and a psychotherapist). De Haan critically reflects on the concept of denialism and furthermore focuses on the problem of indifference to human suffering of distant others and how this can be addressed. With regard to this last aspect, he points to the role that shaming can play because it makes us aware of our indifference and it can thereby motivate us to take constructive action. Bruna Seu's contribution is based on a series of qualitative studies carried out to investigate ordinary people's understanding of, and responses (including actions and inaction) to, information about human rights violations. She proposes a psychosocial model of public denial as a dynamic equilibrium which clarifies the key factors fostering denial. She furthermore presents a psychodynamic model of factors fostering individual 'connectedness' with human rights and humanitarian issues. Lastly, she discusses some important policy implications that follow from this research.

The second part focuses on children's rights and contains James Dwyer's (Professor of Law, William & Mary Law School) keynote paper on diagnosing and dispelling denialism regarding children. His contribution analyses how harmful denialism with respect to children takes many forms and operates at a moral, conceptual, descriptive and empirical level. After having elaborated how denialism operates at these levels, he suggests several strategies for eliminating it. The second contribution in this section is Jan Willems's paper titled 'Too Close to Home. The Denial of Prejudice and Discrimination against Children'. The paper discusses a variety of denial concepts, such as, for instance, elaborated in Dwyer's contribution, and other prejudice and discrimination concepts coined by other authors. Based on this overview, Willems develops the model of the 'juvism onion' and subsequently he presents ten denialisms surrounding the complex field of child maltreatment as an agenda for future research. The third paper is written by Tonny Weterings, who discusses 'denialism at work' in the Netherlands in her paper on the denial of developmental needs of foster children by Dutch youth care services. On the one hand, this is part of the deeply ingrained denialisms discussed in the two preceding chapters; on the other hand, some hope might be derived from the recent testing in the Netherlands of a model the author has developed. In the last paper of this section on children's rights, Elvira Loibl critically reflects on the phenomenon of inter-country adoption. She points out that for various reasons this system has a commercial 'underbelly' where questionable practices are employed to meet the demands of the inter-country adoption market which ultimately results in the placement of children who are not in need of a home or who could have been properly cared for in their native countries. Despite such practices being known due to well documented scandals, many actors deny the widespread existence of the system's 'underbelly'.

The third part of this volume concerns a topic that is probably most readily associated with denial, namely that of genocide denial. The first paper is Roland Moerland's contribution and it addresses the denial of the genocide against the Tutsi, and concerns, in particular, the BBC documentary *Rwanda's Untold Story*. The paper analyses how genocide denial operates in the context of the genocide against the Tutsi and it discusses how crucial elements of the official denial discourse are recycled by other actors who were not implicated in the genocide against the Tutsi, such as scholars and journalists. Lastly, the analysis addresses how the BBC documentary also recycles certain key elements from the official denial discourse and it reflects on the implications thereof. Two papers focus on Holocaust denial. Johannes Keiler's paper addresses the challenge of fighting National Socialist (NS) ideology and Holocaust denial in Austria. It commences with a brief analysis of in how far criminal law can properly be utilised to curb denial and right-wing ideology and extremism. Subsequently, the historical roots of the Austrian NS Prohibition Act are outlined in order to better understand the social background from which it originated and evolved. He furthermore discusses the different criminal offences contained in the Prohibition Act. The contribution of Georgi Verbeeck looks into how the dominant discourse of the Holocaust affects our perception of other genocides, and he addresses the question of why Holocaust denialism is taken so seriously in our society. He critically reflects on scholarly and legal responses to the phenomenon of Holocaust denial. The contribution of Sévane Garibian concerns the denial of the Armenian genocide and in particular it focuses on the *Doğu Perinçek v. Switzerland* case that was brought before the European Court of Human Rights in 2013. The paper more particularly addresses one specific argument of the ECtHR's ruling in the case which concerns the problematic argument of the absence of a 'general consensus' on the 1915 genocide. The author subsequently reflects on the far-reaching implications of the decision and its underlying argumentation. The last paper in this section is Robert Kahn's paper on the question of what is the concrete, practical harm of genocide denial. Although it is generally assumed that genocide denial is harmful, the harm is rarely clearly defined. In his essay, Kahn critically reflects on three potential types of harm that genocide denial might pose: harm to victims, harm to the democratic order, and lastly, harm to the historical record.

The fourth part focuses on (inter)national organisations and it starts off with a contribution by Fred Grünfeld in which he analyses the denial of genocide by bystanders, and in particular, how international actors such as states and the UN fail to intervene. Taking the theoretical elaboration by Irene Bruna Seu in this volume as his main point of reference, he analyses the dynamics of bystander denial in the cases of Srebrenica, Rwanda and Darfur. The second contribution is by Konstantinos Magliveras and his paper addresses how a certain regional intergovernmental institution, the African Union, exhibits denialism in carrying out its mandate. The instances of denialism shown by the organisation concern situations of genocide and crimes against humanity and intra-state and inter-state strife. The paper analyses the underlying causes of such denialism and the far-reaching implications that follow from it. Lastly, Michael Reed Hurtado's contribution focuses on killing through the state in the Columbian war, and is an exploration of organisational crime and its denial. He illustrates how situational and organisational factors play a role in the spread of the sham-KIAs. It is shown how these murders became normalised and routinised revealing different mechanisms of 'denial at work'. Lastly the paper looks into how controlled and partial acknowledgement has been used to contest organisational wrongdoing.

The new penology is the focus of attention in the fifth part. The first paper of Cecil Hunt critically reflects on denial, human rights, and American racialised mass incarceration. Hunt addresses how the massive racialised imprisonment of young black persons, is the result of racist beliefs that have become institutionalised in every aspect of the American criminal justice system. He points out that most Americans are in almost complete denial of this reality in which 'imprisonment ceases to be the fate of a few criminal individuals and becomes a shaping institution for whole sectors of the population'. The second contribution in this section concerns Samantha Williams's analysis of prisoner disenfranchisement in the UK and the denial dynamics at play in that context. It explores the basis of denialism by looking both how and why denialism is perpetrated and justified in the UK by focussing on the ban on prisoners' voting rights as a concrete example of political or functional denialism in practice.

The sixth part of the book brings together a collection of papers on very diverse topics, and includes a selection of the most interesting contributions presented in the remaining conference panels not represented above. The first paper of Gustavo Arosemena reflects on the issues of poverty, just world thinking, human rights law and the relevance of denial for normative legal research. It analyses the problem of global poverty and the deficient response it has received from human rights law from the perspective of just world thinking, and denialism more in general. The analysis is used as a springboard to draw more general conclusions about the relevance of this sort of social-scientific research for law. In doing so it shows both the importance and the limits of the perspective of denialism for normative legal research. Subsequently, Regina Paulose explores the fate of refugees from genocide and issues related to their lack of protection in international law. The analysis addresses the particularities of the 1948 Convention on the Prevention and Punishment of the Crime of Genocide, and the 1951 Refugee Convention. She then discusses how these Conventions neglect, or deny, refugees protection when faced with genocide resulting in a second cycle of genocide denial taking place. She looks into these dynamics by drawing on the case of Bangladesh. Zoi Aliozi addresses the issue of climate change denial and how it undermines the fulfilment of internationally protected human rights like the rights to health and life; rights to food, water, shelter, property; rights associated with livelihood and culture; with migration and resettlement; and with personal security in the event of conflict. She looks into the human rights repercussions of climate change, and how the organisation of international human rights law and knowledge conveys that phenomenon. Aliozi's aim is to 'clarify the confusion covering this area of study, and by examining the relationship between climate change and human rights, an attempt is made to discover, examine and analyse their most essential links. Annelize Nienaber addresses the issue of AIDS denial in the context of South Africa, and more particularly the denialist effects of the criminalisation of the 'intentional' sexual transmission of HIV. The author argues that AIDS denialism is still very present in South Africa. She analyses how this is especially the case in the courts' approach to the 'intentional' transmission of HIV to sexual partners. To this end the paper examines the implications of the North Gauteng High Court decision in *Phiri v. S.* and critically reflects on the appropriateness of the court's decision in the context of public health efforts to curb the HIV epidemic. Finally, the paper of Radka Babjaková et al. concerns the topic of Olympic idealism and human rights infringements, and addresses whether athletes are aware of the human rights violations surrounding the Olympic Games in which they compete, and if so, how these violations have an impact on them and how they deal with them. Before the paper addresses what denial at work looks like in the context of athletes participating in the Olympic Games, the main principles of Olympic idealism are introduced and their implications discussed. After the presentation of the main results of the research, the theoretical implications thereof are discussed.

The concluding chapter of this volume is written by David Nelken (Professor of Comparative and Transnational Law in Context, King's College London). Professor Nelken was invited to act as the conference rapporteur and he was given the challenging task of summarising and integrating the leading threads of the conference and present the results and his reflections during the closing ceremony. Nelken's concluding chapter thus provides a broader reflection on the theme of denialism and human rights based on the conference proceedings and the above-mentioned contributions.

CHAPTER II

DENIALISM AND THE PROBLEM OF INDIFFERENCE

Willem De Haan

In Albert Camus' classic novel *La Peste*, a physician diagnoses the plague. Soon, however, he discovers that the people around him refuse to acknowledge the threat of the contagious disease. When, at last, they can no longer deny the fact that an epidemic has infected them, it is too late.[1]

In recent years, *La Peste* has been read as a comment on denialism of the AIDS epidemic.[2] Traditionally, however, Camus' novel was interpreted as an allegory of how the French population responded to the occupation of France by Nazi Germany. At first, they could not imagine that the German army would force the French army to surrender. Then they wanted to believe that it would be best to submit and live with the *in*evitability of a long-term occupation or to even collaborate with the occupational forces.

Obviously, the meaning readers gave this allegory – in 1947, when the novel was first published – is quite different from the meaning the story has for readers today. As historian Carl Becker has noted:

> 'it is well known that every generation writes the same history in a new way, and puts upon it a new construction. The reason why this is so … is that our imagined picture [of a past event] is always determined … by our own present purposes, desires, prepossessions, and prejudices, all of which enter into the process of knowing it'.[3]

---

1 The example is taken from C. Hamelton, 'What can history teach us about climate change denial?' in: S. Weintrobe (ed.), *Engaging with Climate Change: Psychoanalytic and Interdisciplinary Perspectives*, Routledge, Sussex 2013, pp. 16–32, at pp. 26–27.

2 The denial, against conclusive scientific evidence, that the human immunodeficiency virus (HIV) is the cause of Acquired Immune Deficiency Syndrome (AIDS).

3 C.L. Becker, 'What are Historical Facts?' in: H. Meyerholtt (ed.), *The Philosophy of History in Our Times*, Doubleday Publications, Garden City, New York 1959, pp. 23–24, at p. 24.

In other words, even though the past itself does not change, it will be rewritten by every new generation.[4]

An example of rewriting the past is the debate concerning what the general population in the Netherlands 'knew' about the Holocaust.[5] It is a question that even today, seventy years after the war, continues to create conflict and controversy.

In the 1960s, it was argued that, during the war, the general population did not know about the Holocaust because available information was fragmented, inconsistent and, untrustworthy. In the 1980s, that view was challenged by the argument that people *could* have known but did not *want* to know what was going on. Information about large-scale 'extermination' of Jews was available, but many preferred to deny the facts and remain ignorant.

In his prize-winning but controversial book *Wij weten niets van hun lot* (We know nothing of their fate), historian Bart van der Boom has recently challenged the view that the general population looked the other way when their Jewish neighbours were deported, and were, therefore, complicit in their fate.[6] On the basis of his analysis of more than 100 diaries, Van den Boom concludes, that most people could not know what was going on because they just could not *believe* that the deported Jews would be killed in gas chambers upon their arrival in the concentration camps. Their disbelief was not a matter of denial, but of incomprehension.[7] What happened, simply, was beyond their imagination.

---

4 In fact, each new generation not only has a need, but also a right, to re-interpret history in its own way.

5 Note that the term 'Holocaust' was not in common usage until well into the 1970. In the 1950s, historians started to apply the term 'Holocaust' ('inferno') as an equivalent to the Hebrew term 'shoah' ('catastrophe') when referring to the mass murder of the Jews by the Nazis (1939–1945). However, it was not until well into the 1970s that the term started to become more commonly used. D. Diner, *Beyond the Conceivable: Studies on Germany, Nazism, and the Holocaust*, University of California Press, Berkeley and Los Angeles 2000. Quoted by J.C. Alexander, 'On the Social Construction of Moral Universals: The "Holocaust" from War' (2002) 5 *European Journal of Social Theory* 1, 5–85, at 27.

6 B. Van Der Boom, *Wij weten niets van hun lot*, Boom, Amsterdam 2012.

7 Following influential historians such as A. Herzberg, J. Presser and L. De Jong, F. Bovenkerk has also argued that the existence of extermination camps went beyond the imagination of most of the Dutch population, and that only later, after the war had ended, it became fully clear what had happened in Auschwitz and the other extermination camps. F. Bovenkerk, 'Het Nederlandse aandeel in de jodenvervolging als criminologisch probleem' in: M. Moerings, C.M. Pelser and C.H. Brants (eds.), *Morele kwesties in het strafrecht*, Gouda Quint, Deventer 1999, pp. 11–31, at p. 15. E. Moraal, *Als ik morgen niet op transport ga. Kamp Westerbork in beleving en herinnering*, De Bezige Bij, Amsterdam 2014 has shown that the same applies to Dutch Jews. American Jews could also not believe what they heard about extermination because it was, for them, 'unimaginable'. I.L. Horowitz, *Taking Lives: Genocide and state power*, Transaction, New York 1989, p. 26.

The debate about what the general population 'really knew' about the Holocaust raises many questions[8], including the three which the organisers of this conference on *Denialism and Human Rights* have asked me to address:

(1) What exactly is denial?
(2) What are the implications of denial concerning human rights violations?
(3) And how do we have to deal with them?[9]

1. WHAT IS DENIAL?

As you probably all know, the late Stanley Cohen has been the pioneer in addressing these questions.[10]

In his groundbreaking[11] – and now classic – book *States of Denial: Knowing About Atrocities and Suffering,*[12] he notes that 'denial' is a notoriously elusive concept which can mean many things. But the only 'legitimate use' of the term 'denial' is 'when persons, who, as audiences, bystanders, observers, onlookers, spectators or witnesses, have come to see, hear or know what happened or is going on – either at the time or later, for whatever reason – in good or bad faith – claim not to know'.[13]

Denial can be a personal and private state of mind, but also a public, social and cultural phenomenon. At the personal level, the process of denial 'includes *cognition*

8 For example, questions concerning silence and silencing or concerning the difference between disbelief and denial.

9 The conference is based on the assumption that deeply embedded denialism causes and/or facilitates human rights violations, because the true nature of the problems remains fully or partly unacknowledged and as a result appropriate actions remains absent. More ambitious would, therefore, be trying to answer the question: what social, economic, cultural and political structures provide for denialist defence mechanisms in society? And how do we acknowledge and address this problem of denialism and develop strategies to move beyond it? Answering these questions lies, however, beyond the scope of this essay.

10 Re-reading his book for this occasion has been emotional. It made me aware of how much Stan, who sadly passed away on 7 January 2013, is missed. I have always deeply admired his work, to begin with his chapter on 'Guilt, Justice and Tolerance: Some Old concepts for a New Criminology' published in 1979 in D. Downes and P. Rock (eds.), *Deviant Interpretations*, Martin Robertson, Oxford 1979, pp. 17–51. This chapter has been a great inspiration for writing my book *The Politics of Redress: Crime, Punishment, and Penal Abolition*, Unwin Hyman, London 1990, for which Stan Cohen, kindly, wrote a wonderful Preface.

11 Not many scholars have tried to develop a more general conceptualisation of denial than Stan Cohen. See R. Moerland, *The Killing of Death. Denying the genocide against the Tutsi*, Diss. Maastricht University, Maastricht 2015, p. 87, note 92. Moerland does not, however, mention Eviatar Zerubavel's effort. See: E. Zerubavel, 'The Social Sound of Silence: Toward A Sociology of Denial' in: E. Ben-Ze'ev, R. Ginio and J. Winter (eds.), *Shadows of War: A Social History of Silence in the Twentieth Century*, Cambridge University Press, Cambridge 2010, pp. 32–46.

12 Polity Press, Cambridge 2001.

13 Ibid., p. 9.

(not acknowledging the facts); *emotion* (not being disturbed); [and] *morality* (not recognizing wrongness or responsibility). A person who is in denial will refrain from *action* (will not take any steps in response to the unwanted knowledge)'.[14]

But denial is always a collective effort. People learn from one another what they are socially expected to ignore – that is, not look at, not listen to, not speak about. Collective denial is based on a 'shared reconstruction of reality'[15] in which painful realities are not – or only partially – acknowledged.[16]

Collective denial may emerge as a spontaneous social and cultural phenomenon 'when an entire segment of society ... turns away from reality in favor of a more comfortable lie. But collective denial can also be officially initiated and organized by the state, for example, as in the concerted covering up a record of genocide or other past atrocities' (p. 12).

A well-known example of state-organised denial is the Armenian genocide that took place between 1915 and 1917. The facts are thoroughly documented in official records, survivors' accounts, witness testimonies and historical research. Yet successive Turkish governments have consistently denied that a genocide took place.

This obliteration of the past is an example of what Cohen has called literal denial: asserting that a statement about past reality is, in fact, untrue. It is perhaps the most obvious form of denial which, in this case, is officially organised and 'built into the ideological façade of the state' (p. 10).

State-organised denial, however, concerns not only *literal* denial. In discourses of official denial, we may also find *interpretive* denial. This form of denial 'concedes that something is happening but that this "something" must be seen in a different light'.[17]

An example of *interpretive denial* would be that during the Second World War concepts like 'annihilation', 'elimination', 'eradication' and 'extinction' – which currently mean 'murder upon arrival in the extermination camps' – were believed to refer to death caused by hard labour, hunger and exhaustion.[18]

---

14 Ibid., p. 11.

15 M.A. Milburn and S.D. Conrad, *The Politics of Denial*, MIT Press, London 1996, p. 3.

16 Like, for example, the fact that, from 1945 to 1949, the Dutch military committed 'war crimes' on a considerable scale is still not openly acknowledged. S. Scagliola, 'The Silences and Myths of a "Dirty War": Coming to terms with the Dutch-Indonesian Decolonization War (1945–1949)' (2007) 14(2) *European Review of History* 235–262, 243. Quoted in R. Moerland, *The Killing of Death. Denying the genocide against the Tutsi*, Diss. Maastricht University, Maastricht 2015, p. 97, note 106.

17 S. Cohen, *States of Denial: Knowing About Atrocities and Suffering*, Polity Press, London 2001, p. 22.

18 The example is given by B. Van Der Boom, *Wij weten niets van hun lot*, Boom, Amsterdam 2012. As we have seen, Van den Boom argues that this was not a case of denial but of incomprehension.

A third form of denial, is what Cohen has called *implicatory* denial. This form of denial is *not* about facts, nor about their interpretation, but rather about the moral significance of what has happened or is happening.

A historical example of implicatory denial is that during the Second World War the majority of population in the Netherlands could see with their own eyes how Jews were removed from their jobs, evicted from their homes and deported from their country. However, even though people knew this was happening, they denied the moral *significance* of these events and their own moral responsibility to intervene by helping their Jewish neighbours or colleagues to survive.[19]

What these forms of denial have – or, at least, should have – in common is that they refer to a state of mind that is, at least in part, unconscious.[20]

The reality of what is happening is both acknowledged and, to some extent, hidden from consciousness. While people are vaguely aware of choosing not to look at the facts, they are not quite conscious of what exactly it is that they are trying to evade. It is this intriguing 'paradox of knowing and not knowing' which – according to Cohen[21] – is at the heart of the concept of denial.

2. WHAT IS DENIALISM?

Unlike 'denial', 'denialism' is not a common term.[22] In Cohen's book *States of Denial* the word 'denialism' is not even used once.[23] And, in fact, I have not been able to find a single scientific publication in which the term was actually properly defined.[24]

---

19 This (implicatory) denial of responsibility has been proposed as a possible explanation for the disturbing fact that – of all Western European countries that were occupied by Nazi Germany – the Netherlands had the highest proportion of its Jewish population that did not survive the war. For a scientific explanation of this phenomenon, see P. Griffioen and R. Zeller, *Jodenvervolging in Nederland, Frankrijk en België 1940–1945*, Boom, Amsterdam 2010 (2nd ed.) (1st ed. 2008).

20 Denial in the 'vernacular sense' of declaring something not to be true is not necessarily denial in the 'scientific sense' of an unconscious process. See E.E. Trunnel and W.F. Holt, 'The Concept of Denial or Disavowal' (1974) 22 *Journal of the American Psychoanalytic Association* 775.

21 S. Cohen, *States of Denial: Knowing About Atrocities and Suffering*, Polity Press, London 2001, p. 22.

22 K. Kahn-Harris, 'Unreasonable doubt', *New Humanist* 25.05.2010, pp. 14–17.

23 When Stanley Cohen, in 2011, did use the term in a discussion about climate change, he used it in an ambivalent (or even contradictory) way. On the one hand, he considered denialism as 'yet another variant of generic denial'. But on the other, it was for him 'the polar opposite' of denial. S. Cohen, 'Climate change in a perverse culture' in: S. Weintrobe, *Engaging with Climate Change: Psychoanalytic and Interdisciplinary Perspectives*, Routledge, Sussex 2013, pp. 72–79.

24 In this respect Roland Moerland's doctoral thesis is no exception. In this thesis, which 'deals with the phenomenon of genocide denialism' at p. 15, the term denialism itself is not defined. In a footnote a reference is made to C. Tatz, *With intent to destroy: Reflections on genocide*, Verso, London 2003. However, in this book the term 'denialism' is not defined either. Tatz

The 'ism' of 'denialism' would suggest a philosophical, political or moral system of mutually supportive beliefs. In actual fact, however, denialism is more a form of newspeak. It is used as a polemical term in various contexts,[25] but most prominently in debates about medical and environmental problems like AIDS[26] and climate change.

In these debates, 'denialism' entails rhetorical arguments to discredit and undermine well-established but unwelcome positions in scientific debates.[27] At first glance, it seems as if scientific truth is itself at stake in these debates. At second glance, however, it becomes clear that the aim of denialism is not to engage in legitimate scientific debate, but merely to create the *appearance* of a scientific debate.[28]

As a social and cultural phenomenon, denialism has not been the subject of any sustained analysis, with one notable exception: the American journalist Michael Spector. In his book *Denialism: how irrational thinking hinders scientific progress, harms the planet, and threatens our lives*[29] he explores the ways in which rigorous and open-minded scientific scepticism is being replaced with the inflexible certainty of ideological commitment and conviction.

The kinds of denialism that Spector is concerned with are less extreme than Holocaust denialism. It is not so much the fanaticism of a small minority of active deniers that concerns him, but rather the vulnerability of the general population to plausible and pervasive forms of denialism concerning, for example, food security, public health and evidence-based medicine.

In these contexts, he understands denialism as a natural response to deep-seated fears of losing control and an attempt to cope with social change in a globalising world. As a coping mechanism, denialism seems similar to denial to the extent that both are based on unintentional and – in many circumstances – understandable, if not entirely forgivable, human shortcomings.

We all have moments where we know what is happening, but cannot resist the wishful thought that this cannot possibly be true. In *States of Denial*, Cohen quotes the writer Saul Bellow as saying that the state of knowing and not knowing is one of the most frequent of human arrangements. Cohen agrees with Bellow, but adds that the mental state of denial serves not only those who

merely uses it 'to denote a range of denialist and denial-like behaviors' (R. Moerland, *The Killing of Death. Denying the genocide against the Tutsi*, Diss. Maastricht University, Maastricht 2015, note 1).

25 Other than AIDS and climate change, denialism has been related to such different issues as abortion, circumcision, evolution, Lyme Disease, and vaccinations.

26 Early – if not the first – use of the word 'denialism' was made in the struggle to prevent AIDS by E. Cameron, 'The dead hand of denialism', 2003 *Mail & Guardian* Johannesburg.

27 P.A. Diethelm and M. Mckee, 'Denialism: what is it and how should scientists respond?' (2009) 19(1) *European Journal of Public Health* 2–4, 2.

28 S. Cohen, 'Climate change in a perverse culture' in: S. Weintrobe, *Engaging with Climate Change: Psychoanalytic and Interdisciplinary Perspectives*, Routledge, Sussex 2013, p. 76.

29 Penguin Press, New York 2009.

fear their own suffering (or loss of control). Denial *also* serves perpetrators who inflict suffering on other human beings. And it serves all those who witness or know about the suffering of others but do nothing to intervene.[30] These practices are more pertinent when denialism becomes what Spector calls 'denial writ large'.

It is in these cases, I would argue, that the term 'denialism' is not very helpful. It is even misleading to suggest that there is an equivalence between debates about the Holocaust and, for example, climate change. It is misleading because, as Cohen has put it, the Holocaust refers to a well-documented set of events that happened in recorded history, while climate change is a scientific prediction of what is likely to happen in the future.[31]

In the case of climate change, there is and ought to be room for respectable scientific scepticism, whereas with regard to the Holocaust there is not and ought not to be room for 'reasonable doubt'. It is in this vein, that – at least in some jurisdictions – Holocaust denial is a criminal offence whereas denial of climate change is, at least legally, legitimate under the principle of freedom of expression.[32]

In sum, denialism is an unclear notion. It has *not* been clearly delineated in scientific discourse and, therefore, easily lends itself to misunderstandings in public debate. I believe that in relation to gross human rights violations, we should have serious doubts about the analytical usefulness and political implications of denialism as a concept.

By applying denialism the way the term is currently used, we run the risk that gross human rights violations and crimes against humanity become an object of pseudo-scientific debate about facts and their interpretation, while – if only as an unintended consequence – the moral dimensions of denial are overlooked, i.e. the moral responsibility of acknowledging the facts and the moral obligation to intervene in order to protect.

If you nevertheless persist in using the term denialism with regard to gross human rights violations and crimes against humanity, then use it, at least, in ways that are consistent with how the concept of 'denial' is defined in scientific discourse.[33]

---

30 S. Cohen, *States of Denial: Knowing About Atrocities and Suffering*, Polity Press, London 2001, p. 50.

31 S. Cohen, 'Climate change in a perverse culture' in: S. Weintrobe, *Engaging with Climate Change: Psychoanalytic and Interdisciplinary Perspectives*, Routledge, Sussex 2013, p. 77.

32 Incidentally, it has been proposed that denying HIV as a cause of AIDS ought to be criminalised given the harm caused by denial of AIDS.

33 As 'a mechanism of defense that serves to provide an actor with protection against a reality which is for some reason perceived as too threatening to acknowledge and – when engaged in – results in the paradoxical self-deceptive state of knowing and not knowing at the same time'. R. Moerland, *The Killing of Death. Denying the genocide against the Tutsi*, Diss. Maastricht University, Maastricht 2015, p. 50.

3. INDIFFERENCE

In the remainder of this article, I will limit myself to *implicatory* rather than literal or interpretive denial. And, rather than on past events, I will be focusing on denial of *actual and ongoing* human suffering and even of 'atrocities and suffering that lie ahead'.[34]

More specifically, I will be looking at what has been called 'perhaps the most overwhelming (and the most overwhelmingly obvious) reaction and response to gross human rights violations and crimes against humanity: indifference'.[35] Indifference may be defined as a form of 'moral disengagement whereby people disavow their responsibility for the problem or the solution'.[36]

With regard to atrocities and gross human rights violations, indifference is 'a lack of concern on the part of those who are not the sufferers towards the abuses and affronts, the insults and miseries that are experienced by others'.[37] In other words, we are indifferent if we know that cruelty is being perpetrated upon others and do not care or feel compelled to do anything about it.

Being indifferent is a state of mind that we are all familiar with, even though we probably would rather not admit it. Personally, I often feel totally overwhelmed by the images of human suffering that we are being confronted with day by day. Even though I have a professional interest in these events, there is always more information than one can – cognitively and emotionally – deal with, let alone do something about.

Given that there are always many other things that need to be done, I often feel tempted to ignore – at least part of – the information that – day in, day out – is made available about atrocities and gross human rights violations taking place elsewhere in the world. It is tempting to avoid such disturbing information that invariably feels like an unwelcome interruption of daily life. However, being (half-consciously) aware of the fact that I know but do not (want to) know about what is going on elsewhere in the world also leaves me feeling guilty and, when I look at myself through the eyes of others, even ashamed.[38]

---

34 S. Cohen, *States of Denial: Knowing About Atrocities and Suffering*, Polity Press, London 2001, p. 288.

35 K. Tester, *Moral Culture*, Sage, London 1997, p. 16.

36 C. Hamilton, 'Why We Resist the Truth About Climate Change. A Paper to the Climate Controversies: Science and Politics conference Museum of Natural Sciences', Brussels 28.10.2010, p. 5.

37 K. Tester, 'A theory of indifference' (2002) 1, 2 *Journal of Human Rights* 173–186, 175.

38 After the Second World War, German philosopher K. Jaspers (*The Question of German Guilt*, Dial Press, New York 1947) famously distinguished – amongst others – moral and metaphysical guilt. Moral guilt concerned people who, during the Holocaust, went on with their activities as if nothing happened. In the moral sense, we should also be guilty when today in the face of human suffering elsewhere in the world, we carry on with our business as usual where we could, and, indeed, should, do something to stop or prevent it. In the metaphysical sense, however, we are guilty of the suffering of other human beings regardless of whether we have, deliberately or inadvertently, contributed to it or done nothing to stop or

Uncomfortable feelings of guilt and shame confront us with questions like: how do we decide where and when to look or not to look, to read or not to read, to listen or not to listen and, finally and most importantly, to act or not to act? In other words, how do we maintain a morally viable position *vis-á-vis* an overload of information on human suffering in the world in which we live? Rather than focusing on my own moral inadequacy, I will now turn to a more sociological analysis and critique of indifference.

As social and cultural phenomenon, indifference to the suffering of others is 'an inevitable and inescapable dimension of social relationships and arrangements'.[39] It is a condition, however, that is exacerbated in what sociologist Zygmunt Bauman[40] has called 'liquid modernity', i.e. a world in which social forms and institutions no longer have enough time to solidify and cannot serve as frames of reference for human actions.

Liquid modernity, according to Bauman, 'weakens the pressure of moral responsibility [and] promotes indifference to the plight of the Other which otherwise would be subject to moral evaluation and morally motivated response'.[41] In this context, we all become bystanders of human suffering, while, at the same time, the distinction between bystander and accomplice or accessory becomes increasingly tenuous.[42]

As a result, the phenomenon of indifference becomes 'a serious moral problem'.[43] Not responding to the suffering of others – 'if only by offering them, at least, a spark of hope' – is, in the words of Holocaust survivor Elie Wiesel, to deny their humanity and betray our own.[44]

Most of us are aware of distant human suffering only indirectly, through information provided by the mass media and by professional humanitarian organisations like Amnesty International, Human Rights Watch, and Doctors without Borders (*Médecins Sans Frontières*). As a result of their efforts, our discourse about human suffering 'is largely the product of their moral imagination'.[45]

Sociologists like Stanley Cohen and Zygmunt Bauman are rather pessimistic about the ways in which mass media and human rights organisations are tackling the problem of indifference to human suffering by providing actual information.

prevent it. The other forms of guilt are criminal guilt concerning the responsibility for acts which are 'capable of objective proof and violate unequivocal laws' (p. 31) and political guilt concerning the responsibility for 'the consequences of the state whose power governs me and under whose order I live' (p. 31).

39 K. Tester, 'A theory of indifference' (2002) 1(2) *Journal of Human Rights* 173–186, 175.

40 Z. Bauman, *Liquid Modernity*, Polity Press, Cambridge 2000.

41 Z. Bauman, 'From bystander to actor' (2003) 1(2) *Journal of Human Rights* 137–151, 199.

42 Ibid., p. 139.

43 K. Tester, 'A theory of indifference' (2002) 1(2) *Journal of Human Rights* 173–186, 175.

44 E. Wiesel, 1999.

45 S. Cohen, *States of Denial: Knowing About Atrocities and Suffering*, Polity Press, London 2001, p. 164.

4. THE MASS MEDIA

While academic research can draw some public attention to atrocities and gross human rights violations, journalists can reach much wider audiences and their reports on atrocities taking place elsewhere in the world, can reach us almost in real time.

Yet, despite the fact that today we are better informed about human suffering of distant others than any generation before us, indifference prevails. The mere scale of the atrocities as well as their geographical distance give us a sense that they belong to another world: a 'hyper-reality' which we experience as external and remote. And the constant repetition of images of atrocities by the media only increases our sense of the remoteness of these events from our daily lives.[46]

Instead of becoming consciously engaged with what we see and hear, we tend to sit back and let the images and reports 'wash over us'. And while we sit and watch, we become anaesthetised to any moral impact those images should have upon us.

The main problem with images of human suffering, however, 'is not their multiplicity but their ... *moral distance*'.[47] In his book *Moral Culture,* philosopher Keith Tester claims that we experience distant wars and atrocities in the media as 'completely and utterly banal'.[48]

While there is undoubtedly some truth to this claim, it is too general for at least two reasons.

The first reason is that members of Muslim communities in Western Europe are far from indifferent to the suffering of distant others in counties like Iraq, Afghanistan or Syria – on the contrary.

Their identification with who they see as their 'brothers and sisters' explains why they identify with victims of bloodshed in ways that most non-Muslims cannot or do not show. For most non-Muslims, distant victims of human suffering tend to be 'othered' as belonging to different cultures and religions and, therefore, excluded from the sphere of universal solidarity and human rights.

Tester's claim is also too general, given that massive mobilisation for humanitarian emergencies through the media *is* occasionally successful. In these cases, television viewers *do* seem to be touched by the sight of human suffering and *do* want 'to do something' about it. Some people spontaneously take the initiative to organise help, e.g. by collecting clothing or food and transporting it to emergency situations. This shows that it *is* possible to invoke a moral response to distant human suffering, even though these periodic outbursts of solidarity are seldom and – according to Bauman – a 'sorely inadequate, alternative to the meek acceptance of the state of affairs'.[49]

---

46 Ibid., p. 194.

47 Ibid., p. 194.

48 K. TESTER, *Moral Culture,* Sage, London 1997, p. 28.

49 Z. BAUMAN, 'From bystander to actor' (2003) 1(2) *Journal of Human Rights* 137–151, 148.

In general, however, public engagement is limited to those victims we can somehow identify with. But even then this engagement goes no further than demanding that 'something must be done' whereby it remains totally unclear what this 'something' is that needs to be done. Actually, this should be no surprise as, in fact, 'it is far from evident what (if anything) can be done by us to make a real difference'.[50]

One of the most popular responses to suffering is 'getting someone else to do it for us' by sending money (or counting on the government to do so). The attraction of this 'monetisation of morality' is, that it allows us to claim – unashamedly – that we did what we had to do, that we could not have done more than we did and that, therefore, we should be absolved from our moral guilt.

5. HUMAN RIGHTS ORGANISATIONS

One reason why professional organisations like Amnesty International, Human Rights Watch, and Doctors without Borders fail in their task to move and mobilise people and to create public pressure in order to stop human rights violations, is that they fail to tackle the problem of indifference adequately.

In *States of Denial,* Cohen analyses how these organisations try to move and mobilise us by making moral appeals and inducing feelings of guilt. Guilt is induced by making us 'feel bad' for living our comfortable life as if we do *not* know – what we obviously *do* know – about horrors taking place elsewhere in the world. This strategy does not work because – as Cohen has pointed out – the 'guilt-induction chain' is weak. Instead of moving people to take action, these moral appeals even seem to have the opposite effect. This is because 'the more responsible and "bad" you feel for not doing anything … the less you feel motivated to absorb more information [and] the more likely you are to shut out and switch off'.[51]

A second reason why these organisations fail to move and mobilise people is that the resources for a moral response to the instances of distant human suffering have been exhausted and 'evacuated of any power'.[52] The routine translation of what Bauman has called 'morally pregnant knowledge' into abstract legal and political discourse fails to mobilise people and passes the ownership of a human rights problems into the hands of a – what Cohen has called – 'bureaucratic cartel' of human rights professionals. It may, therefore, be concluded – with a quote from Lawrence Langer – that: 'Until we find a way of toppling the barrier that sequesters mass suffering in other regions of the world

---

50 Ibid., p. 146.

51 S. Cohen, *States of Denial: Knowing About Atrocities and Suffering*, Polity Press, London 2001, p. 216.

52 K. Tester, *Moral Culture*, Sage, London 1997, p. 28.

from the comfort and the safety we enjoy far from its ravages, little will be done to rouse the attention of our political and professional leaders, to say nothing of our own'.[53]

6. TACKLING THE PROBLEM OF INDIFFERENCE

If providing actual information about atrocities is not effective in rousing the attention of people and ending their indifference to human suffering, then what is?

A possible remedy, is to try make people feel ashamed about being uninformed about the suffering of distant others. In *States of Denial*, Cohen has noted that the moral appeal to shame is used much less than the appeals made to guilt which, as we have seen, do not work or even are counterproductive. Instead of inducing guilt feelings, it would, therefore, make more sense to try to induce feelings shame.[54] Shame is a highly uncomfortable feeling to be sure. However, it can make us aware of our indifference and motivate us to do something about it.[55]

It is an uncomfortable feeling that should be welcomed also because it, paradoxically, shows that we are not totally indifferent and, in principle at least, are willing to consider and maybe even do something about the human suffering of distant others. Shame is, therefore, essential in ways that guilt is not.

As a socially productive emotion, shame also appeals to a sense of community and moral interdependence rather than to personal responsibility alone.

The public shaming of indifference does not allow us to 'feel good' about ourselves, individually and collectively. Our feelings of shame challenge us and force us to re-evaluate our ideas and assumptions about ourselves and the world we live in.

Although, as citizens, we tend to defer our judgments on atrocities and gross human rights violations by arguing 'that nothing we can do will make much difference anyway'.[56] Morally, this is, of course, hardly a sustainable position.

As the American philosopher Michael Walzer has noted in his book *Just and Unjust Wars,* when we – as ordinary citizens – 'go along with' the policies and human rights violations that our governments commit, support or condone,

---

53 L.L. Langer, 'The Alarmed Vision: Social Suffering and Holocaust Atrocity' (1996) 125(1) *Daedalus* 47–65, 47.

54 S. Cohen, *States of Denial: Knowing About Atrocities and Suffering*, Polity Press, London 2001, p. 11.

55 This is why indifference can be considered as a form of denial. Avoiding information without acknowledging that we are actually doing so would be an example of 'meta-denial'. Our moral (or metaphysical) is then neutralised by denying the denial. E. Zerubavel, 'The Social Sound of Silence: Toward A Sociology of Denial' in: E. Ben-Ze'ev, R. Ginio and J. Winter (eds.), *Shadows of War: A Social History of Silence in the Twentieth Century,* Cambridge University Press, Cambridge 2010, pp. 32–46, at p. 69.

56 M. Walzer, *Just and Unjust Wars: A Moral Argument with Historical Illustrations,* Basic Books, New York 2000, p. 301.

we are 'collectively liable' for the crimes against humanity that are committed, supported or condoned 'in our name'.[57]

Of course, as ordinary citizens we do not – in any way – cause these crimes and – as such – we are not legally liable for them. But '[w]hile passivity ... is too diffuse to give rise to any meaningful form of legal responsibility, it nonetheless has consequences which raise important issues about [moral] responsibility'.[58] As citizens, we have a collective moral responsibility to ensure that our governments are not a source of unjust harm to others.[59] By remaining passive (or failing to protest), we risk – albeit in only a small way – supporting such wrongdoings and adding to the appearance of their legitimacy.

This also applies when our government supports or condones human rights violations committed by others or fails to comply with the international 'responsibility to protect'.

In these cases, the responsibility to protect, which is usually used as an argument for justified military interventions, may just as well be used as an argument to justify 'a responsibility to protest'[60] against unjustified military interventions in order to prevent the human rights violations that are committed during these interventions and cause human suffering elsewhere in the world.

And this is *exactly* what millions of people in more than 600 cities in sixty countries around the world did on 16 February 2004. They were ashamed of and protested against crimes that were being committed – as they put it – *'Not in Our Name'*. This was a global political protest against the military intervention in Iraq, against the way in which that intervention had been decided, and against the lack of accountability the governments of the US and the UK had demonstrated toward the citizens in whose name these decisions were taken.[61]

It is in this same vein that Crawford[62] argues that, as ordinary citizens we always have a *collective* moral responsibility to deliberate, monitor, and make judgments about such issues. And, I may add, we have a collective moral responsibility to counter the denialism of our governments if they try to deny atrocities and gross human rights violations that are currently occurring or that have occurred in the past.

---

57 In K. Jaspers, *The Question of German Guilt*, Fordham University Press, New York 2002, p. 55, German philosopher Karl Jaspers has argued that the German people were collectively liable for the acts committed by their state. He wrote that: 'we are politically responsible for our regime, for the acts of the regime, for the start of the war in this world historical situation'.

58 L. Farmer (2007) 1 *Criminal Law and Philosophy* 151–156, 154.

59 J. McMahan, *Killing in War*, Oxford University Press, Oxford 2009, p. 215.

60 N.C. Crawford, 'War "In Our Name" and Responsibility to Protest: Ordinary Citizens, Civil Society, and Prospective Moral Responsibility' (2014) 38 *Midwest Studies in Philosophy* 138–170, 148.

61 J. Williams, '"Not in My Name"? Legitimate Authority and Liberal Just War Theory' in: A.F. Lang Jr., C. O'Driscoll and J. Williams (eds.), *Just War, Authority, Traditions and Practice*, Georgetown University Press, Washington DC 2013, p. 75.

62 N.C. Crawford, 'War "In Our Name" and Responsibility to Protest: Ordinary Citizens, Civil Society, and Prospective Moral Responsibility' (2014) 38 *Midwest Studies in Philosophy* 138–170.

7. DENIALISM AND CRITICAL CRIMINOLOGY

Finally, I would like to address the question of what role criminology could play in countering indifference and mobilising support for human rights interventions.

Within the field of criminology, it has been argued that an 'engagement' with human rights is a 'scholarly and moral responsibility'[63] and, as such, 'essential for 21th century criminology'.[64] It is the only way to ensure that the 'next generation' of criminologists 'need never again be bystanders to genocide'.[65]

The call for criminologists to become engaged in this kind of work is, however, based on the presumption that criminology can provide the knowledge of how to create public awareness of atrocities and gross human rights violations and of how to make sure that these crimes against humanity will not happen again.[66]

In his book *Just and Unjust Wars,* Michael Walzer raises the issue of how to get one's fellow citizens to think seriously about these issues, even though he notes that it is 'not easy to know' what sort of actions would need to be taken in order to achieve this.

Although academic research cannot draw as much public attention to atrocities and human rights violations as journalists who reach much wider audiences, at least, 'there is intellectual work to do'.

We must describe, as graphically as we can, the reality of atrocities and human rights violations, what it means to be a victim of these crimes. And we must analyse the nature of our moral and democratic responsibilities to respond to them.

These are not only feasible tasks, but they are morally required of those academics and public intellectuals who are trained to perform the role of what philosopher Herman Shue has called the 'citizen expert'.

The task of the citizen expert – and, thus, the critical criminologist – is to try to develop a consensus on questions of how to respond to atrocities and gross violations of human rights and how to prevent such crimes against humanity from ever occurring again.[67]

---

63 J. Hagan and W. Rymond-Richmond, 'Criminology Confronts Genocide: Whose side are you on?' (2009) 13 *Theoretical Criminology* 503–511, 509.

64 D. Garland in a blurb on the back of J. Savelberg, *Crime and Human Rights: Criminology of Genocide and Atrocities*, Sage, London 2010.

65 J. Hagan and W. Rymon-Richmond, *Darfur and the Crime of Genocide*, Cambridge University Press, New York 2009, p. 222.

66 Ibid., p. 221.

67 N.C. Crawford, 'War "In Our Name" and Responsibility to Protest: Ordinary Citizens, Civil Society, and Prospective Moral Responsibility' (2014) 38 *Midwest Studies in Philosophy* 138–170, 165.

This work is essential because, ultimately, the key to mobilising public support is to 'have ... good arguments, intelligently and energetically advanced'.[68]

Developing these arguments and publicly defending them is what critical criminologists can and should do in order to counter denialism and tackle the problem of indifference to human suffering of distant others.

68 G. Evans, 'Crimes against humanity: overcoming indifference' (2006) 8(3) *Journal of Genocide Research* 325–339.

CHAPTER III

DENIAL AND ACKNOWLEDGMENT IN PUBLIC RESPONSES TO INFORMATION ABOUT HUMAN RIGHTS VIOLATIONS

Irene BRUNA SEU

1. INTRODUCTION

This chapter discusses denial and acknowledgment in public responses to information about human rights violations. It draws on the findings from a series of qualitative studies investigating ordinary people's understanding of, responses to (including actions and inaction), and emotional and cognitive reactions to information about human rights violations.[1] This work complements existing theorisations of denial[2] and offers an empirically grounded formulation of denial and acknowledgment to illustrate the varied and complex modalities in which they find expression in people's behaviours and attitudes.

The first part of the chapter briefly summarises the key features of denial in the original formulations by Freud and then developed by Cohen. In bringing these two formulations together it proposes a psychosocial theorisation of denial as generated by a conglomerate of social and psychological influences.

---

1 A total of 282 participants took part in 3 studies across the UK and the Basque Country between 2001 and 2014. The first of the UK studies and the one in the Basque Country focused exclusively on human rights issues. The third, a nationwide study carried out in the UK, had a wider humanitarian scope. Overall, the participants were mixed in terms of ethnicity, age, nationality, gender, social class, sexual orientation and family formation. In the first UK study 63 participants took part in 12 focus groups, 37 took part in five focus groups in the Basque country, and 182 took part in twenty focus groups in the second UK study. All the studies followed the same format: the participants were given either communications about human rights violations (from NGOs and the media), or about humanitarian and human rights issues. Participants were asked to look at the information and pay attention to their thoughts and emotional reactions. The author, with the help of other researchers, loosely followed a semi-structure schedule of questions while respecting the natural flow of group dialogue.

2 e.g. S. COHEN, *States of Denial: Knowing About Atrocities and Suffering*, Polity Press, London 2001; P. CLARKSON, *The Bystander: An End to Innocence in Human Relationship*, Whurr Publishers Ltd, London 1996; T. VAN DIJK, 'Discourse and the denial of racism' (1992) 3(1) *Discourse and Society* 87–118.

The second part of the chapter is dedicated to 'acknowledgement', the opposite of denial. It introduces the '3M' model delineating the psychosocial factors fostering a 'connectedness' with human rights and humanitarian issues that is manageable, meaningful and sustainable for individuals.

Quotes from the studies' participants will illustrate how people 'do' denial and acknowledgement, how empathy and connectedness with the sufferer is blocked through denial but also how the connectedness can be fostered and integrated into everyday morality, enabling action and ongoing active respect for human rights principles.

Questions about knowledge and action are central to any exploration of denial and acknowledgment. That is, what and how much people know about human rights violations, and what they do in response to that knowledge. Hence, at the core of formulations of denial and acknowledgement is a tension between, on the one hand, knowing and not knowing, and on the other, the self-protective 'switching off' and the intentional 'turning away'. Throughout the chapter I will return to these tensions and the dynamism between what could be paraphrased as 'I wish but I can't' and 'I could but I won't'. The 'I can't' refers to not being able to intervene, viewed here as an automatic self-protective defence mechanism which includes helplessness and disassociation resulting from trauma. The 'I won't' refers to the conscious turning away that has to be justified and accounted for.

The concept of denial, originally coined by Freud and later broadened by Cohen, captures this ambiguity as it describes what Cohen calls the 'twilight zone of knowing and not knowing', in which both the autonomic 'shutting off' and the active 'turning away' from unpalatable truths operate.[3] To properly understand public passivity and acknowledgment we need to engage with both these aspects. Equally, we need to engage with both the individual/psychological and the socio-cultural aspects of these dynamics as they are constantly intertwined, informing and affecting each other. Accordingly, the psychosocial approach to denial and acknowledgment proposed in this chapter is concerned with understanding both the social formation in which the subject lives, relates and is formed, and the biographical experience and psychic life of the individual subject, as well as the relationship between these domains. As such, the theorisation of denial and acknowledgment proposed here attempts to articulate the intertwining of the psychic and the social, of inner and outer worlds. I suggest that members of the public – 'passive bystanders' to the virtual spectacle of human rights violations – should be understood simultaneously as psychologically defended subjects,[4] responding to disturbing information and imagery of human rights violations with psychodynamic defence mechanisms,

---

3 S. Cohen, *States of Denial: Knowing About Atrocities and Suffering*, Polity Press, London 2001.

4 W. Hollway and T. Jefferson, *Doing Qualitative Research Differently. A Free Association, Narrative and the Interview Method*, Sage, London 2000.

as well as morally agentic, crafting acceptable justifications for passivity through the use of socially constructed narratives, what Cohen,[5] drawing on Wright Mills,[6] calls 'good stories'.

2. DENIAL

In psychoanalytic theory denial is one of the key defence mechanisms used to defend ourselves from painful or troubling realities. As is the case with many of Freud's formulations, the concept of denial was changed and refined by him many times. Originally, Freud referred to 'a mode of defence which consists in the subject's refusing to recognize the reality of a traumatic perception'.[7] It is not until later, however, that the true complexity of the term denial (and disavowal) were fully spelled out by Freud when, in describing the paradox of knowing and not knowing, he distinguished between the disavowal of the idea of something unacceptable to the mind, and the repression of the related affect. In 'true' denial, the original perception persists and 'energetic action must be taken to maintain the disavowal'.[8] We can already see, as early as these first formulations, the tension between an automatic defence mechanism in the form of unconscious repression, and the 'energetic action', in the form of repudiation and disavowal, involving agency and some degree of intentionality, investment and action.

Because of the dual processes operating in denial, Freud switched his interest from the object of denial to its workings. He was intrigued by the idea that awkward facts of life could be handled by simultaneous acceptance and disavowal: they are too threatening to confront, but impossible to ignore. The compromise solution is to deny and acknowledge them at the same time. Freud considered this a 'false resolution', as it was a way of protecting oneself from reality rather than learning to confront it. As Steiner pointed out in *Psychic Retreats*[9] 'the subject uses "perverse arguments" to misinterpret the facts – a way of dealing with reality which, in Freud's words, almost deserves to be described as artful'.[10] It was the interest in these artful arguments and their ubiquitous presence in social life that brought Cohen to develop a psychosocial typology of denial.

---

5 S. Cohen, *States of Denial: Knowing About Atrocities and Suffering*, Polity Press, London 2001.

6 C. Wright Mills, 'Situated actions and vocabularies of motives' (1940) 904 *American Sociological Review* 13.

7 J. Laplance and J.B. Pontalis, *The Language of Psycho-Analysis*, The Hogarth Press, London 1985, p. 118.

8 S. Cohen, *States of Denial: Knowing About Atrocities and Suffering*, Polity Press, London 2001p. 27.

9 J. Steiner, *Psychic Retreats: pathological organizations in psychotic, neurotic and borderline patients*, Routledge, London 1993, p. 92.

10 S. Cohen, *States of Denial: Knowing About Atrocities and Suffering*, Polity Press, London 2001, p. 28.

In his ground-breaking work *States of Denial*,[11] Cohen grapples with the cultural, political and psychological factors involved in the complex variety of modes of avoidance we all use to protect ourselves from unpalatable realities and our responsibility towards the suffering of others. Cohen claims that, differently from 'not knowing', simply lying or deliberately choosing not to expose ourselves to certain unpalatable information, we are, sometimes, not entirely aware of switching off or blocking out that information. Denial, therefore, is 'neither a matter of telling the truth nor intentionally telling a lie. … There seem to be states of mind, or even whole cultures, in which we know and don't know at the same time'.[12]

According to Cohen, there are three distinct, although at times overlapping, types of psychosocial denial: literal, interpretive and implicatory. In the first, literal, factual denial, the fact or knowledge of the fact is denied, for example 'my husband could not have done that to our daughter'; 'there was no massacre'.

In interpretive denial, the raw facts are not denied but given a different meaning to that which seems apparent to others,[13] for example 'I am a social drinker, not an alcoholic'; 'this was population exchange, not ethnic cleansing'; 'this was not torture, but robust and legitimate interrogation'. The observer disputes the cognitive meaning given to an event and reallocates it to another class of events by changing words, using euphemisms or adopting technical jargon.[14] Van Dijk calls this form of denial *mitigation*, which involves toning down, minimising or using euphemisms when describing one's negative actions.[15] Finally, implicatory denial refers to those explanations that do not deny the reality of the event, or their conventional interpretation, but deny the 'psychological, political or moral implications that conventionally follow'.[16]

Cohen refers here to 'the multitude of vocabularies – justifications, rationalizations, evasions – that we use to deal with our awareness of so many images of unmitigated suffering'.[17] He argues that these vocabularies are increasing and becoming more convoluted as they are used to attempt to bridge the moral and psychic gap between 'what you know and what you do'.

Crucially, Cohen states that the techniques of evasion, avoidance, deflection and rationalisation should draw on good – that is, believable – stories. He draws on Wright Mills' work,[18] according to which accounts of denial are not mysterious

---

11 Ibid.
12 Ibid., pp. 4–5.
13 Ibid., p. 7.
14 Ibid., p. 8.
15 T. Van Dijk, 'New(s) Racism: A Discourse Analytical Approach' in: S. Cottle (ed.), *Ethnic Minorities and the Media*, UK Open University Press, Milton Keynes 2000, pp. 33–49.
16 S. Cohen, *States of Denial: Knowing About Atrocities and Suffering*, Polity Press, London 2001, p. 8.
17 Ibid., p. 8.
18 C. Wright Mills, 'Situated actions and vocabularies of motives' (1940) 904 *American Sociological Review* 13.

internal states, but typical vocabularies with clear functions in particular social situations. 'Accounts are learnt by ordinary cultural transmission, and are drawn from a well-established, collectively available pool. An account is adopted because of its public acceptability. Socialisation teaches us which motives are acceptable for which action'.[19] Hence, a denial account does not simply give a plausible, acceptable story about an action (e.g. 'this is what I do'), but also provides crucial moral accountability for the speaker ('this is why what I do is all right'). Such moral accounting takes a variety of forms in denial: from the psychological techniques of rationalisation, defence mechanisms and disavowal, to the sociological forms of apologies, normalisation and neutralisation.[20]

While some intra-psychic forms of denial are private, unique to each person and might not be connected to any cultural, organised or political phenomena, other states of denial are public and shared by whole cultures and institutions, and are increasingly referred to as 'cultures of denial' (for example, the police, army, hospitals, government). In his latest writing on denial Cohen introduced the concept of 'denialism', another variant of generic denial, and argued that: 'in a sense denialism is the polar opposite of "in denial". Instead of a personal and private state that might last a lifetime, denialism is expressed in a learned, shared public language; the activities of claim makers and moral entrepreneurs are organised, planned, intentional and – sometimes less obviously – ideological'.[21] For example, with issues of gun control, social redistributive policies, creationism and abortion, denialism correlates with shifts to the right.

In the case of global warming Cohen points out that at first scientists, politicians and the more enlightened middle class worked towards the translation of global warming as a scientific problem into a social problem. Moral entrepreneurs pushed to create new rules to prevent global warming. 'Soon enough, evidence became claims; claims generated counter-claims; some counter-claims became fully-fledged denials – literal, interpretive and implicatory'.[22]

Because of the dialectical nature of these social processes Cohen revisited the idea that forms of denial are used to bridge the moral and psychic gap between what we know and what we do.[23] In his later writing he clarified that instead 'we need a flowing, fluid narrative like this, rather than the static image of "gaps", to study both the internal discourse and how (or whether) this reaches the everyday concerns of ordinary people'.[24] Furthermore, 'the notion of "gap" between

19 S. Cohen, *States of Denial: Knowing About Atrocities and Suffering*, Polity Press, London 2001, p. 59.

20 T. Van Dijk, 'New(s) Racism: A Discourse Analytical Approach' in: S. Cottle (ed.), *Ethnic Minorities and the Media*, UK Open University Press, Milton Keynes 2000, pp. 33–49.

21 S. Cohen, 'Climate change in a perverse culture' in: S. Weintrobe, *Engaging with Climate Change: Psychoanalytic and Interdisciplinary Perspectives*, Routledge, London 2013, p. 76.

22 Ibid., p. 77.

23 Ibid.

24 Ibid.

knowledge and action – useful as it is for rhetorical and pedagogical purposes – makes little psychological sense'[25] as there are no clearly demarcated areas of our brain allocated to 'knowing', 'feeling', and 'acting'.

Additionally, Cohen[26] stressed that a key requirement for a working conception of denial is that it should make sense both in psychological/individual and social/collective terms. There are several ways in which this can happen: one could determine the other or the two could be in a symbiotic relationship, one reinforcing the other. The latter is the model I find most convincing and that which is used in this chapter to offer a psychosocial theorisation which embraces the fluidity and complexity of operations of denial postulated by Cohen, by looking at the intricate intertwining of the psychic and the social, the inner and the outer world, and the mutual interplay of knowledge, emotions and action.

Similarly, vocabularies of denial are not seen as static, rather as fluid and unstable. Various scripts circulate simultaneously in society and are therefore available to individuals to make sense and use as successful explanations and justifications. They are produced and reinforced through governmental attitudes and policies, and the operation of the media. Some become dominant and more stable and recurrent than others.

For those interested in the workings of denial – at individual, cultural and state levels – knowing about these scripts/vocabularies of denial is essential in order to study them and counteract them. Part of the counteraction consists in unmasking their ideological origin and political function. Expressions of denial are multiple, varied and changeable.

Word constraint prevents a full discussion of all forms of denial identified in the empirical studies.[27] What follows is a strategic focus on two types of vocabularies of denial: 'in countries like that' and 'switching off', representing two ways in which people 'do denial'. The first, 'in countries like that', exemplifies a vocabulary of implicatory denial which is particularly potent in the UK at the moment. The second, 'switching off', is discussed as functioning both as a socio-cultural script and an intra-psychic defence mechanism thus illustrating how socio-cultural vocabularies of denial become lived experience and *vice versa*. The two vocabularies were selected because of the frequency in which they were used across the studies and focus groups, and because, as stated by Cohen,[28] these vocabularies work both at psychological/individual and socio/collective level, thus illustrating the symbiotic relationship between individual and socio-cultural expressions of denial.

---

25 Ibid., p. 78.

26 Ibid., pp. 72–79.

27 For a more comprehensive discussion see I.B. Seu, *Passivity Generation; Human Rights and everyday morality*, Palgrave, London 2013.

28 S. Cohen, 'Climate change in a perverse culture' in: S. Weintrobe, *Engaging with Climate Change: Psychoanalytic and Interdisciplinary Perspectives*, Routledge, London 2013, pp. 72–79.

3. SOCIO-CULTURAL VOCABULARIES OF DENIAL: 'IN COUNTRIES LIKE THAT'

Participants across different focus groups often described countries where atrocities are committed as 'countries like that'. This vague definition was never questioned, as if it were common knowledge which countries were 'like that'. Looked at more closely, this trope appeared to be used by participants to make sense of atrocities, to draw symbolic moral boundaries and to justify a passive and self-distancing response to human rights issues.[29]

According to Opotow and Weiss[30] the scope of justice is our psychological boundary for fairness. Norms, moral rules, and concerns about rights and fairness govern our conduct towards those inside our scope of justice and determine who and what counts. Moral concerns are only relevant for those inside the scope of justice. Moral exclusion, in contrast, rationalises and justifies harm for those outside, viewing them as expendable, undeserving, exploitable, or irrelevant. A crucial role in these dynamics of rationalisation and moral exclusion is played by those ideological processes that construct excluded groups as beyond the moral order. These forms of stereotyping naturalise and essentialise characteristics of the excluded group. We have seen examples of this operation throughout history and at present. In a recent article in the British newspaper *The Guardian*, the UN High Commissioner for Human Rights commented how the recent branding of migrants as 'cockroaches' in *The Sun* tabloid is reminiscent of anti-Semitic Nazi propaganda and language used prior to the Rwandan genocide.[31]

For our purposes, placing countries where human rights are violated beyond the boundary of moral responsibility, accounts containing this trope perform a denial operation for the purpose of exonerating audiences from intervening. This operation of moral exclusion interferes with audiences' empathy and compassion by distancing audiences from the victims of atrocities. Thus 'in countries like that' is an act of implicatory denial because it symbolically and ideologically demarcates the boundaries of moral responsibility towards suffering others, and enables people to justify and rationalise their unresponsiveness.

> Tina: 'In so many countries there doesn't seem to be a good side and a bad side. It's kind of, it's like everyone's in there committing these atrocities.'

---

29 For a full discussion see I.B. Seu, '"*In countries like that…*": moral boundaries and implicatory denial in response to human rights appeals' (2012) 16(8) *The International Journal of Human Rights* 1170–1182.

30 S. Opotow and L. Weiss, 'Denial and exclusion in environmental conflict' (2000) 56(3) *Journal of Social Issues* 478.

31 'UN Human Rights chief denounces Sun over Katie Hopkins "cockroach" column' 2015 *The Guardian* <www.theguardian.com/global-development/2015/apr/24/katie-hopkins-cockroach-migrants-denounced-united-nations-human-rights-commissioner>.

By using 'in there' in connection with 'these atrocities', Tina lexically links the atrocities described in the appeals and newspaper article, with countries 'over there'. This move simultaneously locates atrocities in particular countries (and by implication not in others), and distances our country here from countries 'over there'.

Tina further strengthens the differentiation between us and them by drawing a moral boundary on the basis of who is good and who is bad. Using generalisation and referential ambiguity she states that in 'many countries', in essence, everybody is bad. One of the consequences of stating that 'everyone's in there committing these atrocities' is that there is not a 'clean' or, as Reiff (2002) calls it, a 'deserving' victim. What Tina implies is that the victim might also be a perpetrator or somehow implicated in a cycle of violence. Thus whilst reinforcing the moral boundaries that keep her separated from what happens in 'these countries', by negating a differentiation between victim and perpetrator, Tina lumps them together.

If the victims are allegedly implicated in the violations, moral boundaries drawn on grounds of moral purity justify Tina distancing herself from the atrocities.

These extracts show how members of the public hold the belief that human rights violations happen only – or more frequently – somewhere else.

> Leila: 'I think when I was reading about Saudi Arabia I think it was those stories there I was thinking that Q<oh, that kind of thing happens>Q[32] is the story with the woman who was accused of being a prostitute. I think it was only because of one book that I read when it talked a lot about things like that and I just thought, Q<oh well, that's the kind of thing that happens there>Q.'

Responding to *The Guardian* article on Saudi Arabia, which was a prop in one of the studies, Leila implicitly refers to mechanisms of social stereotyping when she tells of the recognition conveyed by 'Oh, that kind of thing happens'. This memory is credited to a book that 'talked about things like that' – like what exactly is unclear: prostitution in general, prostitution being a crime, human rights violations, Sharia law? This important vagueness is carried out into the final sentence, where 'that kind of thing happens' turns into 'Oh well, that's the kind of thing that happens there', where 'the kind of thing' stops being a legal category and becomes representative of a particular country. Truthfulness is not the issue here, but the process of labelling and social stereotyping that is taking place. Vagueness is central to these processes as, by de-contextualising the problem and removing it from its historical and political roots, it feeds into essentialist beliefs about a country and a population. What is implied is an unspoken assumption that this is how *they* are, have been and always will

[32] Q<>Q is used when the speaker makes use of referred speech.

be. Particularly revealing in that respect is Leila's resignation, conveyed by her 'Oh well', and normalisation 'that's the kind of thing that happens there' that contributes to the belief that human rights violations only take place in countries 'like that' and because this is intrinsic to those countries, there is nothing we can do about it.

> Carol: 'I was thinking that erm could this be erm the issue of difference, uhm, between human beings because erm, I usually feel that erm we have not really yet accepted each other, I mean sort of that there is always the other for us. So that maybe, like I'm African, the other for me is maybe a white person. I'm African and Christian, the other for me could be a white person or a Muslim or maybe a Jew, so that erm, or maybe another tribe because in Africa we have our [different tribes] erm so that if it is happening erm to a white person, a Muslim, another tribe, erm, it's no big deal, it's no big deal really for me because it's them, you know that, it's not me, and it's not the people who, it's not what I belong to. So erm, it's easy to disassociate myself and not really feel or really, or maybe not look at the issues as objectively as possible. And maybe feel erm that in my country I come from one tribe and we have a dominant tribe. But the general feeling is usually uhm if it's happening to them then they deserve it because of A, B, C they have done or this sort of thing so I have no business you know, caring for such a purpose ... But er when I sit in my living room in Nairobi it's easy to say when I see Kosovo and everything that's happening, it's easy for me to say Q<ah, look at those Europeans, ah, look at what they are doing and they thought it was Africans who [all laugh] everyday they thought it would happen in Rwanda, yeah? Well, let them deal with this>Q. And it's no big deal for me over there.'

Carol's nuanced intervention explicitly delineates the key stages of drawing moral boundaries through 'us and them' differentiations and prejudicial categorisation, psychosocial processes of moral exclusion and 'just world thinking', according to which people deserve what happens to them, and their use to justify inaction and disconnection. The essence of what Carol says is that whilst we cannot get away from difference and therefore 'the other', as soon as the other is defined, something happens to our emotional and moral responses towards the other's troubles. The resulting attitude could be summarised as 'it has nothing to do with me'. Carol is hinting at the existence of an invisible line of demarcation between what is our business and what is not. What makes 'the other' is not fixed – it could be determined by skin colour, nationality, religious orientation, or, resonant with Freud's 'narcissism of small differences', might be determined by a difference ostensibly so small and yet so important such as belonging to a neighbouring, but different, tribe. However, as soon as the victim is 'the other', as Carol puts it, 'if it's happening to a white person, a Muslim, another tribe, it's no big deal really for me because it's them, it's not me, it's not the people I belong to'. It is acceptable then to turn away and reject any responsibility.

In all the studies socio-cultural categorisations were used by focus groups participants when referring to the distant suffering other to explain when and how they responded to the pleas made on their behalf. Some specific and prejudicial categorisations of the other were recurrent. Three in particular were used with particular frequency and portrayed the other as barbaric, constantly at war with each other and uncivilised; as suffering from arrested development and need us in order to progress; as esoteric, brainwashed and intractable. These characterisations of the Other, whose human rights have been violated, is key to the dynamics of implicatory denial, thus exemplifying one aspect of the tension running through this chapter: 'I could but I won't'.

4. 'SWITCHING OFF' – DENIAL AS SELF-PROTECTIVE DEFENCE MECHANISM

The next section looks at examples of the opposite pole of tension – 'I wish but I can't' - which refers to denial as intra-psychic defence mechanism protecting the subject from overwhelming information.

> Bob: 'Well you tend to shut yourself off from it because it's so, um, appalling. And, um, you sort of feel sick. Your stomach makes you feel that it's really, you don't want to know anything about it. Um, so, it's like, if you see a lot of it you then become, it doesn't become anything … You desensitise yourself. And if you only see little bits of it, you get the opposite effect, where it's repulsion. Alright, so, you see these sort of posters and a lot of the time they're just, you know, make you repulse against it. And you just want to run away from it, you don't want to look at it.'

In the first line Bob uses the idea of a defence mechanism: the information is so appalling that it leads to shutting off. That leaves Bob having to justify his action, not terribly commendable from an ethical point of view: he is told of a fellow human being's suffering and he does not want to know. But how can we blame him if he feels sick? Bob has a stake in convincing us that it is not that he, Bob, does not want to know; it is his stomach that tells him that really he should not know. Agency and responsibility are handed over to the stomach, an involuntary organ. The moral subject is in this way constructed as grappling, struggling with a body or internal dynamics independent of his own will.

Bob is describing something ordinary and familiar. We all recognise the reaction and the cliché: 'I felt sick; it was sickening'. And yet, I suggest, these ordinary commonplaces operate the important ideological function of removing responsibility and blame. They also counter the possibility of alternative action/reaction. The subject is passive, dominated by forces beyond its control. This is simultaneously true and not true. Bob, almost in a 'slip of the tongue' or perhaps in an implied political semi-awareness, at the same time attributes agency to himself. Because, although he says that 'your stomach makes you feel that ... you don't want to know anything about it', at the same time he also acknowledges that '*you* shut yourself off ' and that '*you* want to run away from it, *you* don't want to look at it'. Freud captured the ambiguities and complexities of what happens when we want to run away from a difficult truth, but do not want to be seen as doing that. In his discussion of defence mechanisms in 'Analysis terminable and interminable', Freud makes an analogy with a book containing statements considered undesirable. One way would be for the offending passages to be thickly crossed out. However, if what was desired was not only the disappearance of the passage but also the *intention* of mutilating the book, the best option would be 'if the whole passage would be erased and a new one which said exactly the opposite put in its place ... and it is highly probable that the corrections had not been made in the direction of the truth'. He concludes: 'if the perception of reality entails unpleasure, that perception – that is, the truth, – must be sacrificed'.[33]

On similar lines, I am suggesting that the dilemma of not wanting to know about human rights violations and at the same time not wanting to be seen to be doing so is resolved by resorting to psychological explanations of being desensitised and experiencing compassion fatigue. Different discourses allow different possibilities for subjectivity. Science as objective and mechanistic is, by definition, beyond morality. The type of subjectivity made available by a scientific discourse is one governed by physiological autonomous mechanisms. This allows a translation of the participant's response from a moral and social sphere to an individualistic cognitive/physiological domain, where issues of morality and social responsibility become irrelevant. Psychological and psychoanalytic concepts, or psycho babble, have been incorporated into the vocabulary of valid explanations of human behaviour. At that level they might be stating the obvious, but viewed as rhetorical tools they allow the 'shifting of domains', the re-framing of the problem, the new demarcation of the territory. Furthermore, the employment of this reasonable, self-evident, commonsensical explanation forecloses further investigation of the mechanics of desensitisation and moral apathy. It also pre-empts the possibility of a closer examination of what exactly is defended against. The mechanistic view of human functioning sustains the idea of a threshold of information to which we react. News of horrendous human suffering becomes stimuli we get used to, just as our pupils restrict in bright light (defence mechanism) or we no longer smell a bad smell after being exposed to it for a while (habituation due to overexposure). How can anybody blame our eyes or noses for doing what they are programmed to do – that is, protect us from damage and bad experiences? They cannot help it.

---

33 S. Freud, 'Analysis Terminable and Interminable' in: S. Freud (ed.), *Wild Analysis*, Penguin, London 2002, pp. 236–237.

In the focus groups the evidence that the problem of desensitisation was constructed not as a moral dilemma, but as a simple physiological stimulus–reaction, is very significant. The participants would like to communicate that they simply cannot help it. This involves a process through which the information is reframed and repositioned in a different arena, thus providing justifications and explanations which otherwise would not be possible.[34] Psychological explanations, absorbed into everyday common sense talk, allow the reframing in this case. Ideas of an unconscious mind, mixed with some notions of physiologically based autonomous reactions, are used to support this claim. In short, what I am suggesting is that emotionally based explanations can be used as a powerful vocabulary of denial.

In this example, Bob is considered both as a morally agentic – as such justifying his inaction and switching off – and as autonomically self-protecting from disturbing knowledge, thus illustrating the symbiotic relationship between individual psychological experiences and socio-cultural scripts available to people to make sense of their responses to knowing about human rights violations to themselves and others.

5. ACKNOWLEDGEMENT

According to Cohen, similarly to denial, acknowledgment also covers a range of responses bridging the gap between knowledge and action: 'people respond to the information by getting upset, express sympathy or compassion and do something about it, they intervene, help, become committed'.[35] This second section introduces the '3M' model of acknowledgment according to which 'knowing' leads to 'doing' through manageable emotions, meaningful understanding, and morally significant actions. The three components will be discussed separately and in relation to each other. The model emerged from the data analysis and will be illustrated through a selection of quotes from the focus groups.

6. MANAGEABLE EMOTIONS

Both vocabularies of denial discussed above – 'in countries like that' and 'switching off' – provide explanations and illustration of what results in the viewer's emotional disconnection from victims of human rights violations.

---

34 S. Cohen and I.B. Seu, 'Knowing Enough Not to Feel Too Much: Emotional Thinking About Human Rights Appeals' in: M. Bradley and P. Petro (eds.), *Truth Claims: Representation and Human Rights*, Rutgers University Press, London 2002, pp. 187–201.

35 S. Cohen, *States of Denial: Knowing About Atrocities and Suffering*, Polity Press, London 2001.

Emotions, neutral in themselves, play a vital role both in connecting to and disconnecting people from the sufferer.

There was consensus in all the studies that information about human rights violations and humanitarian crises should be shocking and evoke sadness and some degree of upset.[36] Whether emotions connect or disconnect, however, seems to be determined by two factors: whether the emotions evoked by the knowledge are manageable and whether they are recognised as having integrity of purpose. As the 'switching off' type of denial has illustrated, if emotions are overwhelming people respond by switching off and disconnecting. Equally, if people feel their emotions are manipulated, they also disconnect and, some have claimed, their attitude towards requests for help and involvement hardens. Although people's capacity to manage their emotions varies from individual to individual and at different times in their lives, the data suggest that shock tactics and overly traumatic communications, particularly when de-contextualised or in soundbites, are counterproductive in general. Often these evoke helplessness and result in disconnection.

> Alan: 'I can't stand it, it hurts me so much I just flick away, it makes me feel sick in a way.'

Although Alan took part in a study several years after Bob, their words are almost identical and confirm that if the information is too traumatic, the upset caused in the reader feels unmanageable and leads to self-protective disconnection – 'I just flick away'.

Empathy can be a powerful way of counteracting people's resistance to being drawn in sympathetically towards distant sufferers. Halpern and Weinstein's (2004) definition of empathy is particularly germane as they conceptualise it as the capacity and willingness to 'imagine what it is like to be someone else, to step inside their world and glimpse their concerns, cognitively and emotionally, as if from their perspective'. Cameron's (2011) more recent formulation of empathy dynamics moves away from empathy as a simply emotional response to define it as a dialogical process that might start from a dyad, but echoes and affects larger groups and communities. This nuanced perspective brings hope and empowers individuals and, crucially, builds on a capacity we all have as human beings.

However, there is a fine and unstable line between the need to evoke empathic identification between members of the public and the sufferer, and that identification becoming a threat, as in the example below.

---

36 I.B. Seu, '"*In countries like that...*": moral boundaries and implicatory denial in response to human rights appeals' (2012) 16(8) *The International Journal of Human Rights* 1170–1182; I.B. Seu, *Passivity Generation: Human Rights and Everyday Morality*, Palgrave, London 2013; I.B. Seu and S. Orgad, 'Mediated humanitarian knowledge; audiences' reactions and moral actions' 2014 *Final Report* <www.bbk.ac.uk/psychosocial/FinalReportBruna.pdf>.

> Francine: 'Like that one, this quote, it's like this quote from the kids or there's the quotes from the women saying, so you know then it's come from them themselves. I don't want to read that. It's just too much. Because you're like putting yourself in that position and you start to feel it yourself and it's not fair to play with emotions like that and it's not nice. You can't imagine what they've gone through and you don't want to imagine what they've gone through, so I won't read it.'

In terms of the tension mentioned at the beginning of the chapter, Francine's words are a good example of the complexities underpinning the 'I wish but I can't'. Francine explains that particularly when the sufferer 'speaks to her' through direct quotes contained in the information, she automatically empathises with the sufferer – 'you're like putting yourself in that position'. However, that breaks down the protective distance and the sufferer's pain becomes Francine's pain – 'you start to feel it yourself'. She continues by implicitly criticising NGOs who brought this information to her for playing with her emotions, which will be briefly addressed later on. The complexity of this interaction is captured in the stated ambivalence about knowing and not wanting to know – 'I don't want to read that. It's just too much' – and the tension between her automatic empathic identification and her active turning away – 'you don't want to imagine what they've gone through'. In Francine's case, the ambivalence and tension are resolved by preventing the knowledge – 'so I won't read it'.

Additionally, audiences are sophisticated and media-savvy. Audience reactions should be understood within the highly commercialised context of western societies. People are used to have their emotions manipulated by advertising and have developed sophisticated ways of responding and decoding communications aimed at evoking strong emotions in them. When they detect a manipulative intention, for example in fundraising, their response is fury. So the guilt, which was intended to tap into people moral standards and make them respond sympathetically, backfires and produces further distancing and suspicion (see Seu (2013) and Seu and Orgad (2014) for further discussion). This response was identified throughout all the studies, even in participants who had been staunch supporters of human rights and humanitarian causes over their lifetimes.

> Caroline: 'When I feel they're (NGOS) trying to manipulate my emotions I switch off. … You can't keep hitting the same note, after a bit you get a hardening of attitudes and a backlash.'

Additional to emotions having to be manageable and have integrity of purpose, reparative emotions also played an important role in acknowledgment.

Suski, grappling with the ubiquitous presence of children in humanitarian communications, argues that: 'When adults help children, we are in negotiation with our own childhood, and the line between self and other is blurred, as is the distinction between altruism and self-interest'.[37] Judging from the biographical reasons why people respond to human rights appeals it seems that people are often motivated by a wish to vicariously repair some damage in their own lives (for example, a man whose father was violent, or participants who had been abused as children). So the line between us and the other, at close scrutiny becomes increasingly blurred, which can also illustrate the importance of denial in self-protectively hardening the boundaries between self and others.

For the purposes of connectedness, however, the wish for reparation is a powerful force that can potentially be harnessed in the service of upholding human rights.

7. MEANINGFUL UNDERSTANDING

Participants experienced human rights violations to be so removed from their daily lives that they seemed to be 'happening on another planet'. The horror, sense of disbelief and difficulties in 'getting their head around it' militate against a helpful understanding and the basic capacity to think. It seems difficult to find a language and a way of thinking about unthinkable horror that can fit into everyday experience. The way in which the public is informed about human rights violations, through soundbites and NGO communications, is a double-edged sword – it informs on one hand, but distances on the other. Similar to emotions, information in itself also has neutral valence. It is necessary for acknowledgment but it can easily feed into denial. What came across clearly from all the studies is audiences' widespread cynicism towards media and distrust of the motivation behind NGO communications. People experienced soundbites at best as de-contextualised information, but most often participants talked of feeling bombarded with horrors and requests for donations. For this reason many welcomed documentaries and tried to inform themselves further, but in a society where time is a very precious commodity, it is hard for the ordinary citizen to find the time and the mental space to do so. These difficulties point to the gap between us – rushed and self-preoccupied viewers – and them – the victims of human rights violations. We have seen how easily this gap gets filled with prejudice and stereotypical fantasies about the Other. Hence meaningful understanding is essential, both in enabling members of the public to contextualise and make sense of the horrors they are informed about, and to process emotionally the traumatic content of the information. The extract from Jonathan, in response to the campaign from Amnesty below, exemplifies these processes.

---

[37] L. Suski, 'Children, suffering, and the humanitarian appeal' in: R.A. Wilson and R.D. Brown (eds.), *Humanitarianism and suffering*, Cambridge University Press, Cambridge 2009, p. 2010.

Jonathan: 'I saw that and I thought, I didn't particularly think that was an amazing picture,[38] but obviously, like, it's okay, and then I turned over and saw the thing on the next thing,[39] that artillery destroyer... At first I thought it was, like, fireworks or something, and then I read it and I was like, oh my God!! That's, like, a cluster bomb attack or something, isn't it? And, then you realise these people are running for their lives, and that really hit home, and then that made me want to read all of this, and then what I realised is, as I was reading it, I didn't feel like when I read these things. I didn't feel like it was trying to get money out of me. I felt like it was trying to educate me, and so that made me want to read more. In fact, I didn't finish reading all of it, because I didn't have enough time, so... if you've got a spare one, I'll take it away.'

---

[38] Jonathan is referring to the first image, captioned '*Some people can never forget the horrors they witnessed*'.

[39] Jonathan is referring to the second image, portraying people running.

Here we can see how the understanding gained through reading the communication strengthens and fosters connectedness between Jonathan and the distant sufferer. Although he is emotionally aroused by the information he does not want to switch off – on the contrary, he wants to know more. Others similarly commented on how being able to understand the historical and socio-cultural reasons behind events helped them relate to the information better and enabled them to manage their own emotions and helplessness. This applied not only to specific human rights violations, but also to human rights principles in general.

The data leave no doubt that the Universal Declaration of Human Rights (UDHR) has become universally normative and fully accepted and respected, at least in principle. This in itself is a positive sign and supports Igantieff's optimistic view that human rights have become accepted into ordinary parlance.[40] But it does not necessarily mean that these principles are understood or meaningfully integrated into people's everyday lives. Indeed empirical evidence consistently points to a widespread level of ignorance and confusion about the UDHR.[41] Without this meaningful understanding, it is hard to make sense of human rights violations and to know how to properly respond in acknowledgement. Instead, disjointed thinking is likely to occur which prevents a meaningful reconnection with the historical roots and geopolitical lines of responsibility we are all embroiled in. Current European attitudes (particularly in the UK) towards asylum seekers are a good example of disjointed thinking. A recent article published in the British tabloid *The Sun*,[42] in which refugees fleeing from civil war and the threat of torture are re-framed as 'vermin' flooding Europe to rob us of our benefits, provide a good example of how disjointed thinking interferes with people's capacity for acknowledgment, empathy and connectedness. Disjointed thinking is not a purely cognitive operation. Indeed vocabularies of denial, as well as ideological propaganda, are highly evocative emotionally, evoking public anxiety and feelings of being under threat.

In summary, we can see the illusory nature of a separation between emotions and cognition, as well as self and other. Manageable and empathic emotions, together with meaningful understanding, work in a symbiotic relationship as powerful connectors, supporting each other and fostering acknowledgment.

---

40 M. Ignatieff, *The Rights Revolution*, Anansi, Toronto 2000.

41 K. Ballagan, S. Castell, K. Brough and H. Friemert, *Public Perception of Human Rights*, Equality and Human Rights Commission 2009; I.B. Seu, *Passivity Generation: Human Rights and Everyday Morality*, Palgrave, London 2013.

42 'Rescue boats? I'd gunships to stop migrants' *The Sun* <www.thesun.co.uk/sol/homepage/suncolumnists/katiehopkins/6414865/Katie-Hopkins-I-would-use-gunships-to-stop-migrants.html>.

8. MORALLY SIGNIFICANT

People need to feel they can make a difference. There is ample empirical evidence that proof of efficacy is a key element in motivating people to act but finding actions that can be morally significant for an ordinary person when confronted with human rights violations is particularly challenging. Despite all the problematic, and often in the long term, counterproductive effects of donations[43] to humanitarian causes as a form of action, at least people can see a connection between their 'acknowledgement' and an effect on the situation. The success of the popular Oxfam campaign 'Unwrapped – Gift a Goat'[44]' is due precisely to the clear and visible effectiveness of the action. People are told of a problem and given a simple and manageable solution. Human rights problems do not lend themselves to similarly simple and practical solutions. Petitions and letter writing might have some visible effectiveness but, as many participants said, they are perceived as a little bandage on a very big wound and do not really address the cause of the problem. Unlike humanitarian appeals, which overall offer a recognisable line of connection between individual action (particularly donations) and benefits for the victim, human rights appeals offer a less identifiable line. Human rights NGOs give feedback to their supporters, and their newsletters contain stories of successful interventions, but these are easily overshadowed by new violations and seemingly endless suffering. Bearing this in mind it is understandable that ordinary people tend to feel overwhelmed, hopeless and helpless.

In the recently published *Finding Frames* Darnton and Kirk[45] argue that the public have far-reaching capacity to make a difference, far beyond donations. They talk of the 'impact associated with the public's actions and conversations in the public sphere including those in the media, responding to public concerns. These interventions open up space for the kind of political, socio-economic and pro-environmental change that is necessary to tackle global poverty. The public's role here is more than pressuring the government to accede to campaigning demands, it is about opening up the political and wider societal space to the possibility of deeper change. It is only with deeper change that we can build new institutions and societal norms, which in turn will enable different models of development, and more effective results'. Yet it was clear from the studies that this is not the experience of the majority of people who, on the contrary, feel despondent and that fighting for human rights is hopeless and futile.

---

43 Offering a quick and short term way of connecting with humanitarian problems often followed by guilt-free disconnection.

44 'Oxfam Unwrapped charity gifts' *Oxfam* <www.oxfam.org.uk/shop/oxfam-unwrapped?pscid=ps_ggl_CT_Unwrapped+2014+-+BAU&gclid=CLm888zpoMUCFernwgodkp8AHQ>.

45 A. Darnton and K. Kirk, *Finding Frames: New Ways to Engage the UK Public in Global Poverty*, DFID, Oxfam 2012.

The study on humanitarianism showed that when wanting to alleviate distant human suffering, people tend to apply moral principles and practices of care they are familiar with.[46] In this sense humanitarianism becomes a site for people to rehearse familiar ethics and moral principles. The humanitarian model lends itself to this, not just through donations, but also through more direct relating (e.g. child sponsoring, volunteering, trips, etc.). In this case, empathy and identification help to bridge the distance through a perception of similarity and closeness with the beneficiary. But with human rights violations the identification is often too threatening, partly because of the helplessness that comes with the identification, and because familiar practices of care do not apply. Additionally, people's expressed desire for embodied, close and relational forms of caring can turn into an obstacle to the 'leap of care' necessary to go beyond one's own immediate circle of care when taking responsibility for violations of human rights in distant places. Indeed, although the normative to help suffering others is well established and internalised, it often becomes parochial and concentrates on close circles of care. It is clear from the data that people care for others and tend to respond proactively but overall to causes that fall within their immediate circle of care. The challenge therefore is how to foster the 'leap of care' required to move people beyond their most immediate bonds and identification towards caring for distant Others and fostering a so-called ' identification with all humanity'[47] which has been found to be a key characteristic of people actively supportive of human rights principles.

Some have argued that for this to be possible, the provision of care has to be institutionalised, not only for effectiveness but also because a right of care, as with positive welfare rights in general, cannot convincingly be linked to individual duty.[48] Instead, it might be more helpful to talk of legal responsibility and accountability in regards to the state, while in terms of individuals how to move them from 'tribal' or 'in-group' altruism to 'universal' altruism. According to New, this consists of moving beyond conditional forms of giving and reciprocity towards social practices which create solidarities across the boundaries of place, gender, culture and ethnicity.[49] Hoggett further argues that these practices should be embodied in society in a non-institutional way, with the state and leaders 'leading by example'.[50] Far from this scenario, the vast majority of participants across all the studies repeatedly expressed deep

---

46 I.B. Seu, 'Mediated humanitarian knowledge, audiences' responses and moral actions' 2014 Birkbeck University of London <www.bbk.ac.uk/psychosocial/our-research/research-projects-current/mediated-humanitarian-knowledge-audiences-responses-and-moral-actions>.

47 S. Mcfarland, M. Webb and D. Brown, 'All Humanity Is My Ingroup: A Measure and Studies of Identification With All Humanity' (2012) *Journal of Personality and Social Psychology*, DOI: 10.1037/a0028724.

48 C. Cleent, *Care, Autonomy, and Justice: Feminism and the Ethic of Care*, Westview Press, Oxford 1996.

49 C. New, *Agency, Health and Social Survival*, Taylor and Francis, London 1996.

50 P. Hoggett, *Emotional Life and the Politics of Welfare*, Macmillan, Basingstoke 2000.

disillusionment and distrust of politicians who are experienced at best as corrupt and sometimes as the source of human rights violations. Yet, there were some isolated examples of an internalised ethics of care that is Universalist and makes the citizens feel empowered.

The extracts from Jill from Finland and Dahlia from Sweden, are amongst these rare examples.

> [2] Jill: 'Oh yes, I mean, well, Scandinavia is so ah, we have a very high level of living standards. We don't have people begging on the streets, you just don't see them because the government takes care of them. And then you do see this kind of articles [referring to the focus groups' props] all the time because we are such a small country we can't afford to ignore everybody else so we do get lots of information about what's going on. And it is terrible. I have to admit I'm very proud of my country because we send people to work with, in these crisis areas and even working lots with Amnesty International.'

This account provides important information on what might foster proactive and socially responsible reactions from the public. First, we see the introduction of an ethics of care offered by a government that leads by example and 'takes care' of the vulnerable and needy. Second, in terms of knowledge – similarly to what has been repeated in all focus groups – Jill reports a large amount of information on human rights violations; but unlike the others, she frames this positively and as essential for a small country to be connected to others. In terms of action, Finland actively intervenes in humanitarian crises, which makes Jill proud of her country. There is no sense of helplessness in Jill's account; rather, her narrative upholds the importance of connectedness, and thus the information about atrocities is integrated through this logic and is not felt as threatening. The active and caring stance taken by the government clearly plays a key role in the alternative moral reasoning presented by Jill.

> [5] Dahlia: 'I think also that it depends on where you're coming from as you said because if you come from a country like Sweden where we're from you can't really say, Q<well you need to look in your own back yard>Q, because our problems [laugh] are ridiculous in comparison to this. Our economy is so strong, our country has no problems if you look on an international level, it's seriously it's like, you cannot use that argument coming from that background … if you come from most of Europe our relative problems are very minor. And also I was just thinking when they, when Sweden's economy went down, together with everyone else's I guess, Sweden has always had one per cent given to the third world of the GNI and they made that half. Half a per cent all of a sudden and there was, people were so upset and people were so, there was a large going on and people were like, Q<this is just unbelievable>Q, like this is one of the very, very few years, we've had very left wing government for very long, not very left wing but social democrats in power and those were during the few years that there was a right wing government I think, and people were extremely

upset because of this like, Q<we may have problems, our economy may be in a down period right now but if you look at the third world then we can never ever like defend that kind of actions.>Q'

Jill and Dahlia thus propose a causal explanation for parochialism based on education and political climate. Dahlia's comments in particular provide evidence that if a country leads by example, and leaders foster a climate of social responsibility and universal solidarity, their citizens will internalise those values. Citizens protesting because of governmental cuts to foreign aid seems unimaginable in the context of what is currently happening in Europe, particularly in relation to refugees and asylum seekers, but Dahlia's account explains it as a natural corollary of years of Swedish government taking a responsive approach to Third World problems. A morality of connectedness and contextualisation, rather than individualism and insularity, is key to this script.

Unfortunately, there were no parallel examples coming from UK residents in terms of trust in the nation's leaders. Yet, inspiring leadership was mentioned by participants as a selection criterion when reflecting on what would make them take action. The following campaign by Amnesty International about human rights in Burma depicting marching monks and San Suu Kyi, at that time the leader of the opposition and chairperson of the National League for Democracy (NLD), evoked many positive responses.

Many participants selected this communication amongst the many in the pack. They expressed passionate admiration and respect for San Suu Kyi because she represented dignity in the face of suffering, and peaceful resistance. Many participants commented on what her face expressed: calm but firm and strong, and, crucially, human. A lot seemed to be projected onto this image as well as on the iconic image of the monks' feet signifying how everyday acts, such as walking, can acquire deep political significance and can be powerful acts of acknowledgments.

Rachel: 'Amnesty International, it does pump a lot of money into, obviously, infrastructure, but it also has people like Aung San Suu Kyi, it's just, they have like figureheads that are human. I don't know, like, I really like... not just saying, oh, generally poorer people who are having bad time, but no; this person is having a really bad time. Q<We're going to follow her to see what she's doing when she gets freed, we're going to use her as a figurehead>Q. Like, I really like that, personally.'

For others, San Suu Kyi and her liberation were the living proof of the power of resistance, international solidarity and pressure.

Harold: 'But if you create enough [pressure] ... it works.'
Hal: 'It's not likely though, isn't it?'
Harold: 'She [Aung San Suu Kyi] is out now, isn't it? And that was through public opinion, that was through world...'
UM Outside pressure.
Harold: 'Yes, that's what got her released; it wasn't about... it didn't cost any money to get her released. ... if you find a person that's held accountable and you make enough noise, then it's [possible]'.

9. CONCLUSIONS

People do not respond neutrally or mechanistically to human rights information. On the contrary, human rights information is filtered through a metaphorical psychosocial prism, which is made of beliefs and attitudes originating from various sources: global geopolitical, national and local, personal biographies, emotional and moral. These provide lenses through which the public understand and respond to human rights information.

I propose that instead of looking at public reactions as *either* socially determined, *or* as intra-psychically affected, we should regard denial and acknowledgement as something generated by a conglomerate of social *and* psychological influences. Geopolitical, socio-historical and contingently localised factors frame how the public come to understand human rights and the boundaries of social responsibility and action. These social understandings acquire personal meaning and significance through individual emotional, biographical and intra-psychic trajectories.[51] It is essential therefore to be attentive both to the social confines of discourse, and to personal and affective resonances and emotional stumbling blocks to higher responsiveness. Related to, and underpinning, these, are personal sensitivities and specific personal and biographical experiences.

What emerges from this conceptualisation is a 'troubled subjectivity' – an understanding of the individual as a psychosocial site of conflict where a variety

[51] I.B. Seu, *Passivity Generation: Human Rights and Everyday Morality,* Palgrave, London 2013.

of forces, both socio-cultural and intra-psychic, interact dynamically with each other. Subjectivity is full of ambivalence, instability and discomfort.

The ongoing negotiation between clashing forces – 'internal' and 'external', social responsibility versus self-protective preoccupations, altruism and acknowledgment versus the comfort of ignorance – generate an unstable equilibrium that could move either way; either towards more proactive engagement with human rights issues or become further entrenched in passivity and disconnection. Therefore, conceptualising public responses as a dynamic equilibrium challenges the notion of public passivity as static and fixed and replaces it with a view of an unstable field in which the subject struggles with contrasting and opposing forces. A psychosocial approach, interested in conflict and ambivalence, and attentive to factors originating from 'out there' and 'inside' of people, can offer a thicker and more complex understanding of the conflictual, dynamic and fluid nature of public (un) responsiveness.

This chapter has provided some examples of these complex dynamics and of the symbiotic intertwining of the psychological with the social in processes of denial and acknowledgement. Further empirical research is necessary to gain insight into the multifaceted and ever changing expressions of denial in order to combat them and turn them into acknowledgment.

PART I
CHILDREN'S RIGHTS

CHAPTER IV

DIAGNOSING AND DISPELLING DENIALISM REGARDING CHILDREN

James G. Dwyer

Denialism is a useful lens through which to think about children's legal and social situation. Diagnosing it might also be a relatively effective way of producing progress. By pinpointing explicit or implicit premises in the reasoning of those who would justify unjust treatment of a group and showing the premises entail denial of something demonstrably true, one might make greater headway in converting those others than one might by presenting the case in favour of just treatment. Many people cannot open their minds to others' views until forced to see problems with their own views.

1. FORMS OF DENIALISM REGARDING CHILDREN

I identify below four forms denialism takes in discourse concerning children, or in other words, four types of premises – usually implicit rather than explicit, perhaps even unconscious in most instances – that underlie asserted justifications for treating children in certain ways that, from an objective perspective, are harmful. The four forms of denialism are moral, conceptual, descriptive and empirical. One could categorise or characterise the phenomenon I describe differently; the typology I adopt is not itself important, but simply a means of imposing order on the analysis. The four forms I identify are inter-related and mutually reinforcing.

1.1. MORAL DENIALISM

The problematic moral premise is a denial of children's equal moral status. By 'moral status' I mean the relative position a being occupies, in a moral hierarchy, by virtue of which it commands moral concern. To the extent a being has moral status, moral agents must pay its interests or integrity some regard in their decision making. If a being is of lesser or no moral status, moral agents may give less or no weight to its interests in rational decision making.

The view that children are of inferior moral status relative to autonomous adults, and therefore less worthy of moral regard, used to be explicit, just as a similar view was once explicit regarding slaves, women, and mentally disabled persons. Today it is more commonly implicit. Outwardly almost no one today says children are of lesser moral worth relative to adults. But it seems implicit in many arguments as to why children should not receive certain protections or benefits that they are simply less deserving of moral regard than are adults. In fact, there remains a widespread tendency to view children as possessions of parents, communities, or states, rather than as equal persons. Jan Willems characterises this as 'parentiarchy' or 'transgenerational discrimination', and many of the examples of the phenomenon in this chapter are ones he has highlighted.[1]

This implicit denigration of children is manifest rhetorically in *sui generis* pseudo-reasoning about the laws governing their lives and about how society and individuals may or must treat them. Rarely does one see reference to general principles, applicable to *persons*, that support assertions about what is appropriate or just. Instead, scholars, state actors, and the general public speak as if children were a separate species having nothing in common with adults. For example, in justifying corporal punishment, many assert simply that it is effective in producing desired behaviour, as if that is all one must show to justify hitting children, even though no one would think 'it works' is a sufficient moral basis for using hitting to alter the behaviour of any other group of human beings (or household pets, for that matter), because general principles about when it is appropriate for one person to hit another person simply do not countenance such a justification.

When someone takes a position defensible only on a supposition that children are of inferior moral status, yet claims to accept children's moral equality, one need only show the irrational inconsistency underlying the position. But how would one argue against anyone who explicitly asserted that children *do* occupy a lower moral status, that they simply do not matter as much as adults in moral deliberations? Is it possible to prove the truth or falsity of such an assertion? Likewise, if someone said that some other vulnerable group – defined, for example, by race, gender, disability, sexual orientation, etc. – comprises inferior beings less worthy of moral regard, how could one prove them wrong? A brief digression into moral philosophy provides an answer to these questions.

Several years ago, I undertook to develop a comprehensive theory of what gives rise to moral status in our moral psychology and moral practices, and then

---

1 For further explanation of these concepts, see J.C.M. Willems, 'Principles and Promises in the Convention on the Rights of the Child and the Convention on the Rights of Persons with Disabilities' in: L. Waddington, G. Quinn and E. Flynn (eds.), *European Yearbook of Disability Law*, Intersentia, Cambridge-Antwerp-Portland 2012, pp. 26–28.

apply that theory to children.[2] Much had been written about the moral status of particular entities – in particular, animals and foetuses. But there had been little attempt to look at moral status comprehensively, to develop a general theory, and no attempt to analyse the moral status of children with any rigour.

One basic flaw I exposed in prevailing discussions about moral status is a pervasive assumption that there is only one determinant of moral status, a single criterion for determining who or what matters morally. Advocates for particular positions or for a particular group of creatures identify a criterion for moral status that supports their view and argue for recognising that criterion as a basis for deserving moral regard. What no one had done was to demonstrate that their preferred criterion was the only one – that is, that any other possible criteria are inappropriate or inconsistent with our moral practices.

The criterion with the most currency in the history of philosophy (unsurprisingly, given that philosophy is written by philosophers, whose sense of self-worth depends on the supreme importance of intellectual ability) is higher-order cognitive capacities. Some philosophers have even maintained that non-autonomous persons cannot be said to possess any moral rights. Elevating rational agency above all other traits is obviously self-serving for educated white men wanting to dominate the world and all its inhabitants, and white men have historically justified their domination even over other human adults by depicting those others as having lesser cognitive capacities by virtue of their race or gender.

My book showed that, even if arguments in favour of ascribing moral status on the basis of cognitive capacities are sound, they say nothing about whether other characteristics can also give rise to moral status. I found no rational justification for making rational agency the only, or even the most important, determinant of moral worth. Arguments by animal rights proponents that sentience is a basis for moral status are also plausible. Yet the animal rights proponents likewise fail to establish that their preferred criterion is the only one. There is also purchase to the idea that mere aliveness makes a being worthy of consideration, as Albert Schweitzer maintained.[3]

A complete descriptive account of our moral psychology and practices regarding moral status, I show, supports the view that there are several criteria of moral worthiness. Both our non-rational empathetic responses to other beings and our sense of what makes ourselves worthy of moral consideration support a conclusion that several characteristics of beings make them matter morally and worthy of respect – not just rationality, but also the potential for healthy growth and development, sentience, aliveness, and being an object of concern to others. Only based on a multi-criterion account of moral status can we explain, for

---

2 See J.G. Dwyer, *Moral Status and Human Life: The Case for Children's Superiority*, Cambridge University Press, Cambridge 2011.

3 See A. Schweitzer, *Out of My Life and Thought*, C. Campton, trans. 1961, Henry Holt & Co., New York 1933, pp. 158–59.

example, why an adult human who loses rational capacities nevertheless retains moral status and must be treated with respect.

As to children specifically, the book suggests that on most of these plausible bases for ascribing moral status, children (I focus, for illustrative purposes, on children in the pre-teen years) might actually *exceed* adults (I use middle-aged adults for comparison). Children have more acute senses, manifest more aliveness, are developing cognitively at a far greater rate, and are generally objects of greater concern to particular individuals. Enormous difficulties might face someone attempting a precise calculation of relative moral status, but this multi-criterion account at least provides robust theoretical support for a view that children are at least of equal moral status relative to adults. Thus, their interests are at least as deserving of respect in moral decision making and it is presumptively (but subject to rebuttal) illegitimate to treat children in ways we generally deem improper with respect to adults, or to deny children rights identical or equivalent to rights we adults insist on for ourselves.

In their treatment of persons less than the age of majority, therefore, legal systems should operate on a presumption of equal treatment – as we do with, for example, adults with diminished mental faculties – and allow for some different treatment but only with justification. We should not think of children as belonging to a different and inferior species, but rather as persons, and presumptively apply to them the principles we apply to competent adults and presumptively accord them rights equivalent to those we enjoy. So rather than 'children's rights', I would promote 'extension of *person's rights* to children'. Some difference in treatment among persons based on relative degree of autonomy will surely be warranted, but we should start with an assumption of sameness, not difference, if we are to give children the respect they merit. Some concrete examples will help clarify.

1.1.1. Family Formation

The question arises regarding children at their birth: with whom will they form family relationships? The traditional way of answering presupposes children are not 'persons' but possessions of whoever created them. The proper way of answering it is to think of them as persons, persons who need – like other persons – to have family relationships but who – unlike competent adults but like some other groups of persons, such as incompetent adults – are presently incapable of choosing with whom. By beginning with a view of them as persons rather than property, we should ascribe to them rights equivalent to those which we competent adults possess in connection with family formation – namely, a right to form a relationship with the best available persons, from among those who reciprocate the choice. Persons incapable of making such choices can nevertheless possess this right; they simply need an agent to act as their proxy.

This is, in fact, the model we adopt with incompetent adults who need a caretaker guardian. We could at least approximate this model with newborn children. They have, like incompetent adults, a moral right to the best available caregiver, a right analogous to our right as competent adults to the best available spouse who reciprocates our choice. In practice, there are practical limitations on our ability to operationalise this right, but certainly we could come much closer to the ideal than we do with the current practice of consigning children to custody of biological parents regardless of their capacity for caregiving, at a minimum excluding those manifestly unfit.

1.1.2. Dissolution of Family Relationships

Likewise with getting out of family relationships that turn out to be bad: we should ask not what rights parents have to retain possession of children, or what rights children have to removal from parental custody, but rather what right do *persons* have to exit a relationship when that is in their best interests? We adults believe we should be able to exit a family relationship, such as a marriage, based solely on our determination of what is best for us; it is no longer necessary in western societies to show terrible fault on the part of a spouse, and parents have never needed a justification legally for walking away, in every way other than financial, from a relationship with a child. So, likewise, persons in a dependent relationship should have a right to exit solely because staying in the relationship is not in their best interests. And, again, we find this is the model we already deploy regarding incompetent adults; a court will terminate a guardianship based solely on a best-interests finding. There is no balancing of the ward's interests against those of the guardian, and no requirement of egregious harm against the dependent person.

1.1.3. Authority over Non-Autonomous Persons

A final example is state conferral of control *rights* over children's lives on persons whom the state makes legal parents – that is, not merely authority held as a fiduciary, and as a privilege, but an entitlement of the sort we have also with respect to our house, car, farm animals, and other items of property. Even the vaunted United Nations Convention on the Rights of the Child embraces this notion of parents having an entitlement over children, reassuring state parties in several provisions that the Convention is not meant to diminish the rights of parents and that many of children's rights should be interpreted through a lens of parental sovereignty.

Yet in every other area of law, our legal systems today categorically reject the notion that one person has a right to control the life of another.[4] Western legal systems used to accept this notion in the context of marriages – that is, that

4 For elaboration of this point, see J.G. Dwyer, *Religious Schools v. Children's Rights*, Cornell University Press, Ithaca, NY 1998, Chapter 3.

husbands have an entitlement to control their wives' lives. And some countries used to accept it with respect to humans who were enslaved. But those ways of viewing competent adults have been rejected, and today the idea is also anathema in relation to incompetent adults. The guardian for an elderly ward is not viewed as a right holder, such that if the state imposes unwelcome restrictions or duties the guardian can complain this infringes his or her rights. The guardian must instead object on the grounds, if any, that the imposition infringes a right of the ward, or the guardian could ask to be relieved of the position.

Thus, only children remain objects of others' rights, and this occurs directly because of collective denialism as to children's personhood, which allows for treating children in any way amenable to adults, without need to conform policies or treatment to the way we treat adults, competent and incompetent, nor to cite any general principles in support. This denial of children's distinct personhood is encapsulated in a term as commonly used as it is nonsensical: 'parental autonomy'. Because 'autonomy' means rule of one's self – that is, self-determination, treating parenting as an exercise of autonomy elides children's separate personhood, treats them as appendages of their parents or as objects, control of which is properly viewed as an aspect of parents' self-determination.

Recognising children's equal moral personhood would mean thinking not in *sui generis* terms but instead in more general terms: of *persons* who, like many persons over the age of majority, are unable – or have limited ability – to act in their own behalf at a particular point in time. We should ask what principles apply to such persons, and what rules respect their personhood while taking into account their current relative lack of autonomy, with respect to such life-determining state decisions as who will be a child's legal parents and what legal authority the state will give those parents.

1.2. CONCEPTUAL DENIALISM

A second form of denialism regarding children relates to how we conceptualise conflicts over how children are treated and raised – most commonly, conflicts between state regulation and wishes of parents or cultural communities. An assumption pervades thinking about children's lives, that their situatedness within families and communities and their subjection to the will of certain adults, is 'natural', private, and pre-political, as if babies today are born into a state of nature, or fall out of the sky, with the names of their owners stamped on their foreheads and in their hands a list of all powers their owners possess. Unjust subordination of racial minorities and women, when legal systems treated them as property, was similarly defended as natural and pre-political.

What is denied by this way of conceptualising children's situations is the determinative role the state plays in creating it, which in turn enables denial of the state's responsibility for harms children incur because of parental malfeasance or neglect. Moreover, it is always important to recall that the state is an agent of the collective adult will – that is, of us, so this conceptual denialism spares *us* from acknowledging *our* responsibility for the plight of children in harmful circumstances.

Consistent with this assumption as to the pre-political, private, and natural status of the family, people generally characterise state efforts to protect children from their custodians' harmful choices or behaviours as 'state intervention' – that is, a heavy-handed intrusion into the private realm, presumptively inappropriate, requiring very strong justification, or else deemed a violation of parents' rights (which are sometimes mischaracterised as 'family rights', as if young children are equal participants in collective decisions when, for example, parents send them to an authoritarian, anti-liberal elementary school or beat them in the name of discipline). Such state efforts are sometimes also characterised as violations of community rights – for example, if a state insists all children receive an autonomy-promoting education that might result in some rejecting the belief system of their parents' cultural community.

The falsity of this denialism is easily demonstrated. The obvious reality is that the state is crucially and unavoidably involved from the moment of a child's birth in creating the child's family life and community situation. There are laws dictating who a child's legal parents and custodians will be. There must be such laws, lest there be utter chaos and conflict over who takes possession of newborns. In the absence of state conferral of legal parent status on particular individuals, whether biological parents or not, those individuals would have no legal basis for taking custody of a child and precluding others from doing so. If the doctor who delivered a baby wanted to take the baby home, the birth parents would accomplish nothing by crying out to God or nature; they would need to call the police, and the police would not respond unless the birth parents had legal status conferred by the state.

As it happens, western societies uniformly confer initial legal parent status on a child's biological parents without exception, regardless of their fitness to care for a child. This 'structural disrespect' has many serious and lifelong adverse consequences for many children.[5] Yet because parentage based on nothing other than procreation is so universal and matches what occurred millennia ago in human groupings lacking any form of state apparatus, it appears natural and inevitable. But it is not 'natural' in the sense of being written in the stars and effected without human action; it is today a state-created legal practice that each society collectively chooses and that could be otherwise. It should be subject to examination and assessed in terms of whether it comports with

5 See J.C.M. Willems, 'Principles and Promises in the Convention on the Rights of the Child and the Convention on the Rights of Persons with Disabilities' in: L. Waddington, G. Quinn and E. Flynn (eds.), *European Yearbook of Disability Law*, Intersentia, Cambridge-Antwerp-Portland 2012, pp. 26–28.

children's human rights. Every child is entitled to that assessment, just as every individual adult is entitled to assessment of whether legal rules governing family relationships between adults comport with their human rights.

The obvious reality is that states' blunt decision making regarding parentage and blindness as to the abject unfitness of many biological parents cannot possibly be deemed consistent with newborn children's human rights. The state intervenes in children's lives in the most profound way when it creates legal parent–child relationships and bestows extraordinary powers on the persons whom it makes legal parents, and *that* intervention requires justification. If the state's doing so predictably harms a child, it is unjustified and is just as much a violation of the child's human rights as would be the state's forcing a woman to marry a man with a history of domestic violence.

Again, comparison with the situation of incompetent adults is illuminating. We recognise this principle in creating legal guardian–ward relationships; if the state chose someone with a history of maltreating the elderly, and that guardian ended up abusing the ward, we would charge the state with responsibility for the harm that befell the vulnerable adult. In fact, people actually recognise this to be true also of state-created parent–child relationships whenever the adults involved are not biological parents – in particular, in adoption. If the state selected as substitute parents for a child applicants addicted to drugs who previously maltreated other children, we would deem this outrageous, and a horrible abuse of state power. And if those adoptive parents abused the child we would demand that the state be held accountable. Yet it is no less outrageous when the state does this in creating a child's first family relationship. Denialism as to the state's crucial involvement in creating children's families wrongly spares the state (our agent) from having to justify its often tragically bad choices as to initial parentage. This denialism prevents us from holding the state, and therefore ourselves, accountable.

This myth of family privacy also extends to children's fates after the state has created legal parent–child relationships. What content the legal status of parent entails reflects a choice and action by the state. Unless the state infuses the parental role with special privileges and powers, it contains none; adult and child would stand in the same relationship as that between a child and a neighbour or complete stranger. Children would possess the same rights against parents as against any other person, including rights against being taken into possession, stripped of clothing, being hit for any reason, or being forced to live in a dangerous neighbourhood. And the parents would have no greater power over the child than over a neighbour or a neighbour's child.

To the extent legal parents in any legal system do possess powers to dictate particular aspects of a child's life, such as education, medical treatment, residence, and discipline, it is solely because the state gives it to them. The denial of this reality does great mischief because it absolves the state – and, again, that means us, adult society, whom the state represents – from having to justify conferring these powers and privileges. State actors feel no need to justify empowering parents completely to deny children any schooling, as state laws do throughout the US; or privileging certain adults to hit certain small children, creating an exception to the general human-rights-based legal rule that hitting is a crime; or to justify empowering certain adults to have parts of children's genitals surgically amputated, because no one is pointing out that the state has done that. Instead, the state sits smugly and demands that anyone who thinks things should be otherwise must mount a compelling demonstration that children need the state to restrict parents' liberty or power in order to prevent grievous and observable damage. The burden of proof is in the wrong place and it is excessive.

In this context as well, we see that historically the state subordinated other groups of humans as well by conferring such powers on their oppressors. Today it would be obvious to us that the state is implicated if the law conferred on husbands the power to decide whether and where wives would receive education or privileged husbands to hit their wives, and we would treat this state action as presumptively and egregiously wrong. Likewise if the state changed the legal rules governing guardianship to permit corporal punishment of adult wards with diminished mental capacity – for example, an elderly parent suffering from dementia. That the state itself had deprived the dependent adults of something important would be evident. But somehow there is widespread denial that what parents do to children they do because the state has enabled and empowered them to do it.

Moreover, it is not just parents on whom the state confers potentially harmful powers. Some legal systems in some contexts grant powers over children's lives to cultural communities, entitling those communities to exercise jurisdiction over children's family lives, places of residence, education, and vulnerability to abuse. For example, in the US, the federal government has treated children who have the slightest genetic connection to any Native American tribe, regardless of any social connection with the tribe, as property of Native American tribes, in legislation referring explicitly to children as a tribal resource. As another example: until the 1990s, the law in many states effectively treated black children as the property of 'the African American community' in laws and practices proscribing trans-racial adoption.

This community power over children also came to be seem as natural, rather than as a direct result of state action, as if children enter the world with a group membership or ownership stamped on their sides, branded like cattle, and the state merely recognises this natural fact. But that is false; the state makes children possessions of communities, conferring jurisdiction, imbuing the adults in that community with collectively exercised powers over the children. It could do otherwise, and it should have to justify treating children this way.

This observation applies also at the national level in international law. As currently interpreted, the Children's Rights Convention and the Hague Adoption Convention treat children as national possessions, not free to emigrate for purposes of family formation to the same extent that an adult is – that is, based on a determination that that is in their best interests all things considered. Instead, UNICEF and the Children's Rights Committee interpret these special Conventions for children as conferring on nations the power to confine children within national borders, like prisoners, hundreds of thousands of them in institutional facilities, despite the availability of vastly better lives in loving families in other countries.

This prevailing view of national power over parentless children also illustrates starkly the first form of denialism – that is, denying children's equal personhood, treating them like a completely separate category of human being, not sharing in the human rights of persons. There are other treaties, applicable to all 'persons', that pronounce rights of emigration, conferring on '*all* persons' very strong rights to leave their native country, rights nations may not infringe without compelling reason – namely, the European Convention on Human Rights, Protocol 4 (Art. 2(2)) and the International Covenant on Civil and Political Rights (Art. 12(2)). Yet no one in the world of international adoption thinks of those Conventions as applicable to children. No one has thought to assert those Conventions as a basis for international institutions with real power chastising Russia and other countries that have refused to allow orphaned children to leave to start a new and far better life. Instead, people think only in terms of special Conventions relating to children, as if children have no rights unless we create special rights documents; they have no rights as persons but only possibly as children if the legal community has bothered, out of charity, to create special rights for them.[6]

1.3. DESCRIPTIVE DENIALISM

A third form of denial relates to how adults deliberating about children's lives describe their welfare and needs. In doing so, there is a widespread tendency to impute to children their parents' interests, as if the two persons – parent and child – are a single entity. There are, to be sure, ways in which the interests of parents and children are intertwined and interdependent, just as is true with spouses. For example, it is difficult to enjoy one's own home life if a person with whom one shares that home is miserable, especially if one is completely dependent on care from that other person. But by no means is there a complete unity of interests between two people in any type of relationship; successfully handling conflicts of interest is a virtue constitutive of being a good spouse or a good parent.

Many conflicts of interest between parent and child are routine and minor, not something the state needs to arbitrate. Do you give up a time-consuming

6 See J.G. Dwyer, 'Inter-Country Adoption and the Special Rights Fallacy' (2014) 35 *University of Pennsylvania Journal of International Law* 189.

hobby after having a child, if the child might be better off were you to do so? Do you make your two-year-old endure a five-hour car drive so you can attend a school reunion? Parents face such dilemmas on a regular basis. But other conflicts threaten greater loss of welfare for a child, yet still are often unseen. For example, regarding education, some parents wish to insulate their children from mainstream learning and autonomy-promoting experiences and instead choose to indoctrinate the children in their (the parents) religious worldview, to ensure their children grow up to think just like they do.

Many people reasoning about such cases view the situation as a conflict between the state and 'the family', as if the family is a uniform unit representing one position and the state is representing collective interests. They implicitly deny that the children's interest might be at odds with parents' desires and so fail to see the state's *parens patriae* responsibility to ensure the child receives an education conducive to development toward autonomy as a distinct person. They also fail to see, as noted previously, that the parents' position is not that of holding negative rights against state intervention, but rather that of claiming a positive right to state conferral of an extraordinary and presumptively illicit power – that is, the power to stifle the intellectual growth of another human being.

A related phenomenon likewise illustrating the tendency to elide the distinction between parent and child, or between adults and children in a cultural community, is invocation of 'culture' in conflicts between the position of advocates for children and those who aim to protect parents, communities, and nations against having children removed from them. In discussing certain issues mentioned above, such as international adoption, indigenous communities' jurisdiction over children, and inter-racial adoption, people who are actually concerned only about interests and supposed rights of adults in particular, concerned that adults will feel denigrated or struggling communities will be further weakened by having children removed from them – routinely ascribe to children an interest in 'maintaining their culture'. Then implicitly, without explanation, they treat that supposed interest as more important than anything else, even more important than having a family at all, because the result of their position would be that children remain in orphanages or foster care.

There is some sense to the idea of maintaining one's culture when one is: (a) old enough to have internalised a culture and formed a sense of self based on it, or (b) destined to be labelled by others as a member of that culture regardless of whether one grows up within it. But even for people in one of those two categories, being and remaining immersed in the native culture cannot be of such importance as to override every other consideration, as evidenced by the millions of autonomous adults who choose to leave their places of origin to find better lives in different cultures, with full awareness of what they leave behind. And there is no sense to the idea of 'maintaining one's culture' when one is a newborn or infant, as is generally true of the adoption contexts mentioned above, and where the child will be growing up in a heterogeneous society in which outward appearance does not signal belonging elsewhere. Just as children do not enter the world branded with an owner's name, they also do not enter the world with a culture, and insisting that they do is adult-serving delusion, resting on a denial of children's distinct personhood and interests.

A particularly absurd example of misplaced, adult-centred preoccupation with culture was a case before the United States Supreme Court in 2013, involving application of the Indian Child Welfare Act.[7] The child was born to a Mexican woman. The child's father was 3/128 Cherokee – that is, roughly 2% – but had put his name on the Cherokee nation membership list. Neither birth parent had ever lived in a Cherokee community. But federal law gives tribes the power to decide who their members are, and by Cherokee rules this child, with 3/256 Cherokee ancestry, was a member of that tribe and thus, under federal law, presumptively the tribe's to do with as it wished, because of this trivial ancestral connection.

With astonishing ease, many Americans, including many law professors,[8] supported the transfer of this child from her Italian-American adoptive parents to strangers on a reservation, where poverty and domestic abuse are rampant, invoking the child's supposed need to be connected to her Cherokee culture. The absurdity entirely escaped them that they were declaring 'the culture' of this child – an infant with no experience of Cherokee life, whose ancestry was one percent Cherokee, and who was probably 50% Mexican and 49% European American (perhaps Italian American) – just *is* Cherokee, and that the child would suffer unless raised Cherokee. It escaped them because the welfare of children was not their true focus; they were moved by sympathy for Native American tribes, whose adult members have left in droves to find better lives elsewhere, to use children's lives to serve the perceived interests or desires of (adult) tribe members, refusing to acknowledge that what is best for tribes might not be best for children, whether the children have 1% tribal ancestry or 100%.

Perhaps the most tragic manifestation of this failure to recognise a divergence of interests between adults and children afflicts children born to unfit parents in dysfunctional communities. Regardless of how dangerous the family and community circumstances are that a newborn's biological parents present, the prevailing view is that it is best for the child to have those adults as parents and to restrict the liberty of those adults as little as possible. This is why generation after generation of people from the same families and the same communities are in the child maltreatment system, in delinquency proceedings, in drug rehabilitation, and in prisons. Because of blindness to the stark conflict of interests between newborns and unfit parents, states continue to force children to be in legal relationships with adults destined to harm them, and to empower those adults to force children to

7 *Adoptive Couple v. Baby Girl*, 133 S. Ct. 2552 (2013).

8 See e.g. B. Atwood, 'Hard Facts, Muddled Law: Deciphering the Baby Veronica Decision' (2013) 93 *Boston University Law Review* Annex 3.

live in a hellish environment. This violates basic human rights of children; it is an egregious abuse of state power to force children to endure this horror, when there are millions of qualified adoption applicants in western nations.[9] It is also terribly unwise from a societal perspective, because the vast majority of social pathologies can be traced to bad parentage decisions, to the states subjecting children unnecessarily to dangerous parents and dangerous neighbourhoods.

1.4. EMPIRICAL DENIALISM

Closely related to, and often supporting, the third form of denialism is a denial of children's actual experience, a blindness to the ways children suffer when we make adult-centred and adult-protective decisions. Probably no one is immune to this tendency to deny that one's actions adversely affect others. For scholars, policy makers, judges, and others, it is much easier, and perhaps only possible, to assert a unity of interests between adults and children if they simply ignore children's experience or baldly deny there is anything negative about children's experience, so long as it is consistent with what parents or adult leaders of a cultural community want. It is crucial, therefore, that law and policy rest on sound scientific research regarding children's welfare.[10]

Consider circumcision. The time and energy the United States medical profession has spent trying to find benefits from removing boys' foreskins is remarkable. Almost no time or energy is expended examining possible harms, including the loss of functionality or sensitivity, and highly intelligent people say the most irrational things by way of defending the practice, like 'babies can't feel pain because they don't yet have memory'. An arguably more troubling example is the obliviousness of many people involved in child protection to the impact on infants of instability during the attachment stage.[11]

Moreover, one sees repeatedly in contexts where children's interests appear to be in conflict with those of parents or ethnic community a gross misuse of scientific research by advocates for adults. In the United States, the Casey

9 See e.g. J.C.M. Willems, 'Principles and Promises in the Convention on the Rights of the Child and the Convention on the Rights of Persons with Disabilities' in: L. Waddington, G. Quinn and E. Flynn (eds.), *European Yearbook of Disability Law*, Intersentia, Cambridge-Antwerp-Portland 2012; J.C.M. Willems, 'Children's Rights at a Dignitarian Horizon of Responsible Parenthood' in: J.C.M. Willems (ed.), *Developmental and Autonomy Rights of Children: Empowering Children, Caregivers and Communities*, 2nd ed., Intersentia, Antwerp 2007; J.G. Dwyer, 'A Constitutional Birthright: The State, Parentage, and Newborn Persons' (2009) 56 *University of California, Los Angeles Law Review* 755.

10 Willems emphasises the importance of valid scientific research to counteract the widespread tendency among those operating from an adult-centred perspective to make groundless claims about what is best for children, in 'Too close to home', in this volume.

11 See J.G. Dwyer, 'The Child Protection Pretense: States' Continued Consignment of Newborn Babies to Unfit Parents' (2008) 93 *Minnesota Law Review* 407.

Family Foundation has waged a campaign to eliminate foster care by publicising distorted portrayals of data on incidence of maltreatment, to convince policy makers that child protection agencies should leave children in homes and merely offer voluntary services to parents reported for abuse or neglect, especially if the children are African American.[12]

Another example of this denialism regarding harm inflicted on children, and of corrupt social science, is prison nurseries. These exist throughout the world, and now are spreading in the United States; ten states place newborn babies into prisons to live with their incarcerated mothers. In the US, these are not community-based, home-like residences; rather they are blocks of cells in a maximum security prison. Programmes placing babies in prisons have not come at the behest of children's advocates but at the behest of prisoners' advocates, who see the women suffer when they must hand a newborn baby over to a relative living in the community. They receive support from legislators and prison officials when able to convince them the programmes will reduce criminal recidivism (though no studies demonstrate this is true). So they reflect adult-centred concerns rather than genuine concern for children's welfare.

New York State has had a prison nursery for a century, but until 2010 there had not been a single longitudinal study of outcomes for children whose lives began in prison. No one bothered to ask: is this good for the children? No one worried about babies living in such a stressful environment, surrounded by adults suffering from addictions and mental illnesses, under authoritarian control of hostile guards. No one asked: what happens to a baby who lives in prison with a birth mother for one year and then is separated from her because there is a one year limit for a nursery stay but the mother has more than a year left to serve? No one asked: what usually happens when mother and child leave together and return to the environment that made the woman a criminal, now that, on top of all her previous struggles, she has a criminal record, no place to live, no job, and no one to help her, and when she probably has other children for whom she must resume care?

Finally, about eight years ago, some researchers at Columbia University decided to study outcomes for these babies. But who were these researchers? They were a team of nursing school faculty and students who were providing services to the women prisoners, under a grant-funded programme, and who therefore were advocates for prison nurseries, standing to gain professionally and financially (by continuing to receive grants) if they could show the nursery had positive results. No one questioned the appropriateness of their being the ones to study whether the programme was good or bad. Unsurprisingly, when they published the results of their study, they distorted their data to generate a

12 See E. Bartholet, 'Differential Response: A Dangerous Experiment in Child Welfare' (2015) 42 *Florida State University Law Review* 573; E. Bartholet, 'The Racial Disproportionality Movement in Child Welfare: False Facts and Dangerous Directions' (2009) 51 *Arizona Law Review* 871.

positive report. Though they started by studying 100 babies, they mysteriously reported results for only thirty, and no one asked what happened to the other seventy. Among the thirty, they found indications of secure attachment at the child's first birthday at a rate normal for the general population, and so declared success. Other women's advocacy groups latched on to this uncritically, and soon advocates for women prisoners in many other states were telling legislators that prison nurseries had been proven extremely successful, producing great outcomes for children, citing this study.

I did some digging into the study.[13] I examined the team's publications closely and asked the authors for more information. I determined that the secure attachment rate for the other seventy babies was close to zero. The authors had come up with various unpersuasive reasons for not including those babies in their computations, and could offer no reason for not even mentioning the terrible results for those children. If those children had been included, the study would have revealed an abysmal 20% secure attachment rate. In addition, the authors neglected to mention that even among the 18 out of thirty who showed indications of secure attachment at first birthday, many would separate from the mothers thereafter, resulting in attachment disruption, which is typically traumatic and the cause of lasting psycho-emotional damage. They separated for several reasons: Some mothers had to spend more time in prison, beyond the time limit for babies to stay there. Some mothers left prison with the baby but violated parole or committed another crime and so went back to prison without the baby. Some left prison with the baby but abandoned the baby, returning to drugs, abusive boyfriends, and so forth. Ultimately, only a small fraction of the prison babies remained consistently in maternal custody; most had lives as chaotic as they would have had if they had gone to live with a biological family member in the community right after birth instead of entering prison. Tethering these children legally to an incarcerated birth mother was highly detrimental for the great majority of them.

Tellingly, no one participating in discussions about prison nurseries, until I did, even mentioned the obvious alternative for these newborn persons – namely, immediate adoption. The only alternative to imprisoning babies contemplated is parking children in the temporary and unstable custody of relatives until their 'owners' get out of prison and claim their property. Further, no one, until I did, ever suggested that some competent authority should make an objective assessment, at the time of each child's birth, of what choice regarding legal parenthood is in their best interests, taking into account all facts and all available options. No one considers adoption or urges a best-interests determination at birth because all these forms of denialism come together against these children, most of whom in the US are of minority race: an implicit denial of their humanity and equal personhood; denial that they have human rights against being imprisoned; denial that it is the state causing the tragic fate

[13] See J.G. Dwyer, 'Jailing Black Babies' (2014) 2014 *Utah Law Review* 465.

the vast majority of these children will experience, because it is the state forcing them to be in a legal relationship with an incarcerated woman rather than with adoptive parents, and to be placed in a prison; denial of the conflict of interests these children have with the birth mothers and with the adult members of the dysfunctional community that wants to claim them as members; and denial that there can be anything bad in a child's life experience so long as he or she is in a birth mother's custody.

Prison nurseries are thus a metaphor for the broader phenomenon that our legal systems – from the local to the international – imprison some children in hellish worlds their parents inhabit or create, because adults generally identify more with, and accord greater respect and deference to, adults rather than children. Prison nurseries also epitomise the indifference of laws governing children's lives, from parentage laws to child maltreatment laws to school regulation and beyond, toward children's fundamental, developmental needs and the ways various experiences thwart that development, impoverish their lives, and ultimately prevent them from becoming fit parents themselves.

2. OVERCOMING DENIALISM REGARDING CHILDREN

In thinking about how to realise the human rights of a subordinated group, and how to change popular attitudes and perspectives regarding that group, we commonly look to other groups' experiences for strategies and indications of whether success is possible. Doing that is a mixed bag, however. In many countries, racial minorities and women have made great progress, though they still struggle for full substantive equality. The progress of sexual minorities in recent years has been remarkable.

Those are all groups of competent adults, however – that is, people able to hire lawyers, assert their rights themselves, and convey their experience through myriad media avenues. Rights of persons with disabilities have also come a long way, most recently with an international Convention, but a Convention that appears more protective of persons with physical disabilities than persons with mental disabilities that would prevent someone from participating in creating such a document. It is especially difficult for non-autonomous persons to capture public attention and the power of legal systems, and there is always danger of false advocacy – that is, of people claiming to represent and protect them who actually serve other masters. And there is danger that legal changes ostensibly promoting their good actually disserve it, as the CRC does to children in some ways. Perhaps no group is more in danger of indifference or false advocacy than children, because: (1) they generally are unable to advocate on their own behalf, and (2) many of the greatest harms that befall children are at the hands of the very adults who are assumed to represent their interests and advocate for them in public fora. Societies make custodians the guardians of children's welfare, but if the custodians have a conflict of interests with the children, the children might have no one at all who is concerned about and speaks for them in legislative or adjudicative proceedings.

Yet progress can and sometimes does occur once small steps are taken. The same-sex marriage movement is an example of small steps initiating a process toward large-scale law and policy reform: once one state in the US – Massachusetts – began conferring legal marriage status on same-sex couples, it became imaginable to Americans, and people elsewhere saw that nothing bad resulted, but rather only more happiness for some group of people. Arguably, the first steps in the US were made possible by first steps in Europe, beginning with the Netherlands' recognition of same-sex marriage in the late 1990s (1998, registered partnership open to same-sex couples; 2001, marriage open to same-sex couples). Similarly, the first national ban on corporal punishment – in Sweden – made such a ban imaginable to the rest of the world and changed conversations elsewhere. American opponents of corporal punishment who previously would have been branded lunatics could then speak with greater credibility by couching their position in terms of the challenge: 'If Sweden can do it, why not us?'

The corporal punishment ban is especially noteworthy because it came by legislative action. Real reform by legislation is especially unlikely for children, because they are politically powerless themselves, and on any issue presenting a conflict of interests with parents, the majority of adults who are parents are likely to vote against them. Yet it happened in Sweden by legislative action, not by a rights based complaint to a court. Perhaps more progressive European nations will also initiate other reforms that have spill-over effects in the US – for example, if the Netherlands or Belgium were to adopt the Upbringing Pledge that Jan Willems and Hans Van Crombrugge have proposed.[14]

The same-sex marriage movement, in contrast, took its first steps through litigation, asserting constitutional rights. The advantage of a lawsuit is that courts, unlike legislators, are expected to set out their reasoning in writing, for all to judge, and that constrains arbitrary and prejudicial decision making somewhat; it makes denialism more difficult to maintain in the long run. I believe carefully managed, strategically chosen, and adequately financed lawsuits in US courts, asserting the constitutional rights of children against harmful state action, could have a tremendous impact on state law governing parentage, child protection, and education of children. There might be similar potential in other western nations, but it might be a virtue of United States' law that we do not have a charter of special rights for children, so advocates for children are expected

14 See H. Van Crombrugge, W. Vandenhole and J.C.M. Willems (eds.), *Shared Pedagogical Responsibility*, Intersentia, Antwerp-Oxford-Portland 2008.

to invoke general rights, rights presumptively applicable to all persons, drawing on interpretations of those rights in cases involving adults, and so tending toward robust construal rather than narrow and weak. Accordingly, the burden is in on states' lawyers and judges to explain why children do not enjoy rights comparable to those of adults. They are often quite ingenious in doing just that, but sometimes they simply cannot come up with a good reason for denying that children are entitled to a change in law and practice.

The main obstacle has been the lack of adequately financed children's rights organisations that engage in litigation and that perceive the problem, that recognise the denialism and the ways it harms children. Existing organisations with substantial funding generally accept the adult-centred normative universe and simply plead – with little success – for more funding to help parents, instead of demanding that states respect children's rights now regardless of what impact this has on parents or other adults, just as it must respect adults' rights as to relationships regardless of incidental effects on others. Conversely, organisations that 'get it', that see the way denialism and adult-centred law and attitudes harm children, are small and under-funded, unable to finance impact litigation. Substantial funding comes from large charitable institutions, and such institutions tend to be relatively conservative in outlook, not especially receptive to challenges to fundamental cultural assumptions. That is the thing about denialism; it persists precisely because it is pervasive and backed by power and wealth, so those seeking to expose and eliminate it are likely to be few and under-funded.

The way forward, then, is either to transform the thinking of directors at well-funded child advocacy organisations, to get them to recognise the forms of denialism outlined above and the illicit ways laws and policies harm children, or to secure sufficient funding for the individuals and organisations who have already broken free of the denialism and are intellectually prepared and motivated to advance serious reform efforts. Even if not always successful, such efforts spark public discussions; they lift the curtain to some degree from taken-for-granted practices, exposing the ways in which they reflect a denial of children's personhood, distinct interests, and experience and of the state's role in creating children's suffering and thwarted lives.

CHAPTER V

TOO CLOSE TO HOME?

The Denial of Prejudice and Discrimination against Children

Jan C.M. Willems

'No amount of intellectual sophistication can ground us in reality when our emotional wounds are serious enough.' (Grille 2013)[1]

'In the words of Dr. Robert Block, the former President of the American Academy of Pediatrics, "Adverse childhood experiences are the single greatest unaddressed public health threat facing our nation today." And for a lot of people, that's a terrifying prospect. The scope and scale of the problem seems so large that it feels overwhelming to think about how we might approach it. ... [A]t first I thought that we marginalized the issue because it doesn't apply to us. That's an issue for those kids in those neighborhoods. Which is weird, because the data doesn't bear that out. ... But then, the more I talked to folks, I'm beginning to think that maybe I had it completely backwards. If I were to ask how many people in this room grew up with a family member who suffered from mental illness, I bet a few hands would go up. And then if I were to ask how many folks had a parent who maybe drank too much, or who really believed that if you spare the rod, you spoil the child, I bet a few more hands would go up. Even in this room, this is an issue that touches many of us, and I am beginning to believe that we marginalize the issue because it does apply to us. ... The single most important thing that we need today is the courage to look this problem in the face and say, this is real and this is all of us.' (Burke Harris 2014)[2]

'Given the epidemic of violence against children, the multiplicity of its forms, its cross-border nature, and the fact that children are not safe even in their own homes, the campaign to abolish it is still in its early stages. ... The elimination of all violence against children and freedom from violence in all its forms will ... remain the human

---

1 R. Grille, *Parenting for a Peaceful World*, second edition, Vox Cordis Press, New South Wales 2013, p. 291.

2 N. Burke Harris, 'How childhood trauma affects health across a lifetime' (transcript TED talk September 2014/February 2015) <www.ted.com/talks/nadine_burke_harris_how_childhood_trauma_affects_health_across_a_lifetime/transcript?language=en>.

rights imperative of the next decades to come, if not of the twenty-first century.' (Lenzer 2015)[3]

1. INTRODUCTION

Nazism was aggressive and utterly racist, to a degree unparalleled in human history. After its defeat, in 1945, 'lessons learned' concepts were codified in the Charter of the United Nations. Human dignity and non-discrimination were two of them, but in its Preamble reference was also made to 'equal rights of men and women'.[4] As patriarchy remained aggressive and utterly sexist in some parts of the world, and more or less paternalistic in many other parts, equal rights of men and women became the object and purpose of a special UN Convention, the Convention on the Elimination of all forms of Discrimination Against Women (CEDAW), which was adopted by the General Assembly in 1979. Its universal message: women are subjects of rights, of equal rights and specific rights, and not property of fathers or husbands, or objects of protection. A decade later, the UN also declared children to be subjects of rights, of equal rights and specific rights, and not property of fathers or parents, or objects of protection. On 20 November 1989, another special UN Convention was adopted, the Convention on the Rights of the Child (CRC). Children's new universal status, however, is rather implicit in this instrument. Not until 1992 was their 'parental property' status – in national law and practice – labelled 'parentiarchy'.[5] But also international law does not, until this day, fully acknowledge their status and plight. Although violence against women,[6] as a large-scale and structural phenomenon and a gross and serious human rights violation, is seen as discrimination against women,[7]

---

3 G. Lenzer, 'Violence against children' in: W. Vandenhole, E. Desmet, D. Reynaert and S. Lembrechts (eds.), *Routledge International Handbook of Children's Rights Studies*, Routledge, London-New York 2015, pp. 276–294, at p. 291.

4 UN Charter, first sentence and second preambular paragraph: 'We the peoples of the United Nations determined ... to reaffirm faith in fundamental human rights, in the dignity and worth of the human person, in the equal rights of men and women and of nations large and small'. <www.un.org/en/documents/charter/preamble.shtml>.

5 The term *parentiarchy* (in Dutch *parentiarchie* or *parentiarchaat*) was introduced in 1992 in an article in the Dutch feminist law journal *Nemesis* (J.C.M. Willems, 'Van parentiarchie naar Vadertje Staat; Over 't verwekken, mishandelen en beschermen van kinderen' (1992) 3 *Nemesis* 8–23, 9 and 17 note 22 <www.iiav.nl/ezines/DivTs/Nemesis/1992/nemesis_1992_vadertje.pdf>).

6 See K. Rose-Sender, 'Emerging from the shadows: violence against women and the Women's Convention' in: I. Westendorp (ed.), *The Women's Convention Turned 30. Achievements, Setbacks, and Prospects*, Intersentia, Cambridge-Antwerp-Portland 2012, pp. 453–465. See also (the website of) the Special Rapporteur on violence against women, its causes and consequences <www.ohchr.org/EN/Issues/Women/SRWomen/Pages/SRWomenIndex.aspx>.

7 See CEDAW Committee (<www.ohchr.org/en/hrbodies/cedaw/pages/cedawindex.aspx>), General recommendation 19 (1992), Violence against women <www.un.org/womenwatch/daw/cedaw/recommendations/recomm.htm#recom19>.

violence against children,[8] no less a large-scale and structural phenomenon and gross and serious human rights violation,[9] is not seen as discrimination against children, that is, against children as a group, a specific – and very vulnerable – age group of human beings.[10] The UN Children's Convention (CRC) is not titled 'Convention on the Elimination of all forms of Discrimination Against Children'. Several terms have been proposed in academic literature to label prejudice and discrimination against children. In 2012, Elisabeth Young-Bruehl made a strong plea for the re-introduction of the term *childism*.[11] The terms *transgenerational discrimination* and, in shortened form, *transism* were coined by the present author in 1998 and 2000, respectively.[12] Jack Westman wrote several books and articles on *juvenile ageism* (age discrimination against the young), or in shortened form, *juvism*, a term coined more recently by the present author.[13] Until now, the term *adultism* (adults' abuse of their power over children) is the only one with a page in Wikipedia.[14] However, none of these terms are familiar, or even known, outside of small academic circles. In the meantime, parentiarchy remains aggressive and – through the lens of these respective concepts – utterly childist, or transist, or juvist, or adultist, all over the world, albeit not in all segments of society. As a matter of fact, after centuries of cruel modes of

---

8 See Special Representative of the Secretary-General on violence against children (SRSG) <http://srsg.violenceagainstchildren.org>.

9 For an extensive analysis (in Dutch), see J.C.M. Willems, *Wie zal de Opvoeders Opvoeden?*, PhD Maastricht University 1998, T.M.C. Asser Press, The Hague 1999.

10 Article 2 CRC deals with discrimination against individual or groups of children, listing specific grounds, not with discrimination against children as a group. The CRC does not define discrimination against children, contrary to CEDAW, which defines discrimination against women in Article 1. Article 1, *juncto* preambular para. 9 CRC only defines the age group of children ('before birth' until age 18, without prejudice to national laws regulating abortion).

11 E. Young-Bruehl, *Childism: Confronting Prejudice Against Children*, Yale University Press, New Haven-London 2012.

12 J.C.M. Willems 1998 (*Wie zal de Opvoeders Opvoeden? [Who will Educate the Educators?]*); 2002/2007 (*Developmental and Autonomy Rights of Children*); 2010 (*Children's Rights and Human Development*). The term *transgenerational discrimination* was introduced in 1998 (*Wie zal de Opvoeders Opvoeden?* PhD Maastricht University 1998, T.M.C. Asser Press, The Hague 1999, p. 752, p. 785); the short version *transism* was introduced in 2000 in book publications of conferences in Nijmegen (the Netherlands) and Ghent (Belgium), respectively: see J.C.M. Willems, 'Kindervolkenrecht en Trias pedagogica' in: J.R.M. Gerris (ed.), *Preventie van binnenuit*, Van Gorcum, Assen 2000, pp. 15–30, at p. 17 (16th Family research symposium, Nijmegen University, 25–26 November 1999); and J.C.M. Willems, 'Het belang van het kind, de rechten van het kind, hechting en verwerking: vier katalysatoren in de humanitaire ontwikkeling naar preventieve opvoedingsfacilitering en uitbanning van transisme' in: M. Bouverne-De Bie and R. Roose (eds.), *Opvoedingsondersteuning en jeugdzorg*, Academia Press, Ghent 2000, pp. 5–41, at pp. 7–8 (Ghent University, 12 January 2000).

13 J.C. Westman 1994 (*Licensing Parents*); 2009 (*Breaking the Adolescent Parent Cycle*); 2013 (*Parent Power*). Also see <http://jackwestman.com>, Documents: Parenthood Pledge Brochure. The variant *juvism* was proposed by the present author in an email to Westman on 19 July 2013.

14 See B.A. Lefrançois, 'Adultism' in: T. Teo (ed.), *The Encyclopedia of Critical Psychology*, Springer Reference 2013 (<www.springerreference.com>, Behavioral Science, Encyclopedia of Critical Psychology, Adultism). Also see Wikipedia on adultism and adultcentrism: <https://en.wikipedia.org/wiki/Adultism> and <https://en.wikipedia.org/wiki/Adultcentrism>, respectively.

childrearing – infanticidal, abandoning, ambivalent, intrusive, socialising (that is, violently disciplining) – a more 'helping mode' of childrearing is becoming dominant in the West.[15] But also in the West, violence against children, labelled 'child abuse and neglect' or 'child maltreatment', remains a large-scale and structural violation of fundamental human rights.[16]

When parents are unfit or dysfunctional, the protection of infants against inhuman treatment or, generally speaking, the protection of children's personal integrity hardly seems possible without specific rights. For children, the protection of fundamental rights requires specific rights, especially rights related to prepared, supported and competent parenthood. In that sense, specific rights are more important, certainly in the first years of life, than equal rights to particular freedoms, although equal rights should always be the starting point (as Dwyer stipulates in his chapter in this book). Denying equal rights without justification could be seen as formal discrimination, in light of paragraph 1 ('recognition of ... the equal ... rights of all members of the human family') and paragraph 3 ('everyone is entitled to all the rights and freedoms') of the CRC's Preamble.[17] Denying specific rights could be seen as substantive discrimination, in light of the CRC's preambular paragraph 4: 'childhood is entitled to special care and assistance'.[18] For this reason, 'equal rights for adults and children' is not likely to become a principle with the same humanising and civilising potential as the 'equal rights for men and women' principle.[19] Nor need it be, because the world has a potentially far more powerful principle, namely the paramountcy, or prioritisation, principle of 'the best interests of the child'.[20] This principle appeared twice in the Declaration

15 See R. Grille, *Parenting for a Peaceful World*, 2nd ed., Vox Cordis Press, New South Wales 2013, pp. 27–90. Historically dominant modes still exist, either as dominant modes in some cultures or countries, or as deviant (and even criminal) modes in others. In his historical account, Grille follows Lloyd deMause (editor of the *Journal of Psychohistory*), who, according to Young-Bruehl, 'should be read with great caution' (E. Young-Bruehl, *Childism: Confronting Prejudice Against Children*, Yale University Press, New Haven-London 2012, p. 302). There is no denying, however, that, generally speaking, childrearing has become less cruel over time, although cruel and harmful practices, as well as large-scale child abuse, still exist everywhere.

16 As explained and defended in J.C.M. Willems, *Wie zal de Opvoeders Opvoeden?*, PhD Maastricht University 1998, T.M.C. Asser Press, The Hague 1999.

17 For the full text of the CRC, see <www.ohchr.org/EN/ProfessionalInterest/Pages/CRC.aspx>.

18 The prime specific right is the right to competent parents, on which see preambular para. 6 ('grow up in a family environment, in an atmosphere of happiness, love and understanding'); para. 7 ('be fully prepared to live an individual life in society'); para. 9 ('special safeguards and care ... before as well as after birth'); para. 11: ('special consideration [for] children living in exceptionally difficult conditions'); *juncto (inter alia)* articles 3, 5, 6, 9, 12, 18, 19, 37a CRC.

19 In this contribution, non-discrimination and equal rights are understood as referring to both formal and substantive equality. For a differentiated analysis of these concepts, see R. Oostland, 'The principle of equality' in: *The Women's Convention Turned 30*, above note 6, pp. 67–92.

20 On which see Committee on the Rights of the Child (<www.ohchr.org/EN/HRBodies/CRC/Pages/CRCIndex.aspx>), General comment 14 (2013) on the right of the child to have his or her

of the Rights of the Child, the CRC's precursor instrument, proclaimed by the General Assembly on 20 November 1959.[21] Every decade since shows a new milestone in its development.

- In 1969, the American Convention on Human Rights was adopted in San José, Costa Rica. This regional human rights Convention stated in Article 17(4) that in cases of divorce 'provision shall be made for the necessary protection of any children solely on the basis of their own best interests'.[22]
- In 1979, the best interests principle appeared twice in the UN Women's Convention (CEDAW), in Article 5(b) ('the interests of the children is the primordial consideration in all cases'), and in Article 16(1)(d) ('in all cases the interests of the children shall be paramount').
- In 1989, the best interests principle appeared several times in the CRC, most importantly in Article 3(1) (paramountcy, that is, prioritisation, for state organs and public and private institutions: 'the best interests of the child shall be a primary consideration'), and Article 18(1) (paramountcy, in even stronger terms, for parents and legal guardians: '[t]he best interests of the child will be their basic concern').[23]
- In 1999, an Optional Protocol to CEDAW was adopted which created an international complaints procedure for women before the CEDAW Committee. In *González Carreño v. Spain* (2014) the CEDAW Committee opinioned that, in divorce proceedings, the best interests of the child prevail over equal rights of men and women.[24] In Spain, the opposite appeared to be the case, and this is probably true for most, if not all, other Western states.

---

best interests taken as a primary consideration (Art. 3(1) CRC) <http://tbinternet.ohchr.org/_layouts/treatybodyexternal/TBSearch.aspx?Lang=en&TreatyID=5&DocTypeID=11>.

21 See principles 2 and 7 of the UN Declaration of the Rights of the Child (General Assembly Resolution, 20 November 1959) <www.un-documents.net/a14r1386.htm>.

22 Fifteen years later, another regional instrument, Protocol 7 (1984) of the European Convention on Human Rights, refers to the best interests principle in seemingly much weaker terms, in Article 5: 'Spouses shall enjoy equality of rights and responsibilities of a private law character between them, and in their relations with their children, as to marriage, during marriage and in the event of its dissolution. This article shall not prevent States from taking such measures as are necessary in the interests of the children'.

23 Committee on the Rights of the Child, General comment 14 (2013) on the right of the child to have his or her best interests taken as a primary consideration (Art. 3(1) CRC), para. 3: 'The Convention also explicitly refers to the child's best interests in other articles: Article 9: separation from parents; Article 10: family reunification; Article 18: parental responsibilities; Article 20: deprivation of family environment and alternative care; Article 21: adoption; Article 37(c): separation from adults in detention; Article [40(2)(b)(iii)]: procedural guarantees, including presence of parents at court hearings for penal matters involving children in conflict with the law. Reference is also made to the child's best interests in the Optional Protocol to the Convention on the sale of children, child prostitution and child pornography (Preamble and Article 8) and in the Optional Protocol to the Convention on a communications procedure (Preamble and Articles 2 and 3)'.

24 '[T]he … authorities showed a lack of interest in properly evaluating all aspects of the case … [T]he [CEDAW] Committee in the case *[González Carreño v. Spain]* found that judges

- In 2009, with the entry into force of the Treaty of Lisbon, the EU Charter of Fundamental Rights (2000) became legally binding on EU institutions and national governments; its Article 24 (The rights of the child) refers twice to the best interests of the child.[25]

What could explain the gap between these international legal advancements in the past 55 years (1959–2014) and the reality for children today – a reality of violence and discrimination diametrically opposed to the requirements of the paramountcy principle? Why is this reality largely ignored, or even denied? Which 'hidden' prejudices may be at work to sustain this lack of awareness, or outright denial? As a first step to explore these questions, two brief overviews are presented in this contribution. Taken together, these overviews may be seen as a preliminary agenda for further research. The first overview takes a look at the forms of 'denialism regarding children' in James G. Dwyer's contribution to this book,[26] and their relation, on the one hand, to the forms of denial, *qua* organisation, in Stanley Cohen's standard book *States of Denial*,[27] and, on the other hand, to the above-mentioned prejudice and discrimination concepts. These concepts – childism, parentiarchy, transism (short for transgenerational discrimination), adultism, and juvism (short for juvenile ageism)[28] – have been developed by different authors since the 1970s, and may be understood as forms of 'known-and-unknown' prejudice and discrimination against children. On the basis of this first overview, the model of the 'juvism onion' will be presented, and the term 'denialism', or rather, its plural, 'denialisms', will be introduced. This comprises the following section (section 2) of this contribution. The

are often found to prioritise re-establishing a relationship between a child and an allegedly abusive parent over ensuring a child's protection from the risk of abuse … ignoring the risk of further violence'. (Child Rights International Network <www.crin.org/en/home/what-we-do/crinmail/children-court-crinmail-38#B>). In the CEDAW Committee's own words: 'The administration of the case by the authorities reflected a stereotypical concept of dealing with a parental visit scheme. The best interests of the child always has to be considered in these cases, and the State failed to take this into account in this case.' See CEDAW, Jurisprudence, <http://tbinternet.ohchr.org/_layouts/treatybodyexternal/Download.aspx?symbolno=CEDAW/C/58/D/47/2012&Lang=en> (Final Decision, Communication 47/2012, CEDAW/C/58/D/47/2012, 15 August 2014).

25 See <http://ec.europa.eu/justice/fundamental-rights/charter/index_en.htm> (accessed 20 August 2015). Article 24 of the EU Charter reads as follows: '1. Children shall have the right to such protection and care as is necessary for their well-being. They may express their views freely. Such views shall be taken into consideration on matters which concern them in accordance with their age and maturity. – 2. In all actions relating to children, whether taken by public authorities or private institutions, the child's best interests must be a primary consideration. – 3. Every child shall have the right to maintain on a regular basis a personal relationship and direct contact with both his or her parents, unless that is contrary to his or her interests.'

26 J.G. Dwyer, 'Diagnosing and Dispelling Denialism Regarding Children', in this volume (introductory paragraph).

27 S. Cohen, *States of Denial: Knowing about Atrocities and Suffering*, Polity Press, Cambridge 2001.

28 See above note 5 and notes 11–14.

next section (section 3) presents a short overview of ten suggested denialisms surrounding the complex field of child maltreatment. After this second overview follows the conclusion.

2. THE DENIAL OF JUVENILE AGEISM

In his contribution to this volume, Dwyer does not explicitly define denialism but relates it to the attempt to 'justify unjust treatment of a group [based on] ... premises [that] entail denial of something demonstrably true'.[29] He goes on to identify:

> 'four forms denialism takes in discourse concerning children, or in other words four types of premises – usually implicit rather than explicit, perhaps even unconscious in most instances – that underlie asserted justifications for treating children in certain ways that, from an objective perspective, are harmful.'

Dwyer discusses these four forms under the headings moral, conceptual, descriptive and empirical denialism. In the following four subsections (subsections 2.1–2.4), these four forms of 'denialism' (in Dwyer's understanding of this concept as quoted above) will be linked to the concepts of, respectively, childism, parentiarchy, transism (short for transgenerational discrimination), and adultism. The first three of these forms and concepts will be linked to the three 'organisation' forms of denial discerned by Cohen: personal, cultural, and official denial. The concepts of childism, parentiarchy, transism and adultism are combined in the model of the 'juvism onion' presented in subsection 2.5. The last subsection (2.6) proposes a definition of denialism, or denialisms, in relation to child maltreatment. It is hoped that, in future research, a more in-depth comparison and combination of all these concepts, which have been developed from various disciplines – prejudice studies, philosophy of law, human rights law, history, psychology and sociology – may contribute to a better understanding of the nature and causes of prejudice and discrimination against children, and thus to a more structural approach of the prevention of child maltreatment and other forms of violence against children.

2.1. PERSONAL DENIAL: MORAL DENIALISM AND CHILDISM

Moral denialism refers to seeing or treating children as morally inferior human beings, as once people of colour and women were, and in some countries or

---

29 Dwyer, above note 26.

cultures women still are. Today, seeing or treating people of colour as morally inferior human beings is universally understood as racism. Seeing or treating women as morally inferior human beings is generally understood as sexism. Until recently, seeing or treating children as morally inferior human beings was not acknowledged as a prejudice, let alone, as Jack Westman asserts, a 'prejudice … as virulent as racism and as pervasive as sexism'.[30] According to Westman, this prejudice 'exists when adults use their superior power to mistreat children as inferior persons in order to further their own needs and desires'.[31] In the 1970s, Westman introduced the term *childism* for this prejudice, which he later, 'following the introduction of the term *ageism*', changed into *juvenile ageism*.[32] In 2012, in her book *Childism: Confronting Prejudice Against Children*, Elisabeth Young-Bruehl re-introduced the concept *childism*, defining it as 'a prejudice against children on the ground of a belief that they are property and can (or even should) be controlled, enslaved or removed to serve adult needs'.[33] In her book she explains that these – immature or pathological – adult needs may be of a narcissistic (as in sexism), obsessional (as in anti-semitism) and/or hysterical or histrionic (as in racism) nature.[34]

According to Dwyer (in this volume, section 1.1),

> 'The view that children are of inferior moral status relative to autonomous adults, and therefore less worthy of moral regard, used to be explicit, just as a similar view was once explicit regarding slaves, women, and mentally disabled persons. Today it is more commonly implicit. … [T]here remains a widespread tendency to view children as possessions of parents, communities, or states, rather than as equal persons.'

In my opinion, especially people who abuse, neglect or (otherwise) exploit children bear witness to the 'hidden' – implicit and denied – prejudice described by Dwyer, Westman and Young-Bruehl. Since, generally speaking, perpetrators and bystanders of child maltreatment, and even victims,[35] do not acknowledge this, it may be seen, from an individual perspective, as a form of personal denial as explained by Cohen.[36] Although further research into these concepts and phenomena, the degree to which they overlap and the way they are interrelated, is necessary, I propose to reserve the term *childism* for the individual or personal (denial of) prejudice against children. Personal denial of childism is at the core

30 J.C. Westman, *Licensing Parents: Can We Prevent Child Abuse and Neglect?*, Perseus Publishing, Cambridge 1994, p. 123.
31 J.C. Westman, *Parent Power: The Key to America's Prosperity*, CreateSpace, North Charleston, South Carolina 2013, p. 79.
32 See Young-Bruehl, above note 11, p. 299.
33 Ibid., p. 37.
34 Ibid., pp. 44, 47, 35, 308.
35 On these 'agents of denial' see Stanley Cohen, *States of Denial*, above note 27, pp. 14–18.
36 As one of three organisational forms of denial: personal, cultural and official: ibid., pp. 9–11, at p. 10.

of cultural and official (or rather structural or institutional) denial, as childism itself is at the core of cultural and institutional or structural prejudice against children, as I will suggest below. Childism, as I view it, has to be seen, and further explored, as a (pathologically) exclusionary concept, and as such a child-excluding and child-nonresponsive phenomenon. Unfortunately, and rather confusingly, the term childism is also used in the opposite sense, somehow comparable to the term sexism as opposed to feminism. In his book *Ethics in Light of Childhood*, John Wall elaborates a child-inclusive and child-responsive moral theory, for which he introduces the term childism as an (ethically) inclusionary concept.[37]

2.2. CULTURAL DENIAL: CONCEPTUAL DENIALISM AND PARENTIARCHY

When discussing conceptual denialism, Dwyer writes (this volume, section 1.2):

> 'An assumption pervades thinking about children's lives, that their situatedness within families and communities and their subjection to the will of certain adults, is "natural," private, and pre-political. ... Unjust subordination of racial minorities and women, when legal systems treated them as property, was similarly defended as natural and pre-political.'

Women's legal and social position as subordinated to the 'natural, private, and pre-political' supreme authority of fathers or husbands is called *patriarchy* by both feminists and the public at large. Patriarchy in essence refers to the status of both women and children as property of men. In 1992, the present author introduced the term *parentiarchy* to indicate the increasing emancipation of women, but not of children, from this legal and social status in several parts of the world.[38] Today, in 'emancipated' states, the law does not grant automatic rights of one group of people over another group except when the former are the (legal) parents of the latter. Although, both in international law and in the law of some states, the terminology has changed from parental power or parental authority into parental responsibilities, to my knowledge there is no state in the world that requires parents to be somehow prepared, informed or educated, let alone screened and counselled, before they are granted parental rights by family law.[39] As we will see below, this is only one of several examples of adult legal

---

37 J. Wall, *Ethics in Light of Childhood*, Georgetown University Press, Washington, DC 2010.

38 See above note 5.

39 The present author has discussed this 'automatic rights' privilege in a book chapter in Dutch: J.C.M. Willems, 'Kindisme en anti-kindisme na Korczak: Kinderrechten tussen vooroordeel en SMECC-model' in: H. Brouwers and T. Cappon (eds.), *Het verlangen naar een betere*

and social privileges over children which, on several occasions, are harmful and, thus, contrary to 'the best interests of the child'.

The general lack of awareness of the universal status of children, especially of newborn persons[40] and the very young, as *de facto*, if not *de jure*, parental property may be called cultural denial as described by Cohen.[41] According to Cohen, '[w]hole societies are based on forms of cruelty, discrimination, repression or exclusion which are "known" about but never openly acknowledged'.[42] In this volume, both in Dwyer's contribution and below, in section 3, examples and illustrations of his thesis are presented in relation to children and child abuse and neglect. As I will further discuss in section 2.5 below, I propose to reserve the term *parentiarchy* for the 'hidden' prejudice against children which causes them to be treated as parental possessions; 'hidden', that is known-and-not-known, due to the collective or cultural denial of children's status as adult, and more specifically parental, property.

2.3. OFFICIAL DENIAL: DESCRIPTIVE DENIALISM AND TRANSISM

Describing adults' interests in terms of children's needs or 'best interests' constitutes descriptive denialism. In Dwyer's own words (this volume, section 1.3):

> 'A third form of denial relates to how adults deliberating about children's lives describe their welfare and needs. In doing so, there is a widespread tendency to impute to children their parents' interests, as if the two persons – parent and child – are a single entity.'

After presenting examples regarding education (insulating children from mainstream learning to indoctrinate them in their parents' worldview) and culture (invocation of 'culture' to protect parental, community or national interests), Dwyer continues:

---

wereld: Een hoopvol perspectief voor kinderen en opvoeders in moeilijke situaties, Janusz Korczak Stichting, Amsterdam 2012, pp. 37–55.

40 On which see J.C.M. Willems, 'It takes a SMECC to raise a child; Meeting Basic Developmental Needs of Newborn Persons: Principles and Promises in CRC and CRPD' (updated online version of: J.C.M. Willems, 'Principles and promises in the Convention on the Rights of the Child and the Convention on the Rights of Persons with Disabilities' in: L. Waddington, G. Quinn and E. Flynn (eds.), *European Yearbook of Disability Law - Volume 3*, Intersentia, Cambridge 2012, pp. 59–100) <http://pub.maastrichtuniversity.nl/2bde406f-987e-456e-9463-94453a464143>.

41 Cohen, above note 27, pp. 9–11, at pp. 10–11.

42 Ibid., p. 11.

> 'Perhaps the most tragic manifestation of this failure to recognise a divergence of interests between adults and children afflicts children born to unfit parents in dysfunctional communities. Regardless of how dangerous the family and community circumstances are that a newborn's biological parents present, the prevailing view is that it is best for the child to have those adults as parents and to restrict the liberty of those adults as little as possible. This is why generation after generation of people from the same families and the same communities are in the child maltreatment system, in delinquency proceedings, in drug rehabilitation, and in prisons.'

Perpetuating rather than breaking the transgenerational transmission of childhood trauma, attachment insecurity, domestic violence, poor physical and mental health, crime, poverty, and welfare dependency, caused by state and institutional denial of the best interests of newborn persons, has been labelled *transgenerational discrimination* or, in shortened form, *transism* by the present author.[43] Defining the best interests of the child in terms of children's biological origin ('blood tie'), or their parents' membership of a particular religious or cultural group ('cultural relativism'), rather than in terms of children's wellbeing and developmental needs, may be seen not only as an example of descriptive denialism, or as a manifestation of transism, but also as a form of what Stanley Cohen calls *official denial*. Official denial is characterised by Cohen as a form of 'public, collective and highly organized' denial 'built into the ideological façade of the state'.[44] In this case, however, official denial is not so much part and parcel of an ideological 'façade' but rather a structural or institutional form of denial rooted in the cultural denial of the 'ideology' of parentiarchy. In the same manner as childism serves personal adult interests, descriptive denialism serves organisational interests. The resulting transism reinforces parentiarchy instead of enlightening adults, empowering parents, and emancipating children. It is telling, in this regard, that in our so-called 'risk societies' the political system, and more specifically the child protection system, appear to look away from what may be one of the greatest risks for public health and wellbeing: toxic stress during pregnancy and in the early years of children caused or continuated by insufficiently prepared and inadequately supported parenthood (see below section 3.3).

By obscuring or misinterpreting the best interests of the child, large-scale and structural violations of children's fundamental human rights are perpetuated. At the same time, the best way to expose and 'deconstruct' institutional obscurantism or interpretive denial,[45] I would submit, is to see the best interests principle not only as part of the problem but also as part of the solution. What actually is 'in the best interests of the child' has to be

---

43 WILLEMS 1998/2000 (above note 12) and 2012 (above note 40).

44 COHEN, above note 27, p. 10.

45 On interpretive denial, see ibid., pp. 7–8, and more specifically T. WETERINGS's chapter in this volume.

determined, generally speaking and in the final analysis, by the state of the art in child development science (the science of early childhood), more specifically neuroscience (the science of early brain development) and the science of (infant, adult, and transgenerational) attachment. The key to future social – both cultural and institutional – transformation may very well rest with the merging of the science of child development, as the basis for building adult capabilities and other forms of innovation,[46] with the paramountcy principle of 'the best interests of the child'.

Article 3(1) CRC states the paramountcy, or prioritisation, principle of 'the best interests of the child' in the following terms:

> 'In all actions concerning children, whether undertaken by public or private social welfare institutions, courts of law, administrative authorities or legislative bodies, the best interests of the child shall be a primary consideration.'

The state organs, national, regional and local authorities, and public and private institutions mentioned in this provision, including the professionals working in these institutions, have the power of definition of 'the best interests of the child'. This power is abused if their definition is not rights-based in relation to children's general and specific human rights, science-based in relation to core developmental needs of children, and evidence-based in relation to the measures and programmes listed in Article 19 CRC,[47] including, for instance, child abuse risk assessment in foster care and child custody proceedings.[48] Science and human rights should join efforts to end this abuse of power.

---

46 For key concepts, science-based innovation, theories of change (such as building adult capabilities to improve child outcomes), and other information and documentation, see Harvard University's Centre on the Developing Child at <http://developingchild.harvard.edu/science>. Although Schema Therapy theory provides an interesting additional understanding of the varied adult outcome of underlying childhood trauma and unmet (emotional) developmental needs, it would go too far to elaborate this here. See E. Rafaeli, D.P. Bernstein and J. Young, *Schema Therapy; Distinctive Features*, Routledge, London and New York 2011. Also see International Society of Schema Therapy (ISST), <www.schematherapysociety.org>.

47 According to Article 19 CRC, '1. States Parties shall take all appropriate legislative, administrative, social and educational measures to protect the child from all forms of physical or mental violence, injury or abuse, neglect or negligent treatment, maltreatment or exploitation, including sexual abuse, while in the care of parent(s), legal guardian(s) or any other person who has the care of the child. 2. Such protective measures should, as appropriate, include effective procedures for the establishment of social programmes to provide necessary support for the child and for those who have the care of the child, as well as for other forms of prevention and for identification, reporting, referral, investigation, treatment and follow-up of instances of child maltreatment described heretofore, and, as appropriate, for judicial involvement.'

48 On which see, in relation to foster care (proceedings), T. Weterings' chapter in this volume, and, in relation to child custody and/or criminal proceedings, several of C. De Ruiter's publications listed on <www.corinederuiter.eu>. According to De Ruiter (<http://law.maastrichtuniversity.nl/denialismandhumanrights/wp-content/uploads/2015/03/Abstract-Corine-De-Ruiter.pdf>, Denial of child abuse in child custody proceedings;

2.4. ACADEMIC DENIAL: EMPIRICAL DENIALISM AND ADULTISM

Unfortunately, both 'science' and 'human rights' are practiced by scholars who may be in 'academic denial'. Academic denial, denial of children's inferior legal and social status, and related suffering, in academic research concerning children, women, parents, families, communities and minorities, including human rights research and research on children's human rights, or children's rights, is part of what Dwyer exposes as empirical denialism. Dwyer presents examples of empirical denialism relating to the medical profession (and circumcision of baby boys), to a US family foundation ('publicizing distorted portrayals of data on incidence of maltreatment'), the child protection system ('the obliviousness of many people involved in child protection to the impact on infants of instability during the attachment stage'), and to social science (and babies in prison nurseries). According to Dwyer, 'one sees repeatedly in contexts where children's interests appear to be in conflict with those of parents or ethnic community a gross misuse of scientific research by advocates for adults'.[49] Researchers themselves may contribute to this if they are in academic denial. Although Cohen does not list this as a separate form of organisational denial, that is, related to a separate and different actor, a distinct fourth category seems justified since laws and policies are often initiated on the basis of studies and reports produced by academics. I propose to reserve to term *adultism* to denote the prejudice against children underlying academic denial as a major subcategory of empirical denialism. I will briefly return to academic denial in section 3 below when discussing child abuse denial in human rights research. Adultism, that is, juvism in academic research, may be seen as the outer layer of a denialist onion, as I will submit in the next section.

2.5. THE JUVISM ONION

To guide further research into the concepts mentioned above, and especially their interrelatedness, the model of the juvism onion may be helpful. In this model, which I present here for the first time in academic literature, juvism – that is, juvenile ageism as defined and elaborated by Jack Westman in his book *Parent Power*[50] – is used as the overarching term for all forms of prejudice and discrimination against children, including their denial by researchers, state organs, institutions, professionals, individual perpetrators of violence against

Abstract Maastricht Denialism conference 22–23 January 2015, accessed 22 September 2015), 'The ultimate aim of forensic assessment in child custody cases is to serve the best interests of the child. This aim is currently not being served.'

49 J.G. Dwyer, this volume, section 1.4.

50 Westman, above note 31, pp. 69–101.

children (abuse, neglect and exploitation), and society at large. The juvism onion, then, has the following three layers: adultism, transism, and parentiarchy. After these three layers have been peeled off, one will see childism as defined and elaborated by the late Elisabeth Young-Bruehl in her book, published shortly after her untimely death, *Childism: Confronting Prejudice Against Children.*[51] Childism is the personal and pathological (narcissistic, obsessional, histrionic) denialist core of the juvism onion. Parentiarchy, as introduced and defined in the work of the present author,[52] may be seen as the cultural, traditional and ideological ('newborns as parental property') denialist layer surrounding this core, greatly contributing to the lack of mental health care for parents-to-be and the relative impunity of perpetrators of child abuse. Transism, or transgenerational discrimination, as introduced and defined in the work of the present author as well,[53] may be seen as the institutional and structural denialist layer surrounding parentiarchy. Its denialist nature is especially seen in the 'known-and-unknown' way, rooted in a patriarchal or post-patriarchal ('Western') parentiarchal 'culture of privacy',[54] in which childhood trauma is transmitted from generation to generation through both the action and inaction of state organs and institutions, as discussed by Dwyer and Weterings in this volume.[55] The outer layer of the juvism onion is adultism, academic denial in scientific research.

In his book *Parent Power*, when discussing juvenile ageism in child development research, Westman points at the – denialist – way research questions are framed. According to Westman:

> '[R]esiliency research ... assesses how much neglect and abuse ... young children can tolerate without being permanently damaged. Compare this to research on how much neglect and abuse ... Jews, blacks or elders could tolerate without being seriously damaged .... Research on child neglect and abuse usually asks whether actions and practices harm children rather than whether they are in the developmental interests of children. ... [Research] findings are used ... as if there is an acceptable level of damage to children. ... Research on the effects of childcare on children usually takes for granted the unavailability of parents employed away

---

51 Young-Bruehl, above note 11.

52 See Willems 1992 (above note 5), 1998 (above note 9), 2012 (above note 40).

53 Willems 1998/2000 (above note 12) and 2012 (above note 40). Also see J.C.M. Willems, The Convention on the Rights of the Child: Orientation and Conceptualization of Children's Rights (Trias Pedagogica versus Transism), in Jan C.M. Willems (ed.), *Developmental and Autonomy Rights of Children: Empowering Children, Caregivers and Communities* (second revised edition), Intersentia, Antwerp-Oxford, 2007, pp. 143–186, at pp. 166–167.

54 See Jan C.M. Willems, Child abuse and the culture of privacy, in Fons Coomans *et al.* (eds.), *Rendering Justice to the Vulnerable; Liber Amicorum in Honour of Theo Van Boven*, Kluwer Law International, The Hague (etc.), 2000, pp. 311–322.

55 Although not discussed in this contribution, the content of transist, and probably all juvist, denialism is both literal, interpretive and implicatory as explained by Cohen (Cohen, above note 27, pp. 7–9).

from home and doesn't ask how much non-parental care is in the developmental interests of the children or [the childrearing interests of] the parents. Criminology research focuses on children as offenders – delinquents – rather than as victims of adversity.'[56]

Adultism, that is, juvenile ageism in academic research, perceived as the outer denialist layer of the juvism onion, is rooted in parentiarchy and reinforces transism. The juvism onion, as a whole, is a model that, it is hoped, may contribute to the study of prejudice and discrimination against children, including their denialist nature. Let us have a brief look at this denialist dimension.

2.6. DENIAL, DENIALISM, AND DENIALISMS

According to Roland Moerland in his contribution to this volume:[57]

> 'Denial, as a concept, is difficult to define and although scholars disagree on many aspects, there are two aspects on which there appears to be a consensus. The first aspect is that denial is a defence mechanism that actors use in order to deal with realities that are somehow too difficult to acknowledge. The second aspect on which they tend to agree is that denial involves the paradoxical self-deceptive state of knowing and not-knowing at the same time.'

I would like to submit that denialism is an aggravated form of denial, that is, a form with one or more negative elements added to both, not necessarily always negative, aspects mentioned by Moerland. Three elements could be mentioned. (1) The denial is not only personal but also cultural and/or institutional or official. Bruna Seu, in her contribution to this volume,[58] refers to this as a 'symbiotic relationship'; in this contribution this is illustrated by the model of the juvism onion. (2) The denial serves particular (well-described) economic, political and/or ideological interests or sentiments (note Bruna Seu's reference to the 'ideological origin and political function' of 'scripts/vocabularies of denial',[59] and the references to parentiarchy and other 'juvism onion' concepts above). (3) The denial is related to (past, present and/or future/to be expected) gross human rights violations (such as child abuse and neglect, as mentioned above,[60] and to be further discussed in the next section).

---

56 Westman, above note 31, pp. 99–100.

57 R. Moerland, 'Rwanda's Untold Story: Acknowledging Genocide or Denying It?', in this volume.

58 I. Bruna Seu, 'Denial and Acknowledgment in Public Responses to Information about Human Rights Violations', in this volume.

59 Ibid.

60 See above note 9 and note 16.

In relation to children and children's rights, denialism as conceptualised above concerns both the private and the public sphere. Denialism in relation to the private sphere is not facing or ignoring the cruelty and structural violations of human rights and the rights of children in communities and families where women are suppressed (patriarchy, misogyny, sexism), children learn to hate others (antisemitism, racism, homophobia), or adults lack the empathy and skills to take care of infants and raise children (parentiarchy, automatic parental rights, unprepared parenthood, transism, childism). Denialism in relation to the public sphere (state organs, institutions, universities, professional and other non-governmental organisations, society at large) is not acknowledging and addressing these structural violations through (research on and advocacy of) integrated and comprehensive preventative legislation and policies.[61]

As I have argued in several publications, on the basis of a large and still growing body of evidence from various disciplines,[62] violence against children in the home, that is, child abuse and neglect, also referred to as child maltreatment, or starting in the home and continued in other settings (school, neighbourhood, youth care and juvenile justice institutions, workplace, etc.), is a large-scale gross (serious and structural) human rights violation in both poor and rich states, and a major contributor to crime, welfare dependency, poor physical and mental health, and violence and poverty over the generations. The human, social and economic costs are both enormous and largely preventable – if states were to start addressing the root cause: unprepared parenthood (parents who – according to a minimum normative standard in family law – are not adequately prepared, informed, assisted and screened for specific forms of support), including the related and no less 'harmful tradition' of automatic parental responsibilities at child birth.[63] Even if child maltreatment is high on political agendas, this root cause is completely overlooked, or denied. It is submitted in this contribution that this constitutes child abuse denialism with all three elements mentioned above: personal, cultural, and official; related to gross violations of fundamental human rights, and based on ideological sentiments rather than on rational arguments and scientific research. In the next section, ten sub-forms of child abuse denialism will be presented. These ten sub-forms are labelled 'child abuse

61 On structurally preventative (so-called SMECC) policies, see Willems, above note 40.

62 See, e.g., Willems 1998 (above note 9) and 2012 (above note 40).

63 According to Article 24.3 CRC, states 'shall take all effective and appropriate measures with a view to abolishing traditional practices prejudicial to the health of children'. In the author's view, unprepared parenthood and automatic parental rights/responsibilities could be considered as falling within the scope of this obligation although – not surprisingly – they are not mentioned in the 2014 joint General recommendation 31 of CEDAW (the Committee on the Elimination of Discrimination against Women) and General comment 18 of the Committee on the Rights of the Child on harmful practices. Nor is baby boy circumcision, for that matter.

denialisms'. They should be seen as hypothetical until further research into their denialist nature is conducted.

3. TEN CHILD ABUSE DENIALISMS

In light of several decades of research on early child development – both in relation to emotional development (infant and adult attachment research) and to brain development (neuroscience) – it must be concluded that putting infants in the care of manifestly unfit parents amounts to cruel and inhuman treatment of these infants, with lifelong health and social consequences. Only prenatal (youth) care and (child) protection could prevent this but an ineffective and harmful bureaucratic practice still exists today: intervening in families after children are reported for abuse or neglect. According to a study in the *Lancet*'s Series on Child Maltreatment, one in ten children in high-income countries is maltreated 'but only a tenth of these are investigated and even fewer removed from danger'.[64] Those – relatively few – children who are 'removed from danger' are likely to face new forms of harm, however, through repeated changes in alternative care placement or through placement in institutions. It has been submitted in this and other contributions by the present author that this harmful and ineffective bureaucratic tradition of post-harm intervention in families is related to, if not caused by, family law's granting of automatic parental rights at child birth. Prenatal care and protection should be the rule, not the exception. A paradigm shift is needed from post-harm family intervention to a structural preventative – so-called 'prepared parenthood' – approach on the basis of a minimum normative standard for parental competency in family law.[65] However, denial of, *inter alia*, the family law origins of childhood abuse seems to stand in the way of ending the cruel and inhuman treatment of newborn persons. Further study of child abuse denialism may be the way forward towards the paradigm shift that could, ultimately, change this situation. In this section, I will briefly point at ten specific 'denialisms' that can be discerned in an analysis of child abuse denialism. These ten denialisms relate to what is considered to be child abuse (its scope or definition (denialism 1)), its scale (the number of victims (denialism 2)), its seriousness (its harmfulness or consequences (denialism 3)), its structural or systemic character (denialisms 4 to 9), and the lack of human rights research relating to, or including, child abuse as a violation of fundamental rights (denialism 10). In other words, all the elements of child abuse and neglect (that is, its scope or definition) as a large-scale and gross (that is, serious and

---

64 The *Lancet*'s Series on Child Maltreatment, in Jan C.M. Willems (ed.), *Children's Rights and Human Development: A Multidisciplinary Reader*, Intersentia, Antwerp-Oxford-Portland, 2010, pp. 189–239, at p. 189.

65 Willems, above note 40.

structural) human rights violation (to be researched as such) will be briefly touched upon. Future research will be needed to explore their denialist nature, specifically qua content and organisation.[66]

3.1. DENIALISM 1: DEFINING CHILD ABUSE

All forms of violations of the human rights of children relating to their attachment,[67] dignity,[68] health,[69] and development,[70] more specifically, all forms of preventable damage to children's healthy development, may be considered to fall within the World Health Organisation's definition of child maltreatment:

> 'Child maltreatment, sometimes referred to as child abuse and neglect, includes all forms of physical and emotional ill-treatment, sexual abuse, neglect, and exploitation that results in actual or potential harm to the child's health, development or dignity. Within this broad definition, five subtypes can be distinguished – physical abuse; sexual abuse; neglect and negligent treatment; emotional abuse; and exploitation.'[71]

A similar broad definition may be derived from Article 19 CRC,[72] which aims

> 'to protect the child from all forms of physical or mental violence, injury or abuse, neglect or negligent treatment, maltreatment or exploitation, including sexual abuse, while in the care of parent(s), legal guardian(s) or any other person who has the care of the child.'

Excluding many forms of preventable damage from one's perception of child maltreatment, and only acknowledging the most severe cases as constituting child abuse, may be seen as a form of child abuse denialism not only in light of the definitions above but also of definitions in national laws and national

66 As to denialist organisation, see section 2 above (especially section 2.5 on the 'juvism onion'). The content of child abuse denialisms may be literal, interpretive or implicatory (see Cohen, above note 27, pp. 7–9). Denialist content is not discussed in this contribution.

67 See <www.child-encyclopedia.com/attachment> (accessed 6 October 2015).

68 According to the Committee on the Rights of the Child (in its 2011 General comment 13 on the right of the child to freedom from all forms of violence, para. 3c; see <http://tbinternet.ohchr.org/_layouts/treatybodyexternal/TBSearch.aspx?Lang=en&TreatyID=5&DocTypeID=11>), '[t]he concept of dignity requires that every child is recognized, respected and protected as a rights holder and as a unique and valuable human being with an individual personality, distinct needs, interests and privacy.'

69 See CRC (committee), General comment 15 (2013) on the right of the child to the enjoyment of the highest attainable standard of health.

70 See CRC (committee), General comment 7 (2005) on implementing child rights in early childhood.

71 See <www.who.int/topics/child_abuse/en> (accessed 5 October 2015).

72 For an extensive analysis of Article 19, see CRC (committee), General comment 13 (above note 68).

incidence or prevalence studies, the categories of abuse and neglect covered by the ACE (Adverse Childhood Experiences) Study,[73] and, more specifially the LONGSCAN classification.[74]

3.2. DENIALISM 2: THE SCALE OF CHILD ABUSE

Just to give an impression of the systematic underestimation of the scale of child maltreatment, reference may be made to the Netherlands, where before 2005 incidence was estimated to be 50,000 child victims per year, amounting to 1.4 percent of Dutch children.[75] In 2005, the first Dutch prevalence study (*NPM-2005*) was conducted among professionals working with children, resulting in a number of 107,000 child victims (aged 0–18 years) in that year. This study was repeated in 2010 (*NPM-2010*), resulting in a (10 percent higher) number of 118,000 child victims in that year, amounting to 3.4 percent of Dutch minors.[76] Several indicators, however, point at the fact that this may still be a substantial underestimation. Some of these indicators are:

- The ACE Study – a large collection of research papers based on more than 17,000 mostly white, middle- and upper-middle class, college-educated participants – in the USA reports three or more ACE (Adverse Childhood Experiences, that is, traumatic events in one or more of ten categories, six of which constitute child maltreatment; the other four may be traumatic for other reasons but are likely to largely coincide with different forms of child abuse or neglect) in 20% of patients with all kinds of diseases:

  > 'Childhood abuse, neglect, and exposure to other traumatic stressors which we term adverse childhood experiences (ACE) are common. Almost two-thirds of our study participants reported at least one ACE, and more than one of five reported three or more ACE.'[77]

  In 2010, the Dutch research institute TNO conducted an ACE study in the Netherlands based on data 'collected in a representative sample of

---

73 See for (prevalence and) definitions <www.cdc.gov/violenceprevention/acestudy/prevalence.html> (accessed 6 October 2015).

74 On which see Willems, above note 40, <www.acestudy.org> and <www.cdc.gov/violence prevention/acestudy>, and <www.unc.edu/depts/sph/longscan/pages/maltx/index.htm>, Modified Maltreatment Classification System.

75 In Willems, see above note 9, the present author argued that the minimum number of yearly child victims was likely to be 80.000 (2.2 percent of Dutch minors).

76 See Netherlands Youth Institute, <www.youthpolicy.nl/yp/Youth-Policy/Youth-Policy-subjects/Youth-policy-Youth-Policy-Child-abuse/Child-abuse-figures>. On these and other studies and statistics, (also) see Willems, above note 40.

77 See <www.cdc.gov/violenceprevention/acestudy> and <www.cdc.gov/violenceprevention/acestudy/findings.html> (accessed 5 October 2015).

approximately 2,200 respondents from the Dutch population'. Although more Dutch respondents reported no ACE at all, that is, no traumatic events in any of the ten categories, compared to the American sample (56% *versus* 36%), the prevalence of an ACE score of four or higher was found to be almost equal in the Dutch and American population: 11% and 13%, respectively.[78] An ACE score of four or higher is very likely to fall within any definition or classification of child maltreatment.

- Similar high – or even higher – statistics show up in child maltreatment prevalence studies among (former) victims, both abroad (prevalence of 20%)[79] and in the Netherlands (prevalence of 30%).[80]
- According to the *Lancet*'s studies of 2008,[81] approximately 10% of children in high-income countries are maltreated. This percentage appears to be somewhat in the middle of the outcomes of different types of prevalence or incidence studies, that is, studies – on one or more forms of child maltreatment (sexual, emotional or physical abuse, emotional or physical neglect, or witnessing domestic violence) – among professionals working with children or among (former) victims in high-income states.

In her doctoral thesis, defended in October 2015, Jacqueline Hovens observes:

> 'There is a great deal of uncertainty about estimates of the frequency and severity of child maltreatment worldwide. Childhood trauma remains largely hidden and unreported because of fear and stigma and the societal acceptance of this type of violence .... Discrepancies between child abuse rates reported by official statistics (child-protection agencies) and community studies (self-report) suggest that most incidences of child abuse are not reported to the authorities ... Prevalence rates

78 R.M. Kuiper *et al.*, *A first hypothetical estimate of the Dutch burden of disease in relation to negative experiences during childhood*, TNO Quality of Life, Report and Factsheet, 2010, <http://media.rtl.nl/media/actueel/rtlnieuws/2010/rapportkindermishandeling.pdf> (table 3).

79 See, e.g., a 2011 UK study by the NSPCC according to which '[a] substantial minority of children experience severe maltreatment and abuse at home, in school, in the community, from adults and from peers ... 1 in 5 children have experienced severe maltreatment.' Quoted from <www.nspcc.org.uk/services-and-resources/research-and-resources/child-abuse-and-neglect-in-the-uk-today>. Also see <www.nspcc.org.uk/services-and-resources/research-and-resources/statistics> (accessed 5 October 2015).

80 Francien Lamers-Winkelman *et al.*, *Scholieren Over Mishandeling [SOM]; Resultaten van een landelijk onderzoek naar de omvang van kindermishandeling onder leerlingen van het voortgezet onderwijs*, Faculteit der Psychologie en Pedagogiek VU Amsterdam, PI Research, WODC, Duivendrecht, 2007, <www.wodc.nl/onderzoeksdatabase/1172a-omvang-kindermishandeling.aspx> (accessed 17 November 2015). Some of the conclusions in this study are: 'Over a third of the adolescents appear to have experienced child abuse in the form of serious psychological aggression by parents, domestic violence, perceived physical conflicts between parents, sexual abuse and/or severe neglect at one point in their lives. One out of five adolescents was the victim of (a form of) child abuse during the past year. One out of fifteen adolescents was the victim of a combination of different forms of child abuse during the past year.'

81 See above note 64. Also see <www.thelancet.com/series/child-maltreatment> (accessed 7 October 2015).

from large population-based random samples are probably closest to the true, unobservable rate of childhood abuse.'[82]

This would imply that the Dutch ACE study conducted by TNO in 2010 provides statistics that are more reliable than those from the *NPM-2010*.[83] It is very difficult, however, to find any reference in the Netherlands to other data than those from the *NPM-2010*. Almost always the figure of 118,000 (or 120,000) victims shows up. Would it not be a form of denial, one wonders, by researchers and others, to present oneself as the most objective and neutral if one refers to the lowest statistical data – not acknowledging many other studies and statistics?

3.3. DENIALISM 3: THE SERIOUSNESS OF CHILD ABUSE

Ignoring or outright denying the harmful consequences of child abuse and neglect should become more and more difficult in light of the fast growing body of online and printed information and documentation. According to the ACE Study,[84] child maltreatment results in a multitude of health and social problems. As the number of ACE increase, the risk for the following health problems increases in a strong and graded fashion: lung, heart, liver diseases; alcoholism and alcohol abuse; depression; health-related quality of life; illicit drug use; smoking; suicide attempts; intimate partner violence; obesity; and a reduction of life expectancy by twenty years.[85] Research from several disciplines contributes to a better understanding hereof. Neuroscience explains the effects of early neglect and toxic

82 Jacqueline HOVENS, *Emotional scars: impact of childhood trauma on depressive and anxiety disorders*, Ph.D. Leiden University Medical Center (LUMC), Leiden University, 2015, p. 13; see <https://openaccess.leidenuniv.nl/bitstream/handle/1887/36026/01.pdf?sequence=12> (accessed 18 November 2015).

83 See (in Dutch) <https://www.rijksoverheid.nl/documenten/rapporten/2011/09/30/de-tweede-nationale-prevalentiestudie-mishandeling-van-kinderen-en-jeugdigen>, and <www.leiden-attachmentresearchprogram.eu/wordpress/content/rapportnpm-2010_screen_2nd-ed.pdf>; also see <www.nji.nl/nl/Databanken/Cijfers-over-Jeugd-en-Opvoeding/Nationale-Prevalentie studie-Mishandeling-(NPM)>.

84 See ACE Study findings, above note 77. Also see <www.cdc.gov/violenceprevention/childmaltreatment/consequences.html>, and <http://acestoohigh.com/aces-101>. For the latest developments – 'childhood adversity as as "the root of the root": the source of significant lifelong health issues that exert a massive toll on families and communities [that is, society and the state, JW]' (Nadine Burke Harris), and as a 'public-safety crisis' (Lenore Anderson): the 'root of the root' of violence and crime –, see <http://acestoohigh.com/2015/11/18/california-child-trauma-advocates-eye-policy-impact/#more-4692> (accessed 19 November 2015).

85 Also see, e.g., Robin KARR-MORSE, *Scared Sick; The Role of Childhood Trauma in Adult Disease*, Basic Books, New York, 2012; Donna Jackson NAKAZAWA, *Childhood Disrupted: How Your Biography Becomes Your Biology, and How You Can Heal*, Atria Books, New York (etc.), 2015.

stress on brain development,[86] adult attachment representations research explains the effects of child maltreatment on intimate relationships,[87] etc.

3.4. DENIALISM 4: THE LOVE MYTH

That all parents automatically are attached to and love their children is a myth and a denial of parental envy, hatred and/or self-infatuation. Sometimes parents abuse their children out of an 'envy motive' or a transgenerational form of 'acting out'. As a mother allowing her daughter to be genitally mutilated said: 'If I submitted to this and bore it, then so shall those who follow'.[88] But professional organisations that should know much better also make denialist claims on their websites: 'We know that parents want the best for their children and don't want to hurt them'.[89] Young-Bruehl's book on childism (*Childism: Confronting prejudice against children*)[90] is one of many testimonies to the contrary. More and more often, former victims of childhood abuse, calling themselves experts of experience, are coming out with their stories, and unite in survivors' groups or organisations such as the Dutch foundations *Geheim Geweld* (Hidden Violence) and *Praat* (Talk).[91] Loving one's children is not about saying *how much* you love them but about *how* you love them.

3.5. DENIALISM 5: THE BLOOD-TIE MYTH

Professionals who interpret 'the best interests of the child' as implying that being or staying with his or her parents, or having contact with both of them upon their separation or divorce, is almost by definition beneficial to a child's development, belong to the group of believers in the 'blood-tie myth': they are in denial of attachment security as a basic need in spite of all the evidence to the contrary.[92] In the case of a father who wanted his 7-year-old daughter – who had lived with foster parents since she was a baby – to live with him, experts

86 See <http://developingchild.harvard.edu/science/key-concepts> (accessed 6 October 2015).

87 See David Howe, *Attachment across the Lifecourse; A Brief Introduction*, Palgrave Macmillan, New York, 2011.

88 Willems, above note 9, p. 475.

89 APA (American Psychological Association), International Day on Prevention of Child Abuse (2013), <www.apa.org/pi/prevent-violence/programs/international-day.aspx> (accessed 6 October 2015.

90 See above note 11.

91 See <www.stichtinggeheimgeweld.nl> and <www.praatoverkindermishandeling.nl>. Also see the short video (with subtitles in Engish) at <www.bernardvanleer.org/English/Home/News/News-Archive/Hidden-Violence-(Geheim-Geweld).html>.

92 See James Kenny and Daniel Pollack, 'Bonding' in the child placement process: A psychological and legal perspective, *Policy & Practice* (APHSA), December 2015, pp. 5 and 30–31 (<www.aphsa.org>).

concluded that the blood tie should prevail over the child's attachment to her foster parents and home. In an exceptional verdict, the Court in Groningen did not follow them and ruled that not the child's blood tie but her attachment should prevail.[93] As Weterings observes:

> 'Usually, a parent feels attached to his child because he is born out of the parent, part of him, with some of the same characteristics. The child may awaken feelings of protection in the parent. All those feelings do not exist in the child. The child is only reacting to the kind of care he will get. Adequate care will awaken in the child the wish to be near his caregiver – a natural biological feature, necessary to survive. It has nothing to do with blood-ties'.[94]

3.6. DENIALISM 6: THE RESILIENCE MYTH

Denial of children's vulnerability to trauma often takes the form of what may be called the resilience myth. In his book (co-authored with Maia Szalavitz) with highly enlightening stories from his notebook, child psychiatrist Bruce Perry explains:

> 'Unfortunately, the prevailing view of children and trauma … – one that persists to a large degree to this day – is that "children are resilient." … If anything, children are more vulnerable to trauma than adults …. Resilient children are made, not born. The developing brain is most malleable and most sensitive to experience – both good and bad – early in life. (This is why we so easily and rapidly learn language, social nuance, motor skills and dozens of other things in childhood, and why we speak of "formative" experiences.) Children become resilient as a result of the patterns of stress and of nurturing that they experience early on in life … Consequently, we are also rapidly and easily transformed by trauma when we are young. Though its effects may not always be visible to the untrained eye, when you know what trauma can do to children, sadly, you begin to see its aftermath everywhere.'[95]

3.7. DENIALISM 7: THE CHILD PROTECTION MYTH

Child protection systems have existed for over a century in Western states. The child protection myth concerns the denial of the structural failure of these

---

93 Court Groningen 22 May 2012, <http://uitspraken.rechtspraak.nl/inziendocument?id=ECLI:NL:RBGRO:2012:BW6269>.

94 A.M. (Tonny) WETERINGS, Denial of developmental needs of foster children by Dutch youth care services (chapter in this volume).

95 Bruce D. PERRY and Maia SZALAVITZ, *The boy who was raised as a dog, and other stories from a child psychiatrist's notebook: What traumatized children can teach us about loss, love and healing*, Basic Books, New York, 2006, pp. 38–39.

systems to effectively protect children. As we have seen above, one in ten children in high-income countries is maltreated, 'but only a tenth of these are investigated and even fewer removed from danger'.[96] In other words, the vast majority of abused and neglected children is not seen by the system. But even if the system reaches out to them, they are often not helped by it, or may actually be worse off. According to Dutch research published in 2001 by VU Amsterdam, only one in three children was better off after a measure of child protection, for one in three the situation had deteriorated, for one in three the situation had not improved.[97] In too many cases children have died at the hands of their parents despite the fact that the child maltreatment system was involved with their families – such as the Savanna case in the Netherlands, and the Victoria Climbié and Baby P. cases in the UK.[98] Further investigations would be needed to find out whether and where systematic research has been or presently is being conducted on the effectiveness of child protection systems in high-income states.[99]

3.8. DENIALISM 8: IMMUNITY AND IMPUNITY DENIAL

Several traditional practices amount to parental privileges that are harmful to children and contribute to large-scale violations of children's fundamental human rights. These adult privileges may be explicitly legal under national law or may not lead to prosecution even if children are seriously harmed. This unequal protection under the law is often not acknowledged, thus constituting what may be labeled immunity or impunity denial. In this subsection a non-exhaustive list is presented of (ten) adult privileges which may harm children with impunity or immunity of perpetrators:[100]

96 The *Lancet*'s Series on Child Maltreatment (see above note 64).

97 N.W. Slot *et al.*, *999 Zorgen; Een onderzoek naar de doelmatigheid van de ondertoezichtstelling*, VU University, Amsterdam, 2001; see <www.wodc.nl/onderzoeksdatabase/99.139a-909-zorgen.aspx?cp=44&cs=6802#project-informatie> (accessed 7 October 2015).

98 See <www.theguardian.com/society/2008/dec/01/child-protection-baby-p-netherlands> (accessed 7 October 2015).

99 For a preliminary study outside Europe, see Unicef, *Measuring and Monitoring Child Protection Systems: Proposed Core Indicators for the East Asia and Pacific Region*, Bangkok, 2012, available at <www.unicef.org/eapro/Measuring_and_monitoring.pdf> (accessed 7 October 2015).

100 Several of these privileges are discussed in the academic work of Dwyer, see James G. Dwyer, (books) *The Relationship Rights of Children*, Cambridge University Press, 2006; *Moral Status and Human Life: The Case for Children's Superiority*, Cambridge University Press, 2011; (articles) Symposium, Children's Interests in a Family Context; A Cautionary Note, *Santa Clara Law Review* 1999, pp. 1053–1073, <http://digitalcommons.law.scu.edu/lawreview/vol39/iss4/4>; A Child-Centered Approach to Parentage Law, *William & Mary Bill of Rights Journal* 2006, pp. 843–855, <http://scholarship.law.wm.edu/wmborj/vol14/iss3/4>; The Child Protection Pretense: States' Continued Consignment of Newborn Babies to Unfit Parents, *Minnesota Law Review* 2008, pp. 407–492, <http://scholarship.law.wm.edu/facpubs/25>; A Constitutional Birthright: The State, Parentage, and the Rights of Newborn Persons, *UCLA*

- unprepared parenthood or automatic parental rights privilege (discussed above);
- toxic pregnancy privilege, e.g., smoking and alcohol abuse during pregnancy (in the Netherlands resulting in immunity until the 24th week of pregnancy and impunity until child birth);[101]
- privacy privilege: privacy in the home as almost exclusive right of adults, that is, not including children's personal integrity as privacy's first or core requirement;
- corporal punishment ('reasonable chastisement') privilege (still legal in more than three out of four UN Member States);[102]
- circumcision of (baby) boys' privilege;[103]
- non-immunisation (non-vaccination) privilege (in the Netherlands falling within adults' religious or political freedoms);
- not sending your child to school privilege (home schooling privilege), depriving a child, *inter alia*, of peer contact;
- smoking near child privilege (gradually being challenged in some states);[104]
- inappropriate baby naming privilege;[105] and
- deprivation of identity privilege, through IVF (In Vitro Fertilisation) and other techniques with anonymous donors.

3.9. DENIALISM 9: UNFITNESS DENIAL (AUTOMATIC COMPETENCE MYTH)

Connected with the first privilege listed above, the unprepared parenthood or automatic parental rights privilege, is the denial of absolute incompetence of

Law Review 2009, pp. 755–835, <http://scholarship.law.wm.edu/facpubs/26>; First Parents: Reconceptualizing Newborn Adoption, *Capital University Law Review* 2009, pp. 293–320, <http://scholarship.law.wm.edu/facpubs/27>; Parents' Self-Determination and Children's Custody: A New Analytical Framework for State Structuring of Children's Family Life, *Arizona Law Review* 2012, pp. 79–136, <http://scholarship.law.wm.edu/facpubs/1281>.

101 For a recent advisory report to the Dutch government to change this odd situation (caused by jurisprudential interpretion *per analogiam* of Dutch abortion legislation), see <www.nji.nl/nl/Actueel/Nieuws-over-de-jeugdsector/2015/RSJ-wil-OTS-voor-ongeboren-kind-in-wet> (Raad voor Strafrechtstoepassing en Jeugdbescherming, *Advies Prenatale kinderbescherming en de rol van de overheid*, June 2015).

102 See <http://endcorporalpunishment.org/progress/countdown.html> for the gradual 'countdown to universal prohibition' of hitting children (accessed 7 October 2015).

103 Several NGOs are now active in this field, providing information and/or as advocacy organisation; see, e.g., <www.icgi.org> (International Coalition for Genital Integrity), <www.nocirc.org> (National Organization of Circumcision Information Resource Centers), <www.cirp.org> (Circumcision Information and Resource Pages), <www.genitalautonomy.org> (Genital Autonomy), <www.jewsagainstcircumcision.org>, <www.jewishcircumcision.org>, <www.beyondthebris.com>.

104 See, e.g., <www.inquisitr.com/2342320/smoking-in-cars-with-children-illegal-starting-october-1st-2015>.

105 On which see Michael Sherrod and Matthew Rayback, *Bad Baby Names: The worst true names parents saddled their kids with – and you can too!* Ancestry Publishing, Provo, Utah. 2008.

manifestly unfit parents, particularly in cases of serious psychopathy or other psycho(patho)logical conditions where adults lack the capacities of empathy and critical self-reflection or introspection.[106] This 'unfitness denial' stems from the myth that giving birth to a child automatically implies parental competence. As a result, we more often empathise with a manifestly unfit mother whose child might be 'taken away' than with the newborn baby in her care. It is as if we cannot hear the baby crying: 'My mother can't take care of me. Don't I have rights?'

3.10. DENIALISM 10: DENIAL IN HUMAN AND CHILDREN'S RIGHTS RESEARCH

Newborn persons (infants, pre-schoolers) are possibly the last category of human beings who are not fully included in human rights discourse and research. The virtual exclusion of newborn persons may explain why neither infant attachment security nor the right of newborn babies to prepared and competent parents, including a right to be adopted at birth in case parents are manifestly unfit, are seen, analysed and advocated as fundamental human rights – in spite of all the rhetoric on children's rights. As a matter of fact, not many human rights scholars appear to be conducting research on the intersection of children's human rights and child maltreatment. Is children's rights discourse itself in denial? In her contribution to a recently published *Handbook of Children's Rights Studies*, Gertrud Lenzer, a Professor of Children's Studies, criticises the so-called 'bottom-up' approach to children's rights research because of its almost exclusive focus on participatory or agency rights of children. As Lenzer points out:

> '[T]he data [on child abuse and neglect] make it impossible for children – especially since ... infants and very young children are among the largest cohorts of victims – to organize on their own behalf to achieve any diminution in or remedies for the violence they encounter or are forced to endure. ... [T]he merest possibility of participation, autonomy, emancipation and social justice are denied to these children and young people. No matter how desirable it would be for children to participate in their own liberation, the hard social, economic and legal realities are an iron cage that makes such participation impossible.'[107]

It is submitted here that a bottom-up or liberationist approach in child rights studies is denialist as it ignores, or denies, the basic developmental needs – attachment security in infancy to begin with – that have to be met for children to grow up healthily, including childhood trauma reparation, as the crucial road

---

106 On which see Simon Baron-Cohen, *Zero Degrees of Empathy; A new theory of human cruelty and kindness*, Penguin Books, London, 2012.

107 Lenzer, above note 3, pp. 288–289.

and decisive means to empower them to adequately and fully participate in family, school, community and society.

4. CONCLUSION

According to Article 3(1) of the Convention on the Rights of the Child, the best interests of the child is a uniquely prioritised principle of human rights law. What actually is 'in the best interests of the child' ultimately has to be determined by the state of the art in child development science: the science of attachment, of brain development, of child abuse risk assessment. In spite of decades of research, however, a huge gap still exists between theory and practice in protecting children from abuse and neglect. The power of definition of the best interests of the child is not easily transmitted from adult and organisational interests towards children's rights based and both child development and childhood trauma informed knowledge. The best interests of the child are still to a large degree determined by non-scientific standards. This is facilitated by and made possible through the denial of prejudice and discrimination against children. Further study of the denial of juvenile ageism, or juvism, and of child abuse denialism, and its sub-forms: child abuse denialisms, is necessary to better understand – and then remedy – this state of affairs. But this is not an easy venture. As Burke Harris has stated, it takes courage to look denial in the face: we marginalise the issue because it applies to all of us.[108] Maybe it is easier to study child rights violations far away, or child abuse in 'those neighbourhoods', rather than going through the self-reflection and introspection, and face the personal ghosts, that is needed to study the abuse of children and the violations of their rights under our own noses, including those in our own lives. For many, this may be bringing the issue too close to home.

However, that is probably not the whole story. The situation is compounded by the culture and times we live in. We can see racism and sexism as apparent pollutions in the waters of society. Childism is a pollution that is much more difficult to see. It is covered by parentiarchy, transism and adultism: additional components of a poisonous juvism onion. As a matter of fact, parentiarchy is the water we all swim in, and from which we try to understand adultism, transism and childism. We would have to come out of the water to really see these pollutants. But we swim as fish in the waters of our times. No longer the times of slavery, with the resulting racism. Nor the times of patriarchy, with the resulting sexism. But – still – the times of parentiarchy, with the resulting childism, transism and adultism: caregivers who demean children, professionals who do not protect children, researchers who ignore children's core needs. With

108 Burke Harris, see above note 2.

parentiarchy to hide and protect their, our, personal or institutional – individual or collective – emotional, ideological, economic or political interests. Knowing-and-not-knowing about the existence and our continuation of prejudice and discrimination against children.

CHAPTER VI

DENIAL OF DEVELOPMENTAL NEEDS OF FOSTER CHILDREN BY DUTCH YOUTH CARE SERVICES

A.M. Weterings, in collaboration with Jan C.M. Willems

1. INTRODUCTION

In the two preceding chapters in this volume, explorations and analyses are presented on forms of denialism regarding children (by Dwyer) and their relation to prejudice and discrimination against children (by Willems).[1] Willems argues that violence against children should be seen as a form of discrimination against children for similar reasons and on similar grounds as violence against women is seen as a form of discrimination against women. According to Willems, these reasons and grounds are related to prejudices against children as an age group, such as childism and juvenile ageism, and to exclusion or discrimination perpetuated by cultural denial of harmful adult privileges ('parentiarchy') and, as a consequence thereof, a lack of political will to address the large-scale transgenerational transmission of attachment insecurity and childhood trauma ('transgenerational discrimination' or 'transism'), in both developed and developing states.[2] In this chapter, it is argued that this transgenerational transmission is negatively impacted by interpretive denial within the child protection system. According to Cohen, in interpretive denial, facts are given a different meaning.[3] For the purposes of this chapter, interpretive denial refers in particular to the interpretation and application of the principle of 'the best interests of the child' without acknowledging the state of the art of the science of early childhood and more specifically the research of the past half-

---

1. J.G. Dwyer, 'Diagnosing and Dispelling Denialism Regarding Children'; J.C.M. Willems, 'Too Close to Home: The Denial of Prejudice and Discrimination against Children' (preceding chapters in this volume).
2. J.C.M. Willems, 'Too Close to Home' (section 1, Introduction; section 2.3, Official Denial: Descriptive Denialism and Transism).
3. S. Cohen, *States of Denial; Knowing about Atrocities and Suffering*, Polity Press, Cambridge 2001, p. 7.

century on attachment security. Willems labels this form of denial as 'the blood-tie myth', which he briefly addresses in the section on 'child abuse denialisms'. In this chapter an illustration of this 'myth' will be presented based on the general literature on attachment security and several master theses in which research is reported on the treatment of foster children in the Dutch youth care and child protection system (hereafter: youth care services).

Interpretive denial affects both children and caregivers over the generations. It may thus be seen as a form or expression of transgenerational discrimination, or transism (see Willems's chapter). Transism has deep and complex roots and ramifications in tradition, belief systems, culture, legislation and politics. Nonetheless, it is rather surprising that youth care services, as professional institutions, do not take the lead in transforming the 'blood-tie' paradigm into a 'science of early childhood' approach to child protection in general and to foster care in particular. Many organisational and other interests might prevent this, and many forms of denial could be at work. Social welfare institutions and courts have an enormous power over both children and their caregivers in the interpretation and application of the best interests principle. It is therefore of special importance to scrutinise any prejudice and denial that may interfere with the correct use of this principle, and thus with children's basic emotional developmental needs, of which attachment security, as our first developmental task in life, is the most outstanding one. Especially in relation to foster care children, who often come from vulnerable families, it is of crucial importance that youth care services are both attachment and trauma informed, and act accordingly. The policies of Dutch youth care services do not bear witness to this, as will be illustrated in this chapter. Therefore, Cohen's concept of interpretive denial, as contextualised above, will be used here in order to attempt to shed light on these policies.

As will be elaborated in this chapter, the policies of Dutch youth care services appear to be based on the presumed importance of the parent for the child, that is, the importance of the blood tie between the parent and the child. The question is, however, whether policies based on this presumption actually create better conditions for the healthy development of foster children. For more than four decades the problems of foster children, their parents and their foster parents in the Netherlands have been studied at the Department of Orthopedagogics at Leyden University.[4] Every child needs loving care and guidance in order to grow up and become a well-functioning adult. Neglect of those basic developmental needs is not easy to see by the eye alone. One has to *know* which signs in the

---

4 See P.M. Van Den Bergh and A.M. Weterings (eds.), *Pleegzorg in perspectief*, Van Gorcum, Assen 2010. Masters theses on this theme have been supervised by both editors. In most of these theses, the children were 0–11 years old, entering foster care at an average age of four. They stayed with the same foster parent(s) for an average of two to three years, varying from a few months to ten years. Boys and girls were about evenly divided. None of the statistical analyses showed any gender-related differences.

child's behaviour are to be interpreted as a disturbance in the development of the child, now and/or in the future. A disturbed development affects at least four generations: the neglected child; his[5] parents, who are not able to give proper care to their child; the grandparents of the child, who did not give the child's mother or father proper care; and the child's future children. When the neglected child grows up, he will most likely not be able to raise his own child(ren) adequately because he has not experienced that sufficiently himself. The need to break this transgenerational cycle – lack of proper care and affection from one generation to the next – is obvious. When a child is placed in foster care, the opportunity presents itself to improve his possibilities for an adequate development. Interpretive denial seems to stand in the way of adequately using this opportunity. Several decades of 'attachment science' both internationally and in Dutch settings have not succeeded in changing this situation.

However, a model has been developed which might persuade youth care services to follow a different path. It may be seen as no less than a breakthrough that this model is now being tested by two care services working together (foster care and youth care), operating in three cities in the Netherlands. Therefore, it may be justified to pay attention to this model at the end of this chapter. This will be preceded by five sections following this introduction. In the next section (section 2) some results are presented of the research conducted at the Leyden University Department of Orthopedagogics on the development of foster children for whom Dutch youth care services bear responsibility. In section 3 the relevance of the attachment theory for the development of children is explained. Section 4 deals with research on attachment specifically in relation to foster children. In section 5 a child's loyalty to his caregivers is discussed, and in section 6 contra-indicators for reunification with his parents are listed. In section 7, the above-mentioned model is presented; it is submitted in this section that working according to this model could break the transgenerational cycle of neglect by giving the foster child new opportunities for development. The chapter closes with a short conclusion (section 8).

2. THE START OF A TRANSGENERATIONAL CYCLE AS SHOWN BY RESEARCH ON THE DEVELOPMENT OF FOSTER CHILDREN

Problems in a family may be seen by neighbours, family of the parents, the school, a social worker, another professional, or the parents themselves. Youth care services may be alerted. One of their professionals (hereafter: practitioners)

---

5 To avoid using he/she in every other sentence, the child and his parent will be referred to as 'he'. The parent, mother or father, is always the biological (legal) parent. Foster parents will be named as such.

may then provide some form of support, once or twice a month. The more problems, the more help and support may be given. But with what result?[6]

Extensive knowledge on foster care has been obtained by research on dossiers and second analyses on data acquired by the *Pedagogisch Signalerings-Instrumentarium* (Pedagogical Signalling Instrument, hereafter PSI).[7] The children had lived an average of three quarters of their lives in a (multi-) problem family. Their parents had received help from an average of seven or eight institutions during an average of five and a half years. All this help did not prevent the out-of-home placement of the child.[8] In the PSI questionnaires the foster parents talk about the development of the children in the first few months of their stay. Their development was problematic in many respects, e.g. health (80%), social functioning with peers (62%), or emotional development (95%), and continue to be so, although to a lesser degree.[9]

2.1. DESCRIPTIONS OF THE DEVELOPMENT OF SOME CHILDREN SHORTLY AFTER THEIR ARRIVAL IN FOSTER FAMILIES

- Girl, five years old. She behaved like a three-year-old and did not speak. She could not handle things by herself; was always cheerful but could scream and

---

6 This question was also put – and answered with: 'No benefit for the child' – by E. Monck, J. Reynolds and V. Wigfall, *The role of concurrent planning; Making permanent placements for young children*, BAAF, British Agencies for Adoption and Fostering, London 2003.

7 The PSI was developed by Weterings and Van den Bergh between 1996 and 2012. It consists of 12 to 14 questionnaires with 'semi-structured' (fixed) questions. These questions are asked by the practitioner for a particular (foster) family. The parent, or the foster parent, can give answers in his own words, written down by the practitioner and afterwards scored by a researcher (a psychologist) who does not know the (foster) family or the child. If there are specific problems, one point is given, and if not, zero points. The validity of the PSI as an instrument to make *a risk assessment (taxation)* of the (foster) family's environment has been examined. The development of the child is related to ten different factors (questionnaires). Every questionnaire (factor) correlated significantly with (an average) five of the ten other questionnaires. See A. Sitskoorn, *De validiteit van het PSI voor Pleeggezinnen*, Masters thesis, Department of Orthopedagogics, Leiden University, Leiden 2011.

8 See L.M Kastelein, *Van probleem tot uithuisplaatsing*, Masters thesis, Department of Orthopedagogics, Leiden University, Leiden 2010; and M. Moene, *De beleving van ouders (van het pleegkind) van de problematische opvoedingssituatie*, Masters thesis, Department of Orthopedagogics, Leiden University, Leiden 2011.

9 In the PSI, seven areas of development are questioned: physical development, motor skills, language, contact with peers, social functioning, emotional development, and mental or cognitive disability (the last one was left out in the analyses; in most cases the foster parent was not given much information about the mental abilities of the child, neither of the circumstances of the child when living with his parents). See P.M. Van Den Bergh, *Pleegouders, een investering waard; Een onderzoek naar redenen voor beëindigen van het pleegouderschap*, Dickhoff Design, Amsterdam 2013; and H.J.H. Van Duijn, *Groeien in een pleeggezin*, Masters thesis, Department of Orthopedagogics, Leiden University, Leiden 2009.

cry without reason; displayed strange behaviour. 'Everyday, we [the foster parents] watched her behaviour with astonishment.'

- Boy, 3½ years old. He did not want to eat; uncoordinated movements; did not speak; did not feel pain; struck himself; claimed unlimited attention from everyone; had tantrums.
- Girl, nearly eight years old. She stopped defecation for extremely long periods. Her attitude: 'I am a nobody, so tell me what you want me to do for you.' She could handle things by herself very well: she had had to care for a complete household.

These kind of problems are caused by a lack of affection, attention and care from their parents (and sometimes also in institutional care after out-of-home placement). Another thesis showed that once the problems started (in 50% of the cases when the child was 0–1 years old), the lack of care for the child *continued* over the years, until the out-of-home placement.[10] In an analysis of 150 dossiers, the main reasons for placement in foster care were parent related problems (30–61%), while only in 2–4% of the cases child-related problems were mentioned. And although in 25% of the cases child abuse was suspected or proven, only two of the 150 children were placed out of home explicitly for that reason. Other research on dossiers of 130 foster children showed similar results.[11]

2.2. REFLECTION

The nature and scope of the above-mentioned symptoms of conduct disorders are not simply to be qualified as 'these children are a bit lagging behind' or 'a bit slow'. These disorders are to be considered as a *disruption* in their development. Supporting the parent was necessary of course. But although an approach to give more and more help to the parents seems logical, progress, if any, proved to be slow and took years, at best. Because of the complexity of the family problems, often with roots in the past of the parents, this is to be expected. To continue supporting parents, and interpreting this as being in the best interests of the child, while failing to see that the development of the child worsens, may be seen as *interpretive denial* in relation to the child and his behaviour, minimising or overlooking the well-being of the child. One can understand, of course, the predicament of youth care services, since they have to deal with the parent, who

10 See S. Helder, *De relatieontwikkeling tussen ouder en kind en de zorg in het dagelijks leven bij ouders met een kind in een pleeggezin of in een internaat*, Masters thesis, Department of Orthopedagogics, Leiden University, Leiden 2007.

11 See V.A.C.B. Dalm, *Netwerkpleeggezinnen en bestandspleeggezinnen*, Masters thesis, Department of Orthopedagogics, Leiden University, Leiden 2009; K. Dankaart, *Besluitvorming en het beëindigen van pleeggezinplaatsingen*, Masters thesis, Department of Orthopedagogics, Leiden University, Leiden 2011.

has parental authority and legal rights. The services generally do not confer with the child, who has no power and is not given a voice. After all, 'the parent has the right to raise his child' (although Dutch family law calls this a 'duty and a right' and international law refers to parental 'responsibilities'). This interpretation of the parent–child relationship, as if the child is a parent's extension or 'property', and not a subject of rights, is hampering the development of the child. According to Article 12 of the Convention on the Rights of the Child (New York, UN, 1989), all children should be given a voice. Also the very young are able to express their feelings and needs. Better listening to children would make it easier to see the seriousness of their problems and prevent denialism in this regard.

The problems of foster children are often far more severe than institutions (youth care services, child protection agencies, family courts) are willing or able to see. This may be seen as a sad example of interpretive denial at work. In PSI and dossier research, about 60% of the foster children still had problems in three to six areas of development after an average of two to three years in their foster family. Only after three years in the same foster family did their problems diminish significantly.[12] In the first two years problems declined, but after two to three years they increased (this is understandable since after the first adaption period the child feels gradually accepted and dares to act out his anxieties and frustrations). After three years the problems gradually decreased. Children who stayed up to three years with their foster parents had significantly more problems than children who stayed five years or longer.[13] Foster children clearly benefit from their stay in a foster family. Because their problems usually start in the most vulnerable period of their lives, the pre-school years, they are severe and emotionally profound, and it is to be expected that the children often only benefit after many years in a foster family. Their developmental problems are mainly caused by long-lasting insufficient care by their parents in the child's early developmentally most critical years. Nonetheless, youth care services and courts, as a general policy, based on traditional rather than science-based interpretations of family law, still aim at the reunification of parent and child as the perceived ultimate benefit for the child. This is so in spite of the fact that many reunited children had to be placed out of home again (one out of four or even one out of

---

[12] See A.A.M. Huijg, *Pleegzorg, de ontwikkeling van pleegkinderen, de relatie-ontwikkeling tussen pleegkind en pleegouders en de invloed van het oudercontact*, Masters thesis, Department of Orthopedagogics, Leiden University, Leiden 2010. Examples are: health problems decrease from 80% to 54%; language problems from 66% to 41%; social functioning with peers from 62% to 56%; emotional problems from 95% to 89% (see A.M. Weterings, *Ontwikkeling van pleegkinderen volgens 61 PSI's (in 2008/2009)*, Internal paper, Department of Orthopedagogics, Leiden University, Leiden 2010). Also see P.M. Van den Bergh and A.M. Weterings (eds.), *Pleegzorg in perspectief*, Van Gorcum, Assen 2010.

[13] See H.J.H. Van Duijn, *Groeien in een pleeggezin*, Masters thesis, Department of Orthopedagogics, Leiden University, Leiden 2009.

three children in two different studies).[14] Considering this research on Dutch foster children, one can deduct a considerable emphasis to the parents, and a focus on their needs, while neglecting to look into the signs for an adequate development of the child. Several factors or research data appear to have been overlooked or not taken into account, for instance: years of support of the parents while the child may continue to live in an insecure environment with too little care and attention; problems of the parent as the actual reason for the out-of-home placement of a child; an already very disturbed development of the child when he is finally placed in foster care; the lack of emotional security for the foster child with his foster parents, as youth care services may consider reunification at any time they deem the parent to be fit (based on traditional rather than science-based – and thus denialist – interpretations of family law); the fact that, because of this, foster children, parents and foster parents live in 'endless temporariness'; the fact that no child related indicators call for reunification; the fact that a considerable number of reunited foster children have to be placed out of home again. All of this raises the question as to how youth care services and courts interpret the extensive knowledge on early child development. Let us therefore first take a brief look at the literature on adequate child development.

3. ATTACHMENT SECURITY IS NECESSARY FOR ADEQUATE DEVELOPMENT

For over half a century research has been conducted on the development of deprived children in children's homes, children fostered during the war, and adopted children. This research has clarified the conditions for development. Secure attachment of the child to someone who cares and provides for him on a permanent basis, is the most important factor for stimulating development. Bowlby has conducted extensive research on this subject.[15] Van IJzendoorn[16] and

---

14 See E.J. Peuchen, *Een kind in de pleegzorg: ontwikkeling, relaties en terugplaatsing*, Masters thesis, Department of Orthopedagogics, Leiden University, Leiden 2012 (research on 98 foster children, nearly 25% of reunited children had to be placed out of home again); K. Dankaart, *Besluitvorming en het beëindigen van pleeggezinplaatsingen*, Masters thesis, Department of Orthopedagogics, Leiden University, Leiden 2011 (research on 130 foster children; there were no child related indicators for reunification, and 33% of reunited children were placed out of home again).

15 J. Bowlby et al., *Maternal care and mental health and deprivation of maternal care*, Schocken Books, New York 1966. Bowlby used studies of other researchers on (early) hospitalism as well (e.g. W. Goldfarb, 'Effects of early institutional care on adolescent personality' (1943) *Journal of Experimental Education* 106–129; R.A. Spitz, 'Hospitalism: An inquiry into the genesis of psychiatric conditions in early childhood' (1945) *Psychoanalytic Study of the Child* 53–74), especially in World War II, such as D. Burlingham and A. Freud, *Young children in wartime*, Allen & Unwin, London 1942.

16 M.H. Van IJzendoorn, *Gehechtheid van ouders en kinderen*, Bohn-Stafleu-Van Loghum, Houten 1994; M.H. Van IJzendoorn and F. Juffer, 'Adoption as an intervention' (2006)

Juffer[17] have developed his theory further with research on adopted children. Oosterman[18] has shown in her research that the (secure) attachment of the child to his foster parents is the main factor for developmental success. Bokhorst[19] showed – in a twin study – that the environment, i.e. maternal care, is the main factor in the child's (secure) attachment to the mother, and not his genetics and blood tie.

Attachment is based on the *biological drive* of the fully dependent young child to survive.[20] The young child is not able to survive on his own. He needs care and support from a caregiver. When this caregiver meets the needs of the child, the child will develop 'attachment behaviour' such as smiling and 'crying, clinging and following' in order to get close to that specific person. The brain of a young child, the nerves and the connections between the cells, are yet to be developed. The way the brain will develop depends on the way the signals of the child to get attention for his needs are understood by his carers (sensitivity) and met by them (responsiveness). When the needs of the child are met consistently and the child can rely on his carer, he can develop trust – trust in others and in himself as well (he does the 'right' things to get attention). The child will seek out this caregiver and develop a 'secure selective attachment relationship' with this person. At the same time, the child will 'bid to the whishes' of this caregiver and listen to him in order to keep his attention. That means that the child can be influenced – and thus raised, accepting the given structure, and learn how to control his feelings of greed, anxiety or stress. His experiences will lead to a particular set of mental representations, beliefs and ideas about himself and others, what Bowlby called 'the internal working model'.[21] This is the basis for a mentally healthy personality. The early years are the most important stage in human development, especially also from a neurobiological brain developmental perspective. As child psychiatrist and neuroscientist Bruce Perry explains:

> '[F]rom birth to age four the brain grows explosively. The brain of the four-year-old is 90 percent adult size! A majority of the physical growth of the brain's key neural networks takes place during this time. It is a time of great malleability and vulnerability as experiences are actively shaping the organizing brain. This is a time of great opportunity for the developing child: safe, predictable, nurturing

Journal of Child Psychology and Psychiatry (Emanuel Miller Memorial Lecture) 1228–1245; M.H. Van IJzendoorn, 'Gehecht aan pleegouders' in M. Van Den Bergh and A.M. Weterings (eds.), *Pleegzorg in perspectief*, Van Gorcum, Assen 2010, chapter 2.

17 F. Juffer, *Verbonden door adoptie*, PhD thesis, Utrecht University, Utrecht 1993; F. Juffer, *Beslissingen over kinderen in problematische opvoedingssituaties; Inzichten uit gehechtheidsonderzoek*, Raad voor de Rechtspraak, Research Memoranda no. 6, 2010.

18 M. Oosterman, *Attachment to foster parents*, Ipskamp, Enschede 2007.

19 C. Bokhorst, *Attachment in twins*, Mostert & Van Onderen, Leiden 2004.

20 M.H. Van IJzendoorn, *Gehechtheid van ouders en kinderen*, Bohn-Stafleu-Van Loghum, Houten 1994.

21 See G. Schofield, M. Beek, K. Sargent and J. Thoburn, *Growing up in Foster Care*, BAAF, British Agencies for Adoption and Fostering, London 2005.

> and repetitive experiences can help express a full range of genetic potentials. Unfortunately, however, it is also when the organizing brain is most vulnerable to the destructive impact of threat, neglect and trauma.'[22]

Usually, the main caregiver is the parent. That is why the prevailing idea is that a blood tie is necessary for development. But, as pointed out above, this is not the case. The child should get love, attention and guidance in order to be able to learn how to behave towards others and to control his own wishes and desires. In *interaction* between the child and his main caregiver, now and in the future, the child can build up enough trust to accept his caregiver's guidance. When the parent does not see and meet the needs of the child, the brain will not develop in a consistent way. The connections between the nerves will not be adequate. Brain pictures of severely neglected children (as in the Romanian institutions) show a smaller brain and empty spaces within the brain.[23] Attachment security thus is also the basis of healthy brain development as well as the foundation for lifelong health (see Willems's chapter).

A child who often changes from caregiver to caregiver, does not know how to react and respond to all these different caregivers. It makes him very insecure. Apart from that, the child cannot build up a bond with caregivers because they will change too often. How can a child in those circumstances develop consistent behaviour? His brain develops erratically, with no clear patterns. The child cannot build up trust. After each replacement his problems increase.[24] Foster children without replacements had less problems than replaced children.[25]

Research on the development of children deprived of adequate parental care has made clear that, apart from affection, the parent needs to give the child adequate structure and stimulation. The present author has specified the concept 'attachment' between parent and child (affection and care) by introducing the term 'attachment and parenting relationship' (in Dutch: *gehechtheids-*

---

22 B.D. Perry and M. Szalavitz, *The boy who was raised as a dog, and other stories from a child psychiatrist's notebook*, Basic Books, New York 2007, p. 247.

23 See A. Havermans, C. Verheule and B. Prinsen, *Gehechtheid in beeld*, SWP, Amsterdam 2012.

24 See S.J. Leathers, 'Placement disruption and negative placement outcomes among adolescents in long-term foster care: the role of behaviour problems' (1996) *Child Abuse & Neglect* 307–324; J. Strijker and T.J. Zandberg, 'Breakdown in foster care' (2005) *International Journal of Child and Family Welfare* 76–87; S. Oijen, *Resultaat van pleegzorgplaatsingen*, Rijksuniversiteit Groningen 2010; M. Oosterman, C. Schuengel, N.W. Slot, R.A.R. Bullens and T.A.H. Dorreleijers, 'Disruptions in foster care' (2007) *Children and Youth Care Services Review* 53–76.

25 See E.J. Peuchen, *Een kind in de pleegzorg: ontwikkeling, relaties en terugplaatsing*, Masters thesis, Department of Orthopedagogics, Leiden University, Leiden 2012. Dossiers of 98 foster children. Not re-placed: after 2–3 years 11% had problems in 4–5 areas of development; re-placed: 27% had problems in 4–6 areas. The correlation between 'development' and 'attachment and parenting relationship' of the not re-placed child with his foster parents was high: $r\ (52) = 0.70$. This correlation was lower for the re-placed children, although significant as well: $r\ (24) = 0.55$; $p = < 0.01$.

en opvoedingsrelatie). This was necessary since youth care services mainly focus(ed) on affection (does the parent show, or assert, he loves the child?), while not paying sufficient attention to the kind of guidance and stimulation that is also necessary for an adequate development.[26] Thus, the conditions for the development of a secure attachment relationship are:

- affection (love): the main caregiver reacts sensitively and responsively to the needs of the child to live in a secure world, feeling understood and supported by lasting love, care and attention; and
- guidance: this caregiver gives guidance and structure, 'raises' the child, and is available when needed, now and in the future, so that the child can build up trust.

If the child is securely attached to his caregiver, the loss of this person will shatter his world, because he has lost the person who provided security by love and structure. This loss is a trauma which deeply affects the development of the child. An attachment and parenting relationship of the child with his caregiver can be *seen* in the behaviour of the child:[27]

- the child accepts authority of the caregiver; the child listens to him;
- the affection of the child is *specifically* given to this caregiver; he seeks comfort especially from this person (a selective attachment and parenting relationship); and
- the child expresses himself to this caregiver in an adequate way.

4. THE RELATIONSHIP OF THE CHILD WITH HIS FOSTER PARENTS AND HIS PARENTS

4.1. RELATIONSHIP WITH FOSTER PARENTS

The basic developmental need of and conditions for attachment security now have been discussed. The next question to address is: can a child develop an attachment and parenting relationship with his foster parents and, if so, what effect has such a relationship on his development. Progress in the development

26 See A.M. Weterings, *Het pleeggezin als opvoedingssituatie; Een empirisch vervolgonderzoek naar de ontwikkeling van de opvoedingsrelatie van voogdijpupillen van 15–18 jaar*, PhD thesis, VRB Drukkerijen, Groningen 1977; A.M. Weterings (ed.), *Pleegzorg in balans*, Garant, Leuven/Apeldoorn 1998.

27 The concept of 'attachment and parenting relationship' is operationalised in one of the questionnaires in the PSI and is based on the AACAP as well ('Praktijklijn voor de diagnose en behandeling van kinderen en adolescenten met RHS [Reactieve Hechtingsstoornis] van de zuigelingentijd en vroege kindertijd' (2006) *Kind en Adolescent Review* 225–283).

of a foster child appears to be best predicted by the relationship between the child and his foster parents.[28] A reduction in the amount of problems in this relationship also shows a reduction in the problems of the child. The relationship proved to be a predictor for the development of the foster child as well.[29] The outcome of the *Interaction between the child and his foster parents* questionnaire also correlates significantly with the problems in the development of the child.[30] These findings are in accordance with the literature on attachment.

4.2. INFLUENCE OF 'PARENT CONTACT'

In none of the studies, nor in the literature, was contact of the foster child with his parents found to be beneficial for the child, although in some individual cases it was. In the majority of cases the development of the foster child is influenced negatively by contact with his parents.[31] Huijg analysed the influence of contact of the foster child with his parents.[32] 'Mother contact' caused problems for 70% of the foster children. The correlation between 'mother contact' and 'relationship with foster parents' is significant.[33] Problems mentioned were: the mother does not give sufficient attention to the child; the child does not listen, is avoiding the mother or does not like to be cuddled by her. The more problems in the contact with the mother, the more problems in the relationship between the

---

28 A.A.M. Huijg, *Pleegzorg, de ontwikkeling van pleegkinderen, de relatie-ontwikkeling tussen pleegkind en pleegouders en de invloed van het oudercontact*, Masters thesis, Department of Orthopedagogics, Leiden University, Leiden 2010; A. Sitskoorn, *De validiteit van het PSI voor Pleeggezinnen*, Masters thesis, Department of Orthopedagogics, Leiden University, Leiden 2011; H.J.H. Van Duijn, *Groeien in een pleeggezin*, Masters thesis, Department of Orthopedagogics, Leiden University, Leiden 2009.

29 The relationship with the foster parents and the 'interaction between foster parent and child' predict the development of the child (see A.A.M. Huijg, *Pleegzorg, de ontwikkeling van pleegkinderen, de relatie-ontwikkeling tussen pleegkind en pleegouders en de invloed van het oudercontact*, Masters thesis, Department of Orthopedagogics, Leiden University, Leiden 2010, p. 22).

30 H.J.H. Van Duijn, *Groeien in een pleeggezin*, Masters thesis, Department of Orthopedagogics, Leiden University, Leiden 2009.

31 See M.W.E. Lambermon, 'Onderzoek in de pleegzorg' (2005) 8 *Ouderschap en Ouderbegeleiding* 11–12; A.M. Weterings, W.A. Bloemberg, H. Pruijs and W. Pool, *Pleegzorg in balans*, Garant, Leuven 1998.

32 In 90% of cases the parents do not live together. About 80% of the children had contact with the mother and 45–60% with the father (A.A.M. Huijg, *Pleegzorg, de ontwikkeling van pleegkinderen, de relatie-ontwikkeling tussen pleegkind en pleegouders en de invloed van het oudercontact*, Masters thesis, Department of Orthopedagogics, Leiden University, Leiden 2010; E.J. Peuchen, *Een kind in de pleegzorg: ontwikkeling, relaties en terugplaatsing*, Masters thesis, Department of Orthopedagogics, Leiden University, Leiden 2012). For this reason most of the analysis has been conducted with regard to the mother.

33 Correlation for the whole group is: r (105) = 0.20, p = < 0.05; for the 0–5 years old: r (42) = 40, p = < 0.01 (A.A.M. Huijg, *Pleegzorg, de ontwikkeling van pleegkinderen, de relatie-ontwikkeling tussen pleegkind en pleegouders en de invloed van het oudercontact*, Masters thesis, Department of Orthopedagogics, Leiden University, Leiden 2010).

child and his foster parents. For young children this connection is even stronger. 'Mother contact' – as well as 'father contact' – are significantly correlated with 'development of the child': the more problems in the contact, the more problems in the development of the child.[34]

The *frequency of the contact* does not correlate with any of the variables used and neither does it with the age of the child nor the length of his stay in his foster family. Analysis of the answers of the foster parents revealed that the nature of the visits is the problem. When the visits are just that: a visit, then it is OK. If the visits reactivate previous bad experiences with his parents or are the start of reunification, the relationship between the child and his foster parents will be threatened. When, for example, the mother says that the child will come and live with her in the near future, the child will feel threatened. He is afraid of losing his foster parents, and is also afraid to go and live with his parent, a person he does not know well or with whom he has had nasty experiences.[35] Contact with the parent often makes the child insecure because he does not know what the contact means.[36] This insecurity obviously affects the young child. Often the foster parents referred to the services as 'parent protectors' and 'no child protectors'.[37] The prevailing opinion of these services appears to be: a child is always loyal to his parents and therefore a foster child should have contact with his parents, and eventually be reunited with them (the 'blood-tie myth'). As seen above, respectively nearly 25–33% of reunited children had to be placed out of home again.[38] This raises the question of what 'loyalty to parents' means for the child, and whether this is different for a foster child.

---

34 A.A.M. Huijg, *Pleegzorg, de ontwikkeling van pleegkinderen, de relatie-ontwikkeling tussen pleegkind en pleegouders en de invloed van het oudercontact*, Masters thesis, Department of Orthopedagogics, Leiden University, Leiden 2010; A.M. Weterings, *Het pleeggezin als opvoedingssituatie; Een empirisch vervolgonderzoek naar de ontwikkeling van de opvoedingsrelatie van voogdijpupillen van 15–18 jaar*, PhD thesis, VRB Drukkerijen, Groningen 1977; A.M. Weterings (ed.), *Pleegzorg in balans*, Garant, Leuven/Apeldoorn 1998; S.J. Leathers, 'Parental visiting, conflicting allegiances and emotional and behavioural problems among foster children' (2003) *Family Relations* 53–63.

35 P.M. Van Den Bergh and A.M. Weterings, *Pleegzorg: jeugdzorg voor het kind*, Agiel, Utrecht 2007.

36 Contact in a divorce case is essentially different. In a foster case the parents could not give the child adequate care, which is usually not the case in a divorce.

37 P.M. Van Den Bergh, *Pleegouders, een investering waard; Een onderzoek naar redenen voor beëindigen van het pleegouderschap*, Dickhoff Design, Amsterdam 2013 (research among 444 foster parents).

38 E.J. Peuchen, *Een kind in de pleegzorg: ontwikkeling, relaties en terugplaatsing*, Masters thesis, Department of Orthopedagogics, Leiden University, Leiden 2012; K. Dankaart, *Besluitvorming en het beëindigen van pleeggezinplaatsingen*, Masters thesis, Department of Orthopedagogics, Leiden University, Leiden 2011.

5. LOYALTY OF THE FOSTER CHILD TO HIS PARENTS

Loyalty refers to a kind of bond. Bonds may have a completely different content and quality. In the Dutch youth care and child protection system the concept of loyalty was, and still appears to be, based on the theory of Nagy (Ivan Boszormenyi-Nagy), who claimed, without any research other than his experiences as a family therapist, that a child is always loyal to his parents.[39] Nagy divided 'loyalty' into two concepts: 'existential loyalty' by birth of the child, and 'obtained loyalty' by the parents through their care for the child. Existential loyalty 'by birth' exists in the sense that any child, or adult, would like to know what kind of persons his parents are, or were. Because he is born out of them, he wants to *know* his 'roots' as part of his identity.[40] If there has been no or hardly any care, the parents will not obtain much loyalty from their child (although they might think this is a 'natural' feature). In the experience of the child there was hardly any care, so no feelings of loyalty have been awakened. Therefore, the author of this chapter proposes a third form or dimension of the concept loyalty: emotional loyalty of the child to his parents. When the parents have given the child love and care, the child will get emotionally attached and will *feel* loyal to them. In the theory of Nagy this concept had no place because the children in his therapy lived with their parents. The 'existential loyalty' always had an emotional quality for the child as well – and thus emotional loyalty of the child was not discerned as a separate phenomenon.

'Emotional loyalty of the child' comes into the picture for adoptive and foster children. For those children it is not self-evident that they will feel loyal to their parents, sometimes not even knowing them. When considering an increase in frequency of visits of a foster child to the parent or a reunification with the parent, one should consider *the child's perception* of the parent and of the foster parent. By analysing the PSI Diagram[41] for children from 6 years of age and older, Tamtelahitu discovered that foster children make a clear distinction between their foster parents and their parents.[42] Foster mothers were often more important to them than the mother (or father). When the child did not put his

39 I. BOSZORMENYI NAGY and B.R. KRASNER, *Between give and take*, Brunner Mazel, New York 1986; translated into Dutch by N. BAKHUIZEN, *Tussen geven en nemen*, De Toorts, Haarlem 1994.

40 See P.M. VAN DEN BERGH, A.M. WETERINGS and M. SCHOENMAKERS, 'Gehechtheid en loyaliteit bij pleegkinderen: een analyse vanuit de theorie en de praktijk' (2011) *Tijdschrift voor Orthopedagogiek, Kinderpsychiatrie en Klinische Kinderpsychologie* 128–143.

41 On the PSI, above note 7. The PSI Relationship Diagram consists of four circles around the child, who is in the middle. He can write the person(s) who is (are) most important or valuable to him in the first circle; persons who are next in importance to him in the second circle, and so on.

42 N.J.A. TAMTELAHITU, *De beleving van de nabijheid van ouders en pleegouders door pleegkinderen*, Masters thesis, Department of Orthopedagogics, Leiden University, Leiden 2009.

mother in the Relationship Diagram at all, the relationship of the child with the foster parents was less problematic.[43]

Analysis of sixty Relationship Diagrams showed that the significance of the parent vanishes gradually, while the significance of the foster parent grows over the years, especially when the child came to live with the foster family at a young age or/and stayed with them for many years. Nearly half of the children suffered from loyalty conflicts. Those conflicts were related to the vagueness and insecurity of the foster placement. The foster child did not know if he could stay with his foster parent(s) or would go to his parent(s) eventually. But it was not self-evident that the parent was the most important person in the life of the foster child.[44] Note that the 'parent–child relationship' is not one and the same entity for the parent and the child. The relationship is not equally strong and of equal quality for the parent as for the child. Usually a parent feels attached to his child because he is born out of him. The child may awaken feelings of protection in the parent. Those feelings do not exist in the child. The child is only reacting to the kind of care he gets. A blood tie has no meaning to him. But for the parent it usually does, even when he has taken care of the child for a very short time only. Often, however, the parent's feelings are mixed with feelings of failure and are (thus) mainly self-centred. Such mixed feelings are far from beneficial for the child.

6. CONTRA-INDICATORS FOR REUNIFICATION

Officially, based on tradition and family law, foster care is seen as a temporary support for the parent, until he is able to care of the child himself. This has led to idea that parent–child reunification should be the ultimate aim (see section 2 above). However, the question should be asked if and when a reunification is justified in view of the child's development. An adequate development for the child is the core business for youth care services. The foster child is to be considered first of all as a child, a developing person in his own right. When he enters foster care, his development usually is disrupted by lack of care by his parents. The first question should not be: when can he return to his parents? But: how can his development be stimulated? Since an attachment and parenting relationship of the child with a main caregiver is most crucial for his development, it is necessary to analyse the factors which may hamper the development of such a relationship of the child with his foster parents. Those

---

43 A. Sitskoorn, *De validiteit van het PSI voor Pleeggezinnen*, Masters thesis, Department of Orthopedagogics, Leiden University, Leiden 2011.

44 A.M. Weterings and P.M. Van Den Bergh, 'De stem van het pleegkind' (2012) *Tijdschrift voor Familie- en Jeugdrecht* 12–20.

factors can be considered as contra-indicators for reunification as well. Five main indicators can be deduced from the information given above.

6.1. THE HISTORY BETWEEN THE FOSTER CHILD AND HIS PARENT

The foster child has lived in an environment without sufficient care, no clear rules to set his behaviour, little structure, physical and/or emotional neglect, violence or abuse. It is necessary to know what kind of relationship the child has had with his parents while living with them. He has not had sufficient opportunities to develop a positive 'working model' for dealing with himself and others, resulting in developmental problems and conduct disorders. The longer the child has lived with neglectful parents, the more his behaviour is built on an inadequate base. For foster parents is it is difficult to understand the child and to react sensitively and responsively to his behaviour and needs when they do not know what experiences he has had (which are usually not 'normal' and adequate). Often, information about a child's life before his out-of-home placement is not given because the privacy of the parents prevails. But the kind of relationship the child has had with his parents concerns the privacy of the child as well. Knowing what has happened to the child is necessary for adequate parenting. During the out-of-home placement the child cannot develop a new attachment and parenting relationship with his parent. Therefore, it is by no means self-evident that the child will develop a positive attachment and parenting relationship with his parent after reunification. Before the start of a reunification programme 'the problems which necessitated removal of the child must be identified and well-documented'.[45] An assessment should be made. It must be apparent that the parent will be able to change his former way of life and will be able to take care of the child.

6.2. THE RELATIONSHIP BETWEEN THE CHILD AND HIS FOSTER PARENTS

During his stay the child usually develops an attachment and parenting relationship with his foster parents, particularly when he came to live with them at an early age and/or stayed with them a few years (see above sections 2 and 4). When this child might have to return to his parents, his development will be hampered by the insecurity created. If reunited, he will be traumatised by the loss of his foster parents, who are his 'emotional' parents.

---

45 E. Monck, J. Reynolds and V. Wigfall, *The role of concurrent planning; Making permanent placements for young children*, BAAF, British Agencies for Adoption and Fostering, London 2003, p. 41.

6.3. THE RELATIONSHIP BETWEEN THE CHILD AND HIS PARENT

When reunited, the parent will have to raise a child he does not know well, and who is traumatised on top of that. And the child has to live with a parent he does not know well. Moreover, there will be a considerable change in interaction with him, because his parent is not only 'another person' but – more often than not – his parent was not sufficiently cared for by his own parents. Often, the parent does not know how to communicate with his child ('I love him, but I do not know how to do that'). An attachment and parenting relationship between the child and his parent will be severely hampered.

6.4. REACTIONS OF THE CHILD DURING AND AFTER THE VISITS TO HIS PARENT

The parents have the right to see their child. However, sometimes that right is granted even when, for instance, the child is afraid of his father, and police or other protection is necessary when the father visits the foster family. The question of whether those visits are beneficial for the child is justified. Usually the foster child will be attached to his parent in an insecure way – because there was no one else when he lived at home. A young child needs to become attached in some way or other (secure or insecure) to a caregiver in order to survive. But if there was insufficient care, the relationship of the child with his parent will be disturbed and not secure (insecure or even disorganised attachment). *During* a visit the child may behave properly, reacting to the kind behaviour of the parent, although the child maybe subdued or not paying much attention to the parent. The practitioner who may be present, will report that all is going well. But *afterwards* the impact of the confrontation with his parent might re-awaken bad experiences with the parent in the past and cause fear. The practitioner may prevent uncontrolled behaviour of the parent, but he cannot prevent the negative feelings of the child afterwards.

6.5. THE POLICY OBJECTIVE THAT THE FOSTER CHILD SHOULD EVENTUALLY RETURN TO HIS PARENT

When the child has stayed for some time with his foster parents and his development is improving, it means that an attachment and parenting relationship has started to grow. But the policy objective of youth care services (the child should return to his parents) is obstructing the trust of the child in his foster parents, thus blocking his development. The longer his stay, the more traumatising the loss of his foster parents at reunification will be, because the foster parents may have been the first persons he could trust. The relationship with the foster parents will be hampered as well because they cannot help the child. He will feel abandoned by them.

6.6. AN EXAMPLE OF UNJUSTIFIED REUNIFICATION: BEN, 3½ YEARS OLD

Placed in a foster family by a court order a few months after he was born, Ben grew up to be a cheerful and happy child. After three years Ben's parents wanted to raise him. The family guardian increased the frequency and the duration of the visits to his parents. Ben resisted these visits more and more. After a visit Ben displayed an increasingly difficult behaviour, throwing himself into tantrums for no obvious reason, had nightmares, and behaved as a much younger child, clinging to his foster mother all the time. His parents had said to him that he would come and live with them soon. The foster parents could not reassure him because of the family guardian's policy. The practitioner who supported the parents, said that they did their best and Ben did not cause any problems. Ben went to live with his parents when he was 3½ years old. He could see his former foster parents once a month. After six months the foster parents saw a totally different child. Ben looked miserable, was quiet and did not laugh any more. In a petting zoo, he intentionally stepped on flowers and wanted to harm the animals. The foster parents were shocked by the negative changes in Ben. However, the family guardian felt that the reunification was justified. The practitioners and/or family guardians often have the idea that those reactions are caused by the foster parents, who want to claim the child for themselves and 'begrudge' the parents their child, while *he* would like to live with them.[46] But it is quite unlikely that this behaviour should be interpreted as 'the child is missing his parent so much'. When the child would like to live with his parents, he is telling the foster parents gladly about the visits and there will be no signs of a conduct disorder or behavioural problems after a visit. In the next section a model is presented to tackle the interpretive denial exposed above in order to avoid a reunification that is harmful to the child.

7. BREAKING THE TRANSGENERATIONAL CYCLE OF PARENTAL NEGLECT: THE PEDAGOGICAL DECISION MODEL FOR FOSTER CARE

The transgenerational cycle of parental neglect could be broken if youth care services no longer acted along blood tie and reunification paradigms

46 P.M. Van Den Bergh and A.M. Weterings (eds.), *Pleegzorg in perspectief*, Van Gorcum, Assen 2010; P.M. Van Den Bergh, *Pleegouders, een investering waard; Een onderzoek naar redenen voor beëindigen van het pleegouderschap*, Dickhoff Design, Amsterdam 2013.

but according to the scientific knowledge discussed above. The child needs *existential security,* an emotionally secure base, knowing that he can stay with his parents or with his foster parents, who will take adequate care of him. The reunification programme of the proposed model outlined in this section aims at a definite decision: the child will stay with his parent until he has grown up, or the child will stay permanently with his foster parents. Existential security for the child can be established when a reunification is based on four factors:

- adequate functioning of the parent, no addictions to drugs or domestic violence;
- the existence of a bond between the child with the parent before the out-of-home placement of the child;
- the development of an attachment and parenting relationship between the child and his parent, as *seen* in observations during the programme; and
- an attachment and parenting relationship between the child and his foster parents has not yet developed, and/or his development has not yet improved. The traumatic loss of his foster parents can thus be avoided.

If the child does not accept the attention and guidance of the parent sufficiently, the child should not be reunited with his parents. When it is decided that he will grow up in a foster family, it is necessary that the parental rights come to an end in order to establish security. Otherwise the parent can stop the foster placement, refuse to give permission for a specific treatment, a holiday abroad, or enrolment in a certain school. The termination of parental rights will give the child and his foster parent a future together, necessary for development of a healthy relationship.[47] But it will give the parent a new future as well, not 'fighting' all the time to get his child back but trying to create an emotional bond with his child in a new way.

As stated above in the introduction, a model to obtain existential security for a foster child is now being tested. This model, the Pedagogical Decision Model for Foster Care (PDM), is now part of a project that started in the autumn of 2009 with discussions between youth care services in Tilburg and Goirle[48] and the Expertise Centre on Children in Foster Care.[49] A reunification programme was set up, with a detailed design,[50] and in 2011 the first foster children were

---

47 See E.C.C. Punselie, *Voor een pleegkind met recht een toekomst*, PhD thesis, Leiden University, Leiden 2006.

48 Bureau Jeugdzorg Tilburg; Pleegzorg Kompaan en De Bocht, Goirle, the Netherlands.

49 Stichting Expertisecentrum Kind in de pleegzorg, Voorschoten, the Netherlands (the present author is its Secretary).

50 The PDM programme is designed as follows:
  - An accurate assessment of all aspects of parental (in)adequacy or pathology.
  - A Care Order and the appointment of a family guardian is necessary because otherwise the parent can stop the programme and/or take the child with him at any time.

enrolled. The early results of a programme on the basis of this model will be briefly sketched. As these results are based on a relatively small number of cases, they should be seen as preliminary, however.

7.1. EARLY RESULTS OF THE PDM PROGRAMME

Until December 2014 the data of 43 children were analysed: 31 children of 0–5 years old, and 12 children of 6–11 years old.[51] In all cases with a care order but one, the court followed the advice to either return the child to his parent, or not. The duration of the programme was, on average, four months. Ten children were reunited (but only five of them according to the advice given; for four of the five other reunited children there was no care order); 15 children remained in the

- The PDM can best be started within six months of an out-of-home placement because there may still be an emotional bond between the parent and the child will most probably not yet have an attachment and parenting relationship with his foster parents – which could be a traumatic loss for the child.
- The practitioner who will support parent and child, starts with an assessment of the relationship between child and parent before the out-of-home placement. He interviews the parent about his experiences (PSI Questionnaires are used (see above section 2)).
- The child visits his parent every week at home, two hours to begin with, increasing up to 6–8 hours. During every visit the practitioner supports the parent, observes and reports.
- Another practitioner interviews the foster parents about the development of the child, the interaction between the child and the foster parents, and the contact with the parents (PSI Questionnaires are used).
- After every visit the foster parents fill in an observation form.
- The data of the PSI questionnaires and observations are analysed by an independent reporter, a psychologist who does not know child, parents and foster parents (in this programme, the present author is the independent reporter). The question to be answered is: will reunification be beneficial for the child's development, now and in the future?
- After 4–6 months the situation should be clear enough to give an advise about reunification (yes or no).
- The report and advice of the independent reporter is discussed by the Foster Care Service and the family guardian – who has the authority to decide and to bring his decision to court.
- When the court decides a yes, the child and his parent will receive support for at least six months.
- When the court decides a no, the child will grow up in a foster family – preferably in the same foster family.
- The family guardian will propose to the court to terminate the parental rights.
- One or two years after the decision, the reunification or the foster placement will be evaluated.

51 A.M. Weterings and M. Bakker, 'Pedagogisch Beslissingsmodel bij Terugplaatsing van pleegkinderen; Bestaanszekerheid voor vier generaties', Report, Expertise Centrum Kind in de Pleegzorg, Voorschoten, 2014; and an internal paper, Autumn 2015 (by A.M. Weterings). The project is partly subsidised by the *Kinderpostzegels* Foundation in the Netherlands (SKN, Leiden).

same foster families; 14 children went to other foster families to stay there until their 18th birthdays; three children will go to other foster families where they can stay until they are 18; one child will stay in a semi-residential setting (but the caretakers will change in 2016 or 2017).

The average of positive reactions of the child towards his parents were 80% for the reunited children, and 56% for the children who will stay permanently in a foster families. The difference in positive reactions towards the parent of reunited and not reunited children is considerable. Only one (of the 18 items) was scored positively for nearly all the children: 'Doing things together was pleasant'. This should be noted because in many reunification programmes this item is considered the most relevant observation and an important reason for the family guardian and the court to decide on reunification.

Existential security was obtained for two thirds of the children, that is, for five children, who were reunited with their parent according to the advice; and for 24 children who can stay with their foster families until they are 18 (with termination of the parental rights of their parents). The PDM also gave existential security in other ways. Eight foster children were enlisted for the programme, but as the parent could not meet the conditions, was not able to lead a regular life, and cancelled appointments, the court decided that these children should permanently stay with their foster families. Six foster children showed severe regression in conduct after visits to their parents. The practitioners and the family guardians took notice of this behaviour, and the programme was stopped after two to three months. The court decided that these children should also permanently stay with their foster parents.

7.2. AN EXAMPLE: LISA, 1 YEAR AND 4 MONTHS OLD

Lisa did not react to any attempt of the foster mother to form a bond with her. She did not cry, did not make any sound, she hardly moved. The foster mother did not know what she needed. Lisa seemed mentally disturbed. After three months of affectionate care the girl 'came alive'. After a year she proved to be a 'normal' child, although easily unsettled. When she was three years old, the mother wanted the child back. The court approved a PDM reunification programme. After each visit to the mother, Lisa became more and more disturbed, had nightmares, didn't eat, cried, and didn't speak anymore. 'It was terrible to see her suffering', the foster mother said. The youth care service stopped the programme and Lisa stayed with her foster parents.

7.3. FIRST EVALUATION OF THE PDM PROGRAMME WITH THE PSI QUESTIONNAIRES

In 2013/2014 an evaluation has been started for six foster children and two children who had returned to their mother (siblings).[52] All foster children still had problems in many areas of their development. Yet the problems had clearly diminished. The behaviour of three children had improved in a spectacular way. The development of one of the two reunited children had clearly improved, the younger one had not had many problems. They were placed out of home for only six months when the programme started. A remarkable result was that for *all* eight children the attachment and parenting relationship had improved and for four of them this was especially clear. The contact with the father had improved for two foster children, three children did not have contact and for one child the contact caused more problems. All six foster children had contact with the mother. The contact had improved for one child only.

7.4. CONCLUDING REMARKS

The PDM is designed for decision making in accordance with the best interests principle in the Convention on the Rights of the Child, more specifically its Articles 3(1) (prioritisation of this principle for, *inter alia*, youth care services and courts), 18(1) (the best interests of their child as the basic concern of his parents), and 20 (continuity in a child's upbringing in case of foster placement, adoption or other care for a child who, in his own best interests, cannot stay with his parents).[53] In order to cut down the 'endless temporariness' for all persons concerned, a definite decision about either living with the parents or living in a

---

52 This evaluation is independently conducted according to a method described in A.M. Weterings, *Het Draaiboek voor het Pedagogisch Beslis-Model voor (terugplaatsing van) Pleegkinderen*, Expertise Centrum Kind in de Pleegzorg, Voorschoten, 2015 (section 8).

53 When making decisions concerning reunification, youth care services should pay attention to the following indicators and observations.
Indicators for the start of a reunification programme:
- The parent leads a stable life and can run a household.
- No drug or alcohol addiction and no violence.
- The parent has experienced some positive care from his own parent (experience of parenting).
- The child has experienced some positive care from his parent as a basis for the development of an attachment and parenting relationship with his parent.
- The PDM for reunification can be best started within (half) a year after the out-of-home placement.

Observations during the visits:
- The child shows positive emotions towards his parent (glad to see him; asking to be cuddled).
- He seeks his parent for comfort and help.
- He accepts the authority of the parent.

foster family should be made in about one year after the out-of-home placement of a child, including the termination of parental rights when the child will stay with a foster family. A recent study clearly shows the positive effect of this legal support, especially when the foster child will be adopted. When a foster child is adopted, his situation is much more stable, with far less disruptions, than just a 'permanent' foster placement.[54]

8. CONCLUSION

The objective of youth and foster care is, or should be, to give the deprived child an opportunity to develop adequately – to his benefit and the benefit of society. Often that child is raised in a family where neglect is passed on from one generation to the next. It is necessary to break that vicious circle, and therefore to end youth care services' interpretive denial. Youth care services should do so by a research-based reappraisal of their prevailing opinion, namely, that child and parent belong together (the 'blood-tie myth'). This is most evident in foster care. The child is sent to foster parents because of neglect or abuse by his parents, but youth care services are still acting on the principle that the child should return to his parents, although this might never happen. The child is saddled with insecurity, not knowing who will take care of him in the near and far future. This insecurity hampers his abilities to develop and causes conduct disorders. In order to develop healthily, a child needs existential security, living with caregivers who he can trust and rely upon. Acknowledging this is the first step towards policies that are in accordance with Articles 3(1), 18(1) and 20 of the Convention on the Rights of the Child.

- After approximately six months in the PDM programme, the parent is able – increasingly so – to understand the behaviour of the child and to act accordingly.
- The child does not show conduct disorders after visits to his parent.

54 See J. Selwyn, D. Wijedasa and S. Meakings, *Beyond the adoption order*, UK Department of Education, BAAF, London 2014.

CHAPTER VII

CRIME IN THE INTERCOUNTRY ADOPTION INDUSTRY

Towards a Broader Definition of Child Trafficking

Elvira LOIBL

1. INTRODUCTION

In Western countries, the demand for adoptable children, especially healthy infants, has been considerably high for several years. Rising infertility rates, liberal abortion politics, the widespread use of contraception, and the increasing acceptance of unmarried motherhood are factors that have decreased the number of infants available for domestic adoption in the United States, Canada and Europe. As a consequence, numerous involuntarily childless couples and individuals turn to intercountry adoption as viable alternative to have a child of their own. However, the continuing demand for children far outpaces the supply of orphans with the desired characteristics.[1]

The imbalance between the number of prospective adopters and the children available for international adoption results in long waiting lists and high prices. The inordinate sums of money involved in the intercountry adoption system have created a commercial 'underbelly' where unethical and illicit practices are employed to provide the intercountry adoption market with adoptable children. Thus, children that are not in need of a home or that could have been properly

1 A. FLEISHER, 'The Decline of Domestic Adoption: Intercountry Adoption as a Response to Local Adoption Laws and Proposals to Foster Domestic Adoption' (2003) 13 *Review of Law and Women's Studies* 1, 171, 174–175; R. RIOS-KOHN, 'Intercountry adoption: An international perspective on the practice and standards' (1998) 1 4 *Adoption Quarterly* 3, 6–8; R. HÖGBACKA, 'The quest for a child of one's own: Parents, markets and transnational adoption' (2008) 39 *Journal of Comparative Family Studies* 3, 311, 311–314.

cared for in their native countries are being placed internationally to meet the growing demand for intercountry adoptions.[2]

Despite numerous well-documented adoption scandals, many promoters of intercountry adoption deny the widespread existence of the system's underbelly. They perceive that illicit adoption practices occur only rarely and consider decisions by sending countries to restrict or ban intercountry adoptions as 'throwing the baby out with the bath water'.[3] Even those who acknowledge the considerable evidence of illegal adoption practices downplay the profound harm inflicted upon the children, their birth parents as well as the local welfare systems. They argue that the positive aspects of intercountry adoption clearly outweigh any illegal adoption activities.

This article claims that purchasing, abducting and selling children for the purpose of adoption is a serious crime and seeks to explain why the issue and its harmful consequences is being denied by the international legal community, by scholars and the wider public. For this purpose, Henry and Lanier's 'prism of crime' is applied to illustrate the dimensions of the intercountry adoption system's underbelly. The article explains how the illegal adoption practices create profound individual and social harm, which, however, remains invisible in the majority of cases. In addition, it draws on Cohen's states of denial to assess the public disagreement on the seriousness of purchasing, abducting and selling children for the purpose of adoption. Finally, this article shows why the probability of a severe social response to this crime is generally low.

Section 2 describes the various forms of illegal adoption practices and aims to define the full scope the intercountry adoption system's 'underbelly'. Section 3 explains Henry and Lanier's 'prism of crime' by outlining its five dimensions, and section 4 applies this conceptual framework to examine the different dimensions of purchasing, abducting and selling children for the purpose of adoption. Section 5 concludes by proposing a broader definition of child trafficking, covering not only the transfer of a child for the purpose of sexual exploitation, forced labour and organ removal, but also the purchasing, kidnapping and selling of children for the purpose of adoption.

---

2 F. Fuentes, H. Boéchat and F. Northcott 'Investigating the Grey Zones of Intercountry Adoption' (2012) *International Social Service, International Reference Centre for the Rights of Children Deprived of their Family* 22.

3 E. Bartholet, 'International adoption: The child's story' (2007) 24 *Georgia State University Law Review* 333, 375.

2. THE INTERCOUNTRY ADOPTION SYSTEM'S UNDERBELLY

Cases of illegal adoption practices have been uncovered in many countries. According to Smolin, these countries usually are characterised by two factors: (1) a large proportion of the population lives in poverty, and (2) the country has become a significant sending nation.[4] Thus, stealing and selling children has been observed, for instance in Peru, Brazil, Paraguay, Colombia, Honduras, Sri Lanka, Romania,[5] Guatemala[6], India[7], Haiti[8], and Cambodia.[9] However, also in China, a developed country, illegal adoption practices have been uncovered.[10] The actors involved in the intercountry adoption system's underbelly employ a variety of *modi operandi* to generate adoptable children. Often real cases are a combination of these methods.[11]

In some sending countries attorneys, orphanage directors, and independent agents establish a system for *purchasing* children from their birth parents. These systems, Smolin describes, 'usually involve persons at the head of a criminal network who possess the language, literacy skills and the financial and social position to interact with adoption agencies and prospective adoptive parents in the sending countries'.[12] They send out unofficial intermediaries or 'recruiters', typically of a lower social status, to approach vulnerable pregnant women or birth mothers – most often young, impoverished and unmarried – and to incite them to give up their future or newborn child.[13] Consent to relinquishment is

4 D.M. Smolin, 'Child Laundering: How the Intercountry Adoption System Legitimizes and Incentivizes the Practices of Buying, Trafficking, Kidnapping, and Stealing Children' (2006) 52 *The Wayne Law Review* 113, 126.

5 J.L. Carro, 'Regulation of intercountry adoption: Can the abuses come to an end?' (1994) 18 *Hastings International & Comparative Law Review* 121, 131–140.

6 D.M. Smolin, 'Child Laundering: How the Intercountry Adoption System Legitimizes and Incentivizes the Practices of Buying, Trafficking, Kidnapping, and Stealing Children' (2006) 52 *The Wayne Law Review* 113, 163–170.

7 D.M. Smolin, 'The Two Faces of Intercountry Adoption: The Significance of the Indian Adoption Scandals' (2004) 35 *Seton Hall Law Review* 403; A. Dohle, 'Inside Story of an Adoption Scandal' (2008) 39 *Cumberland Law Review* 131.

8 S. King, 'Owning Laura Silsby's Shame: How the Haitian Child Trafficking Scheme Embodies the Western Disregard for the Integrity of Poor Families' (2012) 25 *Harvard Human Rights Journal* 1.

9 T. Maskew, 'Child Trafficking and Intercountry Adoption: The Cambodian Experience' (2004) 35 *Cumberland Law Review* 619.

10 B.H. Stuy, 'Open Secret: Cash and Coercion in China's International Adoption Program' (2003) 44 *Cumberland Law Review* 355.

11 D.M. Smolin, 'Child Laundering: How the Intercountry Adoption System Legitimizes and Incentivizes the Practices of Buying, Trafficking, Kidnapping, and Stealing Children' (2006) 52 *The Wayne Law Review* 113, 118.

12 Ibid.

13 Ibid.

usually not given freely but induced by psychological pressure and financial or material rewards.[14]

Another method to illegally obtain children is the *deception of biological parents to obtain their consent to adoption*. Here biological parents are intentionally provided with false information about the consequences of an adoption in order to obtain their consent.[15] They may be told that their child is only going away for educational purposes or on a temporary basis. Or they may be promised that they can keep contact with their child, receive payments from the adoptive parents or will be allowed to follow their child to the Western nation once the child has grown up.[16] In other cases birth parents are urged to sign paperwork relinquishing their parental rights without understanding the concept of 'relinquishment' that is based on a culturally foreign, exclusivist nuclear family model.[17]

Also, there are cases where children are being obtained through *kidnapping or abduction*. The children are being kidnapped either from the streets, schools, or their homes[18] or abducted from orphanages or hostels where they have been placed into temporarily by their parents for purposes of education or care.[19] Poor families commonly use these institutions as a safety net without, however, intending to sever their parental rights or ties.[20] Furthermore, there are incidences

---

14 Pregnant women or birth mothers may be told that they are not the most suitable person to bring up a child properly and that they should give their future or new born children the opportunity to have a better life than themselves. Such pressure is often reinforced by the reward of free pre- and postnatal care or of money or goods, resulting in an actual purchase of the child (UNICEF International Child Development Centre, 'Intercountry adoption' (1998) UNICEF, Florence (Innocenti Digest no. 4), 6). In other incidences, birth mothers are being forced to give up their baby in payment of a debt. Some involve women who are not able to pay the costs of childbirth; others involve moneylenders who indebt vulnerable women and then propose or prompt them to place their child into an orphanage (D.M. Smolin, 'Child Laundering: How the Intercountry Adoption System Legitimizes and Incentivizes the Practices of Buying, Trafficking, Kidnapping, and Stealing Children' (2006) 52 *The Wayne Law Review* 113, 124.).

15 UNICEF International Child Development Centre, Intercountry adoption, (1998) UNICEF, Florence (Innocenti Digest no. 4), 6; D.M. Smolin, 'Child Laundering: How the Intercountry Adoption System Legitimizes and Incentivizes the Practices of Buying, Trafficking, Kidnapping, and Stealing Children' (2006) 52 *The Wayne Law Review* 113, 121.

16 D.M. Smolin, 'Child Laundering: How the Intercountry Adoption System Legitimizes and Incentivizes the Practices of Buying, Trafficking, Kidnapping, and Stealing Children' (2006) 52 *The Wayne Law Review* 113, 121.

17 D. M. Smolin, 'Intercountry adoption and poverty: A human rights analysis' (2007) 36 *Capital University Law Review* 413, 442–443.

18 D.M. Smolin, 'Child Laundering: How the Intercountry Adoption System Legitimizes and Incentivizes the Practices of Buying, Trafficking, Kidnapping, and Stealing Children' (2006) 52 *The Wayne Law Review* 113, 126.

19 Ibid., p. 119.

20 They either place their children into the institution on their own initiative for a period of time during which they are not able to care for them due to financial or other reasons; or the children are deliberately recruited into such an institution based on false pretenses. Scouts, for instance, prompt birth parents to send their children to an institution, which were being

where birth mothers are fooled into thinking that their newborn children were stillborn or died shortly after birth, while in reality the babies are being abducted from the hospitals or maternity clinics.[21] Finally, there is the scenario of child abduction in the aftermath of a natural disaster or in a conflict situation where 'lost' or 'missing' children are being placed for intercountry adoption without any efforts having been made to find their birth parents or relatives.[22]

After the children have been illegally obtained from their birth families through purchase, deception or abduction, birth certificates or any other documents necessary for an adoption are falsified by intermediaries, employees in child care institutions or bribed government officials to hide the illegal conduct and to identify the illegally obtained children as legally abandoned orphans.[23]

In other incidences, the official adoption act is maliciously avoided altogether by *processing a purchased or abducted child as* the adoptive parents' own *'biological child'*. Cases emerged where biological mothers registered in a maternity clinic using the adoptive mother's name, where the doctors falsely issued birth certificates with the name of the adoptive parents as biological parents or where the adoptive fathers untruthfully acknowledge the paternity of an allegedly 'illegitimate' child.[24]

The intercountry adoption system's underbelly does not only involve purchasing or kidnapping children from their intact families, but also purchasing and selling actual orphans. Cases were uncovered where adoptive parents, adoption agencies or their intermediaries *bribe government officials* or *grant financial or material rewards to employees of a childcare institution* to secure a steady supply with orphaned children by circumventing the subsidiary

promoted as boarding schools (D.M. Smolin, 'Child Laundering: How the Intercountry Adoption System Legitimizes and Incentivizes the Practices of Buying, Trafficking, Kidnapping, and Stealing Children' (2006) 52 *The Wayne Law Review* 113, 120).

21 UNICEF International Child Development Centre, Intercountry adoption, (1998) UNICEF, Florence (Innocenti Digest no. 4), 6.

22 D.M. Smolin, 'Child Laundering: How the Intercountry Adoption System Legitimizes and Incentivizes the Practices of Buying, Trafficking, Kidnapping, and Stealing Children' (2006) 52 *The Wayne Law Review* 113, 121–122.

23 F. Fuentes, H. Boéchat and F. Northcott 'Investigating the Grey Zones of Intercountry Adoption' (2012) *International Social Service, International Reference Centre for the Rights of Children Deprived of their Family* 80–86.

24 UNICEF International Child Development Centre, Intercountry adoption, (1998) UNICEF, Florence (Innocenti Digest no. 4), 6; Commission on Human Rights, Report of the Special Rapporteur on the Sale of Children, Child Prostitution and Child Pornography, Ms Ofelia Calcetas-Santos, UN Doc E/CN.4/1999/71 (29 January 1999), paragraph 61. Often these approaches were already prearranged prior to the children's birth, involving psychological pressure and/or payments to the pregnant mother. In other cases birth certificates were issued with the names of the adoptive parents while the biological mothers were told that their newborn babies were stillborn or died shortly after birth (G. Wuttke, 'Ein Kind um jeden Preis? Eine Studie zum Adoptionskinderhandel', terre des hommes Deutschland e.V., Osnabrück 1996, 36–38).

principle as enshrined in the United Nations Convention on the Rights of the Child[25] and the Hague Convention on the Protection of Children and Co-Operation in Respect of Intercountry Adoption.[26] The orphaned children are thus placed internationally even though the available childcare options in the children's country of origin have not been exhausted.[27]

It is often difficult to distinguish between legal payments and the illegal purchase of a child. In most cases monies or goods are not granted as explicit considerations for the child. Rather, financial or material means are exchanged that might seem legitimate at first glance. Some adopters, for instance, provide money or gifts to the birth parents to enable them to care properly for the rest of the family.[28] Moreover, adopters or adoption agencies donate money or goods to the orphanage that provided the child for adoption.

But when does well-intentioned assistance to birth families or donations to childcare institutions transcend into the illicit sale of children? In the majority of cases assistance to birth parents is not given due to pure compassion or kindness[29] but implicitly conditioned on the relinquishment of the child.[30] For extremely poor families (by Western standards) small financial or material support that is conditioned on relinquishing the child will have the effect of actually inducing relinquishment.[31] Even assistance provided after consent has been given can be seen as the fulfilment of an expectation that in itself induced relinquishment.[32]

The same basically applies to monies and goods that are donated to childcare institutions. In developing countries the very existence of many childcare institutions relies heavily on donations. Monies or goods that are donated not independently but only in the context of an intercountry adoption, create an incentive for childcare institutions to circumvent the subsidiarity principle by placing an orphan internationally without having tried to find a foster or adoptive family in the child's country of origin.

Therefore, when assistance to deeply impoverished families or donations to childcare institutions relying on external funds are granted only with regard

25 United Nations Convention on the Rights of the Child, GA Res. 44/25, UN GAOR, 44th Sess., Supp. No. 49, at 166, UN Doc. A/44/736 [1989], hereafter UNCRC.

26 Hague Convention on Protection of Children and Co-Operation in Respect of Intercountry Adoption, 29 May 1993, 32 ILM 1134, hereafter Hague Convention.

27 S. Hoelgaard, 'Cultural determinants of adoption policy: A Colombian case study' (1998) 12 *International Journal of Law, Policy and the Family* 2, 202, 216–219.

28 D.M. Smolin, 'Intercountry adoption as child trafficking' (2004) 39 *Valparasio University Law Review* 2, 281, 312.

29 If assistance were given for the mere sake of compassion or kindness, families would presumably not need to relinquish their children due to extreme poverty, thereby rendering intercountry adoptions obsolete.

30 D.M. Smolin, 'Intercountry adoption as child trafficking' (2004) 39 *Valparasio University Law Review* 2, 281, 311.

31 Ibid., p. 312.

32 D.M. Smolin, 'Intercountry adoption and poverty: A human rights analysis' (2007) 36 *Capital University Law Review* 413, 434.

to an adoption, there is much to suggest that there is causality between the assistance and donations and the resulting international adoption of the child. The illicit payment was a *conditio sine qua non* for the resulting intercountry adoption and constitutes the purchase of a child.

Summa sumarum, the underbelly of the intercountry adoption system includes all those cases where a child (non-orphan or a true orphan) is kidnapped or purchased from her birth family, childcare institution or hospital and sold for the purpose of adoption. A child is being purchased and sold for the purpose of an intercountry adoption when there is a causality between the assistances given to deeply impoverished families, the donations provided to childcare institutions, and the bribes offered to government officials and the resulting intercountry adoption.

The Intercountry Adoption System's Underbelly			
	Scenario 1	Scenario 2	Scenario 3
Obtaining a child	– child is purchased from her birth family; – birth family is deceived to obtain consent for adoption; or – child is kidnapped or abducted from streets, school, home, childcare institution	– child is purchased from her birth mother; or – child is kidnapped from hospital, maternity clinic	– government official is bribed to legitimise an international adoption of an orphaned child; – orphaned child is purchased from childcare institution
Falsifying/ falsely issuing documents	child's birth certificate/ other official documents are falsified	child's birth certificate is falsely issued with the names of the adoptive parents as biological parents	child's adoption documents falsely state that no adequate family could have been found in the child's country of origin
Effect	official adoption process can be used to 'launder' the child as 'orphan' and then adoptee	adoption process is avoided by processing the child as the adoptive parent's own 'biological child'	subsidiarity principle is violated

3. MOVING BEYOND A LEGAL DEFINITION OF CRIME – HENRY AND LANIER'S 'PRISM OF CRIME'

Numerous criminologists have criticised the strict legal definition of crime – as acts or omissions in violation of criminal law – for being too limited in its scope. This traditional concept, critics claim, takes no account of harms covered by administrative law and considered regulatory violations.[33] It ignores the historical and cultural relativity of criminal law since what is defined as criminal by law can vary over time and between different societies and jurisdictions.[34] Moreover, criminal law is shaped by the interests of powerful groups with the ability to influence legislation, whereas powerless groups are generally the victims of oppressive laws.[35]

Over the course of time, differing definitions of crime have been presented that reflected particular disciplinary perspectives.[36] In the late 1990s, Henry and Lanier incorporated the seemingly contradictory views of crime into a comprehensive concept that takes into account not only what is considered criminal by law but also a range of behaviours that are potentially liable to criminal law. They did this by developing a conceptual framework to define the full spectrum of dimensions that constitute 'crime'.[37]

The first dimension of crime is the *individual or social harm* that an act inflicts. It refers to direct individual harm, where the offender has specifically targeted the victim. 'The most harmful crimes here include those in which the victims are killed and those in which they become permanently injured and maimed; through crimes that are harmful through some temporary loss of capability, money, property, or position; to those that might offend moral sensibilities but not directly result in personal loss'.[38] However, this dimension also refers to less direct social harm and injuries by offences of powerful groups against the powerless.[39]

---

33 E.H. Sutherland, 'White-Collar Criminality' (1940) 5 *American Sociological Review* 1.

34 G. Nettler, *Explaining Crime*, McGraw-Hill, New York 1984, 1; G. Barak, *Integrating Criminologies*, Allyn and Bacon, Boston 1998, p. 21.

35 E.H. Sutherland, 'White-Collar Criminality' (1940) 5 *American Sociological Review* 1, 1; R. Quinney, *The Problem of Crime*, Dodd, Mead, New York 1970.

36 E.H. Sutherland, 'White-Collar Criminality' (1940) 5 *American Sociological Review* 1; G. Barak, *Integrating Criminologies*, Allyn and Bacon, Boston 1998; T. Sellin, 'Culture Conflict and Crime' (1938) 44 *American Journal of Sociology* 1, 97; E.H. Sutherland, 'White-Collar Criminality' (1940) 5 *American Sociological Review* 1; G. Nettler, *Explaining Crime*, McGraw-Hill, New York 1984; H. Schwendinger and J. Schwendinger, 'Defenders of Order or Guardians of Human Rights' (1970) 5 *Issues in Criminology* 123; H. Bianchi, *Position and Subject-Matter of Criminology: Inquiry Concerning Theoretical Criminology*, North Holland Pub. Co., Amsterdam 1956; R. Quinney, *The Problem of Crime*, Dodd, Mead, New York 1970.

37 S. Henry and M. Lanier, 'The Prism of Crime: Arguments for an Integrated Definition of Crime' (1998) 15 *Justice Quarterly* 609.

38 S. Henry and M. Lanier, 'The Prism of Crime: Toward an Integrated Definition of Crime' in S. Henry and M. Lanier, *What is Crime? Controversies over the Nature of Crime and What to Do about It*, Rowman & Littlefield Publishers, Lanham 2001, p. 232.

39 H. Schwendinger and J. Schwendinger, 'Defenders of Order or Guardians of Human Rights' (1970) 5 *Issues in Criminology* 123; S. Cohen, 'Human Rights and Crimes of the State: The Culture of Denial' (1993) *Australian and New Zealand Journal of Criminology* 26, 97; R.J. Michalowski, *Order, Law, and Crime: An Introduction to Criminology*, Random House, New York 1985; A. Von Hirsch and N. Jareborg, 'Gauging Criminal Harm: A Living-Standard Analysis' (1991) *Oxford Journal of Legal Studies* 2, 1.

The second dimension of crime is the *degree of social agreement about the wrongfulness of an act* that can vary from greatest agreement, through moderate agreement, apathy or disinterest, to high disagreement, or extreme conflict.[40]

The third dimension is the *probability of severe social response* that refers to the likelihood that a convicted offender will actually receive a severe response provided by the law. This dimension may range from the 'high probability of severe sanctions for convicted offenders (e.g., death penalty or life imprisonment), through moderate sanctions (e.g., short-term sentences, fines, or probation), to a high probability of mild sanctions (e.g., community service, counselling, or public condemnation)'.[41]

Another dimension of crime, according to Henry and Lanier, is the *extensiveness of victimisation*.[42] The number of victims of a criminal act influences the public's perception of its seriousness. Thus, a crime that only harms one person is somehow qualitatively different from acts of violence that harm many people (e.g. terrorist attacks, school rampages). However, the perception of a crime's seriousness is not only shaped by the absolute number of victims, but also by the victims' social and political status.[43]

The last dimension of crime is the *visibility of crime* which is linked to the public's awareness that a particular behaviour is harmful and thus needs to be criminalised.[44] Some crimes may be extremely harmful yet victims might never, or only after a long time has passed, realise that they have actually been harmed (e.g. government or corporate crime). Crime may thus 'range from "being "obvious" or "readily apparent" to "relatively hidden" and, finally, so "obscure" that it is accepted by many as normal, even though it harms its victims (e.g. environmental crimes, racism, and patriarchy)'.[45]

To visualise the continuous spectrum of the five dimensions of crime, Henry and Lanier designed the 'prism of crime'. Its upper half of prism represents the highly visible crime, typically committed in public by the powerless and including acts that are widely agreed as wrongful and that are likely to receive severe societal response. Its lower half represents the less visible crimes. These include a variety of crimes by the powerful and are often met with apathy

40 S. Henry and M. Lanier, 'The Prism of Crime: Toward an Integrated Definition of Crime' in S. Henry and M. Lanier, *What is Crime? Controversies over the Nature of Crime and What to Do about It*, Rowman & Littlefield Publishers, Lanham 2001, pp. 229–230.

41 Ibid., p. 231.

42 S. Henry and M. Lanier, The Prism of Crime: Arguments for an Integrated Definition of Crime' (1998) 15 *Justice Quarterly* 609, 620.

43 Ibid.

44 Ibid., p. 619.

45 S. Henry and M. Lanier, 'The Prism of Crime: Toward an Integrated Definition of Crime' in S. Henry and M. Lanier, *What is Crime? Controversies over the Nature of Crime and What to Do about It*, Rowman & Littlefield Publishers, Lanham 2001, p. 228.

and disinterest or disagreement about their wrongfulness and are likely to be moderately or mildly sanctioned.[46]

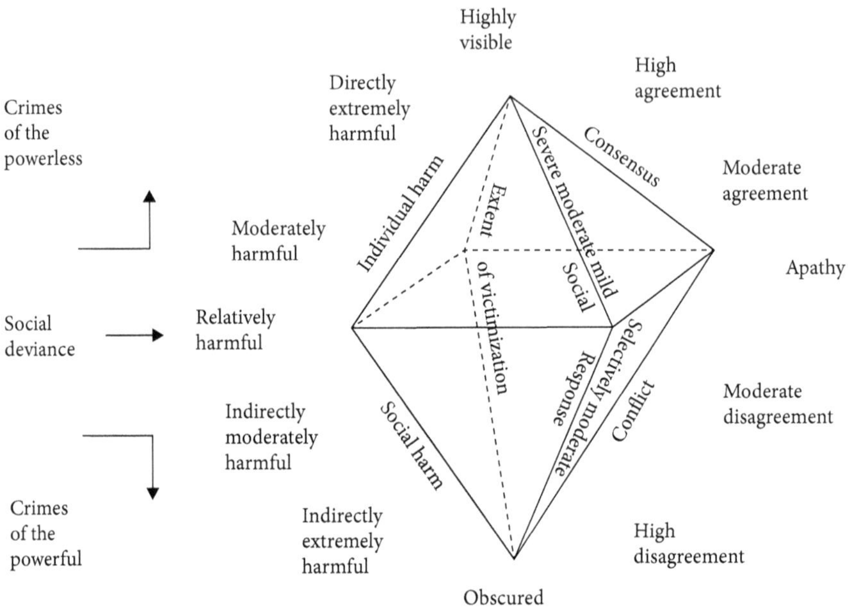

Source: S. Henry and M. Lanier, 'The Prism of Crime: Arguments for an Integrated Definition of Crime' (1998) 15 *Justice Quarterly* 609, 622.

4. THE PRISMATIC ANALYSIS OF THE DIMENSIONS OF CHILD TRAFFICKING FOR THE PURPOSE OF ADOPTION

4.1. INDIVIDUAL AND SOCIAL HARM

The illegal practices employed to serve the market with adoptable children result in a profound interference with these children's rights. The intercountry adoption system's underbelly involves a large network of different individuals or organisations (typically unknown to each other). The actors engaged in illegal adoption practices may be state actors, like judges or government officials, but may also be private agents, ranging from recruiters looking for vulnerable pregnant women and birth families, orphanage directors, doctors, nurses or lawyers.[47] The system's underbelly might, thus, not always involve state agents,

46 Ibid., p. 229.

47 UNICEF International Child Development Centre, Intercountry adoption, (1998) UNICEF, Florence (Innocenti Digest no. 4), p. 6.

which is why not all illegal adoption activity is technically speaking a violation of human rights. Nevertheless, to demonstrate the seriousness of the harm created by the intercountry adoption system's power, it is useful to reflect on the children's basic rights that are being interfered with.

Basically, every legitimate international adoption involves a degree of interference with the child's rights. Children that are placed with an adoptive family of a different race in a different country undoubtedly have their right to identity preservation affected. Article 8 of the UNCRC provides the child with the right to preserve her identity that does not only include nationality, name and family relations but also other aspects, such as the child's culture, religion and language. In light of Article 8, Article 20(3) states that when considering a childcare solution for an unparented child 'due regard shall be paid to the desirability of continuity in the child's upbringing and to the child's ethnic, religious, cultural and linguistic background'.

The Convention's Preamble also stresses the need of all young children for a family by asserting that the family is 'the fundamental group of society and natural environment for the growth and well-being of all its members and particularly children' and that 'the child, for the full and harmonious development of her personality, should grow up in a family environment, in an atmosphere of happiness, love and understanding'. Accordingly, the Handbook of the UNCRC clarifies that the priority should be to place the unparented child into her wider family[48] or in a foster or adoptive family in the child's country of origin, institutional care being considered the destination of last resort.[49]

In relation to the principle of identity preservation as well as to the need of a child to grow up in a family, Article 21(b) determines that intercountry adoption 'may only be considered as an alternative means of child's care if the child cannot be placed in a foster or an adoptive family or cannot in any suitable manner be cared for in the child's country of origin'. Thus, placing the child in a permanent family in the country of origin is clearly to be prioritised over placing the child internationally. But this raises difficult questions. For example, what should happen if a domestic foster or adoptive family cannot be found? Should institutional care in the child's country of origin be considered a suitable childcare measure, one to be prioritised over intercountry adoption? Should the child's right for a family environment override the child's right to preserve her identity or *vice versa*? The UNCRC does not provide an explicit answer, which has resulted in a lack of consensus among experts.

It is arguably not possible or even necessary to provide a definite answer. Each case requires a careful examination of the child and the available childcare

48 R. Hodgkin and P. Newell, *Implementation Handbook for the Convention on the Rights of the Child*, UNICEF, Geneva 2007, p. 281.

49 Ibid., p. 285.

options, in which the child's interests are to be given paramount consideration.[50] Tearing an older child who has already gained a deep sense of cultural and cultural identity out of her familiar environment to place her in an adoptive family in another country is arguably not in the child's best interests and thus violates her basic rights. However, for an unparented infant with special medical needs or a stigma (e.g. being the child of a prostitute) that cannot be placed in an adoptive or foster family in her native country, intercountry adoption might indeed be preferred to institutional care. Young children's developmental needs require a permanent care giver and a family in a developed country might be in a better position to provide proper medical care. The child that is being transferred to another country for the purpose of adoption is obviously ripped out of her ethnic and cultural background. However, the interference with the child's right to identity preservation can be justified by the goal to place him or her into a permanent family environment. The intercountry adoption, thus, ultimately serves the best interests of the child.

The illegal adoption practices outlined in section 2 result in an interference with the children's fundamental rights that cannot be justified whatsoever. The child is affected in her right to identity preservation and – in those cases where she is being removed from her intact families through purchase, abduction or the birth parent's deception – in her right to a family (Articles 7 and 9 UNCRC). Contrary to the example just presented, this infringement does not ultimately serve the best interests of the child. The institution of intercountry adoption is stripped of its humanitarian *rationale* and is being abused by the powerful of the system – adopters, orphanage directors, lawyers, government officials, etc. – to serve their own interests. Intercountry adoption's primary purpose is not to find a family for an unparented child. Rather, intercountry adoption is being misused as a remedy for involuntarily childless couples in Western societies who wish to have their own child as well as a source of capital for those involved in the system that provide adoptable children.

The child is not seen as a unique person with needs, interests and basic rights. Rather, the child is being denied humanity and reduced to a marketable commodity. Her characteristics as healthy and young are being exploited by adoptive parents who want their desire for a child to be fulfilled no matter the price and by individuals and organisations involved in the adoption system that

---

50 See also R.R. Carlson, 'The Emerging Law of Intercountry Adoptions: An Analysis of the Hague Conference on Intercountry Adoption' (1994) 30 *Tulsa Law Journal* 243, 258; and D.M. Smolin, 'Intercountry adoption and poverty: A human rights analysis' (2007) 36 *Capital University Law Review* 413, 424, arguing that this approach is reflected by Article 3(1) UNCRC which asserts that '[I]n all actions concerning children … the best interests of the child shall be a primary consideration.' The UNCRC 'child's best interests' standard is also mirrored in Article 4(b) of the Hague Convention that asserts that an intercountry adoption shall take place only if the competent authorities have determined, after considering the childcare possibilities in the country of origin, that an intercountry adoption is in the child's best interests.

want to gain financially from the intercountry adoption. The child is arguably not being placed for an international adoption because she was in need of a home and the measure has been considered carefully as the best possible childcare option for him or her. The child is being adopted internationally primarily because monies or goods – probably disguised as 'donations' or 'assistance' – were provided.

Removing a child from her intact family through purchase, abduction or deception of the parents (scenario 1 or 2) does not only deeply harm the child but also her birth family. In many sending countries families are discriminated against and marginalised on the basis of their status, including poverty, race, religion, sex, mental and physical disabilities, HIV/AIDS or other serious illnesses, birth out of wedlock, and other socio-economic stigmas. Impoverished birth parents, ethnic minorities and unmarried mothers are often considered as inferior and unworthy of keeping their children that are deemed, however, highly valuable. In the intercountry adoption system's underbelly, their status as the child's family, their responsibilities and capacities for the upbringing and development of their child are systematically being denied. By illegally taking their children, marginalised birth parents are being misused as a breeding unit whose fertility but also extreme powerlessness is exploited. In an intercounty adoption system that is being shaped and influenced by the powerful, discriminated often uneducated birth parents do *de facto* neither have a voice nor the capacities to effectively defend themselves against illegal practices.

Granting financial or material rewards to an employee of a childcare institution or bribing government officials to secure a ready supply with orphaned children (scenario 3) that result in the circumvention of the subsidiary principle does not only result in direct individual harm to the children. It also causes indirect social harm by disrupting and destroying the social welfare system in the sending country.[51] The inordinate sums of money or goods provided with regard to an intercountry adoption make any domestic childcare solution an uneconomic and, thus, unattractive option. Integrating children into their birth or wider families, promoting domestic adoption or foster care programmes or establishing appropriate childcare institutions require ample financial means. Intercountry adoption would, on the other hand, yield huge amounts of money.[52]

Childcare institutions will prefer to place the children internationally rather than assist their birth families or seek a suitable family in the children's country of origin. Government officials will approve an intercountry adoption even though not all domestic childcare solutions have been exhausted. This leads to the paradox whereby children are put up for international adoption even when

---

51 D.M. Smolin, 'The Two Faces of Intercountry Adoption: The Significance of the Indian Adoption Scandals' (2004) 35 *Seton Hall Law Review* 403, 447–448; R. Post, *Romania – for Export Only: The Untold Story of the Romanian 'Orphans'*, EuroComment Diffusion, Netherlands 2007; S. Hoelgaard, 'Cultural determinants of adoption policy: A Colombian case study' (1998) 12 *International Journal of Law, Policy and the Family* 2, 202.

52 Ibid.

waiting lists for domestic adoptive or foster families are lengthening.[53] The illicit payments made in connection with the intercountry adoption of an orphaned child undermine the fundamental principles of the UNCRC and the Hague Convention that prioritise reintegrating the child into her (extended) family or finding a domestic childcare solutions.[54] However, they not only subvert the subsidiarity principle but also incite childcare institutions or other organisations or individuals to secure 'adoptable children' (scenario 1).

4.2. INVISIBILITY OF HARM

As has been shown, the illegal practices employed to serve the market in adoptable children create profound individual and social harm. However, this harm is difficult to trace and thus often remains invisible to the victims or the wider public or both. In cases where employees of childcare institutions or government officials are paid to secure the ready supply of an orphaned child the causal connection between the bribes or 'donations' and the resulting intercountry adoption is often ambiguous. In many developing countries extra payments for services or approvals are common. In corrupt systems it can be virtually impossible to establish whether the illicit payments resulted in an actual circumvention of the subsidiarity principle or whether they have just caused the government official or the orphanage personnel to provide a proper approval or service more quickly than would otherwise be the case.[55] Thus, illicit payments can very well result in an intercountry adoption that is ultimately in the best interests of the orphan and does not, thus, constitute an illegal purchase of the child.

In those incidences where children are purchased or kidnapped from their intact birth families, the illegal practices always cause profound harm to the children and their biological parents. However, the harm usually remains hidden. The majority of adoptive children taken from their families are infants that do not conceive the illegal circumstances of their placements and, therefore, do not realise that they have been victimised.[56] In addition, their birth mothers might not notice that they have been harmed in cases where they were falsely told that their newborn children were stillborn or died shortly after birth. Yet, even if birth parents realised that they have been victimised, the harm caused by the illegal practices remains invisible to the wider public in the majority of

53 D.M. Smolin, 'The Two Faces of Intercountry Adoption: The Significance of the Indian Adoption Scandals' (2004) 35 *Seton Hall Law Review* 403, 474.

54 Preamble of the Hague Convention; Article 21(b) UNCRC.

55 D.M. Smolin, 'The Two Faces of Intercountry Adoption: The Significance of the Indian Adoption Scandals' (2004) 35 *Seton Hall Law Review* 403, 448.

56 D.M. Smolin, 'Child Laundering: How the Intercountry Adoption System Legitimizes and Incentivizes the Practices of Buying, Trafficking, Kidnapping, and Stealing Children' (2006) 53 *The Wayne Law Review* 113, 160.

cases. Due to their extreme powerlessness, vulnerable birth parents usually lack the voice and the capacity to effectively report the purchase or abduction of their children.[57] An additional problem is the fact that the offenders often remain obscured as they are in legitimate, even honourable positions. They do not personify conventional criminals but are doctors, lawyers, government officials, orphanage directors or nuns.

Adding to these layers of insularity is a decision on an illegal adoption made in a court of law that bears all the hallmarks of a perfectly legal adoption procedure. Cantwell asserts: 'The "illegality" of that decision could thus result from situations where, variously, the required procedures have not been followed, documents have been falsified, the child has been declared adoptable without due cause or as a result of manipulation, money has changed hands ... but if it is truly an adoption, rather than some other form of transferor removal, it will necessarily and by definition have been approved by a judge. It follows that all events and acts that would make it "illegal" must therefore have taken place up to and including, but not after, the judgement. "Illegal international adoptions", therefore, are not the same as "illegally moving children abroad": in cases of the former, children are moved abroad legally following an adoption process that contains illegal elements'.[58] A decision made by a judge, thus, imparts the illegal adoption an ostensibly lawful form. The child illegally obtained for an intercountry adoption is, as Smolin vividly describes, 'laundered' through the legal adoption system, 'analogous to a criminal organization engaged in money laundering which obtains funds illegally but then "launders" them through a legitimate business'.[59]

All traces of the illegal adoption practices might be wiped out perfectly at the time the child enters the receiving country to live with her new adoptive family. The adoptive parents, the adoption agencies, and the government authorities may in most cases plausibly deny knowledge of illegal practices overseas and adhere to the idea that the intercountry adoption was a humanitarian deed saving a child from her terrible circumstances in the country of origin. However, the long chain of corruption may also extend to the receiving countries, where adoption agencies are available to place the trafficked children and where adoptive parents tolerate or ignore malpractice in order to secure an adoption. In either case, the rhetoric of charity will disguise the harm that has been caused to the adopted child, her birth parents, and the social welfare system's in the sending country.

57 Ibid., p. 200.

58 N. Cantwell, 'Is intercountry adoption linked with trafficking for exploitation?' (2005) 11–12 *Monthly Review of the International Reference Centre for the Rights of Children Deprived of their Family (ISS/IRC)* 1–2.

59 D.M. Smolin, 'Child Laundering: How the Intercountry Adoption System Legitimizes and Incentivizes the Practices of Buying, Trafficking, Kidnapping, and Stealing Children' (2006) 52 *The Wayne Law Review* 113, 115.

4.3. LACK OF PUBLIC AGREEMENT ON SERIOUSNESS

No comprehensive study of the numbers of children purchased, kidnapped and sold for the purpose of intercountry adoption has ever been undertaken. Given that the illegal adoption practices remain invisible in the majority of cases, it is impossible to present official statistics on their incidence. Nonetheless, prominent adoption scandals indicate the existence of the intercountry adoption system's commercial underbelly and there is much to suggest that they only represent the tip of the iceberg. However, despite reoccurring adoption crimes having harmed thousands of children, their birth families as well as the social welfare systems in the children's country of origin, there is a lack of agreement on the illegal practices' seriousness. Opponents to intercountry adoption that promote restrictive state regulations to limit the number of intercountry adoptions and to eliminate abuses are facing a powerful pro-adoption lobby, including politicians, adopters, lawyers and conservative think tanks, that deny the significance of the system's underbelly.[60]

King, having analysed the discourse on intercountry adoption in law review articles in the United States, illustrates the recurrent tropes and commonplaces that proponents of intercountry adoption use to downplay the incidence of illegal adoption practices: 'reports of child trafficking from sending countries are often qualified in law review articles as "rumors of," "scandals of," "tales of," and at times are explicitly described as misrepresentations or exaggerations by the media of sending countries that hurts children who need adoption'.[61] Wardle, for example, claims: 'Concerns about baby-selling are exaggerated ... [S]tories of baby-selling, baby-napping, and "black market adoptions," are given greatly exaggerated air time by the sensationalizing media. They sell newspapers and attract viewers, and thus are given excessive attention by profit-seeking media producers'.[62] Similarly, Chadwick downplays adoption scandals by arguing: 'Pre-existing suspicion, coupled with the large sums of money exchanged in an international adoption, have fueled the rumor mills which continue to churn out allegations of baby selling rings'.[63] Berger uses the word 'alleged' to describe baby selling and asserts that 'the media has found some instances of baby-selling and made the most of them'.[64]

---

60 R. Post, *Romania-for Export Only: The Untold Story of the Romanian 'Orphans'*, EuroComment Diffusion, Netherlands 2007.

61 S. King, 'Challenging Monohumanism: An Argument for Changing the Way We Think About Intercountry Adoption' (2008) 30 *Michigan Journal of International Law* 413, 438.

62 L.D. Wardle, 'Parentlessness: Adoption Problems, Paradigms, Policies, and Parameters' (2004) 4 *Whittier Journal of Child & Family Advocacy* 2, 323, 347.

63 K.A. Chadwick, 'Politics and Economics of Intercountry Adoption in Eastern Europe, The' (1999) 5 *Journal of International Legal Studies* 113, 121.

64 D. Berger, 'Improving the Safety and Efficiency of Foreign Adoptions: US Domestic Adoption Programs and Adoption Programs in Other Countries Provide Lessons for INS Reform' (1995) 5 *Cornell Journal of Law and Public Policy* 33, 38–39.

Opponents to intercountry adoption are often demonised and their responses to abusive adoption practices depicted as an overreaction and a threat to the children's best interests. Decisions by sending countries to restrict or oppose intercountry adoption due to serious incidents of child trafficking are described as irrational and disproportional responses 'due to public shame, fear of imperialism, nationalistic pride, or xenophobic attitudes toward Westerners' and as severe infringements of children's rights.[65] Chadwick, for instance, claims that 'stoic national pride has led countries such as the Ukraine and Georgia to impose bans on intercountry adoptions. These moratoriums are almost entirely economical and political decisions that neglect the best interests of the children'.[66] Liu dismisses developing countries' opposition to intercountry adoption 'as a result of their history of colonialism. ... They do not see the practice as being one of love for the child, but one used to satisfy the greediness and selfishness of others'.[67] McMillan criticises Latin American countries for often being 'reluctant to allow foreign adoption because of their own ethnocentric bias, ... [they] do not want to appear to the rest of the world as unable or unwilling to care for their own children'.[68] Marx portrays Romania's ban on all international adoptions as 'overly sweeping and restrictive ... [it] is a blatantly self-serving move aimed at achieving its own political and economic goals. Sadly, this comes at the expense of the children's best interests. Romania is hiding behind the best interest standard promulgated in international treaties and using is it to justify its own narcissistic policies'.[69]

Proponents of intercountry adoption do not only deny the frequency of adoption scandals, they also downplay the harm inflicted upon the children and their birth parents. Bartholet, one of the most visible advocates of intercountry adoption, provides a particularly explicit example. Talking about stealing and selling children, she claims: 'if we really care about children, we should be prepared to see even these evils in perspective. They are by no means the worst things that are happening to children or their parents today, and they occur relatively rarely'.[70] She also denies the harmful consequences that the monies involved in intercounry adoptions have on the welfare systems in the sending

65 S. King, 'Challenging Monohumanism: An Argument for Changing the Way We Think About Intercountry Adoption' (2008) 30 *Michigan Journal of International Law* 413, 434.

66 K.A. Chadwick, 'Politics and Economics of Intercountry Adoption in Eastern Europe, The' (1999) 5 *Journal of International Legal Studies* 113, 114.

67 M. Liu, 'International Adoptions: An Overview' (1994) 8 *Temple International & Comparative Law Journal* 187, 194–195.

68 M.A.C. McMillan, 'International Adoption: A Step Towards a Uniform Process' (1993) 5 *Pace International Law Review* 1, 137, 140.

69 M.S. Marx, 'Whose Best Interests Does It Really Serve – A Critical Examination of Romania's Recent Self-Serving International Adoption Policies' (2007) 21 *Emory International Law Review* 373, 411.

70 E. Bartholet, *Family bonds. Adoption and the politics of parenting*, Houghton Mifflin, Boston 1993, pp. 154–155.

countries by qualifying them as 'significant new funds to poor orphanages in sending countries'[71] that relieves the children's home countries of the burden of support.[72] Bartholet's blindness to the profound individual and social injuries caused by adoption crimes leads her to propose that restrictive state regulations and bureaucratic hurdles should be lifted. Also she promotes private adoptions – believed to provide fertile ground for abusive practices as they are directly arranged between the adoptive and birth parents – to ensure that as many children as possible can be placed for international adoption.[73]

When considering the broad range of narratives of denial around the illegal adoption practices, Cohen's states of denial are useful. Cohen described three varieties of denial.[74] The first variety is the *literal denial*, the assertion that something did not happen or is not true.[75] Here the fact or the knowledge of the fact is being denied.[76] The second state of denial is the *interpretive denial*, where not the facts themselves but their meaning is denied.[77] *Implicatory denial* is the third variety. Here neither the facts nor the conventional interpretation are denied but the 'psychological, literal or moral implications that conventionally follow'.[78] Promoters of intercountry adoption do not literally deny the illegal adoption practices, rather they give these practices and the reactions to them a different meaning. They interpret reports of stealing and selling children as exaggerations by the sensationalising and profit-seeking media and construe bans and restrictions as irrational responses due to public shame, ethnocentric bias, narcissism, or xenophobic attitudes. With regard to the harm that is caused by the illegal adoption practices, proponents either literally deny or justify them by claiming that there are by far worse things happening to children and their birth parents.

What are the reasons for the lack of public conviction about the seriousness of the illegal adoption practices? Why do so many legal scholars that ought to be as advocates of justice and guardians of human rights deny the illegal adoption practices and their harmful consequences? The denial is essentially due to the Western cultural mindset about the developing countries in general and about intercountry adoptions in particular that enables promoters of intercountry adoption to perceive this social practice as the ultimate humanitarian act. Western societies, post-colonial critics claim, tend to identify themselves, their

71 E. Bartholet, 'International adoption: Thoughts on the human rights issues' (2007) 13 *Buffalo Human Rights Law Review* 152, 186.

72 Ibid., p. 185.

73 E. Bartholet, 'International adoption: Thoughts on the human rights issues' (2007) 13 *Buffalo Human Rights Law Review* 152, 355–356.

74 S. Cohen, *States of Denial: Knowing About Atrocities and Suffering*, Blackwell Publishers, Oxford 2001.

75 Ibid., p. 7.

76 Ibid.

77 Ibid.

78 Ibid., p. 8.

culture and their knowledge as superior in comparison with non-Western people and their cultures.[79] In contract, the non-Westerns, particularly the people from countries in which the United States or European countries previously had colonies, are being identified as 'the others' and their culture, knowledge and discourse is being excluded or debased. The narratives in Western literature, films, legal practices, jurisprudence, and political discourse, critics claim, reflect this post-colonialist mindset and allow to subscribe universality to the Western culture and knowledge and its 'supporting institutions, vocabulary, scholarship, imagery, [and] doctrines'.[80]

King refers to the post-colonial way of thinking about intercountry adoption as 'MonoHumanism' in which 'children are not seen in the context of their family, community, and culture, but instead, narrowly as the potential children of Western adults. In other words, children are seen through a narrative of identity in the United States, which I am calling *MonoHumanism*, to the exclusion of knowledge and discourse with its origins in the lives, cultures, and vocabulary of the children themselves'.[81] This conception of intercountry adoption, King believes, does not only exist in legal scholarship, but also in other scholarship on adoption, in the media, and in reports of governmental and non-governmental organisations.[82] MonoHumanism is, thus, generally prevalent in public discourse on intercountry adoption. Western society has painted a picture of intercountry adoption that is shaped by their own view on themselves on non-Western people and that suits their own interests and needs.[83] In this picture the children's countries of origin and their birth families are being portrayed as inferior and degenerated. Intercountry adoption, though primarily serving as a remedy for involuntarily childless couples, is depicted as the only viable childcare option serving the children's best interests.

The children's countries of origin – many of them formerly colonised by the West – are described as suffering from impregnable conditions, such as economic collapses, political instability, civil wars, natural disasters, diseases, over-population, and widespread poverty from which children need to be rescued as soon as possible.[84] If the birth parents are acknowledged at all in the legal literature, they are commonly described as 'dead, sick, incapacitated, impoverished, desperate, neglected, addicted to drugs and alcohol, or shamed into abandoning their children'.[85] Western societies portray them as inferior,

---

79 E.W. Said, *Culture and imperialism*, Vintage, New York 1993; E.W. Said, *Orientalism*, Vintage Books, New York 1979.

80 E.W. Said, *Orientalism*, Vintage Books, New York 1979, p. 2.

81 S. King, 'Challenging Monohumanism: An Argument for Changing the Way We Think About Intercountry Adoption' (2008) 30 *Michigan Journal of International Law* 413, 415.

82 Ibid., p. 416.

83 Ibid., p. 425.

84 Ibid., p. 432.

85 Ibid., p. 443.

unworthy of keeping their children, or selfish as they deliberately relinquish their rights for a small amount of money.[86] Intercountry adoption is being conceptualised as the best solution, a charitable, humanitarian deed that saves children from their immediate circumstances and their neglectful families and offers them a 'better life' in a Western county with advanced medicine, better educational institutions, and so-called Western conveniences.[87] The 'best interest of the child' is being established as meaning to grow up in a Western family environment, whereas any child not living in such an ideal family environment is being identified as an 'orphan' in these narratives. 'Law review articles create this narrative by freely interchanging the word "orphan" with "abandoned," "street," "homeless," and "needy". The dominant narrative in law review suggests that an expanding discourse of who is adoptable has broadened the concept of who is adoptable'.[88] The idea that intercountry adoption might cause harm to the children is absolutely contrary to the Western conception of this social practice as the ultimate humanitarian deed.

That denial of the harm inflicted upon the birth families might be the result of an 'othering process' that people in non-Western countries undergo. In Western societies the abduction or purchase of children, e.g. by a parent/guardian or by a stranger for the purpose of adoption, usually shocks the common conscience and produces moral outrage in people. Yet the sale of children from developing countries often seems to offend the collective consciousness considerably less. As Henry and Lanier explain, '[t]his distinction is related to differences in importance attached to human life, based on people's social and political status in a hierarchically ordered society and on the social distance and divisions that complex societies create between human beings. In short, it pertains to socially constructed differences created between those with whom we can identify and "others" with whom we cannot'.[89] The material division between the rich (industrialised) and poor (developing) countries has constructed social distance between the Western people and the – often formerly colonialised – non-Western people. We, the Western society, define ourselves as superior and attach primary importance to the pursuance of your needs and interests. Yet the non-Western people are considered as the lesser 'others' with whom we cannot identify. This detachment allows us to ruthlessly exploit their resources, their labour, their bodies, as well as their children. Whereas we are appalled when cases emerge where 'our' children or families have been harmed, we disavow or deny the harm that our practices cause to the children of the 'others'.

86 Ibid.
87 Ibid., p. 440.
88 Ibid., pp. 444–445.
89 S. Henry and M. Lanier, 'The Prism of Crime: Arguments for an Integrated Definition of Crime' (1998) 15 *Justice Quarterly* 609, 620.

4.4. LOW PROBABILITY OF SEVERE SOCIAL RESPONSE

As has been shown, the chances that adoption scandals are being detected are slim. However, even if cases of kidnapping, purchasing and selling children for the purpose of intercountry adoption are being uncovered, the probability that the actors involved receive a serious official response designed to punish the unjustness involved in the illegal adoption practices is low. The people of a criminal network usually either go unpunished or are only convicted for relatively minor criminal offences, such as visa fraud, forging of documents or money laundering, not, however, for trafficking in human beings.[90] This is because kidnapping, purchasing and selling children for the purpose of intercountry adoption is not considered a form of human trafficking, according to the most important treaty in the field of transnational crime: the Protocol to Prevent, Suppress and Punish Trafficking in Persons, Especially Women and Children, supplementing the United Nations Convention AgainstTransnational Organised Crime.[91]

The Trafficking Protocol is the first global legally binding instrument with an agreed definition on trafficking in persons, especially in women and children. According to its Article 3(a), trafficking in persons has three constituent elements: (1) the recruitment, transfer and receipt of the person; (2) by the use of fraudulent means, including threat or use of force, coercion, abduction, fraud, deception, abuse of power or vulnerability, giving payments or benefits to a person in control of the victim; (3) for an exploitative purpose. However, in cases where children under the age of 18 are recruited, transferred and received for the purpose of exploitation, no fraudulent means need to be involved to be regarded as trafficking in persons.[92]

The Trafficking Protocol does not provide a definition of the term 'exploitation' but lists specific forms of it in Article 3(a), namely prostitution, sexual exploitation, forced labour, slavery and the removal of organs. Adoption is not included in the list of exploitative forms, however, the phrasing 'at a minimum' basically indicates that the list is to be understood as non-exhaustive that leaves room for a wider interpretation and permits the addition of unnamed or new forms of exploitation.[93] The *travaux préparatoires* to the Trafficking Protocol attempt to clarify as to when illegal adoption is to be considered a

---

90 D.M. Smolin, 'Child Laundering: How the Intercountry Adoption System Legitimizes and Incentivizes the Practices of Buying, Trafficking, Kidnapping, and Stealing Children' (2006) 52 *The Wayne Law Review* 113, 190–192.

91 Protocol to Prevent, Suppress and Punish Trafficking in Persons, Especially Women and Children; Supplementing the United Nations Convention Against Transnational Organized Crime, GA Res. 55/25, UN GAOR, 55th Sess., Supp. No. 49, at 60, UN Doc. A/45/49 (2001), hereafter Trafficking Protocol.

92 Trafficking Protocol, Art. 3(c).

93 A.T. Gallagher, *The International Law of Human Trafficking*, Cambridge University Press, Cambridge 2010, p. 40.

form of exploitation. They state: '[w]here illegal adoption amounts to a practice similar to slavery as defined in article 1, paragraph (d), of the Supplementary Convention on the Abolition of Slavery, the Slave Trade, and Institutions and Practices Similar to Slavery it will also fall within the scope of the protocol'.[94]

According to Article 1(d) of the Supplementary Convention on the Abolition of Slavery, the Slave Trade, and Institutions and Practices Similar to Slavery,[95] the term 'institutions or practices similar to slavery' includes, *inter alia*, '[a]ny institution or practice whereby a child or young person under the age of 18 years, is delivered by either or both of his natural parents or by his guardian to another person, whether for reward or not, with a view to the exploitation of the child or young person or of his labour'. Thus, just as the Trafficking Protocol, the Supplementary Slavery Convention requires an exploitation of the child, does, however, neither define the term 'exploitation', nor clarify whether the parents, an intermediary, the legal guardian or the receiving parents must have the intention to exploit the child.[96] The Trafficking Protocol's reference to the Supplementary Slavery Convention does, as Smolin claims, create a 'a problem of circular definitions': the Trafficking Protocol defines illegal adoption as a form of exploitation when it amounts to a practice similar to slavery, whereas the Supplementary Convention defines practices similar slavery as the transfer of a child for purposes of exploitation.[97]

Although the Trafficking Protocol's list of exploitative forms is open-ended, the claim that illegal adoption amounts to a form of exploitation is difficult to justify.[98] Even if a child has been purchased or abducted from her birth parents or from a childcare institution and consequently transferred to another country for the purpose adoption, the ultimate objective is the permanent placement of the child into a family which is perfectly legal and seems to be absolutely contrary to the concept of exploitation, the third constituent element of human trafficking.[99] The Trafficking Protocol's mere reference to the Supplementary Slavery Conventions also seems to support the view that adoption *per se* is not a form of exploitation. Therefore, only cases of illegal adoption that resulted in an actual exploitation of the child, e.g. sexual exploitation, forced labour or organ removal, fall within the scope of the Trafficking Protocol.[100]

---

94 United Nations Office on Drugs and Crime (UNODC), 'Travaux Prépartoires of the negotiations for the elaboration of the United Nations Convention against Transnational Organized Crime and the Protocols thereto', New York 2006, p. 347.

95 Supplementary Convention on the Abolition of Slavery, the Slave Trade, and Institutions and Practices Similar to Slavery, 07.09.1956, 18 UST 3201, 266 UNTS 3, hereafter Supplementary Slavery Convention.

96 A.T. Gallagher, *The International Law of Human Trafficking*, Cambridge University Press, Cambridge 2010, p. 40.

97 D.M. Smolin, 'Intercountry adoption as child trafficking' (2004) 39 *Valparasio University Law Review* 2, 296.

98 Ibid.

99 Ibid.

100 Ibid.; A.T. Gallagher, *The International Law of Human Trafficking*, Cambridge University Press, Cambridge 2010, p. 41.

5. TOWARDS A BROADER DEFINITION OF CHILD TRAFFICKING

There is widespread consensus among people within and across cultures that child trafficking carried out for the purposes of prostitution, pornography, organ removal, and forced labour is a serious crime which creates profound harm to the children affected. Societal response and moral outrage to uncovered child trafficking cases are immediate and pointed. In recent years the issue has climbed the political agenda, resulting in a number of international and regional treaties[101] as well as national criminal laws which are designed to react to and combat one of the fastest growing forms of transnational organised crime. Law enforcement agencies commonly devote all available resources and assemble specific task forces to deal with this particular crime. People involved in running the trafficking network are usually punished severely. Therefore, child trafficking for the purpose of prostitution, forced labour and organ removal would be placed on the top of Henry and Lanier's 'prism of crime'.

In contrast, there is social disagreement on the seriousness of purchasing, kidnapping, and selling children for the purpose of adoption. Proponents of intercountry adoption downplay the significance of the illegal adoption practices as well as the harm caused by them. In the discourse in law review articles on intercountry adoption, Cohen's states of denial could have been identified. Reports of stealing and selling children were interpreted as exaggerations by the sensationalising and profit-seeking media. Sending countries' decisions to ban or restrict intercountry adoption due to incidents of child trafficking are construed as irrational responses due to public shame, ethnocentric bias, narcissism, or xenophobic attitudes. With regard to the harm that is caused by the illegal adoption practices, proponents either literally deny or justify them by claiming that there are by far worse things happening to children and their birth parents.

The lack of public conviction about the seriousness of the illegal adoption practices is due to the Western cultural mindset about intercountry adoption that identifies this social practice as the ultimate humanitarian deed always saving children from poverty and starvation in the developing countries. The idea, however, that intercountry adoption might cause harm to the children is absolutely contrary to our post-colonial way of thinking about intercountry adoptions. This cultural mindset seems to be reflected in the Trafficking Protocol, the first and most important international legal instrument with an

---

101 e.g. ILO Convention No. 182 on the worst forms of child labour (1999); Protocol to Prevent, Suppress and Punish Trafficking in Persons, Especially Women and Children (2000); United Nations Convention Against Transnational Organized Crime (2000); Optional Protocol to the CRC on the Sale of Children, Child Prostitution and Child Pornography (2000); Council of Europe Convention on Action against Trafficking in Human Beings (2005); Council of Europe Convention on the Protection of Children against Sexual Exploitation and Sexual Abuse (2007).

agreed definition on the trafficking of persons, especially women and children. This Protocol does not consider the purchasing, kidnapping, and selling of children for the purpose of adoption a form of human trafficking, as adoption *per se* does not amount to exploitation, the third constituent element of human trafficking. The Trafficking Protocol's definition of child trafficking is, in turn, mirrored in the national criminal laws that themselves fail to provide criminal prohibitions and responses designed to punish the kinds of wrongs involved in the purchasing, kidnapping, and selling of children for the purpose of adoption. Even when cases of illegal adoption practices are detected, the probability that the criminal actors receive a serious official response designed to punish the kinds of wrongs involved in the illegal adoption practices is low. The people in the criminal network usually either go unpunished or are only convicted of relatively minor criminal offences, such as visa fraud, forging documents, or money laundering.

This paper demonstrated how the illegal adoption practices employed to serve the market in children create profound individual and social harm. Removing a child from her intact family through purchase, abduction or deception of the parents exploits the child and her birth family and interferes with their fundamental human rights. This cannot be justified as ultimately serving the child's best interests. The institution of intercountry adoption is being stripped of its humanitarian *rationale* and is being abused by the powerful in the system – adopters, orphanage directors, lawyers, and government officials – to serve their interests. The child is not seen as a unique person with needs, interests, and basic rights. Rather, the child is being denied humanity and reduced to a marketable commodity. Her characteristics as healthy and young are being exploited by adopters who want their desire for a child to be fulfilled at any price and by individuals and organisations that want to gain financially from intercountry adoptions. Additionally, the child's birth parents are being denied humanity and the status of the child's family. They are degraded to a breeding unit whose fertility but also extreme powerlessness is being exploited. Illicit payments made to facilitate the intercountry adoption of an orphaned child create profound social harm by disrupting and destroying the social welfare system in the child's country of origin and by inciting childcare institutions or other organisations or individuals to secure 'adoptable children'.

The harm caused by illegal adoption practices is however difficult to trace and, thus, often remains invisible to the victims or the wider public or both. The majority of adoptive children who are taken from their families are infants who cannot conceive the illegal circumstances of their placements. Their vulnerable birth parents usually lack the voice and the capacities to report the purchase or abduction of their children effectively. After the child has been obtained illicitly, any decision on an illegal adoption is made in a court of law that bears all the hallmarks of a perfectly legal adoption procedure and that 'launders' the child through the adoption system as 'orphan' and then adoptee. Purchasing, kidnapping, and selling children for the purpose of adoption would, therefore, be located in the lower half of the 'prism of crime'.

It is time for the international community and the national legislators to stop turning a blind eye to the profound individual and social harm caused by the intercountry adoption system's underbelly and to rethink the traditional definition of child trafficking. The concept of child trafficking should no longer cover only those cases where children are being transferred for the purpose of prostitution, forced labour or organ removal but also those cases where a child (non-orphan or a true orphan) is kidnapped or purchased from her birth family, a childcarc institution or a hospital and sold for the purpose of adoption. In practices it is difficult to distinguish between legal payments and the illegal purchase of a child because monies or goods are often not granted as explicit considerations for the child. This paper claimed that a child is being purchased and sold for the purpose of an intercountry adoption if there is a causality between the assistance given to deeply impoverished families, the donations provided to childcare institutions, the bribes offered to government officials and the resulting intercountry adoption. In short, child trafficking for the purpose of intercountry adoption incudes all illegal practices serving the intercountry adoption market with children that would not otherwise been put there.

PART II

GENOCIDE

CHAPTER VIII
THE BBC DOCUMENTARY 'RWANDA'S UNTOLD STORY'
Acknowledging Genocide or Denying It?

Roland MOERLAND

1. INTRODUCTION

On 1 October 2014, the BBC broadcasted the documentary 'Rwanda's Untold Story', which, '[t]wenty years on from the Rwandan genocide, reveals evidence that challenges the accepted story of one of the most horrifying events of the late 20th century'.[1] The documentary investigates 'evidence of Kagame's role in the shooting down of the presidential plane that sparked the killings in 1994 and questions his claims to have ended the genocide. It also examines claims of war crimes committed by Kagame's forces and their allies in the wars in the Democratic Republic of Congo and allegations of human rights abuses in today's Rwanda'.[2] It is, of course, legitimate to critically investigate past crimes for which Kagame and the Rwandan Patriotic Front (RPF) are responsible and it is also legitimate to critically reflect on problematic aspects of the contemporary socio-political situation in Rwanda. Such issues warrant serious attention and they have been investigated before.[3] Furthermore, to revision complex conflict

---

1 The documentary is part of the BBC This World current affairs series and was made by Jane Corbin and John Conroy.

2 J. CORBIN, 'Rwanda's untold story' 2014 *BBC* <www.bbc.co.uk/programmes/b04kk03t>.

3 For investigations into these crimes see, for instance, Amnesty International, 'Rwanda: Reports of Killings and Abductions by the Rwandese Patriotic Army, April – August 1994' 1994 *Amnesty International* <www.amnesty.org/en/library/info/AFR47/016/1994/en> accessed 14.10.2015; Human Rights Watch, '"Leave None to Tell the Story": Genocide in Rwanda' *Human Rights Watch*, New York 1999; International Panel of Eminent Personalities, 'Rwanda: The Preventable Genocide' 2000 *Organization of African Unity*; G. PRUNIER, *Africa's World War: Congo, the Rwandan Genocide, and the Making of a Continental Catastrophe*, Oxford University Press, Oxford 2009. In this context Adelman, who also reflected on the BBC documentary, notes that the story of RPF crimes has not simply been unreported as he and his co-author Suhrke documented these charges of atrocities in their work. They found that crimes were indeed perpetrated, but that the scope was 'grossly

histories, including Rwanda's history of violence, is a legitimate exercise. However one should be careful that such critical revisionism does not amount to denial, which instead of acknowledging the complex reality of conflict obfuscates it. It is because of this last aspect that the approach taken in the BBC documentary towards revisioning Rwanda's conflict history has raised serious concerns amongst a variety of actors. Instead of seriously reflecting on the role of Kagame and the RPF in the violence with respect for rigor and factual evidence, substantial parts of the documentary raise doubt about the history of the genocide perpetrated against the Tutsi and confusion is created with regard to the nature and the direction of the violence that took place. It furthermore questions the number of Tutsi victims killed during the genocide and it makes doubtful claims as to who is responsible for downing the airplane of former president Habyarimana, which is said to be the 'spark that lit the fire of the genocide'.[4] These issues have caused a variety of actors to express their concern with the BBC.[5] The umbrella association for genocide survivor organisations in Rwanda (IBUKA) has appealed to the BBC and in its letter it stated that the documentary is a 'blatant denial of the Genocide against the Tutsi'.[6] Meanwhile in Rwanda an official inquiry by the government-appointed Rwanda Utilities

---

exaggerated'. Adelman concludes that: 'If that was the main charge, then the BBC story, whether accurate or not in the body of the piece, was not accurate in entitling the narrative, 'Rwanda: The Untold Story'. H. Adelman, 'The Rwandan Genocide Revisited: Part I the Context of a Recent BBC Report' 2014 <http://howardadelman.com/2014/10/14/fathers-and-sons-part-ii-review-of-the-judge/>. For a critical analyses of the contemporary socio-political situation in Rwanda see, for instance, Amnesty International, 'Unsafe to Speak Out: Restrictions on Freedom of Expression in Rwanda' 2011 <www.amnesty.org/en/library/info/AFR47/002/2011>; L. Waldorf, 'Revisiting Hotel Rwanda: Genocide, Ideology, Reconcilliation, and Rescuers' (2009) 11(1) *Journal of Genocide Research* 101–125; B. Ingelaere, 'Do We Understand Life after Genocide? Centre and Periphery in the Knowledge Construction in/on Rwanda' (Working Paper), Institute of Development Policy and Management, Antwerp 2009.

4 It also raises doubt about the nature of the Interahamwe militia and it questions whether the RPF stopped the genocide. For an inventory of inaccuracies and other problematic issues concerning the documentary see 'Rwanda's Untold Story: Letter to the Director-General of the BBC' 2014 <www.lindamelvern.com>.

5 In a reaction to the criticism, Professor Reyntjens who also featured in the documentary stated that: 'The arguments were predictable: those critical of or opposed to the Rwandan regime applauded the film, those supporting it, and of course the Rwandan regime itself, vehemently attacked the BBC.' (F. Reyntjens, '"Rwanda: The Untold Story": Facts and Fabrication' 2014 *Open Democracy* <https://www.opendemocracy.net/filip-reyntjens/rwanda-untold-story-facts-and-fabrication>) Professor Reyntjens makes it seem that all the commentators belong to a certain party in the (political) conflict. This, however, omits the possibility that commentators could also have expressed their concern because they are sincerely troubled by the issue of genocide denial without trying to meet certain favourable political ends. The analysis developed throughout this article certainly has implications for actors, but it is not *a priori* in favour of a certain group, but it concerns the problematic phenomenon of genocide denial and how it operates in the context of the genocide against the Tutsi.

6 J. Nishimwe, 'Ibuka Genocide Survivors Call on BBC to Stop Broadcasting Rwanda's Untold Story' 2014 *Jambonews.net* <www.jambonews.net/en/news/20141014-ibuka-genocide-survivors-call-on-bbc-to-stop-broadcasting-rwandas-untold-story/>.

Regulatory Authority has also concluded that the documentary amounts to genocide denial and in its report it urged the government to take action against the BBC because genocide denial is a criminal offence in Rwanda. The report furthermore advised the Rwandan government to terminate its contract with the BBC to broadcast in Rwanda, which the government subsequently did.[7] More notably, in an unprecedented effort initiated and led by Linda Melvern,[8] a group of 48 scholars, researchers, journalists, etc. expressed their grave concern at the denialist elements contained in the documentary,[9] first in a letter to BBC Director-General Lord Tony Hall, and later in a 15-page document to the BBC's Editorial Complaints Unit which outlined their concerns in greater detail.[10] Actors included Cornelio Sommaruga (former president of the International Committee of the Red Cross), Senator Roméo Dallaire (Force Commander, United Nations Assistance Mission for Rwanda), Senator Alain Destexhe (Secretary General of *Médecins Sans Frontières* in 1994), Barbara Mulvaney (Former Senior Trial Attorney United Nations International Tribunal for Rwanda) and Professor Gregory H. Stanton (President of Genocide Watch) as well as the author of this chapter.

---

7 For the report of the Rwandan authorities visit <http://rwandabbcinquiry.rw/>. See also D. Baird, 'Rwanda Places Indefinite Ban on BBC Broadcasts over Genocide Documentary' 2015 *The Guardian* <www.theguardian.com/media/2015/jun/01/rwanda-places-indefinite-ban-on-bbc-broadcasts-over-genocide-documentary>. Whether criminal prosecution or termination of the contract with the BBC will solve the problem of genocide denial is questionable. It does not address the root cause of the denial and it is very likely that it strengthens the deniers in their belief that their 'truth' about what happened is being covered up.

8 Melvern has written extensively on the genocide against the Tutsi and she also published two books on the subject: L. Melvern, *A People Betrayed. The Role of the West in Rwanda's Genocide*, Zed Books, London 2000 and L. Melvern, *Conspiracy to Murder: The Rwandan Genocide*, Verso, London-New York 2006.

9 See <www.lindamelvern.com/> for the initial letter of complaint to the Director-General of the BBC Lord Tony Hall of 12.10.2014. See also D. Baird, 'BBC Rejects Complaint over Controversial Rwanda Genocide Documentary' 2015 *The Guardian* <www.theguardian.com/media/2015/apr/10/bbc-rejects-complaint-rwanda-genocide-documentary>. The rest of the correspondence with the BBC is being kept confidential until the complaint process has been finalised after which the documentation will be made publically available.

10 From the various reactions to the letter it becomes clear that our concerns about the denialist content of the documentary are often interpreted as a manoeuvre to silence critique and diverging opinions concerning what happened. That is certainly not the intent. We are seriously and solely concerned about the history of the genocide and we do not write on behalf of the 'Kagame power-lobby' as has been insinuated. The letter even states that the signatories 'accept and support that it is legitimate to investigate, with due diligence and respect for factual evidence, any crimes committed by the Rwandan Patriotic Front (RPF), and to reflect on the contemporary political situation in Rwanda.' In the letter of complaint to the BBC's ECU of 16.03.2015, the signatories again made clear that: 'We do not intend to silence legitimate critique or dissent, and we do not seek to impede critical journalistic investigation.' The signatories furthermore made clear that there is no relation to the earlier mentioned inquiry performed by the Rwandan authorities (letter, 16.03.2015, BBC ECU Provisional findings reply 2015 Rwanda's Untold Story, p. 1).

In its responses, the BBC has noted that it deplores the above-mentioned critique and it has defended its decision to broadcast the documentary by arguing that it had 'a duty to investigate difficult and challenging subjects' and that the documentary made 'a valuable contribution to the understanding of the tragic history of the country and the region'. The BBC refutes the accusation that any part of the programme constitutes genocide denial.[11]

Despite the fact that the documentary raised great controversy not many actors have attempted to analyse its content by drawing on the body of scholarly work available on the phenomenon of genocide denial in the field of genocide studies. Most critical reflection is predominantly descriptive and concerns the omissions and inaccuracies of the documentary and its lack of proper context. A more theory-driven analysis of the documentary which enables people to understand what genocide denial entails and as a result makes people able to better comprehend the controversy surrounding the BBC documentary is currently lacking. Therefore the following analysis will provide for a more theory-driven analysis of the documentary.

The analysis sets out to address the following elements. Firstly, the concept of genocide denial will be discussed and the role that denial plays in the process of genocide will be clarified. Subsequently, the analysis addresses more specifically how genocide denial operates in the context of the genocide against the Tutsi. This section outlines the general discursive structure of the official denial discourse that the perpetrators of the genocide developed in order to obscure the true nature of their genocidal enterprise. The third part of the analysis will discuss how crucial elements of the official denial discourse are recycled by other actors who were not implicated in the genocide against the Tutsi, such as scholars and journalists. Here Herman and Peterson's work on Rwanda will serve as a case illustration. Lastly, the analysis addresses how the BBC documentary also recycles certain key elements from the official denial discourse and it reflects on the implications thereof.[12]

---

11 D. Smith, 'Rwanda Calls for BBC to Be Banned over Controversial Documentary' 2014 *The Guardian* <www.theguardian.com/world/2014/oct/23/rwanda-calls-bbc-banned-over-controversial-documentary>.

12 The article is based on the author's PhD research entitled *The killing of death. Denying the genocide against the Tutsi*, which has been published by Intersentia. (R. Moerland, *The killing of death. Denying the genocide against the Tutsi*, Intersentia, Cambridge 2016) and research conducted in the context of the letters written to the BBC by the earlier mentioned group of signatories and especially the report annexed to the letter, 16.03.2015, BBC ECU Provisional findings reply 2015 Rwanda's Untold Story. The analysis of the case of Herman and Peterson has also featured in an article in the Dutch journal for cultural criminology (C.A.R. Moerland, 'Verzet of Collaboratie? Hoe De Strijd Tegen Genocide Kan Bijdragen Aan Genocide' (2014) 4(1) *Tijdschrift over Cultuur & Criminaliteit* 80–96.).

2. DENIAL IN THEORY

2.1. GENOCIDE, DENIAL AND ANNIHILATION

The concept of genocide was coined in 1944 by Raphael Lemkin who defined genocide as 'a coordinated plan of different actions aiming at the destruction of essential foundations of the life of national groups, with the aim of annihilating the groups themselves'.[13, 14] Lemkin's use of the term *annihilation* signifies the specific nature of genocide. The term has its roots in the Latin word *nihil*, which means 'nothing' and to annihilate means to 'blot out of existence' or to 'reduce to nothing'. Genocide thus renders a people inexistent. Significant about Lemkin's pioneering work is furthermore that it makes clear that genocide involves more than the act of killing. According to him, the techniques of genocide operate in various fields: the political, social, economic, cultural, religious, biological, etc.[15] Therefore the violence of genocide can vary from economic crippling and cultural marginalisation to eugenic social engineering and physical extermination. The range of techniques also makes clear that what genocide tries to achieve is not just the physical or biological death of a people, but their social death as it tries to annihilate a people's social power.[16] On this aspect Shaw notes that a people as an entity is a 'social construction' that 'can neither be constituted nor destroyed simply through the bodies of their individual members'.[17] It is furthermore important to understand that what sets genocide apart from other crimes, such as war crimes or crimes against humanity, is the intention informing the violence. The (individual) acts of violence are undertaken with the ulterior motive or special genocidal intention to annihilate the groups themselves.[18] However, in order for genocidal annihilation to be complete, the manifestations of the process of genocide need to be destroyed to the extent that nothing acknowledges or reminds us of the victims and the process by which they were victimised.[19] Annihilation is complete only when the event

13 R. Lemkin, *Axis Rule in Occupied Europe: Laws of Occupation – Analysis of Government Proposals for Redress*, Carnegie Endowment for International Peace, Washington DC 1944, p. 79.

14 Letter, 16.03.2015, BBC ECU Provisional findings reply 2015 Rwanda's Untold Story, Annexe A, genocide denial, pp. 1–3.

15 R. Lemkin, *Axis Rule in Occupied Europe: Laws of Occupation – Analysis of Government Proposals for Redress*, Carnegie Endowment for International Peace, Washington DC 1944, p. 79.

16 M. Shaw, *What Is Genocide?*, Polity Press, Cambridge 2007, p. 22.

17 Ibid., p. 106. See also C. Card, 'Genocide and Social Death' (2013) 18(1) *Hypatia* 63–79. For Card genocide is about 'loss of social vitality' because it is about 'loss of identity and thereby of meaning for one's existence'.

18 In the process of genocide, violent acts against individuals are thus a means to the end of the overarching aim of annihilating the collective.

19 Y. Ternon, 'Négationnisme, régles générales et cas particuliers' in: K. Boustany and D. Dormoy (eds.), *Génocide(S)*, Emile Bruylant, Brussels 1999, pp. 143–160, at p. 149.

of annihilation, the genocide itself, is annihilated and it is genocide denial that performs this last action.[20] Scholars therefore argue that genocide attacks truth, history and memory as its last victims. As a result, genocide constitutes a double victimisation: first the central elements of a people's existence are targeted, followed by the destruction of the remembrance of that violence.[21] Huttenbach therefore concludes that '[d]enial has become an integral part of genocide; not to take this aspect into consideration is to fail to comprehend a major component of the dynamics of extermination'.[22] Smith, Markusen and Lifton argue that genocide denial ought to be seen as a 'contribution to the genocidal violence in its own right'.[23] From this follows that denial does not simply occur after genocide has been perpetrated. Instead, denial is a crucial part of the genocide and it constitutes the last stage in the process of perpetration.[24] This also means that, as long as there is denial, the genocidal process continues.[25] Genocide does not stop

---

20 In order to complete the process of annihilation of a people, genocide ultimately unleashes its violence also upon itself with the aim to erase itself from reality. This is done by physically destroying the weapons and other means used to perpetrate the genocide, or by destroying the bodily remains of its victims. However, due to its magnitude it is virtually impossible to destroy all the physical evidence of the genocide and that is why the perpetrators also utilise discursive violence and engage in genocide denial. Events are reinterpreted in order to change their reality: what happened was not genocide but war. So, in addition to physical destruction of the crime's physical evidence, history and memory are also targeted by the violence. To this end words are used as weapons to discursively destroy the genocidal reality. C.A.R. Moerland, *The Killing of Death: Denying the Genocide against the Tutsi*, PhD thesis, Maastricht University, Maastricht 2015, p. 131.

21 J-P. Dupaquier, 'Rwanda: le révisionnisme, poursuite du génocide par d'autres moyens' in: R. Verdier, E. Decaux and J-P. Chrétien (eds.), *Rwanda: Un Génocide du Xxe Siècle*, L'Harmattan, Paris 1995, pp. 127–136, at p. 129; R.G. Hovannisian, 'Denial of the Armenian Genocide in Comparison with Holocaust Denial' in: R.G. Hovannisian (ed.), *Remembrance and Denial: The Case of the Armenian Genocide*, Wayne State University Press, Detroit 1999, pp. 201–236, at p. 229; S. Totten and W. S. Parsons, 'Introduction' in: S. Totten, W.S. Parsons, and I.W. Charny (eds.), *Century of Genocide: Critical Essays and Eyewitness Accounts*, 2nd ed., Routledge, London 2004, pp. 1–13, at p. 2.

22 H.R. Huttenbach, 'The Psychology and Politics of Genocide Denial' in: A. Jones (ed.), *Genocide*, Sage, Los Angeles 2008, pp. 306–316.

23 R.W. Smith, E. Markusen and R.J. Lifton, 'Professional Ethics and the Denial of the Armenian Genocide' in: R.G. Hovannisian (ed.), *Remembrance and Denial: The Case of the Armenian Genocide*, Wayne State University Press, Detroit 1999, pp. 271–295.

24 G.H. Stanton, 'The 8 Stages of Genocide' (paper was originally written in 1996 and was presented as the First Working Paper (Gs 01) of the Yale Program in Genocide Studies in 1998), 1998 *Genocide Watch* <www.genocidewatch.org/genocide/8stagesofgenocide.html>. See also I.L. Horowitz, *Taking Lives: Genocide and State Power*, Transaction Publishers, New York 1989 and J.-M. Lecomte, *Teaching About the Holocaust in the 21st Century*, Council of Europe Publishing, Strasbourg 2001.

25 This conceptualisation has implications with regard to how events of genocide are perceived. In this conceptualisation the techniques of genocide are broad and not only involve killing, it moves beyond the 'physical' and also encompasses violence that operates in social, economic, political, cultural, religious fields as well. This means that when we look at the genocide against the Tutsi, we cannot simply reduce it to the 100 days of killing. The process of genocide started much earlier. C.A.R. Moerland, *The Killing of Death: Denying the Genocide against the Tutsi*, PhD thesis, Maastricht University, Maastricht 2015, pp. 95–97.

when the killing stops. As a result, genocide does not only consist of the *killing of life*, it also entails the *killing of death*.[26] This too provides insight as to why genocide survivors have such trouble with the denial of their victimisation. It is not only about incitement of hatred or traumatisation. It is about the existential threat that denial poses to them and their people due to the fact that genocide denial is an intrinsic element of the perpetration of the crime of genocide: as long as there is denial, they as a people continue to be annihilated.[27]

2.2. GENOCIDE DENIAL

Denial is thus the primary mechanism operating in the last stage of the genocide where it contributes to the genocide in its own right and in that case can thus be seen as an *act of genocide*. However, we should be careful not to reduce the role of denial to the last stage of genocide because denial also performs important functions at earlier stages in the process of genocide. Spencer even notes that denial is 'rarely absent from any part of the process'.[28] In order to make clear that genocide serves different roles throughout the process, I have made the following distinction. In my research I differentiate between 'genocide denial' and 'denial of genocide'. Following Nichanian's observation that genocide encompasses both the *killing of life* and the *killing of death*, I argue that 'genocide denial' constitutes or facilitates the *killing of death* and that 'denial of genocide' facilitates the *killing of life*.[29] 'Denial of genocide' thus facilitates the perpetration of other acts of genocide, such as mass killings. In contrast to such 'denial of genocide', which I will discuss in greater detail in the next section, 'genocide denial' does not primarily enable other acts of genocide, but it is an act of genocide in its own right. With regard to 'genocide denial', roughly two types can be distinguished: 'primary genocide denial' and 'secondary genocide denial'. The most important difference between the two types is the intention informing the denial. 'Primary genocide denial' requires a genocidal intention and this is the case when an act of genocide denial is undertaken with the

---

26 M. Nichanian, 'The Truth of the Facts: About the New Revisionism' in: R.G. Hovannisian (ed.), *Remembrance and Denial: The Case of the Armenian Genocide*, Wayne State University Press, Detroit 1999, pp. 249–270; M. Nichanian, 'Between Genocide and Catastrophe' in: D.L. Eng and D. Kazanjian (eds.), *Loss. The Politics of Mourning*, University of California Press, Berkeley 2003, pp. 125–247; M. Nichanian, *The Historiographic Perversion*, Columbia University Presss, New York 2009.

27 C.A.R. Moerland, *The Killing of Death: Denying the Genocide against the Tutsi*, PhD thesis, Maastricht University, Maastricht 2015, p. 135.

28 P. Spencer, 'Genocide Scholars and Legislating to Outlaw the Denial of Genocide' 2012 *Genocide Prevention Now* <www.genocidepreventionnow.org/Home/tabid/39/ctl/DisplayArticle/mid/1161/aid/664/Default.aspx>.

29 C.A.R. Moerland, *The Killing of Death: Denying the Genocide against the Tutsi*, PhD thesis, Maastricht University, Maastricht 2015, p. 137.

intention to finalise the process of genocide. Here acts of genocide are denied in order to deliberately continue and conclude the process of genocide. 'Primary genocide denial' is a means to the end of annihilation of a people. In contrast, 'secondary genocide denial' is not informed by such a genocidal intention and because of this 'secondary genocide denial' facilitates the process of annihilation because it contributes to the denial dynamic on which the genocidal process thrives. By denying genocide, one carries out acts that support the finalisation of the process of genocide.[30] For instance, perpetrators can engage in denial to safeguard the bigger genocidal cause, but perpetrators can also deny acts of genocide in order to ward off personal responsibility for these crimes. The first instance amounts to 'primary genocide denial', the second instance concerns 'secondary genocide denial'.

2.3. DENIAL OF GENOCIDE

At earlier stages in the genocidal process denial serves a different purpose and instead of being an act of genocide in itself, its purpose is to facilitate other acts of genocide which concern the killing of life of a people. Inflicting genocidal violence on a people causes considerable psychological strain. It conflicts with empathetic feelings and societal norms and values. Denial helps actors to overcome these barriers, allowing them to engage in such behaviour for the first time. This is what I refer to as 'primary denial of genocide'. By, for instance, denying the humanity of their victims, perpetrators are able to overcome the inhibitions against violence and it enables them to engage in violence against their fellow human beings.[31] Empathetic and ethical distance towards the victims is created by depicting the victims as sub-human and/or as vermin posing a threat to society. Human subjects that would normally fall within our universe of moral obligation and who demand respect are through processes of dehumanisation turned into objects fit for destruction because moral obligations towards them no longer exist.[32] Such 'primary denial of genocide' basically neutralises inhibitions before the acts are perpetrated. In contrast, 'secondary denial of genocide' helps to rationalise acts of genocide after they have been performed. 'Secondary denial of genocide' helps to legitimate and justify the actions afterwards and when perpetrators succeed in rationalising their

30 Ibid., p. 139.

31 H.C. Kelman, 'The Social Context of Torture: Policy Process and Authority Structure' in: R.D. Crelinsen and A.P. Schmid (eds.), *The Politics of Pain: Torturers and Their Masters*, COMT, Leiden 1993, pp. 21–38. See also H.C. Kelman and V.L. Hamilton, *Crimes of Obedience*, Yale University Press, New Haven 1989.

32 A. Alvarez, 'Adjusting to Genocide: The Techniques of Neutralization and the Holocaust' (1997) 21(2) *Social Science History* 139–178, 167.

behaviour and empathetic and ethical barriers have been overcome, the way for further violent criminal action is often cleared.[33]

2.4. 'DENIAL' IN EFFECT

Denial, as a concept, is difficult to define and although scholars disagree on many aspects, there are two aspects on which there appears to be a consensus. The first aspect is that denial is a defence mechanism that actors use in order to deal with realities that are somehow too difficult to acknowledge.[34] The second aspect on which they tend to agree is that denial involves the paradoxical self-deceptive state of knowing and not-knowing at the same time. This is the paradox of denial, because in order to deny a reality one first has to acknowledge that reality in order to be able to deny it.[35] However, it has been argued by scholars in the field of genocide studies, such as Charny that the continuum of denial already runs from 'a position where the person denying the genocide really or largely does not know the facts'. He gives the example of university students who truly do not know of a specific genocide.[36] However, if people are truly (and not wilfully) ignorant, it is questionable whether they are in denial. If there is no awareness, there is nothing to deny. If this is the case, it would be incorrect to define such behaviour as denial and as a logical consequence Charny's continuum should start with wilful ignorance, and not ignorance. This does, however, not mean

---

33 C.A.R. Moerland, *The Killing of Death: Denying the Genocide against the Tutsi*, PhD thesis, Maastricht University, Maastricht 2015, p. 139. The violence that is subsequently inflicted dehumanises the victims even more, contributing to the denial of their humanity which in turn facilitates the infliction of further violence. From the analysis above it becomes clear that denial plays a role during genocide and at the end of the process. However, denial also plays a role before these stages, at the beginning of genocide. The denial of previous genocidal crimes committed against peoples can be a prerequisite for re-victimisation and therefore one could even argue that denial is not the final, but the first stage in the genocidal process. By denying past genocides, the seeds of future genocides are planted. This argument can be illustrated with reference to Hitler's Obersalzburg speech in which he stated that: 'Who after all is today speaking of the destruction of the Armenians?' Hitler's speech reveals that denial of victimisation (Armenian Genocide) facilitates victimisation (Holocaust). Ibid., p. 98.

34 Actors can engage in denial out of sincere coping, but it can also serve Machiavellian manipulation.

35 C.A.R. Moerland, *The Killing of Death: Denying the Genocide against the Tutsi*, PhD thesis, Maastricht University, Maastricht 2015, pp. 103–108. For an elaborate investigation into the phenomenon of denial and its implications see; S. Cohen, *States of Denial: Knowing About Atrocities and Suffering*, Polity Press, Cambridge 2001; E. Zerubavel, *The Elephant in the Room: Silence and Denial in Everyday Life*, Oxford University Press, Oxford 2008; E. Zerubavel, 'The Social Sound of Silence: Toward a Sociology of Denial' in: E. Ben Ze'ev, R. Ginio and J. Winter (eds.), *Shadows of War: A Social History of Silence in the Twentieth Century*, Cambridge University Press, Cambridge 2010, pp. 32–44; and I.B. Seu, *Passivity Generation: Human Rights and Everyday Morality*, Palgrave Macmillan, New York 2013.

36 I.W. Charny, 'Innocent Denials of Known Genocides: A Further Contribution to a Psychology of Denial of Genocide' (2000) 1(3) *Human Rights Review* 15–39, 21.

that ignorance is not problematic, because ignorance does contribute to the denial dynamic on which genocide thrives as it also does not acknowledge genocide. It is therefore that in my research I do not define ignorance as denial, but as '"denial" in effect', which includes other actions than 'denial of genocide' or 'genocide denial' that do not acknowledge genocide and as a result facilitate the denial dynamic on which genocide thrives. So, in addition to 'primary' and 'secondary genocide denial', other behaviour than denial, such as ignorance, but also erosion of memory, non-recognition, indifference, ethno-centrism, lack of empathy, etc., can facilitate the denial dynamic on which the process of genocide thrives.[37]

2.5. GENOCIDE DENIALISM

The above analysis clarifies that in the context of genocide we are not dealing with a single type or act of denial. Instead we are dealing with a more elaborate and multifaceted process of genocide denialism that encompasses a variety of denialist and denial like acts which all play a role in the process of genocide.[38] Now scholars mainly use the term 'genocide denial' to denote all these different instances (states of denial), which is problematic because it obscures their particular nature and hinders a better understanding of how denial precisely operates in the context of genocide.[39]

2.6. THE OBJECT OF DENIAL

Scholars often define denial in terms in what is being denied: the object of denial. For instance, in his work Cohen identifies three major forms of denial: literal denial, interpretative denial, and implicatory denial.[40] Genocide denial also tends to take these forms. Firstly, in cases of 'literal' or 'factual denial' the facts or the reality as such are denied: 'No genocide is taking place, what you say did not happen'. Secondly, 'interpretative denial' acknowledges that indeed something

37 C.A.R. Moerland, *The Killing of Death: Denying the Genocide against the Tutsi*, PhD thesis, Maastricht University, Maastricht 2015, p. 143.

38 Ibid., pp. 28 and 135.

39 In addition to the above-mentioned types of denial that play a role in the context of genocide, I also note that such denialist speech can be insulting and traumatising to the victims and it can incite (re)new(ed) violence. Therefore in my genocide denialism typology these effects of denial are referred to as 'denial related consequences'. Ibid. p. 145.

40 S. Cohen, 'Human Rights and Crimes of the State: The Culture of Denial' (1993) 26(2) *Australian and New Zealand Journal of Criminology* 97–115; S. Cohen, 'Government Responses to Human Rights Reports: Claims, Denials, and Counterclaims' (1996) 18 *Human Rights Quarterly* 517–543; S. Cohen, *States of Denial: Knowing About Atrocities and Suffering*, Polity Press, Cambridge 2001.

happened, but the meaning of the events is reinterpreted and its reality is changed: 'This is not what you think it is. It is not genocide, but civil war or interethnic violence'. Lastly, in case of 'implicatory denial', the event is acknowledged, maybe even its meaning, but the consequences that normally follow from it are denied: 'Yes, there was violence, yes we targeted that group of people, but we acted out of legitimate self-defence. So, what we did was not wrong.'[41] This list of denials is also illustrative of the chronological order that denial often follows, because once the worldview of deniers is challenged, they are likely to engage in further denial in order to keep up their alternative version of reality.[42] Payne therefore concludes that 'denial does not disappear or erode over time; it escalates and spirals'.[43] Denial thus tends to be progressive which makes it a challenging phenomenon to constructively deal with. In the specific context of genocide this also means that due to its progressive character actors can move along a spectrum from '"denial" in effect', to 'secondary genocide denial' and from that stage even to 'primary genocide denial'. This dynamic aspect of denial is also important to take into account when reflecting on the documentary and the reactions of the BBC. However, before we start to analyse 'denial at work' which will be the focus of the analysis in the following sections, it is relevant to briefly mention one other important aspect of denial, which is its interpersonal character.[44] Denial is very much a collective effort, because unless supported by others, a state of denial often cannot successfully be maintained.[45] This can result in a situation in which actors, in order to keep up their denial, join others with similar (denialist) worldviews because it provides them with the much needed collusive and non-threatening environment. Denial is thus not simply an individual exercise, but

41 In theory these distinctions are easy to draw, but in practice these forms of denial can often not easily be separated as their use might coincide and in extensive denial discourses all different forms can be used. Parts of the reality can be literally denied, while other facts concerning that reality are acknowledged. These facts are subsequently reinterpreted and afterwards the implications are not accepted.

42 C.A.R. Moerland, *The Killing of Death: Denying the Genocide against the Tutsi*, PhD thesis, Maastricht University, Maastricht 2015, p. 119. When confronted with a threatening reality, actors first tend to literally deny that something happened and once this is no longer tenable because of the mounting evidence, actors claim that the world misunderstands what really happened and they subsequently reinterpret the events. Once this also becomes hard to keep up, actors acknowledge what happened, but they subsequently play down the consequence that would ordinarily follow from such events. So when one confronts actors with their denial it is very likely that they will engage in further denial.

43 L.A. Payne, *Unsettling Accounts: Neither Truth nor Reconcilliation in Confessions of State Violence*, Duke University Press, Durham 2008, p. 162.

44 C.A.R. Moerland, *The Killing of Death: Denying the Genocide against the Tutsi*, PhD thesis, Maastricht University, Maastricht 2015, pp. 110 and 125. In earlier conceptualisations denial was mainly presented as an intra-psychic or intrapersonal phenomenon. Later scholarship has however highlighted the interactional dynamics of denial and it has shown that the content (what) and the techniques and practices (how) of denial are learned through social interaction.

45 L. Goldberger, 'The Concept and Mechanisms of Denial: A Selective Overview' in: S. Breznitz (ed.), *The Denial of Stress*, International Universities Press, Inc., New York 1983, pp. 83–95, at p. 87.

an interpersonal project involving many more actors.[46] Also this interpersonal dimension of denial is relevant with regard to the question whether parts of the BBC documentary are problematic in terms of genocide denialism.

3. DENIAL AT WORK

3.1. AN OFFICIAL GENOCIDE DENIAL DISCOURSE

In the wake of the genocide against the Tutsi in Rwanda, authorities involved in the planning, organisation and implementation of the genocide developed a sophisticated ideological discourse that aimed at denying the true nature of their criminal and genocidal enterprise.[47] When one analyses the discourse of the implicated former Rwandan authorities, such as the interim government[48] and the military,[49] it becomes clear that their propaganda concerning the events tends to follow a similar discursive structure. While not able to literally deny the existence of a violent episode, their discourse aims at denying the genocide by

---

46 E. Zerubavel, *The Elephant in the Room: Silence and Denial in Everyday Life*, Oxford University Press, Oxford 2008, p. 4. In my research I furthermore explain how Zerubavel refers to this as a 'conspiracy of silence', a mutual denial, in which multiple actors 'collaborate to jointly avoid acknowledging something.' Although the phrase 'conspiracy of silence' points out that denial is socially organised, the term might actually also give a wrong impression, because denial is very often not the result of simply remaining silent. The alternative reality that is less threatening, is often constructed through talk and narratives. In that sense, denial is not about being silent, but about speaking out. Zerubavel (p. 8) concludes that '[b]eing silent thus involves more than just absence of action, since the things about which we are silent are in fact actively avoided.' We tend to believe that when people talk they reveal and acknowledge, but talk and text can conceal as much as they reveal. C.A.R. Moerland, *The Killing of Death: Denying the Genocide against the Tutsi*, PhD thesis, Maastricht University, Maastricht 2015, p. 110.

47 J.-P. Chrétien, 'Le génocide du Rwanda: un négationnisme structurel' 2010 *LDH Toulon* <http://ldh-toulon.net/Jean-Pierre-Chretien-Le-genocide.html>; J.-P. Chrétien, *Le défi de l'ethnisme: Rwanda et Burundi*, Karthala, Paris 2012; J-P. Dupaquier, 'Rwanda: le révisionnisme, poursuite du génocide par d'autres moyens' in: R. Verdier, E. Decaux and J-P. Chrétien (eds.), *Rwanda: Un Génocide du Xxe Siècle*, L'Harmattan, Paris 1995, pp. 127–136; M. Fierens, *Le négationnisme du génocide des Tutsi au Rwanda*, Golias, Villeurbanne 2009; J. Semujanga and J.-L. Galabert (eds.), *Faire face au négationnisme du génocide des Tutsi*, Éditions Izuba, Saint-Jean 2013.

48 See, for instance, the following documents written by the former Minister of Justice: A. Ntamabyaliro, 'Cover Letter Document Le Peuple Rwandais Accuse…', 1994 *Republic of Rwanda Ministry of Justice* and the report A. Ntamabyaliro, 'Le Peuple Rwandais Accuse…', Interim Government of Rwanda, Bukavu 1994. Documentation on file with author. In the book S. Cohen, *States of Denial: Knowing About Atrocities and Suffering*, Polity Press, Cambridge 2001, p. 10, Cohen also uses the term official denial to denote state and governmental denial that aims to cover up human rights abuses.

49 See, for instance, the report written by the former Rwandan Armed Forces: Rwandan Armed Forces Command in Exile, 'Contribution of Raf to the Search for the Truth on the Rwandan Tragedy', 1995. Documentation on file with author.

changing the meaning of the event and thereby its reality.[50] This official denial discourse can briefly be summarised as follows.[51] According to the discourse of the former Rwandan authorities the world has greatly misunderstood what happened in Rwanda and this misunderstanding is caused by the propaganda of the Tutsi-led RPF and their Western supporters. Subsequently, the Tutsi are presented as the root cause of an age long interethnic conflict. In early history they invaded Rwanda and enslaved the Hutu population, who, after years of serfdom, managed to oust the Tutsi from power during what they refer to as a 'social revolution'. It is argued that in their quest to regain power the Tutsi have been willing to use all means necessary including violence. Also, during the war that broke out in October 1990 when the RPF invaded the country, the Tutsi are again presented as alien invaders who attempt to regain power at the cost of the Hutu population. The former authorities claim that the extreme violence that the world witnessed in 1994 was the result of the Tutsi war effort and their quest for power. During this episode of violence interethnic massacres occurred in which both groups attacked each other. The Hutu did use violence against the Tutsi, however, not because they had planned to exterminate them, but because they spontaneously defended themselves and their country against this overwhelming and superior Tutsi force. Moreover, according to the former authorities what happened was justifiable and legitimate self-defence.[52] The former authorities furthermore claim that in contrast to what people generally believe, it was not the Hutu who planned to kill the Tutsi. In contrast to such knowledge, the Tutsi led RPF is presented as a power hungry anti-revolutionary and anti-democratic indiscriminate killing machine. The discourse even claims that in an ultimate attempt to gain power Kagame and the RPF downed the airplane of president Habyarimana. The most extreme forms of the official denial discourse accuse the Tutsi and the RPF of perpetrating genocide against the Hutu. Furthermore, in the official denial discourse of the former Rwandan authorities, the majority of the victims are Hutu and not Tutsi. Lastly, the former authorities assert that the Tutsi-led RPF received substantial support from other states, such as Uganda, the United States, the United Kingdom, and Belgium. These powers, together

50 For a discussion of this discourse see: C.A.R. Moerland, *Verzet of collaboratie? Hoe de strijd tegen genocide kan bijdragen aan genocide* (C.A.R. Moerland, *The Killing of Death: Denying the Genocide against the Tutsi,* PhD thesis, Maastricht University, Maastricht 2015). When analysing the discourse of the former authorities it becomes clear that they initially engaged in 'literal' denial, but due to the mounting evidence, such denial quickly became untenable and their discourse advanced involving a more complex mixture of interpretative and implicatory denial.

51 Letter, 16.03.2015, BBC ECU Provisional findings reply 2015 Rwanda's Untold Story, Annexe A, An official denial discourse, pp. 3–4.

52 The claim of self-defence is highly questionable, taking into account the fact that the violence also indiscriminately targeted old men, women, children and (unborn) babies. Furthermore, the extreme nature of much of the violence falsifies the claim of a justified self-defence as it is not proportional. The fact that these people were targeted is indicative of the genocidal nature of the violence.

with the current power holders in Rwanda, are described both as co-responsible for the killings in Rwanda in 1994, and for the allegedly flawed justice meted out at the International Criminal Tribunal for Rwanda (ICTR), which supposedly constitutes victors' justice.

From this brief outline of the discourse of the former authorities it becomes clear that it mixes interpretative and implicatory denial. The discourse reinterprets the events and constructs an alternative reality concerning what happened, while the consequences that follow from that reality are denied. In effect, the official genocide denial discourse turns the perpetrator and victim roles around.

That those who were somehow implicated in the genocide deny their crimes is not surprising because that is what perpetrators generally tend to do. What is however intriguing, but also worrying, is that crucial elements of the official genocide denial discourse of the perpetrators are being reiterated by other actors who initially were not involved in the genocide against the Tutsi. A much more complex picture thus starts to emerge, in which not only perpetrators deny, but their message is recycled by various other actors as well.

3.2. RECYCLING OFFICIAL GENOCIDE DENIAL

Probably the most well know case in this respect concerns the work of Professor Edward S. Herman and journalist David Peterson on Rwanda.[53, 54] In 2010 Herman and Peterson co-authored the book *The politics of genocide*.[55] The book aims to address the issue of the political (ab)use of genocide which is a problem that certainly warrants our attention as it leads to a denial of human suffering, because for certain political reasons genocidal episodes remain unacknowledged. The problem is, however, that their work on Rwanda presents an alternative reading of events that in its discursive construction recycles many of the core discursive elements that are central to the above discussed official denial discourse. Their section on Rwanda ultimately results in a brazen denial of the genocide against the Tutsi. Herman and Peterson's work on Rwanda merges in many ways with the official denial discourse.[56] Both discourses claim that the events in Rwanda are greatly misunderstood

---

53 Herman is a Professor Emeritus at the Wharton School of Business of the University of Pennsylvania. He has written extensively on economics, political economy, foreign policy, and media analysis. David Peterson is a writer, independent journalist and researcher based in Chicago.

54 Letter, 16.03.2015, BBC ECU Provisional findings reply 2015 Rwanda's Untold Story, Annexe A, Recycling official genocide denial, pp. 4–5.

55 E.S. Herman and D. Peterson, *The Politics of Genocide*, Monthly Review Press, New York 2010.

56 For an analysis of this process of recycling see C.A.R. Moerland, *The Killing of Death: Denying the Genocide against the Tutsi*, PhD thesis, Maastricht University, Maastricht 2015.

due to a misleading propaganda campaign by the RPF and its Western allies. Both discourses obscure the true nature of events and assert that the violence against the Tutsi was unplanned and a justified self-defence against an RPF effort to take over power by any means. Moreover, both discourses imply that the RPF effort to take over power involved a planned and organised genocide against the Hutu that is ongoing. Herman and Peterson also engage in a numbers game when discussing the victim rates and they draw on the work of professors Christian Davenport and Allan Stam[57] in order to claim that the vast majority of victims were Hutu and that the only major killing force in Rwanda was the Tutsi-led RPF and not the extremist Hutu regime. Lastly, both discourses claim that the justice meted out by the ICTR is biased and serves the interests of the Tutsi-led RPF and its Western backers. Western states, mainly the US, are not presented as bystanders to genocide, but were actively involved in this.

The case of Herman and Peterson has been critically addressed by Rwanda experts and experts in the field of genocide studies and they concluded that their work on Rwanda constitutes a brazen denial of the genocide against the Tutsi.[58] Like the official denial discourse, the discourse of Herman and Peterson also involves a mixture of interpretative and implicatory denial as the meaning of the events is reinterpreted and an alternative reality concerning what happened is constructed. Subsequently, the consequences that follow from that reality are denied.

Although Herman and Peterson's discursive construction of the events is very similar to that of the official denial discourse of the former authorities, there are also significant differences between the two discourses. In the official denial discourse the Tutsi are presented as the root cause of an age long inter-ethnic conflict. In contrast, Herman and Peterson present the nature of the conflict as a Western-syndicated proxy war. This reveals a significant divergence from the official denial discourse. The official denial discourse is driven by a

---

57 Christian Davenport is Professor at the Department of Political Science of the University of Michigan Institute for Social Research. Allan C. Stam was Professor at the Gerald R. Ford School of Public Policy of the University of Michigan and currently Dean of the Frank Batten School of Leadership and Public Policy and Professor of Public Policy.

58 For discussions on the denialist nature of Herman and Peterson's work on Rwanda see: G. Caplan, 'Sources and Testimonies: A Response to Herman and Peterson' 2010 *Pambazuka News* <www.pambazuka.net/en/category/features/65974/print> accessed 17.09.2015; A. Jones, 'On Genocide Deniers: Challenging Herman and Peterson' 2010 *Pambazuka News*; A. Jones, 'Denying Rwanda: A Response to Herman and Peterson' 2010 *Genocide Study Media File* <http://jonestream.blogspot.nl/2010/11/denying-rwanda-response-to-herman.html>; G. Monbiot, 'Genocide Denial: Expert Assessments' 2010 <www.monbiot.com/2012/05/21/genocide-denial-expert-assessments/>; M. Shaw, 'Book Reviews. The Politics of Genocide. Edward S. Herman and David Peterson. New York: Monthly Review Press, 2010' (2011) 13(3) *Journal of Genocide Research* 353–387; M. Shaw, 'The Politics of Genocide: Rwanda & DR Congo' 2010 *Open Democracy* <https://www.opendemocracy.net/martin-shaw/politics-of-genocide-rwanda-and-dr-congo>.

racist and genocidal anti-Tutsi ideology, while for Herman and Peterson, the case of Rwanda turns out to be mainly a means to an end to criticise the foreign policy of the US and its allies.[59] Herman and Peterson's denial discourse thus appears to follow from a radical anti-US/imperialist ideology. This indicates that Herman and Peterson initially did not intentionally recycle the official denial discourse.[60] Although their discourse was not inspired by a genocidal ideology, it nonetheless remains problematic. By reiterating significant elements from the discourse of the perpetrators, the aforementioned actors facilitate and empower the denial of the genocide against the Tutsi and thereby basically contribute to the implementation of the last stage in the genocide. The significance of such reiterations of the official denial discourse becomes clear when you take into account that denial is interpersonal. In order for the perpetrators to successfully maintain their alternative reality it is required that others collude or collaborate with them in this process. Because of their professional status Herman and Peterson provide the denial discourse with intellectual, scholarly and journalistic credibility.[61] The interpersonal nature of denial also appears to determine to what extent actors engage with other relevant scholarly material

---

59 They draw on the earlier discussed framework of the politics of genocide to develop their criticism, but how the analytical concept of the politics of genocide that they present in their work is applied reveals a particular way of looking at and making sense of massive conflicts in the world, including the conflicts in the Great Lakes Region. For them the US or other major Western powers are to blame for what is happening. The politics of genocide encompasses the denial of human suffering by those responsible for that suffering in order to safeguard their positions and/or to consolidate their power with the result that these powerful actors enjoy impunity for what they have done. Herman and Peterson apply this framework with a focus on the US and its allies. That the RPF is responsible for perpetrating gross human rights violations during the conflict in Rwanda in the 1990s, but also in later conflicts in neighbouring Congo, cannot be denied and these crimes do deserve our attention. However, it appears that instead of being an analysis of the politics of genocide in case of Rwanda and which acknowledges the specific nature and seriousness of all perpetrations by all parties in the conflict, Herman and Peterson engage in the politics of genocide themselves. They minimise the crimes perpetrated by Hutu Power and they maximise the crimes perpetrated by the RPF to unrealistic proportions. In their analysis acknowledgment of the crimes perpetrated by the RPF thus comes at the cost of a denial of the crimes perpetrated by Hutu Power. C.A.R. Moerland, *The Killing of Death: Denying the Genocide against the Tutsi*, PhD thesis, Maastricht University, Maastricht 2015, pp. 245–253.

60 Ibid., pp. 245–253.

61 In the context of an analysis of the denial of the Armenian genocide, Mamigonian has observed that an 'alternative corpus of competing literature on the events' is being developed that 'draws deeply from the well of denialist tropes'. He explains that 'we can observe the conscious and unconscious adoption of denialist rhetorical framing by academics and mainstream journalists'. He adds that: 'The efforts partially described in this paper have had a cumulative effect; they have helped to normalize the presentation of denial of the Armenian Genocide within academia in much the same way that denials of other scientific phenomena have made inroads. It is because of this relative success and the prestige value of "academic denial" that it is a key element of the larger denialist project inasmuch as it lends an unsavoury undertaking a necessary air of respectability.' M.A. Mamigonian, 'Academic Denial of the Armenian Genocide in American Scholarship: Denialism as Manufactured Controversy' (2015) 9(1) *Genocide Studies International* 61–82, 72 and 77.

on the case of Rwanda. In their work Herman and Peterson do not seriously engage with the massive volume of work on Rwanda. If they do address it, they downplay its significance and they attempt to discredit the authors. Moreover, instead of drawing on well-known and authoritative research they tend to rely on what according to them is 'suppressed' information.[62] As will become clear throughout the following sections, when it comes to the BBC documentary similar issues are at play.[63]

4. THE BBC DOCUMENTARY 'RWANDA'S UNTOLD STORY'

4.1. VANTAGE POINT

In the same vein as the official denial discourse and the narrative of those who recycle this denial, the BBC documentary discursively constructs a rhetorical vantage point which attempts to create a legitimate ground for the questionable content that follows.[64, 65, 66] To illustrate this aspect, it is insightful to reiterate what discursively happens during the opening scenes of the BBC documentary.

62 One of these suppressed pieces of information that Herman and Peterson, but also the BBC documentary, relies on is the so-called Gersony report, it has not been officially published, but it was not suppressed. Its content is widely known and discussed. Herman and Peterson claim that it is because of Kagame's and Western powers that the report was never officially published. Others, however, argue that the method was problematic and the outcomes therefore unreliable. Adelman, for instance, notes: 'The conclusions of the Gersony Report of occurrences within Rwanda could possibly have been true, but the evidence we examined undermined the credibility of those conclusions and fit in too well with the Hutu revisionist claim that, on the one hand, denied the genocide, and, on the other hand, claimed that it was Kagame that had perpetuated a genocide.' H. Adelman, 'The Rwandan Genocide Revisited: Part I the Context of a Recent BBC Report' 2014 <http://howardadelman.com/2014/10/23/part-iii-the-bbc-report-the-downing-of-habyarimanas-plane/>.

63 These elements were also addressed by the earlier mentioned group of complainants in their letters to the BBC.

64 Letter, 16.03.2015, BBC ECU Provisional findings reply 2015 Rwanda's Untold Story, Annexe A The BBC documentary Rwanda's Untold Story, pp. 5–6.

65 Like in the approach taken by Herman and Peterson, the documentary also 'reveals evidence that challenges the accepted story' and instead of engaging with the massive body of work on Rwanda they mainly refer to obscure sources. The message that is communicated to the audience is that they have misunderstood the events and that the documentary will show 'evidence' that remedies this misunderstanding. This rhetorical vantage point attempts to create a legitimate basis for the questionable claims that follow and which reiterate crucial elements of the official denial discourse.

66 Adelman observed: '[T]he BBC Report said that, "Up until now, in Western media, scholarship, and commentary, the Hutus as a community have been held solely responsible for the Rwandan genocide of 1994, and Kagame held up as Rwanda's saviour." Neither we, nor any of the scholars with which I was associated, held that the Hutus as a community were responsible for the genocide. Rather, we all insisted that it was an extremist group of Hutus and definitely not the Hutu community as a whole.' H. Adelman, 'The Rwandan

First, producer Jane Corbin, who also narrates the documentary, makes the following opening statement: 'A Country dominated by its dark history. The senseless barbarity of the genocide still shocks us. We think we know the story. But do we?' This is followed by a remark of Professor Allan Stam who claims that 'What the world believes, and what actually happened, are quite different.' Subsequently, RPF defector General Kayumba Nyamwasa and Professor Filip Reyntjens accuse Kagame of being a 'serial killer' and being 'the most important war criminal in office today'. The introduction to the subject matter of the documentary ends with Corbin questioning: '20 years on from the genocide, what is the truth about Rwanda?'

Such statements make the audience wonder what exactly it is that they do not know or what exactly they have misunderstood.[67] To further highlight the significance of such statements, it is insightful to refer to Marc Mamigonian's observations which he made with regard to the denial of the Armenian Genocide. Mamigonian observed that nowadays genocide denial often presents itself as a 'manufactured controversy' noting that 'a growing body of critical scholarship and documentation of the Armenian Genocide has rendered traditional strategies of silencing and denial increasingly untenable'. He adds that, '[l]ike the tobacco industry lobbyists of the 1950s, apologists for the "Turkish position" now labour to construct denialism as a legitimate intellectual position within a historical debate.'[68] Mamigonian refers to a memo written in 1969 by a tobacco executive in which it is stated that '[d]oubt is our product since it is the best means of competing with the "body of fact" that exists in the mind of the general public. It is also the means of establishing a controversy.'[69] The idea is promoted that there still is no consensus on what happened and a debate over the facts and interpretations is thus still legitimate and necessary to get to the real truth.[70] The above opening statements reveal that is also the sentiment that the documentary taps into.

The remainder of the documentary attempts to further convince the audience that the public has greatly misunderstood what happened in

Genocide Revisited: Part I the Context of a Recent BBC Report' 2014 <http://howardadelman.com/2014/10/23/part-iii-the-bbc-report-the-downing-of-habyarimanas-plane/>.

67 In another discussion on a case of questionable reporting on the genocide against the Tutsi, Smith pointed out that to the unsuspected reader, such an the introduction leaves 'nagging doubts on the details, which in turn calls into question the established facts.' S.D. Smith, 'The Fine Line of Genocide History' 2014 *Huffington Post* <www.huffingtonpost.com/stephen-d-smith/the-fine-line-of-genocide_b_4719666.html>. See also: L. Melvern and G.H. Stanton, 'The Rwandan Genocide' 2014 *The New York Times* <www.nytimes.com/2014/01/22/opinion/the-rwandan-genocide.html?_r=0>.

68 M.A. Mamigonian, 'Academic Denial of the Armenian Genocide in American Scholarship: Denialism as Manufactured Controversy' (2015) 9(1) *Genocide Studies International* 61–82, 62.

69 Ibid., p. 77.

70 Ibid., p. 62.

Rwanda.[71] That what the world according to the documentary knows is the 'official history' or 'the government version' of the conflict and the genocide which in the documentary is questioned and even claimed to be 'wrong' and 'made up'. Halfway through the documentary Corbin interviews Professors Davenport and Stam and she introduces them and their research as follows: 'The world knows what happened in Rwanda during the genocide against the Tutsis, but when two American academics came to the country and conducted exhaustive field research up and down Rwanda, they found a different side to the story.' Corbin notes that 'They found the government's version of events was repeated everywhere.' Stam explains: 'Every person we talked to their story was exactly the same. That told us that something was wrong … with the story … that the story was made up. … As we looked more closely, a totally new understanding of what had taken place became very clear.' Generally in scholarly research, the fact that many individuals tell the same story tends to be taken as a sign that what they are telling is probably true. For Davenport and Stam, however, this appears to prove the opposite. If you were to ask Holocaust survivors, or victims of other genocides, what happened to them and their relatives, they would also come up with a similar story about their persecution, which is not strange because that is what collectively happened to them. To take this as proof of the opposite, as Davenport and Stam apparently do, is highly questionable.[72] One could, of course, argue that in the wake of the conflict Kagame and the RPF have been able to control the national discourse concerning what happened and that the official history of the violence excludes much of the crimes perpetrated against the Hutu population by the RPF, while predominantly focusing on the genocide against the Tutsi. However, the fact that the crimes perpetrated against the Hutu tend to be ignored does not automatically make acknowledgments of the crimes perpetrated against the Tutsi 'wrong' or 'made-up'.

71 See also 16.03.2015, BBC ECU Provisional findings reply 2015 Rwanda's Untold Story.

72 Letter, 16.03.2015, BBC ECU Provisional findings reply 2015 Rwanda's Untold Story, Conclusion, p. 15. It also puts the victims in an extremely dire situation as they somehow have to prove their own deaths and this is exactly what the perpetrators of genocide want as Nichanian observed. According to Nichanian, the genocide creates an unimaginable catastrophe for the survivor: 'In the very moment when the first survivor has uttered a word of testimony, at the very instant the first sound came out of his mouth to tell his cavalry of his observations, the archive has already seized his speech. That is the catastrophe for the survivor. From the beginning, before the beginning even, the murderer is here, facing me, and he tells me: Prove it! Prove it then if you can! And I, for ninety years, I have stood up and proven it. … I answer to the injunction of the executioner. For ninety years, by proving, by making testimony function as proof, I answer to the call and injunction of the executioner. For that is what he wanted from the beginning is it not? To kill, to eliminate, to exterminate? Of course, he wanted that too, but, above all, he wanted me to prove – and prove again.' M. Nichanian, *The Historiographic Perversion*, Columbia University Press, New York 2009, p. 123.

4.2. NATURE AND DIRECTION OF VIOLENCE

The documentary furthermore tends to obscure the nature and the direction of the violence.[73] The documentary relies heavily on the research of Professors Davenport and Stam and this is the same research on which Herman and Peterson rely in their analysis. In the documentary Stam claims that: 'Violence was committed in 1994 by almost every side and every participant in this war and breakdown of social order. Random violence happened and hundreds of thousands of people died for no particular purpose.' To simply state that violence was committed 'by almost every side' obscures the direction of the violence.[74] Note that the official denial discourse designates the violence as 'interethnic massacres' which conveys the idea that the violence was mutual. Moreover, Stam's claim that it was a 'war and breakdown of social order', with 'random violence' and people died for 'no particular reason' obscures the nature of the genocidal violence. Genocide, because of its scope, is by definition planned and organised and to define it as 'war', 'breakdown' or 'random violence' is to deny its specific and orchestrated nature. We also see this approach in the official denial discourse of the perpetrators of the genocide, which promotes the idea that due to the RPF war effort there was a '*colère totale*' that ultimately resulted in spontaneous and uncontrolled violence against the Tutsi people. The way Davenport and Stam lump together all kinds of specific violent events under the same heading of political violence obscures the different nature and direction of these events.[75]

4.3. NUMBER OF VICTIMS

One of the most questionable aspects of the documentary concerns the discussion of the number of individuals that were victimised during the

73 Letter, 16.03.2015, BBC ECU Provisional findings reply 2015 Rwanda's Untold Story, section 1. Our claims of Genocide Denial, pp. 2–6.

74 They mix up the so called 'conflict triangle' and the 'atrocity triangle' which structures the relationships between the actors (perpetrator, victim and bystander) involved.

75 In their research they furthermore tend to reduce the violence to acts of killing. By focusing predominantly on killings, Davenport and Stam tend to reduce genocide to the physical destruction of people by murder. They reduce it to mortality rates, battle map simulations, etc. The problem is however that genocide is a process that involves multiple stages of violent marginalisation that include a wide variety of genocidal techniques. So when Davenport and Stam make insightful, who did what to whom, by solely focusing on killing, they are missing the bigger genocidal picture and it is exactly that 'bigger picture' of what happened that audiences need in order to understand the difference between genocide, war crimes and crimes against humanity and to understand what actors engaged in which crimes. C.A.R. Moerland, *The Killing of Death: Denying the Genocide against the Tutsi*, PhD thesis, Maastricht University, Maastricht 2015, p. 280.

genocide against the Tutsi.[76] Following the above statements, Stam makes the following claim: 'If a million people died in Rwanda in 1994, and that's certainly possible, there is no way that the majority of them could be Tutsi. ... Because there weren't enough Tutsi in the country. ... If a million Rwandans died and two hundred thousand of them were Tutsi that means that 800,000 of them were Hutu.' Corbin subsequently notes: 'That's completely the opposite of what the world believes happened in the Rwandan genocide.' But according to Stam '[w]hat the world believes and what actually happened are quite different.' As noted earlier, according to Stam, this story as we know it is 'made up' and 'wrong'. Such a reversal of the victim rates not only contradicts virtually all expert research on the death toll of the genocide, it moreover confirms what the official denial discourse has been promoting, namely that the real victims are the Hutu and not the Tutsi.[77] Davenport and Stam's conclusion concerning the death toll creates considerable confusion, because they do not explain where the very high number of Hutu victims actually originated from.[78] Many Hutu have indeed been killed by the RPF, but Davenport and Stam's estimate is much higher than the highest estimate on RPF killings of Hutu. This is problematic

---

76 Rwanda's Untold Story: Letter to the Director-General of the BBC 12.10.2014, p. 2. See also Letter, 16.03.2015, BBC ECU Provisional findings reply 2015 Rwanda's Untold Story, section 3. The number of Tutsi people murdered, pp. 8–11.

77 The perpetrators of the genocide namely attempt to tip the balance and to overshadow the suffering of the Tutsi.

78 In a reaction to an article of Shaw on the issue of the BBC documentary one commentator insightfully observed: 'Davenport and Stam tend to focus upon data that emphasizes three points: a) low Tutsi population numbers by 1994, b) high numbers of Tutsi survivors, and c) high number overall killed. ... In their original "What Really Happened in Rwanda" (2009) Davenport and Stam claim that the 1991 Rwandan census pegged the number of Tutsi at 600,000 (C. Davenport and A.C. Stam, 'What really happened in Rwanda', 2009 <www.psmag.com/navigation/politics-and-law/what-really-happened-in-rwanda-3432/>; Prunier (1995) had previously analysed the same census figures, but came up with the much higher figure of 930,000 Tutsi alive by April 1994. Prunier accounts for three factors Davenport and Stam miss: Rwanda's high growth rate (3.2%), intentional underreporting, and Tutsi with Hutu identities. As for the number of Tutsi that survived the genocide, they use Ibuka's figure of 300,000. This is a far cry from Prunier's 130,000 survivors. Nonetheless, ever if Ibuka's number is closer to the truth, subtracting it from Prunier's interpretation of the census data leaves us with 630,000 Tutsi victims. These numbers far exceed the 300,000 Tutsi that Davenport and Stam calculate to have been slain. If we use Human Rights Watch's number of 800,000 overall deaths, and subtract Prunier's 630,000 Tutsi deaths, then that leaves us with 170,000 Hutu victims. Davenport and Stam however seem to prefer high end estimates of overall deaths, including one that's as high as 1,260,000 (1998 govt survey). By juxtaposing these high estimates of overall deaths with low level of Tutsi killed, Davenport and Stam can claim Hutu deaths of between 500,000 to over a million. Through arithmetical chicanery, Davenport and Stam invent Hutu victims while obscuring the number of Tutsi deaths. While their later work utilizes a "Baysian technique" in order to draw from as many sources as possible, they tend to read these sources in such a way as to reinforce their particular viewpoint.' Remarks to Shaw <http://martinshaw.org/2014/10/18/bbc-you-cant-indict-rwandas-government-by-denying-the-1994-genocide/#comments>. See also the research of Verpoorten on the number of victims and how Davenport and Stam are wrong to claim that 200,000 Tutsi died. M. Verpoorten, 'Rwanda: Why Claim That 200,000

as Jones explains, because unless we take the view that 'in fact the RPF did butcher hundreds of thousands of Hutus without anyone noticing at the time, we can only explain that Holocaust of Hutus as inflicted by Hutus themselves'.[79] Davenport and Stam's conclusions discussed above challenge virtually all of the scholarly work on the genocide in Rwanda and it raises the question whether such dramatic conclusions should be drawn when thorough explanations are lacking, the research has never been published in a peer reviewed journal and more importantly if the results, to use their own words, were ultimately 'an educated guess' based on 'an estimate'.[80, 81]

Tutsi Died in the Genocide Is Wrong – by Marijke Verpoorten' 2014 *African Arguments* <http://africanarguments.org/2014/10/27/rwanda-why-davenport-and-stams-calculation-that-200000-tutsi-died-in-the-genocide-is-wrong-by-marijke-verpoorten/>.

79 A. Jones, 'Rwanda and the Politics of Genocide Denial', *The 9th Biennial Conference of the International Association of Genocide Scholars (IAGS)*, Buenos Aires, Argentina 2011. Paper on file with author.

80 C. Davenport and A.C. Stam, 'What Really Happened in Rwanda?', Millar McCune 2009. Interestingly, Reyntjens (who, himself, also featured in the documentary) in a reaction to the critique mentioned earlier stated that: 'I do not need to dwell on the second claim considered untenable by the signatories. I agree with them that the figures provided by Professors Stam and Davenport on Tutsi and Hutu killed in 1994 do not appear to be based on solid research. At least the data they have published (not in a scientific journal or book, but merely on their website <http://genodynamics.weebly.com>) are insufficient to support their claim, which flirts with genocide minimisation or denial.' F. Reyntjens, 'Rwanda's Untold Story. A reply to "38 scholars, scientists, researchers, journalists and historians" – by Filip Reyntjens' 2014 *African Arguments* <http://africanarguments.org/2014/10/21/rwandas-untold-story-a-reply-to-38-scholars-scientists-researchers-journalists-and-historians-by-filip-reyntjens/>. For more analysis of Davenport and Stam's work see H. Adelman, 'The Rwandan Genocide Revisited: Part IV: the BBC Report – Genocide Denial – A' 2014 <http://howardadelman.com/2014/10/27/the-bbc-report-genocide-denial-a/>.

81 What makes the above-mentioned discussion of victim rates even more questionable, is that it in the documentary directly follows a section in which Corbin visits a genocide memorial in Murambi where she talks to genocide survivor Gaspard who is also the groundskeeper of the museum. Corbin narrates that: 'In Rwanda today, it all seems peaceful on the roads where the militias once separated out and killed the Tutsis. But Paul Kagame keeps the flame of genocide burning at memorial sites across the country. These places reinforce the official story that it was overwhelmingly Tutsis who died, and Hutus who killed him.' Corbin's last remark also makes clear that instead of seeing the memorial sites as places which attempt to commemorate what happened, she simply portrays them as political tools; as means to the end of the 'official story'. At Murambi 50,000 people were killed and Gaspard shows Corbin the 'rooms in which bodies of victims, many of them, especially women and kids, were killed by machetes and clubs.' Confronted with the terrible image of mummified bodies Corbin asks: 'Why is it important to keep these bodies? People would find this macabre and strange.' Gaspard answers that 'There are those people who do not want that proofs can be seen. So these are tangible proofs of the genocide committed, perpetrated against the Tutsi in 1994.' The content of this section in which Gaspard talks about the genocide against the Tutsi is automatically challenged by the discussion that follows on the victims rates. The argument that Stam unfolds sheds serious doubt on what Gaspard has previously been telling. It leaves the audience with the following dilemma: is what Gaspard has been telling the truth or simply the 'official story' which according to Stam is 'made up' and 'wrong'. It also casts doubts on the events of commemoration that the documentary featured in the beginning of the documentary.

4.4. THE DOWNING OF THE PLANE

In the documentary it is alleged that Kagame and the RPF shot down the plane of former president Habyarimana.[82] The documentary treats this allegation as entirely credible and in this context it refers to the indictment of French investigative judge, Bruguière, and the allegations of defected former RPF members, such as the already mentioned General Kayumba Nyamwasa. However, the documentary does not address the criticisms concerning Jean-Louis Bruguière's investigation and the evidence on which it is based. It does not mention that investigations of other French investigative judges, Marc Trévidic and Nathalie Poux, who worked on the dossier after Bruguière, have resulted in other ideas about, for instance, the location from which the missiles could have been fired. Their research also still leaves much unanswered, but it shows that we cannot take Bruguière's report as fact. Moreover, the documentary does not call into question the accusations of the former RPF members, such as Nyamwasa, who claim to have the knowledge and proof that Kagame is responsible for downing the plane. Although Nyamwasa states that he was 'in a position to know', his claims remain unverifiable and superficial.[83] It is actually telling that those who accuse Kagame and the RPF of having assassinated Habyarimana have not been able to produce any direct or otherwise substantial evidence for their accusations. The documentary also does not mention that the actions of these RPF defectors, who are now part of the political opposition abroad, could be politically motivated. The subject matter is thus less clear cut and straightforward than it is being presented in the documentary.[84] However, the most important aspect in the context of this discussion on the issue of denial is that the allegations that feature in the documentary have been a key element in the official denial discourse of the genocide perpetrators. They use this accusation of the downing of the plane to argue that the violence that was perpetrated against the Tutsi was not organised but rather a spontaneous public reaction to the death of the president. The logical consequence of such reasoning is that ultimately the RPF and the Tutsi are responsible for whatever suffering they endured; they triggered their own annihilation. By giving such accusations a platform while letting them go unchallenged, the documentary has empowered this denialist discourse. The reality concerning the downing of the plane is that,

---

82 Rwanda's Untold Story: Letter to the Director-General of the BBC 12.10.2014, p. 2. See also Letter, 16.03.2015, BBC ECU Provisional findings reply 2015 Rwanda's Untold Story, section 4. The Assassination of Habyarimana, pp. 11–14.

83 Full Nyamwasa quotation: 'I know. I was in a position to know and he knows I was in a position to know.'

84 For more other omissions and further decontextualisations see H. Adelman, 'The Rwanda Genocide Revisited: Part III the BBC Report – the Downing of Habyarimana's Plane' 2014 <http://howardadelman.com/2014/10/23/part-iii-the-bbc-report-the-downing-of-habyarimanas-plane/>.

although authoritative experts on Rwanda often see it as part of a *coup d'état* by Hutu extremists (and much of the evidence indeed supports that thesis), we do not know who shot down the plane and to claim otherwise is speculation.[85]

5. RWANDA'S UNTOLD STORY – ACKNOWLEDGING GENOCIDE OR DENYING IT?

The analysis shows that the documentary recycles elements that are central to the official denial discourse of the genocide perpetrators.[86] This aspect of recycling also makes clear that, contrary to what the title of the documentary suggests, the 'story' featured in the documentary is not 'untold'. It has been told many times before in the propaganda of the perpetrators and this story has been repeated by them in court where they stand trial for their crimes.[87] As a result, the presented views concerning the nature and the direction of the violence, the victim rate, the downing of the plane, etc. are thus not simply 'alternative perspectives' with regard to what happened. Instead, they make up key discursive elements of a political and criminal discourse that aims to deny the genocide against the Tutsi. In the context of genocide the notion of an 'alternative perspective' is highly problematic. Najarian explains that by presenting another side to the story deniers reduce an indisputable historical event to a conflict between two opposing sides with the regard to what happened (a manufactured controversy) and in doing so 'deniers have constructed a linguistic ground where none existed before'. Najarian concludes that: '[To break genocidal events] into opposing camps is already to deny its reality, even before one starts making excuses … To begin to argue numbers and sides is already to give in to denial. It is our own decorum, our fascination with the paraphernalia of objectivity that makes denial possible.'[88] The crime of genocide, as Nichanian explains, tries to erase itself as a fact.[89] This specific nature of the crime of genocide has implications for our critical investigation into such events because we should be careful not to facilitate and empower their denial. Genocide research thus comes with great responsibility. Care is warranted that critical and revisionist analyses

85 The investigations of the French investigative judges Marc Trévidic and Nathalie Poux also do not make clear who the responsible actors are.

86 The analysis above focused on three elements, but others have also raised concern as to how the Interahamwe militia is portrayed and how the documentary questions whether the RPF stopped the genocide.

87 Rwanda's Untold Story: Letter to the Director-General of the BBC 12.10.2014, p. 1. See also Letter, 16.03.2015, BBC ECU Provisional findings reply 2015 Rwanda's Untold Story, pp. 1–2.

88 J. Najarian, 'Gnawing at History: The Rhetoric of Holocaust Denial' (1997) *The Midwest Quarterly*.

89 M. Nichanian, *The Historiographic Perversion*, Columbia University Press, New York 2009.

of the events do not end up mimicking the narrative of those who perpetrated the crime, because that would empower their denial and the continuance of the crime. This does not mean that there is a moratorium on genocide research.[90] On the contrary, the more we are able to reveal the complexity of genocide, the less vulnerable it becomes to denial. Discussions on issues such as the number of victims, precipitation of events, the role of third parties, etc. are relevant and still continuing, but one should be careful that such critical analysis and revisionism does not turn into an attack on the event as such.[91]

In their reactions to the criticism the BBC has noted that it 'strongly refutes the suggestion that any part of the programme constitutes a "denial of the Genocide against the Tutsi."' They furthermore stipulate that '[t]here are repeated references to the mass killings of Tutsis by Hutus in 1994 and that this constituted genocide.' The documentary indeed contains references to the genocide against the Tutsi, but the reasoning that the documentary cannot amount to genocide denial because of these references is flawed.[92] The genocide against the Tutsi is predominantly framed as the 'official story' or the 'official narrative' of the genocide. Moreover, at the beginning and throughout the documentary it is made very clear that 'evidence' will be presented which 'challenges' that 'accepted story of the Rwandan genocide' and even depicts it as 'made up' or 'wrong'. This conveys the message that there is something mistaken about the history of the genocide as we know it. To make matters worse, the 'evidence' concerns the above-mentioned questionable 'alternative perspectives' that obscure the reality of the genocide.[93] Terms such as 'genocide against the Tutsi' are indeed used in the documentary, but the meaning and reality that these terms generally convey is fundamentally challenged. The perpetrators of the genocide and others who deny the genocide against the Tutsi also make occasional reference to the genocide against the Tutsi. They, however, subsequently deny it by reducing it to an 'official' version of what happened that has its roots in the propaganda of the RPF and which obscures what really happened. Such a reference is not a truthful acknowledgment of the genocide, but a means to the end of denial.

90 Adelman noted: 'There have been a number of academic disputes about the genocide, though no scholarly denials that the genocide took place.' H. Adelman, 'The Rwandan Genocide Revisited: Part I the Context of a Recent BBC Report' 2014 <http://howardadelman.com/2014/10/14/fathers-and-sons-part-ii-review-of-the-judge/>.

91 To depict it as shocking but serious revisionism is giving it too much credit, because elements are extremely problematic from the perspective of genocide denial.

92 Letter, 16.03.2015, BBC ECU Provisional findings reply 2015 Rwanda's Untold Story, Annexe A, Provisional finding of the Editorial Complaints Unit, p. 7. The documentary also does not clearly explain what genocide entails. The genocidal intent of wiping out the Tutsis completely is not addressed nor does the documentary shed light on the underlying ideology that is essential to the perpetration of genocide. It is noted that violence against the Tutsi was orchestrated, but the virulent genocidal nature of it is not clarified.

93 It is important to understand that the history that the documentary challenges is not simply an 'official' history, but a history that is acknowledged in scholarly articles, books, expert reports and witness statements and in the legal rulings of the ICTR.

Not only does the documentary recycle key elements of the denial discourse of the perpetrators of the genocide against the Tutsi, but because the BBC is a renowned and trustworthy media outlet, it has also significantly empowered the denial.[94] This is an important aspect especially when one takes into account the interpersonal character of denial. The perpetrators can only keep up their denial when other actors knowingly collude or unintentionally collaborate in the process of denial. However, the BBC has not only enhanced the credibility of their denial by broadcasting such a documentary in a prime time slot, it has also empowered the denial by how it has reacted to criticism. Instead of taking the concerns seriously, the BBC has directly refuted the accusation that any part of the programme constitutes genocide denial.[95] It is, of course, possible that the BBC and the producers of the documentary were initially not aware of how sensitive certain elements contained in documentary were in terms of genocide denialism. It is indeed not always easy to recognise the denial of the genocide against the Tutsi due to the complex ways in which it operates. Moreover, in order to recognise the problem of recycling, one has to be intimately familiar with the discourse of the perpetrators. The problem is, however, that even if the actions are unintentional, the lack of intent does not mitigate or undo the negative consequences. Such acts still have dire implications because 'denial' in effect also facilitates the broader denial dynamic on which genocide thrives. However, as explained earlier, denial is a dynamic and often progressive process and in this case it is illustrated by how the BBC has further reacted to the concerns raised with regard to the documentary. Note that after its broadcast, the documentary was immediately picked up by extremist elements and presented as a proof of their perverted version of history. How the BBC reacts is thus of crucial importance. Despite being made aware of the problems concerning the documentary and their implications in terms of denial, the BBC has refused to take any constructive action which addresses the problems pointed out to them.[96] Because the BBC is aware of the implications of their actions, as they

94 Rwanda's Untold Story: Letter to the Director-General of the BBC 12.10.2014, pp. 1 and 3. See also See also Letter, 16.03.2015, BBC ECU Provisional findings reply 2015 Rwanda's Untold Story, Conclusion, p. 15. And Letter, 16.03.2015, BBC ECU Provisional findings reply 2015 Rwanda's Untold Story, Annexe A, Provisional finding of the Editorial Complaints Unit, p. 8.

95 The BBC, furthermore, noted that 'a duty to investigate difficult and challenging subjects' and that the documentary made 'a valuable contribution to the understanding of the tragic history of the country and the region.' It is, however, highly doubtful whether the programme is a 'valuable contribution'. The story presented has already been told before, it lacks context, is riddled with omissions, and it is one-sided. Moreover, if one seriously wanted to reflect on the RPF crimes, the role of Kagame and the contemporary situation in Rwanda, there are more appropriate ways to do this and should not have come at the cost of the genocide against the Tutsi.

96 On 1 June 2015, nine months after its broadcast, in a reaction to the ban on BBC broadcast in Rwanda a BBC World Service spokesperson said: 'We are extremely disappointed by the decision of the commission to indefinitely suspend the BBC Kinyarwanda programme. The BBC World Service reaches an audience of over 2 million in Rwanda who rely on the BBC

have been pointed out to them, they cannot maintain that their inaction is unintentional. So, instead of unwillingly collaborating, the BBC now appears to be wilfully colluding in the process of denial and as a result they have moved from '"denial" in effect' to 'secondary genocide denial'.[97]

6. CONCLUDING REMARKS

The above analysis aims to contribute to a better understanding of the denial of the genocide against the Tutsi and the problematic nature of the documentary in that regard. It is not the intention to question the BBC's investigative role, nor does it aim to defend the RPF and the government of Rwanda against allegations concerning human rights violations. Parts of the BBC documentary raised attention to the crimes perpetrated by Kagame's RPF and it raised questions concerning the contemporary socio-political climate in Rwanda. Both of these issues have implications in terms of human rights and are therefore important and legitimate areas of investigation. Furthermore, these realities should not be denied, but thoroughly investigated. However, a critical investigation into these issues should not come at the cost of the genocide against the Tutsi. That is unacceptable. These crimes should not become a means to the end of the denial of the suffering of the Tutsi people.[98] Nor

for impartial news and information. We stand by our right to produce our independent journalism and strongly reject any suggestion that the documentary Rwanda's Untold Story constitutes genocide denial.' D. Baird, 'Rwanda Places Indefinite Ban on BBC Broadcasts over Genocide Documentary' 2015 *The Guardian* <www.theguardian.com/media/2015/jun/01/rwanda-places-indefinite-ban-on-bbc-broadcasts-over-genocide-documentary>.

97 Adelman, however, doubts whether it amounts to denial: 'Using the difficulty of the subject matter as a cover for a terribly flawed process is no excuse. Freedom of inquiry does not account for terribly sloppy research. The presentation was a travesty against objectivity. But did it constitute genocide-denial?' He concludes that: 'The BBC broadcasters and American academics do not appear to be genocide deniers, but they are, at the very least, genocide minimalizers. And they put their position forth by using many of the same arguments, the same type of evidence, the same approach and the same illogic of the deniers.' It seems that Adelman has a very narrow perception of genocide denial, but one which he does not clearly define in his articles. As explained before, genocide denial can take several forms. The facts can be denied or they can be reinterpreted, but denial can also take the form of minimisation or even trivialisation when genocide and other events are placed on equal footing or when genocide is put in the shadow of other events. This way the implications that would normally follow when such events occur are mitigated. C.A.R. Moerland, *The Killing of Death: Denying the Genocide against the Tutsi*, PhD thesis, Maastricht University, Maastricht 2015, pp. 145 and 219.

98 Shaw captures it well in his reaction to the documentary: 'The truth about genocide in Rwanda does not belong to the opponents of the RPF regime any more than to President Kagame. Acknowledging the crimes of the RPF should not mean minimising or denying the Hutu Power genocide – or the fact that Kagame's victory ended it, whatever new horrors it led to in the Congo. The catastrophic 1994 events were certainly the outcome of a political struggle in which the RPF was far from innocent, but that movement was not its perpetrator. Nothing the RPF has done since can justify the journalistic revisionism that the BBC allowed

should the genocide perpetrated against the Tutsi people be used to minimise the crimes suffered by the Hutu at the hands of the RPF. Safeguarding the history of the genocide also relies on an acknowledgement of RPF crimes and serious research into this matter, so that deniers cannot abuse and inflate these crimes for their political purposes. It is important that all parties come to understand that denialist narratives are disrespectful to all those who have suffered, because the reality, the histories of their victimisation are ultimately only (ab)used as means to questionable political ends. All victims of violence deserve justice no matter to which group they belong, who the perpetrator is or by which type of violence they have been victimised.

Lastly, in addition to the various issues addressed in the previous analysis, there is another aspect that I think is important to mention at the end of this paper. Namely, that the BBC documentary is illustrative of the fact that the denial of the genocide against the Tutsi is apparently becoming more accepted and mainstream. This is worrisome, especially when taking into account that, in contrast to Holocaust denial or the denial of the Armenian genocide, the denial of the genocide against the Tutsi receives virtually no scholarly attention. Without such research to inform the public, people and institutions remain unaware of the problem and its seriousness. The implications are profound, because the perpetrators and their denial are well served by this scholarly and public ignorance.

out on October 1st.' M. Shaw, 'BBC: You Can't Indict Rwanda's Government by Denying the 1994 Genocide' 2014 <http://martinshaw.org/2014/10/18/bbc-you-cant-indict-rwandas-government-by-denying-the-1994-genocide/>.

CHAPTER IX

FIGHTING NS IDEOLOGY AND HOLOCAUST DENIAL IN AUSTRIA

Past and Present Perspectives

Johannes KEILER

1. INTRODUCTION

Denial has become a common concept in our everyday lives as well as in everyday language and appears to be something that we are generally familiar with. Terminally ill patients who fail to acknowledge the severity of their illness, alcoholics who deny that they have a problem and claim that after all they are just social drinkers; politicians who reject responsibility for a disaster, and society turning a blind eye to the catastrophic situation of asylum seekers, may all be situations which can be classified as states of denial.[1] Despite the common nature and familiarity of the concept, a uniform scholarly definition is, however, hard to come by. It seems that we know denial when we see it but beyond that 'denial is a presence that evaporates, the nearer you get to defining it'.[2]

Despite its elusive character there are serval features of the concept on which there seems to be academic consensus. First, denial is generally seen as a defence or coping mechanism which helps people to protect themselves against painful and threatening internal (emotions) and/or external realities (situations).[3] Ultimately, denial is thus about the need to be free from a troubling recognition.[4]

---

1 See: S. COHEN, *States of Denial: Knowing About Atrocities and Suffering*, Polity Press, London 2001, pp. 1–6.

2 Ibid., p. 49. See also R. MOERLAND, *The Killing of Death. Denying the genocide against the Tutsi*, Intersentia, Cambridge 2016.

3 R. MOERLAND, *The Killing of Death. Denying the genocide against the Tutsi*, Intersentia, Cambridge 2016.

4 S. COHEN, *States of Denial: Knowing About Atrocities and Suffering*, Polity Press, London 2001, p. 25.

As a concept the mechanism of denial is in itself neutral. Depending on the circumstances it can, however, carry positive or negative connotations. On the one hand it functions as a coping mechanism which we all use to deal with traumatising events, threatening realities, etc.[5] On the other hand denial can also be used as an intentional tool of collusion, cover ups, propaganda and political manipulation.[6] In other words, the concept of denial 'serves not only those who suffer. It is indispensable for those who deliberately inflict terrible suffering on their fellow human beings – and for others who come to know about this'.[7]

In any case, the very core of the concept of denial can be found in the paradoxical state of knowing and not knowing at the same time.[8] For the defence mechanism to function, one first needs to be aware of a certain stimulus, a threatening reality, in order to subsequently be able to turn a blind eye to it or to reinterpret the situation as a less threatening one.[9] To deny a reality some awareness of it is paradoxically necessary. If we were truly ignorant of a threatening reality, denial would be superfluous. Denial is also a progressive phenomenon which can evolve over time. The desire to avoid knowing the unacceptable often initially prompts literal denial (it did not happen), but as this becomes harder to maintain, more sophisticated denial mechanisms (e.g. reinterpretation of facts) are used to block out the threatening reality.[10]

Finally, denial can function on a variety of levels. Denial can, for instance, be individual, personal or shared, collective, social or cultural.[11] In this article we will be concerned with two of those in the context of Austria, namely denial (of the Holocaust) by individuals on the one hand, and a broader, collective social or cultural denial (of responsibility) on the other.

The former nowadays constitutes a serious criminal offence in Austrian criminal law. As will become apparent below, the latter state of denial (i.e. the collective and cultural denial of responsibility) began to be replaced by acknowledgment in the early 1990s, but nevertheless played an important role in shaping the fight against the former. In this sense the two forms of denial are thus connected in the case of Austria. The initial social or cultural denial constitutes the vantage point of Austria's path of coming to terms with the horrors of the past. The fight against Holocaust denial, even by means of criminal law, arguably constitutes a milestone in the transition from denial to

5 Ibid., p. 6.
6 Ibid., pp. 58–68.
7 Ibid., p. 50.
8 Ibid., pp. 22, 44.
9 Ibid., pp. 21–50.
10 R. Moerland, *The Killing of Death. Denying the genocide against the Tutsi,* Intersentia, Cambridge 2016.
11 S. Cohen, *States of Denial: Knowing About Atrocities and Suffering,* Polity Press, London 2001, pp. 9 et seq. See also: R. Moerland, *The Killing of Death. Denying the genocide against the Tutsi,* Intersentia, Cambridge 2016.

acknowledgement and the moral realisation that the atrocities committed by the Third Reich must never again be repeated.

At first sight the use of criminal law to prevent and tackle denial may seem crude. However, while these laws may admittedly not be able to change social attitudes and sentiments they may work towards influencing behaviour and individual conduct. Traditionally, criminalising denial derives from the broader use of criminal law against incitement to hatred and discrimination.[12] The scope and purpose of the Austrian law is, however, much broader. As will subsequently be shown, the offence of Holocaust denial is but one element of a broader legal strategy to tackle, prevent and minimise Neo-Nazism, NS ideology and right-wing extremism.

Frequently denial manifests itself in the form of speech acts or other forms of expression. This, however, causes friction with several fundamental principles of criminal law, such as the harm principle, as well as human rights and civil liberties. This article will therefore commence with a brief analysis of the extent to which criminal law can be utilised properly to curb denial and nip right-wing ideology and extremism in the bud (section 2). Subsequently, the historical roots of the Austrian NS Prohibition Act will be outlined in order to better understand the social context in which it came about and later evolved (section 3). Having established the historical background, the focus will shift to analysing the different criminal offences contained in the Prohibition Act (section 4). Finally, some general conclusions and critical reflections will be provided (section 5).

2. CRIMINALISING DENIAL AND EXTREMIST IDEOLOGY

In a liberal, democratic society values and principles such as respect for human dignity, equality, the rule of law, freedom of thought and freedom of expression are of paramount importance. Despite the fact that these principles and values arguably 'constitute one of the essential foundations of a democratic society, one of the basic conditions for its progress and for each individual's self-fulfilment', they are not, however, sacrosanct and can be restricted provided certain requirements are fulfilled.[13]

Limitations may, for instance, be imposed by employing criminal law. Yet, liberal criminal law generally does not apply to thoughts, attitudes, opinions, let alone ideologies. This makes applying criminal law to any form of extremism, dangerous ideologies, or even more so to denial as an inherently psychological

12 S. Cohen, *States of Denial: Knowing About Atrocities and Suffering*, Polity Press, London 2001, p. 268.

13 *Handyside v. UK*, no. 5493/72. §49, ECHR 1976, ruling on Art. 10 ECHR (freedom of expression) and denial of the Holocaust.

mechanism, particularly challenging and problematic. Any form of extremism such as a person's attitude or opinion can thus *prima facie* never be subject to criminal sanctions. Rather, criminal law focuses instead on (potentially*) harmful conduct*. What, however, qualifies as harmful conduct is open for debate and is in every penal system also to a large extent socially and historically determined.

As is well known, the costs of the application of criminal rules are high – not just the social or financial cost of the criminal justice system in general, but also the costs for offenders who are subjected to the state's most intrusive and coercive measure, i.e. punishment.[14] This is why the use of criminal law as a means of regulating conduct is generally thought to require special justification and should only be used as a last resort.[15] The traditional starting point thereby is the 'harm principle' which essentially holds that the state may only criminalise conduct that causes or threatens harm to others.[16] Yet in the context of fighting National Socialist (NS) ideology and Holocaust denial this already poses a problem. Thereby often forms and means of expression are criminalised and it may not be immediately apparent how expressions may cause or threaten harm to others. Yet, there are arguably good reasons to think that they do.

First, the harm caused by expression may be direct in cases of racial insults, humiliation or intimidation. Direct speech, but also graffiti spray painted in public places, or pamphlets delivered by mail, may all act towards that end.[17] In this sense (hate) speech may create fear, mistrust and hostility among the members of society.

Secondly, expressions may also produce indirect harm through the mediation of attitudes and (racial) prejudices as well as the reinforcement of shared ideology on the part of the audience other than the target group itself.[18] Often these forms of expression for instance allege the inferiority of the target group and may thereby contribute to the unequal social status of minorities as well as create and fuel hostility, harassment and discrimination.

In case the expressions either imply or openly encourage the use of violence against certain segments of society the linkage to harm becomes more tenable.[19] In any case, the two are often interlinked in practice and can also for this reason be considered dangerous and harmful. For instance, history has arguably shown

---

14 L.W. Sumner, 'Criminalizing expression: Hate speech and obscenity' in: J. Deigh and D. Dolinko (eds.), *Oxford Handbook of Philosophy of Criminal Law*, Oxford University Press, New York 2011, p. 17.

15 See, for instance: A. Ashworth and J. Horder, *Principles of Criminal Law*, Oxford University Press, Oxford 2013, pp. 22–43.

16 Ibid., pp. 28 et seq.

17 L.W. Sumner, 'Criminalizing expression: Hate speech and obscenity' in: J. Deigh and D. Dolinko (eds.), *Oxford Handbook of Philosophy of Criminal Law*, Oxford University Press, New York 2011, p. 25.

18 Ibid., pp. 24 et seq.

19 Ibid. For a more restrictive view see: S. Wallerstein, 'Criminalising remote harm and the case of anti-democratic activity' (2007) 28(6) *Cardozo Law Review* 2697–2737.

that in the process of gross human rights violations public humiliation and dehumanisation of the target group often precedes the use of violence. In other words, verbal violence may often precede physical violence.

While from a doctrinal point of view it thus seems possible to justify criminalising expressions of NS ideology, etc., it should not be overlooked that values such as humanity, tolerance and respect for fundamental rights can of course never be superimposed on a society by the means of criminal law. It may, however, as the example of Austria shows, be invoked to help keeping radical elements and extreme factions in check.[20] Austrian criminal law namely prohibits certain forms of *conduct* which express right-wing extremist attitudes and which are considered especially dangerous for society.[21] The central legal instrument thereby is the Prohibition Act, which is nowadays frequently applied to combat re-engagement in NS activity. In this sense, criminal law is now part and parcel of a social and political counter-strategy to tackle re-engagement in NS activities as well as Holocaust denial.[22]

Even this legitimate goal is, however, subject to limitations in a liberal society based on the rule of law. In the case of fighting right-wing ideology and Neo-Nazism a well-balanced approach is needed as modern criminal law ought not to treat offenders with the same arbitrariness and harshness as the NS regime did. Were it otherwise the state would arguably threaten to undermine its own credibility.[23] It would then turn a blind eye to (i.e. deny) the past and simply replace one oppressive regime with another and thereby also lay the foundation for another web of denial.

3. THE NS PROHIBITION ACT OR THE LONG AND ROCKY ROAD TO COMING TO TERMS WITH THE PAST

The NS Prohibition Act was introduced immediately after the end of World War II on 8 May 1945 and enjoys constitutional status.[24] It was initially seen as a

20 W. Platzgummer, 'Die strafrechtliche Bekämpfung des Neonazismus in Österreich' (1994) 22 *ÖJZ*, pp. 753 et seq.

21 H. Gallhuber, 'Rechtsextremismus und Strafrecht' in: Stiftung Dokumentationsarchiv des Österreichischen Widerstandes (ed.), *Handbuch des österreichischen Rechtsextremismus*, 2nd ed., Deuticke, Wien 1994, pp. 625–646.

22 B. Bailer, 'The "Ban on Re-Engagement in National Socialist Activity" as a Social and Political Counter-strategy in Austria' in: R. Melzer and S. Serafin (eds.), *Right-Wing Extremism in Europe,* Druck und Verlagshaus Zarbock, FES, Berlin 2013, pp. 281–305.

23 H. Gallhuber, 'Rechtsextremismus und Strafrecht' in: Stiftung Dokumentationsarchiv des Österreichischen Widerstandes (ed.), *Handbuch des österreichischen Rechtsextremismus*, 2nd ed., Deuticke, Wien 1994, pp. 625–646.

24 This fact already expresses the special status of the Act as it is the only criminal law Act in Austria which enjoys constitutional status.

means of retaliation for those who had suffered under the NS regime against the Nazis and for the crimes they had committed against Austria and its citizens.[25]

From a legal viewpoint its aim primarily was to protect and safeguard the democratic development of Austria and to expunge any remaining pockets of National Socialism. From a political perspective the new law was an important prerequisite on Austria's path from an occupied country towards independence. It was part and parcel of the denazification process initiated by the Allied powers at the end of the war in Europe. However, while in Germany the Allied powers themselves carried out the denazification, this task fell to the provisional government in the case of Austria. The reason for this was that in the Moscow Declaration which was signed on 30 October 1943, Austria was (perhaps surprisingly) granted victim status. It was established that Austria was considered the first free country to fall victim to Hitlerite aggression and should be liberated from German domination.[26]

In its original version the Prohibition Act ordered the registration of all National Socialists. Failing to register carried a sanction of up to five years' imprisonment.[27] It thus did not only apply to direct perpetrators but also stigmatised opportunists, conformists and tag-alongs which created a lot of distrust and bitterness in large segments of society. For some the law may even constitute a motive to re-engage in NS activities today.

Approximately 550,000 people were officially registered. Adding family members to that figure, it can be said that in 1945 roughly a quarter of the Austrian population were officially listed as National Socialists.[28] Being listed could also have far reaching implications spanning from confiscation of assets and pensions, exclusion from elections and higher education to forced labour.[29] After regaining its independence in 1955 these special measures and sanctions were, however, abolished by means of a general NS amnesty.[30]

Since its introduction in 1945, the NS Prohibition Act has been amended several times, most notably in 1947, 1957 and 1992, but its impact remained initially limited. Convictions on the basis of the Prohibition Act proved difficult to achieve. One reason for this may be seen in the draconic minimum and

---

25 During the early parliamentary debates it was proposed to name the new law 'Retaliation Act' (*Vergeltungsgesetz*) but the name was later dropped and the term Prohibition Act adopted. See: S. Hirt, *Vom "Vergeltungs-" zum Verbotsgesetz*, Master's thesis, University Vienna, Vienna 2008 <http://othes.univie.ac.at/2786/>.

26 Ibid., p. 19.

27 W. Platzgummer, 'Die strafrechtliche Bekämpfung des Neonazismus in Österreich' (1994) 22 *ÖJZ* 753 et seq.

28 S. Hirt, *Vom "Vergeltungs-" zum Verbotsgesetz*, Master's thesis, University Vienna, Vienna 2008, p. 53 <http://othes.univie.ac.at/2786/>.

29 W. Platzgummer, 'Die strafrechtliche Bekämpfung des Neonazismus in Österreich' (1994) 22 *ÖJZ* 753 et seq.

30 S. Hirt, *Vom "Vergeltungs-" zum Verbotsgesetz*, Master's thesis, University Vienna, Vienna 2008, pp. 93 et seq. <http://othes.univie.ac.at/2786/>.

maximum sentences which the Act initially prescribed and which may have prompted juries to reach a verdict of not guilty.[31]

In addition, it should, however, also be noted that for some time the Prohibition Act simply did not really have the backing of society either. Certain parts of society, at least until the 1990s, primarily perceived the Act as a law superimposed on Austria by the occupying powers.[32] Furthermore, the general social attitude at that time seemed to be more favourable towards the perpetrators and against the victims of the NS regime. This attitude arguably reflected the then quite common collective, social or cultural denial by Austrians. Many claimed that people had just been following orders and that hardly anyone knew at the time what was happening, let alone the magnitude of the crimes committed. Many had decided to rather see no evil and hear no evil despite the more than obvious 'writing on the wall'.[33]

Finally, it should not be overlooked that the state apparatus remained interspersed with civil servants which before had willingly and very keenly served the NS regime.[34] This practice of application (or rather non-application) of the NS Prohibition Act as well as denial of the underlying problem and responsibility for the past lasted for more than a decade.[35]

A pertinent example of this unsatisfactory state of affairs can be found in the case of the Neo-Nazi and Holocaust denier Walter Ochsenberger. Ochsenberger was publisher, Chairman and author of the Neo-Nazi newspapers *Sieg* (Victory), *Top Secret,* and *Phoenix,* which published anti-Semitic articles. In addition, in these journals the existence of gas chambers, etc. was regularly denied. He was prosecuted under the NS Prohibition Act in 1979 and 1983 but was acquitted on both occasions. On a third occasion he tried to hijack the trial and to convert it into a trial about the existence of the Holocaust itself. When the jury

---

31 H. Gallhuber, 'Rechtsextremismus und Strafrecht' in: Stiftung Dokumentationsarchiv Des Österreichischen Widerstandes (ed.), *Handbuch des österreichischen Rechtsextremismus*, 2nd ed., Deuticke, Wien 1994, pp. 625–646; W. Platzgummer, 'Die strafrechtliche Bekämpfung des Neonazismus in Österreich' (1994) 22 *ÖJZ* 753 et seq.; LÄSSIG in *Wiener Kommentar zum Strafgesetzbuch,* VG Vorbem 2006, Mn 4.

32 See also: B. Bailer, 'The law against national-socialist activities in Austria – NS Verbotsgesetz' (2011) *Vienna J. on Int'l Const. L.* 42, and B. Bailer, 'The "Ban on Re-Engagement in National Socialist Activity" as a Social and Political Counter-strategy in Austria' in: R. Melzer and S. Serafin (eds.), *Right-Wing Extremism in Europe,* Druck und Verlagshaus Zarbock, FES, Berlin 2013, pp. 281–305.

33 See: S. Cohen, *States of Denial: Knowing About Atrocities and Suffering,* Polity Press, London 2001, pp. 148–156. See also: M. Janowitz, 'German reactions to Nazi atrocities' (1946) *The American Journal of Sociology* 141–146; and G. Horwitz, *In the shadow of death: Living outside the gates of Mauthausen,* The Free Press, New York 1990.

34 H. Gallhuber, 'Rechtsextremismus und Strafrecht' in: Stiftung Dokumentationsarchiv des Österreichischen Widerstandes (ed.), *Handbuch des österreichischen Rechtsextremismus,* 2nd ed., Deuticke, Wien 1994, pp. 625–646.

35 See also: B. Bailer, 'The "Ban on Re-Engagement in National Socialist Activity" as a Social and Political Counter-strategy in Austria' in: R. Melzer and S. Serafin (eds.), *Right-Wing Extremism in Europe,* Druck und Verlagshaus Zarbock, FES, Berlin 2013, pp. 281–305.

again returned with a verdict of not guilty he classified it as an 'acquittal for Germany'.[36] In 1991 Ochsenberger was finally convicted and sentenced to three years' imprisonment, and in 2002 again to two years' imprisonment (of which 16 months were suspended on probation).

The conviction of Ochsenberger in 1991 arguably signals and reflects a change in Austrian public opinion – a move from the state of denial to acknowledgment – which culminated in an amendment of the Prohibition Act in 1992. Thereby the high minimum sentences were reduced. Furthermore, life imprisonment became confined to particularly dangerous offenders, and for the rest, was replaced by sentences ranging from ten to twenty years' imprisonment.[37] Most importantly however, the legislator introduced §3h into the Prohibition Act which made denial of National Socialist crimes a criminal offence.

The reasons for this change in public opinion leading to the 1992 amendment and the criminalisation of Holocaust denial are certainly manifold. Three, however, stand out and will be briefly discussed.

One reason can certainly be found in the steady increase and resurgence of revisionism since the 1970s. Shortly after the war NS atrocities were still fresh in the mind of the people, and denying the facts seemed perhaps absurd. Yet, spurred on by public attention generated by for instance the trial against the virulent Holocaust denier Ernst Zündel in Canada in 1988, the revisionist movement gained momentum. The passage of time since the end of the war may have certainly also helped the revisionist cause. As the international network of revisionists and the intensity of their propaganda however grew, denying the problem became unacceptable and the need for a legislative response arguably became more pressing.[38]

Moreover, legal developments abroad may have been influential as well. Israel had, for instance, criminalised the denial of NS crimes in 1986 and also in Germany reforms to make the prosecution of Holocaust deniers easier and more effective already started in 1982.[39] Influenced by the aforementioned developments the Austrian legislator also decided to tighten measures to combat Holocaust denial in particular and re-engagement with NS activity in general.

---

36 B. SCHAGER, *Holocaustleugnung in Österreich. Die Leugner und ihr Umfeld. Eine Analyse*, Master's thesis, University Vienna, Vienna 2011, p. 16 et seq., available at: <http://othes.univie.ac.at/16692/>.

37 H. GALLHUBER, 'Rechtsextremismus und Strafrecht' in: STIFTUNG DOKUMENTATIONSARCHIV DES ÖSTERREICHISCHEN WIDERSTANDES (ed.), *Handbuch des österreichischen Rechtsextremismus*, 2nd ed., Deuticke, Wien 1994, pp. 625–646; W. PLATZGUMMER, 'Die strafrechtliche Bekämpfung des Neonazismus in Österreich' (1994) 22 *ÖJZ* 753 et seq.; LÄSSIG in *Wiener Kommentar zum Strafgesetzbuch,* VG Vorbem 2006, Mn 4.

38 B. SCHAGER, *Holocaustleugnung in Österreich. Die Leugner und ihr Umfeld. Eine Analyse*, Master's thesis University Vienna, Vienna 2011, p. 17 et seq., available at: <http://othes.univie.ac.at/16692/>.

39 Ibid., p. 18.

On the other hand, the political dynamic as well as public opinion in Austria also changed due to the so-called 'Waldheim affair'. Kurt Waldheim was a former Secretary of the United Nations and became Austrian President in 1986. He had, however, concealed in his biography his war past as former officer in an SA corps which had, *inter alia*, been involved in the deportation of the Jewish population in Greece. National and international newspapers reported widely on the affair which in Austria triggered for the first time a public debate about Austria's role and responsibility for NS atrocities.[40] The previously prevalent state of collective, cultural denial based, *inter alia*, on the perception of Austria as the first victim of NS aggression could no longer be maintained and instead the debate shifted towards acknowledgement of co-responsibility and co-perpetratorship.[41] In the wake of this affair public, political and media awareness concerning Neo-Nazi activities in general and Holocaust denial in particular also grew. This change in political and social climate certainly made it easier for the legislator as well as for the judiciary to address and tackle Neo-Nazism and denial of NS crimes.

4. FIGHTING RIGHT-WING EXTREMISM, NS IDEOLOGY AND DENIAL OF THE HOLOCAUST: PRESENT PERSPECTIVE

To fight right right-wing extremism, NS ideology and denial of the Holocaust, Austrian law has a toolkit consisting of various laws at its disposal. Three of those are criminal laws and two are administrative offences. The first and most important of these is the NS Prohibition Act (*Verbotsgesetz*). Another important provision in this context is §283 of the Austrian Criminal Code which proscribes incitement to hostile action against religious or ethnic groups.[42]

Furthermore, the Insignia Act prohibits wearing, displaying, depicting or disseminating insignias, emblems, symbols and signs of an organisation prohibited in Austria (§1 (1) Insignia Act). The prohibition also applies to insignia

40 Austria had also refused to pay compensation to Nazi victims, and, as described above, from 1970 onwards refused to investigate Austrian citizens who were senior Nazis. Stolen Jewish art remained public property until after the Waldheim affair. In 1995 a Restitution Act for victims of the NS regime was finally adopted. See 30.06.1995, Bundesgesetz über den Nationalfonds der Republik Österreich für Opfer des Nationalsozialismus, BgBl 1995, 6257.

41 B. Schager, *Holocaustleugnung in Österreich. Die Leugner und ihr Umfeld. Eine Analyse*, Master's thesis, University Vienna, Vienna 2011, pp. 19 et seq. <http://othes.univie.ac.at/16692/>. See also: B. Bailer, 'The "Ban on Re-Engagement in National Socialist Activity" as a Social and Political Counter-strategy in Austria' in: R. Melzer and S. Serafin (eds.), *Right-Wing Extremism in Europe*, Druck und Verlagshaus Zarbock, FES, Berlin 2013, pp. 281–305.

42 Sending a book containing anti-Semitic ideas to 90 persons in one's circle of friends was, for instance, held to constitute public agitation against a religious and ethnic group. See: OGH 4 March 1982, SSt 53/9.

that because of their similarity or their evident purpose are used as substitutes for the ones mentioned above (§1 (2) Insignia Act). Thus, wearing, for instance, a jacket with a swastika sticker on it or the SS runes respectively is punishable by a fine of up to €4,000 or a maximum prison sentence of one month. The same also applies for NS insignias placed on websites, etc.[43] The attempt already constitutes a punishable offence (§3 (3) Insignia Act).

Finally, under administrative law Article IX (1) no. 3 of the Introductory Provisions to the Code of Administrative Procedure (EGVG) prohibits by threat of a fine publicly expressing prejudice against persons on the grounds of their race, colour, national or ethnic origin, religion or creed. Article IX (1) no. 4 on the other hand prohibits disseminating NS ideas in the sense of the Prohibition Act. These two provisions thus aim to address petty crimes with an NS connection.

This brief overview shows that Austrian law applies a variety of different measures and instruments to tackle right-wing extremism and Neo-Nazism. Due to the considerable breadth of the legal framework the following discussion will however confine itself to the main instrument, i.e. the NS Prohibition Act. Subsequently the salient features of the Act will be discussed and its central articles will be systematically assessed and analysed.

4.1. THE NS PROHIBITON ACT: INTRODUCTION

As the NS Prohibition Act causes tensions with constitutionally protected principles such as equality, freedom of assembly and freedom of speech, the Act itself enjoys constitutional status. As a consequence, the Act can only be amended if the formal requirements for drafting constitutional rules are met. More importantly however, its constitutional status protects the Act from any challenges alleging unconstitutionality.[44]

Pursuant to §3j all violations of the Prohibition Act are to be dealt with by jury trial.[45] This once again underlines the special significance, and perhaps also the perceived severity of the transgressions, as generally only the most severe crimes which carry a minimum sentence of five years' up to life imprisonment or political offences, are subject to trial by jury in Austria. The offences of the Prohibition Act due to their severe sanctions as well as their perceived political nature are to be decided by a chamber consisting of three

43 S. Ebensperger, 'Die Verbreitung von NS-Gedankengut im Internet und ihre strafrechtliche Auswirkungen' (2002) *ÖJZ* 137.

44 Lässig in *Wiener Kommentar zum Strafgesetzbuch*, VG Vorbem 2006, Mn 3.

45 Lässig in *Wiener Kommentar zum Strafgesetzbuch*, VG §3j 2006, Mn 1.

professional judges and eight jurors.[46] The jury alone decides the question of the defendant's guilt and will together with the judges also determine the sentence to be imposed.

The provisions of the Prohibition Act often contain normative elements which need to be covered by the intention of the defendant. Consistent with the general approach to *mens rea* in Austrian criminal law, *dolus eventualis* is sufficient for all offences of the Prohibition Act.[47] One pertinent example of a normative offence element is, for instance, the concept of 'acting as a means towards the achievement of National Socialist aims' (*Betätigung im nationalsozialistischen Sinn*).[48] As this element is of particular importance in the context of §3g it will be discussed in more detail there.

§§1–3 of the Prohibition Act do not contain any criminal norms in the strict sense, but rather contain administrative prohibitions. These prohibitions are subsequently fleshed out in the criminal offences of §§3a and b as well as §3d – i. §1 formally dissolves the NSDAP (the National Socialist Workers Party) and all other NS organisations such as the SS and the SA and prohibits their renewal. §2 revokes the mandate of all members of (regional) administrative bodies and professional representation which were directly or indirectly based on proposals from the NSDAP or any other NS organisation. Finally, §3 prohibits any activities by any person in furtherance of the NSDAP or its aims, regardless of whether they take place within or outside NS organisations.

4.2. THE NS PROHIBITION ACT: THE OFFENCES

The offences enshrined in the Prohibition Act can roughly be subdivided into five different categories. First, §§3a–d prohibit the re-establishment of a National Socialist organisation as well as participating in, supporting or promoting such organisations. Second, §§3e and f criminalise acts of violence, carried out as a means to re-engage with National Socialist activity. Third, §3i introduces a general duty to report violations of the Prohibition Act to the authorities. Fourth, §3g contains a broad catch-all clause which prohibits any other acts carried out as a means towards the achievement of NS aims, which are not explicitly covered by the aforementioned offences. Finally, since 1992 §3h criminalises denying, grossly downplaying, condoning or seeking to justify the NS genocide or other NS crimes against humanity. After this cursory overview this article will now proceed to analyse the provisions of the Austrian Prohibition Act in more detail.

---

46 Ibid., Mn 2.
47 Ibid., Mn 2.
48 Ibid.

4.2.1. *Re-Establishing, Participation in, Supporting or Promoting a NS Organisation*

§3a no. 1 proscribes any attempt to maintain or re-establish a NS organisation or any attempt to contact such an organisation or its representatives. As any attempt to maintain or re-establish a NS organisation is prohibited, this article formerly covers any conduct aiming to do so and therefore also covers preparatory conduct. This is in stark contrast to the general approach taken by the Austrian Criminal Code, where preparatory conduct generally cannot trigger criminal liability.[49] With regard to the prohibited conduct of maintaining or contacting an NS organisation or one of its members, it seems that after more than seven decades since their dissolution these forms of conduct have become historically obsolete.[50] The same can unfortunately not be said with regard to re-establishing NS organisations.

§3a no. 2 prohibits founding any association whose aim it is through the actions of its members as a means towards the achievement of National socialist aims to undermine the independence of Austria or to disturb the public peace. The former will be fulfilled in case of conduct aiming to undermine Austria's sovereignty under international law or threatens the existence of its (internal) legal order.[51] The concept of public peace on the other hand refers to fundamental social interests, which will be disturbed if the offender's conduct aims (through acting as a means to achieve National Socialist aims) to unsettle Austria's internal social structure and cohesion.[52]

§3a no. 3 firstly prohibits supporting the consolidation of an organisation outlined in nos. 1 and 2 by recruiting members, providing money or other resources, and secondly equipping the members of such an organisation with weapons, means of transportation or communication or with any other means.

§3a no. 4 finally prohibits producing or obtaining these materials for such an organisation or association as well as keeping them at their disposal. §3a foresees a minimum sentence of ten years, and a maximum sentence of twenty years. In the case of particularly dangerous offenders, life imprisonment can be imposed. Before the 1992 amendment life imprisonment was the only possible sentence here. Despite the reduced sentence range, the sanctions, however, remain drastic especially when juxtaposed with other offences against the state such as, for instance, §246 (1) of the Austrian Criminal Code which criminalises

---

[49] H. Gallhuber, 'Rechtsextremismus und Strafrecht' in: Stiftung Dokumentationsarchiv des Österreichischen Widerstandes (ed.), *Handbuch des österreichischen Rechtsextremismus*, 2nd ed., Deuticke, Wien 1994, pp. 625–646.

[50] Lässig in *Wiener Kommentar zum Strafgesetzbuch*, VG §3a 2006, Mn 3.

[51] Ibid., Mn 5.

[52] Ibid.

the establishment of subversive associations and which carries a prison sentence of six months to five years.[53]

§3b of the Prohibition Act proscribes participating in an organisation or association as outlined in §3a, or supporting it financially or in any other way. To fulfil the element of participation no special activities are required, simple (informal) membership suffices.[54] Under support falls any conduct which aims to strengthen the organisation itself or to bring forward the accomplishment of their goals.[55]

§3c provides that liability pursuant to §§3a and b can be removed in case of active repentance by the offender. This will be the case when the offender voluntarily informs the authorities about an organisation or association and their plans at a time when these were still secret and the harm threatened can be prevented.[56]

§3d deals with the public promotion of prohibited (NS) organisations or associations. In essence §3d thus criminalises preparatory conduct aiming at re-establishing the NSDAP. Publicly inducing, encouraging or inciting someone to conduct prohibited pursuant to §§1 or 3 of the Prohibition Act in print mediums, writings or pictorial representations, especially if for that end the aims of the NSDAP, its institutions or measures are glorified or promoted, is punishable by a prison sentence of five to ten years. In the case of particular dangerousness of the offender an aggravated sentence of twenty years may be imposed. Attaching stickers of the NSDAP/AO which next to the swastika contained slogans such as 'Don't buy from Jews', 'Jews out' and 'Foreigners out' may, for instance, trigger liability pursuant to §3d.[57] With regard to *mens rea*, intention in the form of *dolus eventualis* is sufficient.

It follows that any (public) exercise of influence on others to violate the prohibitions of §§1 and 3 is prohibited under the Prohibition Act.[58] §3d thus constitutes a criminal provision that covers the announcement and dissemination of right-wing extremist or NS content.[59] The question as to the precise meaning of the defendant's utterances is considered a question of fact to be answered by the jury.[60] In their assessment jurors ought not only to evaluate

---

53 W. Platzgummer, 'Die strafrechtliche Bekämpfung des Neonazismus in Österreich' (1994) 22 *ÖJZ* 753 et seq.

54 Lässig in *Wiener Kommentar zum Strafgesetzbuch*, VG §3b 2006, Mn 1.

55 Ibid., Mn 2.

56 W. Platzgummer, 'Die strafrechtliche Bekämpfung des Neonazismus in Österreich' (1994) 22 *ÖJZ* 753 et seq.; Lässig in *Wiener Kommentar zum Strafgesetzbuch*, VG §3c 2006.

57 H. Gallhuber, 'Rechtsextremismus und Strafrecht' in: Stiftung Dokumentationsarchiv Des Österreichischen Widerstandes (ed.), *Handbuch des österreichischen Rechtsextremismus*, 2nd ed., Deuticke, Wien 1994, pp. 625–646.

58 Lässig in *Wiener Kommentar zum Strafgesetzbuch*, VG §3d 2006, Mn 1; W. Platzgummer, 'Die strafrechtliche Bekämpfung des Neonazismus in Österreich' (1994) 22 *ÖJZ* 753 et seq.

59 Lässig in *Wiener Kommentar zum Strafgesetzbuch*, VG §3d 2006, Mn 2.

60 Ibid.

the objective wording of an expression but also take account of the context in which the statement was made. This means that the common parlance, practices and level of education of the defendant and the recipients of the statement ought to be taken into consideration as well.[61]

Once again, compared to the general rules on public incitement pursuant to §282 (1) of the Austrian Criminal Code, which carries a maximum sentence of two years, the sanctions of §3d seem stiff particularly as §282 (1) also applies to any offender acting in the interest of other totalitarian political systems. Neo-Nazis are thus subject to exceptional treatment which may be understandable given the harm and devastation caused by NS ideology but which may in practice just as well have the counterproductive effect of glorifying offenders as political martyrs.[62]

4.2.2. Acts of Violence, Carried out as a Means to Re-engage with NS Activity

§§3e and 3f deal with the commission of NS motivated acts of violence. These provisions try on the one hand to learn lessons from the interwar period where terrorist actions were a popular means to disturb public peace and undermine the sovereignty and independence of Austria. On the other hand, they are based on the memory of the extreme and brutal violence against dissidents, Jews, Gypsies and members of other subdued (ethnic) groups which became the norm after the accession of Austria to the Third Reich. In a sense, these provisions in particular and the Prohibition Act in general thus try to prevent history from repeating itself.

§3e (1) covers preparatory conduct and prohibits *conspiring* to commit certain felonies such as murder, robbery, arson or the aggravated destruction of property as a means towards the achievement of NS aims.[63] The latter element is for instance fulfilled if the offender(s) agree to commit aggravated destruction of property by spray-painting swastikas or slogans such as 'Foreigners out' or '*Sieg Heil*' on walls, vehicles, etc. Should the offence be consummated, then liability pursuant to §3f will arise. §3e (2) again provides for a possible exemption from liability in the case of active repentance. Violations of §3e (1) carry a sanction of imprisonment for between ten and twenty years. In the case of particular dangerousness of the offender life imprisonment may be imposed.

While §3e deals with preparatory conduct, §3f prohibits the attempt or respectively the commission of the aforementioned felonies (such as murder, robbery, arson, aggravated destruction of property), as a means to achieve NS aims. Spray painting NS or right-wing extremist slogans or symbols (e.g. NS

61 Ibid.
62 W. Platzgummer, 'Die strafrechtliche Bekämpfung des Neonazismus in Österreich' (1994) 22 *ÖJZ* 753 et seq.
63 Lässig in *Wiener Kommentar zum Strafgesetzbuch*, VG §3f 2006, Mn 2.

instead of US) in public places, monuments, cemeteries, etc. can, for instance, be subsumed here. Likewise, vandalising so-called stumbling stones[64] can trigger liability pursuant to §3f.[65]

§3f is thus the logical expansion of §3e. Yet it seems slightly inconsistent that both provisions carry exactly the same punishment. This is particularly so as preparatory actions are usually considered less harmful and therefore sanctioned less severely than attempted or consummated offences respectively.[66]

§3i finally imposes a duty to report offences pursuant to §§3a, b, d or e to the police. Intentionally failing to report an undertaking pursuant to §§3a, b, d or e to the police after having gained credible knowledge of it at a time when the harm could have been prevented is punishable by imprisonment for between one and ten years. Liability will, however, be excluded if the person by reporting the undertaking to the police would have exposed himself or his close relatives to danger.

4.2.3. The Catch-All Provision of §3g

§3g in turn introduces a broad catch all clause which underlines and highlights the legislator's goal to nip any form of re-engagement with NS aims and ideology in the bud.[67] It prohibits, in broad terms, the commission of any acts other than those enshrined in §§3a–f as a means toward the achievement of NS aims. As no specific modes of conduct are required by §3g it also applies to acts committed via the Internet.[68] Violations of §3g carry a prison sentence of between one and ten years. In the case of particularly dangerous offenders an aggravated sentence of up to twenty years may be imposed.

The normative offence element 'as a means towards the achievement of NS aims' (*Betätigung im nationalsozialistischen Sinn*) has been further fleshed out by jurisprudence. It covers any (objective) conduct that seeks to revive, publicise and thus refresh the aims of the NSDAP. Any impertinent, one-sided

64 A stumbling stone (*Stolperstein*) is a monument created by the German artist Gunter Demnig which commemorates a victim of the Holocaust. *Stolpersteine* are small, cobblestone-sized memorials for an individual victim of Nazism. They commemorate individuals – both those who died and survivors – who were consigned by the Nazis to prisons, euthanasia facilities, sterilisation clinics, concentration camps, and extermination camps, as well as those who responded to persecution by emigrating or committing suicide.

65 Several young adults were, for instance, sentenced to imprisonment for between six months and five years for, *inter alia*, vandalising approximately sixty of those stumbling stones in the city of Salzburg. See: <http://salzburg.orf.at/news/stories/2692330/> accessed 20.08.2015.

66 Generally see: J. Keiler, *Actus reus and participation in European criminal law*, Intersentia, Cambridge 2013, pp. 321–435.

67 OGH 14.7.2004, 13 Os28/04. See also: 13 Os 135/92.

68 S. Ebensperger, 'Die Verbreitung von NS-Gedankengut im Internet und ihre strafrechtliche Auswirkungen' (2002) *ÖJZ* 136.

or propagandistic depiction of NS measures and aims is considered sufficient. Hence an explicit approval is not necessary.[69]

Accordingly, any attempt to justify, trivialise, whitewash, deny or approve NS crimes and atrocities can be subsumed here.[70] This means that, for instance, publishing or disseminating writings that deny or trivialise NS crimes (e.g. an article entitled 'The Hoax of the 20th Century – the End of the 6 Million Lie') can give rise to liability under §3g.[71] Likewise, publishing journals that, *inter alia*, contain anti-Semitic and xenophobic propaganda, as well as articles that express support for and describe convicted Neo-Nazis and Holocaust deniers as patriots and scapegoats has been subsumed here.[72]

Yet the scope of liability is even broader as it is not required for 'as a means towards the achievement of NS aims' that one publishes or disseminates such writings. Collecting NS propaganda material such as NS songbooks and swastika insignias[73] or advertising the aforementioned publications will already trigger liability.[74]

Furthermore, it is not necessary that the offender pursued all the aims of National Socialism. Rather, the advancement of individual NS ideas and programme points, such as the persecution and mass killing of the Jews and the brutal elimination of dissidents in concentration camps suffices.[75] Likewise, glorification of Adolf Hitler and his life's work or the accession of Austria to the Third Reich has been accepted by the courts as constituting a means towards the achievement of NS aims. The same goes for demanding unification and freedom for the entire German nation and the propagandistic use of NS slogans such as '*Heil Hitler*' (Hail Hitler), '*Sieg Heil*' (Hail Victory), or symbols such as the swastika. Likewise, the ostentatious singing of the Horst-Wessel song in public[76] has been subsumed here.[77] Insufficient are however (isolated) comments such as

---

69 Lässig in *Wiener Kommentar zum Strafgesetzbuch*, VG §3g 2006, Mn 4; W. Platzgummer, 'Die strafrechtliche Bekämpfung des Neonazismus in Österreich' (1994) 22 *ÖJZ* 753 et seq.; H. Gallhuber, 'Rechtsextremismus und Strafrecht' in: Stiftung Dokumentationsarchiv des Österreichischen Widerstandes (ed.), *Handbuch des österreichischen Rechtsextremismus*, 2nd ed., Deuticke, Wien 1994, pp. 625–646.

70 OGH 18.10.1990, 12 Os 57/90, OGH, 13.01.1999, 13 Os 169/98.

71 OGH 27.09.1978, 10 Os 136/78. See also W. Platzgummer, 'Die strafrechtliche Bekämpfung des Neonazismus in Österreich' (1994) 22 *ÖJZ* 753 et seq.

72 OGH 14.7.2004, 13 Os 28/04.

73 OGH 09.12.1993, 15 Os 155/93.

74 OGH 25.06.1986, 9 Os 132/85.

75 Lässig in *Wiener Kommentar zum Strafgesetzbuch*, VG §3g 2006, Mn 4; H. Gallhuber, 'Rechtsextremismus und Strafrecht' in: Stiftung Dokumentationsarchiv des Österreichischen Widerstandes (ed.), *Handbuch des österreichischen Rechtsextremismus*, 2nd ed., Deuticke, Wien 1994, pp. 625–646. See also: OGH 14.7.2004, 13 Os 28/04.

76 Lässig in *Wiener Kommentar zum Strafgesetzbuch*, VG §3g 2006, Mn 6. See also: OGH 13.09.200, 13 Os 45/00, OGH 04.12.2003, 15 Os 80/03.

77 See also: OGH 18.12.2012, 14 Os 117/12f, where singing: 'we're going to build a subway from L**** to Auschwitz' during a soccer match with 5,200 spectators was considered to constitute a 'means towards the achievement of NS aims' and was subsumed under §3 g.

Rudolph Hess would deserve the Noble peace price and that Hitler was not that bad and created many jobs.[78]

Recently Ulrich Seidl's documentary '*Im Keller*'[79] ('In the basement') was the cause of a trial based on §3g which nicely demonstrates the breadth of the article.[80] In the movie the defendant and four friends[81] sit around a table in a basement filled with various NS devotional objects such as swastika flags and sculptures of the Third Reich's eagle. In the background a portrait of Adolf Hitler (which the defendant describes as his most precious wedding gift) and a mannequin wearing an NS uniform can be seen. The men drink and sing together. The 58-year-old owner of the basement was found guilty pursuant to §3g and sentenced to a conditional prison sentence of ten months for his participation and showcasing of NS devotional objects in the movie.[82]

It can be deduced from the foregoing examples that §3g, doctrinally speaking, functions as an abstract endangerment offence.[83] Accordingly no harm needs to have been manifested, nor is it necessary that a concrete endangerment has taken place. As an abstract endangerment arises out of any conduct which seeks to revitalise or to propagandise aims of the NSDAP, the offence of §3g is already committed once, for instance, a person starts with the necessary *mens rea* collecting NS propaganda materials.[84]

With regard to *mens rea*, it is required that the offender's intention also covers the normative offence element 'as a means towards the achievement of NS aims' (*Betätigung im nationalsozialistischen Sinn*).[85] *Dolus eventualis* will be sufficient. Accordingly, the mere possession of NS propaganda materials (such as CDs and data files with xenophobic and NS propagandistic content) without any further intent, will regardless of the offender's general disposition, not give rise to liability pursuant to §3g.[86] The assessment of the normative offence element 'as a means towards the achievement of NS aims' as well as questions concerning the precise meaning of the utterances made is again considered a question of fact to be answered by the jury.[87]

---

78 Lässig in *Wiener Kommentar zum Strafgesetzbuch*, VG §3g 2006, Mn 7.

79 See: <http://im-keller.at> accessed 20.8.2015.

80 See: '"Nazi-Keller"-Prozess: Zehn Monate bedingt' <http://burgenland.orf.at/news/stories/2719020/> accessed 20.08.2015.

81 Two were local politicians and members of the municipal council. The charges against them were dropped but they had to step down from their jobs and also resign from their political party (the Christian democrats – ÖVP).

82 '"Nazi-Keller"-Prozess: Zehn Monate bedingt' <http://burgenland.orf.at/news/stories/2719020/> accessed 20.08.2015.

83 Lässig in *Wiener Kommentar zum Strafgesetzbuch*, VG §3g 2006, Mn 8.

84 Ibid. See also: OGH 25.06.1986, 9 Os 132/85.

85 Lässig in *Wiener Kommentar zum Strafgesetzbuch*, VG §3g 2006, Mn 9; see also: OGH 13.09.2000 13 Os 45/00.

86 Ibid., Mn 9; see also: OGH 27.5.2004, 15 Os 49/04.

87 Ibid., Mn 17.

It is noteworthy here that in line with settled ECtHR case law the Austrian Supreme Court considers the systematic mass extermination of Jews under the NS regime to constitute a 'clearly established historical fact' and any evidence to the contrary will accordingly be inadmissible in court.[88] The rejection of any evidence of this fact is consequently neither thought to violate the accused's right to an adequate defence nor his rights under Article 6 ECHR.[89] This cuts off any debate about the (non-)existence of the Holocaust in the courtroom and prevents that the criminal trial becomes a platform for the revisionist movement and their feeble-minded theses.

The law thus clearly protects the prevalent historical view regarding the NS genocide by circumscribing fundamental defence rights. It, however, remains an open question why only the NS genocide and not any other genocide is considered a 'clearly established historical fact'. In the case of Austria this approach can certainly be explained by practical considerations as well as its past and historical responsibility, but whether it can be justified in general remains open for debate.

4.2.4. Denial of the NS Holocaust and Other NS Crimes

Based on and further developing the line of thought that the NS genocide constitutes a clearly established historical fact the legislator introduced §3h in 1992 which criminalises the denial of the NS genocide and other NS crimes against humanity, which again underlines that these historical facts need not be proven in court.

§3h criminalises denying, grossly trivialising, approving or seeking to justify the NS genocide or other NS crimes against humanity in a publication, broadcast or other media or in any other public form accessible to many people. This thus also covers denial via the internet.[90] The provision covers the three classic forms of denial: denying the facts (the Holocaust is a myth), their interpretation (there was no genocidal machinery – people simply died from malnutrition) and any justification of NS atrocities.[91] The prescribed sanction is imprisonment for between one and ten years. In the case of particular dangerousness of the offender an aggravated sentence of up to twenty years may be imposed.

Before the 1992 amendment such acts were punishable under §3g as interpreted by the courts. Yet, as already mentioned, convictions proved difficult to achieve, especially as §3g requires proof of an intent to act 'as a means towards

---

88 Ibid., Mn 16.

89 OGH 18.10.1990, JBl 1991, 464. See also *Witzsch v. Germany*, no. 7485/03.

90 S. Ebensperger, 'Die Verbreitung von NS-Gedankengut im Internet und ihre strafrechtliche Auswirkungen' (2002) *ÖJZ* 136.

91 S. Cohen, *States of Denial: Knowing About Atrocities and Suffering*, Polity Press, London 2001, p. 269.

the achievement of NS aims' (*Betätigung im nationalsozialistischen Sinn*).[92] §3h now dispenses with this requirement, giving special status to the offence of Holocaust denial.[93] Any public denial of the NS crimes and the Holocaust, even without intent to act 'as a means towards the achievement of NS aims', will now give rise to criminal liability.

The case of the technician Walter Lüftl illustrates nicely the difference made by the 1992 amendment. Lüftl had published an article in which he doubted the technical feasibility of mass murder by poisonous gas. He was prosecuted under the old version of the Prohibition Act but his case was dropped as an intent to act as a means towards the achievement of NS aims could not be proven. However, the amendment made it possible afterwards to convict the editor of the journal for publishing the article.[94]

The focus of §3h thus rests on the objective conduct of the offender. Accordingly it covers conduct preceding the explicit aim of 'acting as a means towards the achievement of NS aims' and can therefore in the context of the NS Prohibition Act be seen as a type of preparatory offence.[95] The mass murder of millions of people is the heaviest accusation against National Socialism. The only way of reviving NS ideology is by minimising or denying those crimes. Furthermore, the offence certainly also aims to convey a symbolic message and furthermore underlines the legislator's aim to counteract any form of resurgence of National Socialism at the earliest possible stage. This aim arguably seems justifiable given that denying, approving or seeking to justify the Holocaust only aims to rehabilitate National Socialism and to reduce reservations concerning its inhuman ideology.[96] Finally, §3h may also be perceived as a preparatory offence as denying, trivialising or justifying NS crimes can also be seen as an ideological gateway drug which can create a risk of committing further or even more far reaching offences under the Prohibition Act.

Denying in the context of §3h requires a denial of essential elements of the NS genocide or other NS crimes and not just of border areas. Serious scientific publications which seek, for instance, to shed new light on the amount of victims of the NS regime are thus exempt from liability.

---

92 See: B. Schager, *Holocaustleugnung in Österreich. Die Leugner und ihr Umfeld. Eine Analyse*, Master's thesis, University Vienna, Vienna 2011, p. 16 <http://othes.univie.ac.at/16692/>.

93 Lässig in *Wiener Kommentar zum Strafgestzbuch*, VG §3h 2006, Mn 5; H. Gallhuber, 'Rechtsextremismus und Strafrecht' in: Stiftung Dokumentationsarchiv des Österreichischen Widerstandes (ed.), *Handbuch des österreichischen Rechtsextremismus*, 2nd ed., Deuticke, Wien 1994, pp. 625–646.

94 B. Bailer, 'The law against national-socialist activities in Austria – NS Verbotsgesetz' (2011) *Vienna J. on Int'l Const. L.* 46.

95 H. Gallhuber, 'Rechtsextremismus und Strafrecht' in: Stiftung Dokumentationsarchiv Des Österreichischen Widerstandes (ed.), *Handbuch des österreichischen Rechtsextremismus*, 2nd ed., Deuticke, Wien 1994, pp. 625–646.

96 Ibid.; B. Schager, *Holocaustleugnung in Österreich. Die Leugner und ihr Umfeld. Eine Analyse*, Master's thesis, University Vienna, Vienna 2011, pp. 4 et seq. <http://othes.univie.ac.at/16692/>.

The *actus reus* of §3h contains two modalities for committing the offence. Succinctly put, denial can take place via the media or in any other public form. In case the denial takes not place in a publication, broadcast or other media, the requirement that it must be accessible to many people is interpreted as requiring roughly thirty persons.[97] However, as the word 'accessible' already indicates, it is not required that the denial, etc. was effectively communicated to thirty persons. It suffices that a concrete danger of such communication can be proven.[98] It follows that regarding the offence mode of denial in media §3h functions as a conduct crime, while with regard to the mode in 'any other public manner', §3h takes the form of a result crime.[99]

Regarding *mens rea*, §3h requires intention as to the denying, grossly trivialising, approving or justificatory nature of one's statement(s). *Dolus eventualis* is sufficient. As already mentioned, proving intent to act 'as a means towards the achievement of NS aims' is not necessary. Should such intent nevertheless be present, liability pursuant to §3d or §3g may arise.

An infamous example of the application of §3h can be found in the trial of the British historian David Irving. In 1989 Irving had given two speeches in which he denied the Holocaust. He, *inter alia*, claimed that the Holocaust was a myth and the gas chambers were a lie.[100] On 20 February 2006 Irving pleaded guilty to the charge of trivialising, grossly playing down and denying the Holocaust and was sentenced to three years' imprisonment of which he served 13 months.

Also the engineer and former Freedom Party (FPÖ) politician Wolfgang Fröhlich publicly claimed that the use of gas chambers was 'scientifically impossible' by arguing that Zyklone-b was ineffectual and too expensive for this task. He had, *inter alia*, sent CDs and pamphlets to Austrian politicians and other members of the public. He was convicted several times for violations of the Prohibition Act. In total he received a prison sentence of 11 years.[101]

It seems clear that particularly in the context of §3g and §3h tensions with the right to freedom of speech arise. Austria's experiences in the past may certainly explain the broad provisions and harsh sanctions of the Prohibition Act outlined above. History has shown that democracies can be undermined gradually. Denial of the Holocaust as well as any other conduct enshrined in the Prohibition Act is therefore, for one, outlawed due to its anti-democratic tendencies. In addition it can be argued that for Austria, given its special historical responsibility, denying the Holocaust is unacceptable as it diminishes the dignity of the victims

---

97 Lässig in *Wiener Kommentar zum Strafgestzbuch*, VG §3h 2006, Mn 3.

98 Ibid.

99 Ibid.

100 'David Irving jailed for Holocaust denial' 2006 *The Guardian* <www.theguardian.com/world/2006/feb/20/austria.thefarright> accessed 20.08.2015.

101 B. Schager, *Holocaustleugnung in Österreich. Die Leugner und ihr Umfeld. Eine Analyse*, Master's thesis, University Vienna, Vienna 2011, p. 4 <http://othes.univie.ac.at/16692/>. See also: OGH 22.08.2008, 12 Os 39/08i.

and their descendants. Any attempt to deny or relativise the Holocaust also undermines the memory of unspeakable atrocities which must not be forgotten. Without these memories we may just run the risk of eventually making the same mistakes again.

5. CONCLUDING REMARKS

The Austrian Prohibition Act covers a wide variety of offences driven or inspired by NS or right-wing extremist ideology reaching from offences criminalising certain forms of expression to the destruction of property, arson, murder to the (attempted) (re-)establishment of NS organisations and the denial of NS crimes. The scope of liability created by the Act is to be considered broad, as even certain forms of preparatory conduct are prohibited. In addition, many offence definitions remain vague, which grants much leeway to public prosecutors and courts with regard to the prosecution of conduct covered by the Prohibition Act as well as the interpretation of certain offences.

In any case, as outlined above, the Prohibition Act essentially introduced a special law and treatment for (Neo-)Nazis, NS crimes and NS ideology. Next to a broad scope of liability the Act also introduced a stiff sentencing regime. While these high sentences may be an expression of the perceived gravity of the offences and an acknowledgement of Austria's responsibility for the past, they can, nevertheless, be considered problematic from a criminal policy perspective as it risks glorifying Neo-Nazis as political martyrs.[102]

Despite its shortcomings the Prohibition Act can be seen as one of the most powerful weapons against all forms of Neo-Nazi propaganda and activists in Austria. Still, right wing extremist groups as well as politicians, not surprisingly situated predominately on the right side of the political scale, continue to demand the abolishment of the Act as it, so they claim, undermines the right to freedom of expression.[103]

The Act is, however also sometimes criticised by liberal academics and journalists who claim that in a liberal democratic society a 'marketplace of ideas' ought to exist. The underlying idea of this economic analogy essentially is that the truth will emerge from the competition of ideas in free, transparent public discourse. A solid liberal democracy should be strong enough to deal with nonsense such as Holocaust denial, rendering involvement of the criminal justice system redundant.[104] The best test of truth is the power of the thought

102 See also: W. Platzgummer, 'Die strafrechtliche Bekämpfung des Neonazismus in Österreich' (1994) 22 *ÖJZ* 753 et seq.

103 B. Bailer, 'The law against national-socialist activities in Austria – NS Verbotsgesetz (2011) *Vienna J. on Int'l Const. L.* 47.

104 See for instance: L. Pech, 'The law of Holocaust denial in Europe: Towards a (qualified) EU-wide criminal prohibition', *Jean Monnet Working Paper 10/09*, p 4, Fn 6.

to get itself accepted in the competition of the market, so the argument runs. This, however, raises questions regarding the political and democratic stability or maturity of a liberal state.

Be that as it may, in the case of Austria, recent statistical evidence reveals a steady increase with regard to violations of the Prohibition Act. Since 1992 the number of reported violations of the Prohibition Act has risen constantly. In 2013 alone an increase of 26% was reported, bringing the total of right-wing-extremist, racist or anti-Semitic offences up to 574.[105] These figures arguably, on the one hand, show the unchanged importance of the Prohibition Act and on the other may also be seen as a cause for concern. However, these statistics certainly ought to be assessed with care as the increase in reported offences may also be related to an increase in public awareness and a more stringent application of the Prohibition Act in general. In addition, the figures may simply express a reduction of the dark figures of violations of the Act rather than a concrete rise in transgressions.[106] Nevertheless, these figures arguably show a worrying trend with regard to the spread of right-wing extremism and NS ideology throughout society. A further cause of concern is the current trend in right-wing circles to make a bogeyman out of Muslims. The PEGIDA[107] movement arguably bears witness to the dangers that this xenophobic and anti-Islamic ideology entails. In the face of the current asylum seeker crisis a relapse or return of Europe to the old inhuman ideologies and patterns of conduct seems at least conceivable. Civil vigilance and courage seems certainly called for, especially since ideologies, just like the concept of denial, can adapt to social currents and fears and evolve to return – be it in a slightly different form – but equally destructive.

Yet the dilemma that the Prohibition Act and the application of criminal law to right-wing-extremist offences faces is that although in everyday social life an increase in conduct and activities informed by xenophobia, every day racism, bigotry and references to NS rhetoric and propaganda can be detected, the Prohibition Act targets primarily explicit political ideological conduct rather than subtle socio-ideological processes. The offences of the Prohibition Act mainly target the core and key figures of the right-wing extremist scene but reach its limits with regard to more contemporary, mundane and subtle manifestations of extremism.

To curb this more subtle and creeping (re-)ideologisation of society is not what the Prohibition Act was designed to achieve in the first place and furthermore is neither a task that can easily be achieved by the means of criminal law. Criminal law may be able to influence human behaviour but cannot change hearts and minds. Education programmes, measures that increase social stability

---

105 Bundesministerium für Inneres, 'Verfasungsschutzbericht 2014' <www.bmi.gv.at/cms/BMI_Verfassungsschutz/BVT_VSB_2014_V20140613_online.pdf> pp. 21 et seq.

106 Ibid.

107 Pegida is the German acronym for: Patriotic Europeans Against the Islamisation of the West.

and tolerance as well as socio-economic measures creating future perspectives for the youth will arguably work much better towards this end rather than any threat of criminal punishment. As a means of last resort (*ultima ratio*) criminal sanctions should remain reserved for the severest manifestations of ideologically influenced conduct.

CHAPTER X
THE HOLOCAUST AND ITS DENIAL
A Paradigm in our Historical Culture

Georgi VERBEECK

The Holocaust not only represented a tragic historical episode in itself, but it rapidly started to serve as a central point of reference and comparison by which to judge the essence of other genocidal practices – committed either before or after the Jewish catastrophe. It delivered a standard measure for our understanding and awareness of other major crimes and wrongdoings, either in the past or in the present day. 'Holocaust awareness' therefore has become one of the cultural pillars upon which an official postwar European identity was constructed. What is true for its acknowledgement necessarily also applies to its denial. They are equally indicative for our moral standing. The Holocaust and the way we pronounce upon it serve as a template for other acts of mass violence, and so does Holocaust denial. This chapter will look into how a dominant discourse of the Holocaust affects our notion of other genocides. And why is it that Holocaust denialism touches such a raw nerve in our society? The final question will be to what extent Holocaust denial provides a draft of a wider phenomenon of denialism comprising other genocides.

1. HISTORY AND MEMORY

In his internationally acclaimed book *Postwar. A History of Europe since 1945* Tony Judt once convincingly pointed at the importance of the Holocaust and its commemoration for present-day European citizens.[1] He called to mind German poet Heinrich Heine (1797–1856), who at the start of 19th century concluded that conversion to Christianity provided Jews the only opportunity to gain access to the community of European nations. However, this specific role of baptism in Heine's day and age has been taken over by *extermination* after

[1] T. JUDT, *Postwar. A History of Europe Since 1945*, The Penguin Press, New York 2005, pp. 803–834 (Epilogue: From the House of the Dead, An Essay on Modern European Memory).

1945. The extermination, or rather its universal *acknowledgment,* has become the admission ticket to the community of civilised European nations. Those who call into doubt or who do not fully acknowledge the genocide of the Jews in the Third Reich condemn themselves to the role of international pariah. Denying or belittling the Holocaust is equal to placing oneself beyond the pale of civilised public discourse. 'Auschwitz', in other words, has become the benchmark for post-war European identity.

After the crimes committed by the Nazis became known, the Holocaust has figured as point of reference in the assessment of other crimes against humanity as well. Since the end of the Second World War, all other genocides and large-scale violence in history began to be measured against the fate of the Jews in the Nazi death camps. Whether this should be welcomed in itself or not is another issue, yet it is hard to ignore that the Holocaust has established itself in the heart of our public memory. As Tony Judt eloquently put it, 'the memory of Europe's dead Jews has become the very definition and guarantee of the restored humanity on the European continent'.[2]

Judt's argument underscored the sensitivity of the memory of the Holocaust in today's political culture. It is generally accepted that all those who question this memory in whatever way undermine the spiritual foundation of a democratic society.[3] If one may regret this development (and it is true, there has been increasing criticism of this turning of the past into an icon), it is also a fact that denial of the extermination of the Jews continues to trigger fierce reactions. Affirmation or denial of the Holocaust is closely linked to acceptance or rejection of Europe's post-war political order and the rules of international law. It shows that historical understanding is more than just an academic engagement with the past. It touches the core of how we position ourselves in our own time. Mostly, our memory is guided by the external factors rather than involving a spontaneous process.

The political, social and cultural construction of memory has become a central topic in the expanding field of 'memory studies'. The study of the 'politics of history' is one of the key components within this field.[4] There is a growing awareness now that memory is always a mirror of the time in which this memory emerges. But memory is also tied to a specific framework in time and location. Increasingly, people have begun to wonder which external factors have contributed to our dealing with the past. This has involved actors that have had nothing to do with the profession or field of history itself, such as politicians, courts, the media, international institutions and diverse interest groups. History always reveals itself to be a construction of the past. Scholars in the field speak of

2 Ibid., p. 804.

3 G. Verbeeck (ed.), *De verdwenen gaskamers. De ontkenning van de Holocaust*, Acco, Leuven 1997, pp. 7–14.

4 S. Troebst, 'Geschichtspolitik', *Docupedia-Zeitgeschichte*, 4 August 2014.

and make a distinction between communicative and cultural memory. The first is realised by the interactions about what contemporaries have gone through; the second is shaped by various institutions that determine the content of our official collective memory from the outside.[5]

A crucial example of historical (re-)construction concerns the Nazi genocide of the Jews. Its representation and its denial directly touch the nerve of our collective identity building.[6] It explains why the Holocaust, much more than any other historical episode, remains in the centre of political and ideological controversy. As a rule, the denial of the Holocaust evokes fierce reactions. In recent years many countries therefore have felt urged to take legal measures. In Western Europe Holocaust denial has been around for several decades, but it is only since the last decade of the 20th century that political institutions have been proactive. In the countries of Central and Eastern Europe this same phenomenon came to the surface with the dismantling of communism. In these countries' public memories of the Holocaust, first the effects of the forty-year rule of the dominant Socialist ideology needed to be erased. Ever since then, the coming to grips with the Holocaust and World War II has had to compete with the traumas of communist rule. Much less than in the West, there is no taboo here on juxtaposing communism and fascism.[7] The Holocaust, then, has taken on emblematic value in Eastern Europe to a lesser extent; it functions less as an exclusive memory and 'warning for the future'. How a specific country remembers the Holocaust and responds to those who deny it tells us much about this country's particular historical culture.[8]

2. HOLOCAUST DENIAL

Holocaust deniers often tend to present themselves as the iconoclasts of history writing. In this respect, it is relevant to refer to the confusing distinction between 'revisionism' and 'negationism'. Holocaust deniers often present their theory about the so-called 'lie of Auschwitz' in a broader historical account

5 J. Assmann, 'Communicative and Cultural Memory' in: A. Erll and A. Nünning (eds.), *Cultural Memory Studies. An International and Interdisciplinary Handbook*, De Gruyter, Berlin-New York 2008, pp. 109–118.

6 M. Fulbrook, *Gernan National Identity and the Holocaust*, Polity Press, Cambridge 1998.

7 G. Link and L. Neumayer (eds.), *History, Memory, and Politics in Central and Eastern Europe. Memory Games*, Palgrave Macmillan, Basingstoke-New York 2013, pp. 1–22.

8 T. Judt, *Postwar. A History of Europe Since 1945*, The Penguin Press, New York 2005, pp. 820–826. G. Verbeeck and M. Hausleitner, 'Cultural Memory and Legal Responses: Holocaust Denial in Belgium and Romania' in: B. Kosmala and G. Verbeeck (eds.), *Facing the Catastrophe. Jews and non-Jews in Europe during World War II*, Berg Publishers, Oxford-New York 2011, pp. 229–260.

that aims to revise the conventional view of the history of World War II.[9] Thereby they cash in on the positive connotation of the term 'revisionism'. Revisionism applies to the putting up for discussion and re-interpretation of established scholarly insights. This is a strategy aimed at lending scholarly credibility to deniers and confusing the general public. In this latter case they certainly succeed in setting the agenda. Those who lack real expertise view the controversy involving deniers as a scholarly dispute between two 'equal' interpretation models. Holocaust denial commonly pertains to the *singular* denial of the National Socialist genocide on some 6,000,000 Jews (negationism). In a broader sense, this singular denial is embedded in a strategy aimed at rewriting the history of World War II, in particular the specific responsibility of Nazi Germany (revisionism). Often this leads to a *multiple* denial of various aspects of the Nazi regime (war crimes, racist geopolitics, euthanasia, etc.). In the latter case, one has to distinguish between controversial yet scholarly accepted views that produce new historical insights on the one hand and explicit apologies that boil down to a glorification and justification of National Socialism on the other. In both cases revisionism, in its critical and destructive sense, centres on the historical question of guilt. Revisionism in history writing is always somehow tied to reversing or removing historical responsibility.[10]

3. SCHOLARLY AND LEGAL RESPONSE

Scholarly responses to Holocaust denial can be roughly divided into three categories: Most academics would simply refuse to engage Holocaust deniers or their arguments at all, on grounds that doing so would ultimately lend them unwarranted legitimacy. A second group of scholars, mostly academics who engage with the phenomenon of negationism as a subject of study in itself, have tried to raise awareness of the methods and motivations of Holocaust denial without legitimising the deniers themselves. American scholar and leading authority in the field Deborah Lipstadt belonged to this group of critical analysts.[11] A third group of historians tends to respond to arguments and claims made by Holocaust denial groups by pointing out inaccuracies and errors in their evidence.[12]

---

9 R.J. Evans, *In Defense of History*, Norton, New York 1999; R.J. Evans, *Lying About Hitler: History, Holocaust, and the David Irving Trial*, Basic Books, New York 2002; D. Lipstadt, *Denying the Holocaust: The Growing Assault on Truth and Memory*, Plume, New York 1993; T. Bastian, *Auschwitz und die 'Auschwitz-Lüge'. Massenmord und Geschichtsfälschung*, Beck'sche Reihe, Munich 1994.

10 G. Verbeeck (ed.), *De verdwenen gaskamers. De ontkenning van de Holocaust*, Acco, Leuven 1997, pp. 7–14, 161–178.

11 D. Lipstadt, *Denying the Holocaust: The Growing Assault on Truth and Memory*, Plume, New York 1993.

12 G. Van Den Berghe, *De uitbuiting van de Holocaust*, Anthos, Antwerp-Amsterdam 2001.

In various countries politicians and legislators decided to take legal measures against the dissemination of the so-called *Auschwitz Lüge* (denying the historical fact of the Holocaust).[13] Inspired by previous international examples, Belgian lawmakers decided in 1995 to introduce legislation to ban public Holocaust denial: 'He is sentenced to imprisonment ... who denies, grossly minimizes or tries to justify or approve the genocide committed during World War II by the German National Socialist regime under one of the circumstances listed in section 444 of the Penal Code. To apply the previous section, the term genocide must be understood in the sense of section 2 of the International Treaty of 9 December 1948 concerning the prevention and punishing of genocide. In case of recurrence, moreover, the convict can be sentenced to disfranchisement in accordance with section 33 of the Penal Code.'[14] Since the final decade of the 20th century various European countries have introduced equal measures to repress the dissemination of Holocaust denialism.

4. DEFENCE

Anti-Holocaust denial legislation inevitably provoked a sharp discussion between proponents and critics of a legal limitation of free speech.[15] Proponents of the law generally make the argument that the law has only a restrictive character, and that the risk of an instrumental misuse of the law is therefore minimal. The reference to the section in the Penal Code is meant to ensure that expressions of opinion could only be made punishable if they have a 'subverting' character. Moreover, merely negationist views expressed in a public space – and whereby thus persons are involved who might feel offended – are subject to criminal law. In its use of the term 'genocide' the law also refers to the definition that was adopted by the UN Convention of 1948. This has the benefit that everyone is deemed to know which definition of genocide is used. It is also meant as a measure to prevent the legislator putting himself in the place of the historian. Which genocide has to be protected against denial and which not is therefore a discussion that is prevented. The law incriminates only the denial of events which have already served as basis for convictions that have already been ruled by international courts, in this case in the post-war Nuremberg trials. It

---

13 G. Verbeeck (ed.), *De verdwenen gaskamers. De ontkenning van de Holocaust*, Acco, Leuven 1997, pp. 175–177.

14 G. Verbeeck and M. Hausleitner, 'Cultural Memory and Legal Responses: Holocaust Denial in Belgium and Romania' in: B. Kosmala and G. Verbeeck (eds.), *Facing the Catastrophe. Jews and non-Jews in Europe during World War II*, Berg Publishers, Oxford-New York 2011, pp. 229–260, at pp. 240–241.

15 K. Raes, 'Vrijheid van meningsuiting en de revisionistische geschiedvervalsing' in: G.A.I. Schuijt and D. Voorhoof (eds.), *Vrijheid van meningsuiting, racisme en revisionisme*, Academia, Ghent 1995, pp. 31–78.

has never been the intention, then, to provide a summing-up of a series of facts that possibly need to be investigated with the help of historical method. There has always been a clear reference to the Nazi genocide, as defined in 1948, which has already been the subject of a legal verdict.[16]

5. CRITICISM

5.1. GENERAL

Inevitably, however, sharp response was elicited.[17] From the start the suggestion to legally ban Holocaust denial prompted critical comments. It could be pointed out, for instance, that the legislator made no difference between *descriptive* speech acts (denying and minimising) and *normative* acts (justifying or approving). Because, basically, the latter never occurs (who *approves of* genocide or how can genocide be *justified* by those who argue that it has never taken place?), it soon became clear that the legislator tended to see denial and minimising as normative acts. This confusion of normative and descriptive dimensions posed is already quite relevant in and of itself. The legislator also referred explicitly to a penal code section that referred to the act of insulting persons. It means that the law treats any negationist view as an offensive expression of opinion by definition, which can however be seriously questioned.

Also questionable remains the exclusive definition of genocide by the law limiting it to the Nazi genocide of the Jews during the Third Reich. The denial of other genocides, then, was not seen as punishable by law. This shows the very clear political intention of the law: namely the safeguarding of a specific historical 'truth', in this case the extermination of the Jews as a core historical experience in European memory. Attacks on this truth seemingly need to be held off by use of legal means. The underlying idea is that the collective memory of a society needs protection so as to 'prevent recurrence of history'. To be sure, this did not apply to history in general, but only to a well delineated episode of it. It relates directly with the notion of the Holocaust as a seemingly absolutely unique historical experience. The memory of the Holocaust receives, in this way, official political status and legally ensured protection.

16 D. Voorhoof, 'Racismebestrijding en vrijheid van meningsuiting in België: wetgeving en jurisprudentie' in: G.A.I. Schuijt and D. Voorhoof (eds.), *Vrijheid van meningsuiting, racisme en revisionisme*, Academia, Ghent 1995, pp. 155–192.

17 G. Verbeeck and M. Hausleitner, 'Cultural Memory and Legal Responses: Holocaust Denial in Belgium and Romania' in: B. Kosmala and G. Verbeeck (eds.), *Facing the Catastrophe. Jews and non-Jews in Europe during World War II*, Berg Publishers, Oxford-New York 2011, pp. 229–260, at pp. 241–244.

5.2. ROLE OF HISTORICANS

It is particularly historians that voiced substantial criticism against legalised oppression of Holocaust denial.[18] Most historians would feel uneasy and uncomfortable with an officially sanctioned historical truth. It ties in with a growing criticism against an implicit sacralisation of the Holocaust, which is the inevitable result of an interpretation of the Shoah as absolutely unique and exceptional, incomparable to any other mass destruction of human life.[19] It is exactly against this sacralisation of the Holocaust that Holocaust denial reacts. And it is exactly here that denialism can gain ground, as it cleverly exploits a certain Holocaust fatigue among the public at large. This is what frequently happens if the claim to uniqueness is endlessly repeated. Holocaust denialism, in other words, touches a nerve that reaches much further than the historical narrative about *x* number of victims. It rips open a wound linked to a specific commemoration culture as well as fundamental political-ideological choices.

One may justifiably ask, then, whether a law may put a taboo on a historical debate, in which various legitimate viewpoints can be defended. Negationists have shrewdly exploited the semantic confusion between historical revisionism and negationism.[20] The first involves legitimate historical method, the second does not. It becomes hard to ask a judge to rule on where revisionism is justified and where negationism represents a legal offence. In short, legislation has turned that which is part of the core of the historian's profession into a legal and political affair. By definition historians do not feel at home in the role of a judge.[21]

Banning Holocaust denialism also obstructs a public and scholarly discussion of the Holocaust in another way. There are some gaps and misconceptions in our conventional knowledge of the Holocaust. Some of these misconceptions and exaggerations, and minor distortions (for instance, the widespread misconception that *all* Jews were killed in gas chambers) are manipulated by negationists to deny the genocide as such. These can only be seriously addressed in a critical discussion on some of the arguments of Holocaust deniers. What is needed is a deep knowledge of the historic events and facts in order to refute

---

18 G. Van Den Berghe, 'Een oorlog die, omdat hij nooit meer gebeuren mocht, blijft duren. Revisionisme en negationisme herzien' in: G. Verbeeck (ed.), *De verdwenen gaskamers. De ontkenning van de Holocaust*, Acco, Leuven 1997, pp. 15–48.

19 A.S. Rosembaum (ed.), *Is the Holocaust Unique? Perspectives on Comparative Genocide*, Westview Press, Boulder 2000.

20 G. Verbeeck (ed.), *De verdwenen gaskamers. De ontkenning van de Holocaust*, Acco, Leuven 1997, pp. 7–13.

21 G. Verbeeck, 'Coming to terms with the (post-)colonial past in Belgium: the inquiry into the assassination of Patrice Lumumba' in: H. Jones, K. Östberg and N. Randeraad (eds.), *Contemporary History on Trial. Europe since 1989 and the Role of the Expert Historian*, Manchester University Press, Manchester-New York 2007, p. 59.

negationism. This is exactly what an historian can offer, rather than the strong arm of the law.[22]

5.3. FREEDOM OF SPEECH

A more fundamental dimension in the discussion has to do with the restriction of freedom of speech, even regarding utterly unacceptable and nonsensical ideas. An often expressed view stems from the Voltairean tradition: pretending 'that Auschwitz is a lie' is just an opinion, and opinions should be fought only by means of other opinions. Inevitably, therefore, anti-denialism legislation, no matter how well intended from the angle of its proponents, *kuriert am Symptom*; it does not get to the heart of the matter and comes with the danger of mounting censorship of socially unaccepted, hurting and unpleasant views. In the long term one could argue that this ultimately weakens the democratic right to freedom of speech, which is a necessary condition for a democracy, and, so the reasoning goes, who meddles with it automatically puts democracy at risk.[23]

5.4. TACTICS

In addition to objections of a more principle quality, it is possible to bring forward considerations of a rather tactical nature. The main one concerns the aspect of efficiency. Does the law not give more attention to Holocaust deniers than they in fact deserve?[24] One can argue that legal persecution causes the media to concentrate on negationists inordinately. This forces them into an underdog position that can only generate more public sympathy for them. Does one-sided attention sufficiently do justice to the sensitivities of victims and their surviving relatives of other genocides? By making Holocaust denial punishable by law, victim chauvinism and an inappropriate suggestion of 'hierarchy' of human suffering will increase rather than decline. Is the law a useful weapon in the struggle against the extreme right in the digital era? More importantly, what is the risk that the application of this law will turn into a single case issue? In many countries, indeed, application of the law seemed to have been merely directed against notorious individuals: Robert Faurisson in France, Ernst Zündel in Canada, the Verbeke

---

22 G. Van Den Berghe, 'Een oorlog die, omdat hij nooit meer gebeuren mocht, blijft duren. Revisionisme en negationisme herzien' in: G. Verbeeck (ed.), *De verdwenen gaskamers. De ontkenning van de Holocaust*, Acco, Leuven 1997, pp. 15–48, at pp. 43–45.

23 L. Abicht, 'Moet het negationisme bestreden worden? Persoonlijke en filosofische beschouwingen' in: G. Verbeeck (ed.), *De verdwenen gaskamers. De ontkenning van de Holocaust*, Acco, Leuven 1997, pp. 57–58.

24 Ibid., pp. 59–60.

case in Belgium, David Irving in Germany and Austria. Finally, does tabooing the subject hamper the public and scholarly debate rather than enhance it?

5.5. SPEECH ACT

For many, one of the main weak points in anti-Holocaust denial legislation is the assumed intentional character of voicing negationist opinions. Does Holocaust denial, in other words, involve a harm-causing intent, is it offensive in itself? One needs to distinguish here between individuals (survivors, or surviving relatives of Holocaust victims) and society at large. The latter applies to the fundamental values of a democratic society. Can one attribute harmful consequences to an opinion based on content-related grounds? Is Holocaust denial necessarily an insulting act to Holocaust victims and their descendants?[25]

Most democratic societies will tend to agree on a limitation of the right to freedom of speech where the fundamental values of democratic society are at stake. In the case of Holocaust denial a sense of bad faith is assumed. It is assumed that those who deny the Holocaust implicitly justify an ideology that is reprehensive and essentially incompatible with democracy. Democratic societies principally seem to struggle with two competing principles: the freedom of speech which should protect the right to express any opinion, regardless of the content of the statement, and the obligation to protect individuals and society from harm-causing effects of certain opinions. There is a central ambiguity which remains unclarified. The letter of the law itself suggests the centrality of the content of a claim. According to various interpretations by legal experts however the law could only be invoked when such claim causes harm and, consequently, is clearly meant to insult.

Proponents of the law, such as the highest Belgian court, will claim that the content of a standpoint and its implied intentions are in fact one and the same, or at least result from each other. 'The legislator', the court argued, 'did not punish the opinions involved for their content as such, but for their disadvantageous effects on others and on democratic society as such.'[26]

This interpretation comes very close to Tony Judt's previously described observation. The memory of the Holocaust is directly tied to a specific view of democracy. Protecting this 'historical truth' with legal measures is considered an admission ticket to democratic society. It is essentially part of a 'combative

---

25 C. Calvert, 'Hate Speech and its Harms. A Communication Theory Perspective' (1997) 47 *Journal of Communication* 4–19.

26 G. Verbeeck and M. Hausleitner, 'Cultural Memory and Legal Responses: Holocaust Denial in Belgium and Romania' in: B. Kosmala and G. Verbeeck (eds.), *Facing the Catastrophe. Jews and non-Jews in Europe during World War II*, Berg Publishers, Oxford-New York 2011, pp. 229–260, at p. 243.

democracy' (in the Federal Republic of Germany: a *streitbare Demokratie*).[27] A democratic constitutional state is seen as more than a system that derives power from a mere accidental mathematical majority. It is based on particular values. It presents itself as having the right to limit the liberties of those who are deemed to form a threat to democracy. It explains why anti-Holocaust denial legislation only comes into operation in a specific political context. Individual opinions as such are not targeted in the first place. Someone who claims 'the 6 million dead Jews' to be 'a lie', or someone who, based on historical study, arrives at the conclusion that the conventional image of history should be revised will most likely not be targeted by the law. Anti-Holocaust denial legislation is primarily meant as a political weapon against political extremism, against structural networks that undermine the cultural memory of our common past.[28]

6. USE AND ABUSE OF THE HOLOCAUST PARADIGM

The fierce public and intellectual reactions to Holocaust denialism directly ties in with the centrality of the Shoah in our present day's historical culture. Seventy years after the end of the Second World War the Holocaust remains firmly entrenched within the consciousness of the West.[29] Rather than receding, academic investigations as well as popular representations have increased to the point where those not familiar with this event are a distinct minority. That the Holocaust has become ever-present within Western culture is beyond doubt, but what remains debatable, however, is the degree to which this increased awareness of literally the worst crime of our age is necessarily desirable. British scholar David Patrick, for instance, expressed serious criticism of the omnipresence of the Holocaust trope in our political discourse and cultural imagination.[30] Following his argument, questions can be raised concerning: (1) the political and ideological use of the Holocaust; (2) the inappropriate expectations regarding the lessons that can be learned; and (3) the often unintended moral and pedagogical consequences of an over-representation of the Holocaust. Criticism against an over-representation of the Holocaust should *not* be equalled with a plea to erase the Holocaust from our collective memory, but rather perceived as a call to critically engage with some problematic aspects of Holocaust education and

---

27 G. Flümann, *Streitbare Demokratie in Deutschland und den Vereinigten Staaten. Der staatliche Umgang mit nichtgewalttätigem politischem Extremismus im Vergleich*, Springer, Wiesbaden 2015.

28 Bundesamt für Verfassungsschutz, *Rechtsextremistischer Revisionismus. Ein Thema von heute*, Bundesamt für Verfassungsschutz, Cologne, Köln 2001.

29 G. Hartman, *The Longest Shadow: In the Aftermath of the Holocaust*, Palgrave, London 2002.

30 D. Patrick, *Keep the Truth Small: Has the Use of the 'Holocaust' Diluted Its Impact?*, retrieved on 09.07.2013 (n.p.).

remembrance and an attempt to promote another and better understanding of the past.

6.1. POLITICAL USAGE

In politics and society, particularly in the arena of power politics, the Holocaust has gradually acquired the status of an unquestionably moral reference point. When it is politically useful to do so, few politicians will refrain from using the Shoah to obtain support for political goals. Justification of many wars serves as a good example here, with the enemy's crimes (Saddam Hussein, Slobodan Milošević, Bashar al-Assad) often being highlighted as being of the same nature as those of the Nazis. The Holocaust narrative certainly played an important role in the legitimation of the conflicts in the Balkans – where Serbian prison camps were equated with Auschwitz, or where the Croats were depicted as the resurfaced Ustasha. Peter Novick described the Holocaust as the 'yardstick of evil' and, certainly since the early 1990s, various political and societal players have frequently invoked Holocaust images in an attempt to win internal public support.[31] The basic problem, however, with repeated references such as these, is that they can easily lead to an (unintended?) degree of trivialisation.[32] Indeed, when used in an inappropriate context, utilising the Holocaust in this manner can actually weaken someone's argument, rather than strengthening it. By becoming universally recognised as the symbol of suffering, the Holocaust has come to be instrumentalised in a vast number of political and ethical causes. The best-known examples are the radical opponents of abortion who refer to abortion as 'Baby caust'; animal rights activists who describe the treatment of animals in the agricultural and food industry in terms of an 'Animal-caust', an 'Auschwitz for animals'; and the radical pacifists and environmentalists who predict the horrors of a looming 'nuclear Holocaust'. It is highly questionable whether these labels and comparisons actually help gathering support for these (just) causes. It remains to be seen whether the equating the fate of animals, unborn babies with the victims of the Nazi extermination camps has any positive effect on these campaigns. Could a deeply troublesome consequence of this 'abuse' of the Holocaust paradigm not be a form of trivialisation, ultimately leading to moral indifference? If everything is linked to the Holocaust, it loses its warning capacity. If the term is heard too often and frequently used in an unreflective manner, it may weaken the argument of the speaker and lose the impact for which it was intended.

---

31 P. Novick, *The Holocaust in American Life*, Mariner Books, New York 2000, p. 197.

32 D. Patrick, *Keep the Truth Small: Has the Use of the 'Holocaust' Diluted Its Impact?*, retrieved on 09.07.2013 (n.p.).

The same applies to the scholarly debate. Activist historians tend to link their subject of study to the history of the Shoah, suggesting a fundamental similarity between the fate of their subject under study and the Jews under Nazi persecution. In this way, the notion of the Holocaust is expanded to the 'Armenian Holocaust' during the First World War; the 'Indian Holocaust' during the conquest of the West in North America; the 'Black Holocaust' as a result of African slave trade and slavery in the New World; or finally the 'Red Holocaust' as a reference to the crimes under the Stalinist regime in the Soviet Union. Suggesting a similarity between the Holocaust and other genocides in modern history, has serious methodological and conceptual consequences. Stressing the uniqueness of the Jewish Holocaust leads to overestimating the exclusive and incomparable fate of the Jews, and finally makes every lesson to be drawn essentially impossible. Because one cannot learn from something that will never recur. If, on the other hand, one tends to underline the universal dimension of the Holocaust, linking it to other genocides, there is a lurking danger of trivialising its horrific characteristics. 'Uniqueness' or 'comparability' constitutes the constant dilemma that each discourse on the Holocaust has to reckon with.[33]

6.2. 'LESSONS FROM THE PAST'

Can lessons be drawn?[34] Many scholars and educators will defend the position that a widespread representation of the Holocaust is necessary on the grounds that 'a number of lessons can be learned from it'.[35] Students are told that engaging with the Holocaust will make them more tolerant towards other people and that they will be better suited to respond to new human rights abuses and mass atrocities in our time. One only has to look at the recent past's various failed responses to genocide, however, to realise that this is no more than misplaced optimism. It has been repeatedly claimed that remembering the Holocaust is an intrinsically redemptive activity. The quick and easy assumption that more awareness will automatically lead to a more proactive response to future instances of genocide is grossly misplaced. It overlooks the clear discrepancy between awareness and action.[36] Engaging with the past does not necessarily make people better.

---

33 A.S. Rosenbaum, *Is the Holocaust Unique? Perspectives on Comparative Genocide*, Westview Press, Boulder 1995.

34 D. Patrick, *Keep the Truth Small: Has the Use of the 'Holocaust' Diluted Its Impact?*, retrieved on 09.07.2013 (n.p.).

35 G. Verbeeck, 'Lessen uit het verleden? Historische analogie als antifascistisch wapen' in: H. De Witte (ed.), *Bestrijding van racisme en rechts-extremisme. Wetenschappelijke bijdragen aan het maatschappelijk debat*, Acco, Leuven-Amersfoort 1997, pp. 133–154.

36 D. Patrick, *Keep the Truth Small: Has the Use of the 'Holocaust' Diluted Its Impact?*, retrieved on 09.07. 2013 (n.p.).

If the Holocaust is presented as the preeminent genocide, it may easily lead to the thought that genocide can only take the form that the Nazi extermination of the Jews actually took, namely death camps and gas chambers. In other words, for many the Holocaust serves as the only 'real' example of genocide. This is perhaps one reason why so many practices of genocide have remained virtually unnoticed by the Western powers and their public opinion. Notorious examples are the Killing Fields in Cambodia, precisely at a time when the Western world was experiencing its first wave in Holocaust awareness, or Rwanda's mass murders in 1994, only a few weeks after *Schindler's List* was at the centre of a whirlwind of international media publicity. Indeed, if one stresses the very unique nature of the Holocaust itself, it makes the application of lessons almost impossible. Especially for lessons that should be applied to *our times*, what can then indeed be learned from a rather exceptional industrialised attempt *in history* to exterminate an entire race?[37]

6.3. DESENSITISATION

A final point that should be addressed here is the idea that increasing familiarity with the Holocaust may have produced the unintended effect of making people less sensitive to new forms of massive injustice.[38] It has been suggested indeed that what was once a shocking experience no longer holds our collective attention. This can be examined by comparing the images after 1945 with our responses to Bosnia or Rwanda in the late 20th century. Commentators have spoken of a gradual process of desensitisation to genocide. By being exposed to conventional images of the Jewish tragedy for so long, subsequent atrocities and mass crimes no longer necessarily carry the same shock effect as they otherwise would have done. 'There seem to be no circumstances and conditions of life which a man cannot get accustomed, especially if he sees them accepted by everyone around him' (Leo Tolstoy). This could explain why, in a world full of images related to the historic Holocaust, contemporary societies have persistently failed to appropriately and timely react to genocide in the present day. In the same sense, it is also probable that this particular form of desensitisation has occurred as the ultimate effect of constant attempts to compare subsequent atrocities to the historic Holocaust. Since 'the Holocaust is the emblematic horror against which all other horrors are measured' (Peter Novick), it means that most other occurrences of mass violence, even those of a quantitatively massive scale, have problems 'competing' with this emblem.[39] By focusing on the

37 S. Friedländer, 'The Shoah between Memory and History' (1990) 37 *The Jewish Quarterly* 11.

38 D. Patrick, *Keep the Truth Small: Has the Use of the 'Holocaust' Diluted Its Impact?*, retrieved on 09.07.2013 (n.p.).

39 P. Novick, *The Holocaust in American Life*, Mariner Books, New York 2000, p. 255.

iconic figure of six million victims the Holocaust is virtually unbeatable in terms of its death toll and, as a result, the popular consensus is that any other genocide *must* therefore equate with millions of deaths. This is of course a questionable response, but in view of the comparison with the fixed and massive proportions of the Shoah many spectators can easily find ways to rationalise the lack of response to a contemporary atrocity. In terms of numbers and intrinsic nature, few genocidal practices can actually stand up to comparison with the Holocaust, and this may lead to an inappropriate examination and response to more recent developments.

7. EPILOGUE

Legal measures to combat Holocaust denialism are rarely inspired by the ambition to secure history as such, but rather motivated by a political agenda to determine a crucial cultural and ideological symbol of contemporary society. The struggle for the memory of history coincides with the struggle against the enemies of liberal democracy. Not only do internal considerations play a role, but equally pivotal is the wider international context. The state of Israel has certainly played a role in elevating the Shoah to a central episode in the history of humanity. Without the power and the influence of the Jewish state, which views itself as a safeguard against a possible recurrence of the history, the Shoah would certainly have not become as solidly anchored in collective memory. Political, economic and military developments in the Middle East have contributed to what citizens worldwide consider important to commemorate and remember. Polemical writings have mentioned specific machinations by the state of Israel and Jewish lobby groups influencing our historical sensitivities.[40] This should not be readdressed here again. Yet it is evident that collective memory does not emerge out of the blue, nor does it result from a spontaneous process of memory, but that it is influenced by external factors such as political power. The very existence of the state of Israel has caused Holocaust memory to acquire a separate status, particularly in Western Europe and North America. Holocaust denial is seen as a radical attack against putting the historic tragedy of the Jewish people centre-stage in a democratic society's collective memory. This is precisely what Holocaust denial defies: the widespread conviction that crimes and errors in the past should be acknowledged and remain remembered for the sake of civic health today.

Public attention to the Holocaust – in research and teaching, through the media and public education – remains unchallenged. This may be an effect of the

[40] N. Finkelstein, *The Holocaust Industry: Reflections on the Exploitation of Jewish Suffering*, Veso, London 2003; T. Cole, *Selling the Holocaust: From Auschwitz to Schindler, How History is Bought, Packaged and Sold*, Routledge, New York 2000.

fact that the number of survivors is rapidly decreasing, with those who actually remember the Jewish genocide soon to disappear. The Holocaust remains one of the most extensively studied topics in modern history, and Holocaust related memorial activities are still on the rise. It may be applauded for political reasons, but one cannot necessarily assume that these educational campaigns will achieve anything more than providing the general public with a greater knowledge of the Holocaust. The idea that such information can lay the foundations of a better society is highly questionable and a belief that it could actually prevent atrocities in the future rests upon wishful thinking. One should however look for alternative manners of engaging with the Holocaust in order to help achieving these goals but it remains very unclear as to what form this would take and only very few fresh ideas have emerged in recent years. If the process of saturation and desensitisation is to be stopped, historians and the wider public must find new narratives and imaginations, as new and dramatic challenges can be foreseen, and there is no reason to believe that future conflicts will be less destructive as the last ones. New global dynamics (global warming, overpopulation, inequality, and the scramble for energy sources) can easily lead to new local conflicts, potentially leading to genocide. In order to stop and properly respond to such developments it is recommended that the popular notion that extensively dealing with the Holocaust will automatically prevent the awaking of the ghosts of the past be left behind. The conventional wisdom, that those who refuse to learn from history are bound to repeat it, is unconvincing. *Knowing* and *learning* are not necessarily exchangeable.

The final question needs to be addressed now: should the denial of the Holocaust provide the template for a more universal pattern of denialism, related to different forms of genocide? The answer is balanced. Following Judt's argument it may become comprehensible why events such as the Armenian genocide or the act of ethnic cleansing during the civil war in former Yugoslavia carry such a political charge – and the reason why Europe has invested itself with the responsibility to make sure that attention is paid to them and to define Europeans as people who do pay attention to them – is because they are partial instances of the pivotal crime of the Holocaust, which was an attempt by one group of Europeans to exterminate every member of another group of Europeans, on European soil, and still within the boundaries of communicative ('living') memory. The Holocaust therefore continues to play the role as a central point of reference and comparison by which to judge the essence of other practices of genocide and mass crime. It delivers a standard measure for our understanding and awareness of other major crimes and wrongdoings, either past or present. It is in this sense that the Holocaust – but also its denial, and the responses to its denial – presents a master model for our historical culture and moral understanding.

But the opposite option might hold truth as well, since there is a widespread consensus, in academic scholarship as among the wider public as well, on the unicity of the Holocaust, and the centrality of this aspect in our collective memory. It is hard to imagine that an equal amount of intellectual efforts would be invested to preserve and protect the memory of other genocides, as is the case with the Holocaust. Holocaust memory is much more closely interwoven with European identity, which explains the firm responses to its denial. A comparable political and cultural charge in the Armenian, Cambodian, Bosnian and Rwandan cases (notwithstanding the numbers involved) is less self-evident and similar measures to be taken being taken, as in the case of Holocaust denial, cannot be expected. Various attempts have been made to extend the scope of the law to the denial of other genocides, mostly in vain. It has been suggested in this chapter that legal actions against Holocaust denial are already problematic and questionable enough in itself. What is needed is caution and utmost restraint before a possible extension of legal measures to other fields is considered.

CHAPTER XI

CAN THE LAW UNDERSTAND THE HARM OF GENOCIDE DENIAL?

Rob KAHN*

1. INTRODUCTION

What's so bad about genocide denial? Several countries (largely in Europe) have banned denial of the Nazi crimes against the Jews. French Armenians have tried repeatedly to pass legislation banning Armenian genocide denial. Rwanda has banned denial of its genocide. The European Union Framework Decision calls on Member States to ban denial of genocide and crimes against humanity. Statutory violations can be enforced with prison sentences. One must add to this a general loathing of genocide denial. Even those who would tolerate genocide denial, describe it as offensive, vile and disgusting. This often comes with a call for non-legal responses to genocide denial ranging from education and counter-speech to 'informal censorship' (i.e. when libraries, social media outlets, newspapers, and other non-state actors refuse to engage with genocide deniers).[1]

While there is a consensus that genocide denial is harmful, the harm is rarely spelled out.[2] Instead, the focus is on the genocide denial bans. Reactions

* The author wishes to thank Jacqueline Baronian for her helpful comments. The paper benefited greatly from informal conversations at the Denialism and Human Rights conference with Eric Heinze, Uladzislau Belavusau, Sévane Garibian, Marloes van Noorloos, Roland Moerland and Luigi Cajani. I would also like to Thomas Hochmann, as well as my colleagues at the University of St. Thomas School of Law. In particular, I would like to thank Joel Nichols, Greg Sisk, Teresa Collett, Virgil Wiebe, Wulf Kaal, and Mitchell Gordon.

1 For an early study of how informal censorship applies in the context of Holocaust denial, see R. KAHN, *Holocaust Denial and the Law: A Comparative Study*, Palgrave, New York 2004, pp. 119–52.

2 For two notable exceptions, which I will address later, see U. BELAVUSAU, *Freedom of Speech: Importing European and US Constitutional Models in Transitional Democracies*, Routledge, New York 2013, pp. 166–201; F. SCHAUER, 'Social Epistemology, Holocaust Denial, and the Post-Millian Calculus' in: M. HERZ and P. MOLNAR (eds.), *The Content and Context of Hate Speech: Rethinking Regulation and Responses*, Cambridge University Press, Cambridge

include shock ('how can a free society ban a view about the past?'), assertions of the importance of history,[3] and well-intentioned efforts to cabin the problem by narrowing the zone of acceptable genocide denial bans. These last efforts take two forms. Either one creates a hierarchy of genocides in which some killings (i.e. the Holocaust) become more important than other genocides. Or one makes an argument based on geography: given the deportation of 80,000 Jews during the occupation, France can (possibly) ban Holocaust denial;[4] but the Ottoman genocide against the Armenians is another matter entirely since it did not occur on French soil.[5]

These attempts to justify legal toleration of genocide denial make it easy to pass over a central question of the Denialism and Human Rights conference: what is it about denial that poses harm? For some of the types of denial discussed at this conference, the harm is relatively easy to see. For example, denial of global warming encourages states, corporations and individual consumers to make decisions that will exacerbate climate change. Likewise, the South African government's denial of AIDS led it to restrict access to anti-AIDS drugs. The harms here are immediate and visceral.

By contrast, what is the concrete, practical harm of denying that an act of mass murder took place decades or centuries in the past?[6] Historians debate competing views about what happened in the past; interested parties sometimes exaggerate or lie about the past.[7] But these lies, exaggerations

---

2012, pp. 129–44. Both works are sophisticated treatments of denial that advance our understanding of the problems posed by genocide denial legislation.

3 This trend is notable on the *Liberté pour l'Histoire* website. See P. Nora, 'Historical Identity in Trouble' 2008 <www.lph-asso.fr/index.php?option=com_content&view=article&id=152&Itemid=182&lang=en> accessed 28.04.2015; R. Remond, 'History and the Law' 2006 <www.lph-asso.fr/index.php?option=com_content&view=article&id=149&Itemid=176&lang=en> accessed 28.04.2015. For a notable exception, see P. Lobba, 'Criminalizing Negationism beyond the Holocaust' 2013 <www.lph-asso.fr/index.php?option=com_content&view=article&id=184%3Acriminaliser-le-negationnisme-au-dela-de-lHolocauste&catid=53%3Aactualites&Itemid=170&lang=en> accessed 28.04.2015. Like me, Lobba takes the position that restricting genocide denial bans (and memory laws) to situations in which there is a discriminatory intent (what he calls 'racist denial') is an improvement over the current situation.

4 See T. Garton Ash, 'This is the moment for Europe to dismantle taboos, not erect them' *The Guardian*, 18.10.2014.

5 For a critique, see R. Kahn, 'Should it matter where genocide denial is banned? A Critique of the Nexus Argument' University of St. Thomas Legal Studies Research Paper, No. 14–31, posted to the Social Science Research Network, 07.10.2014.

6 If the denial concerns events in the very recent past, then denial might prevent concrete acts of justice such as punishing perpetrators or compensating victims. As the killings recede into the deeper past these types of practical concerns also fade away. For example, it may be harmful to deny the killing of Jewish communities in Germany during the First Crusade, but the harm does not rest on the inability to bring the perpetrators to justice.

7 In 1898 a Swedish immigrant living in Minnesota discovered the Kensington Runestone which – according to legend – was inscribed by Viking explorers to the state in 1362. There has been a vigorous 'debate' over the stone's authenticity. See R. Gilman, 'Kensington Runestone Revisited: Recent Developments, Recent Publications' 2006 *Minnesota History*, pp. 61–65.

and denials are not generally seen as harmful.[8] What makes genocide denial different?

There have been varied responses to this question. Deborah Lipstadt, in *Denying the Holocaust: The Growing Assault on Truth and Memory*, saw denial as a way to spread racism and anti-Semitism.[9] Taking a different tack, Lawrence Douglas sees an acceptance of 'the facticity of the Holocaust' as 'a litmus test of one's willingness to participate in the thinnest version of the discursive community', a willingness that denial threatens.[10] This recalls what Hannah Arendt refers to as the compulsion of historical truth.[11] To deny, for example, that on 4 August 1914 Germany invaded Belgium 'would require ... a power monopoly over the entire civilized world'.[12] One might, then, see genocide denial as an attempt to seek out this power monopoly; once the deniers attained it, they could resume their past acts of hate.[13]

Others have questioned the legal harm posed by genocide denial. In *Freedom of Speech: Importing European and US Constitutional Models in Transitional Democracies*, Uladzislau Belavusau has argued that 'historical revisionism', a category that for him includes genocide denial, is not hate speech because it does not target a specific victim.[14] By treating genocide denial as a form of historical revisionism, Belavusau returns us to the question of what makes genocide denial unique.

The efforts to answer this question operate at too high a level of generality. Either genocide denial is *always* an expression of racist or anti-Semitic hate speech, or it *never* has this quality. What is missing is an appreciation of how a given speech act, in this case genocide denial, can change its meaning depending on its precise content and the context in which it arises.[15] Some forms of

8 To continue the previous example, it is hard to see how denying the Runestone's authenticity – or denying the opposing view that the stone is a hoax – harms anyone.

9 D. Lipstadt, *Denying the Holocaust: The Growing Assault on Truth and Memory*, Penguin, New York 1994, p. 217.

10 L. Douglas, 'Policing the Past: Holocaust Denial and the Law' in: R. Post (ed.), *Censorship and Silencing: Practices of Cultural Regulation*, Getty Research Institute for the History of Art and the Humanities, 1998, p. 71.

11 H. Arendt, 'Truth and Politics' in: *Between Past and Future: Eight Exercises in Political Thought*, Penguin, New York (enlarged edition 1968), pp. 239–40.

12 Ibid., p. 239.

13 I made a similar argument a few years ago. R. Kahn, 'Holocaust Denial and Hate Speech' in: L. Hennebel and T. Hochmann, *Genocide Denials and the Law*, Oxford University Press, Oxford 2011, pp. 75–108.

14 U. Belavusau, *Freedom of Speech: Importing European and US Constitutional Models in Transitional Democracies*, Routledge, New York 2013, pp. 166, 171.

15 It is equally important to examine the forms that genocide denial might take. As Stanley Cohen has observed, there are three types of denial – literal (factual), interpretive and implicative (or moral) denial. See S. Cohen, *States of Denial: Knowing About Atrocities and Suffering*, Polity Press, Cambridge 2001, pp. 7–9. In the genocide denial context one most readily thinks of denial of specific *facts* – such as the claim that no Jews were gassed at Auschwitz, or there was no Ottoman plan to exterminate the Armenians. But one can also

genocide denial might pose harm; others might not. Indeed, the same statement might pose different harms when repeated in different contexts – something increasingly likely given the global spread of social media.

In this essay, I focus on three potential types of harm genocide denial might pose.[16] First, genocide denial might *harm a specific set of victims*. Second, genocide denial might encourage others to act in ways that *pose a threat* to the free democratic order. Finally, the *deliberate falsity* of genocide denial might cause social harm similar to the type caused by false advertising or the rejection of a connection between cigarette smoking and lung cancer. Because of time and space limitations, I will focus largely on the first question: who – if anyone – is victimised by genocide denial?

Taking a fine-grained approach to the potential harm posed by genocide denial helps us evaluate genocide denial bans. Writing from the United States, I have some scepticism about the effectiveness of broad bans on genocide denial, even if they convey a useful symbolic message about society's acknowledgement of a given act of genocide. But the justification of such laws might not be merely symbolic. A case-by-case analysis might suggest that *some* specific acts of genocide denial pose enough concrete harm to justify legal prohibition even if others do not. When these harmful denials arise with sufficient frequency, a ban on genocide denial could be justified – at least in a country that normally punishes hate speech.

From civil libertarian perspective a recognition that genocide denial can sometime harm others might ironically strengthen the argument against general blanket bans of genocide denial. To reject out of hand the possibility that denying a genocide might harm a survivor or member of the targeted group opens the door to accusations that the opponent of bans is 'denying the harm of denial' – especially in light of those forms of denial that seem especially egregious (as, for example, when a Holocaust denier contacts Holocaust survivors asking for proof that the Holocaust happened).

The civil libertarian can avoid this problem by conceding that some – perhaps very few – instances of genocide denial harm specific groups of people. This

deny the *interpretation* of these facts as a genocide. (For example, one could say that what happened to the Armenians was tragic, but not a genocide.) While the second, interpretive form of genocide denial sounds innocent (since it carries the implication that the underlying facts have not been denied), it can also serve as a shorthand for denying everything. 'What happened to the Jews was not a Holocaust' is very close to 'The Holocaust never happened'. Cohen's third, implicative type of denial arises when one accepts the facts of the situation, and their characterisation, *but denies a need to do anything about it*. While this is an important issue, and one that plays out while the genocidal acts are underway, it carries less weight in the aftermath of the genocide (at least when it comes to legal regulation of genocide denial).

16 There is also an additional harm. One of the few 'benefits' of genocide is the recognition that individuals, groups and societies are capable of cruel, violent, 'inhumane' acts. Denial robs us of this hard-earned knowledge. While this harm is real – and worth exploring at length – I do not take it up here because it would not likely justify banning genocide denial.

could pave the way to a more constructive debate, even if the civil libertarian was unwilling to punish these 'aggravated' forms of genocide denial. At a minimum, non-legal responses to genocide denial (such as public repudiation of the denier) would make more sense if they were informed by a deeper, more nuanced understanding of when genocide denial is harmful.

In what follows, I first focus on the harm genocide denial might inflict on *genocide survivors* before turning to the impact of denial on the *groups targeted by the genocide*. I then turn to context – i.e. the possibility that the same act of denial may be more harmful in one situation than in another. After that, the essay briefly examines two other potential harms: (i) the threat denial poses to the post genocidal social and political order and (ii) the possibility that genocide denial is harmful because it is false. In the conclusion, I briefly suggest what the context-sensitive approach advanced here means for the legal regulation of genocide denial.

2. SURVIVORS

2.1. WHO DOES GENOCIDE DENIAL HARM?

Does genocide denial have a victim? Uladzislau Belavusau argues that genocide denial bans are not justifiable because they lack 'an individual addressee, attribution of inferiority … [or] incitement to violence'.[17] Rather, most denial sticks to 'racially neutral rhetoric' and avoids 'explicit appeals for aggression' towards 'target groups'.[18]

The lack of an addressee on one level makes perfect sense. Because genocide involves killing, its greatest offence is inflicted against someone who doesn't care – because he or she is dead. While many societies, like Germany, have rules for respecting the dead, these concepts (avoiding offence, venerating the deceased, honouring memory, etc.) have much in common with the type of blasphemy prosecutions out of fashion in both Europe and the United States, outliers like the *Otto-Preminger-Institut* case notwithstanding.[19] Therefore, harm to the dead cannot justify genocide denial bans.

---

17 U. Belavusau, *Freedom of Speech: Importing European and US Constitutional Models in Transitional Democracies*, Routledge, New York 2013, p. 171.

18 Ibid.

19 In *Otto-Preminger-Institut v Austria*, no. 13470/87, ECHR 1994, the European Court for Human Rights held that Austria could ban as blasphemy the showing of a satirical movie about the Holy Family at a small arts theatre. The case has been roundly criticised. See R. Kahn, 'A Margin of Appreciation for Muslims? Viewing the Defamation of Religions Debate through *Otto-Preminger-Institut v. Austria*' (2011) 5 *Charleston Law Review* 401, 431–433.

The harder questions involve those who, despite the best efforts of the genocide killers, managed to survive. According to Belavusau, survivor harm is a difficult way to justify denial bans for two reasons. First, in the Jewish tradition, only a direct victim can forgive, something that undermines the logic of Holocaust denial bans as a symbolic 'apology' to survivors.[20] Second, as Holocaust survivors pass away, justifying denial bans based on survivor harm will require 'a legal fiction' in which the offspring of survivors stand in for their parents and grandparents.[21]

Here, Belavusau takes up the idea of 'surrogate mourning'. He quotes a passage from J.H.H. Weiler about how, given the lack of mourners, the community must appoint surrogates who 'are treated by the community as if they had actually suffered loss'.[22] Because '[n]obody is in psychological need we go through the communal motions of mourning'. In other words, genocide denial bans harm genuine reconciliation by forcing Jews (and the society at large) to 'go through the motions' of mourning.

There is much to agree with here. A genocide denial ban – or prosecution of a genocide denier – should not rest on a symbolic 'apology' to the survivors be they former camp residents, descendants of the dead, or members of the target ethnicity. Any set of criminal prohibitions on speech, even on the most offensive speech, should rest on a specific showing on harm to the human dignity of a specific, living person (or group of persons). To put it another way, the harm flowing from a specific act of genocide denial should be equivalent to the harm that justifies hate speech prosecutions.

Ideally, conceptualising the harm of Holocaust denial (and the suitability of legal sanctions) should be a two-step process. First, one assembles a broad cross section of genocide denial speech acts. At this stage, the question should be: Which, if any, of these statements harm the human dignity of a survivor, descendant or member of the target group? Second, assuming some genocide denial acts have this quality, do they occur frequently enough to justify denial bans? Or should deniers be prosecuted under traditional hate speech laws?

2.2. HUMAN DIGNITY AS A MEASURING STICK

In the paper, I approach this through the lens of human dignity. The choice of human dignity is provisional – there are other ways to measure the harms of hate speech that do not involve assaults against human dignity. (For example,

20 U. Belavusau, *Freedom of Speech: Importing European and US Constitutional Models in Transitional Democracies*, Routledge, New York 2013, p. 172.

21 Ibid., p. 173.

22 Ibid. (quoting J.H.H. Weiler, 'Epilogue: Europe's Dark Legacy Reclaiming Nationalism and Patriotism' in: C. Joerges and N. Singh Ghaleigh (eds.), *Darker Legacies of Law in Europe: The Shadow of National Socialism and Fascism over Europe and its Legal Traditions*, Hart Publishing, Portland, Oregon 2003, pp. 390–91).

many countries punish insulting speech.) I also recognise that human dignity is a vague concept, one all too often synonymous with 'punishable'.[23] My interest with human dignity is narrower. I simply want to use it as a convenient way to compare the harms of genocide denial with the harms of traditional hate speech.

In *The Harm in Hate Speech*, Jeremy Waldron describes a Muslim father who, passing an anti-Muslim sign on a New Jersey street corner ('Muslims and 9/11! Don't serve them, don't speak to them, don't let them in'), is asked by his ten-year-old daughter: 'Papa, what does it mean?'[24] According to Waldron, the poster conveys two messages. First, it tells the family that, despite appearances: 'You are [not] welcome.' In this regard, the poster proclaims that: 'You and your families will be shunned, excluded, beaten and driven out[.]'[25] Second, the poster tells those who are not Muslim, and who feel that Muslims are 'dirty' or 'dangerous', that they are 'not alone' that, despite what the government says: 'There are enough of us around to make sure that these people are not welcome.'[26]

I will discuss Waldron's second idea of encouragement (or incitement) to hateful acts later. For now, let us focus on the idea by promoting feelings of exclusion can rob the subjects of their human dignity.[27] Waldron defines dignity as a person's 'social standing' including 'the fundamentals of basic reputation' that 'entitle' people 'to be treated as equals in the basic operations of society'. Hate speech undermines human dignity by 'associating ascriptive characteristics like ethnicity, race, or religion with conduct or attributes that should disqualify someone from being treated as a member of society in good standing'.[28]

At first glance, Waldron's definition appears to exclude genocide survivors and their descendants from hate speech since, as Belavusau would point out, they are not a category based on 'ethnicity, race or religion'. Nor does most genocide denial call for violence against the victim group of the 'alleged' genocide, or engage in name calling. Rather, the tone of genocide denial is often mild and (pseudo)scientific.[29] However, Waldron, describing the harm to the Muslim family, does not stop at future threats of exclusion, and beatings. The poster also makes a statement about past harm: 'Don't get too comfortable. Remember what has happened to you and your kind in the past. Be afraid.'[30]

---

23 I thank Thomas Hochmann for this point.
24 J. Waldron, *The Harm in Hate Speech*, Harvard University Press, Cambridge, MA 2012, p. 3 (internal quotations omitted).
25 Ibid.
26 Ibid.
27 Ibid., p. 5.
28 Ibid.
29 See U. Belavusau, *Freedom of Speech: Importing European and US Constitutional Models in Transitional Democracies*, Routledge, New York 2013, p. 171.
30 J. Waldron, *The Harm in Hate Speech*, Harvard University Press, Cambridge, MA 2012, p. 3.

2.3. HARMS TO VICTIMS

Given this, might genocide denial sometimes ignite a similar fear? Imagine another Muslim family, this time in Sarajevo. They encounter a poster that reads: 'No Muslims were killed in Srebrenica' or, to take justification, a theme particularly notable in Armenian genocide denial: 'The Muslims in Srebrenica attacked us first.' The sign is clearly offensive. But depending on the context, it could also send the following message: 'Be even less comfortable. We can exclude, maim or kill your type in the future and deny it ever happened. Just like we did in the past.' What if the parent is also a survivor of Srebrenica – one of the lucky few to escape? What will he say when his daughter asks: 'Papa, what really happened?'

This example shows how, theoretically, genocide denial could harm a survivor. But this argument proves too much: if any statement of denial can harm any survivor, the resulting genocide denial ban will be very broad. Given that restrictions on expression involve balancing competing interests, one might reasonably insist on a more specific link between genocide denial and harm to human dignity. In other words, some forms of genocide denial may be harmful (and worthy of classifying as hate speech) in some contexts – but genocide denial is not always harmful.

Yet I wonder about Belavusau's effort to separate the 'hate speech' aspects of genocide denial, from the 'historical revisionism' aspects of it.[31] For better or worse, some acts of genocide denial are both statements about history, as well as speech acts that (sometimes intentionally) harm members of victim groups. Moreover, statements of this nature strike me as quite different from the type of revisionism involved in arguing that Herbert Hoover, despite being blamed for worsening the Great Depression, was a very good President of the United States.[32] Whatever one thinks of the arguments for and against Hoover, it is hard view them as hateful.[33]

Let me next turn to Belavusau's argument about 'surrogate mourning'. Let us assume that, in the Jewish tradition, apologies must be made to, and accepted by,

---

31 U. Belavusau, *Freedom of Speech: Importing European and US Constitutional Models in Transitional Democracies*, Routledge, New York 2013, p. 171. For example, the *Protocols of the Elders of Zion* is full of stereotypes about Jewish greed and power and, as such is a classic example of anti-Semitism. At the same time, however, the *Protocols* contains statements about history.

32 See P. O'Brien and P. Rosen, 'Hoover and the Historians: The Reconstruction of a President' in: M. Dodge (ed.), *Herbert Hoover and the Historians*, Herbert Hoover Presidential Library Association, West Branch, Iowa 1989, pp. 40–85.

33 For example, in the 1950s one historian referred to Hoover as the 'Great Failure' – harsh language, to be sure, but nothing that would suggest harm to a given group. See P. O'Brien and P. Rosen, 'Hoover and the Historians: The Reconstruction of a President' in: M. Dodge (ed.), *Herbert Hoover and the Historians*, Herbert Hoover Presidential Library Association, West Branch, Iowa 1989, p. 43.

the direct victim – in this case those who were murdered. Even if true, however, two sticking points remain. First, genocide is a global phenomenon. Victims come from a wide variety of groups, including (potentially) some that might take a different view of mourning and apologies.

Second, in some contexts genocide denial his highly likely to harm to specific survivors. For example, consider the *sonderkommandos* who cleaned out the gas chambers after each act of killing. They may experience a statement 'it didn't happen' very directly. For the *sonderkommandos*, and others like them, the statement 'there were no homicidal gas chambers at Auschwitz' conveys the following message: 'You are lying about acts of horrendous cruelty, acts that are likely a defining moment of your life.' To a lesser extent, anyone who survived a death camp – and wondered if they would live or die – suffered harm to their human dignity. For these survivors, the mourning is 'actual' rather than 'surrogate'.[34]

To be fair, this group of 'direct' victims of genocide denial is small; and I agree with Belavusau that, with the passage of time, survivor experiences can no longer justify bans on genocide denial. Indeed, were this the only harm posed by genocide denial, the bans might well merit only a limited period of viability. Not only that, using harm to the *sonderkommando* to justify broad bans gives speakers little guidance on what speech acts are allowed. If I put up a poster saying 'The Holocaust Never Happened', should my legal penalty depend on whether a former *sonderkommando* or death camp victim saw it? In other words, even if I am correct that 'bare' Holocaust denial – i.e. denial without any circumstances that add an anti-Semitic tinge to it – can harm the human dignity of some Holocaust survivors, is this a compelling enough reason to ban it?

Maybe not. But not all denial is bare. Often denial comes with a context, one that supplies the missing element of harm that could justify prohibition. This case is strongest when the deniers abandon their veneer of neutrality and add a statement targeting a specific group: 'The Holocaust was a Zionist lie.' This type of statement has been prosecuted as hate speech. In addition, sometimes a bare statement of genocide denial can harm vulnerable survivors. For example, when the Institute for Historical Review mailed flyers to Holocaust survivors promising $50,000 for proof that Jews were gassed at Auschwitz, they engaged in an assault on the dignity of those survivors.[35] While there is not a statement of racial inferiority, or a specific call for violence against a victim group, there is

34 At one level further removed are those survivors who without facing execution suffered horribly under camp conditions. For these, the direct impact of genocide denial is more limited. But to the extent that genocide denial also involves denial of great suffering – even if it does not lead to death – one might have a limited claim to harm here as well.

35 For an example of this, see M. Mermelstein, *By Bread Alone: The Story of A-4685 Mel Mermelstein, A Survivor of the Nazi Holocaust*, Auschwitz Study Foundation, Huntington Beach, California 1993; R. Kahn, *Holocaust Denial and the Law: A Comparative Study*, Palgrave, New York 2004, pp. 22–24.

a harm that goes beyond mere offensiveness, one that could – with appropriate restrictions – justify legal prohibition, at least in countries that routinely punish hate speech.[36]

3. JEWS, ARMENIANS AND TUTSI (AMONG OTHERS)

Nor are survivors the only potential victims; to this category also belongs the ethnic, racial or religious group targeted by the genocide. To group members, genocide denial (even 'bare' denial) can, in the right context, send a message of exclusion. Sometimes this wraps around to indirect glorification of genocide. ('Hitler did not kill the Jews; but he should have.') Here, Belavusau makes a helpful distinction between the land of the perpetrators (where statements of denial can be very troubling) and other contexts (in which they have less impact).[37] Thus, from a Jewish perspective it is more troubling to hear a German deny the Holocaust because such a denial raises questions about whether Germany has moved on from its Nazi past. Likewise, an Armenian would be especially concerned with Turkish denial, a Tutsi with Hutu denial, or – to take an example from the United States – an African American with a white American's statement that accounts of police brutality against African Americans (as happened in Ferguson, Missouri) were a 'lie'.[38]

This explains why Holocaust denial has been punished more vigorously in Germany and Austria than in other European countries. As the German Federal Supreme Court stated in its 1979 ruling that Holocaust denial is a 'direct attack' on the 'self-conception' of Jews living in the Federal Republic.[39] Significantly, the

---

36 It is an open question whether – in a country tolerating hate speech bans – one should do this under traditional hate speech bans, or under very narrowly construed genocide denial laws. Let me observe that some of the most difficult problems of Holocaust denial litigation – such as the propensity for the accused to use the trial to promote Holocaust denial, and the tendency to make martyrs of deniers – did not go away with genocide denial bans. Moreover, the specific problems genocide denial bans address (such as denier attempts to present evidence denying the Holocaust and judicial unease in rendering judgments about history) could be cured by less drastic measures. For example, instead of banning all Holocaust denial, one could enact a rule of evidence preventing deniers from using the 'truth' of genocide denial as a defence to hate speech prosecutions.

37 U. Belavusau, *Freedom of Speech: Importing European and US Constitutional Models in Transitional Democracies*, Routledge, New York 2013, p. 193.

38 In Ferguson Missouri a white police officer shot an unarmed African American who, according to witnesses, had his hands up. The shooting led to a polarisation of opinion along racial lines, in which many white Americans sought to justify the shooting and deny the systematic nature of racism in suburban police forces across the United States. See M. Apuzzo, 'Ferguson Police Routinely Violate Rights of Blacks' *The New York Times*, 03.03.2015.

39 *BGHZ* (*Entscheidungen des Bundesgerichtshofes in Zivilsachen*) 75 (1979): 160 (quoted in R. Kahn, *Holocaust Denial and the Law: A Comparative Study*, Palgrave, New York 2004,

court traced this reading of denial to the Holocaust itself, which placed a duty on German citizens to provide Jews living in Germany with a 'guarantee against repetition' which is 'an essential condition for their life in the Federal Republic'.[40] Fears of repetition are naturally greater in the land of the perpetrators; so, potentially, is harm to human dignity.

Yet it goes too far to take a strictly geographic approach to assessing the harm of genocide denial.[41] In a global media age, national boundaries are less relevant in marking out different regimes of speech protection.[42] This makes it harder to keep genocide denial out of the lands of the perpetrators. Germany and Austria can ban Holocaust denial within its borders; Rwanda can do the same with its genocide. If they are vigilant, they can prevent outside deniers from entering the country.[43] But they cannot prevent denial from seeping in from Facebook, Twitter and other websites.[44] A Jewish family living in Germany who receives a tweet, sees a Facebook update, or visits a website denying the Holocaust may feel insecure, perhaps not as insecure as if the tweet, update or website originated in Germany, but insecure enough to raise doubts about the viability of their future life in Hamburg, Berlin, or Munich.

Second, as Aleksandra Gliszczynska-Grabias argues, Holocaust denial is 'an unprecedented phenomenon present all over the world', one closely linked to anti-Semitism.[45] This connection highlights dangers of restricting the harms of genocide denial to the countries of the perpetrators. For example, Holocaust denial is problematic in Iran, a country with no direct link to the Nazi crimes against the Jews, but where the government sponsored a contest to draw cartoons denying the Holocaust. Gliszczynska-Grabias sees the connection

p. 18). The quote came in a case holding that Holocaust denial violates Section 185 of the German Penal Code, which outlaws insulting speech.

40 Ibid.

41 I previously had more sympathy with this view. See R. Kahn, 'Holocaust Denial and Hate Speech' in: L. Hennebel and T. Hochmann, *Genocide Denials and the Law*, Oxford University Press, Oxford 2011, p. 96 (seeking to establish a relationship between a country's experience with the Holocaust and the presence Holocaust denial laws).

42 R. Kahn, 'Should it matter where genocide denial is banned? A Critique of the Nexus Argument' University of St. Thomas Legal Studies Research Paper, No. 14–31, posted to the Social Science Research Network, 07.10.2014.

43 See U. Belavusau, *Freedom of Speech: Importing European and US Constitutional Models in Transitional Democracies*, Routledge, New York 2013, p. 198 (describing 2009 visit of David Duke to the Czech Republic).

44 The problem of transnational flows of genocide denial was always present. One of the reasons for prosecuting Ernst Zundel in Canada were complaints from West Germany about his mailings. For more, see R. Kahn, 'Should it matter where genocide denial is banned? A Critique of the Nexus Argument' University of St. Thomas Legal Studies Research Paper, No. 14–31, posted to the Social Science Research Network, 07.10.2014, pp. 3–7.

45 A. Gliszczynska-Grabias, 'Some Remarks on Holocaust Denial Penalization in Europe – Analysis, Anti-Israelism, Anti-Semitism', Scholars for Peace in the Middle East, 2013 <http://spme.org/spme-research/some-remarks-on-holocaust-denial-penalization-in-europe/15863/> accessed 28.04.2015.

between Holocaust denial and anti-Semitism as the strongest reason for banning it,[46] a perspective shared by Justices Elizabeth Evatt and David Kretzmer who, in a concurring opinion in *Faurisson v. France*, justified the Gayssot Law on this basis.[47] To the extent they are correct, they raise a concern about genocide denial that is global in scope.

Moreover, the use of Holocaust denial by anti-Semites raises the possibility that, under some circumstances, Holocaust denial can be a marker for anti-Semitism (i.e. the phrase 'the Holocaust never happened' actually sends the message 'down with the Jews'). This coded meaning, moreover, is understood as such both by the deniers and those most likely to take offence – Jews and Holocaust survivors. In this situation, genocide denial looks less like a form of 'historical revisionism' and more like hate speech, not that different from the swastika (a symbol of Nazi Germany) or the burning cross (a symbol of white supremacy in the United States).[48] But when is genocide denial a symbolic marker for hate speech?

This is not an easy question to answer. One might start with the deniers themselves. Does a given denier sincerely believe that 'only lice were gassed at Auschwitz'? Is he or she making historical arguments about it? In other words, are they doing something that approximates the activities of the genuine historical revisionist who is constructing a coherent view of the past – albeit an unpopular one? Or is the denier using the sentence as an epithet, just as people earlier referred to Jews as 'Christ Killers'? If enough Holocaust denial is expressed as coded slogans, one starts to appreciate the position of Deborah Lipstadt, who in *Denying the Holocaust* argued Holocaust denial is inherently anti-Semitic.[49] Or to return to Waldron's example, a Jew who hears a Holocaust denial slogan may reasonably conclude that the speaker (or poster) seeks to exclude her, and all Jews, from the larger human community.

One might ask if the link between Holocaust denial and anti-Semitism is an outlier, or if other forms of genocide denial also serve as coded language for group hatred. I am not an expert on the denial of the Armenian, Rwandan or Bosnian genocides. However, nothing in the nature of genocide forecloses such a possibility. Indeed, the notions of racial superiority and ethnic hatred that made the original genocide possible could find subliminal expression as denial in a post-genocide era in which blatant expressions of group hatred are no longer politically acceptable.[50]

---

46 Ibid.

47 *Robert Faurisson v. France*, No. 550/1993 UN Doc. CCPR/C/58/D/550/1993 (1996).

48 For more, see R. Kahn, 'Offensive Symbols and Hate Speech Law: Where to Draw the Line? An American Perspective' in: A. Koltay (ed.), *Media Freedom and Regulation in the New Media World*, Wolters Kluwer, Budapest 2014, pp. 441–57.

49 D. Lipstadt, *Denying the Holocaust: The Growing Assault on Truth and Memory*, Penguin, New York 1994. To return to the Hoover example, both critics and defenders support their claims about Hoover with evidence as opposed to using statements about Hoover to send coded messages about vulnerable groups in society.

50 See R. Kahn, 'Should it matter where genocide denial is banned? A Critique of the Nexus Argument' University of St. Thomas Legal Studies Research Paper, No. 14–31, posted to the

4. WHICH SPEECH ACTS ARE HATEFUL?

The link between anti-Semitism and Holocaust denial, however, does not establish that a given speech act is anti-Semitic. Nor are all statements denying the Ottoman-era atrocities against the Armenians necessarily be a manifestation of anti-Armenian hatred, or all Rwandan genocide denial coded hate against the Tutsi. We return to the original dilemma: sometimes genocide denial is hateful but sometimes it is not. Some acts of deniers are laden with racism, deliberately provocative, or arise in a context that threatens or harms survivors or the target group. Other acts of denial lack this quality.

Here I agree with Paolo Lobba that genocide denial bans should require an intent to spreading racism, or harming the human dignity of a survivor or member of a racial, ethnic or religious group targeted by the act of genocide.[51] Some laws, such as Swiss genocide denial ban, do this; others, such as the Gayssot Law, do not.[52] Indeed, the Gayssot Law is so broad that it could ensnare the uneducated American college sophomore who, when asked whether the Holocaust happened, replies innocently: 'I don't think it did'.

While an improvement to the existing 'either or' approach to genocide denial, the case-by-case method cannot account for the strange overlap in which what looks like a neutral statement about an historical event, stated in modest, scientific language – the statements that Belavusau treats as historical revisionism, and the *Liberté pour l'Histoire* scholars protect in the name of defending History – are also be symbols of a hateful doctrine, or riddled with anti-Semitic premises. It is easy to accept, as a German court did in a 1994, that a speech denying the Holocaust that referred to 'problem Jewish elements' and included a joke about the gas chambers harmed the human dignity of Jews, especially given that the defendant in the case was National Democratic Party leader, Günter Deckert.[53]

Social Science Research Network, 07.10.2014, pp. 12–15. If true, my argument suggests the ironic possibility that the global regime against hate speech has spurred the development of genocide denial.

51 P. Lobba, 'Criminalizing Negationism beyond the Holocaust' 2013 <www.lph-asso.fr/index.php?option=com_content&view=article&id=184%3Acriminaliser-le-negationnisme-au-dela-de-lHolocauste&catid=53%3Aactualites&Itemid=170&lang=en> accessed 28.04.2015. Requiring intent may go too far given the difficulty of seeing into someone else's mind. It might be easier to rely on an objective standard here. See T. Hochmann, 'The Denier's Intent' in: L. Hennebel and T. Hochmann, *Genocide Denials and the Law*, Oxford University Press, Oxford 2011, pp. 279–319. As Hochmann points out, a focus on intent suggests that the denier is punished for lying, rather than for a specific harm that arises from the denial. ibid., p. 317.

52 See Swiss Penal Code Art. 264-bis (genocide denial to be punished must be done 'in a way that which undermines human dignity'; Art. 24 of the Law of the Press of 29 July 1881 (France) (prohibiting questioning of the Holocaust).

53 For an overview of the Deckert case, see R. Kahn, *Holocaust Denial and the Law: A Comparative Study*, Palgrave, New York 2004, pp. 70–77. Interestingly, the same court that had little difficulty finding Deckert guilty used the sentencing part of the ruling to express sympathy for Deckert (to whom it gave probation) for standing up to the 'wide reaching claims ... of a financial type arising out of the persecution of the Jews'. Ibid, p. 72 (quoting

But what about the statement that there were no gas chambers within the territory of the Third Reich? Or a poster that reads: 'Auschwitz, 125,000 deaths!?'[54] Are these statements hate speech, historical revisionism or something else?

The difficulty goes to the nature of speech acts – especially those that are recorded. The same poster, blog post or newspaper article will have different meanings for different audiences that encounter it. For example, in 1994 German Neo-Nazis set up a telephone answering service. If you dialled the number and pressed '88' you got a message complaining about how 'Spielberg the Jew' was 'showered with Oscar awards' for *Schindler's List*, because 'a film by Spielberg on principle obtains an Oscar'. The message characterised the film as a 'shoddy effort' directed against Nazi Germany that 'kept the Auschwitz myth alive'. However, despite 'media propaganda', only '300,000' people in Germany had seen the film, as opposed to *Otto: The Film* which had 'over three million viewers'.[55]

Because of the reference to the 'Auschwitz myth', the operators of the answering service were prosecuted under Germany's then new law banning denial or trivialisation of the Holocaust.[56] The court acquitted the defendants, holding that the term 'Auschwitz myth' had many different meanings, including some that did not trivialise the Holocaust.[57]

The decision was criticised, especially given the right-wing context in which the message was recorded. But consider the message as a whole. Suppose the message appeared not on a right wing phone service, but in the newspaper of a small city in the United States. One might then read it as a film review – albeit a harsh one. The recording's statement that 'a film by Spielberg on principle obtains an Oscar' could have been written by anyone who, in the mid-1990s, noted his success as a film director. Perhaps *Otto: The Film* was a better movie than *Schindler's List*. While the phrase 'Auschwitz myth' is a bit off-putting, an American audience might not know of that phrase's meaning in German right-wing circles. Read this way, the phone message is a poster child for the argument that bare genocide denial is not hate speech.

But the statement did not appear in Peoria, Illinois, or Knoxville, Tennessee – it was made in Hamburg, Germany. To access the message one had to type '88' (a symbol for 'Heil Hitler' both words of which start with the eighth letter of the

---

Neue Juristisiche Wochenschrift (NJW) (1994): 2494). The result was an uproar: two of the judges who wrote the opinion were forced into early retirement; the opinion was reversed on appeal. Ibid, pp. 74–77.

54 Both examples are drawn from early litigation under the Gayssot Law. See R. Kahn, *Holocaust Denial and the Law: A Comparative Study*, Palgrave, New York 2004, pp. 113–115. The statement about the absence of gas chambers in the former Third Reich violated the Gayssot Law because the uniformed reader could have imagined the statement to include Auschwitz (which was outside the boundaries of the Reich). In the second case, the trial court acquitted on the number of deaths but was reversed on appeal.

55 Ibid., p. 78 (quoting the ruling of the Hamburg Administrative Court, NJW (1995): 1038)).

56 Ibid.

57 Ibid.

alphabet). The reference to Spielberg 'the Jew' could intimidate a Jewish German citizen who stumbled across the message: Why is Spielberg's ethnicity relevant? The reference to 'media propaganda' could easily be read to mean 'Jewish' media propaganda. Finally, the use of the phrase 'Auschwitz myth' might be startling to the German Jewish listener who is aware of the phrases meaning in right wing circles. Overall, the listener who accidentally stumbles across this message may leave with the message that she should 'be afraid'.

Here lies the crux of the problem: One speech act has two possible readings – each plausible. From a legal perspective, the difficulty is surmountable. Judges, courts and legislators routinely draw lines. A genocide denial ban that covered every conceivable offense would greatly burden freedom of expression. To avoid this result, judges will draw lines – even if some hateful acts of denial remain unpunished. But as analysts of genocide denial bans, we do not have such an easy out. Moreover, in an internet age, a message originating in a small American town (say Lincoln, Nebraska)[58] might well end up being read in Hamburg or Dresden. As the post-modernists point out, this is true of all literature. But the irreducibility of a text to a single message poses a particular difficulty with genocide denial, where one of the readings can be potentially very harmful, especially when, as in the case of Holocaust denial, there is a practice of using denial of the Nazi mass murder of the Jews in the past to justify hatred of the Jews in the present.

5. ADDITIONAL HARMS OF GENOCIDE DENIAL: THREATS AND FALSITY

Harm to a survivor or target group is not the only type of harm genocide denial may cause. As noted above, genocide denial may threaten society at large by encouraging others to act out against the targets. Alternatively, denial may also pose a harm to the extent people come to believe it. This section will briefly take up each harm.

5.1. THREATS TO SOCIETY AT LARGE

Does a statement of denial cause harm if no one else hears it? Perhaps, like a tree in the forest, it doesn't. But when statements of denial are heard, they

58 Lincoln, Nebraska was the home of Gary Lauck who, in the 1972, founded the *NSDAP Aufbau- und Auslandsorganisation,* a right-wing extremist group with connections to German Neo-Nazis. On a trip to Denmark in 1995 he was arrested, extradited to Germany and sentenced to four years in prison. M. Lee, *The Beast Reawakens: Fascism's Resurgence from Hitler's Spymasters to Today's Neo-Nazi Groups and Right-Wing Extremists,* Routledge, New York 1999, p. 343.

cause harm, and not just to victim groups. The harm also falls on society, either because the act of denial encourages supporters of the previous genocidal regime to speak out, or because – more generally – it undermines the legitimacy of the post-genocide regime.

On this view, Holocaust denial threatens the legitimacy of the German and Austrian states, just as Karl Loewenstein saw Nazi uniforms, marching, and other expressive activities as threats to European democracies in the 1930s.[59] The same is true of genocide denial more generally – especially if the legitimacy of the post-genocide order is in doubt. Critical here is proof denial has acquired a symbolic meaning that undermines the state. Although line drawing would be difficult, in theory such a position is little different from the current situation in Germany which bans the swastika and the Nazi national anthem.

The key is the level of threat required. One might ban (or remove from Facebook or Twitter) statements that embolden potential perpetrators by reassuring them that 'they are not alone'. But do all acts of genocide denial have this quality? Consider in this light the debate between United States Supreme Court Justices Sandra Day O'Connor and Clarence Thomas in *Virginia v. Black* over whether cross burning by its very nature intimidates another person.[60] While Justice Thomas, writing in dissent, eloquently describes how the burning cross has only one meaning for African Americans,[61] some of the examples raised by Justice O'Connor in her majority opinion – including a cross burning at a wedding between a member of the Ku Klux Klan and the American Nazi party[62] – are hard to categorise in this way.

There is another problem. What if genocide denial is sending a slightly different message? Rather than 'you are not alone', what if the message is 'you did not do anything wrong' or, to as time passes by, 'your parents and grandparents were not guilty'. For example, during the late 1990s this sentiment arose in Germany, in response to public debates over crimes against humanity committed by Wehrmacht forces (which unsettled the comfortable stereotype that the Holocaust was solely the work of the SS). This message is unsettling; but does it pose the same type of threat of Nazi revival as a work like Ernst Zundel's, *The Hitler We Loved and Why*?[63]

---

59 See K. Loewenstein, 'Legislative Control of Political Extremism in European Democracies I' (1938) 38 *Columbia Law Review* 591; K. Loewenstein, 'Legislative Control of Political Extremism in European Democracies II' (1938) 38 *Columbia Law Review* 725.

60 538 U.S. 347 (2003). For a discussion, see R. Kahn, 'Did the Burning Cross Speak? Virginia v. Black and the Debate between Justices O'Connor and Thomas over the History of Cross Burning' in: A. Sarat (ed.), *39 Studies in Law, Politics, and Society*, 2006, pp. 75–90.

61 *Virginia v. Black*, 538 U.S. at 347, 388 (Thomas, J., dissenting).

62 Ibid., p. 356 (majority opinion).

63 Zundel wrote the book under the pseudonym Christof Friedrich. To take an American example, does denial of police violence against African Americans reflect support for that violence, or simply a wish that the entire problem would go away? The answer to this question will depend on the context of the specific speech act.

Here one might reply that, even in their milder forms, calls to be 'left alone' are themselves socially harmful. This applies to calls for Germany must 'get over' the Holocaust, and African Americans to 'get over' slavery. Replacing the past with promises of a colourblind future is quite unsatisfying given the role of mass murder, or racial oppression in the case of slavery, in creating the present. But calls to end affirmative action in the United States, or for Germany abandon its Holocaust complex, differ from explicit rehabilitation of the perpetrators themselves.

On top of that, how could one show that a particular given act of denial actually eased the guilt feelings of the perpetrators? Indeed, there are other ways to justify a status quo arising out of an unjust past besides genocide denial (or denial of slavery). For those most invested in normalisation, denial can be embarrassing, which why in the 1950s and 1960s, as the Klan revitalised itself, the strongest support for bans on Klan masks, hoods, and crosses came from conservative white elites fearful that the Klan would make white supremacy look bad.[64]

There is one context where the threat posed by Holocaust denial does appear plausible – namely in its connection to anti-Semitism. In a society that in the name of political correctness rejects explicit statements of racial superiority, or tropes about Jewish power and world domination of the sort portrayed in the *Protocols of the Elders of Zion*, Holocaust denial is a powerful symbolic alternative, one that lets anti-Semites to express their hatred of the Jews indirectly, by questioning their genocide. Here may be a context in which a society that bans hate speech might also prosecute acts of genocide denial.

5.2. GENOCIDE DENIAL AS HARMFUL FALSITY

Another potential harm from genocide denial involves falsity. In an interesting essay, Frederick Schauer challenges the conventional view that society has an interest in protecting speech acts because, the 'truth' will win out in the marketplace of ideas.[65] While others have questioned the marketplace of ideas as a means to reach the truth, or carved out exceptions for especially egregious speech acts (such as genocide denial) Schauer takes the further step of asking whether a society benefits from truth testing ideas that are most likely demonstrably false. What if certain falsehoods persist despite the proving ground of free debate? What if, for example, people still believe 'that President Obama was born in Kenya and that President Bush knew in advance about

64 For more, see R. Kahn, 'Did the Burning Cross Speak? Virginia v. Black and the Debate between Justices O'Connor and Thomas over the History of Cross Burning' in: A. Sarat (ed.), *39 Studies in Law, Politics, and Society*, 2006.

65 Schauer, 'Social Epistemology, Holocaust Denial, and the Post-Millian Calculus' in: M. Herz and P. Molnar (eds.), *The Content and Context of Hate Speech: Rethinking Regulation and Responses*, Cambridge University Press, Cambridge 2012.

the 9/11 attacks?' Under these circumstances, John Stuart Mill's normative argument from truth appears less compelling.[66]

At the core of Schauer's argument is the idea that 'unsuppressed falsity' can cause harm.[67] In academic settings, the 'dangers of unsuppressed falsity' are diminished because falsity is more likely to be quickly identified and remedied; outside the ivory towers, however, 'truth' is a less effective remedy for the suppression of false beliefs.[68] In this regard, Schauer asks whether 'Holocaust denial is simply a dramatic example of widespread resistance of popular (and sometimes academic) opinion to argument and factual demonstration'.[69] In deciding whether to tolerate the 'hate-based falsity' that is genocide denial, Schauer concludes that a society compare it to the harm posed by false statements a society restricts.[70]

Schauer's conclusion that falsity is more troublesome in popular as opposed to academic discourse has a certain logic when applied in service of a contextual approach to genocide denial. A doctoral thesis, monograph or scholarly article that denied an act of genocide, subject to the scholarly rules of peer review and academic rigour, might never see the light of day and consequentially have little if any impact on the scholarly debate over the genocide in question. For example, the pseudo-academic efforts of Armenian genocide deniers have large failed to challenge the scholarly consensus that the Armenian genocide took place.[71]

Given this, one might tolerate 'scholarly' denial while still punishing the slogans, pamphlets and other denial materials are much closer to hate speech. On one level, this is a matter of form – a scholarly press is simply unlikely to publish an article replete with racist arguments or anti-Semitic arguments.

But it is also because of substance. If Schauer is right that in 'the rarefied precincts of academic inquiry' falsehood is more quickly exposed, it is because an article or book full of falsehoods cannot get published by an academic press or a peer-reviewed journal. Either way, under Schauer's scheme denial runs a good risk of exclusion – if it is populist history, the dangers of 'unsuppressed falsity' appear to justify restriction (at least in a society that punishes false statements that harm the public); if deniers go the academic route, they will be censored by literary agents and unnamed anonymous reviewers. The process will be different, but the result the same.

---

66 Ibid., p. 140.

67 Ibid.

68 Ibid., p. 141.

69 Ibid., p. 142.

70 Ibid., p. 143.

71 On the other hand, Schauer's confidence may depend on assumptions about the neutrality of the academic community. To the extent the scholarly community is ideologically top heavy in a given direction, denial of 'unpopular' genocides may sneak through. I thank Teresa Collett for this point.

What is more, Schauer has something in common with Pierre Nora, Réne Rémond and the French historians of *Liberté pour l'Histoire*: They both put a special emphasis on academic discourse as something that needs to be protected from the marketplace of ideas. For the *Liberté* historians, history is protected from the masses who, in the name of political manipulation and ethnic solidarity, have sullied the law books with memory restrictions.[72] Likewise, Schauer argues that – in some instances – academia does a better job than the marketplace of ideas in delivering what society needs. While the French historians fear that memory laws – justified or not – will prevent historians from their professional role as 'guardians of history', Schauer expects historians (and other academics) to root out falsity.

This curious overlap between Schauer and the French historians suggests a compromise of sorts. On the one hand, defenders of history might, as part of their role, energetically root out falsity from academia. In return, memory law supporters would limit their efforts to rooting out denialist discourse in popular culture. Where genocide denial is not history but rather coded messages of hatred, historians should acknowledge this – even if, as citizens, they oppose genocide denial bans as a matter of civil liberties or because they think the laws are simply a dumb idea. In other words, opponents of genocide denial laws (and memory bans more generally) should not let their eagerness to protect history from its enemies deny the hurtful nature of many denial acts.

For their part, supporters of genocide denial bans might focus their energies on popular expression of genocide denial letting slide that rare 'sincere' denier who, for whatever reason, takes a contrary view about genocide. The sincerity of such a denier would turn on a good faith engagement of the sources demonstrating the existence of the genocidal act in question. Since this can be difficult to demonstrate, an easier solution is to limit punishment to genocide denial to those acts that threaten an identifiable victim or are used to spread coded messages of hate. As we have seen, Lobba has already taken a very similar position in an article on the *Liberté* website. So, convergence may be in the offing.

6. CONCLUSION: THE IMPORTANCE OF CONTEXT

To conclude, in at least some instances genocide denial poses tangible harms to society. It does this even when it does not directly target victims or contain the

72 For example, Françoise Chandernagor refers to 'specific groups' who, 'charged with emotion', become the 'clientele' of demagogic politicians. See F. Chandernagor, 'The Historian at the mercy of the law', available on the *Liberté pour l'Histoire* website 2008 <www.lph-asso.fr/index.php?option=com_content&view=article&id=150&Itemid=179&lang=en> accessed 28.04.2015.

racist appeals ('bare denial') traditionally associated with hate speech. Not only that, Belavusau is correct that memory laws can – in certain instances – stifle the emergence of counter-xenophobic ways of dealing with the past.[73] This is especially true of broad bans like the French Gayssot Law.

But while not every statement of genocide denial is hateful, there is something about the denial of acts of mass murder based on race, religion and ethnicity that distinguishes genocide denial from other types of historical revisionism. Denying the slaughter of the Tutsis is not the same thing as coming up with a new interpretation about why Robert E. Lee lost the battle of Gettysburg; nor is rehabilitating Herbert Hoover the same thing as rehabilitating Adolf Hitler. Even if it is not always punished, denial is not casual, garden variety historical revisionism.

So when should denial be punished (or removed from social media)? The only way forward is a context-laden approach in which legislators, judges, and scholars in the field evaluate speech acts on a case-by-case basis: Who sent the message? What type of language was used? Who was the intended audience? Only by asking these questions can we begin to sort out when genocide denial is hateful or racist.

This effort should come with a recognition of limitations. The law is imperfect and so are we. There will be hard cases, situations in which a statement of genocide denial will mean different things to different people. In these situations, one could do worse than the Hamburg Administrative Court judge who, faced with competing meanings of the phrase 'Auschwitz myth', issued an acquittal under the old maxim: *in dubio pro reo*.[74]

---

73 U. Belavusau, *Freedom of Speech: Importing European and US Constitutional Models in Transitional Democracies*, Routledge, New York 2013, p. 200.

74 See R. Kahn, *Holocaust Denial and the Law: A Comparative Study*, Palgrave, New York 2004, p. 79 (quoting NJW (1995): 1038). In *dubio pro reo* means 'in doubt for the defence'.

CHAPTER XII

ON THE BREAKING OF CONSENSUS

The Perinçek Case, the Armenian Genocide and International Criminal Law

Sévane GARIBIAN*

The 100th anniversary of the Armenian genocide is also the year of the revision by the Grand Chamber of the *Doğu Perinçek v. Switzerland* judgment rendered by the European Court of Human Rights (ECtHR) on 17 December 2013. We will focus here on one of the arguments set forth by the ECtHR in 2013, which disfavours the Swiss criminal jurisdictions in this case of genocide denial: the problematic argument of the absence of a 'general consensus' on the 1915 genocide. This contribution aims to shed light on the paradoxes and consequences of such an argument that calls, notably, for a historical perspective – and demands, in particular, that we look back on the history of international criminal law.

> '[T]hey will persist. And you won't yet have come to their real plan: they do not, in spite of what they say, intend to make history, but rather modify *irreversibly* what happens when a community consents.'[1]

---

* The author wishes to thank Philomène May for her editing work; Katia Villard, Vincent Fontana and Uladzislau Belavusau for their comments; and Jonathan Hensher for his translation. This article was originally written and published in French in a slightly shorter version ('De la rupture du consensus. L'affaire Perinçek, le génocide arménien et le droit pénal international' in *Le génocide des Arméniens. Un siècle de recherche (1915–2015)*, Armand Colin, Paris 2015, pp. 212–221). It should be noted that at the time of writing (August 2015), the Grand Chamber was yet to rule on this case. It did so on 15 October 2015. The final judgment confirms the Chamber's conclusion by a very short majority (ten votes to seven), yet abandoning the argument of the absence of a 'general consensus' on the 1915 genocide (see interview published in *Agos* on 27 October 2015: www.agos.com.tr/en/article/13158/svane-garibian-the-polarization-in-grand-chamber-is-important).

1 *'[I]ls persisteront. Et vous n'aurez pas encore atteint leur véritable projet: ce n'est pas de l'histoire qu'ils entendent faire, malgré leurs dires, mais modifier irréversiblement ce qui se passe quand une communauté consent.'* P. LORAUX, 'Consentir' (1989) 22 *Le Genre Humain* 151, 152–153.

The year which marks the centenary of the Armenian genocide is also the year which sees a legal challenge against the ruling of 17 December 2013 by the ECtHR in the case of *Doğu Perinçek v. Switzerland*.[2] In this ruling, the Court (by five votes to two) found Switzerland guilty of having violated the applicant's freedom of expression guaranteed by Article 10 ECHR. The holder of a law doctorate who 'considers himself as an historian and writer',[3] Perinçek is the Chairman of the Turkish Workers' Party (recently renamed 'Homeland Party' – *Vatan Partisi*) and the founder of the Talaat Pasha Committee, the aim of which is to rehabilitate and defend the memory of the principal instigator of the 1915 Armenian genocide – the 'Ottoman Hitler'.

Among the various arguments presented by the ECtHR in support of its overruling of the Swiss courts in this genocide denial case, one stands out as deserving particular attention here. According to the Court, the denial expressed by Doğu Perinçek when he described the Armenian genocide specifically as an 'international imperialist lie' poses no problem from the point of view of human rights, as it supposedly only denies the legal characterisation of the genocide (rather than the facts themselves): a characterisation which, in this particular case, is apparently not the subject of 'general consensus'.[4] This is in spite of the fact that the Swiss judges had reached the opposite conclusion in the very same case.[5] The ECtHR justifies this argument by declaring that 'the present case is clearly distinct from those cases which related to the denial of the crimes of the Holocaust'[6] for the following reasons: (1) 'convictions for crimes committed by the Nazi regime … had a clear basis in law, namely Article 6, subsection (c) of the Charter of the Nuremberg International Military Tribunal, set out in an annex to the London Agreement of 8 August 1945'; and (2) 'the historical facts challenged by the defendants had been judged to have been clearly established by an international jurisdiction'.[7]

After the request by the Swiss government to refer the case to the Grand Chamber was granted on 2 June 2014, the second appeal hearing took place in Strasbourg on 28 January 2015. It gave the Grand Chamber the chance to rule on genocide denial in relation to human rights law, a judgment awaited by many. Indeed, the ECtHR had previously ruled on genocide denial once

---

2 *Doğu Perinçek v. Switzerland*, no. 27510/08, ECHR 2013-II (hereafter 'Perinçek case').

3 Ibid., §112.

4 Ibid., §114.

5 Cf. the ruling of 9 March 2007 by the Lausanne Police Court, upheld on 18 June 2007 by the Court of Cassation of the Canton of Vaud. The Federal Court (the highest legal chamber in Switzerland) subsequently upheld the rulings of these lower courts in its verdict of 12 December 2007 (the most relevant extracts from which are reproduced in Perinçek case, §13).

6 Perinçek case, §117. Cf. the view of the United Nations Human Rights Committee on the case of *Robert Faurisson v. France*, 8 November 1996 (Communication no. 550/1993, doc. CCPR/C/58/D/550/1993 (1996)); and *Roger Garaudy v. France*, no. 65831/01, ECHR 2003-IV.

7 Perinçek case, §117.

before, in the famous 2003 *Roger Garaudy v. France* case,[8] but without any referral to the Grand Chamber being requested. It is important to bear in mind that in the latter case, the ECtHR considered that denial or rewriting of 'clearly established historical facts, such as the Holocaust, ... undermines the values on which the fight against racism and anti-Semitism are based and constitutes a serious threat to public order'; 'such acts are incompatible with democracy and human rights because they infringe the rights of others' and 'run counter to the fundamental values of the Convention, as expressed in its Preamble, namely justice and peace'. The Court hence excluded genocide denial from any protection by the Convention, in accordance with its Article 17 (prohibition of abuse of rights). It considered that Roger Garaudy attempted 'to deflect Article 10 of the Convention from its real purpose by using his right to freedom of expression for ends which are contrary to the text and spirit of the Convention'. It concluded that 'denying crimes against humanity is therefore one of the most serious forms of racial defamation of Jews and of incitement to hatred of them'.

Furthermore, this comprehension of genocide or other crimes against humanity denial as 'aggravated denial' – i.e. as a kind of hate speech 'directed against a group of persons or a member of such a group defined by reference to race, colour, religion, descent or national or ethnic origin'[9] likely to have harmful consequences – is predominant in Europe. Nevertheless, *denial* describes many types of expression[10] and its forms evolve constantly.[11] In any case, we do believe that denial 'does not constitute historical research', the 'real purpose being to rehabilitate [a political] regime and, as a consequence, accuse the victims themselves of falsifying history'.[12] Genocide denial is, above all, an *ideology* aiming at destroying facts and manipulating history.[13] Lastly, even though *denial* (or *denialism*) as the common translation of the French neologism *négationnisme* (initially created in 1987 by historian Henry Rousso) is, in our view, debatable,[14] such a discussion falls outside the scope of this paper. We will thus refer here to the term 'denial' as it is also the one used in the English version of the ECtHR rulings.

---

8 *Roger Garaudy v. France*, no. 65831/01, ECHR 2003-IV.

9 See Article 1 of the Council Framework Decision 2008/913/JAI of 28 November 2008 on combatting certain forms and manifestations of racism and xenophobia by means of criminal law.

10 See L. Hennebel and T. Hochmann (eds.), *Genocide Denials and the Law*, Oxford University Press, New York 2011, introduction pp. xix ff, in particular on the distinction between *bare* and *aggravated* denial.

11 Cf. I. Charny, 'A classification of denials of the Holocaust and other genocides' in: S. Totten and P.R. Bartrop (eds.), *The Genocide Studies Reader*, Routledge, New York 2009, pp. 517.

12 *Roger Garaudy v. France*, no. 65831/01, ECHR 2003-IV.

13 See also S. Garibian, 'Taking Denial Seriously: Genocide Denial and Freedom of Speech in French Law' (2008) 9(2) *Cardozo Journal of Conflict Resolution* 479, 486.

14 Notably in light of existing distinctions in French between *négation/dénégation/déni*.

Whatever one thinks of the Perinçek December 2013 ruling and its effects, the aforementioned argument of the absence of a 'general consensus' regarding the Armenian genocide is a surprising one. This contribution aims to shed light on the paradoxes and consequences of such an argument. Indeed, the latter calls notably for a historical perspective and demands, in particular, that we look back on the history of international criminal law, following some introductory remarks on the disputable presumptions contained in the analysed argument. The contribution ends with summarised conclusions.

1. INTRODUCTORY REMARKS

The ECtHR argument of an absence of consensus provides an opportunity both to clarify some important points and to consider the problem posed by the three glaring presumptions, which this argument contains.

The first presumption (and a very shaky one at that) is that a distinction exists between the denial of the characterisation of a crime as genocide and the denial of historical facts. Such a distinction is nonsensical: denying a crime's legal characterisation as genocide amounts precisely to denying the *specific intent*, which defines this crime (namely the intention to destroy the entirety or a part of a national, ethnic, racial or religious group). And denying this specific intent amounts, in this particular case, to denying the 'reality of clearly established historical facts' (quoting the *Garaudy* case).[15] The second, erroneous, presumption is that only a 'general consensus' regarding said legal characterisation as *genocide* would allow a sentence to be imposed in a denial case: neither Swiss law[16] (nor other national legal systems such as, for example, French law)[17] nor, indeed, the 2008 EU framework decision[18] on this subject

---

15 When his case came before the ECtHR, Roger Garaudy had argued, to no avail, that he did not deny the existence of the crimes of the Nazis.

16 Doğu Perinçek had been found guilty in Switzerland on the basis of Article 261*bis* of the country's Penal Code, targeting (paragraph 4) 'any person who has publicly … insulted or discriminated against, in a way which infringes on human dignity, a person or group of persons on account of their race, ethnic origin or religion, or who, for the same reason, *denies, unduly downplays, or seeks to justify a genocide or other crimes against humanity*' (emphasis added).

17 Law no. 90-615 of 13 July 1990 enabling the prosecution of all racist, anti-Semitic or xenophobic acts (known as the Gayssot Law) refers to 'crimes against humanity as defined in Article 6 of the Charter of the [Nuremberg] International Military Tribunal'.

18 Council Framework Decision 2008/913/JAI of 28 November 2008 on combatting certain forms and manifestations of racism and xenophobia by means of criminal law (which refers to crimes of genocide, crimes against humanity and war crimes, as well as 'crimes against humanity as defined in Article 6 of the Charter of the [Nuremberg] International Military Tribunal'). Cf. also the Report from the Commission to the European Parliament and the Council COM(2014) 27 final of 27 January 2014 regarding the implementation of this framework decision.

set such a stringent condition. The third presumption, which is questionable at the very least, is that only legal language, and more specifically a *judicial*, not to mention *international*, decision, would allow the existence or otherwise of a consensus regarding a historical fact to be established. This is all the more problematic given the degree to which, as we know only too well, the implementation of international justice is governed by the vagaries of politics. Such a presumption amounts to dismissing out of hand the importance of – and need for – the work of historians 'on events such as those considered here, given that', as the ECtHR informs us, 'historical research is by definition debatable and open to question, and is ill-equipped to reach definitive conclusions or establish objective and absolute truths'.[19] Fortunately, however, no serious lawyer or historian would see fit to question the existence of the genocide, as such, of the Jewish people, despite the fact that no international judgement has ever characterised the Holocaust in these exact terms.[20] Nor, indeed, is it clear why and exactly how the work of a judge would take precedence over the (quite distinct and complementary) work of the historian, or *vice versa*; nor why judicial truth, while presumed to be valid – and certainly absolute in terms of its effects – should not be relative and debatable from an epistemological point of view.

With respect to this question, I will briefly make three points, which I have had the opportunity to set out more thoroughly elsewhere.[21] Firstly, and contrary to what is often stated, it is not the role of judges to rule one way or the other over the historical facts as such in the trials of those accused of crimes against humanity or genocide (the primary aim of which is to establish the guilt or otherwise of the defendants, a process involving the application of legal characterisation)[22] or in the trials of genocide deniers (where judges rule on the methods used by deniers and their intentions, not on their opinions as such regarding the truth of the events in question). Judges may, however, use the work of historians to assist them in their own tasks, *pace* the objections raised by proponents of the relativistic theory developed out of the 'linguistic turn':[23] this

19 '*[S]ur des événements tels que ceux qui sont en cause ici, étant donné que la recherche historique est par définition controversée et discutable et ne se prête guère à des conclusions définitives ou à des vérités objectives et absolues.*' Perinçek case, §117.

20 See also the dissenting opinion expressed by Judges Vučinić and Pinto de Albuquerque (hereafter 'dissenting opinion'), §§17–18.

21 S. Garibian, 'La mémoire est-elle soluble dans le droit? Des incertitudes nées de la décision n° 2012-647 DC du Conseil constitutionnel français' (2013) 2/66 *Droit et Cultures* 25, 49.

22 Such a characterisation, while it involves an implicit acknowledgment of the facts, does not aim to establish these *per se*, but rather to evaluate 'facts in order to settle disputes which have arisen regarding them' ('*choses pour trancher les disputes nouées à leur sujet*'). Y. Thomas, 'Présentation' (2002) 6 *Annales HSS* 1425, 1426. On the 'efficient force' ('*pouvoir efficace*') of the legal characterisation of facts by the 'authentic authority' ('*l'autorité authentique*') represented by a judge, see O. Cayla, 'Ouverture: la qualification, ou la vérité du droit' (1994) 18 *Droits* 3, 3–18.

23 An intellectual current chiefly represented by the Californian historian and literary critic Hayden White, who argues that history is fiction, and that no defined limit separates the

is how law apprehends historical fact, which forms the basis of its treatment of a past event with respect to its consequences in the present. Accordingly, we have seen the mass crimes of 1915 form the subject of various practices of judicial 'recognition'.[24] On the one hand are those which appeared in the context of the trials conducted in Turkey from 1919 onwards[25] or of the Tehlirian trial (for the killing of Talaat Pacha) in 1921 in Berlin,[26] and, more recently, those which have arisen from trials for genocide denial, particularly in Europe.[27] On the other are those which have been produced by 'alternative', *sui generis* judicial mechanisms that have had to fill the vacuum left by the absence of any international criminal tribunal due to the stubborn facts of *Realpolitik*, amnesty and the death of the perpetrators: one could cite such examples as the ruling passed by the Permanent Peoples' Tribunal in April 1984,[28] or that pronounced by a federal judge on 1 April 2011 in the context of a 'trial for the truth' (*juicio por la verdad*) in Argentina (the Hairabedian case).[29] Lastly, an analysis of both the ECtHR case law related to freedom of expression and the text of the EU framework decision mentioned above confirm that the force of *res judicata*[30] (i.e. the pre-existence of a judicial decision attesting the criminal fact) is not a precondition for the prosecution of genocide deniers: the former insofar as it does not predicate the recognition of 'clearly established historical facts' upon the existence of a legal ruling;[31] the latter insofar as, according to Article 1(4) of its text, it allows states, if they so wish, to restrict the scope of indictments for denial 'to crimes which have been established by a final decision of a national court of [the] Member State and/or an international court' – showing that, far from being a necessary precondition, this is rather an option left to the discretion of sovereign states.

two disciplines, thus reducing the study of history to a linguistic study lacking any objective character (H. White, *Metahistory: the Historical Imagination in Nineteenth-Century Europe*, Johns Hopkins University Press, Baltimore-London 1973). His main critic is the Italian historian Carlo Ginzburg, to whom a special issue of the journal *Critique* (n° 769–770, 2011) has recently been devoted, returning in particular to the key issues of the famous White/Ginzburg controversy.

24 For a summary of international political and legal recognition of the genocide, see dissenting opinion, §§8–10.

25 See dissenting opinion, §9 and below notes 47 and 51.

26 See dissenting opinion, §9. On the trial, see below note 58.

27 Cf. dissenting opinion, §9 and S. Garibian, 'La mémoire est-elle soluble dans le droit? Des incertitudes nées de la décision n° 2012-647 DC du Conseil constitutionnel français' (2013) 2/66 *Droit et Cultures* 25, 49–50.

28 An opinion tribunal established 24 June 1979 in Bologna. Its judgment relating to the Armenian genocide was published following its 11th session, held at the Sorbonne (Paris) between 13 and 16 April 1984.

29 On the Argentine 'trials for the truth' and the Hairabedian case, see S. Garibian, 'Ghosts Also Die. Resisting Disappearance Through the 'Right to the Truth' and the *Juicios por la verdad* in Argentina' (2014) 12(3) *Journal of International Criminal Justice* 515, 515–538.

30 Which implies the presumption that 'the thing judged is taken to be the truth' (*Res judicata pro veritate habetur*).

31 Cf. the case of *Lehideux and Isorni v. France*, no. 24662/94, ECHR 1998 (the European Court was in this instance referring to the Holocaust).

However one looks at it, it is history and the *archives* which reveal the reasons behind and the judicial-political context of the successful creation in 1945 of the International Military Tribunal (IMT) in Nuremberg, and of its legal authority, both of which are referred to by the European judges in their 2013 ruling in order to explain, by means of a counter-example, exactly *why* consensus exists regarding the crimes of the Nazis (in contrast to the crimes of the Ottomans). It is precisely this history of international criminal law that allows us to understand the legacy of the Armenian Question, its treatment following the First World War and its role in the difficult elaboration of a new form of international justice, which would, a quarter of a century later, revolutionise traditional concepts of law and the state.

The argument that there is no 'general consensus' regarding the 1915 genocide, and the use of this argument by the judges of the ECtHR, make it necessary to adopt a historical perspective on this question in the light of two important facts.[32] Firstly, the mass crimes, deportations and exterminations committed by the Ottoman Empire against its Armenian population were the original reason for the creation and definition of the concept of crime against humanity and subsequently, in conjunction with the persecution of the Jewish people, for that of the crime of genocide. Secondly, these historical facts are at the heart of the first, abortive attempt to set up an international tribunal for the prosecution of the mass violations in question, before this became a reality in 1945.

2. A 'CLEAR BASIS IN LAW': REVISITING THE ORIGINS OF THE NUREMBERG STATUTE

While the world's attention was focused on the First World War, the Young Turk government was implementing its radical plan for the 'Turkification' of the Ottoman Empire through the systematic deportation and extermination of Turkey's Armenian population. On 24 May 1915, France, Great Britain and Russia issued a warning in the form of a Joint Statement. Their condemnation was unambiguous:

> 'In view of those *new crimes of Turkey against humanity and civilisation*, the Allied Governments announce publicly to the Sublime Porte that they will hold personally

[32] The overview which follows is developed in greater detail in the opening chapter of S. Garibian, *Le concept de crime contre l'humanité au regard des principes fondateurs de l'Etat moderne. Naissance et consécration d'un concept*, Schulthess-LGDJ-Bruylant, Geneva-Paris-Brussels 2009. See also S. Garibian, 'From the 1915 Allied Joint Declaration to the 1920 Treaty of Sèvres: Back to an International Criminal Law in Progress' (2010) 52(1–2) *Armenian Review* 86, 86–103. Some of the points raised in this section are also referred to in the dissenting opinion (§§6–7).

responsible for these crimes all the members of the Ottoman Government and those of their agents who are implicated in such massacres'.[33]

This was a highly significant event: it was the first time that the concept of *crimes against humanity* had appeared at an international level – recent international criminal tribunals have acknowledged this in their rulings.[34] Although the Allies' condemnation was political in nature, it was nevertheless revolutionary insofar as, for the first time, acts by a government targeting its own citizens, independently of the wartime context, were described as 'crimes against humanity and civilisation', thus also raising the question of its criminal responsibility.

Concrete attempts to prosecute the Turkish leadership would be made a few years later in Paris, during the Paris Peace Conference organised following the Great War. As part of the conference, which began on 18 January 1919, the group known as the Commission of Fifteen, led by the American Secretary of State Robert Lansing, had the job of examining individuals' responsibility for breaches of the laws and customs of war. Alongside its work in preparation for the trials of German war criminals, it envisaged prosecuting Turkish officials for 'crimes against the laws of humanity' committed against the Armenian population of the Ottoman Empire outside the scope of the international armed conflict.[35] In a report dated 5 March 1919, the Commission specified the breaches in question: systematic terrorism, murders and massacres, violations of the honour of women, confiscation of private property, looting, confiscations of property belonging to communities or educational and charitable institutions, wanton destruction of public or private property, deportation and forced labour, executions of civilians on false allegations of war crimes and violations against civilian and military personnel.[36] Contained in this list are the fundamental underpinnings of the legal definition of a crime against humanity as set out in Article 6(c) of the Charter of the Nuremberg IMT of 8 August 1945.

It must be noted here that the Charter of the Nuremberg Tribunal, and consequently its judgements, contain no reference to the crime of *genocide*, a

---

33 *'En présence de ces nouveaux crimes de la Turquie contre l'humanité et la civilisation, les Gouvernements alliés font savoir publiquement à la Sublime Porte qu'ils tiendront personnellement responsables desdits crimes tous les membres du Gouvernement ottoman ainsi que ceux de ses agents qui se trouveraient impliqués dans de pareils massacres'.* Note from the French Ministry of Foreign Affairs to the Havas news agency, 24 May 1915: Archives du Ministère des Affaires étrangères, Guerre 1914–1918, *Turquie*, tome 887, folio 127; reproduced in A. Beylerian, *Les grandes Puissances, l'Empire ottoman et les Arméniens dans les archives françaises (1914–1918)*, Publications de la Sorbonne, Paris 1983, p. 29.

34 See in particular the judgement *Dusko Tadic*, IT-94-1, §618, ICTY, Trial Chamber II, 1997; also the Judgement *Jean-Paul Akayesu*, ICTR-96-4, §565, ICTR, Trial Chamber I, 1998.

35 Here, again, the rulings of the ICTs contain explicit references to the work carried out in 1919. See the judgements cited *supra* from the ICTY (§663) and the ICTR (§565).

36 V. Dadrian, *Histoire du génocide arménien* (trans. Marc Nichanian), Stock, Paris 1996, p. 483.

concept that did had yet to be formulated in legal terms at this time.[37] The latter expression had, it is true, been coined in 1944 by Raphael Lemkin[38] in order to designate policies of extermination such as those carried against the Armenians and the Jews, as its creator himself confirmed in an interview given to CBS in 1949,[39] as well as in his recently published autobiography.[40] But it would be four years before the legal theorist would manage to convince the General Assembly of the United Nations to adopt the Convention on the Prevention and Punishment of the Crime of Genocide on 9 December 1948, on the eve of the adoption of the Universal Declaration of Human Rights, thus laying down the first legal definition of the crime in question.[41] This explains why there are no international judgements referring to the 'genocide' of the Jewish people, as the IMT of 1945 was the only international criminal jurisdiction with the authority to rule on the crimes of the Nazis, by means of a retroactive application of the new Nuremberg Statute drawn up by the Allies.[42]

The fact remains, though, that the debates held during the 1919 Peace Conference in general, and the final report of the Commission of Fifteen dated 29 March 1919 in particular,[43] laid the foundations for the necessary preliminaries to the Nuremberg tribunal and paved the way for an approach based on three main legal innovations: the conceptual distinction between war crimes ('grave offences against the laws and customs of war' in the context of an international armed conflict) and crimes against humanity ('grave offences against the laws of humanity' committed independently of a situation of war); the principle of the individual criminal responsibility of agents of states for such crimes; and the recognition of the need for judicial intervention in

---

37 It should be noted that the word 'genocide' appears, albeit rather covertly, in the List of Charges from 18 October 1945 under Charge no. 3 relating to *war crimes* (*Trial of the Major war Criminals before the International Military Tribunal 14 November 1945–1 October 1946*, vol. I, International Military Tribunal, Nuremberg 1947, p. 46). It would also be used by the British prosecutor Sir Hartley Shawcross in his summing-up (*supra*, vol. XIX, pp. 518 and 521).

38 R. Lemkin, *Axis Rule in Occupied Europe. Laws of Occupation, Analysis of Government, Proposals for Redress*, Carnegie Endowment for International Peace, Washington 1944, pp. 79–95.

39 The dissenting opinion also refers to this (§29). A short extract from the interview is accessible at: <http://youtu.be/dzAexRmeZFs> accessed 11.11.2014.

40 D.-L. Frieze, *Totally Unofficial. The Autobiography of Raphael Lemkin*, Yale University Press, New Haven-London 2013.

41 Cf. Article 2 of the Convention of 1948. On Lemkin's role in having this Convention accepted, see T. Elder, 'What you see before your eyes: documenting Raphael Lemkin's life by exploring his archival Papers, 1900–1959' (2005) *Journal of Genocide Research* 469, 480 ff.

42 On the issues raised by this retroactive application of these laws and the consequences of the use of the concept of crimes against humanity in the judgements of the IMT, see S. Garibian, *Le concept de crime contre l'humanité au regard des principes fondateurs de l'Etat moderne. Naissance et consécration d'un concept*, Schulthess-LGDJ-Bruylant, Geneva-Paris-Brussels 2009, pp. 133 ff.

43 *Violation of the Laws and Customs of War* (Reports of Majority and Dissenting Reports of American and Japanese Members of the Commission of Responsibilities), Conference of Paris, Carnegie Endowment for International Peace, Washington DC 1919, p. 19.

order to prosecute and judge the accused. The diplomatic conference held on 20 October 1943 at the Foreign Office in London would put the finishing touches to the official formation of the United Nations Commission for War Crimes first announced in 1942 by the United States and Great Britain. This would be something of a 're-run' of the 1919 Commission of Fifteen, whose conclusions it would reprise – with the important difference that the political context was now favourable to the concrete implementation of the innovative ideas produced in the aftermath of the Great War. The most spectacular shift occurred in the position of the American government, which in 1943 executed a 'U-turn'[44] with respect to the reticent attitude it had shown in 1919: this time the Americans were determined to set up an international criminal tribunal, even though the strictly legal obstacles were identical to those encountered a quarter of a century earlier in Paris.[45]

Yet the 1920s had already seen an important change in the general climate, in particular with the work of the League of Nations and the emergence of the idea of a new legal world order in order to protect human rights. And all this had occurred following the first, abortive, attempt to establish an international tribunal for the prosecution and judgement of those responsible for the 'massacres' of the Armenians.

3. 'FACTS ... CLEARLY ESTABLISHED BY AN INTERNATIONAL COURT': AN OVERVIEW OF THE FIRST ATTEMPT AT INTERNATIONAL PROSECUTION

Before the work of the Peace Conference had even begun, the Allies had, in order to avoid intervening directly through judicial action against the Turkish leadership (owing amongst other reasons to a lack of appropriate legal

44 T. Taylor, *Procureur à Nuremberg* (trans. Marie-France De Paloméra), Seuil, Paris 1995, p. 45.

45 Some ascribe this shift in position to a feeling on the part of the Americans that their refusal to join the League of Nations and take firm measures against German aggression had helped cause the catastrophe of the Second World War (see, for example J.F. Willis, *Prologue to Nuremberg. The Politics and Diplomacy of Punishing War Criminals of the First World War*, Greenwood Press, Connecticut 1982, p. 174). The active role played by Lemkin in bringing about this new sense of responsibility in the United States following his arrival in America in April 1941 is to be noted. See S. Power, *'A Problem from Hell'. America and the Age of Genocide*, Harper Perennial, New York 2003, pp. 26 ff. On his contribution to the debate surrounding legal doctrine on these issues, see D.M. Segesser and M. Gessler, 'Raphael Lemkin and the international debate on the punishment of war crimes (1919–1948)' (2005) *Journal of Genocide Research* 453, 453–468.

instruments),[46] suggested that Turkey should set up an 'extraordinary national tribunal' with the objective of prosecuting those responsible for the 'crimes against humanity and civilisation' denounced in May 1915. A court martial was duly set up in Constantinople in order to judge the Turkish cabinet and the leadership of the *Ittihad ve Tiraki* (the Union and Progress Committee, or Young Turk party, which held power in the Ottoman Empire during the First World War).[47] Its stated aim was to judge crimes which had 'revolted all humanity',[48] were 'of a nature that would forever cause the conscience of humankind to quiver with horror'[49] and were contrary to the 'rules of law and of humanity'.[50] The chief culprits (including Talaat Pacha) were sentenced to death *in absentia*, while lower-ranking *Ittihadists* were given prison sentences of 15 years with hard labour, and some former ministers were acquitted. The archives from these trials contain an extraordinary wealth of documentation, bringing together evidence both of the intention to exterminate the whole of the Armenian population and of the concerted plan drawn up to this end by the Young Turk government.[51] On 13 January 1921, the newly-formed Kemalist regime abolished all the courts martial and passed their jurisdiction over to regular military tribunals. In the meantime, most of the criminals had already fled or been released. Yet, as much as they illustrate the limitations of a system of national justice hastily drawn up in a period of political transition, with the clear aim of obtaining more favourable treatment from the Allies at the Paris Peace Conference,[52] these trials are nonetheless of undeniable historical and legal importance.

By taking the mass crimes committed against the Armenians into account in its definitive report of 29 March 1919, the Commission of Fifteen would facilitate

46 The treaties authorising the European powers to intervene in the Ottoman Empire *in the cause of humanity* had, from 1914 onwards, been annulled by Turkey. See V. Dadrian, *Autopsie du génocide arménien* (trans. Marc and Mikaël Nichanian), Complexe, Paris 1995, pp. 67–68.

47 Parallel trials were also set up to judge lower-ranking defendants, in particular in Yozgat, Trebizonde and Kharpert (see V. Dadrian, *Autopsie du génocide arménien* (trans. Marc and Mikaël Nichanian), Complexe, Paris 1995, pp. 132 ff and R. Kévorkian, 'La Turquie face à ses responsabilités. Le procès des criminels Jeunes-Turcs (1918–1920)' (2003) 177–178 *Revue d'histoire de la Shoah* 166, 195 ff).

48 Statement by the new Grand Vizier Damat Ferid, sworn enemy of the *Ittihad*, reproduced in V. Dadrian, *Autopsie du génocide arménien* (trans. Marc and Mikaël Nichanian), Complexe, Paris 1995, p. 127.

49 Note from Grand Vizier Damat Ferid dated 17 June 1919 addressed to the Paris Conference (A. Mandelstam, *La Société des Nations et les Puissances devant le problème arménien*, 2nd ed., Edition des Universitaires Arméniens, Lebanon 1970 (1926), p. 23).

50 Statement by a Turkish deputy during preliminary enquiries and investigations prior to the trials (V. Dadrian, *Autopsie du génocide arménien* (trans. Marc and Mikaël Nichanian), Complexe, Paris 1995, p. 113).

51 See V. Dadrian and T. Akcam, *Judgment at Istanbul. The Armenian Genocide Trials*, Berghahn Books, New York and Oxford 2011.

52 In a political/media context favourable to the prosecution of Young Turk officials – all of whom were discredited at this time.

the subsequent insertion of several articles into the Treaty of Sèvres of 10 August 1920 calling for the prosecution of Turkish officials by an *international tribunal*. The legal implications of the Treaty of Sèvres, which was imposed by Article 22 of the Covenant of the League of Nations of 28 June 1919, were considerable in a number of respects.[53] Firstly, it declared all conversions of non-Muslim Ottoman subjects to Islam void 'in view of the terrorist regime which has existed in Turkey since November 1, 1914', and demanded the 'delivrance of all persons … who have disappeared, been carried off, interned or placed' since that date, '[i]n order to repair so far as possible the wrongs inflicted on individuals in the course of the massacres perpetrated … during the war' (Article 142). Secondly, it required the restoration of 'any movable or immovable property' to 'Turkish subjects of non-Turkish race' who had survived the 'massacres', and demanded that they be allowed to return to their homes (Article 144). More specifically, the Treaty of Sèvres required the Ottoman government to 'hand over to the Allied Powers the persons whose surrender may be required by the latter as being responsible for the massacres committed during the continuance of the state of war on territory which formed part of the Turkish Empire on August 1, 1914', adding that the Allied Powers 'reserve to themselves the right to designate the tribunal which shall try the persons so accused, and the Turkish Government undertakes to recognise such tribunal'. The tribunal in question could, it was stated, be the one created by the League of Nations if this was done in sufficient time (Article 230). This was a first in international law.

None of the provisions relating to the Armenian Question in general, and the 'massacres' perpetrated in the Ottoman Empire in particular, would be included in the Treaty of Lausanne, signed between Kemalist Turkey and the Allies on 24 July 1923.[54] This new Treaty rendered the Treaty of Sèvres null and void for reasons of international *Realpolitik*, in a climate of growing tension between the French, Italians and British caused by the support given by the first two of these powers to the new national policy in Turkey from 1920 onwards.[55] The resulting *tabula rasa*, which in many ways represented the 'official' launch of the Turkish state's policy of denial, was made all the more complete by the fact that this international agreement began with the statement that the 'relations [between the signatories] must be based on respect for the independence and sovereignty of States', and ended with an annex containing a declaration granting amnesty

53 For the full (French) text of the Treaty of Sèvres, see H. Triepel, *Nouveau Recueil général de Traités* (continuation of the *Grand Recueil* by G.F. de Martens), series III, vol. XII, Librairie Theodor Weicher, Leipzig 1923, pp. 664 ff.

54 For the full (French) text of the Treaty of Lausanne, see H. Triepel, *Nouveau Recueil général de Traités* (continuation of the *Grand Recueil* by G.F. de Martens), series III, vol. XIII, Librairie Theodor Weicher, Leipzig 1924, pp. 342 ff.

55 V. Dadrian, *Autopsie du génocide arménien* (trans. Marc and Mikaël Nichanian), Complexe, Paris 1995, p. 140.

to the Turkish leadership for all crimes committed between 1914 and 1922.[56] It is crucial, then, not to lose sight of the reasons behind the failure to establish the international tribunal as initially envisaged, and of the direct link between this infliction of impunity and the scale of the 'industry of denial'[57] – the only one of its kind – that has been organised ever since by the Turkish state.

It is also interesting to place this radical removal of the Armenian Question from the international scene in the otherwise extremely active context of the 1920s. At the international level, on the one hand, this decade saw the flourishing of a doctrine centred on the construction of a system of international criminal law and universal human rights law, with its basis in a new world order whose primary constituents were no longer states, but rather the 'international community'. At the national level, too, it witnessed the highly publicised trial of Soghomon Tehlirian, a survivor of the genocide of the Armenians, for the assassination of Talaat Pasha (who, having been condemned to death *in absentia* at the Constantinople trials, had fled to Germany) and his subsequent acquittal by the German Court of Assizes on 3 June 1921.[58] At each of these levels emerged two famous legal minds whose thinking, later to prove decisive in the development of international human rights law and international criminal law, was deeply affected by the realisation of the impunity that would henceforth characterise the genocide of the Armenians.

The first was André Mandelstam, a passionate supporter of the League of Nations and from 1921 onwards a permanent member of the *Institut de droit international* (International Law Institute, or ILI) where he coordinated the activities of the *Commission de la protection internationale des droits de l'homme, du citoyen et des minorités* (International Commission for the Protection of Human Rights, the Rights of Citizens and of Minorities). He drew directly on the Armenian Question in several of his works as a means of enriching his thinking on the fundamental rights of the human individual at the most universal level.[59] He had already, in his 1917 book *Le sort de l'Empire ottoman* ('The Fate of the

56 It should be noted that the validity of amnesties for the most serious international crimes (crimes not subject to a statute of limitations) has now been brought into question in international law, as the two dissenting judges point out (dissenting opinion, §7).

57 To use an expression coined by the historian Taner Akcam. See T. Akcam, *Un acte honteux: le génocide arménien et la question de la responsabilité turque* (trans. Odile Demange), Denoël, Paris 2008.

58 For more details on this unusual trial, the archives and testimony that it brought to light in Europe, and the role of *independent third party* played by the German judicial authorities, which unwittingly became a *secondary witness* to the genocide, see S. Garibian, '"Ordonné par le cadavre de ma mère". Talaat Pacha, ou l'assassinat vengeur d'un condamné à mort' in: S. Garibian (ed.), *La mort du bourreau. Réflexions interdisciplinaires sur le cadavre des criminels de masse*, Pétra, Paris forthcoming 2016.

59 A full description of the main aspects of his thinking is given in A. Mandelstam, 'La protection internationale des droits de l'homme' (1931) *Recueil des cours de l'Académie de droit international* 125, 129–229.

Ottoman Empire'),[60] denounced the 'crimes of treason against humanity'[61] of which the Armenians had been the victims, arguing that these acts ought to be sanctioned by a universal humanitarian law which would place them outside the arbitrary purview of nation states.[62] He later proposed the drafting of a universal convention for the protection of human rights and the rights of the citizen which would, after various setbacks, eventually result in the adoption by the ILI on 12 October 1929 of the *Déclaration des droits internationaux de l'homme* (Declaration of the International Human Rights). The second of these jurists was Raphael Lemkin. While the vast majority of the press hailed Tehlirian's acquittal as an 'act of justice bringing honour upon the new Germany',[63] the young Lemkin, born in Belarus but at that time a student at the University of Lwów, was struck by these events: 'why is the killing of a million a lesser crime than the killing of an individual?',[64] wrote the man who would become the father of the concept of genocide and an advisor to Robert H. Jackson, the American prosecutor at Nuremberg. Left deeply affected by this case[65] that, on its own, encapsulated the key problem with which legal doctrine was struggling at this time, and tormented by the question of impunity, he embarked upon a study of state crimes and their international prosecution; a study that would be provided with grim new 'material' by a policy of extermination that was far closer to home, and more pressing – that pursued by Nazi Germany.

4. CONCLUSION

While the Armenian Question and the international prosecution of the mass crimes committed by the Ottoman Empire disappeared from the political agenda with the signing of the Treaty of Lausanne, the legal attempts made to deal with them in the aftermath of the First World War were, and remain, crucial to a better understanding of the genealogy of the concepts of crimes against humanity and genocide – and, more generally, of the birth of international criminal justice.

---

60 A. Mandelstam, *Le sort de l'Empire ottoman*, Payot, Paris 1917.

61 *'[C]rimes de lèse-humanité'.*

62 See the study by D. Kévonian, 'Exilés politiques et avènement du "droit humain": la pensée juridique d'André Mandelstam' (1869–1949)' (2003) 177–178 *Revue d'histoire de la Shoah* 245, particularly 259 ff for more on this point.

63 '[U]n acte de justice honorant la nouvelle Allemagne'. *Justicier du génocide arménien. Le procès de Tehlirian*, Editions Diasporas, Paris 1981, pp. 21.

64 D.-L. Frieze, *Totally Unofficial. The Autobiography of Raphael Lemkin*, Yale University Press, New Haven-London 2013, p. 19.

65 On Lemkin and the Tehlirian case, see. Power, *'A Problem from Hell'. America and the Age of Genocide*, Harper Perennial, New York 2003, pp. 17 ff; S.L. Jacobs, 'Raphael Lemkin and the Armenian Genocide' in: R. Hovannisian (ed.), *Looking Backward, Looking Forward: Confronting the Armenian Genocide*, Transaction Publishers, New Brunswick 2003, pp. 125–135; T. Elder, 'What you see before your eyes: documenting Raphael Lemkin's life by exploring his archival Papers, 1900–1959' (2005) *Journal of Genocide Research* 469.

It is surprising, then, that not only the historical facts themselves, but also their legacy in the gradual construction of a system of international criminal law *in progress* have both been declared the subject of a lack of 'general consensus', when they in fact constitute a documented reality, a *stock* forming the germ of the legal concepts created to take this reality into account.

The paradox underpinning the argument that there is an absence of consensus over the genocide of 1915, as discussed earlier, thus becomes clear. And it itself serves to mask another, doubly problematic paradox. For, by adopting this line of argument, the European judges are unwittingly echoing the well-known *demand for proof* so characteristic of denialist rhetoric, thus flying in the face of sound existing historical research in constant development.[66] They fall instead into the aporia in which we find ourselves locked by the essential underlying argument, indefensible on several counts, based on the absence of the force of *res judicata* (i.e. based on the absence of a judicial international decision establishing the genocide, in other words based on impunity) – a familiar argument, to which the French Constitutional Council had already given succour in 2012.[67] Yet this same impunity should be seen as a further reason to take a serious view of genocide denial – which impunity assists by providing it with a solid footing – rather than being used as a means of justifying negationism. The European Court is, furthermore, contributing to the *competitive victimhood* which so often feeds – or is fed by – denialist discourse: for they have established a double standard[68] (Holocaust/Armenian genocide), an inequality that Swiss law avoids by recognising no hierarchy either between different genocides, or between genocides and crimes against humanity. It is rather surprising that the application of a Swiss anti-racism measure aimed at preventing discrimination and incitement to hatred a law, in other words, which expresses solidarity between human beings and is the basis of the very principle of their equality – should give rise to a judgment by the ECtHR which carries such an inequality. An inequality of treatment that ought, at least, to be subjected to close scrutiny.

To sum up, then, the argument based on the lack of 'general consensus' regarding the Armenian genocide runs counter to the spirit of the European Convention on Human Rights (1950) which was drawn up following the ravages of the Second World War: it marks a victory for negationist ideology. This ideology of the 'specialists of the interruption of consent' ('people ... – as says French philosopher Patrice Loraux – whose aim is to make you ashamed

66 Valeria Thus argues that the ECtHR embodies a new form of denial: V. Thus, 'Armenian Genocide: Perinçek case. Does the European Court of Human Rights embody a new form of denial based on trivialisation?', *Journal of Armenian Genocide Studies*, forthcoming.

67 See S. Garibian, 'La mémoire est-elle soluble dans le droit? Des incertitudes nées de la décision n° 2012-647 DC du Conseil constitutionnel français' (2013) 2/66 *Droit et Cultures* 25, 46.

68 See dissenting opinion, §22.

for having acquiesced too soon, without having demanded further proof')[69] disrupts democratic consensus through its manipulative U-turns and the distortion of facts that it creates. For consent, explains Loraux in his strong analysis of genocide denial, is the act by which 'one stops the *hyperbolic* motion of the demand for proof at the threshold of what we perceive through our "sensus communis"'.[70] By taking this point of view, and whatever might happen in the future, we can better grasp the importance of the referral of the Perinçek case to the Grand Chamber of the ECtHR by the Swiss government: a powerful rejection of the idea that the negationist project is irreversible.

---

69 *'[S]pécialistes de l'interruption du consentement', 'des gens ... dont l'intérêt est de vous faire honte pour avoir trop tôt acquiescé sans avoir demandé un supplément de preuve.'* P. Loraux, 'Consentir' (1989) 22 *Le Genre Humain* 151, 155.

70 *'[O]n arrête le mouvement hyperbolique de la demande de preuve au seuil de l'expérience des "sensibles communs".'* P. Loraux, 'Consentir' (1989) 22 *Le Genre Humain* 151, 156. The author derives the notion of '*sensus communis*' from Aristotle.

PART III

(INTER)NATIONAL ORGANISATIONS

CHAPTER XIII

DENIAL OF GENOCIDE BY BYSTANDERS IN INTERNATIONAL POLITICS

Fred GRÜNFELD

1. INTRODUCTION

What is the role of bystanders on denialism in situations of gross human rights violations? Not the denials of the perpetrator as the usual approach but the role of denials by the bystanders will be addressed in this chapter. It is, in particular, the bystander who can play a crucial role in allowing to continue the perpetrator with these crimes but it is also the bystander that has the ability to prevent, stop or end the atrocities of the perpetrators towards the victims. When the gross human rights violations are very severe the repression makes opposition and resistance from the direct targeted victims in that society almost impossible.

Denying of the gross human rights violations by the bystanders precludes any action to prevent or stop the atrocities and makes for the rescue of the victims by any third party impossible. The bystander matters and the external international bystanders matter very much.

The theoretical elaboration by Irene Bruna Seu in this volume is my reference.[1] What she has described for the individual and group level of analysis will here be applied to actors at the international level. Her study focuses on knowledge and action and she has put forward the question of how much people know about human rights violations and what they do in response to that knowledge. I replace 'people' with 'international bystanders'. The questions in my research were who received what messages at what time, to whom the messages were forwarded, and which (non-)decisions were taken in response to the alarming reports on atrocities. The focus is on the knowledge and action of the international bystanders as the important decision makers in situations

1 I. BRUNA SEU, 'Denial and Acknowledgement in Public Responses to Information about Human Rights Violations', in this volume.

of genocide. The use of denial as a defence mechanism to turn away from the events by international bystanders with disastrous consequences in situations of genocide will be demonstrated from our studies on Rwanda (1994), Srebrenica (1995) and Darfur (since 2003).[2]

We will elaborate the crucial role of bystanders at different levels of analysis in the second section. The role of the UN – as the worldwide international bystander making use of the mechanism of denialism for failing to act or taking limited action – is put forward in section 3. In sections 4 and 5 I will make use of the theoretical approach of Irene Bruna Seu in this book. The groundwork of this approach was made by Stanley Cohen in his extraordinary, revealing studies that have opened new broad interdisciplinary horizons in this field of research.[3] The more comprehensive concept of denialism as introduced by Stanley Cohen will be used and illustrated with a very clear recent example in section 5 of the decision making in the Security Council of the United Nations in summer 2015, denying the genocide in Srebrenica that occurred twenty years previously.

The acting and non-acting of bystanders at state and international level is studied by analysing the decision-making process. When the information on the atrocities was available to the bystanders, the question is why they preferred to be passive onlookers, keeping silent instead of speaking out and acting in employing the available instruments? The explanation was often that there was a lack of political will to act. In this chapter, however, I will assert that denialism was at work in an open or hidden form to circumvent their responsibility. Knowledge and action as the central focus in the studies of Stanley Cohen and Irene Bruna Seu is applied here again and we will demonstrate that denying and distorting the information (knowledge) and not bringing the available information to the attention of the highest decision makers (i.e. Security Council members) made inaction possible. My conclusion will be that deliberately denying the knowledge about impending genocide led to inaction in the three cases of genocide whereas acting against genocide was required.

In section 6 we observe that situations of genocide are deliberately not labelled as such. In section 7 the misinterpretation because of the socio-psychological prism will be shown, as happened with bystanders during the Shoah but also in Rwanda, Srebrenica and Darfur. Believing the unbelievable and accommodating the previously held views prohibits a shift of perception which is needed to act against the atrocities in the world. At the end of this chapter we will draw conclusions on the pattern of denialism by state and international bystanders in the investigated situations of gross human rights violations.

---

2 F. Grünfeld and W.N. Vermeulen in cooperation with J. Krommendijk, *Failure to Prevent Gross Human Rights Violations in Darfur, Warnings to and Responses by International Decision Makers (2003–2005),* Brill-Nijhoff, Leiden-Boston 2014, in particular chapter 3 case studies, pp. 31–49 and chapter 11 conclusions 218–231.

3 S. Cohen, *States of Denial. Knowing about Atrocities and Suffering,* Polity Press, Cambridge 2001.

2. BYSTANDERS AT NATIONAL AND INTERNATIONAL LEVEL

In all atrocities there are perpetrators and victims. A third group of actors, being neither the perpetrators nor the victims, are the bystanders. The level of analysis of all these actors in international relations and genocide studies can be divided into the following: (1) individual level, (2) societal or sub-national level, (3) national or state level, and (4) international or global level.[4] The targeted victims are defined, isolated, persecuted and killed. Actors may change roles during the period of atrocities or in other situations. For instance, abducted child soldiers (being victims) are often compelled to commit atrocities and crimes against others (acting as perpetrators). Apart from these two roles of actors there is the third party. The third party is not directly involved in or affected by the atrocities but can make a choice for the perpetrators (the so-called collaborators) or for the victims (the so-called rescuers). However, they can also prefer not to take the side of one of the two parties in non-acting, watching and passing by. This role is often erroneously seen as impartial and neutral.

In my view this indifferent onlooker is the bystander who facilitates the perpetrator to continue to commit atrocities; in short in being informed about the atrocities or genocide and not trying to intervene, then the bystander is no longer neutral but is complicit.

This complicity at state level has been mentioned by the International Court of Justice in the genocide case of *Bosnia-Herzegovina v. Serbia Montenegro*: 'responsibility is incurred if the state manifestly failed to take all measures to prevent genocide which were within its power, and which might have contributed to preventing the genocide, a state's obligation to prevent, and the corresponding duty to act, arise at the instant that the state learns of, or should normally have learned of, the existence of a serious risk that genocide will be committed'.[5]

The knowledge of the atrocities will be elaborated in section 4 but we can now already assert that modern information technology means it is no longer possible to use ignorance as a defence for inaction at state and international levels.[6] States and international organisations are nowadays fully aware of atrocities elsewhere in the world. In my research all decision makers at state and international level affirmed that they were not only aware of the genocide right from the start but also received the warnings before about the impending genocide. This means

4 A. Smeulers and F. Grúnfeld, *International Crimes and other Gross Human Rights Violations. A Multi- and Interdisciplinary Textbook*, Nijhoff, Leiden-Boston 2011, pp. 331–356.

5 International Court of Justice of 27 February 2007, *Bosnia and Herzegovina v. Serbia and Montenegro*, Judgment, ICJ Reports, paragraph 430–431.

6 F. Grünfeld, 'Do Bystanders Exist?' in: P.A.M. Malcontent (ed.), *Facing the Past: Finding Remedies for Grave Historical Injustices*, Intersentia, Antwerp 2016.

that it is not a lack of information on the part of the international bystanders that causes the failure to take action to prevent, stop or end the gross human rights violations in Rwanda, Srebrenica or Darfur. This was later acknowledged in the inquiry reports of the United Nations.[7]

3. RESEARCH RESULTS OF THE ROLE OF BYSTANDERS IN GROSS HUMAN RIGHTS VIOLATIONS

In order to understand the position of the victim you should have knowledge of the intentions, behaviour and actions of the perpetrator. A focus solely on the victim is not enough for our understanding and for the prevention of future atrocities. Studying the different stages of repression by the perpetrator makes it possible to understand the situation. 'Where authority fails, repression begins', this famous expression from Hannah Arendt has been elaborated by Marjo Hoefnagels in which she makes clear that at a certain stage, because of the violent repression by the perpetrators, any opposition or resistance in that society is no longer possible.[8] When the victims in that society are isolated and silenced, the final opportunity to stop the atrocities belongs to the third parties in that society or outside that society.

One of the lessons of the Shoah is that most neighbours stood silently and idly by when the Jews and Sinti and Roma were deported and killed. This attitude of passivity and inertia in those days was not only demonstrated by bystanders in those occupied societies but also by the international bystanders outside that society. The allied powers were primarily interested in winning the Second World War by conquering Berlin first and they were not focused on saving Jews or attacking extermination camps or obstructing the train transport to those camps.[9] With the 'Never Again' credo in mind, we focus on the role of national and international bystanders to prevent or stop genocide in the post-Cold War period and selected the cases of Rwanda, Srebrenica and Darfur.

The pattern we discovered in all these cases is that serious warnings of an emerging genocide were denied and not taken into account in the decision-making. Warnings are the proximate causes to prevent atrocities and were present in all three situations. Moreover, in all the situations the instruments to prevent or stop atrocities were available to bystanders, for instance, in

---

7 S/1999/1257, *Report of the independent inquiry into the action of the United Nations during the 1994 genocide in Rwanda*, 15 December 1999. A/54/549, *Srebrenica Report*, Report of the Secretary General pursuant to General Assembly Resolution 53/35 (1998), 15 November 1999.

8 M. Hoefnagels (ed.), *Repression and repressive violence*, Swets & Zeitlinger, Amsterdam 1977.

9 F. Grünfeld and A. Huijboom, *The failure to prevent genocide in Rwanda: The role of bystanders*, Nijhoff, Leiden-Boston 2007, pp. 3–8.

Rwanda with 2,500 UN peace-keepers and 1,700 well-armed American, French, British, Belgian and Italian elite troops. Besides, we observed that the real perpetrators (Hutu Power, Bosnian Serbs, Bashir government with Janjaweed) were not condemned and proposed interventions to help the victims were not undertaken. Again, the denial and obscuring of the genocide was characteristic in all situations, whereas the first two (Rwanda and Srebrenica) cases were even not discussed by the members of the Security Council of the United Nations. Yes, again a vanishing world in practice because of ignoring reality in international politics.

4. KNOWLEDGE AND ACTION

The central question in the contribution of Irene Bruna Seu surrounds 'what and how much people know about human rights violations and what they do in response to that knowledge'.[10] This is also the focus in my research, where I investigated, in particular the warnings to the decision makers and the way they have processed this information in the decision-making process.

Based on the defence by bystanders for not acting to rescue the victims during the Shoah, the reasoning based on four arguments is as follows:

(1) 'We did not know of what was going on'. The so-called knowledge question of awareness of the severity of the gross human rights violations is then at stake. A debate in the Netherlands has recently started based on research from a study on the diaries of Jews and Gentiles (based on the premise) that if the Dutch population had known that the final aim of the deportation was annihilation, many more Gentiles would have offered hiding places and many more Jews would have sought sanctuary in hiding places.[11] I do not agree with this argumentation because in the Netherlands during the deportation period finding hiding places was very difficult, in particular for most Jews who lived in abject poverty and who could not pay for hiding places, and the resistance movement was not well organised to help in this period of the war. Moreover, betrayal took place in the Netherlands on a large scale, and being arrested from a hiding place meant being directly transported to an extermination camp for the Jews, and those hiding Jews were punished but not executed, as was the case in Eastern Europe.

The Dutch situation is very different from the situation in Denmark, where the whole population was engaged in providing hiding places on the first day of the planned mass arrests which was leaked by the Germans to the government

10 I. Bruna Seu, in this volume.

11 B.E. Van Der Boom, *Wij weten niets van hun lot; gewone Nederlanders en de Holocaust*, Boom, Amsterdam 2012.

who in turn informed those providing hiding places and Jews. Moreover, the support of many in Denmark for shipping almost all Jews to neutral Sweden and the non-interference of the Germans because of the special position of Denmark, agreed at the moment of occupation, resulted in the remarkable situation that the knowledge – the warnings of arrest – was responded to with effective action in rescuing almost all Danish Jews in a short time.[12]

With regard to the knowledge on the Shoah in the Netherlands during the war, Willem de Haan has referred in this book to the concept of incomprehension. Perhaps for the Dutch population at large the extermination of Jews was unbelievable, but they – as Willem de Haan has put forward – could see the banning of Jews from society but denied the moral significance because they did not help.[13] This is implicatory denial. In my research on the three cases we have ascertained that the international bystanders (states and international organisations as actors) were fully aware of what there was going on.

(2) Had we known about it, according to the second argument, we could not have responded because we did not have the appropriate instruments for action. This is the so-called availability of means question. We concluded that all kinds of military (forces taking enforcement action, intervention, peace keeping, but also the international robust evacuation force sent to Rwanda in April 1994), economic (sanctions) and diplomatic (mediation, humanitarian assistance) instruments were available and often already in place but were mostly not used or used in a limited way.

(3) A response would likely have counterproductive effects is the third argument. In the period after the Cold War – when the fear and risk of a nuclear confrontation no longer existed – we could state for our cases that acting was less harmful than not acting, although we are aware that any military and non-military action would be painful anyway.

(4) The last excuse for not acting, after we have determined that the international bystanders did know what was happening, did have the instruments to act, and acting was less harmful than not acting, is that the political will to act was lacking. Indeed, that is the empirical reality, but in our view the concept of political will is rather vague and general just like the concept of national interest. In trying to unravel this concept and to identify this obstacle for acting we have focused – as Irene Bruna Seu – on domestic internal influences on the decision makers and taking into account the cognitive and psychological mechanism in analysing the foreign policy making of the international bystanders.[14]

---

12 B. Lidegaard, *Countrymen*, Knopf, New York 2013.

13 W. De Haan, 'Denialism and the Problem of Indifference', in this volume.

14 F. Grünfeld and W.N. Vermeulen in cooperation with J. Krommendijk, *Failure to Prevent Gross Human Rights Violations in Darfur, Warnings to and Responses by International Decision Makers (2003–2005)*, Brill-Nijhoff, Leiden-Boston 2014, p. 2.

In our research we found that in all cases the warnings about genocide were available. We consider warnings as proximate causes to prevent atrocities. Taking into account that the instruments were available, the conclusion is that the bystanders (third parties) at international level could have prevented the genocide. However, in all cases the genocide was not prevented. This is the conscious turning away, indicated as 'I won't'. The denial is considered as a self-protecting defence mechanism. The warnings did not lead to action when the decisions were made. At that moment the previous 'never agains' are forgotten. Denial is not only present in the last stage of genocide as part of the covering up evidence as Stanton has argued, but denial is present during all stages of genocide.[15]

5. DENIALISM: LITERAL, INTERPRETIVE AND IMPLICATORY DENIAL

A very recent illustration of literal denial of the genocide in Srebrenica is the Russian veto in the Security Council on 8 July 2015 on the draft resolution because of the following text: 'Condemns in the strongest terms the crime of genocide at Srebrenica as established by judgements of the ICTY and ICJ and all other proven war crimes and crimes against humanity in the course of the conflict in Bosnia and Herzegovina.'[16] Calling the Srebrenica massacre a crime of genocide was observed as confrontational and politically motivated by the Russian Ambassador and it was asserted that it would doom this region to tension.[17] The resolution aimed the opposite, as it continued: 'Agrees that acceptance of the tragic events at Srebrenica as genocide is a prerequisite for reconciliation, calls upon political leaders on all sides to acknowledge the fact of proven crimes as established by the courts, and in this context, condemns denial of this genocide as hindering efforts towards reconciliation and recognizes also that continued denial is deeply distressing for the victims.'[18] The Russian veto is a denial of a well-established fact, said the British Ambassador: 'It (i.e. the veto) is denial, and not this draft resolution that will cause division. Denial is the final insult to the victims.'[19] The implications of this resolution is, according to the Russians, to 'doom this region to tension', but in the resolution it is stated that recognition is 'a prerequisite for reconciliation'. This example is an illustration of both literal (facts established by international courts) and implicatory (its consequences) denial.

---

15 G.H. Stanton, 'The 8 Stages of Genocide' 1998 *Genocide Watch* <www.genocidewatch.org/aboutgenocide/8stagesofgenocide.html>.

16 S/2015/508 p.2.

17 *The New York Times*, 08.07.2015.

18 S/2015/508 pp. 2–3.

19 *The New York Times*, 08.07.2015.

The interpretive denial (to attribute a different meaning) is the most common method of denial in international politics; interpretive denial is the defence for inaction. For instance, leaders in Washington and New York have stated: in countries like these there are always struggles among and between different tribes, so this is civil war and not genocide. Moreover, contrary to the situation on the ground in Rwanda, international bystanders continued to pretend that the transitional government would be established and be facilitated with UN peacekeepers, whereas in reality at that moment, direct aggression including genocide was being planned by Interahamwe. Justifications for not acting, by focussing on the danger posed to peacekeepers (in both Rwanda and Srebrenica) and humanitarian workers (in Sudan), and as a consequence of this, withdrawing peacekeepers and humanitarian workers, is not only an interpretive denial of genocide but also constitutes facilitating the perpetrators to commit genocide. As has been elaborated by Irene Bruna Seu in this volume, the defence of non-action with a reference to 'in countries like that' is also implicatory denial, justifying a passive and self-distancing response. This response to the three situations of genocide we have studied, is very clearly visible in the behaviour of states and international organisations, the international bystanders.

6. LABELLING GENOCIDE REJECTED

The process of labelling situations differently (not as genocide but civil war) in combination with social stereotyping (these things happen in tribal Africa) enhances the indifferent attitude taken by the Western leaders and international decision makers and hinders the mobilising of domestic groups to pressure their governments to take action.

When the special rapporteur on extra judicial executions of the UN Commission on Human Rights, Bacré Waly Ndiaye, wrote, in 1993, about attacks on Tutsis, targeted solely because they belonged to an ethnic group, and therefore used the word 'genocide', he was pressured in the UN to delete that G-word because it was inappropriate and could threaten (Arusha) the peace process: international decision makers in the UN Human Rights Commission deny genocide in Rwanda.[20]

When the UN Resident Coordinator in Sudan, Mukesh Kapila reported in 2003 about the imminent ethnic cleansing or genocide in Darfur to the UN Secretariat in New York he was ordered by the DPA (Department of Political Affairs) to restrict his activities to his humanitarian mandate instead of peace and security affairs. A debate on the situation in the Security Council on Darfur was prohibited in the first year of the atrocities. The Secretary General did not

20 F. Grünfeld and A. Huijboom, *The failure to prevent genocide in Rwanda: The role of bystanders*, Nijhoff, Leiden-Boston 2007, pp. 71–72.

react at all for one full year (March 2003–April 2004) whereas the Resident Coordinator who was dissatisfied with the lack of outcry on Darfur decided to blow the whistle in a BBC radio interview talking about ethnic cleansing and comparing the situation in Darfur with the Rwandan genocide of ten years previously. He had to leave his post without any backing in the UN.[21] For a full year of the atrocities in Darfur (February 2003–April 2004) the UN Security Council, the UN Secretariat and the Secretary General (Kofi Annan) remained silent, did not discuss or raise the issue. It is denial of genocide by the highest UN decision makers, the international bystanders.

We have explained this behaviour in making use of theories in international relations developed by Graham Allison on different perspectives in decision-making:[22] (1) Rational Policy Model, (2) Organisational Process Model, and (3) Bureaucratic Politics Model.[23]

In the Rational Policy Model actors have a prefixed rank of preferences. The decision makers can differentiate between alternatives and their consequences and they will choose the alternative with the highest pay-off. It is a rational decision and the outcome of the costs and benefits calculation of alternative modes of action. It is the fixed national interest for each state which directs the weighing up of alternatives, and it is not linked to the person or their organisation in the decision making. We will give two examples. The first illustrates that priority was given to inaction on Darfur in a rational reasoned weighing and calculation of the consequences. It was decided that the lasting North-South conflict in Sudan, in which more than 1.5 million people were killed, should be resolved first. Because of this priority, acting on the genocide in Darfur was secondary. The UN and the USA and UK prioritised the North-South (Naivasha) peace talks and they took very seriously the Sudanese presidential threat that there would be no progress in this area should there be any interference on Darfur. In the other cases, the perpetrators of genocide were not hindered because they were able to distort the situation, denying (imminent) genocide and persuading the international decision makers of this. Another example of the rational decision making is to focus primarily on national interests. National concerns – killing Belgian peacekeepers in Rwanda or taking French military hostage in Bosnia, and threatening Dutch peacekeepers in Srebrenica – in combination with a concern that the reputation of their own UN (Peacekeeping Operations) Department should not be damaged, resulted in the decision that acting with all instruments against genocide was no option.

---

21 F. Grünfeld and W.N. Vermeulen in cooperation with J. Krommendijk, *Failure to Prevent Gross Human Rights Violations in Darfur, Warnings to and Responses by International Decision Makers (2003–2005)*, Brill-Nijhoff, Leiden-Boston 2014, pp. 96–113.

22 G.T. Allison and P. Zelikov, *Essence of Decision: Explaining the Cuban Missile Crisis*, Pearson Publishers, New York 1999.

23 F. Grünfeld and W.N. Vermeulen in cooperation with J. Krommendijk, *Failure to Prevent Gross Human Rights Violations in Darfur, Warnings to and Responses by International Decision Makers (2003–2005)*, Brill-Nijhoff, Leiden-Boston 2014, pp. 26–28.

The organisational process follows past decisions and behaviour developed as standard operating procedures. Routines with impersonal procedures and objectives with impartiality and neutrality as ends in themselves allow only incremental and minor changes as, for instance, the UN Department of Peacekeeping Operations in our three cases. The routine decision making neglect (i.e. denying) in the case of emerging genocide means that a shift to a different perspective from neutral peacekeeping to taking a side in countering the aggressor and perpetrator is excluded. The Peacekeeping Operations Department left no room for other departments in the decision making. Their view, based on implementing the peace process with peacekeepers in Rwanda (blue helmets), precluded another view of struggling against emerging genocide with enforcement forces (green helmets).

The bureaucratic politics model is characterised by an internal struggle regarding which department or section is allowed to influence the decision-making. It differs from the rational policy model, according to which, the state is not a unitary actor with only one national interest of that state. Political bargaining between various bureaucracies and its individuals is the decision-making process that mentioned phrased by Allison: 'where you stand, depends on where you sit.' In this way they want to protect their own unit, to maximise these interests including financial resources and expertise in the competition with other units or bureaucracies. The UN Department of Peacekeeping Operations – headed by Kofi Annan – did not want to endanger its own administrative unit by responding in Rwanda ('do not respond, the problem does not exist') or give a false impression on Srebrenica to, for instance, the Security Council which would result in the denying of fear of an emerging genocide. They did not act to prevent or counter the gross human rights violations. On the contrary, the UN peacekeepers were withdrawn from Rwanda (at the start of genocide in April 1994), UN humanitarian workers were withdrawn from Darfur (during the worst period of December 2003 until February 2004), military action by the air force on Srebrenica was delayed and cancelled (July 1995). In denying the impending genocide these international bystanders facilitated the perpetrators in these genocides.

However, public opinion and pressure of the many organised pressure groups can make a difference. This happened in the USA and other Western countries on Darfur (but not on Rwanda and Srebrenica) and led to the labelling of the situation in Darfur as genocide by the American Secretary of State in September 2004. The domestic factors changed the British and American attitude on Darfur in the Security Council. The people in the USA and Europe felt that they could make a difference with many demonstrations against the Olympics in China (as a veto power member on Darfur in the Security Council), influencing governments and members of parliament and making Darfur an issue in elections and in politics in general. This feeling is needed to make a difference. As Irene Bruna

Seu has argued, when people see a connection between their acknowledgement and an effect on the situation, they are able to act.[24] Morally significant actions (see Seu's model of acknowledgement in which knowing leads to doing) including a possible identification with groups or individuals as the victims of atrocities enhance action and awareness. For instance, commemoration by the installation of the stumbling stones in Europe (*Stolpersteine*) at a local level for individual victims of the Shoah facilitates identification and understanding.[25] It is also a way of combating Holocaust denial.

7. SOCIO-PSYCHOLOGICAL FILTER

In accordance with the conclusion of Irene Bruna Seu: 'People do not respond neutrally or mechanistically to human rights information. On the contrary, human rights information is filtered through a metaphorical psychosocial prism, which is made of beliefs and attitudes.'[26] We will illustrate this prism for our cases.

The decision makers filter information through previously held views and expectations. It is difficult to believe the unbelievable or the unimaginable. The annihilation of the Jewish people during the Second World War is the classical example. Moreover, in this case winning the war was the priority for the Allied powers and thus decision makers avoided and discounted information that was inconsistent with their prior views and would require to adjust their views. Reaching Berlin was the objective and not bombing Auschwitz, to put it bluntly. Counter information is neglected, thus denied. In particular the information that would lead to action is not forwarded. Inaction was preferred in Rwanda, Srebrenica and Darfur.

It is unbelievable that your neighbour in the Security Council in 1994 is the *génocidaire* in Rwanda, but that is what happened. The wishful thinking with a naïve trust in diplomacy was reinforced. Moreover, the normalisation technique that tribal and civil wars are usual in Africa ('in countries like that') is deliberately expressed by international decision makers on Rwanda and Darfur. Depicting the situation as very confused precludes taking sides with the oppressed in a genocide. In particular, perceiving the situation and events as confusing where in the cycle of violence over a period of time the victim might also be a perpetrator – as the situations in Rwanda, Srebrenica and Darfur were presented inside and outside the UN – leads to indifference and inaction by the bystanders. That blocks action, whereas identification with the victims of the genocide helps to close the gap. The Security Council

---

24 I. Bruna Seu, in this volume.

25 See <www.stolpersteine.eu> and <www.struikelsteentjes-maastricht.nl>.

26 I. Bruna Seu, in this volume.

was misinformed at the time of the attack of the Bosnian-Serbian army on Srebrenica, whereas previous information on the intentions of the Serbian Bosnians was kept secret by permanent members of the Security Council in the UN and not forwarded to those countries that were on the ground with peacekeepers, such as the Netherlands.

In all cases a shift in perception was needed from promoting peace to countering the emerging genocide.

Burying one's head in the sand was a way of describing the Dutch population during the Shoah but it is also a characterisation of the international bystanders towards genocide not only during the Shoah, but also in Rwanda, Srebrenica and Darfur. The more comprehensive concept of denial will encompass this turning away as well.

8. CONCLUSIONS

Denialism of impending genocide by international bystanders in the decision-making and its consequences has been studied in this chapter. The bystander matters and the external international bystanders matter very much because they are able to prevent or stop genocide in states under severe repression.

We focused on the link between knowledge and action. Denying the knowledge precludes making decisions to take action. Denying deliberately the knowledge about impending genocide led to inaction in the three cases of genocide whereas acting against genocide was required. We have differentiated between forms of denial: literal, interpretive and implicatory denial. All three forms were illustrated from our three case studies. Not a lack of information being supplied to the international bystanders, but their literal, interpretive or implicatory denial was due to the inaction to prevent, stop or end the gross human rights violations in Rwanda, Srebrenica or Darfur.

Moreover, we tried to understand these denials in making use of decision-making models. Studying decision making aims to analyse the link between knowledge (information and warnings on the impending genocide) and action or inaction to prevent and stop genocide. The different models explain the behaviour of the international bystanders (rational weighing up based on priority or national interests, organisational motives making routine decisions and in combination with bureaucratic concerns maximising the interests of their own unit) but in all situations denialism took place. The international decision makers always denied the impending genocide and that is why the available instruments were not used to prevent or stop genocide. Moreover, events were presented as something different from genocide and by creating distance from the atrocities identification with the victims was hindered. Famous expressions such as 'in countries like these' or 'it is not genocide but regular civil wars that happen there' were the socio-psychological prisms through which to filter the incoming information. This all resulted in inaction, whereas a shift in perception was needed to change from diplomacy, mediation and peacekeeping to a policy of confrontation in attacking the perpetrators and defending and rescuing the victims in a genocide. In all cases a shift of perception was needed from promoting peace to countering the emerging genocide. In denying the impending genocide these international bystanders facilitated the perpetrators in these genocides. It was the denial of genocide by the highest UN decision makers, the international bystanders.

Denialism afforded the international decision makers the option of inaction. Denialism is an important underlying factor in the genocides in the recent decades in Rwanda, Srebrenica and Darfur not being prevented or stopped by international bystanders. Denial is not only involved in the last stage of genocide to cover up evidence, as has been argued, but denial is present during all stages of genocide, and in particular during the decision making by the international bystanders.

CHAPTER XIV

INTERNATIONAL ORGANISATIONS AND DENIALISM

The Case of the African Union

Konstantinos D. MAGLIVERAS*

1. INTRODUCTION

It might sound oxymoronic that the concept of denialism could be applied to, and discussed in, the context of international organisations and institutions. Denialism is understood as a behaviour (or behavioural pattern) which primarily concerns individuals or groups of people. Its content could be extended to additionally cover sovereign states. However, even in such cases it would principally be the population of a state exhibiting denialism as a form of personal conduct when dealing with a specific issue or when trying to avoid dealing with it. Indeed, it is in the nature of people, either individually or in unison, to refuse to accept facts, events or beliefs which are widely held by others, even when they are objectively regarded as being true, accurate and scientifically correct. In such instances denialism could be perceived as a means of self-preservation. To have done otherwise could have led to facing new realities contradicting what was understood as the absolute truth for many decades or even for centuries.

The above considerations also apply to states. Particularly so when to deny facts or events is used for domestic consumption promoting the agenda of the government of the day or when it has reached the stage of becoming official state policy. In the latter case denialism will influence foreign relations and dealings with third countries. Often the acceptance by one state of an event or historical situation vehemently denied by another state could lead to breakdown in diplomatic relations.[1]

---

* The author would like to thank the Editorial Board for their comments on an earlier draft.

1 The example of Turkey's reaction to those states recognising the Armenian genocide stands out; see for example, Deutsche Welle, 'Turkey threatens "total rupture" with France over

While individuals and states exhibit the attributes of denialism and could spend time, energy and money to promote and to defend their position, international organisations do not *prima facie* have the characteristics associated with denialism. Here lies the oxymoron: during the exercise of their mandate and the implementation of their goals, as laid down in the constitutive instrument and interpreted through their action (or inaction), international organisations may exhibit denialism in the sense of deliberately refusing to do one or both of the following, which fall within their legitimate powers and functions: (a) adopt specific measures; and (b) order Member States to follow a particular behaviour or to abstain from it.

International organisations are still regarded as subsidiary structures and as secondary players in the international field. The principal reason is that they are created by states, which happen to be the prime players in the global community. Notwithstanding this limitation, they do constitute the most advanced form of multilateralism. To that extent, international organisations could be regarded as the amalgamation of the actions and reactions pursued by their members. Despite the fact that individual Member States could have very strong beliefs in a number of issues culminating in exhibiting denialism, very seldom would these situations influence the overall operation of an international organisation. These are, and will remain, domestic matters, which could, as has been mentioned, affect inter-state relations. On the other hand, international organisations have a life of their own, distinct from their Member States. This is invariably manifested in the fact that they are given a separate legal personality and are endowed with organs with their own volition. This fact could entail international responsibility for the international organisations should they happen to act unlawfully (or fail to act) resulting in harm being caused.[1]

While the institutional structure of international organisations differs considerably among them, each one has a (more or less developed) decision-making mechanism through which its various aims and goals are materialised and implemented. These objectives are closely related to the needs of Member States and, if the principle of constitutionalism applies to international organisations,[2] they should reflect the aspirations of their populations as well. More specifically, states chose to entrust certain functions to an international organisation and for this reason they endow it with specific powers. Thus, international organisations are an exact image of their (original) Member

Armenian genocide bill', 24 January 2012 <www.dw.de> accessed 04.03.2016. The denial of the Armenian genocide is state policy of Turkey, see P.R. Bartrop, *Genocide: The Basics*, Routledge, Abingdon 2015.

1 See UN International Law Commission, *Draft articles on the responsibility of international organizations*, 2011, available with commentaries at: <http://legal.un.org/ilc/texts/instruments/english/commentaries/9_11_2011.pdf> accessed 04.03.2016.

2 Cf. A. Peters, 'The Constitutionalisation of International Organisations' in: N. Walker, J. Shaw and S. Tierney (eds.), *Europe's Constitutional Mosaic*, Hart, Oxford 2011, p. 253.

States. They are created as their membership wished them to be: weak with only a few powers and limited functions or strong with a full array of weapons at their disposal. But all international organisations have duties and obligations towards their Member States, which are a correlation of the duties and obligations owed by the Member States to them.[3] On the whole, most international organisations observe most of their covenants most of the time – in short they are not in denial as regards fulfilling their responsibilities. And if they were to fail to do so, this could be for different reasons, including procedural stipulations (the example of the Big Five exercising the veto power in the UN Security Council). However, not all international organisations are the same. Regional organisations in particular could show signs of divergence, which could be explained by the particular circumstances which are prevalent in a given region.

The purpose of this chapter is to demonstrate how a certain regional intergovernmental institution, the African Union, the organisation with a political, economic, social and collective security mandate bringing together almost all African nations, differs from others by examining a number of instances where it has exhibited denialism in carrying out its mandate and, by doing so, fulfilling the aspirations of African peoples. In this chapter denialism in the context of international organisations is understood as consistently and deliberately avoiding adopting and carrying out measures, even though they fall into their mandate and have the required powers to do so. In other words, willingly and for long periods of time refusing to act according to responsibilities, which are not only recorded in their constitutive instrument but also derive from their resolutions and declarations. Naturally, it is far more difficult to detect and prove denialism in the acts or omissions of an international organisation compared to an individual or even to a state. There, the process of denial is far more personalised; one could deny something simply because he/she wants to follow an ideology. But international organisations are not run by ideologies (with the possible exception of organisations with very limited membership or institutions which were set up during the Cold War to further an ideology). Indeed, processes in international organisations are considerably more complex as they involve different actors (the various organs of the organisation and its Member States) with different dynamics and often pursuing dissimilar policies.

However, the instances of denialism shown by the African Union and which will be analysed in this chapter touch upon situations which are not of peripheral importance but concern almost the whole continent. They include genocide and crimes against humanity, intra-state and inter-state strife, the

3 See K. Magliveras, 'Membership in International Organisations' in: J. Klabbers and A. Wallendahl (eds.), *Research Handbook on International Organisations*, Edward Elgar Publishing, London 2011, pp. 84, 90 et seq.

systematic violation of human rights, impunity, etc. These are issues which have plagued Africa since its independence from colonial rule and continue to pose severe obstacles to its emancipation and to the full realisation of the important advances achieved, *inter alia*, in the economy and in democratic governance.

2. WHY THE CASE OF THE AFRICAN UNION IS DIFFERENT

The African Union (AU) and the predecessor Organisation of African Unity (OAU), which it replaced in 2002,[4] arguably constitute special cases among intergovernmental institutions. The OAU was formed in the early 1960s when the continent was still fighting its way out of the centuries' long colonialism. Apart from cementing African nations' statehood, it had to address internal scourges, such as racial discrimination and apartheid. To that extent, the establishment and the evolution of the OAU diverged from intergovernmental institutions in other parts of the world. Having started its operation with the first thirty independent African countries, its membership grew in the 1970s and in the 1980s with the accession of new states as they acquired their independence from the European colonial powers.

Currently the AU has 54 Member States and the dream of Pan-Africanism has long been materialised. From the beginning of its existence, the AU has portrayed itself as the institution uniting the whole continent and acting as its single representative on a global scale.[5] True as this might be, it is of some importance to note the existence of another group of African multilateral institutions, the so-called Regional Economic Communities (RECs). These are players of sizeable actorness and have developed links with other international institutions.[6] However, they are organisations of a sub-regional nature (their membership comes from only parts of the continent) and therefore the AU continues to enjoy a position of dominance and often of norm-setting. Since the AU has conducted itself as the sole spokesman for the entire continent, it could be argued that it has reached the stage of unopposed primacy among

4 For the process of transformation, see K. Magliveras and G. Naldi, *The African Union: Institutions and Activities*, Wolters Kluwer, Alphen aan den Rijn 2014, pp. 77 et seq.

5 Cf. Centre for Conflict Resolution and Friedrich Ebert Stiftung, *The African Union at Ten: Problems, Progress and Prospects*, International Colloquium Report, Berlin, August 2012, pp. 28 et seq. <www.fes.de/afrika/content/downloads/AU_Report_FINAL.pdf> accessed 04.03.2016.

6 The relationship between the AU and RECs is based on an agreement dating from 2007: Protocol on Relations between the African Union and the Regional Economic Communities (RECs) <www.afrimap.org/english/images/treaty/AU-RECs-Protocol.pdf> accessed 04.03.2016. See further R.F. Oppong, 'The African Union, The African Economic Community and Africa's Regional Economic Communities: Untangling a Complex Web' (2010) 18 *African Journal of International and Comparative Law* 92.

African stakeholders and has also acquired a status of monopoly. Indeed, the AU's status is almost unrivalled compared to regional intergovernmental institutions in other parts of the world, including the Organization of American States and ASEAN.

3. THE INTENSE PROBLEMS FACING AFRICA AND THE ENSUING CHALLENGES POSED FOR THE AU

This position of primacy affords to the AU advantages and benefits and it could be used constructively to tackle the complex situations affecting Africa. But, at the same time, it also entails considerable responsibilities, which go beyond the duties that most other intergovernmental organisations are expected to fulfill. And this because at stake are problems and issues which have for very long affected the whole of the continent and, it should be emphasised again, have negated its ability to partake in the global political, economic and technological evolution. One could spend a lot of time determining the root causes of these problems and which factors have exacerbated them. However, this reality does not diminish the fact that the AU, as the sole pan-continental organisation with a political, economic, social, and collective security mandate, is under a clear obligation to address them promptly and effectively. It follows that the AU has the responsibility not only to attempt to tackle them but also to adopt pertinent measures and policies to combat them, always aiming at their eradication.[7] The list of these problems is a long one; by no means are they restricted to Africa (some of them are present even in Europe) but it is their intensity and persistence which makes them stand out in the black continent.

Suffice to mention the following issues: systematic denial of the rule of law; mass violations of human rights and of humanitarian law, not infrequently leading to ethnic cleansing, crimes against humanity and genocide; systemic corruption in both the public and private sectors; endemic impunity; large-scale embezzlement of state funds and revenues, which sentences the population of countries with very rich resources to recurring poverty and underdevelopment; and undemocratic governance, electoral rigging and *coups d'état*. Regarding democratic ideals, even though international law and principles of self-determination teach that the population of a state should be left free to determine

7 See the Solemn Declaration on the 50th Anniversary of the OAU/AU, where the AU has taken full responsibility for the realisation of an 'integrated, prosperous and peaceful Africa ... representing a dynamic force in the international arena', Assembly/AU/Decl. 3 (XXI), 26 March 2013. All Assembly decisions and declarations are available at <www.au.int> accessed 04.03.2016.

the political system and this rule still holds, it should be noted that the AU Charter cites them as guiding principles.[8]

The AU has been endowed with a wide ranging array of organs. Indeed, its institutional architecture is quite impressive even among advanced regional organisations. The Assembly of Heads of State and Government is the highest ranking body. It directs the policy of the other organs and addresses resolutions to Member States which have a binding effect and must be carried out on pain of sanctions being imposed.[9] It often urges Member States to pursue a specific course of action or to adopt certain behaviour. The Assembly has aimed at creating uniform positions which will be regarded by outside actors as representing the African stance.[10] Thus, it transpires that the Assembly speaks in the name of the population of all Member States and it does so in order to fulfill pan-African aspirations and goals.

However, by the same token, when the Assembly fails to act in a given case, it is as if the whole continent neglects its duties or, worse, refuses to comply with them. Considering that these duties may involve upholding fundamental human rights, which have long been regarded as global values, they are not only owed to African populations but arguably to the international community as a whole. On the other hand, the AU expects solidarity from the international community and financial assistance in order to carry out the majority of its programmes.[11] It follows that it would not be unreasonable for the international community to equally expect that the AU obeys those peremptory rules transcending countries, regions and continents.

Based on these considerations and assumptions, it will be argued that over the years the AU has shown behaviour which amounts to denialism in addressing – as it has the obligation to do so – grave situations involving hundreds of thousands of Africans and perpetuating the ethos of impunity which has plagued the continent. Of these situations, the following two will be examined: the chronic inaction in the case of the genocide in the Darfur region of Sudan and the deplorable delay in bringing to justice a former dictator, Hissène Habré of Chad. Finally, the argument will be made that in order to address its inactivity in handling mass violations of human rights, humanitarian law and other breaches of transnational criminal law and at the same time preventing the International Criminal Court (ICC) from exercising its jurisdiction, the AU

8 See Article 4 of the Constitutive Act, 2158 UNTS 3.

9 Ibid., Article 23(2).

10 In June 2015 the Assembly requested the development of a common position for Africa to be presented at the Valletta Conference on Migration, which was organised by the European Union in Malta on 11–12 November 2015, see Assembly, *Declaration on Migration*, AU Doc. Assembly/AU/Decl. 6 (XXV), 15 June 2015.

11 Note that other international organisations as well as individual states contribute more than half of the AU budget; see Assembly, *Decision on the Budget of the African Union for the 2016 Financial Year*, Assembly/AU/Dec. 577 (XXV), 15 June 2015.

decided to set up a criminal law chamber within its judicial organ, the African Court of Justice and Human Rights, which is still not in operation.

4. THE GENOCIDE IN DARFUR AND THE CASE OF HISSÈNE HABRÉ

Denialism can be synonymous with refusing to accept responsibility for acts and for omissions. Originally the OAU and thereafter the AU have never expressly recognised their share of responsibility in the genocides and the other organised violations of humanitarian law that have taken place under their watch. The genocide in Rwanda in 1994 should be considered as the prime example of denialism showed during the OAU era.[12] However, it was not the first time: some 20 years earlier a little noticed genocide between Hutus and Tutsis had taken place in Burundi.[13] In those instances overarching duties and obligations were completely neglected with tragic consequences. Unfortunately, the new epoch that the AU was supposed to bring in did not alter the situation. This is best evidenced by the repeated denialism that the AU has shown in the case of the genocide in Darfur since the beginning of this century. There warfare and killings have long exceeded the perpetration of war crimes or crimes against humanity and have reached the level of genocide with hundreds of thousands of the local population being systematically negated their right to life and the right to live in a humane manner.

The fact that so far only one state (the United States of America)[14] has confirmed that genocide was committed does not diminish this conclusion, which has been shared by the Prosecutor of the ICC. In any event, the situation in Darfur did not constitute what the AU Assembly chose to regard it, namely a deteriorating humanitarian situation which was to be tackled by entrusting the protection of the civilian population to its arch enemy, the government of Khartoum.[15] In February

12 To exonerate itself of any responsibility, the OAU established, with characteristic delay, in 1998 the International Panel of Eminent Personalities to Investigate the 1994 Genocide in Rwanda and the Surrounding Events. Its Report of July 2000 concluded that the genocide was preventable and recommended, *inter alia*, that the OAU establish appropriate structures to enable it to respond effectively in conflict situations <www.refworld.org/pdfid/4d1da8752.pdf> accessed 04.03.2016. Its recommendation was not implemented.

13 See J.-P. Chretien and J.-F. Dupaquier, *Burundi 1972: Au bord des génocides*, L'Harmattan, Paris, 2007.

14 See the Darfur Peace and Accountability Act of 2006, Public Law 109–344, imposing, *inter alia*, sanctions against individuals responsible for genocide, war crimes, and crimes against humanity in Darfur <https://www.congress.gov/bill/109th-congress/house-bill/3127> accessed 04.03.2016. Generally, see S. Totten in: S. Totten and E. Markusen (eds.), *Genocide in Darfur: Investigating the Atrocities in Sudan*, Routledge, Abingdon 2006, pp. 199 et seq.

15 See Assembly, *Decision on Darfur*, Assembly/AU/Dec. 54 (III), 8 July 2004; K. Magliveras and G. Naldi, *The African Union: Institutions and Activities*, Wolters Kluwer, Alphen aan den Rijn 2014, paras. 40–41.

2015, during an UN Security Council debate on the role of the UN Charter in peace and security maintenance, Canada made the allegation that the mass rapes occurring in Darfur had been covered up by the Sudanese government.[16] As held by the International Criminal Tribunal for Rwanda (ICTR), rape constitutes an act of genocide, if committed with the intent to destroy, even in part, an ethnic group.[17] Finally, the International Commission of Inquiry on Darfur reached, in January 2005, a rather diplomatic conclusion: while the Sudanese government had not pursued a policy of genocide, the crimes against humanity and war crimes committed in Darfur may be more serious and heinous than genocide.[18]

The AU could also be accused of double standards, another form of expressing denialism, as regards the right of the people of Darfur to self-determination, especially taking into account the different treatment in respect of South Sudan. In particular, the AU took a proactive stance in the question of South Sudan's independence by aiding the local population to break away from the oppressive regime in Khartoum and choose its future freely.[19] Based on this and other precedence,[20] the question may validly be put as to why the AU continues to deny the people of Darfur their inalienable right to self-determination. Although self-determination has different meanings, the one applicable here is what Jean Charpentier has termed as '*le droit des peuples à se libérer d'une domination qui les opprime*'.[21] In effect we are not here concerned with the 'subjugation of peoples to alien subjugation, domination and exploitation', to cite the UN Declaration on the Granting of Independence to Colonial Countries and Peoples,[22] but with the domination that one group exercises over another group within the same state negating their fundamental rights. Arguably, this was the nature of self-determination when the people of South Sudan were asked at a referendum in January 2011 whether they wanted to secede from the Republic of Sudan.[23]

---

16 See UN Security Council, S/PV.7389, 7389th Meeting, 25 February 2015, p. 61.

17 ICTR, *The Prosecutor v. Jean-Paul Akayesu*, Case No. ICTR-96-4-T, Judgment of 2 September 1998. See further UN Security Council Resolution 1820(2008), 19 June 2008; and Report of the Secretary-General, *Conflict-related sexual violence*, UN Doc. A/66/657-S/2012/33, 13 January 2012.

18 It was created pursuant to Security Council Resolution 1564(2004), 18 September 2004. For the Report see <www.un.org/news/dh/sudan/com_inq_darfur.pdf> accessed 04.03.2016.

19 Cf. Assembly, *Solemn Declaration of the Assembly of Heads of State and Government of the African Union on Sudan*, Assembly/AU/Decl. 3 (XVI), 31 January 2011.

20 The AU has long pressed the UN General Assembly to determine a date for holding a self-determination referendum for the people of Western Sahara, see Assembly, *Decision on the Report of the Peace and Security Council on its Activities and the State of Peace and Security in Africa*, Assembly/AU/Dec. 583 (XXV), 15 June 2015, para. 18.

21 See J. Charpentier, 'Autodétermination et décolonisation' in: *Le Droit des peuples à disposer d'eux-mêmes: Méthodes d'analyse du droit international – Mélanges offerts à Charles Chaumont*, Editions A. Pedone, Paris 1984, p. 117.

22 Adopted by General Assembly Resolution 1514(XV), 14 December 1960.

23 See S. Dersso, *International law and the self-determination of South Sudan*, Institute of Security Studies, Paper No. 231, February 2012.

This specific aspect of self-determination is additionally in line with Article 20 of the African Charter on Human and Peoples' Rights, the regional instrument for the promotion and protection of fundamental freedoms adopted in June 1981.[24] It stipulates that all peoples not only have the right to existence, which culminates in the 'unquestionable' right to self-determination, but, if they happen to be 'oppressed peoples', they also have the right to liberate themselves 'from the bonds of domination' and they may employ 'any means recognised by the international community'. Thus far the AU has arguably denied that the people of Darfur have a separate and distinct right to self-determination. Whether the population will exercise it and, if it exercises it, whether it will lead to the creation of another independent state and the further disintegration of what has been left of the Republic of Sudan (there is even talk about its becoming a new Yugoslavia), are legitimate worries. However, they are not related to the primary consideration, namely that the population of Darfur should be entitled to exercise self-determination and that the AU should not continue to deny it.

The other example of the AU's denialism to enforce the rule of law and to combat impunity to be examined is the way it has treated the prosecution of Hissène Habré, a former dictator of Chad.[25] Based on well-documented evidence, Habré and his entourage were accused of committing, *inter alia*, large-scale torture. He fled to Senegal and lived there peacefully until Belgian prosecutors invoked the principle of universal jurisdiction, brought criminal charges against him and presented Senegal with this dilemma: either prosecute him locally or extradite him to Belgium. In July 2006, the AU Assembly took the situation into its own hands and mandated Senegal to prosecute and try Habré on behalf of Africa.[26] The decision by an intergovernmental organisation to mandate a Member State to try a former head of state (but not a citizen of that state) on behalf of the whole membership (which in this case was a whole continent) was of immense consequences.

Moreover, the decision put to rest the myth that somehow former heads of state may never be answerable for criminal acts perpetrated during their time in office and that there exists an indefinite immunity from persecution. Finally, the decision should also be viewed from the following two perspectives. First, as a manifestation of the AU's motto 'African solutions to African problems',[27] which means exactly what it says: Africa should take ownership of its own problems,

---

[24] 1520 UNTS 217.

[25] For analysis, see K. Magliveras, 'Fighting Impunity Unsuccessfully in Africa: A Critique of the African Union's Handling of the Hissène Habré Affair' (2014) 22 *African Journal of International and Comparative Law* 420.

[26] Assembly, *Decision on the Hissène Habré Case and the African Union*, Assembly/AU/Dec. 127 (VII), 2 July 2006, para. 5.

[27] It was expressly cited in the Declaration on the 50th Anniversary of the OAU/AU, Assembly/AU/Decl. 3 (XXI), 26 March 2013.

deal with them and solve them as it sees it fit. Second, as a manifestation of the so-called African renaissance, namely the emancipation and re-birth of the continent.[28] In particular, renaissance denotes the process of leaving behind the idea that the AU operates as a dictators' club, as the predecessor OAU arguably did, and engulfing the rule of law and the principles of democratic governance.

All euphoria created by this progressive and extraordinary decision soon evaporated because Senegal failed to give effect to its mandate. In turn, the AU did precious little to counteract Senegal's denying of its duty, which, as will be recalled, was owed to Africa at large.[29] In the meantime Belgium took, without delay, its case before the International Court Justice, which stated what was obvious to any student of international law: Senegal had breached its duty under the UN Torture Convention[30] to either prosecute Habré through its own courts or extradite him.[31]

With the Habré case becoming a disastrous state of affairs and painting an extremely negative picture of its true commitment to fight impunity and uphold the rule of law, the AU was finally forced to take prompt and concrete action.[32] Thus in late 2012 the Extraordinary African Chambers within the court system of Senegal were established to try Habré.[33] These Chambers bring to mind the case of Cambodia and the prosecution of the Khmer Rouge leaders,[34] but there are important differences. In the case of Habré a whole

---

28 See M. Mbeki, 'The African Renaissance' (1998/1999) 3 *South African Yearbook of International Affairs* 120.

29 In early 2009, the AU even implied that his trial had not started because the European Union had not provided the recourses needed for the prosecution: Assembly, *Decision on the Hissène Habré Case*, Assembly/AU/Dec. 240 (XII), 3 February 2009.

30 See Article 7 of the UN Convention against Torture and Inhuman or Degrading Treatment, 1465 UNTS 85.

31 International Court of Justice, *Democratic Republic of the Congo v. Belgium*, Judgment of 14 February 2012, (2012) *ICJ Reports* 3.

32 Lest it be forgotten, there are other African leaders who had effectively been given immunity by the OAU, while the AU continues to deny that there are crimes for which they should be answerable. And this despite the growing tendency to refuse the validity of statutes of limitations *vis-à-vis* gross violations of human rights law and of humanitarian law constituting crimes under international law; cf. *Basic Principles and Guidelines on the Right to a Remedy and Reparation for Victims of Gross Violations of International Human Rights Law and Serious Violations of International Humanitarian Law*, adopted under UN General Assembly Resolution 60/147, 16 December 2005.

33 The Statute of the Extraordinary African Chambers within the Courts of Senegal created to prosecute international crimes committed in Chad between 7 June 1982 and 1 December 1990, was annexed to the Agreement between the government of Senegal and AU signed in August 2012, reproduced in (2013) 52 ILM 1020. See also the Additional Agreement of 24 July 2014 <www.hrw.org> accessed 04.03.2016. For analysis, see S. Williams, 'The Extraordinary African Chambers in the Senegalese Courts. An African Solution to an African Problem?' (2013) 11 *Journal of International Criminal Justice* 1139; R.O. Savadogo, 'Les Chambres africaines extraordinaires au sein des tribunaux sénégalais: quoi de si extraordinaire?' (2014) 45 *Études internationales* 105.

34 Generally, see K. Magliveras, 'Difficulties and Status of Efforts to Create an International Criminal Court in Cambodia' (2002) 3 *Asia-Pacific Journal on Human Rights and the Law* 105.

continent, acting through its representative intergovernmental organisation, the African Union, undertook to prosecute a former head of state for allegedly being criminally responsible for committing inhumane acts, and appointed Senegal to act as their agent. For almost six years, the AU and its Member States failed to act upon their duty, not because they faced unsurpassable legal obstacles (the creation of the Extraordinary African Chambers shows that it was feasible for it to have been established years ago) but because they preferred inaction, which culminated in denying fulfilling their responsibilities and commitments.

On 20 July 2015, almost two and a half years after the Extraordinary African Chambers had become operative, the criminal trial against Habré began. After being adjourned until 7 September 2015 to allow the court appointed defence lawyers to prepare,[35] the trial resumed. Does the commencement of the proceedings mean that it should no longer be regarded as a case of denialism by the AU? Even though this development is definitely a move towards acknowledgment and certainly the AU could not interfere with the proceedings, for the following reasons it will be submitted that it still represents a case of denialism. First, the proceedings have barely started and at this stage it is not known if, when and how they will be concluded. Second, the AU continues to fail to discuss the issue of bringing to justice former heads of state and high ranking officials against whom credible allegations for committing crimes have been brought. Third, there has been a recent development which shows that, if there is adequate will, African states could tackle the difficulties inherent in setting up a criminal mechanism to bring to justice alleged perpetrators avoiding impunity. The case concerns the Central African Republic (CAR), which overcame the many and complex internal problems and with the assistance of the international community created in February 2015 a Special Criminal Court (SCC), competent to investigate and prosecute serious violations of international humanitarian law committed in its territory since 2003.[36] The majority of the 27 judges to sit at the SCC will be from the CAR with the remaining judges coming from third states.[37] The law creating the SCC was promulgated in June 2015.[38]

---

35 See 'Chad's Hissène Habré forced to appear in court' *BBC*, 21 July 2015 <www.bbc.com/news/world-africa-33607843> accessed 04.03.2016.

36 According to UN Security Council Resolution 2217(2015), 28 April 2015, the SCC's jurisdiction is consistent with the country's international human rights law obligations.

37 See <www.pgaction.org/car-centralafricanrepublic-criminalcourt.html> accessed 04.03.2016.

38 See K. Magliveras, 'The Special Criminal Court of the Central African Republic' (2016) 32 *International Enforcement Law Reporter* 69.

5. THE INTERNATIONAL CRIMINAL LAW SECTION OF THE AFRICAN COURT OF JUSTICE AND HUMAN RIGHTS AS A FURTHER EXAMPLE OF THE AU'S DENIALISM

In the summer of 2014, the AU took a very bold move in its institutional structure by adopting a Protocol adding an International Criminal Law (ICL) Section[39] to its judicial organ, the African Court of Justice and Human Rights (ACJHR).[40] This project had been in the pipeline for a number of years.[41] Although it is meant to cement the rule of law and the fight against impunity, it will be argued that it is another example of the AU denying fulfilling its role and mandate. It should be explained from the outset that the prospects of the ICL Section ever becoming operative are limited, if not negligible. As a matter of fact, even the operationalisation of the ACJHR is not expected to happen in the foreseeable future. And this because the Statute of the ACJHR[42] has received only five out of the 15 ratifications required to enter into force.[43] Regarding the Protocol establishing the ICL Section, it has been signed by eight Member States but with no ratifications yet.[44]

What prompted the AU to create the ICL Section was a combination of reasons, the most prominent being the perceived unfair targeting of Africa by the ICC;[45] the issuance of ICC arrest warrants against African dignitaries, including the serving Presidents of Sudan and Kenya; and the abuse of the principle of universal jurisdiction by Western countries accompanied by

---

39 Protocol on Amendments to the Protocol on the Statute of the African Court of Justice and Human Rights, signed on 24 June 2014 <http://au.int/en/treaties/protocol-amendments-protocol-statute-african-court-justice-and-human-rights> accessed 04.02.2016. See V.O. Nmehielle, '"Saddling" the New African Regional Human Rights Court with International Criminal Jurisdiction: Innovative, Obstructive, Expedient?' (2014) 7 *African Journal of Legal Studies* 7; G. Naldi and K. Magliveras, 'The African Union's International Criminal Court: An Appraisal' (2015) 21 *African Yearbook of International Law* (forthcoming).

40 For analysis, see G. Naldi and K. Magliveras, 'The African Court of Justice and Human Rights: A Judicial Curate's Egg' (2012) 9 *International Organizations Law Review* 387.

41 See C.B. Murungu, 'Towards a Criminal Chamber in the African Court of Justice and Human Rights' (2011) 9 *Journal of International Criminal Justice* 1067; A. Abass, 'The Proposed International Criminal Jurisdiction for the African Court: Some Problematic Aspects' (2013) 60 *Netherlands International Law Review* 28.

42 It was adopted on 1 July 2008 <www.au.int/en/treaties/protocol-statute-african-court-justice-and-human-rights> accessed 04.03.2016.

43 According to the official AU list of signatures and ratifications <www.au.int/en/sites/default/files/treaties/7792-sl-protocol_on_statute_of_the_african_court_of_justice_and_hr_0.pdf> accessed 04.04.2016.

44 See <www.au.int/en/sites/default/files/treaties/7804-sl-protocol_on_amendments_to_the_protocol_on_the_statute_of_the_african_court_of_justice_and_human_rights_19.pdf> accessed 04.03.2016.

45 The ICC was established under the Rome Statute, which came into force on 1 July 2002, 2187 UNTS 90.

the non-observance of traditional rules of international law, for example the absolute immunity from prosecution of heads of state and government.[46] The following extract from an Assembly decision adopted in January 2015 is revealing of both the strength of the AU–ICC antiparathesis and the insistence that common positions agreed at AU level must be observed by all Member States:

> 'The Assembly …
> Expresses … its deep concern regarding the conduct of the Office of the Prosecutor [of the ICC] and the [International Criminal] Court and the wisdom of the continued prosecution against African Leaders …
> Reiterates the imperative need for all African States Parties [to the Rome Statute of the ICC] to ensure that they adhere and articulate commonly agreed positions at the African Union in line with their obligations under the Constitutive Act of the Union …'[47]

To counteract this perceived anti-African sentiment demonstrated by the ICC, the AU, acting through the behaviour and norms setting Assembly, has resorted to a number of actions. Two events merit particular attention. The first was the convening in October 2013 of an extraordinary Assembly session to discuss the continued relationship between African states and the ICC. Before it, the AU had played with the idea of an *en masse* withdrawal of African states from the Rome Statute.[48] As they constitute the largest group of contracting parties (34 at the time of writing), this move would have had devastating effects on the operation of the ICC and would have probably hampered the ICC's drive to achieve universality. In the event, no such radical measure was officially discussed.[49] But even having an international organisation contemplating dictating to its membership what its attitude should be towards another transnational institution is an act clearly exceeding its mandate.

---

46 Generally, see G. Werle, L. Fernandez and M. Vormbaum (eds.), *Africa and the International Criminal Court*, Asser Press-Springer, Berlin 2014; K. Magliveras and G. Naldi, 'The International Criminal Court's Involvement with Africa: Evaluation of a Fractious Relationship' (2013) 82 *Nordic Journal of International Law* 417.

47 Assembly, *Decision on the Progress Report of the Commission on the Implementation of Previous Decisions on the International Criminal Court (ICC)*, Assembly/AU/Dec. 547(XXIV), 31 January 2015.

48 See 'African Union summit on ICC pullout over Ruto trial' *BBC*, 20 September 2013 <www.bbc.com/news/world-africa-24173557> accessed 04.03.2016.

49 See Assembly, *Decision on Africa's Relationship with the International Criminal Court (ICC)*, Ext/Assembly/AU/Dec. 1, 12 October 2013; K. Magliveras and G. Naldi, *The African Union: Institutions and Activities*, Wolters Kluwer, Alphen aan den Rijn 2014, pp. 73–74.

The second event concerns the Assembly Decision of July 2009 directing Member States not to comply with, or give effect to, the arrest warrants issued (or to be issued) by the ICC against African dignitaries.[50] Again, it is highly irregular for an international organisation to dictate to Member States which stance they should pursue *vis-à-vis* another multilateral institution, especially when the latter has no links to the AU. That the defiance towards lawfully issued ICC arrest warrants has become official AU policy is evidenced by the fact that the Assembly has praised those Member States which purposely denied fulfilling strict duties as contracting parties to the Rome Statute. Thus, in January 2015 it commended the Democratic Republic of Congo (DRC), one of the first states to join the ICC in April 2002, for complying with its 2009 Decision and refusing to cooperate with the ICC in arresting and surrendering the Sudanese President al-Bashir.[51] There are two outstanding arrest warrants against al-Bashir; the second accuses him of acts of genocide.[52]

This unacceptable state of affairs has been going on for too long. Even though in December 2011 the ICC rendered a decision against Malawi, another early party to the ICC, where it put forward a clear legal reasoning why serving heads of state are not immune from arrest when a warrant is outstanding,[53] an unsavoury situation has emerged: African contracting parties deny their obligations with the acquiescence of the AU[54] but, at the same time, they do not withdraw from the ICC. Furthermore, in those cases where the ICC has assumed jurisdiction on the basis of an UN Security Council decision (as

50 Assembly, *Decision on the Meeting of African States Parties to the Rome Statute of the International Criminal Court (ICC)*, Assembly/AU/Dec. 245 (XIII), 3 July 2009. For discussion, see D. Tlad, 'The African Union and the International Criminal Court: The Battle for the Soul of International Law' (2009) 34 *South African Yearbook of International Law* 57.

51 See Assembly, *Decision on the Progress Report of the Commission on the Implementation of Previous Decisions on the International Criminal Court (ICC)*, Assembly/AU/Dec. 547(XXIV), 31 January 2015.

52 It was issued on 12 July 2010 <www.icc-cpi.int/iccdocs/doc/doc907140.pdf> accessed 04.03.2016.

53 See 'Prosecutor v. Omar Hassan Ahmad al-Bashir, Decision Pursuant to Article 87(7) of the Rome Statute on the Failure of the Republic of Malawi to Comply with the Cooperation Requests Issued by the Court with respect to the Arrest and Surrender of Omar Hassan Ahmad al-Bashir', Corrigendum, P.-T. Ch. I, ICC-02/05-01/09, 12 December 2011, reproduced in (2012) 51 ILM 393. For discussion, see K. Magliveras and G. Naldi, 'The ICC Addresses Non-Cooperation by State Parties in Arresting President al-Bashir: The *Malawi* Decision' (2013) 6 *African Journal of Legal Studies* 1.

54 The ICC has also held that the DRC deliberately refused to arrest and surrender al-Bashir, see 'Prosecutor v. Omar Hassan Ahmad al-Bashir, Decision on the Cooperation of the Democratic Republic of the Congo Regarding Omar al-Bashir's Arrest and Surrender to the Court', P.-T. Ch. II, ICC-02/05-01/09, 9 April 2014, <www.icc-cpi.int/iccdocs/doc/doc1759849.pdf> accessed 04.03.2013; for commentary, see N. Boschiero, 'The ICC Judicial Finding on Non-cooperation Against the DRC and No Immunity for al-Bashir Based on UNSC Resolution 1593' (2015) 13 *Journal of International Criminal Justice* 625.

is the case against al-Bashir),[55] it has been the turn of the Security Council to show denialism in putting teeth to its commitment to end impunity. In her December 2014 Report to the Security Council on the situation in Darfur, the ICC Prosecutor (herself an African) put it bluntly:

> 'Without stronger action by the Security Council and State Parties [to the ICC], the situation in Sudan is unlikely to improve and the alleged perpetrators of serious crimes against the civilian population will not be brought to justice',[56]

while in her next Report she has castigated the Security Council for its continuing inaction to make African states face the consequences, on the one hand, for serious and inexcusable violations of their obligation to cooperate with the ICC and, on the other hand, for not respecting its own Resolutions.[57]

The reason why the ICC has been involved in African situations is exactly because the AU has been in incessant denial concerning its duties. These duties derive from the Constitutive Act and from the African populations' aspirations that impunity will be eradicated and that they will live in an environment where the rule of law is observed.[58] Naturally, the AU is fully within its rights to create any new entity that it likes, including a criminal tribunal with international remit. But to establish a legal entity in order to cover up the persistent inability to address what the AU itself has recognised as chronic problems[59] should be dismissed as unacceptable, especially when it is fully aware that the judicial entity in question may never come into existence.

6. ARE THERE MITIGATING FACTORS FOR THE DENIALISM SHOWN BY THE AU?

In defence of the AU, it could be argued that it should not be accused of denialism because, as an intergovernmental organisation, it cannot grasp the issues, their complexities and their consequences. Therefore it is unable to address them. This submission could be justified on the premise that denialism presupposes that the

---

55 See Security Council Resolution 1593(2005), 31 March 2005.

56 See *Twentieth Report of the Prosecutor of the International Criminal Court to the UN Security Council Pursuant to UNSC 1593 (2005)*, 15 December 2014, p. 9 <www.icc-cpi.int/iccdocs/otp/20th-UNSC-Darfur-report-ENG.PDF> accessed 04.03.2016.

57 See *Twenty-first Report of the Prosecutor of the International Criminal Court to the UN Security Council Pursuant to UNSC 1593 (2005)*, 29 June 2015, p. 10 <www.icc-cpi.int/iccdocs/otp/21st-report-of-the-Prosecutor-to-the-UNSC-on-Dafur_%20Sudan.pdf> accessed 04.03.2016.

58 Note that the AU is one of the very few intergovernmental organisations able to intervene in Member States when war crimes, genocide or crimes against humanity have been committed; see Article 4h of the Constitutive Act.

59 Cf. Solemn Declaration on the 50th Anniversary of the OAU/AU, Assembly/AU/Decl. 3 (XXI), 26 March 2013.

situations at hand are fully understood and, despite this fact, deliberately no action is taken to deal with them in a positive way. It follows that the AU does not exhibit denialism, in the form of deliberately omitting to act in an affirmative manner.

This line of argument cannot be sustained. Moreover, it is not possible to submit that the same set of objective events can have two opposing views: one being the AU's perspective and the other being that of Western states or of the ICC. To exemplify this, reference will be made to the situation in Darfur, where the ICC has opened investigations leading to arrest warrants against both members of the al-Bashir regime and leaders of the insurgents.[60] If the AU had created an independent and trustworthy judicial mechanism to look into these allegations, it would have denied the involvement of the ICC. This conclusion is based on the principle of complementarity, which has found expression in Article 17(1) of the Rome Statute. It reads that the ICC will consider a case to be inadmissible, if it is being investigated or prosecuted by a state which has jurisdiction over it. Presumably a legal construction will have to be made here because the AU is not a state. However, taking into account that in the past, as has been explained, the AU asked Senegal to try Habré on behalf of the whole continent, a similar construction could have been devised in relation to Darfur. In order to fight impunity the AU could have undertaken the following actions: ask any willing Member State(s) to carry out the investigation and prosecution of the crimes allegedly committed in Darfur; set up an *ad hoc* judicial body of its own to carry out this task;[61] or, propose to the UN Security Council to expand the jurisdiction of the ICTR, whose lifeline is coming to an end,[62] to cover the alleged crimes in Darfur. But the AU has chosen to take no concrete action to uphold its duties. On the contrary and despite the fact that, as has been mentioned, the AU has a very shaky budget, in June 2015 it was decided to allocate resources to finance activities promoting its antiparathesis with the ICC.[63]

If, for the sake of argument, it was argued that the alleged perpetrators be tried before the aforementioned ICL Section of the ACJHR (assuming that it had become operative), that would have only been a half true submission. And this because the Statute of the ICL Section envisages jurisdictional immunity for serving heads of state or government as well as for senior officials.[64] Thus,

---

60 For details on the ICC investigations, see <www.icc-cpi.int/en_menus/icc/situations%20and%20cases/situations/situation%20icc%200205/Pages/situation%20icc-0205.aspx> accessed 04.03.2016.

61 Note that Article 5(2) of the Constitutive Act allows the Assembly to set up any organ it thinks fit. Taking advantage of this provision, the African Peace and Security Commission was established in 2003.

62 See UN Security Council Resolution 1966(2010), 22 January 2010.

63 See Assembly, *Decision on the Update of the Commission on the Implementation of Previous Decisions on the International Criminal Court*, Assembly/AU/Dec. 586(XXV),15 June 2015.

64 See G. Naldi and K. Magliveras, 'African Union Establishes an International Criminal Court' (2014) 30 *International Enforcement Law Reporter* 430, 432–433.

al-Bashir and his co-defendants before the ICC would not be prosecuted for as long as they remain in power, while there would be no bar in indicting the leaders of the insurgents. That the AU has been asking Member States not to give effect to the ICC arrest warrants should be regarded as morally bankrupt behaviour leading to very serious repercussions. It is this attitude that has armed the hand of those accused of heinous crimes who, after being unopposed for so many years, now claim the moral high ground.

More specifically, in the closing months of 2014, al-Bashir demanded that all UN peacekeeping forces leave Sudan while the government appears to have continued its bombing campaign in Darfur. In the course of 2014, the number of victims and those displaced almost reached half a million Darfurians.[65] The denialism which the AU has shown in tackling this situation has contributed to the Sudanese authorities' audacity. This is unacceptable. It also raises hurdles to the AU's efforts to secure a place of importance on the international plane. Much to the disappointment of victims and their families, by denying accountability and by not fighting impunity in the cases illustrated above the AU has not lived up to its lofty principles.

7. CONCLUSION

The question of denialism being exhibited by international organisations has not been investigated in literature. The present chapter is an attempt to show that international institutions can be in denial in realising their goals and carrying out their responsibilities. The African Union is a prominent case of an organisation, which has shown denialism in accepting truths and facts, and in ensuring that the aspirations of a whole continent are fulfilled. Of course a lot could be said about other organisations as well, not least about the United Nations and its Security Council. However, the very close links between the AU membership and the fact that the AU represents a whole continent are adequate reasons to argue that its actions (or inactions) and its policies (or lack of them) could be interpreted as being instances of (often deliberate) denial. A number of such cases have been analysed in this chapter. One of them, the prosecution of Hissène Habré, is currently in progress as it should, but with considerable delays and an uncertain future. But the situation in Darfur remains unresolved. With the ICC unable to go ahead with the proceedings, partly because African contracting parties are unwilling to fulfill their duties in apprehending and

---

65 See S. Sengupta and J. Gettleman, 'U.N. Set to Cut Force in Darfur as Fighting Rises' *The New York Times*, 25 December 2014 <www.nytimes.com/2014/12/26/world/africa/united-nations-set-to-cut-force-in-darfur-as-fighting-rises.html?ref=topics> accessed 04.03.2016.

surrendering those allegedly involved in genocide and crimes against humanity,[66] it is high time that the AU overturned its denialism and confronted the challenges it faces. These are not of secondary importance but touch upon the very essence of humanity. When the life and the personality of millions of people have been negated for so long, the very intergovernmental organisation, which has taken it upon itself to respect the sanctity of human life,[67] cannot continue to deny doing the obvious. Over the years the international community has come up with various tools and instruments to address extraordinary situations. The AU should put them into good use.

66 The list of such states is growing: in June 2015 the Republic of South Africa failed to arrest al-Bashir who was in the country attending the 25th Ordinary Assembly Session, see S. Msimang, 'South Africa's Human Rights Hypocrisy' *The New York Times*, 17 June 2015 <www.nytimes.com/2015/06/19/opinion/south-africas-human-rights-hypocrisy.html> accessed 04.03.2016.

67 Cf. Article 4(o) of the Constitutive Act.

CHAPTER XV

KILLING THROUGH THE STATE IN THE COLOMBIAN WAR AND GETTING AWAY WITH MURDER

An Exploration of Organisational Crime and Its Denial

Michael Reed Hurtado*

Killing the enemy in combat is generally not considered to be a crime when committed by the state militias; however, executing a combatant that has been captured or deposed weapons is cold-blooded murder. Slaying civilians is also a prohibited act. When these homicides get camouflaged as acts of war it is difficult (but not impossible) to uncover misdeeds. When those transgressions are widespread and denial is the active and official response, organisational responsibility is engaged and no longer is the only concern the establishment of individual responsibility for the crime of murder. Organisational facilitation and cover-up of a widespread criminal conduct lead to collective dimensions of responsibility. The consequences of organisational offending within the state are dire; however we know very little of such acts and their collective dynamics because of the immense capacity built into state processes to deny this type of offending. Denial is written into the planning, perpetration and cover-up of state crime. Denial is part of the conspiracy and an important element of organisational offending. This paper explores such criminal conduct and its denial in the context of a recent killing spree by the Colombian Army (COLAR).

COLAR's success in the counterinsurgent war effort has been publicised stateside and abroad. However, a not negligible portion of the feat appears to be shamefully written with the blood of sham combat deaths. 'Kills in action' (KIAs) were used as an indicator of military effectiveness in the war effort in

* I am deeply thankful to a group of Colombian men and women who have shared my motivation to unmask state crime; they will remain unnamed. They all know who they are. The content of this paper is entirely my responsibility.

Colombia. Responding to organisational pressure to show results, military units (and their commanders) throughout Colombia resorted to extended deviance to achieve death quotas: they abducted victims to produce the needed bodies and killed them in cold blood. To present the kill as an operational result they staged combats, including the fabrication of all legal and administrative documents to support phoney military operations; manipulated the crime scene; colluded with crime scene investigators, judges and prosecutors to ensure impunity; and viciously obstructed justice. Whilst the death tally grew, dirty warriors received commendations and praise; and COLAR peddled a triumphant image.

The expression 'sham-KIA' will be used to refer to this contrived practice. It involves the act of killing, but also comprises preparation, conspiracy, orders, tips, smokescreens, whitewash and denial. The shorthand expression is used to denote the entire scope of activity involved in this practice that aimed at plausible deniability. Sham-KIAs, as will be exposed, are almost imperceptible: they occurred in the fog of war and are shielded by COLAR's remarkable capacity to keep their operations secret and outside the purview of external control mechanisms.

Sham-KIAs are known in Colombia as the 'false positive scandal'. Addressed as a bounded affair, the scope and implications of the practice have not been publicly acknowledged; and hierarchical and organisational responsibility resulting from the official stimulus and facilitation of the kills is emphatically disavowed. Each murder has been addressed as an isolated incident. Existing convictions give credence to the official story pointing to soldiers and a few officers as bad apples in a tidy barrel.[1]

Though some of the abuses have been craftily acknowledged, the official and collective implications are disowned. As will be demonstrated, body counting and killing-by-incentive descended into an officially sanctioned slaughter. In other wars, such as the US war in Vietnam, this kill-results-based logic degraded into the killing 'of anything that moves' in order to produce the corpses that were presented as KIAs.[2] Decades after the 'litany of atrocities' committed by US troops in Vietnam in order to satisfy the body count,[3] a similar murderous logic took over the official war effort in Colombia.

Literal denial hovers over a large, still undetermined, portion of the killings by COLAR; interpretative denial is embedded in the social understanding of the sham-KIAs; and implicatory denial thrives as only 'bad apples' are called

1 P. Zimbardo, *The Lucifer Effect. Understanding How Good People Turn Evil*, Random House Trade Paperbacks, New York 2007.

2 Nick Turse described the noxious effects of the state promoted pressure to kill in war, in N. Turse, *Kill Anything that Moves: the Real War in Vietnam*, Metropolitan Books, New York 2013. He depicts 'a system of suffering' put in place in the mid-1960s by the US Department of Defense through the 'body count' as '*the* measure of success' in the Vietnam War. Ibid., pp. 41–75.

3 Ibid., pp. 108–143.

to bear the responsibility.[4] This paper examines the success of the 'false positive scandal' formulation as a means to conduct controlled acknowledgement, whilst attaining plausible deniability for organisational wrongdoing and shielding higher-ups from responsibility. In addition to exemplifying some of the more common manifestations of denial through the ways the sham-KIAs were rationalised and covered-up, this paper emphasises the role played by conformity in the organisational spread and the denial of the practice. Though conformity 'is widely used, highly plausible and makes obvious empirical sense' it has not received sufficient attention as one of the basic drivers of institutional denial.[5] In the context of the military, conformity with atrocity turns to institutional connivance, as commanders strive to remain 'fully uninformed.'[6] As Stan Cohen puts it: 'Careful management is needed to sustain the convenient fiction that those in charge knew nothing of what was going on.'[7] Through concrete examples, this paper contributes to flesh out some of the implications of 'conformity' in the perpetration and denial of atrocities. As Cohen highlighted '"conformity" does not have the resonance of "obedience to authority", but deserves equal attention.'[8]

After providing an overall description of the practice of sham-KIAs, in the first section, the paper illustrates how situational and organisational factors promoted and facilitated the spread of the sham-KIAs throughout tactical units in COLAR.[9] This second section illustrates how these murders became normalised and routinised within COLAR, and also reveals different mechanisms of 'denial at work'. The third section addresses the way in which controlled and partial acknowledgement has been used to contest organisational wrongdoing. The paper ends with a word in conclusion aimed at underscoring the organisational implications of the sham-KIAs. As denial endures as the official response to the sham-KIAs, deception and mendacity take over as collective values in COLAR. Lies and murder have become business as usual.

---

4 S. Cohen, *States of Denial: Knowing about Atrocities and Suffering*, Polity Press, Cambridge 2001. This paper uses the categories of denial mechanisms and rhetorical included in Stan Cohen's basic framework on denial in order to analyse denial practices, as it is convenient, though not without flaws. Ibid., pp. 51–116.

5 Ibid., p. 91.

6 The expression is taken from Stan Cohen's work on denial of atrocities.

7 Ibid., p. 68. He continues: 'The key to successful conspiracy ... is that the higher-ups do not ask what's going on, and the lower-downs do not tell.' This is the route to constructing 'genuine deniability.'

8 Ibid., p. 91.

9 The analysis is based on official documents and sealed records that offer insight into the organisational dimensions of the killing spree. All original documents are in Spanish. The portions cited were translated to English by the author. Many of these documents can be found in copious criminal case files, most of them resting, dusty or mouldy, in file cabinets of the 'competent authorities'. Others are part of active prosecutions or already-decided criminal cases. Where needed in order to protect the source or not damage an ongoing investigation, the respective document will be coded to permit verifiable attribution without putting the source at risk or damaging an ongoing case.

1. A GLIMPSE INTO THE COLAR SHAM-KIAs

Under pressure to produce tangible results whilst confronting an elusive enemy, COLAR became a well-oiled body-counting machine, seemingly increasing its combat effectiveness, according to the reported KIAs, particularly between 2002 and 2008.[10] These kills responded to organisational dynamics: enemy deaths were aggressively ordered down the chain of command; covered corpses were exposed in local news media as war trophies; commanders rewarded units reporting KIAs; kill ratios were used to compare the effectiveness of different tactical units; young officers were pitted against each other and promoted based on KIAs; rewards and decorations were granted based on enemy kills; and KIAs were reported by the Colombian Ministry of Defence (MoD) as *the* indicator of the results-based war effort. The official death tallies demonstrate the impact of the pressure to kill: whereas in 1999, the armed forces reportedly 'defused' 818 guerrillas and 35 paramilitary; by 2002 the yearly toll of reported KIAs had more than doubled – a total of 1,690 guerrillas and 85 paramilitaries were reportedly neutralised in action by the armed forces.[11]

This section provides a brief description of sham-KIAs. First, the practice is examined in the context of the overall kill rates reported by the MoD and numerical approximations to the sham-KIAs are presented. The second subsection offers a qualitative approximation to the killing spree and introduces categories in order to describe the variation noted in the caseload of sham-KIAs, as a result of differences observed in the modalities of commission and the selection of victims (targeting).

1.1. KILLING IN THE COLOMBIAN WAR AND SHAM-KIAs

Death is not as common in Colombia's counter-insurgent warfare as most people would expect.[12] Even at their height, reported combat kills were a small proportion of the overall lethal violence recorded. Most killing in the country

---

10 The expressions used in Colombian military jargon to refer to an enemy killed in action are: '*abatidos*', '*bajas*' and '*positivos*'. These translate literally to: 'defused', 'losses or casualties' and 'positives'.

11 Ministerio de Defensa Nacional, 'Resultados Fuerza Pública, actualizado Mayo 14, 2010' Resultados Operacionales, Dirección de estudios sectoriales, Viceministerio para la estrategia y la planeación, Bogota 2010.

12 Except for specific war fronts, in the south-western part of Colombia, some mountainous regions (Cauca, for example), and the north-western border territory with Venezuela (Norte de Santander), combats are sporadic and without much strategic importance. The nature of the guerrillas, the presence of strong paramilitary forces, and the vulnerabilities of a large military force moving by land render combat an elusive reality in Colombia. The war experience for most COLAR soldiers is about monotonously waiting, and aimlessly marching, generally at night, and waiting some more. Physical and psychological conditions

takes place outside the context of combat; for example, in 2011, the MoD reported 406 enemy KIAs,[13] whereas, the national forensic authority reported 16,554 homicides nationwide.[14] This proportion is merely indicative, as underreporting needs to be considered.[15]

Conveniently for this analysis, the universe of official KIAs is delineated by the fact that there is an account of every event, through the respective bureaucratic documentation, the production of the body, and the tally that reports positive results in the Colombian war effort. COLAR members committed other types of killings and egregious violations, under the radar; however, these incidents are not part of the official scorecard and are not part of this analysis.[16]

The yearly evolution of the overall kill numbers, as reported by the MoD, is represented in figure 1: enemy KIAs are reported according to armed group membership (guerrilla or paramilitary).[17] The line graph provides the overall context for the moment when the sham-KIAs burgeoned. COLAR's kill rates start rising in 2000, with a sharp increase observed in 2002, doubling 1999 totals. As can be observed in the graph, the peak for the kill indicator was reached in 2007, which was followed by a striking drop in 2008.

---

of this routine are austere; food is often lacking, illness is negligently treated, and civic-military relations are jittery. Morale is low and social tensions in the ranks are disturbing; hierarchical abuse is extended.

13 According to the Ministry of Defence (MoD), the annual casualties on the state side are less than 500 per year. For 2011, it reports that 350 members of the military were murdered. The circumstances of the death are not specified.

14 Instituto Nacional de Medicina Legal y Ciencias Forenses (INMLCF), 'Comportamiento del homicidio. Colombia, 2011' 2012 *INMLyCF* <www.medicinalegal.gov.co/documents/10180/34616/2-F-11-Homicidios.pdf/01a6b108-57cd-48bc-9e9b-dcdba0d918a2> accessed 10.10.2014; and Ministerio de Defensa Nacional 2010, 'Resultados Fuerza Pública, actualizado Mayo 14, 2010' Resultados Operacionales, Dirección de estudios sectoriales, Viceministerio para la estrategia y la planeación, Bogota 2010.

15 Recorded murders, whether by the National Police or the forensic authority, are all subject to underreporting. See P. Ball and M. Reed Hurtado, 'Cuentas y mediciones de la criminalidad y la violencia' in INMLCF, *Forensis 2014: Datos para la vida*, Imprenta Nacional, Bogota 2015, pp. 529–546, analysing the problem of missing data in official murder statistics.

16 Though this analysis is circumscribed to official KIAs, many other forms of violence (such as other types of executions, disappearances, torture, rape and displacement) occur in the Colombian context.

17 Notice the considerable difference in kill ratios: paramilitary groups were seldom confronted and war casualties from these armed groups were scarce. Once the paramilitary demobilisation concluded in 2006, the MoD officially vanished these groups from the tally; and, in 2007, reported the use of lethal force against the offspring of those groups. The MoD terms these 'enemies' as 'criminal gangs.' They have been re-labelled as neo-paramilitary groups to underscore some elements of continuity with paramilitary groups (including conformation, structure, state-complicity and activities), still recognising some new elements that rise in the process of reconfiguration.

Figure 1. KIAs Reported by the Ministry of Defense

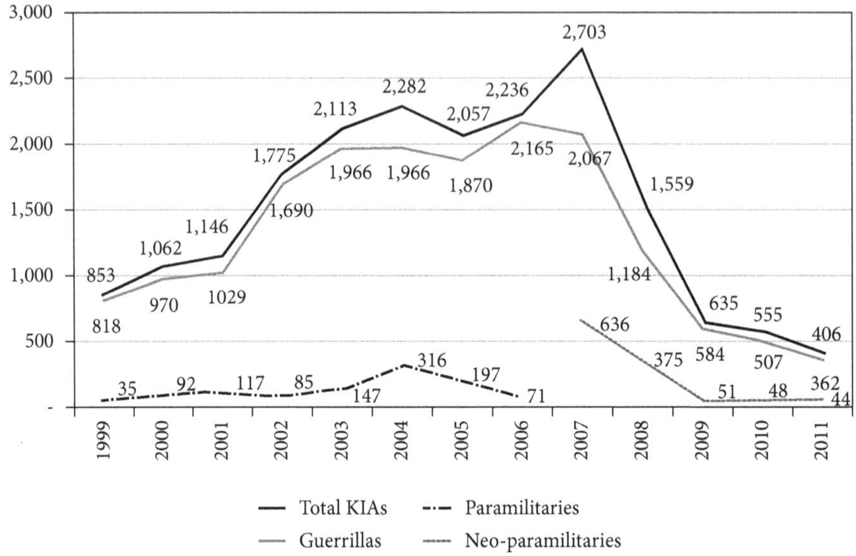

As the peak in the killing spree is of interest, the dramatic drop in KIAs recorded after 2008 is as relevant to understand the configuration of organisational offending. The sharp decline in the use of lethal violence by COLAR is a clear demonstration of the type of negative control that can be asserted in a total institution, such as the military: when the order to stop was given, the killing stopped – at least the great bulk of it!

The sharp drop in the kill curve can only be explained by the effect of official, but controlled and partial, acknowledgement of a few cases of sham-KIAs within COLAR that took place in late 2008. After family members of victims from an urban locality neighbouring Bogotá (*Soacha*) denunciated the slaughter of their loved ones, then President, Álvaro Uribe Vélez, was forced to publicly recognise in late October 2008 that 'members of the Armed Forces may have been involved in assassinations as a result of substandard compliance with procedure, protocols, and supervision'.[18] The understated assessment of the problem was made when absolute literal denial was untenable. Based on a secret administrative inquiry into these cases, then Minister of Defence and current President, Juan Manuel Santos, concluded that 'serious indicia of negligence at different levels of command' were found that 'could have facilitated the collusion

18 Presidencia de la República de Colombia, 'Comunicado No. 191' 2009 *Secretaría de Prensa, Comunicados* <http://historico.presidencia.gov.co/comunicados/2008/octubre/191.html> accessed 14.10.2014. The statement was based on the findings of an *ad hoc* Commission created by the Ministry of Defence through Resolution 4342 of 3 October 2008 (concentrating on 'the alleged disappearances in the *Soacha* district and … alleged homicides in the jurisdiction of the 2nd and 7th Divisions of COLAR').

of some members of COLAR with criminal elements ... in exchange for their support in attainment of irregular results'. The scandal was officially addressed through the administrative purge of 27 commissioned and non-commissioned officers, who were presented as bad apples in a tidy barrel. The three devices presented by Cohen in cases of partial acknowledgement can easily be identified: spatial isolation (this was not systematic); temporal containment (this happened in the past, not now) and self-correction (measures have been adopted).[19]

The partial acknowledgment was skilfully designed. One of the vetted generals summarised the process: 'with the removal of three generals public opinion calms down and ... the government shows that it is doing something'.[20] After the partial recognition of the problem, as the general predicted, further official action has been scarce. Though the findings of the military administrative inquiry pointed to severe flaws in intelligence, operations and control cycles within COLAR, the subject was not integrally addressed. In fact, the report of the inquiry commission continues under seal.[21]

The proportion of cases that amount to sham-KIAs within the official combat death counts is subject to intense and active contestation.[22] Colombian human rights non-governmental organisations (NGOs) have produced lists of sham-KIAs with the identification of the respective victims. For example, a coalition of NGOs compiled a list of 3,345 fully identified victims of sham-KIAs between 2002 and 2008, roughly representing 22% of the total KIAs reported by the MoD.[23] Another important source of information that allows the preliminary

19 S. Cohen, *States of Denial: Knowing about Atrocities and Suffering*, Polity Press, Cambridge 2001, pp. 113–114.

20 Statement by ret. General José Joaquín Cortes, then commander of COLAR's 2nd Division. The statement can be heard in: S. Bruno and D. Carrillo (directors), *Falsos positivos*, Mediakite 2009 at 28'40".

21 Ministerio de Defensa Nacional, 'Informe comisión transitoria. Resolución No. 4342 de 3 de octubre de 2008. OAP No. 0106 del 6 de octubre de 2008', Reservado, Bogota 2008, 73.

22 Early denunciation of the sham-KIAs was quickly turned on its head, as COLAR was presented as a calamitous victim of false accusations and juridical warfare. See, for example, J. McDermott, 'Toxic Fallout of Colombian Scandal' 2009 *BBC News* <http://news.bbc.co.uk/2/hi/americas/8038399.stm> accessed 28.07.2014, containing consonant declarations by then president Alvaro Uribe Velez and then Minister of National Defence (now President) Juan Manuel Santos. When faced with growing tension, then-president Alvaro Uribe attacked and declared on 25 July 2007 that the false positive scandal was the product of a smear campaign: 'the strategy of the guerrilla has changed. Now, each time a guerrilla is killed in action, immediately, they mobilize their *coryphaei* in the country and throughout the world to denounce that it was an extrajudicial execution.' S. Bruno and D. Carrillo (directors), *Falsos positivos*, Mediakite 2009 at 10'57". Denial of the murders, their interpretation and implications continue to be at stake.

23 Federación Internacional de Derechos Humanos (FIDH), *Colombia. La guerra se mide en litros de sangre*, FIDH y CCEEU, Bogota 2012, p. 16. A similar attempt has been conducted by a Jesuit human rights organisation, CINEP (*Centro de Investigación y Educación Popular*). This organisation produces an impressive record of alleged human rights violations in Colombia; after reviewing thousands of cases of executions, it compiled a list of cases coded as executions perpetrated by COLAR, under the 'false positives'

mapping of incidence (over time and space) of the sham-KIAs attributed to COLAR is Office of the Prosecutor General (FGN, *Fiscalía General de la Nación*). After filtering tens of thousands of records, based on information related to the alleged perpetrator, victim and circumstances of commission (including modality, time and place), 2,046 cases of homicides (many involving multiple victims) against members of the armed forces can be identified. All existing lists of sham-KIAs represent different universes and incorporate problems related to convenience bias and underreporting; nonetheless, importantly, all lists consistently shadow the overall kill rates reported by the MoD, marking the 2002 increase, the 2007 spike and the 2008 virtual disappearance of the phenomenon.

A useful numeric representation of the overall tendency of sham-KIAs is produced by comparing the information reported by the MoD and the total number of identified victims in homicide investigations against members of COLAR reported by the prosecutorial authority. By subtracting the number of homicide victims from the body count reported by the MoD, the impact of the currently questioned deaths in combat over the total combat deaths is palpably revealed in figure 2.

Figure 2. Reported KIAs by MoD, excluding number of victims in ongoing homicide investigations against members of COLAR (FGN)

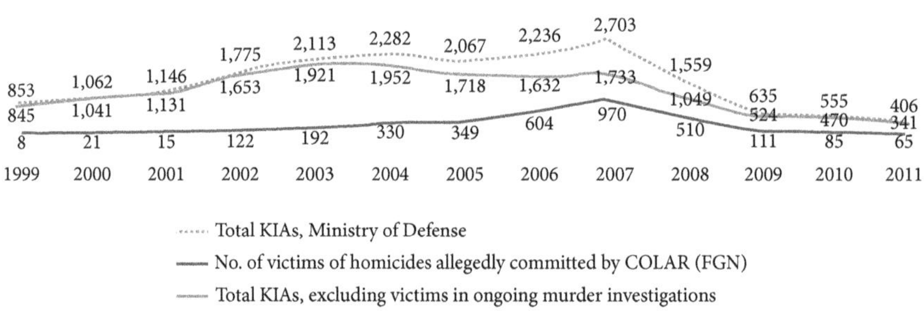

The juxtaposition of these numeric values supports the formulation of a strong inference regarding the salience of the sham-KIAs in the total results reported by the MoD, and thus urges an explanation that moves beyond the elucidation of individual cases and turns to the imbrication of organisational dynamics leading to the killing spree.

A final word of caution regarding the numeric approximation presented: all lists have virtually ignored exploration of foul play in cases in which the victim has not been identified. The subset of unidentified bodies within the KIAs is mostly unexplored, given the inherent difficulties of questioning or censuring cases with anonymous corpses. Only one sham-KIA case of a *non nominatum*

typology. CINEP accounts for 1,263 false positives attributed, between 1999 and 2011. This record mirrors the overall KIA curve: ascent starting in 2002, maximum peak reached in 2007 and sharp decent in 2008.

victim has been successfully investigated and tried.[24] Though it is feasible to conceive that combatants killed in action might not be identified, as they may never have received legal identity documents, in most cases lack of identification is related to a purposeful obfuscation or destruction of identity.[25] An unidentified body has proven to be one of the best ways to bury a sham-KIA in the cold case archives of the military criminal justice authority, thus effectively shielding all of those implicated from prosecution: many cases of murder can easily be literally denied as a result of the lack of identification of the bodies.

Sham-KIAs have a protracted history in COLAR operations;[26] undoubtedly, what changed in the period under examination was the extent to which this

---

24 It implicates a unit of *Batallón de Artillería No. 2 'La Popa'*, a tactical unit with a high rate of sham-KIAs. In this particular case, the unit reported a KIA as a result of Tactical Mission *Mito* (OPORD *Fénix*), after reportedly sustaining a thirty-minute combat on 9 March 2008, a few minutes after midnight, in an isolated site in Valledupar, Cesar. The reported enemy casualty was a young unidentified male, who was said to belong to the ELN (*Ejército de Liberación Nacional*). The bogus combat was poorly staged and the victim was a bad fit for the clothes used to dress him: standing over 6'2" and weighing over 260 lbs, the cadaver was dressed with a 28-inch waist camouflaged pant. The case is known among criminal investigators as '28 Waist' (*Talla* 28). In addition to the odd-sized pants, many aspects of the scene did not make sense. For example, the body was dragged behind a tree, leaving a visible trail, before investigators arrived on the scene. The purported combatant had reportedly sought shelter from the tree during the thirty-minute combat, from where he fought against 16 well-armed soldiers with a 38 calibre handgun. The John Doe did not test positive for gunshot residue and was shot dead from a distance of ten metres. The corporal and four soldiers directly implicated in the death of '28 Waist' were convicted. All elements that led to unearthing this sham-KIA and convicting the direct perpetrators can be found in: Juzgado Penal del Circuito Especializado, *'Homicidio Talla 28', Condena*, Valledupar, 22.07.2011; and Tribunal Superior del Distrito Judicial de Valledupar, *'Talla 28': Segunda Instancia*, Rad. 20016001074200880244, Valledupar, 07.09.2011.

25 For example, consider the case of Anderson Bladimir Monsalve Vinasco. He was initially reported as a John Doe killed in action on 4 June 2007, together with two other persons, in the municipality of Nariño (Antioquia). The three deaths were added to the body count of Counterguerrilla Battalion No. 4 'Granaderos' of COLAR's 4th Brigade. Ministerio de Defensa, Dirección Ejecutiva Justicia Penal Militar, Juzgado 11 de Instrucción Penal Militar, Rad. No. 103/2009, 2009. Though identification of the body could have been immediate, the fingerprints were not run through the Automatic Fingerprint Identification System (AFIS) until two years after the fact, on 30 November 2009. Ibid., p. 340. The other two bodies could not be identified because the fingerprint impression was not deemed suitable for comparison. Monsalve had been reported missing to the FGN on 18 October 2007; the delay in submitting the post-mortem fingerprints for comparison was purposeful. Though an obvious consequence, it is worth underlining that family members of a victim cannot intervene in a judicial proceeding until the victim is positively identified. Similar situations are readily observed in cases involving John Does that are processed by the military courts. Blatant cases of obstruction of justice by those working in the military courts can be documented in many cases.

26 Sham-KIAs have been documented as a part of COLAR's operational dynamic, at least since the 1990s. Episodic 'legalisations' of the murders of detained combatants and alerts about the risks for abuses that derived from a body-counting system are antecedents documented in the old declassified US documents. The National Security Archive, a Washington-based NGO, has uncovered the antecedents of the 2002–2008 upsurge of cases. For example, a 1990 cable approved by US Ambassador Thomas McNamara refers to a reported combat in Ramal, Santander, on 7 June 1990, in which COLAR had publicised nine KIAs. US Embassy in Bogota, 'Human Rights in Colombia: Widespread Allegations of Abuse by the Army',

practice spread throughout various tactical units and acquired higher frequency. Approximately 25% of the total KIAs reported by the MoD, between 2002 and 2008, are suspect. The proportion of illegally tainted cases is likely to be greater, considering that many deaths in combat have not been subject to any independent review.

Sham-KIAs are not identical throughout the country; variation in modality is detected in the offending patterns of different tactical units and even a few individuals.[27] The characteristics of the victims and the modality of commission of the murders vary over time and space, sometimes responding to new targeting criteria set by a commander, a 'new technique' brought to a tactical unit by a newly transferred officer, or a learned mechanism to perfect the sham or ensure proper cover-up.[28] The next section describes how this variation manifests itself through different types of commission.

declassified, US Department of State, July 1990 at 16. However, the administrative and criminal investigations suggested that the nine corpses, all members of the same family, were executed first, and then dressed in fatigues. According to the investigators, the cable states, 'there were no bullet holes in the military uniforms to match the wounds in the victims' bodies.' McNamara was concerned with the 'embarrassment' this and other cases would bring to COLAR. A Central Intelligence Agency (CIA) memorandum, also declassified pursuant to the NSA's efforts, underscored the effect of an unwritten 'take-no-guerrilla-prisoners' rule. Central Intelligence Agency, 'Colombian Counterinsurgency: Steps in the Right Direction', Intelligence Memorandum, Directorate of Intelligence, Office of African and Latin American Analysis, 1994, at 4. A 1994 cable cleared by the US Ambassador to Colombia (at the time) links the body count to the officer-promotion system within COLAR, and underscored the propensity for abuse. US Embassy in Bogota, 'MoD invites A/S Shattuck to visit Colombia', declassified, Department of State, October 1994 at 5. The existence of the body count system and the illegal ramifications of its sustenance were also documented by the US Department of Defense in an informational report. Department of Defense. 'Doc Id: 178798311, Cashiered Colonel talks freely about the Army he left behind'. Information Report, 1997 at 3.

27 Amongst so many cases the imprint of particular killers can also be identified. For example, squad leaders detected soldiers that were willing to follow any order and kill anybody. A young lieutenant who has turned state's evidence has described a soldier of a unit as 'great; he killed all of them'. Though individual and dispositional elements can explain some murders and particular forms of violence, those elements are insufficient to explain the overall pattern of sham-KIAs.

28 For example, the soldiers participating in the murders apparently discussed the minutia of setting up the staged KIAs. Evidence of such considerations is spread throughout depositions. Consider the testimony found in the files related to the murder of Hamilton Rivera perpetrated by COLAR troops in Meta in August 2006. Rivera was held and tortured for one day before being killed and presented as a KIA. The soldiers recall that at dinnertime they discussed whether they should feed the detainee and decided not to do so because they believed that the food they would find in his stomach during the autopsy could contradict the combat version. FGN, *Declaración no. 45*, reservada, Villavicencio 2013. Comparable discussions on how to ensure that investigators would not discover the fabrication of the crime scene refer to: the type of weaponry that should be used; ways of setting up the bodies; determination of the quantities of bodies; quality of the rain boots placed on the cadavers; type of clothing that should be used; best characteristics of a target; and proper fabrication of intelligence files.

1.2. SHAM-KIAs IN 2002–2008: THE VARIATION IN MODALITY

Extrapolating from cases of confirmed sham-KIAs occurring in COLAR tactical units between 2002 and 2008, five variants of this particular form of killing were detected.

The first modality is the execution of guerrilla members *hors de combat*. The victims of these homicides are persons protected under international humanitarian law; however, due to prejudice and shared values that justify these kills, their victim status is often denied. These cases are seldom investigated, as a fully identified guerrilla member is presumed a legitimate target of combat violence and the official version of the KIA is not questioned. Jurisdiction on these cases tends to be ceded to military courts, where the cold-blooded murder hypothesis is never investigated. For purposes of cover-up these persons are the perfect victims: the intelligence department within the tactical unit is likely to have sufficient information to construct a criminal profile for the kill. Combatants *hors de combat* are a distinct category of protected persons and their assassination after being detained is a war crime.

The second modality relates to the execution of land peasants and local civic leaders accused of being guerrilla collaborators. These cases mirror the first type, as they are predicated on the logic of dirty war; however, the victims are not combatants, though they are often included in intelligence annexes describing the conformation of local guerrilla fronts. The dynamics of these sham-KIAs respond to the following design: small COLAR units using informants (demobilised guerrillas) march into rural areas, apprehend persons identified by the hooded informant to be enemy sympathisers, transfer them to an isolated area, execute them and present the kill as a combat death. In these types of cases, as a result of the repeated use of the same informant, the persons killed construct a devastating trail of family ties and friendship. To illustrate: special groups (termed Delta Groups) from at least three different tactical units were assigned directly to the command of the 16th Brigade, in Casanare. These special groups worked with snitches provided by the presidential intelligence agency (DAS, *Departamento Administrativo de Seguridad*) to 'rid the region of militias and sympathisers'. A commander of one of those Delta Groups recognised a long list of murders committed pursuant to information provided by an informant known as Pastrana, reportedly a member of a guerrilla group (ELN, *Ejército de Liberación Nacional*) who had been previously captured by COLAR. In one instance, on 16 March 2007 the Delta Group troops killed an old man and his 16-year-old son (Daniel and Roque Torres), identified by Pastrana as guerrilla militias.[29] Roque, the son, had been a witness of the sham-

[29] Juzgado Segundo Penal del Circuito, *Sentencia anticipada, homicidio en personas protegidas*, Rad. 85001-31-04-002-2011-0015-00, Casanare, Yopal. 26.06.2013.

KIA of a friend of his in the same locality in late 2005.[30] This is not an isolated case.

These first two modalities of sham-KIAs have a well-documented past in COLAR's internal dynamic. Both are forms of denial of the victim that are loaded with ideological justifications.[31] Both of these types of kills were described to the author by a retired major, now working in the private security sector, as 'legalisations' that were part of COLAR's standard operating procedure.

The third modality is the transmission of bodies (mostly dead) by paramilitary groups to COLAR units to be presented as official KIAs. Again this modality has antecedents in the 1990s, but the period examined (2002–2008) demonstrates a rise. The most paradigmatic example of this type of collusion took place in Cesar by troops ascribed to *Batallón de Artillería No. 2 'La Popa'* (Battalion La Popa), under the 2002–2003 command of Lt. Col. Hernan Mejía. In October 2002, the unit presented a nationally acclaimed operation against the ELN, in which 19 guerrillas were reportedly killed in a single operation led by a 14-man squad.[32] COLAR's General Command praised the results. The investigation into the operation uncovered that Mejía had colluded with a paramilitary commander and the victims were members of the paramilitary group that had been internally disciplined to death and were dressed up as guerrillas and served to COLAR. Further investigations have revealed that the colonel created a special group within the battalion, called *Zarpazo* (an expression that means a swipe or a blow), which used paramilitary kills to increase its own body count. There is record of this type of collusion in most tactical units with jurisdiction in rural areas controlled by the paramilitary groups.

The fourth modality relates to the execution of persons with ties to criminal organisations or armed groups. The modality has two particularities that structure denial in these types of cases: the victims generally have a criminal background and are killed in the context of an active criminal plan. Both elements make the official combat death account more believable and more easily subject to denial: the victim is a 'usual suspect' that dies in a context that, though fabricated, is criminal in nature. The anti-extortion and anti-kidnapping units (GAULAs, *Grupos de Acción Unificada por la Libertad Personal*) throughout the country practiced this type of façade. For example, in Tolima, GAULA operatives had infiltrated several criminal rings or posed as their counterpart. In 2008, GAULA operatives put in motion a series of criminal plans that led their co-conspirators to death traps executed by troops of the Jaime Rooke Battalion, ascribed to the

30 Homicide of Hugo Edgar Araque Rodriguez, Alto del Triunfo, Aguazul Casanare, October 10, 2005 by a special group of another battalion ascribed to the 16th Brigade (*Batallón de Infantería No. 44 'Coronel Ramón Nonato Pérez'*).

31 S. Cohen, *States of Denial: Knowing about Atrocities and Suffering*, Polity Press, Cambridge 2001, pp. 61 and 82–83.

32 'La dura condena al coronel Hernán Mejía' 2013 *Semana.com* <www.semana.com/nacion/articulo/condena-coronel-hernan-mejia-paramilitarismo/357056-3> accessed 29.04.2015.

6th Brigade. The GAULA would initiate the criminal activity providing insider information to a group of criminals and then feed the information to the Rooke Battalion operatives so that they would neutralise the subjects. The GAULA got credit for the intelligence that led to the KIAs. The shams were near perfect as COLAR neutralised real criminal threats. However, the family members of the slain criminals detected the farce and denounced the army units.[33] Prosecutors have moved slowly on the cases; according to open sources this type of operation was conducted by GAULA-Tolima in thirty cases between 2006 and 2008, reaching a body count of eighty persons.[34] This modality appeals to the social convention through which criminals are stripped of their rights to facilitate denial.[35]

The fifth modality is the type of sham-KIA that has been partly exposed and partially acknowledged through the *Soacha* disappearance and killings, which gave rise to the 'false positive scandal'. It entails some criminal design and victim profiling, and was premeditated to break the link between the victim and the geographic space where the combat is staged, in order to avoid or delay the identification of the body. Under this modality, persons are intentionally recruited or lured away from their place of residence, generally with a prospect of employment, and then turned to carnage. Since it involves deception to lure subjects to their slaughter, these cases are full of micro-level dynamics that show vile human behaviour and criminal ingenuity. In some areas of Colombia, the killing apparatus was so demanding that houses were set up to serve as holding places for the would-be-victims, while the killing sites and operations were made ready to receive them, for example in Ocaña (Norte de Santander) and Pereira (Risaralda). Complex rings were set up to entice, recruit and transport young men from the Atlantic Coast to the border zone with Venezuela. Soldiers lured intimate friends to their assassination, as a result of a personal disagreement. And, in the process of constructing the perfect victim for this type of sham-KIAs, COLAR soldiers, officers and recruiters made evident their social prejudices: in addition to intentionally seeking homeless persons, drug users, alcoholics, petty thieves, gang members, they picked men with mental disabilities.[36] For

33 This narrative is based on a case file documenting the death José del Carmen Escoria Marimón and, his son, Humberto Junior Escoria in May 2008, in San Luis, Tolima.

34 I. Ramírez Suárez, 'Brigada de la muerte' 2012 *Cofradía.com* <www.revistacofradia.com/articulo/brigada-de-la-muerte/sec/noticias> accessed 22.10. 2014.

35 S. Cohen, *States of Denial: Knowing about Atrocities and Suffering*, Polity Press, Cambridge 2001, pp. 60–61 (used by perpetrators as a form of neutralisation).

36 Several soldiers that have testified confirm this type of profiling. For example, a soldier that served in Casanare reports that his commanding officer ordered him to: 'pick up any strays or pushovers (*ñanga*) that you can find ... for example, junkies, a street dweller or a person that nobody will claim.' FGN, Reservada, Yopal. This type of prejudice was also at play in the selection of at least one of the victims of the *Soacha* disappearances. Amongst the 16 victims lured from the locality south of Bogota in early 2008 to Norte de Santander, recruiters took Fair Leonardo, a young man who experienced a mental disability. He was delivered on 11 January 2008 to troops of the 15th Infantry Battalion 'General Francisco de Paula Santander'. Fair Leonardo was assassinated and reported as an unidentified KIA. He

example, 'Yolito', Erlín Javier Ortiz, a mentally challenged 17-year-old boy, was killed by the *Manosalva* Battalion in Quibdó on 2 February 2005 and presented, next to Octavio Espinoza, as ELN combatants that were killed in action. 'Yolito' was known throughout Quibdó, a relatively small town in the Pacific region of Colombia. His death sparked a local protest. As with most sham-KIA cases, procedural advances in this homicide investigation are nil.

Because this last modality has attracted public attention, it has been used as the general reference for the practice and, thus, public knowledge is incomplete. The other four modalities are as prevalent but are more easily denied and concealed; and have not been exposed. Victims of the fifth modality are portrayed as innocent and, thus, worthy of protection. Victimhood in other cases is often denied. For example, cases involving combatants *hors de combat* are openly dismissed as not meriting investigation, because the persons killed were guerrillas. Attributing victimhood based on attributes of the victim is in itself a deep form of denial and prejudice that is embedded in social life (which needs to be confronted).[37] It denies that atrocity is configured by acts against a person; not by the status of the person against whom those acts are directed.

One final element of the qualitative characterisation of sham-KIAs is intrinsic to the denial of the practice, but also shows its prevalence. The language used by those involved in the sham-KIAs is extended, and plagued with euphemisms and macabre absurdity. This use of language is in itself proof of routinisation and an inherent component of the denial of these atrocities, particularly at the micro level.[38] Perpetrators created their own language to deny the barbarity of their acts. The persons killed were referred to as dolls, dummies, steers, or packages. The language used is revealing of repetition and imitation in the organisation, as it is also evidence of dehumanisation of the victims.[39] Weapons, ammunition and explosives place on the bodies were popularly referred to as 'toys' or

was buried as a John Doe in the local cemetery. Due to the incessant search by his mother and the relatives of the other young men who had been taken from Soacha, his body, together with others, was exhumed; Fair Leonardo was positively identified on September 2008. When the bodies were uncovered, President Uribe attacked: 'They didn't go to pick coffee; they were there with criminal purposes'. 'Uribe dice que desaparecidos de Soacha murieron en combate' 2008 *El Espectador* <www.elespectador.com/noticias/judicial/articulo-uribe-dice-desaparecidos-de-soacha-murieron-combates> accessed 27.10.2010. Later that year, in October, during the controlled acknowledgement ritual, president Uribe was forced to rescind this initial stance. Fair Leonardo's direct killers were convicted. Tribunal Superior del Distrito Judicial de Cundinamarca, *Desaparición forzada y otros, Fair Leonardo Porras,* Case no. 54498-60-01-135-2008-80006-05, decision adopted 30.07.2013. The case continues to be officially addressed as an isolated incident.

37 This mechanism is replete with social prejudice, but becomes effective as official denial capitalises on cultural patterns of discrimination and exclusion. This type of denial includes a cultural component. See S. Cohen, *States of Denial: Knowing about Atrocities and Suffering,* Polity Press, Cambridge 2001, pp. 10–11.

38 See S. Cohen, *States of Denial: Knowing about Atrocities and Suffering,* Polity Press, Cambridge 2001, pp. 79–80 and 90.

39 H.C. Kelman and L. Hamilton, *Crimes of Obedience,* Yale University Press, New Haven 1989.

'decorations'. Whenever the operation implied the use of an informant to single out the victims, that person would be referred to as the 'lamp' or the 'flashlight'. Gruesome humour or institutionalised cynicism in relation to sham-KIAs can also be detected in the organisational language: for example, a squadron known for its effectiveness in killing sprees was named *Thanatos*; or a tactical mission for which soldiers received R&R leave after killing a John Doe on Christmas Eve 2007 was termed Operation Rest or Break (*Misión fragmentaria no. 150 'Descanso'*).[40] The production of this jargon demonstrates how the practice was assimilated into the organisation.[41]

Having illustrated these qualitative elements, the next section explains how the collective dynamic drove the practice.

2. TURNING ON THE HEAT: BODY COUNTING AND KILL QUOTAS

'I don't want blood spatters, I want rivers of blood.'[42] This incitement to kill is attributed to Major General Mario Montoya, a highly decorated warrior, representative of army hardliners, and accused of maintaining links with paramilitary groups.[43] Montoya has not been indicted by the justice system and refutes all accusations. He denies having used language that called for illegal kills. Likewise, the MoD and COLAR deny the existence of institutional pressure, the body count policy, or the existence of any type of institutional wrongdoing.

---

40 This case was reassigned in 2012 to the FGN after sitting cold in a military court for five years. Consejo Superior de la Judicaura, *Colisión de competencias 'Operación Descanso'*, Rad. 110010102000201200296 00, decision adopted 06.06.2012. The case refers to the homicide of an initially unidentified male killed, on December 25, 2007, in the outskirts of Valledupar, Cesar, by a squad belonging to Battalion *La Popa*. As with most cases, the combat took place at midnight, with no witnesses. The unidentified assailant used a shotgun to sustain a ten-minute combat, before being killed. The body and the crime scene were severely manipulated.

41 Rhetorical devices are evidence of normalisation and also demonstrate perpetrators' attempts to cope with their acts. See S. Cohen, *States of Denial: Knowing about Atrocities and Suffering*, Polity Press, Cambridge 2001, pp. 76–116.

42 The phrase is attributed (by Lt. Col. González) to General Mario Montoya. RCN Noticias, *Entrevistas con el coronel Robinson Gonzalez*, 09.06.2014 <www.noticiasrcn.com/tags/robinson-gonzalez-del-rio> accessed 02.10.2014. Montoya would reportedly use this type of phrase in the radio programmes with all major and minor unit commanders. Several officers have backed Gonzalez's version.

43 Montoya commanded Antioquia's 4th Brigade (2001–2003) and COLAR's 1st Division (2003–2005); both jurisdictions are plagued with sham-KIAs during his leadership. He also served for a brief period (December 2005–March 2006) as the first superior of a Joint Command set up in northern Colombia (*Comando Conjunto del Caribe*) before ascending to COLAR's General Command of COLAR from March 2006 until November 2008, when sham-KIAs were at their peak. Montoya is considered a loyal server to former president Alvaro Uribe and one of the architects of the success of his national security policy.

Refuting the official version, this section examines some elements that show that a body count policy was organisationally established and that sham-KIAs were either directly promoted by commanding officers or sanctioned through expressed conformity with the practice. It starts with a brief yet needed stipulation on killing in war, in order to assist the reader in understanding why denial of murder is so plausible in these events. The second subsection examines the ways in which the practice was instituted and routinised within the military operation. And the third subsection reveals exceptional (and still concealed) evidence of the results-driven killing spree.

2.1. BUREAUCRATIC KILLING AND DENIAL

An important stipulation is required to emphasise an obvious, though often ignored, aspect of killing in war by state militaries. Denial of sham-KIAs is, in part, effective because it relates to a form of violence that is legitimate in the operations of any official army, including COLAR killing. Uncomfortable as it may seem in writing, killing in war is normalised, which, inherently, produces denial.[44]

Killing the enemy in a civil war can be a part of state-organised and -sanctioned violence. Enemy fatalities produced by state militias are often deemed positive results in the war effort. Death is normalised to the extent that it is reflected as an indicator of the effectiveness of the military. It becomes part of a bureaucratic-administrative process, as death is regulated, ordered, planned, executed, reported, monitored and evaluated, all with official seal. As long as the fatality involves an alleged combatant, the lethal violence exercised is generally assumed to be legitimate. Criminal liability is not usually attached to these kills – either because the act is considered justified, or because the conduct is considered to not be criminal.

Incidents of death are tallied on a mortal score board. The numeric representation of death in war is consonant with the supposed anonymity of combat; lethal events are turned into figures and represented generically as friend or foe. The fog of war wraps individual deaths in facelessness and ambiguity. The particulars of killing are not examined. Consequently, society is sheltered from the burden of the killing mandate; and the military can go about the official business of killing under a protective cloak of mystery and secrecy.[45]

---

[44] See S. Cohen, *States of Denial: Knowing about Atrocities and Suffering*, Polity Press, Cambridge 2001, pp. 51–52 (presenting the implications of normalisation on mechanisms of denial).

[45] This type of lethal violence is hidden from scrutiny, with the argument of sheltering society from the gruesome act of killing, whilst freeing the specialists of violence to conduct their business in a privatised fashion, which grants secrecy and minimises independent control. This comment is based on Norbert Elias' observations on the privatisation of disturbing events or the removal of 'the distasteful from the sight of society'. It has been applied to 'the spectacle of suffering' and to the modern institution of punishment and regulated violence. D. Garland, *Punishment and Modern Society: a Study in Social Theory*, University of Chicago Press, Chicago 1990, pp. 213–247. In reference to state-sanctioned violence, Garland

Nonetheless, the dire consequences on the humanity of soldiers caused by the brutal demand to kill on behalf of the state should not be dismissed.[46]

Commanders stimulating or tolerating sham-KIAs did not necessarily give illegal orders; when they asked for kills they were within their regulated sphere of action. Commanders were not asking soldiers to torture, rape or disappear. They were asking for kills; and, within reasonable limits, the order to kill could be legally transmitted down the chain of command. The orders to disappear or rape could not.

Sham-KIAs are premised and structured on the perfect organisational defence for commanders: troops were ordered to capture the enemy; if met with armed resistance, soldiers were authorised to respond with force. In every simulated case, this reasoning is used to hide the premeditated murder; additionally, the operation is bureaucratically wrapped in official paperwork. Each kill is embedded in a prim trail of paperwork and official procedure, including: all documents in preparation for the military action – an Intelligence Report (that serves as the annex motivating the mission), an Operation Order (OPORD), followed by a Tactical Mission; all documentation concerning the engagement – Patrol Report, Radiogram on results, Certification of Material Seized, Certification of Ammunition Used; all documentation leading to formal inquiry – Report by First Respondent on Crime Scene, Technical Inspection of the Corpses, Report of Event to Military Judge, Decision by the military judge to open an investigation, sworn statements by soldiers and officers involved in the tactical mission; and the documentation flowing from the positive result – Commendation Request, Notations in professional files of those involved, Army Lessons Learned, and Certification of Award to Informants, amongst others. The paper trail is long and ludicrous, but organisationally significant.

The existence of the administrative documentation supporting each sham KIA is one of the factors that generates organisational responsibility and illustrates how the criminal practice was implanted in COLAR's internal processes. In addition to killers, sham-KIAs needed officers to produce documentation and commanders to sign-off on the operations to mask the murders in organisationally acceptable terms. The following insider testimony from an officer that served in COLAR's 14th Brigade reveals the bureaucratic process involving several branches of the military unit:

> 'Once we had secured a victim, the intelligence officer … and … the company commander would speak with the battalion commander … so that he would back

holds: 'violence … is usually removed from the public arena, and sanitized or disguised in various way, often becoming the monopoly of specialist groups such as the army, the police, or the prison staff which conduct themselves in an impersonal, professional manner, avoiding the emotional intensity which such behaviour threatens to arouse.' Ibid., p. 223.

46 'War is not only becoming more lethal in terms of its ability to kill and maim; it is far more destructive in its ability to drive soldiers mad.' R.A. Gabriel, *The Painful Field: the Psychiatric Dimension of Modern War*, Greenwood Press Inc., Westport, CT 1988, p. 7.

the operation. Then, the operations branch … designed the tactical mission so that a special group could carry it out. The mission defined the number of troops that would participate but in reality this was fake; because, for example, if the tactical mission said it would be 01–02–10 (i.e. one officer, two non-commissioned officers, and ten soldiers) that was a lie, because only those who were going to do the job would go; sometimes they would go in civilian attire. After the KIA was reported, (the tactical unit commander) coordinated with the judicial authorities for the inspection of the body.'[47]

Corroborating versions of the way the sham-KIAs were administratively legalised are available in copious documentary evidence.[48] All the testimonies concur in stressing that the paperwork had nothing to do with the way the war was fought, but that it was a necessary element in the criminal scheme. A lieutenant describes it succinctly: 'those OPORDs do not reflect what in reality was done, the real operations were defined by the verbal orders we received from [the commander].'[49]

Notwithstanding this practical understanding, the paperwork in each case is ceremoniously reviewed by military courts and most prosecutors as the primary source of evidence, as if bureaucratic records could not lie. Bound by presumptions of legality and legitimacy, heaps of ritualistic records are used to deny murder and bar independent scrutiny of killing in war. In this way, the paper trail successfully serves as a denial mechanism based on legalism – a powerful form of interpretive denial,[50] almost becoming part of what Cohen describes as a 'vital lie'.[51]

---

47 Procuraduría General de la Nación (PGN), 'Diligencia de queja suscrita por Edgar Iván Flórez Maestre' Medellín, 15.12.2009, pp. 3–4.

48 In a different operational context, a professional soldier assigned to a Joint Task Force operating in the Atlantic Coast (FTC, *Fuerza de Tarea Conjunta-Sucre*) provided a sworn deposition that similarly described the procedure and the involvement of the various branches. Describing the legalisation of the murders of two men committed on 1 November 2007, in Galeras, Sucre, under OPORD 'Excalibur', he declared: 'The guys from the (operations branch) drafted the OPORD; the guys from the intelligence branch did the intelligence report; with that information the Colonel was the one that directly communicated with the squads and coordinated the kills … To get the guns sometimes the counter guerrilla units put the money together and bought the guns; other times the money came directly from the FTC … For example, if we had to produce a KIA and the cost was two million (pesos), sometimes the company raised a million and the rest came out of the expenses of the FTC. This money was delivered to a member of the (intelligence branch) who was in charge of going to buy the guns or arranging for it; the guns were delivered to whoever was going to make the kill.' FGN, 'Declaración de Iván Darío Contreras Pérez', *Escrito de Acusación, homicidios Fabio Alberto Sandoval y Eleonais Manuel González*. 01.11.2007, pp. 11–12.

49 Juzgado Segundo Penal del Distrito Judicial, *Acta de audiencia*, Yopal, Casanare 18.05.2012.

50 S. Cohen, *States of Denial: Knowing about Atrocities and Suffering*, Polity Press, Cambridge 2001, pp. 107–108.

51 Ibid., pp. 64–68.

2.2. KILL, TAKE NO PRISONERS: CONNIVANCE AND CONFORMITY

Officers point to unwritten communication as the source of the relentless pressure to satisfy death quotas. For instance, the following testimony belongs to a colonel who arrived in 2007 as the commander of a Joint Task Force in the department of Sucre (FTC, *Fuerza Tarea Conjunta*-Sucre), an experimental rollout unit that was supposed to counter mounting insecurity in that region. Prior commanders had produced significant results. The colonel stated:

> 'Approximately two months after [assuming command of the FTC] I found out that some of the KIAs from prior years, and those I had accounted for as commander, had been staged and were actually false positives. After that I became a part of the illegal organization. First because, well, I preferred to keep quiet, and, I don't know, for fear of my life and my family's; and second out of fear of being kicked out of the Army. Because in a meeting in April in Corozal, well, Minister [of Defence, at the time] Santos, responding to a lot of complaints from the cattle-ranchers, had told me that if this wasn't fixed, he would kick me out of the Army. Basically for these two reasons, I kept quiet and stayed on with the army as a result of the illegal activity.'[52]

Several other officers recall the extreme pressure to produce KIAs coming down from Major General Montoya and others top military and civilian authorities. For example, Adolfo Guevara, an army captain that went rogue and joined paramilitary forces, affirms: 'those were the policies of [Gen.] Mario Montoya: "kill them, kill them. Don't bring me detainees. If you don't have KIAs, figure out what to do".'[53] Guevara confessed to directly perpetrating several sham-KIAs as a member of an anti-kidnapping unit of the military (GAULA) on the Atlantic coast.

Testimonies from COLAR members of all ranks ratify the existence of the official pressure. Kills were demanded at any cost and by any means; sham-KIAs, though not officially accepted, were not rejected. Retired Major Juan Carlos Rodriguez, who is now turning state's evidence, stressed that dead bodies were the only metric of success for commanders. This rogue officer, with extensive links to paramilitary groups in Valle del Cauca, declared:

> 'Detainees were of no use to a commander. The person that brought a detainee was seen as a mediocre fighter. It was the KIAs, the bodies that were useful to us. The more kills you had the more admired you were amongst the troops, the more medals you would get, and the greater amount of leave you would be allowed to have.'[54]

52 FGN, UNDH-DIH, 'Indagatoria a Luis Fernando Borja A', Bogota, 20–21.12.2010.

53 A.E. Guevara Cantillo interview by Gonzalo Guillen, 2013 at 40'32" (copy on file with the author). Guevara reportedly refers to Montoya during the time when he commanded COLAR's 1st Division.

54 M. Del R. Arrázola, 'Las confesiones de Zeus' 2014 *El Espectador* <www.elespectador.com/noticias/judicial/confesiones-de-zeus-articulo-501494> accessed 10.10.2014.

The pressure to kill created a take-no-prisoners rule. Major Rodriguez recalled that his commander protested when he turned in three guerrilla members alive.[55] He recounted his superior's response: 'Why did you bring them in alive? The intelligence officer also recalled that this type of reaction was also prevalent outside the military institution: 'When I took them to the FGN, the prosecutors themselves said: "Why would you bring them in alive?" So after a while you would get the message; it was a system where everybody wanted kills and it seemed normal to me to turn them in dead, even if they were alive when I had captured them.'[56]

In response to the body count pressure, tactical unit commanders turned to their troops and stimulated the killing through incentives and provided assurances that their conduct would not be subject to external review.[57] Most soldiers, on record, state that their incentive was not monetary but rather determined by leave granted by their commanders.[58] According to the caseload

---

55 Ibid.

56 Ibid. The effects of the take-no-prisoner rule are confirmed in tactical units throughout the country, not only by officers but also by soldiers. As baked by the sworn statements of a sergeant and a soldier from Casanare's 16th Brigade in: FGN, 'Ampliación de indagatoria a sargento', *Reservada Casanare 61,* Bogota, 2010. See also FGN, Fiscal Seccional No. 87, *Constancia,* Código Único de Investigación 05-736-60-00348-2007-80162, 29.08.2007; and FGN, *Declaración 45*, reservada, Villavicencio 2013.

57 This driver reveals criminal design by commanders who attempted to manipulate the justice system and prevent civilian authorities from assuming jurisdiction. Additionally, it shows some level of rationalisation by soldiers who committed crimes under the belief that the military courts – their peers – would shield them. Abundant testimony from soldiers corroborates both of these postulates. For example, the commander of the urban special forces of Medellin (AFEUR No. 5) assured his troops that they needed not worry about the justice system, because all cases would remain in the military courts and there would be no investigation. FGN, *Acta de sentencia anticipada SLP 4*, Reservada, Bogota 2013. In the same sense, see: FGN, *Ampliación de diligencia de indagatoria SLP 16*, Reservada, 2011; and FGN, *Ampliación de indagatoria Sargento 61*, Reservada, Casanare 2010. In some cases, commanders also attempted to control the ordinary criminal justice system, through complacent or colluded crime scene investigators, prosecutors or judges. Furthermore, legal counsel was secured to coach soldiers on how to present the official version, whether to military courts or prosecutors. SLP-BCG29, *Declaración Libre*, reservada, 2011. This mechanism initially thought to be an absolute safeguard has not proven completely true, at least for soldiers. Officers, especially in the senior ranks, do remain as untouchables.

58 An economic incentive was added to the body count logic through a financial reward mechanism instituted by Permanent Ministerial Directive No. 29 of 2005 – also secret, though this document was leaked to the press. Ministerio de Defensa Nacional, 'Directiva Ministerial Permanente No. 29/2005, *Política ministerial que desarrolla criterios para el pago de recompensas,* Bogota 17.11.2005. This directive's content is fairly standard; it replaced a similar document from 1998, and, in turn, it was replaced in 2008, with a few minor changes. The directive sets up an economic incentive table and monetary rewards for information that leads to different operational results, including KIAs. The regime discusses the use of relatively obscure funds within COLAR – termed reserved funds (*gastos reservados*) – that have a wide discretionary margin and are protected by legal confidentiality. A lot of speculation has surrounded the abuse of these funds as a driving force for the sham-KIAs. The funds are subject to little control and the entity charged with the oversight has not conducted rigorous audits; the audits, too, are secret. Contraloría General de la República, *Informe auditoría especial gastos reservados. Dirección Inteligencia Ejército Nacional. Pago*

analysed, the most common organisational drivers for soldiers were as follows: the threat of sanction or dismissal (negative incentives) if results were not produced; the promise of promotions or access to special courses; and the use official and informal leave, R&R, assignment to light tasks and extension of flexible schedules. In some cases, leave from military duty was a cherished commodity and one that pitted soldiers against each other, especially in tactical units stationed in isolated areas.[59] More commonly, soldiers went along with the killing because they were afraid of losing their job.

Command connivance and institutional conformity with the sham-KIAs are not expressed in illegal orders to commit murder; they are manifested through regular toleration of illegal activity, the bureaucratic cover-up of each one of the homicides, and the neutralisation of (internal and external) controls that are supposed to limit or contain illegal action. The practice did not spread because an evil commander ordered persons to be killed in cold blood; rather, it extended its grip because the top-down pressure to kill greeted cold-blooded murder with conformity.

2.3. SNATCHING THE BODY COUNT POLICY

COLAR's record was (mostly) wiped clean of KIAs being treated as metrics of success. There is some public evidence of when the metric was changed from killing to demobilisations and detentions. However, the official record was sealed and intentionally purged of the original documents structuring the institutional pressure and the incentive system to produce KIAs. However, unearthed secret documents and records confirm that an official body counting policy did exist within COLAR. Through command connivance and institutional conformity, sham-KIAs became a part of standard operating procedure within COLAR,

---

de información y recompensas. Vigencia 2007 y 2008, Reservado, Bogota 2008. Though hints of financial malfeasance exist, the flexibility in the structure of these funds, improper bookkeeping and the overall secrecy of the procedures have not allowed a more rigorous exploration of the economic benefits behind sham-KIAs. Based on the testimony of soldiers, the monies appear to not be behind their explicit motivations. Often monies recovered from rewards were directed to a fund that fuelled other sham-KIAs, in order to purchase weapons or cover the costs of transporting the victims. A few and scarce testimonies point to the funds being used for celebrations after certain sham-KIAs were committed.

59 As illustrated by a group of soldiers stationed in an isolated locality in the department of Meta: in order to decide who went on leave, they would simply draw straws to determine who got to participate in the upcoming sham-KIA. The soldier with the longest straw was assigned to the squad (in the advanced combat post) that would execute an operation with a staged KIA. FGN, *Documento reservado*, Villavicencio, 2008. The confessions regarding this scheme demonstrate the normalisation of killing to the extent that it gets treated as the ticket for a few days out of the bush.

unchecked until October 2008, when the false positive scandal led to partial acknowledgement.[60]

Then President Uribe underscored COLAR's commitment with human rights and indicated the cases should be assumed as actions of isolated soldiers that had deviated from formal procedure. President Uribe carefully declared: 'members of the Armed Forces may have been involved in assassinations and failures in terms of procedure, protocols, and supervision.'[61] He emphasised: 'the High Commanders, the Ministry of Defence, and the Administration have sought to be good examples in terms of the rigorous observance of the respect for human rights.'[62] Organisational wrongdoing was not accepted; on the contrary, he stressed: 'the primordial interest of the Ministry of Defence and the Commander General of the Armed Forces is to secure the integrity, morality and legitimacy of the military organisation, as has been reflected in the various policies, orders and directives. Amongst others, Directives Nos. 10 and 19 of 2007 by the Ministry of Defence and Permanent Directive No. 300–18 of 2007, emanating from the General Command of the Armed Forces.'[63]

Those documents were adopted at the height of the practice of sham-KIAs. They stand for calculated attempts to shield the highest military and civilian echelon from responsibility for a practice that had spread throughout the organisation. The MoD's Directives Nos. 10 and 19 of 2007 reiterate the obligations for competent authorities to enforce the law and avoid homicides of protected persons according to international humanitarian law. Permanent Directive 300–18 of the General Command of the Armed Forces, revealingly, introduces a 'new way' of measuring operational results, prioritising demobilisation and detentions over KIAs, except in the case of guerrilla leaders.[64] It generates a new metric of success, implicitly recognising a problem with the old metric, but not revealing the old metric nor addressing its organisational implications.

An uncovered military monograph conducted in 2006 in Colombia's Military War College (*Escuela Superior de Guerra*) by three COLAR majors offers a missing link in setting out the body count policy.[65] The officers explained

60 S. Cohen, *States of Denial: Knowing about Atrocities and Suffering*, Polity Press, Cambridge 2001, pp. 113–116.

61 Presidencia de la República de Colombia, Comunicado No. 191' 2009 *Secretaría de Prensa, Comunicados* <http://historico.presidencia.gov.co/comunicados/2008/octubre/191.html> accessed 14.10.2014. Acknowledgement was contained to specific incidents of sham-KIAs reported in the jurisdiction of the 2nd and 7th Divisions of COLAR.

62 Ibid.

63 Ibid.

64 Ministerio de Defensa Nacional, Comando General de la Fuerzas Militares, 'Directiva Permanente Nr. 300–18/2007', Bogota 20.11.2007.

65 J.F. Sabogal Moreno, L.E. Vargas Tovar and K. Soler Linares, *Cómo prevenir las infracciones al derecho internacional de los conflictos armados cometidas por militares en situaciones fuera de combate*, Tesis, Escuela Superior de Guerra, Fuerzas Militares de Colombia, Bogota 2006. This document was discovered by *Noticias Uno*, a Colombian television newscast.

that their objective in writing the paper was to address anomalous situations or internal mechanisms that gave were giving rise to IHL violations within COLAR, such as the executions reported in Antioquia's 4th Brigade. The officers designed and applied in July of 2006 a rudimentary survey to sixty commissioned and non-commissioned officers – majors, captains and sergeants. They wanted to examine the consequences of having a single metric of success within COLAR KIAs.[66] All surveyed officers confirmed that they had received incentives to produce operational results, KIAs; 94% of the sergeants manifested that they had been threatened with a negative notation in their career record if they did not produce results.[67] 75% of the officers stated that they had pressured troops under their command to produce KIAs.[68] Positive incentives contemplated to stimulate the results were: medals and other types of commendations; official R&R (including paid vacations); and assignments to foreign posts (mainly the Sinai Peninsula). As incentives were offered to the soldiers and officers having the best results, the majors concluded that the incentives were being granted to those demonstrating the highest level of kills.[69] According to the three majors, the pressure to kill was generating distortions in COLAR's internal dynamics. Though the results of the survey are not generalisable, the 2006 findings of this internal monograph should have raised institutional concerns, as the paper explicitly identifies the organisational harm generated by the pressure to kill.

An additional and, until recently, missing piece of institutional information that can be derived from the War College paper is that the system structured to grant military honours and promote officers throughout their careers was directly linked to the body count.[70] The commendation for 'Distinguished Services in Public Order' has a long tradition in COLAR's counterinsurgency campaign: it was created in 1963 and, though reformed periodically, it has been maintained since then. The mechanism became progressively more important during the first decade of 2000, and a central piece in instituting the organisational pressure and incentive regime that led to the implantation of sham-KIAs to satisfy killing quotas. The internal administrative documents that regulate this regime are secret: Permanent Directives Nos. 17 of 1996 and 50 of 1999; and COLAR's Operations Branch Circular No. 62162/CE-JEOPE-CO-122 of 1996, providing orders to COLAR's Director of Operations and to commanders of major units, respectively. Tellingly, on April 2008, commanders throughout COLAR received the order from the General Commander of the Army, Maj. Gen. Mario Montoya, to 'incinerate' both documents.[71]

66 Ibid., p. 61.
67 Ibid., p. 63.
68 Ibid., p. 64.
69 Ibid., p. 68.
70 Ibid., pp. 70–71.
71 Ejército nacional, documento reservado, April 2008.

The banned administrative ordinances contain the organisational policy that spurs superior and organisational responsibilities in the killing spree. The administrative circular set up a body count regime, differentiated by type of unit, in order to achieve merit. Including detentions, the 'tangible results' demanded by the command structure were as follows:

Unit	KIAs	Detentions
Division	300	1000
Brigade	150	500
Regular tactical units and BCGs	50	250
BAEVVs, tactical units guarding infrastructure,	30	100
Company commanders	15	80

The administrative directive underscores that the results go hand in hand with the public perception of security. It demands that soldiers – not only officers – should be considered for commendations. From the records available, it seems that the recommendation to consider soldiers for rewards was not applied; most soldiers were rewarded with leave and time-off, not with distinctions. The specification of the tangible results expected does, however, unmistakably explain why battalion commanders were always pressing for fifty kills or why twisted competitions took place at the end of a year between units nearing the 150 mark.

The veiled documents exposed in this section serve as the organisational backdrop for the operational demands that were passed down COLAR's line of command. In addition to structuring the numeric benchmarks that each officer relied upon to supervise the 'tangible results' of the war effort, these administrative orders provided the tools used to positively or negatively promote killing.

They provide the standard organisational logic in any chain of production: pressure for results gets turned on from top to bottom, with clear numeric targets, and the pressure is scaled down to the lowest production unit to ensure targets are met. Enhanced production is stimulated; reduced production is shunned and subject to reprimand. Higher-ups are not engaged in the mechanics, they just press the system for more and better results; their concerns are formal (ensuring that the regulatory framework is publicly acceptable), and dynamic (confirming that the system operates smoothly, with no observable deviations). Faith in the control mechanisms written into the system and shared organisational values that lead to active constraints – supervisors assume – will put any significant deviation from procedure or protocol in check. The difference between this ideal organisational dynamic and COLAR's operational environment is that the outcomes demanded were not thingamajigs manufactured as a result of a carefully regulated process in a controlled production line, but rather kills (the gruesome taking of human life) produced by members of a total institution, isolated from independent control and oversight, in the context of messy war conditions, in which the means available to attain results were scarce or absent.

In this type of operational environment, a combination of coercion and stimulus over members of the organisation to achieve the death quotas, coupled with a 'go get em' mentality and a twisted interpretation of the three mystic apes' slogan – see no evil, hear no evil, speak no evil – was conducive to the implantation of the sham-KIA practice to comply with the body count. Most senior officers did not directly commit the act of killing nor did they explicitly order an execution; likewise, staged-combat deaths were seldom ordered. The practice was promoted casually, through unwritten organisational parameters engrained in COLAR's culture, operational dynamics and surreptitious mechanisms. An illegal practice in an organisation that tends to overregulate to achieve calculated disorder (like COLAR) does not survive on the books, it survives and thrives based on a cycle of execution-acceptance, repetition-tolerance, and binge-connivance. While officially sanctioned (either by action or omission) during its perpetration or its ongoing cover-up, the practice changes the way business is conducted and taints the *habitus* of the organisation, and its values.

3. CONTROLLED ACKNOWLEDGEMENT + INDIVIDUAL RESPONSIBILITY = SUCCESSFUL DENIAL!

When forced to acknowledge the *Soacha* cases in October 2008, the government also calculatedly transferred the process of accountability to the 'competent authorities'. Parallel to announcing the administrative dismissal of the officers, the government declared that this action was 'without prejudice to the results that the criminal and disciplinary proceedings would yield'.[72] Criminal and disciplinary proceedings are managed in a fragmented way, case-by-case, according to the division of subject matter and regional jurisdictions that is established to distribute caseloads in the criminal justice system. Consequently, related cases – sharing common elements, including victims, perpetrators or modes of commission – often run parallel to each other and even go in opposite directions.

Most of the ongoing criminal investigations into the killing of more than 4,200 persons have gone cold; only one third of the cases are procedurally active and criminal indictments are directed in 90% of the cases against the low rank-and-file members of the army.[73] In addition to this already large caseload of

72 Presidencia de la República de Colombia, 'Comunicado No. 191' 2009 *Secretaría de Prensa, Comunicados* <http://historico.presidencia.gov.co/comunicados/2008/octubre/191.html> accessed 14.10.2014.

73 Avocats sans Frontières (ASF) – Canada, 'The Principle of Complementarity in the Rome Statute and the Colombian Situation: A Case that Demands More than a "Positive" Approach'

alleged sham-KIAs, many more cases are buried deep in the Executive Direction of Military Criminal Justice (MCJ) apparatus, an administrative dependency of the Ministry of Defence that purports to have jurisdiction over more than 1,500 homicide cases (many of them encompassing multiple victims).

Nearly 750 individual convictions have been reached in about 200 homicide cases, mostly of soldiers, non-commissioned officers and a few junior officers.[74] As of May 2014, 520 soldiers had been convicted of homicides related to the sham-KIAs. The justice system has overcome many obstacles to achieve these convictions. However, the lack of strategy in prosecuting and adjudicating such a complex caseload leads to sentences that concentrate on the reconstruction of a crime scene and the determination of subjective responsibility of those persons directly engaged. Little or no consideration is given to collective dynamics, organisational drivers, hierarchical structures, or examination of the specific incident in a wider context that might show recurrent *modus operandi* or criminal agents engaged in multiple events. Most convictions tend to disavow the official military story and find that a homicide was committed late at night in an isolated place by men who happen to be members of COLAR; but no consideration is given to crucial organisational elements, such as: the commission of crimes occurred while the men were on official duty; their ranked structure and logic imply dependency on a superior; or the fact that the homicide being examined is rapped in an administrative record (which implies planning, supervision, reporting and evaluation, after its commission).

Take the example of the thirty-year prison sentence against a sergeant and a corporal for the aggravated homicide of Humberto Antonio Zapata, established on 12 August 2010, by the mixed subject-matter jurisdictions court (*juzgado promiscuo*) in the small town of Antioquia.[75] Zapata, a peasant, was presented in January 2008 as a KIA resulting from the OPORD '*Majestad*'.[76] According to the official record, each of the non-commissioned officers commanded a squad; when they reached an isolated village in Segovia (Antioquia), they heard noises and bellowed the military salute, after which 'a (subject) started to run, they heard a shot coming from behind, and, at that moment, the soldiers opened

Special Report, ASF-Canada, Quebec 2012, pp. 24–42; and Caracol Radio, 'Fiscalía investiga 4212 casos de "falsos positivos"' 2014 <www.caracol.com.co/noticias/judiciales/fiscalia-investiga-4212-casos-de-falsos-positivos/20140926/nota/2434110.aspx> accessed 21.10. 2014.

74 Caracol Radio, 'Fiscalía investiga 4212 casos de "falsos positivos"' 2014 <www.caracol.com.co/noticias/judiciales/fiscalia-investiga-4212-casos-de-falsos-positivos/20140926/nota/2434110.aspx> accessed 21.10. 2014.

75 Juzgado Promiscuo del Circuito de Segovia, Antioquia, *Sentencia primera instancia no. 077-038*. Rad. CUI: 05-736-60-00000-2009-00001, decision taken 12.10.2010.

76 Ejército Nacional, Batallón Especial Energético Vial No. 8, 18 de enero de 2008, Orden de operaciones fragmentaria No. 0005 'MT Emperador' a la orden de operaciones 'Majestad'. No. 0005/DIV07-BR14-BPEEV 8-S3-375.

fire'.[77] Hours later, 'at one thirty in the morning', they found the victim injured; he later died. A military court initially secured the case; however, due to the intervention of a lawyer representing the interests of Zapata's family, the FGN regained jurisdiction and successfully led the case through trial. The conviction was upheld on appeal.[78] Without minimising the importance of countering the official KIA version and the convictions of the individual killers, the criminal sentence does not explain why the sergeant and the corporal killed Zapata and it does not explore the responsibility of the commanders. The two non-commissioned officers are presented as scoundrel murderers. This conviction speaks to the mechanics of homicide, as most do; but does not address the system of atrocity that was grounded in COLAR's operational dynamic.

After the soldiers, the bulk of convictions are of non-commissioned officers: 116 corporals and sergeants have been convicted. Commissioned-officer convictions mostly apply to lieutenants, as expected, given their role in overseeing the killing squads; as of May 2014, 65 young officers had been sentenced for their roles in particular sham-KIAs. Only seven colonels (mostly tactical unit commanders) have been convicted; most of them based on personal confessions.[79] Convictions are stockpiled, as were the sham-KIAs; links are not drawn and overarching explanations concentrate on individual deviants who abused COLAR's good faith. High-ranking officers continue to successfully deny involvement, and organisational responsibility is not discussed.

Faced with the growing amount of convictions for the sham-KIAs, the MoD continues to reject any insinuation of organisational ties. In 2012, it stated: 'There is no directive, policy or command by the Ministry ... or any other official institution, at any level, that can stimulate or prompt the commission of gross human rights or IHL violations. On the contrary, the [MoD] has an integral human rights and IHL policy that serves as the guiding route for the behaviour of all members of the Armed Forces.'[80]

---

77 Juzgado Promiscuo del Circuito, *Sentencia primera instancia no. 077-038*. Rad. CUI: 05-736-60-00000-2009-00001, Segovia, Antioquia, 12.08.2010.

78 Tribunal Superior de Antioquia, Sala de Decisión Penal, *aprobado mediante acta no. 072, homicidio agravado*. Rad. CUI: 05-736-60-00000-2009-00001, Medellín 08.09.2011.

79 Wilson Javier Castro Pinto was the first colonel convicted as a result of a full-fledged criminal trial. His conviction was confirmed on appeal. See Juzgado Tercero Penal del Circuito Especializado de Bucaramanga con funciones de conocimiento, Rad. No.: 68190600013920080039, Sentencia condenatoria contra Castro Pinto y otros por los delitos de doble homicidio agravado y otros, Bucaramanga, 15 July 2011. Of the officers depicted in this paper: Col. Borja of the FTC-Sucre pled guilty, as a result of overwhelming evidence against him. Col. Mejía, the commander of *La Popa* Battalion, was recently convicted; an appellate decision is pending. Most colonels remain silent, challenging the prosecution, while under military arrest. To date, no generals have been formally charged for sham-KIAs.

80 D.C. Durán Nuñez, 'Informe de la Corte Penal Internacional' 2012 *El Espectador* <www.elespectador.com/noticias/judicial/falsos-positivos-si-han-sido-politica-de-estado-articulo-389506> accessed 16.10.2014.

Criminal convictions of material killers are necessary but insufficient for confronting organisational crime. Superiors need to be brought to account for the killing; the material killers were on a mission, an official mission. Some of them might have had independent motivations and could have benefitted from the crimes; however, the bulk of the soldiers doing the killing responded to organisational direction. The following statement by a professional solider who served in a tactical unit in the Atlantic Coast candidly provides a synthesis of the inadequacy of an accountability strategy that concentrates on soldiers in cases of organisational offending:

> 'A soldier cannot mobilise a battalion to plan or execute operations. The commander knows everything that goes on. A commander knows that if a unit produces 50 enemy kills, well, soldiers will get injured in that process. Well, in our battalion there was only one injury caused by a [anti-personnel] mine and zero deaths ... Any general has to know that something is not right. ... Additionally, the commander was always granting special leaves for those kills ... He had to know.'[81]

When offending responds to organisational goals and institutional resources are used to commit atrocities and ensure impunity, individual criminal responsibility is a necessary but yet a partial response. The implications of the organisational involvement in the commission of atrocities require additional action to dismantle the system of killing embedded in COLAR.

4. A WORD IN CONCLUSION: ACCOUNTING FOR ORGANISATIONAL ENGAGEMENT

This paper has centred on the organisational implications of an offending pattern that has been understated by the Colombian government. Three elements exacerbate the situation: the ongoing aggressive whitewash (including the destruction of evidence); violent harassment of those working to reveal the extent of higher-up complicity in the sham-KIAs (including the killing of witnesses and intimidation of activists); and an ongoing official denial of any organisational wrongdoing.

Common sense dictates that pressure to produce results cannot be equated with an order to kill in cold blood. But there is nothing common about military sense, especially in war. When killing the enemy is expressed as an organisational goal of a total institution officially mandated to kill in war, and the enemy is not around to be killed, innovation is an easy ride to obtaining

81 Juzgado de Instrucción Penal Militar, *Indagatoria de soldado profesional, identidad reservada*, Reservado, 2012.

organisational goals.[82] War produces exceptional situations; war is in itself an exceptional situation that breeds contempt for the law and houses anomie. The anonymous soldier is expected to do the unspeakable in the dark penumbra of the state of necessity, as he, in turn, is promised (by his leaders and the organisation) protection from having to account for actions conducted in the name of the nation. The total nature of the military organisation also contributes to erect a wall to prevent external constraints and controls (whether formal or informal) from entering the equation.

The killing-the-enemy logic structured an arrangement of drivers (motivation and opportunity) at all levels of action (micro, meso and macro) to achieve the organisational results. Additionally, the organisation ensured that constraints and controls in relation to the killing were weakened or neutralised. In this operational or situational context, an incitation to get creative in meeting death quotas becomes a criminogenic element, either by coercion or facilitation.[83] Also, the neutralisation of controls becomes an element of the offending pattern, which engages collective forms of responsibility.

The official incitement to kill coupled with toleration of illegal conduct – conveyed through every day acceptance derived from superiors looking the other way or actively obstructing justice – can easily give way to a binge, especially in an organisational environment driven by ritualism and routine, as is any military organisation. In this way, a sham-KIA (conventionally proscribed) became the habitual effective means to obtain the much-demanded result: a combat kill. Sham-KIAs became 'open secrets'.[84]

For soldiers, the process of killing in this way is part of the nonsensical horrors of war. The material killers are a reduced number; most soldiers have to endure the process of knowing about atrocity, not committing it. For young officers, killing in this way was a horrific but often intoxicating induction into the way things got done. It, too, became a mechanism for personal advancement. For non-commissioned officers, sham-KIAs were just part of being a dog of war; some assumed it enthusiastically others eschewed the practice. Lastly, for senior officers the practice was in their warrior past, maybe not as extended, but ever present. Some senior officers never condoned the practice; however, they remained, and remain, silent. At the height of the sham-KIAs (2002–2008), not a single officer can claim ignorance of the practice; maybe they disapproved and did not actively embrace it, but conformity and passive connivance was extensive. This conformity is a form of complicity, which can manifest itself in

---

82 R.K. Merton, 'Social Structure and Anomie' (1938) 3 *American Sociological Review* 672–682.

83 Most literature exploring organisational crime relates to corporate settings. However, it offers a promising starting point to reflect on organisational dynamics of state crime. See for example M.L. Needleman and C. Needleman, 'Organisational Crime: Two Models of Criminogenesis' (1979) 20 *The Sociological Quarterly* 517–528.

84 S. Cohen, *States of Denial: Knowing about Atrocities and Suffering*, Polity Press, Cambridge 2001, p. 79.

many ways, as illustrated by Cohen: 'virtual blindness', 'not needing to know', 'not wanting to know, refusing to know',' 'compartimentalisation' or 'moral ambivalence'.[85] Though apparently passive, 'conforming to authority is itself an ideological value'.[86]

As with other cases of state offending, the sham-KIAs perpetrated by COLAR members are crimes that are not easily brought to account. The offending pattern is not explained by the accumulation of all known cases, nor is accountability achieved by determining the criminal responsibility of each individual killer. Powerful agents (both public and private) intervened in the organisational process, enabling or tolerating the horrific, but organisationally useful practice. Most were not engaged in the commission of atrocity, just in its knowledge. If left untouched, the practice of sham-KIAs within COLAR will continue to reflect on its values and operational environment.

Emphasis placed on organisational connivance in relation to atrocity does not imply that COLAR is a criminal organisation or that all members of COLAR are criminals.[87] However, it does imply that 'the permissive attitude' with atrocity needs to be confronted and addressed. Any organisational element that guided the implantation of sham-KIAs as a customary or tolerated practice within COLAR needs to be exposed and disassembled. As part of the needed organisational change, all officers and civilian authorities engaged in the promotion or cover-up of the sham-KIAs need to be purged from duty.

Conformity with atrocity within an official institution has organisational implications: ideologically it justifies atrocity; from a criminal standpoint, it shields perpetrators. If not addressed, the conditions that led to cold-blooded murder being officially sanctioned in COLAR are being wilfully allowed to persist. Organisational offending demands organisational reform, which can only start by official acknowledgment of the atrocities committed and their implications. Otherwise, official denial triumphs and atrocity is endorsed.

85 Ibid., pp. 85–87.

86 Ibid., p. 90.

87 As presented by Osiel, '[a]trocity by connivance often occurs by means of what the Official Report on the My Lai massacre referred to [as] "permissive attitude" on the part of commanders "toward the treatment and safeguarding of non-combatants"'. He continues: 'troops are simply given to understand, through winks and nods of acquiescence' that atrocities will not be penalised. M. Osiel, *Obeying Orders: Atrocity, Military Discipline and the Law of War*, Transaction Publishers, New Brunswick 1999, p. 188.

PART IV

NEW PENOLOGY

CHAPTER XVI

JIM CROW 3.0

Denial, Human Rights, and American Racialised Mass Incarceration

Cecil J. Hunt, II

'[W]e will not end mass incarceration without a recommitment to the movement-building work that was begun in the 1950's and 1960's and left unfinished. A human rights nightmare is occurring on our watch. If we fail to rise to the challenge, and push past the politics of momentary interest convergence, future generations will judge us harshly.'[1]

1. INTRODUCTION

Denial can be powerfully toxic on the social and political soul of a nation and its people. Right now, the United States of America is lost in a thick fog of denial regarding the uncomfortable truths about racialised mass incarceration.[2] The United States has only '5% of the world's population, but houses 25% of the world's prisoners.'[3] Among that 25%, 'blacks and Hispanics, together account for about two thirds of the state prison population',[4] and this figure does not even include those in local jails, and federal prisons. Considering the total number of the nation's incarcerated, blacks alone account for, 'more than 40% of the current prison population, while making up only 12% of the U.S. population.'[5] It is clear that the practice of racialised mass incarceration has dramatically changed

1 Professor Michelle Alexander, *New York Times*, 05.14.2011.

2 See below note 44.

3 G.C. Loury, *Race, Incarceration, and American Values*, Boston Review Books, Boston 2007, p. 5.

4 B. Western, *Punishment and Inequality in America*, Russel Sage Foundation, New York 2006, p. xii.

5 D. Pager, Marked: *Race Crime, and Finding Work in an Era of Mass Incarceration*, University of Chicago Press, Chicago 2007, p. 3.

'the racial and economic caste of the prison population.'[6] Something is wrong with this picture; and America is 'just beginning to reflect upon the political and cultural meaning of this new [prison] institution, upon what it means for America to be a mass imprisonment society.'[7]

The issues of race, mass incarceration, and human rights in the United States, is beginning to get some academic attention, as it should.[8] A new report from the Economic Policy Institute concluded that, in America, '[t]he disproportionate incarceration rate of minorities in general, and blacks in particular, is one of the most pressing civil rights issues of our time.'[9] Thus, it is clear to many scholars that racialised mass incarceration in the American criminal justice system has become a debilitating 'modern plague'[10] on the social, political, and economic fabric of America. But the plague of mass incarceration is not simply about putting large numbers of people behind bars, but rather, 'it's about law enforcement using the power of criminal sanctions to target, isolate, demonize, and oppress an entire group of people and their communities based simply on race. Imprisonment becomes mass imprisonment when it ceases to be the incarceration of individual offenders and becomes the systematic imprisonment of whole groups of the population. In the case of America, the group concerned is, of course, young black and brown males in large urban centers. For these sections of the population, imprisonment has become normalized. It has come to be a regular, predictable part of experience, rather than a rare and infrequent event.'[11] Therefore, the primary drivers of mass incarceration in America are race and class. For poor urban black and brown youths, 'imprisonment has become one of the social institutions that structure this group's experience. It becomes part of the socialization process. Every family, every household, every individual in these neighborhoods has direct personal knowledge of the prison – through

---

6 B. Western, *Punishment and Inequality in America*, Russel Sage Foundation, New York 2006, p. xii.

7 D. Garland, *Mass Imprisonment: Social Causes and Consequences*, Sage Publications, London-Thousand Oaks-New Delhi 2001, p.3.

8 For primary examples of this literature, see generally, M. Alexander, *The New Jim Crow: Mass Incarceration in the Age of Colorblindness*, The New Press, New York, 2010. D. Garland, *Mass Imprisonment: Social Causes and Consequences* Sage Publications, London, Thousand Oaks, New Deli, 2001; M. Gottschhalk, *The Prison and the Gallows: The Politics of Mass Incarceration*, Cambridge University Press, Cambridge 2006; B. Western, *Punishment and Inequality in America*, Russell Sage Foundation, New York 2006; T.C. Pratt, *Addicted to Incarceration: Corrections Policy and the Politics of Misinformation in the United States*, Sage Publications, London 2009; P. Butler, *Let's Get Free: A Hip-Hop Theory of Justice*, The New Press, New York, 2009.

9 'Mass Incarceration Is One of the Most Pressing Civil Rights Issues Today' 2015 *Economic Policy Institute* <www.epi.org/press/mass-incarceration-is-one-of-the-most-pressing-civil-rights-issues> accessed 3.15.2015.

10 E. Drucker, *A Plague of Prisons: The Epidemiology of Mass Incarceration in America*, The New Press, New York 2013, p. 40.

11 D. Garland, *Mass Imprisonment: Social Causes and Consequences*, Sage Publications, London-Thousand Oaks-New Delhi 2001, p. 2.

a spouse, a child, a parent, a neighbor, a friend. Imprisonment ceases to be the fate of a few criminal individuals and becomes a shaping institution for whole sectors of the population.'[12] It has not always been like this; the prison boom in America began in the 1970s[13] and has continued apace to the present day. As one scholar observed, '[t]he prison boom opened a new chapter in American race relations … [t]he punitive turn in criminal justice disappointed the promise of the civil rights movement and its burdens fell heavily on disadvantaged African Americans.'[14]

It is important to note that, the racialised imprisonment of hundreds of thousands of young black and brown men, is not the result of individual racist beliefs by so-called, 'guilty perpetrators'. Rather, it is institutionalised in every aspect of the American criminal justice system. But most Americans are in almost complete denial of the reality that their entire criminal justice system is infected with institutionalised racism. But such denials melt in the face of reality. Stanley Cohen has described such denial 'as an unconscious defense mechanism for coping with guilt, anxiety, or other disturbing emotions aroused by reality. The psyche blocks off information that is literally unthinkable or unbearable … [w]e are vaguely aware of choosing not to look at the facts, but not quite conscious of just what it is we are evading. We know, but at the same time we don't know.'[15]

2. JIM CROW IN AMERICA

The current racialised mass incarceration threatens to re-impose many of the same social and political burdens that were characteristic of a period of American history commonly referred to as 'Jim Crow'. The origins of this term are lost to history.[16] Historically, the American era of Jim Crow began soon after the end of the American Civil War in 1865, during what was widely known as 'Reconstruction'. Reconstruction is a term used to describe the ten or so years after the end of the American civil war, 1865–1877. During this period newly freed slaves and free blacks were lifted up from their previous condition of slavery and subservience, and were allowed to run for public office, sit on juries and testify in court against white men, start businesses, build homes and engage

12 B. Western, *Punishment and Inequality in America*, Russel Sage Foundation, New York 2006, p. 12.

13 Ibid., p. 13 (pointing out that '[f]rom 1975, the imprisonment rate began to rapidly increase').

14 Ibid., p. 7.

15 S. Cohen, *States of Denial: Knowing About Atrocities and Suffering*, Polity Press, Cambridge 2001, p. 5.

16 But we do know that in 1832 a man named Thomas D. Rice wrote a minstrel song and dance called 'Jim Crow' and the term had become an adjective by 1838, that was frequently used to describe the inferior nature of slaves in the old American South. Citing C. Vann Woodward, *The Strange Career of Jim Crow, A Commemorative Edition*, Oxford University Press, Oxford 2002, p. 7.

in all of the civil rights accorded to free citizens of the United States. However, Reconstruction ended in 1877 when the election for President of the United States essentially ended in a tie. Southern Democrats then made a deal with Northern Republicans, which essentially said that the Republican candidate could be elected as President in exchange for the government moving all federal troops out of the South, and to then let the whole problem of the Negro 'be left to the disposition of the dominant Southern white people.'[17] The period after Reconstruction was referred to by white southerners as Redemption, referring to their efforts to 'redeem' the south from northern oppression, which regarded the freed slaves as wards of the nation, whose civil and political equality were enforced by federal troops.

During the early stages of the Jim Crow period white southerners engaged in all forms of physical and psychological terrorism, involving murdering, burning out, and lynching[18] innocent blacks in order to enforce the common white resolve that the south, 'shall be and remain a white man's country'.[19] To drive home this message, with the sanction of the law, a whole series of laws were enacted throughout the south with the express purpose of driving the newly freed blacks completely out of southern society. They erected, 'public symbols and constant reminders of [black's] inferior position … and ostracism that extended to churches and schools, to housing and jobs, to eating and drinking … to all forms of public transportation, to sports and recreations, to hospitals, orphanages, prisons, and asylums, and ultimately to funeral homes, morgues, and cemeteries.'[20] Under Jim Crow laws and customs, the 'Negro was made painfully and constantly aware that he lived in a society dedicated to the doctrine of white supremacy and Negro inferiority.'[21] Jim Crow became 'synonymous with a complex system of racial laws and customs … that ensured white social, legal, and political domination. Blacks were segregated, deprived of their right to vote and subject to abuse, discrimination, and violence without redress in the courts.'[22] This period was epitomised by a plethora of 'White Only' signs on virtually every form of public convenience. This period of legalised Jim Crow in the South, and Jim Crow by custom in the North, lasted from 1877 to 1964, with the congressional passage of the Civil Rights Laws of 1964 and the Voting Rights Bill of 1965. These two revolutionary congressional laws were the direct result of what has come to be known as the Civil Rights Movement which began in the

17 Ibid., p. 6.

18 Lynching involved the capture of innocent black men and women by mobs of whites who then hung the blacks from trees, and burned the bodies on large bonfires, after which the mobs would engage in the butchery of cutting off pieces of the burned bodies to save as souvenirs.

19 C. Vann Woodward, *The Strange Career of Jim Crow, A Commemorative Edition*, Oxford University Press, Oxford 2002, p. 8.

20 Ibid., p. 7.

21 Ibid., p. 18.

22 R. Wormser, *The Rise and Fall of Jim Crow*, St. Martin's Press, New York, 2003, p. xi.

1940s. Despite many states' efforts to get around or avoid enforcement of these laws, for the first time in over 100 years, black people could legally come out of the social, political, and economic shadow of legalised white supremacy.

As Michelle Alexander wrote, despite the absence of specific intent, racialised 'mass incarceration is metaphorically, the New Jim Crow.'[23] She goes on to argue that: 'The popular narrative that emphasizes the death of slavery and Jim Crow and celebrates the nation's "triumph over race" with the election of Barak Obama, is dangerously misguided. The colorblind public consensus that prevails in America today – i.e. the widespread belief that race no longer matters – has blinded us to the realities of race in our society and facilitated the emergence of a new caste system … [t]he new caste system lurks invisibly within the maze of rationalizations we have developed for persistent racial inequality.'[24] She goes on to explain that 'there is no inconsistency whatsoever between the election of Barack Obama to the highest office in the land and the existence of a racial caste system in the era of colorblindness. The current system of control depends on black exceptionalism; it is not disproved or undermined by it.'[25] She goes on to explain that 'racial caste systems do not require racial hostility or overt bigotry to thrive. They need only racial indifference.'[26] Because of racialised mass incarceration and the extremely damaging effects that it has not only on the individuals who serve time but on their families and communities, she observes that '[a] human rights nightmare is occurring under our watch.'[27]

Under this 'new caste system', the message to young black and brown males who have served their time and been released from prison, is that as a convicted felon, you are now exiled from civil society. The significance of this exile is that you cannot rejoin society as a full citizen; you cannot participate in society by voting in local, state or national elections; you cannot serve on juries; you cannot receive social government benefits and if you live with someone who does, they will be cut off of whatever programme they are on; you cannot improve your prospects or your station in life by getting federal loans to go back to school to obtain the education or skills that you need to improve your chances of getting a job. These are sobering messages indeed to send to the hundreds of thousands of young black and brown men who get out of prison every year.[28] In fact, 'in many respects, release from prison does not represent the beginning of freedom

23 M. Alexander, *The New Jim Crow: Mass Incarceration in the Age of Colorblindness*, The New Press, New York-London 2010, p. 11.

24 Ibid., p. 14.

25 Ibid., p. 14.

26 Ibid., p. 14.

27 Ibid., p. 15.

28 E. Drucker, *A Plague of Prisons: The Epidemiology of Mass Incarceration in America*, The New Press, New York 2013 (he notes that as recently as 2009 over '700,000 individuals were discharged from prisons': p. 39. And that is not an unusual number of annual discharges from prison. Since 70% of prison inmates are black and brown, it is reasonable to presume that the same racial percentages are reflected in the prisoners released from prison as the prisoners

but instead a cruel new phase of stigmatization and control. Myriad laws, rules, and regulations discriminate against ex-offenders and effectively prevent their meaningful re-integration into the mainstream economy and society … the shame and stigma of the "prison label" is, in many respects, more damaging to the African American community than the shame and stigma associated with Jim Crow. The criminalization and demonization of black men has turned the black community against itself, unraveling community and family relationships, decimating networks of mutual support, and intensifying the shame and self-hate experienced by the current pariah caste.'[29] The real life consequences of racialised mass incarceration has clearly reintroduced the reality of racial caste back into American society, and created what amounts to a permanent underclass – a new class of untouchables – with devastating effects on both them and their communities.

3. DENIAL AND MASS INCARCERATION

America lectures the world on correcting and preventing international human rights abuses and punishes those countries it perceives as having violated those standards. It also enters into conventions and treaties to ban and discourage such abuses. Simultaneously America turns a blind eye to the massive human rights abuses in its own criminal justice system at home. Despite all of the racial progress in America over the past fifty years, the issue of race remains an open wound in American social and political discourse. It is still a difficult conversation for many American people to have. Many whites, both personally and institutionally refuse to engage in candid conversations regarding the existence, implications, and costs of the serious issues that result from the continuing 'problem of … the color line'[30] in America. As a consequence, America is either willfully ignorant, willfully callous, or in deep and 'collective denial'[31] regarding the systemic, stunning, and deeply distressing human rights abuses that are inflicted on whole communities of racial minorities all over the country, through its national policies of predatory racialised mass imprisonment.

This collective cultural denial of the human rights abuses inherent in racialised mass incarceration is not particularly benign. Instead, as Stanley Cohen has observed, 'denial is indeed conscious. Self-deception refers to keeping secret from ourselves the truth we cannot face. … [O]ne has to assume that

already in prison. This is truly a startling number of disenfranchised and marginalised young men of colour that re-enter society every year.).

29 M. Alexander, *The New Jim Crow: Mass Incarceration in the Age of Colorblindness*, The New Press, New York-London 2010, p. 17.

30 W.E.B. Debois, *The Souls of Black Folks*, Dover Publications Inc., New York 1994, p. 9.

31 S. Cohen, *States of Denial: Knowing About Atrocities and Suffering*, Polity Press, Cambridge 2001, p. 6.

she knew or knows about what it is that she claims not to know ... we notice and simultaneously don't notice.'[32] This is important because there can be little doubt that 'the phenomenon of mass incarceration has filtered into the public consciousness through cycles of media coverage and political debates.'[33]

Although some academics have written about the phenomenon of racialised mass incarceration, the vast majority of people and politicians in America have chosen to turn a blind eye to the suffering of young black and brown men that is occurring right in front of them. Cohen observed that, 'the psychology of "turning a blind eye" or "looking the other way" is a tricky matter. These phrases imply that we have access to reality but choose to ignore it, because it is convenient to do so.'[34] While denial is a very powerful personal and cultural force, Cohen describes this phenomenon in a way that tends to mitigate against intentionality. He writes that: 'Denial may neither be a matter of telling the truth nor telling a lie. The statement is not wholly deliberate and the status of "knowledge" about the truth is not wholly clear. There seems to be states of mind, or even whole cultures, in which we know and don't know at the same time.'[35]

This dichotomy is part of the phenomenology of mass cultural denial. How can the whole American culture, 'know and not know' about the plague of mass incarceration 'at the same time'? Cohen describes this as the, 'denial paradox'.[36] He explains by observing that, 'this might be simple fraud: the information is available and registered, but leads to a conclusion that is knowingly evaded.'[37] By this logic, the American criminal justice system and much of its white citizens, 'knowingly evade' the truth about the vast personal and community devastation caused by racialised mass incarceration. He goes on to observe that this kind of 'mass denial [is] characteristic of repressive, racist and colonial states. Dominant groups seem uncannily able to shut out or ignore the injustice and suffering around them. In more democratic societies, people shut out the results not because of coercion but out of cultural habit.'[38] Cohen goes on to describe this paradox theory 'in terms of cognitive psychology and decision making. This approach emphasizes the normality of the process, and lays down its emotional component. [From this perspective] [d]enial is a high-speed cognitive mechanism for processing information, like the computer's command to "delete" rather than "save".'[39] He also suggests that this process could be explained by the 'neurological phenomenon of "blindsight" as a model: one

---

32 Ibid., p. 6.

33 D. Pager, Marked: *Race Crime, and Finding Work in an Era of Mass Incarceration*, University of Chicago Press, Chicago 2007, p. 4.

34 S. Cohen, *States of Denial: Knowing About Atrocities and Suffering*, Polity Press, Cambridge 2001, p. 5.

35 Ibid.

36 Ibid.

37 Ibid.

38 Ibid.

39 Ibid.

part of the mind can know just what it is doing, while the part that supposedly knows, remains oblivious to this. More obviously, information is selected to fit existing perceptual frames and information which is too threatening is shut out altogether. The mind somehow grasps what is going on-but rushes a protective filter into place. Information slips into a kind of "black hole of the mind," a blind zone of blocked attention and self-deception.'[40]

A nation cannot credibly claim to try to solve a problem, the significance and implications of which, it will neither fully acknowledge nor face. Regardless of any feigned sense of a good will discussion of this problem, by a few liberal whites, and some 2016 presidential candidates, as a whole a nation cannot hit a target that it either cannot or refuses to see; and it cannot see the target without opening its social, political and legal eyes. In fact, in some ways the more they know about this problem the more they pretend not to know. This psychological phenomenon is what Cohen described as 'knowing and not knowing at the same time'.[41] Denying that such a serious social problem even exists much less is a cause of pressing national concern, or tentatively approaching it with eyes wide shut is not a strategy for success, but rather a guarantee of failure and the perpetuation of a distressing status quo that has already created a lost generation of young black and brown men and threatens more to come. Any meaningful cure to this plague will require America, as a people and as a nation, to wake-up and face the truth about its denial of the existence, significance, implications and costs of racialised mass incarceration. It will have to reconcile the two halves of its national brain, to gain access to the 'blind zone', that Cohen described.

4. RACIALISED MASS INCARCERATION

The term 'mass incarceration' was originally coined by David Garland, who wrote that this relatively recent social phenomenon is characterised by two essential features: '[o]ne is sheer numbers. Mass imprisonment implies a rate of imprisonment and a size of the prison population that is markedly above the historical and comparative norm for societies of this type'.[42] However, Loic Wacquant has taken exception to the use of the term 'mass incarceration.' Instead he argues that the term 'mass incarceration, is 'a mischaracterization ... mass incarceration suggests that confinement concerns large swaths of the citizenry ... But the expansion and intensification of the activities of the police, courts, and prison over the past quarter-century have been finely targeted by class, ethnicity,

40 Ibid., p. 6.

41 Ibid., p. 5.

42 D. Garland, *Mass Imprisonment: Social Causes and Consequences*, Sage Publications, London-Thousand Oaks-New Delhi 2001, p. 2.

and place.'[43] This analysis has led Wacquant to conclude that mass incarceration is 'better referred to as the *hyper*-incarceration of one particular category, lower-class black men in the crumbling ghetto. He observes that the rest of society – including middle-class blacks – is practically untouched.'[44]

As Michelle Alexander observed '[t]he United States now has the highest rate of incarceration in the world.'[45] This unprecedented increase in the American carceral state has been characterised by many scholars as 'mass incarceration'. But because of the hyper concentration of black and brown young men in prison, I qualify this term and add 'racialised', so the term I use throughout this paper to describe this phenomenon is 'racialised mass incarceration'.[46] As Loury goes on to note, '[m]ass incarceration has now become a principal vehicle for the reproduction of racial hierarchy in [American] society.'[47] Michele Alexander has written that: 'The racial dimension of mass incarceration is its most striking feature. No other country in the world imprisons so many of its racial or ethnic minorities. The United States imprisons a larger percentage of its black population than South Africa did at the height of apartheid.'[48]

The brute facts about the scale of racialised mass incarceration in America are 'stark … today a total of 7.3 million individuals are under the control of the U.S. criminal justice system: 2.3 million prisoners behind bars, 800,000 parolees, and another 4.2 million people on probation. If this population had their own city, it would be the second largest in the country.'[49] However, it is important to note that 'in 2010, after thirty-five years of relentless growth … we see the first decline in the U.S. prison population – a sign that this phase of the epidemic may have peaked.'[50] Maybe. But the verdict is still out on this one.

From 1968 to the early 2000s, the amazing speed and significance of 'mass incarceration in the United States … in fact emerged as a stunningly comprehensive and well-disguised system of racialised social control that functions in a manner strikingly similar to Jim Crow.'[51] As Professor Alexander has noted, the changes in American society since the end of the Jim Crow

---

43 L. Wacquant, in: G.C. Loury, *Race, Incarceration, and American Values*, Boston Review Books, Boston 2007, p. 59.

44 Ibid., p. 59.

45 M. Alexander, *The New Jim Crow: Mass Incarceration in the Age of Colorblindness*, The New Press, New York-London 2010, p. 8.

46 This is my own term to describe the phenomenon of mass incarceration in America, and does not appear anywhere in the literature.

47 G.C. Loury, *Race, Incarceration, and American Values*, Boston Review Books, Boston 2007, pp. 36–37.

48 M. Alexander, *The New Jim Crow: Mass Incarceration in the Age of Colorblindness*, The New Press, New York-London 2010, p. 8.

49 E. Drucker, *A Plague of Prisons: The Epidemiology of Mass Incarceration in America*, The New Press, New York 2013, p. 38.

50 Ibid., p. 40.

51 M. Alexander, *The New Jim Crow: Mass Incarceration in the Age of Colorblindness*, The New Press, New York-London 2010, p. 4.

segregation rules 'has less to do with the basic structure of our society than with the language we use to justify it. In the era of colorblindness, it is no longer socially permissible to use race, explicitly, as a justification for discrimination, exclusion, and social contempt. So we don't. Rather than rely on race, we use our criminal justice system to label people of color as "criminals" and then engage in all the practices we supposedly left behind.'[52]

Professor Alexander's characterisation of racialised mass incarceration as the new Jim Crow, is a sobering and insightful analysis. In addition, it does ring true, because as Loic Wacquant has observed, '[u]like Jim Crow … the ghetto was not dismantled by forceful government action. It was left to crumble onto itself, trapping lower-class African Americans in a vortex of unemployment, poverty, and crime, abetted by the joint withdrawal of the wage-labor market and the welfare state. … As the ghetto lost its economic function and proved unable to ensure ethnoracial closure, the prison was called upon to help contain a population widely viewed as deviant, destitute, and dangerous. In so doing it returned to its original historical mission: not to stem crime, but to manage dispossessed and dishonored populations marginalized by economic transformation.'[53]

However, this is not to suggest there was some type of explicit white conspiracy, where white people – still caught in the thrall of their perceived sense of the natural order of white supremacy, righteousness and social segregation – got together and hatched a plan of racial suppression disguised as a war on crime. It was not as conscious and deliberate as that. Rather, it was an evolving social and political response, resistance, and resentment to judicially imposed racial equality in America. It can be fairly characterised as a form of what I term 'racial revenge' exacted for the loss of the power of explicit white supremacy. This suggests that denial can also manifest itself when a dominant group has lost social and political control of a minority group. To be sure, as David Garland points out '[m]ass imprisonment was not a policy that was proposed, researched, costed, debated, and democratically agreed. America did not collectively decide to get into the business of mass imprisonment, in the way that it decided to build the institutions of the New Deal, or the Great Society, or even the low-tax, low spending, free-market institutions of Reaganomics. Instead, mass imprisonment emerged as the over determined outcome of a converging series of policies and decisions. Determinate sentence structures; the war against drugs; mandatory sentencing; truth in sentencing; the emergence of private corrections; the political events and calculations that made everyone tough on crime – these developments built upon one another and produced the flow of prisoners into custody. These developments may have been a part of a general realignment of

52 Ibid., p. 2.

53 L. Wacquant, in: G.C. Loury, *Race, Incarceration, and American Values*, Boston Review Books, Boston 2007, p. 65.

politics and culture … America has drifted into this situation, with voters and politicians and judges and corporations willing the specific means without anyone pausing to assess the overall outcome',[54] and turning a blind eye to the consequences of these policies.

Garland observed that racialised mass imprisonment 'may have been a part of a general realignment of politics and culture',[55] and is worthy of particular note, because of the timely juxtaposition between the end of the civil rights movement and the beginning of America's prison boom, and a pattern of racialised hyperincarceration. As Bruce Western concluded, 'the prison boom helps us understand how racial inequality in America was sustained, despite great optimism for the social progress of African Americans. From this perspective, the prison boom is not the main cause of inequality between blacks and whites in America, but it did foreclose upward mobility and deflate hopes for racial equality.'[56]

In addition, racialised mass incarceration has been a colossal fiscal drain on the nation. It has been estimated that the average cost of maintaining one inmate in prison is 'over $25,000 per year or about $60 billion annually … with several billion more to build all these prisons.'[57] Only recently has the enormity of the financial burden on the states and localities to maintain a racialised system of mass incarceration begun to filter into the consciousness of the taxpaying public. As a result, there has been a noted movement in many states to engage in various forms of disincarceration, to limit the size of their prison population. However, despite the current trend to lessen the cost of incarceration by finding alternative diversion options short of prison, it is important to note that even if these efforts bear some fruit, the individuals involved will still be legally characterised as convicted felons. As Devah Pager has concluded, 'within the employment domain, the criminal credential has indeed become a salient marker for employers, with increasing numbers using background checks to screen out undesirable applicants. The majority of employers claim that they would not knowingly hire an applicant with a criminal background, [and this] … mark of criminality … [is] accessible to employers, landlords, creditors, and other interested parties … and can be used as the official basis for eligibility determination or exclusion … the "credential" of a criminal record, like educational or professional credentials, constitutes a formal and enduring classification of social status, which can be used to regulate access and

---

54 D. Garland, *Mass Imprisonment: Social Causes and Consequences*, Sage Publications, London-Thousand Oaks-New Delhi 2001, p. 2.

55 Ibid., p. 2.

56 B. Western, *Punishment and Inequality in America*, Russel Sage Foundation, New York 2006, p. 7.

57 E. Drucker, *A Plague of Prisons: The Epidemiology of Mass Incarceration in America*, The New Press, New York 2013, p. 46.

opportunity across numerous social, economic, and political domains.'[58] So even if diversion or disincarceration programmes are successful, while that may result in fewer black and brown bodies in prison, having the 'mark of criminality' by virtue of being a convicted felon, can be a virtually disqualifying condition to get a job, housing, credit, and a host of other important assets to be able to participate fully in organised society.

5. DRIVERS OF MASS INCARCERATION

5.1. THE WAR ON DRUGS

The overwhelming majority of black and brown men that have been caught up in America's obsession with racialised mass incarceration have been imprisoned for minor and non-violent low level drug offences as part of this nation's so-called 'War on Drugs'. The timing of the declaration of America's War on Drugs is very interesting and very telling. Although some scholars attribute the beginning of the war to President Ronald Reagan in 1982, the more accurate account is that this War on Drugs began in 1968 with President Richard Nixon's speech to Congress, officially declaring America's War on Drugs. The year 1968 also marks the end of the civil rights struggle for racial equality in America. Glenn Loury observed that this incredible expansion of the black prison population has been significantly fuelled by the so-called War on Drugs. He notes that 'the incarceration rate for violent crime almost tripled, despite the decline in the level of violence. The incarceration rate for non-violent drug offenses increased at an even faster pace: between 1980 and 1997 the number of people incarcerated for non-violent offenses tripled, and the number of people incarcerated for drug offences increased by a factor of eleven ... and none of the growth in incarceration between 1980 and 1996 can be attributed to more crime ... the growth was entirely attributable to a growth in punitiveness.'[59] Marc Mauer has observed that 'on a proportional basis [between violent crime and drug offenders] the increase in incarcerated drug offenders is more dramatic, with a 546 percent rise during [the period 1985–2000].'[60] Michelle Alexander observed that '[a]lthough the majority of illegal drug users and dealers nationwide are white, three fourths of all people imprisoned for drug offenses have been black or Latino.'[61] She goes on to say that 'people of all races use and sell illegal drugs

---

58 D. Pager, Marked: *Race Crime, and Finding Work in an Era of Mass Incarceration*, University of Chicago Press, Chicago 2007, pp. 4–5.

59 G.C. Loury, *Race, Incarceration, and American Values*, Boston Review Books, Boston 2007, p. 29.

60 M. Mauer, *Race to Incarcerate*, The New Press, New York-London 2006, p. 18.

61 M. Alexander, *The New Jim Crow: Mass Incarceration in the Age of Colorblindness*, The New Press, New York-London 2010, p. 97.

at remarkably similar rates. If there are significant differences in the surveys to be found, they frequently suggest that whites, particularly white youth, are more likely to engage in illegal drug dealing than people of color.'[62] One national study on the racial dynamics of drug use found that 'white students use cocaine at seven times the rate of black students, use crack cocaine at eight times the rate of black students, and use heroin at seven times the rate of black students.'[63]

This racial dimension in racialised mass incarceration is so stark that Marc Mauer observed that, 'for African American males, the rates of incarceration can only be described as catastrophic.'[64] America's prisons are literally, 'overflowing with black and brown drug offenders. In some states, black men have been admitted to prison on drug charges at rates twenty to fifty times greater than those of white men, despite the fact that we know that whites and blacks use drugs in roughly the same percentages. In light of that, what explains this vast disparity in imprisonment rates? It can only be understood through a racial lens. And in major cities wracked by the drug war, as many as 80 percent of young African American men now have criminal records and are thus subject to legalized discrimination for the rest of their lives.'[65] Bruce Western has also observed that '[t]he black – white disparity in imprisonment is especially large. Black men are six to eight times more likely to be in prison than whites.'[66]

Just a few years after President Nixon's declaration of a war on drugs, as Marc Mauer observed, 'the number of inmates in U.S. state and federal prisons … skyrocketed from 196,000 in 1972 to 1,410,000 by 2004, a 600 percent increase. At the local jail level, the numbers have similarly escalated from 130,000 to 714,000 for a total of more than 2.1 million inmates. Thus there are now six times as many U.S. citizens locked up as there were thirty years ago, for an overall rate of incarceration of 726 inmates per 100,000 population, or about one of every 138 Americans.'[67] Mauer goes on to conclude that 'in [America's] zeal to imprison … in 1994 … half of the more than one million people imprisoned … were African American', which was the 'price to be paid for the economic and social changes that the nation [was] undergoing in the late twentieth century.'[68]

Some have argued that the dramatic rise in the 'rate of incarceration in itself might merely be a reflection of a high crime rate … [However] [a]n analysis of the growth in the use of prisons from [the 1980s] until the present undermines the contention that the continuing race to incarcerate in the United States is a

62 Ibid., p. 97.
63 National Institute on Drug Abuse, 'Monitoring the Future, National Survey Results on Drug Use' 1975–1999, vol. 1.
64 M. Mauer, *Race to Incarcerate*, The New Press, New York-London 2006, p. 13.
65 M. Alexander, *The New Jim Crow: Mass Incarceration in the Age of Colorblindness*, The New Press, New York-London 2010, p. 8.
66 B. Western, *Punishment and Inequality in America*, Russel Sage Foundation, New York 2006, p. 6.
67 M. Mauer, *Race to Incarcerate*, The New Press, New York-London 2006, p. 20.
68 Ibid., p. 22.

result of higher rates of violent crimes.'[69] In fact, 'research has demonstrated that changes in criminal justice policy, rather than changes in the crime rates, have been the most significant contributors leading to the rise in state prison populations.'[70] In fact, it has been observed that 'both official crime rates and prison rates may be affected by the level of punitiveness in a society.'[71] It has been decisively concluded by many experts in the field that '[t]he correlation between incarceration and crime is statistically insignificant. Statistics like these have led some commentators to 'discount any relationship between crime and punishment.'[72] However, one commentator makes the case for the disassociation between hyperincarceration and any increase in the crime rate, more 'bluntly,' when he wrote that, 'the explosion in the number of prisoners in the USA cannot be explained as "caused by crime". It has to do with penal policy.'[73] This analysis helps to explain why the vast increase in incarceration 'is concentrated among the disadvantaged and the large race and class disparities in imprisonment reinforce lines of social disadvantage. High incarceration rates among less educated, less skilled, and financially disadvantaged, and minority men is unmistakable.'[74] 'The black–white disparity in imprisonment is especially large. Black men are six to eight times more likely to be in prison than whites.'[75] These numbers and their social implications are striking, unprecedented, and politically unacceptable to most of the Western world.

5.2. RACIAL PROFILING

The current national tragedy of mass incarceration, especially of young men of colour, is intimately bound up with contemporary stop and frisk policies of urban policing, racial profiling, and human rights. The deliberate targeting by the police of black and Hispanic young men as being criminally suspicious, otherwise known as 'racial profiling', is nothing new in America. It has been official state policy in some form that dates back to Reconstruction, when vast numbers of young black men were arrested for the 'crime' of vagrancy and idleness. However, what has changed in recent years is that this policing tactic has grown tremendously in its predatory intensity, personal invasiveness, demeaning effect, and in its ability to act as a direct pipeline for massive numbers of young black and Hispanic men to state and federal prisons for relatively

69 Ibid., p. 30.
70 Ibid. p. 33.
71 Ibid. p. 37.
72 B. Western, *Punishment and Inequality in America*, Russel Sage Foundation, New York 2006, p. 15.
73 Ibid., p. 35.
74 Ibid., p. 35.
75 M. Alexander, *The New Jim Crow: Mass Incarceration in the Age of Colorblindness*, The New Press, New York-London 2010, p. 8.

minor, non-violent crimes, and for longer periods of incarceration than their similarly situated white counterparts.

Deliberate state-sanctioned racial profiling of young men of colour has been a virtually universal experience by most young black and brown men who live in the urban core, and many others who do not. Although the experience of being stopped usually only takes only a few minutes, when you are singled out as criminally suspicious on the basis of race, it is a demeaning and humiliating, affront to personal dignity, and social respect – that rightly creates a feeling of anger, or even rage, over what is essentially a type of 'public shaming'. The experience of racial profiling is so widely shared that, most black men of whatever socio-economic status has a story to tell. In fact on Tuesday 16 July 2013, in an address to the national convention of the NAACP, then Attorney General Eric Holder related several similar incidents in his life when he was stopped by the police for no other reason than being what the police considered to be a 'suspicious black man'. In the first two incidences, Holder described himself as driving at the speed limit and breaking no traffic laws and twice he was stopped on the New Jersey turnpike and his car searched. In the third incidence, Holder described himself as 'simply running to catch a movie, in Georgetown, in Washington D.C.', and said that, 'at the time', I was a federal prosecutor.'[76] As Bruce Western observed on this point: 'In the era of mass imprisonment, to be young, black, and male, even if never having gone to prison, is to arouse suspicion and fear.'[77]

A New York Federal Court Judge recently ruled that such targeted practices, known as 'stop and frisk,' as practiced by the New York City police, as an officially sanctioned and encouraged policy, 'violated their constitutional rights in two ways: (1) they were stopped without a legal basis in violation of the Fourth Amendment [of the American Constitution], and (2) they were targeted for stops because of their race in violation of the Fourteenth Amendment [of the American Constitution].'[78] As a result, the judge did not order the police department to end its practice of stop and frisk, but instead ordered them to stop conducting the programme in a racially discriminatory way. She also 'ordered the installation of the department's first ever independent monitor to oversee changes to its practices.'[79] Even though, by its terms the ruling only affects the New York City Police Department, it is expected to be a wake-up call to police chiefs all around the country. As evidence of the racialised nature of the way stop

76 E. Holder, 'Remarks on Trayvon Martin at NAACP Convention' 2013 *The Washington Post* <www.washingtonpost.com/politics/attorney-general-eric-holders-remarks-on-trayvon-martin-at-naacp-convention-full-text/2013/07/16/dec82f88-ee5a-11e2-a1f9-ea873b7e0424_story1.html> accessed 16.07.2013.

77 B. Western, *Punishment and Inequality in America*, Russel Sage Foundation, New York 2006, p. 30.

78 *D. Floyd et. al. v. The City of New York*, Opinion and Order, 08 Civ. 1034 (SAS). Judge Shira A. Scheindlin, 08.12.2013.

79 S. Gardiner, *The Wall Street Journal*, 13.08.2013, p. 1.

and frisk was being used in New York to racially profile black and brown youth, the judge noted that the evidence showed that, 'the NYPD made 4.4 million stops between January 2004 and June 2012. Over 80% of these … were of blacks or Hispanics.'[80] In a fashion evocative of Cohen, Judge Scheindlin observed in her opinion that: 'I also conclude that the City's highest officials have *turned a blind eye* [emphasis added] to the evidence that officers are conducting stops in a racially discriminatory manner. In their zeal to defend a policy of targeting "the right people," is racially discriminatory and therefore violates the United States Constitution.'[81] She also observed that some members of the New York Police Department were in such denial about the unconstitutionality of their stop and frisk policies that: 'One NYPD official has even suggested that it is permissible to stop racially defined groups just to instill fear in them that they are subject to being stopped at any time for any reason – in the hope that this fear will deter them from carrying guns in the streets. The goal of deterring crime is laudable, but this method of doing so is unconstitutional.'[82]

On 14 April 2013 in the midst of a national uproar over the shooting death of an unarmed young teenager named Trayvon Martin, Brent Staples published an editorial in the *New York Times* that featured a picture of a torso of a dummy with a hoodie over its head, and a bull's eye on its chest. The article observed that many white people in America experience young black males as the other, and it noted that: 'Society's message to black boys is – we fear you and view you as dangerous – and is constantly reinforced. Boys who are seduced by this version of themselves end up on a fast track to prison or the graveyard. But even those who keep their distance from this deadly idea are at risk of losing their lives to it. The death of Trayvon Martin vividly underscores that danger.'[83] In fact, one of the primary drivers of the prison boom in the last thirty years in America, is due to what, Devah Pager describes as the 'widespread assumptions about the criminal tendencies among blacks affects far more than those actually engaged in crime.'[84] Pager went on to observe that '[b]lacks in this country have long been regarded with suspicions and fear … [and] associations between race and crime have changed little in recent years. Survey respondents consistently rate blacks as more prone to violence than any other racial group, with the stereotype of aggressiveness and violence most frequently endorsed in ratings of African Americans.'[85] She then concludes dramatically that '[t]he stereotype of

80 *Floyd*, p. 1.
81 *Floyd*, pp. 13–14.
82 *Floyd*, p. 14.
83 J. Capeheart, 'Trayvon Martin and the Stolen Youth of Black Children' 2013 *The Washington Post* <www.washintonpost.com/blogs/post-partison/wp/wp/2013/07/trayvon-martin-and – the-stolen-youth-of -black-children> accessed 18.07.2013.
84 D. Pager, *Marked: Race Crime, and Finding Work in an Era of Mass Incarceration*, University of Chicago Press, Chicago 2007, p. 3.
85 Ibid., p. 3.

blacks as criminals is deeply embedded in the collective consciousness of white Americans, irrespective of the perceiver's level of prejudice or personal beliefs.'[86] She might well have added, 'and degree of denial'. This is a clear example of what Cohen described as 'cultural denial'.

As Loic Wacquant has observed, 'the relatively recent mass incarceration of black men and boys is no longer based on a white supremacist sense of black "unworthiness", but [on] dangerousness, that stamps the hegemonic biased cognition about blacks, precisely because the prison has become the primary machine for signifying and enforcing a class-graduated conception of race in the country.'[87] Illustrating this recent racial phenomenon, CNN recently reported that a high school psychologist tweeted to his friends that 'young black thugs should be put down like the dogs they are. We have been invaded by an army of young black thugs who are holding our country hostage.'[88] As a consequence, young black males are targeted as potential criminals not only by society at large, but also by the police and the entire American justice system. As Jonathan Capeheart, has observed following the iconic shooting of Trayvon Martin by a local vigilante, who was later acquitted of murder by a jury in Florida '[o]ne of the burdens of being a black male is carrying the heavy weight of other people's suspicions.'[89] Capeheart concluded by noting that 'the ... acquittal now makes it clear that justice for an innocent black child killed, requires proof that he lived his life beyond reproach at all times.'[90] He goes on to accurately observe that, just as occurred in the Trayvon Martin case, 'once black boys go out in public, they are profiled as "up to no good" or are pursued and confronted by unidentified strangers. In the eyes of the defense, those children never have the emotions, reactions or fears of children. They are presumed guilty the moment they leave the safe confines of home.'[91] This contemporary white narrative regarding the inherent dangerousness of black and brown young men, is one of the primary factors that led to and continues to fuel the great American tragedy of racialised mass incarceration. As a result of this 'class-graduated conception of race' in which young black and brown males are considered dangerous predators, the focus of America's obsession with incarceration is targeted at young black and brown men.

In addition, it is of particular note that the American public has essentially tolerated and thereby ratified the contemporary connections between race and mass incarceration. One of the most important reasons for this public toleration

---

86 Ibid., p. 3.

87 G.C. Loury, *Race, Incarceration, and American Values*, Boston Review Books, Boston 2007, p. 67.

88 *CNN News*, 22 May 2012.

89 J. Capeheart, 'Trayvon Martin and the Stolen Youth of Black Children' 2013 *The Washington Post* <www.washintonpost.com/blogs/post-partison/wp/wp/2013/07/trayvon-martin-and – the-stolen-youth-of -black-children> accessed 18.07.2013.

90 Ibid.

91 Ibid.

is, as was observed earlier, the association between black men and criminal dangerousness, and thereby that they are considered to be a threat to public safety. Moreover, although it is more subtle, the public fear, held mostly by the white American public, is also tied inextricably to what I term as a sense of white racial revenge or a white backlash[92] to the Civil Rights Movement of the 1960s and its accomplishments in achieving unprecedented levels of racial equality and a dismantling, at least publically, of the social, political, educational, and cultural dominance of white privilege in American society. Most importantly the widespread tolerance of most white Americans in the devastation wrought by racialised mass incarceration is due to the fact that as Stanley Cohen noted: 'Dominant groups seem uncannily able to shut out or ignore the injustice and suffering around them ... out of cultural habit.'[93] Unfortunately, 'shut[ting] out or ignoring ... injustice and suffering around them'[94] is a deeply embedded cultural habit of most white Americans when it comes to the suffering of black people,[95] and has continued from almost the first arrival of African slaves to the American colonies, in 1619, continues to the present day.

6. CONCLUSION

It is way past time for the American public and political elite to stop looking the other way denying the human rights plague of racialised mass incarceration and acknowledge its insidious and destructive effects on the dignity and human rights of millions of its black and brown citizens. As a nation, America must, 'come to terms with its past'[96] and its present social, political, and economic sin of racialised mass incarceration. For too long it has, 'circumvented the issue with the narrative skills befitting a psychopath'.[97] America's mass denial of this terrible reality clearly has not worked as either a political or social strategy and has only exacerbated an already destructive, insidious, and distressing reality, which in turn incurs another great cost of this terrible domestic policy against its racial minorities, in the form of the disapproval and disrespect of the rest of the civilised industrial world for whom respect for the human rights of a nation's ethnic minorities has become an increasingly categorical imperative.

---

92 I.F.H. Lopez, 'Post-Racial Racism: Racial Stratification and Mass Incarceration in the Age of Obama' (2010) 98 *Cal. L. Rev.* 1026, 1023.

93 S. Cohen, *States of Denial: Knowing About Atrocities and Suffering*, Polity Press, Cambridge 2001, p. 5.

94 Ibid., p. 5.

95 This process of insensitivity to pain and suffering of black bodies began during slavery (1619–1865); and Jim Crow laws and segregation in all forms of public life (1877–1965); and now continues with racialised mass incarceration (1975–2015).

96 C.A. Brkic, 'The Wages of Denial' *The New Times*, 11.07.2005, p. A21.

97 Ibid., p. A21.

This widespread and massive national denial regarding the reality and social costs of racialised mass incarceration, has already cost America a generation of young black and brown men, and the destruction of countless black and brown families and communities. It now threatens to destroy yet another generation of young black and brown men, their families and communities with little or no hope for any relief in the foreseeable future. If America is to make any headway in even beginning to solve this problem, it must first open its collective social, political, and societal eyes and free itself from its willful racial blindness, and from what Stanley Cohen describes as 'the mass denial so characteristic of repressive, racist ... states.'[98]

Founding father and former President of the United States, Thomas Jefferson, while contemplating the state of slavery in America, is apocryphally known to have said, '[w]hen I consider that God is just, I weep for my country'. Until America, as a people and as a nation, ceases to deny and ignore the reality of racialised mass incarceration and the vastness of its destructive power to human lives and human rights, we should all weep for human rights nightmare that is occurring America.

98 S. Cohen, *States of Denial: Knowing About Atrocities and Suffering*, Polity Press, Cambridge 2001, p. 5.

CHAPTER XVII
JUSTIFYING ACTS OF DENIALISM
The Case of Prisoner Disenfranchisement in the UK

Samantha MORGAN-WILLIAMS

1. INTRODUCTION

This paper will explore the case of prisoner disenfranchisement in the United Kingdom[1] as a concrete example of political denialism and human rights. It will explore the basis of denialism and human rights, from two approaches, asking both *how* and *why* denialism is perpetrated and justified in the UK. Initially seeking to challenge *how* the blanket ban on prisoner voting is justified at a domestic level. The paper will then identify *why* political denialism is contentious within the concrete example that prisoner disenfranchisement provides, determining the conceptual and legal basis and subsequent political support for the prisoner voting ban.

In examining how political actors, such as the UK Government,[2] justify continued denial of rights at the expense of their obligations under the ECHR, this paper highlights the prisoner voting rights case as concrete example of political or functional denialism in practice. It therefore affords an excellent example within which to address why denialism is committed and consequently how a state can justify continued human rights violations. In looking beyond the act of denialism and addressing the justifications themselves, this paper contributes to deepening understanding of situations where the state power is the main perpetrator of denialism.

---

1 For the purpose of this paper the 'United Kingdom' is used in direct reference to the executive, judiciary and legislative (Parliament) unless indicated otherwise.

2 For the purposes of this chapter, Government refers exclusively to Her Majesty's Government, commonly referred to as the UK Government, which is currently formed of Members of Parliament from the Conservative Party, led by Prime Minister David Cameron.

2. DENIALISM AND HUMAN RIGHTS: POLITICAL DENIALISM

Scholars working within this field have largely drawn upon the works of Stanley Cohen in identifying the forms of denial.[3] At the conference associated with this collection of papers, entitled 'Denialism and Human Rights',[4] a number of forms of denialism where thus identified. The most notable of these was given by Prof. Eric Heinze[5] who outlined the forms which denial has been recognised to take within the field of human rights.[6] These were identified as factual, normative, justifiable and political denialism.[7]

The first of these, factual denial, occurs where a series of events or conduct is questioned as to ever having existed. A key example of such would be Holocaust or more generally genocide denial. Secondly, denialism within human rights can be normative in form, where it is disputed whether a norm can be considered as a human right. An example of this would be the denial of rights to certain groups of minority or even unfavourable groups. Normative denialism is therefore normally characterised as the refusal to grant certain classes of citizens their human rights.[8] Thirdly, justifiable or defensible denialism is a form of denialism present within human rights when the perpetrator seeks to justify a derogation or denial of human rights. A core example is found within the European Convention on Human Rights system (ECHR or Convention) where certain rights are 'derogable' in times of emergency or state crisis for the protection of state security.[9] The fourth and

---

3 For more on this see S. Cohen, *States of Denial: Knowing about Atrocities and Suffering*, 2nd ed., Polity Press, Stafford BC 2010.

4 'Denialism and Human Rights', Maastricht University Faculty of Law, 22 and 23 January 2015.

5 Prof. Eric Heinze, Professor of Law and Humanities, Queen Mary University of London.

6 E. Heinze, presentation entitled 'Functional Denial and the Politics of Human Rights', given at 'Denialism and Human Rights', Maastricht University Faculty of Law, 22 and 23 January 2015. Heinze's presentation and his identification of four forms of human rights denial are representative of existing research into this area, for more on Heinze's own work in the area of politics and human rights see; E. Heinze, 'Even-handedness and the Politics of Human Rights' (2008) 21 *Harvard Human Rights Journal* 7–46 and E. Heinze and R. Freedman, 'Public Awareness of Human Rights: Distortions in the Mass Media' (2009) 12 *International Journal of Human Rights*.

7 In his recent publication, *After Sustainability: Denial, Hope, Retrieval*, John Foster, draws exclusively upon the work of Stanley Cohen in identifying the forms of denialism prevalent within climate change denialism. He notes that these are literal, interpretative and implicative denial. For more on this see; J. Froster, *After Sustainability: Denial, Hope, Retrieval*, Routledge, London 2015.

8 The debate surrounding the legitimacy of the right to development, or even the validity of human rights for animals could serve as an example of normative human rights.

9 Article 15 ECHR allows states to derogate from certain rights guaranteed by the Convention in time of 'war or other public emergency threatening the life of the nation'. Permissible derogations under Article 15 must meet three substantive conditions: there must be a public emergency threatening the life of the nation; any measures taken in response must be 'strictly

final example of denialism often present within human rights is political or functional denialism. Political denialism occurs where an act which results in a denial of rights is seen by a political power as necessary or intrinsic to values.[10]

The latter form, 'political or functional denialism,' is that which this paper concerns itself with, and is arguably the rarest in practice within the field of human rights. This is owing to a number of factors. These draw extensively from the general and driving principles behind human rights, which recognise that basic rights and fundamental freedoms are inherent to all human beings, inalienable, applicable to all regardless of gender, sex or race, and that everyone be treated equally in dignity and rights. Within Europe in particular, there is a clear consensus that upholding human rights and honouring human rights standards is key to a state's standing and this is represented by the reputation of the Council of Europe's Convention on Human Rights and the associated European Court of Human Rights.[11] Thus, states are often unwilling to be seen as complicity or knowingly committing acts of denial of human rights

A central theme when addressing denialism is often that the nature of the denial itself remains either fully or partly unacknowledged.[12] However, in instances of political or functional denialism, the denial of human rights is not only acknowledged by the offending political power, but even widely supported and its continuation justified, as is the case within the prisoner disenfranchisement debate. In the case of political denialism of human rights, it is rare for a state to openly and consistently flout or 'deny' its human

---

required by the exigencies of the situation', and the measures taken in response to it, must be in compliance with a state's other obligations under international law.

10 However, a point to consider here is the nature of human rights itself. Is it more a matter of us not previously regarding political denialism as a form of denialism? Given a number of factors such as human rights systems allowed (to some extent) for derogations and excuses for denying in limited circumstances and given that states rarely directly admit to denying but may only comply in very limited or superficial ways. Could it be said that political denialism is in fact present within all human rights enforcement regimes? Given that considering more controversial issues such as implementation of socio-economic rights as opposed to civil and political rights are seen to be more aspirational rather than intrinsic?

11 Although it must be noted here, that as the case study of this paper shows that this does not mean that in a system where the is largely, strong respect for human rights that human rights abuses and derogations from human rights standards do not occur. Rather, that where a strong system exists, within which there is a functioning consensus that human rights be respected and upheld, that this acts as a sort of 'peer-pressure' mentality, acting as a deterrent. No state therefore wishes to be thought of as a state which does not respect human rights.

12 For more on this see C.A.R Moerland, conference presentation entitled 'The killing of death – The BBC documentary Rwanda's untold story and the denial of the genocide against the Tutsi', given at 'Denialism and Human Rights', Maastricht University Faculty of Law, 22 and 23 January 2015; and also 'Meaning in Motion and Merging Discourses: How Scholars and Journalists Recycle the Ideological Denial of the Genocide Against the Tutsi', Siena, Italy, 10th Biennial Conference of the International Association of Genocide Scholars.

rights duties and obligations. However, in the UK the denial of voting rights for prisoners is a widely supported stance within both political, public and media spheres, which it is argued by proponents is 'enshrined in British democratic tradition.'[13] The legal and conceptually basis for this blanket ban will now be addressed before the justifications for the ban itself are examined.

2.1. PRISONER DISENFRANCHISEMENT IN THE UK

Under domestic law, section 3 of the Representation of the People Act 1983[14] indiscriminately disenfranchises all prisoners. This act creates a blanket ban under which prisoners serving a custodial sentence do not have the right to vote during their incarceration, and only those on remand may partake in elections:

> '(1) A convicted person during the time that he is detained in a penal institution in pursuance of his sentence [or unlawfully at large when he would otherwise be so detained] is legally incapable of voting at any parliamentary or local government election.'

Under this legal provision, prisoners are barred from exercising the right to vote, which is a well-documented basic civil liberty and widely recognised in international law. Protection for this right is expressly provided under in a variety of international and regional systems including Article 21 of the Universal Declaration of Human Rights, as well as Article 25 of the International Covenant on Civil and Political Rights, the ECHR Article 3 Protocol No. 1.[15] Article 3 Protocol No. 1 of the ECHR dictates that states belonging to the Council of Europe, must guarantee 'free elections … under conditions which will ensure the free expression of the opinion of the people in the choice of the legislature.'[16]

---

13 See both D. Grieve, MP (2011) 523 *HC Deb.* 511 and D. Cameron, MP, (2010) 517 *HC Deb.* 921.

14 Section 3 of the Representation of the People Act 1983 as amended by the Representation of the People Act 1985 and 2000.

15 Other International Legal Instruments which protect the right to vote include but are not limited to: the Charter of the Organization of American States, the African (Banjul) Charter on Human and Peoples' Rights and many other international human rights documents Organisation for Security and Cooperation in Europe (OSCE) International Standards of Elections (1990), European Union (EU) Council Regulations 975/99 and 976/99 (1999), Organization of American States (OAS) American Convention on Human Rights (entered into force 1978) see <www.oas.org/> for all OAS documents. Inter-American Convention on the Granting of Political Rights to Women (entered into force 1954) Article 23 of the American Convention on Human Rights and Article 20 of the American Declaration of the Rights and Duties of Man guarantee the right of citizens to vote and be elected in genuine periodic elections. African Union (Formerly Organisation of African Unity), African Charter on Human and Peoples' Rights (1981), Article 13(1) of the African (Banjul) Charter on Human and Peoples' Rights provides that every citizen shall have the right to participate freely in their government.

16 Full text of the Convention and Protocols available at: <www.echr.coe.int/Documents/Convention_ENG.pdf>.

The current blanket ban on prisoner disenfranchisement in the UK under domestic legislation has been found contrary to the ECHR as section 3 of the Representation of the People Act conflicts with Article 3 of Protocol No. 1 of the Convention's provisions. As a result, the UK has been found to be in violation of its treaty obligations and is obliged to align domestic legislation with the relevant ECHR provisions (preamble ECHR, and Article 46).[17] This resulted in a number of cases coming before the ECtHR (*Hirst*,[18] *Greens & M.T.*,[19] *Scoppola*,[20] *Firth*,[21] and *McHugh*)[22] where the Court found the blanket ban to constitute a direct violation of the UK's human rights obligations.

Yet the UK has failed to apply these judgments and amend the current legislation. This refusal to follow the ECtHR clearly demonstrates tensions in the UK between politics and human rights protections, as the UK is purposefully failing in its obligations to uphold minimum human rights standards, denying not only prisoners the rights owed to them under the Convention's provisions, but also denying the supremacy of the Court itself in matters of human rights.

2.2. PRISONER DISENFRANCHISEMENT CASE LAW BEFORE THE ECtHR

On 30 March 2004, the ECtHR gave its judgment in the case of *Hirst v. the UK*.[23] Seven judges at the ECtHR ruled that the UK's ban on prisoners' voting

17 Article 46 Binding force and execution of judgments: 'The High Contracting Parties undertake to abide by the final judgment of the Court in any case to which they are parties. 2. The final judgment of the Court shall be transmitted to the Committee of Ministers, which shall supervise its execution. 3. If the Committee of Ministers considers that the supervision of the execution of a final judgment is hindered by a problem of interpretation of the judgment, it may refer the matter to the Court for a ruling on the question of interpretation. A referral decision shall require a majority vote of two thirds of the representatives entitled to sit on the committee. If the Committee of Ministers considers that a High Contracting Party refuses to abide by a final judgment in a case to which it is a party, it may, after serving formal notice on that Party and by decision adopted by a majority vote of two thirds of the representatives entitled to sit on the committee, refer to the Court the question whether that Party has failed to fulfil its obligation.'

18 *Hirst v. the United Kingdom*, no. 74025/01, ECHR 2005-II.

19 *Greens and M.T. v. the United Kingdom*, no. 60041/08, ECHR 2010.

20 *Scoppola v. Italy*, no. 126/05, ECHR 2012-III.

21 *Firth and Others v. the United Kingdom*, no. 47784/09, ECHR 2014.

22 *McHugh and Others v. the United Kingdom*, no. 51987/08, ECHR 2015.

23 *Hirst v. the United Kingdom*, no. 74025/01, ECHR 2005-II. In the case John Hirst, a prisoner serving a life sentence for manslaughter had challenged the ban on prisoners' votes after previously losing the case in the High Court. Although this was the first time the issue of prisoner disenfranchisement was brought before the ECtHR in a British context, there had been challenges to the validity of the RPA under the ECHR at a domestic level. *R v. (1) Secretary of State for the Home Department (2) Two Election Registration Officers, ex parte (1) Pearson (2) Martinez: Hirst v. HM Attorney General* [2001] EWHC Admin 239. Hirst had

breached the ECHR. The Government subsequently appealed the decision.[24] Upon appeal, the Grand Chamber of the Court held, by a majority of 12 to five that a blanket ban preventing all convicted prisoners from voting, irrespective of the nature or gravity of their offences, constituted a violation of Article 3 of Protocol No. 1 ECHR.[25]

> 'There was, therefore, no question that prisoners forfeit their Convention rights merely because of their status as detainees following conviction. Nor was there any place under the Convention system, where tolerance and broadmindedness were the acknowledged hallmarks of democratic society, for automatic disenfranchisement based purely on what might offend public opinion.'[26]

The Court accepted the UK's argument that Member States should have a wide discretion as to how they regulate a ban on prisoners voting. '[B]oth as regards the types of offence that should result in the loss of the vote and as to whether disenfranchisement should be ordered by a judge in an individual case or should result from general application of a law.'[27]

It recognised, however, that due to a violation of the above Protocol, that reform was necessitated in this instance. Although it advocated legislative change, the court did not give any detailed guidance as to the steps that the UK should take to make its law compatible with Article 3 of Protocol No. 1. Stating that it was for each Member State of the Council of Europe to decide on its own rules under the margin of appreciation, as is the norm under the Convention rules of interpretation.[28, 29]

---

first challenged the ban in the High Court, but lost in 2001 when the court ruled that it was compatible with the European Convention for prisoners to lose the right to a say in how the country was governed.

24 Under Article 43 the Case may be referred to the Grand Chamber, however, the parties have a three-month deadline following the delivery of a Chamber judgment to request referral of the case to the Grand Chamber for fresh consideration. Requests for referral to the Grand Chamber are examined by a panel of judges which decides whether referral is appropriate.

25 *Hirst v. the United Kingdom*, no. 74025/01, ECHR 2005-II.

26 Ibid.

27 Ibid.

28 This position was reiterated in *Frodl v. Austria*, no. 20201/04, ECHR 2010 reference where a breach of Article 3 Protocol No. 1 was found against Austria as his objective disenfranchisement denied him the rights afforded to him under this Article. The applicant, who was convicted of murder and sentenced to life imprisonment in 1993 in Austria, alleged that his disenfranchisement constituted a breach of his rights under Article 3 of Protocol No. 1 because he was serving a term of imprisonment of more than one year. The fact that there was no subjective decision on the matter and that the matter was not decided on a case to case basis but instead amounted to a blanket ban meant that the judgment of the European Court of Human Rights, which became final on 4 October 2010, held that there had been a breach of Article 3 of Protocol No. 1.

29 This was again reiterated post-Scoppola in a press release by Registrar of the Court of ECHR 222 (2012) 22.05.2012. For more see: <http://hudoc.echr.coe.int/sites/eng-press/pages/search.aspx?i=003-3953519-4581929#{'itemid':['003-3953519-4581929']}>.

> 'The Court accepts that this is an area in which a wide margin of appreciation should be granted to the national legislature in determining whether restrictions on prisoners' right to vote can still be justified in modern times and if so how a fair balance is to be struck. In particular, it should be for the legislature to decide whether any restriction on the right to vote should be tailored ... It cannot accept however that an absolute bar on voting by any serving prisoner in any circumstances falls within an acceptable margin of appreciation.'[30]

The breach of Protocol No. 1 was again brought before the court in *Greens & M.T*[31] after the UK failed to implement the *Hirst* judgment. The applicants in this instance complained that the refusal to enrol them on the Electoral Register for domestic and European elections was in violation of Article 3 of Protocol No. 1. In its Chamber judgment of 23 November 2010, the European Court again found a violation of the right to free elections against the UK. Finding that the Government of the UK had failed to amend the blanket ban legislation, or even attempted any means of legislative reform, bringing domestic law in line with the ECHR as required under previous judgment *Hirst.*[32] The Court held that the Government should immediately bring forward legislative proposals to amend the law and to enact the legislation within a period decided by the Committee of Ministers.[33]

> 'Applying its pilot judgment procedure, the Court has given the UK Government six months from the date when Greens and M.T. becomes final to introduce legislative proposals to bring the disputed law/s in line with the Convention.'[34]

Initially the UK was given a six-month time frame by the Committee of Ministers within which to bring forward proposals.[35] This was extended, however, by *Scoppola v. Italy (No. 3)*[36] when the UK intervened as a third party.[37] In this instance the Court held that there had been a breach of Article 3

30 *Hirst v. the United Kingdom*, no. 74025/01, ECHR 2005-II, §41.
31 *Greens and M.T. v. the United Kingdom,* no. 60041/08, ECHR 2010.
32 *Hirst v. the United Kingdom*, no. 74025/01, ECHR 2005-II.
33 The Committee of Ministers (CM) is the executive arm of the Council of Europe which supervises the implementation of the Court's judgments. Once a judgment becomes final, it is transmitted to the CM for supervision of its implementation. Further information about the implementation process can be found here: <www.coe.int/t/dghl/monitoring/execution>.
34 ECHR press notice 23 November 2010.
35 See 1157th meeting notes, *Hirst* No. 2 Group, decision 6 at <https://wcd.coe.int/ViewDoc.jsp?id=2013315>.
36 The applicant, Franco Scoppola was sentenced in 2002 to life incarceration for a multitude of serious crimes. Under Italian law, his life sentence entailed a lifetime ban from public office, amounting to permanent rescinding of his right to vote. Scoppola subsequently complained that the ban on public office imposed as a result of his sentencing had amounted to a permanent forfeiture of his entitlement to vote which constituted a violation of Article 3 of Protocol No. 1.
37 The extension gave the United Kingdom six months from the judgment date within which the implement either proposals or affect legislative change, making the deadline 22 November 2012.

Protocol No. 1 in the form of the disenfranchisement of Mr Scoppola and reiterated that the position of the UK (as observer state under) was contrary to the ECHR:

> 'The Court reiterated that a blanket ban on the right of prisoners to vote during their detention constituted an "automatic and indiscriminate restriction" on a vitally important Convention right ... falling outside any acceptable margin of appreciation, however wide that margin may be.'[38]

This belligerent refusal has brought the focus of the Committee of Ministers into play; as is standard following an ECtHR ruling, as the case(s) were referred to the Committee as the task of supervising judgment executions is vested with the body under Article 46(2) ECHR.[39] In the UK, little has been done in the case of prisoner voting rights to implement the *Hirst* and *Greens & M.T.* judgments, and the Government has made clear that the topic and the possibility of enforced change is a deeply unpopular one with both itself and the public.[40] It appears here that much of the delay in reform has been premised on the understanding that the disenfranchisement of prisoners has been a consistent feature of the UK's history as a parliamentary democracy, a point tabloids have seized upon.[41]

---

38 *Scoppola v. Italy*, no. 126/05, ECHR 2012-II.

39 The article provides that 'the final judgment of the Court shall be transmitted to the Council of Europe, which shall supervise its execution.' Pursuant to this, Rule 3(a) outlines that respondent states are under a duty in the case of a violation to inform the Committee of measures taken to resolve the circumstances under which the violation occurred. Adversely under Rule 4 of the Committee Rules until the state fully complies with the judgment that the issue will continue to refer back to the Committee's agenda every six months until the above measures and proceedings are satisfied.

40 YouGov survey undertaken by Dr Joel Faulkner Rogers at the Cambridge POLIS Department entitled 'Prisoner voting: viva the "civic death" penalty?'; the finding of said survey available at: <https://yougov.co.uk/news/2015/02/06/update-attitudes-prison-voting-viva-civic-death-pe/> show a continued strong public support for the continuation of disenfranchisement of those incarcerated. The survey finds that this is in line with previous findings in 2010, 2011 and 2012. Fieldwork was conducted online between 25–26 January 2015, with a total sample of 1,656 British adults, and the survey was developed in collaboration with William Warr, currently a student on the Masters in Public Policy at the Cambridge POLIS Department, and his supervisor, David Howarth, who is also Director of the course.
The survey began with a split-sample experiment to compare the effect of describing the ECtHR ruling as coming from either a 'European' or an 'international' court when asking about UK law on prisoner voting. The sample was randomly divided and each sub-sample answered variants of the same question.

41 Specifically over prisoner votes: D. Davis and J. Straw, 'We must defy Strasbourg on prisoner votes' 2012 *The Telegraph* <www.telegraph.co.uk/news/uknews/law-and-order/9287633/We-must-defy-Strasbourg-on-prisoner-votes.html> accessed 13.04.2015.

2.3. DEVELOPMENTS 2014–2015

Recent cases before the Court in both *Firth and Others v. the UK*[42] and *McHugh & Others v. the UK*[43] held that the blanket ban on prisoner voting was contrary to the Convention.[44] Despite finding yet again that the UK continues to violate prisoners' rights to participate in elections, the Strasbourg court declined to order that any of claimants be awarded payment in form of redress finding the ruling to be in itself just satisfaction.

In *McHugh*, the Court held:

> 'there had been a violation of Article 3 of Protocol No 1 because the case was identical to other prisoner voting cases in which a breach of the right to vote had been found and the relevant legislation had not yet been amended ... the finding of a violation constitutes in itself sufficient just satisfaction for any non-pecuniary damage sustained by the applicants ...' It dismissed 'the remainder of the applicants' claim for just satisfaction.'[45]

The Court once again held that states have a broad discretion under the margin of appreciation as to how they could implement Article 3 Protocol No. 1 regarding the rights of those in prison, ultimately holding as it did in previous judgments that there is no means by which a blanket ban can be reconciled with the provisions of Protocol No. 1:

> 'The rights bestowed by Article 3 of Protocol No. 1 are not absolute. There is room for implied limitations and Contracting States must be allowed a margin of appreciation in this sphere. ... There are numerous ways of organising and running electoral systems ... which it is for each Contracting State to mould into their own democratic vision. ... [P]risoners in general continue to enjoy all the fundamental rights and freedoms guaranteed under the Convention save for the right to liberty, where lawfully imposed detention expressly falls within the scope of Article 5 of the Convention [guaranteeing the right to liberty and security]. ... Any restrictions on these other rights must be justified ... There is no question, therefore, that a prisoner forfeits his Convention rights merely because of his status as a person detained following conviction.'[46]

---

42 *Firth and Others v. the United Kingdom*, no. 47784/09, ECHR 2014.

43 *McHugh and Others v. the United Kingdom*, no. 51987/08, ECHR 2015.

44 These were so-called 'legacy cases' that gathered all outstanding prisoner voting cases against the UK pending before the Court.

45 *McHugh and Others v. the United Kingdom*, no. 51987/08, ECHR 2015, §§12–17. The Court also rejected the applicants' claim for legal costs. It did not consider that legal assistance was required to lodge an application, for the reasons given in Firth and Others. The Court's approach to follow-up cases was made clear in that judgment, which was both concise and unambiguous. No legal assistance was required to consider its implications.

46 *Hirst v. the United Kingdom*, no. 74025/01, ECHR 2005-II, §§58–61 and 69–71.

The UK Government, however, has clearly held firm to its position on a continuation of prisoner disenfranchisement. A Ministry for Justice Spokesman reiterated the Government's stance post ruling that: 'The government has always been clear that it believes prisoner voting is an issue that should ultimately be decided in the UK. However, we welcome the court's decision to refuse convicted prisoners costs or damages.'[47]

Commenting on the above and the UK's refusal to amend the Representation of the People Act the Equality and Human Rights Commission stated:

> 'It is for parliament to decide how our laws reflect judgments from the European court of human rights, and today's ruling does not change that. The European court cannot change the UK's laws. It would be for parliament to decide which of the possible convention-compliant approaches is introduced. It is important that the UK complies with the convention not least to reinforce our position when we ask other countries to respect human rights.'[48]

It is clear that the situation in the UK regarding prisoner disenfranchisement and the involvement of the ECtHR is not aided by the current political situation. Where tensions with the Court and perceived interference in what is seen as a central policy decision to disenfranchise incarcerated offenders is particularly provoking for the electorate. Notably the UK Government perceives the ECtHR as overstepping its ambit, infringing upon domestic matters:

> 'In recent years the Court seems to have forgotten that its job is to apply the principles of the Convention as originally intended by those who signed it … As a result, we now find ourselves in a situation where the Court is trying to impose judgments on Britain which would have astonished those who signed the Convention.'[49]

In refusing to implement the current jurisprudence from the ECtHR, the UK is actively engaging in denialism, by not recognising the supremacy of the ECHR system on human rights issues and by denying the incarcerated their right to vote as recognised by jurisprudence from the Strasbourg Court. Speaking on this issue, Sean Humber, legal counsel for some of 554 plaintiffs in *McHugh* stated that:

> 'Despite the European court of human rights having first ruled that the UK government's blanket ban on allowing prisoner voting was unlawful a decade ago, and confirming the unlawfulness of this blanket ban in a succession of further

---

47 Quote taken from O. Bowcott 'UK prisoners banned from voting not entitled to compensation' 2015 *The Guardian* <www.theguardian.com/society/2015/feb/10/uk-prisoner-voting-ban-breached-human-rights-european-court-rules> accessed on 16.04.2015.

48 Ibid.

49 D. Davis and J. Straw, 'We must defy Strasbourg on prisoner votes' 2012 *The Telegraph* <www.telegraph.co.uk/news/uknews/law-and-order/9287633/We-must-defy-Strasbourg-on-prisoner-votes.html> accessed 13.04.2015.

> judgments ever since, the government stubbornly refuses to act … We are in a position where the government appears to take a perverse pleasure in unlawfully breaching the human rights of thousands of its citizens. It should be extremely worrying to all of us that the government seems to have so little regard for its international human rights obligations or the rule of law.'[50]

The next part of this paper will address and highlight the weakness of the UK's justifications for the ongoing disenfranchisement of the incarcerated, evidencing the lack of contextual basis and easily rebuttable nature of this current denialist position.

3. JUSTIFICATIONS FOR THE BAN ON PRISONER VOTING RIGHTS

As is often the case when engaging with denialists and cases of denialism, the basis for the UK's current position and resulting blanket ban is an easily refuted one. Speaking on the usage of denialist tactics Justice of the South African Supreme Court, Edwin Cameron notes that denialists will usually cling to and draw extensively upon easily disproved arguments, employing 'distortions and half-truths.'[51] The current vilification by the UK Government of the 'interfering Court' is clearly a prejudiced view of the Strasbourg body. Cameron notes that such 'misrepresentations of their opposition's position'[52] are often key to denialist tactics, where the perpetrator seeks to establish themselves in an 'us and them' type scenario, where the inference is that the opposition is out of touch or misguided about the principles the denialist advocates.[53] This is certainly the case in the prisoner disenfranchisement debate, as this section will evidence.

The disenfranchisement of prisoners in the UK dates back to the Forfeiture Act 1870 and was linked to the notion of 'civic death', whereby through the crime committed the right to partake in elections is removed through lack of a civic responsibility. The 1870 Act denied offenders their rights of citizenship and any person convicted of treason or a felony sentenced to a term of imprisonment exceeding 12 months lost the right to vote until they had served their sentence and then regained their civic duties. The Representation of the People Act 1969 (RPA) codified the legislation further, permanently introducing a specific provision into electoral law, that convicted persons were legally incapable of voting during the time that they were detained.

50 *McHugh and Others v. the United Kingdom*, no. 51987/08, ECHR 2015.

51 E. Cameron, 'The Dead Hand of Denialism,' edited version of his Edward A Smith Annual Lecture at Harvard Law School's Human Rights Programme on 8 April 2003, *Mail & Guardian (Johannesburg)* <http://ww2.aegis.org/news/dmg/2003/MG030410.html> accessed 16.04.2015.

52 Ibid.

53 Ibid.

The UK has cited many different reasons for the continuation of prisoner disenfranchisement, there are three main points, which provide a basis for the continuation of a blanket ban; the notion of civic death or civic virtue; the social contract theory; and the assumption that denying prisoners the right to vote enhances sentencing aims.

The justifications and reasoning behind these will be examined, alongside the contrary evidence, which will challenge the validity of each of these and their usage as part of the prisoner voting ban.

3.1. CIVIC DEATH ARGUMENT AND HISTORICAL JUSTIFICATIONS

Regarding the notion of 'civic death', Juliet Lyon, Director of the Prison Reform Trust, has said:

> 'People are sent to prison to lose their liberty not their identity. The UK's outdated ban on sentenced prisoners voting, based on the 19th century concept of civic death, has no place in a modern democracy and is legally and morally unsustainable. Experienced prison governors and officials ... believe people in prison should be able to exercise their civic responsibility.'[54]

Although this is the most common justification used to justify the continuation of a blanket ban on voting for those imprisoned, it is undoubtedly the weakest, stemming from the fact that those who utilise the argument have yet to explain its usage. Further, a brief overview of the history of this particular justification serves well to undermine its very practice. The claim of civic death suggests that through the act of their crimes, that prisoners lose their civic virtue, are no longer worthy of being afforded civic duties and as a result befall 'civic death'. It is apparent therefore that the relationship between the individual and the state changes radically when one is found guilty of an offence and incarcerated. The use of civic death as a justification was discredited by Lord Sumption during a recent Supreme Court consideration of the prisoner voting debate, when the judge outlined that depriving prisoners of the vote:

> 'is not and never has been a form of outlawry, or "civil death" (the phrase sometimes used to describe the current state of the law on prisoners' voting rights).

54 Juliet LYON, Director of the Prison Reform Trust, quote sourced at: Government Has Six Months to Overturn Prisoners' Voting Ban: <www.prisonreformtrust.org.uk/Projects Research/Citizenship/BarredfromVoting>.

On the contrary, until the 1960s, it was mainly the incidental consequence of other rules of law.'[55]

The very term 'civic death' conjures forth draconian ideas of having damaged the democratic process and as a result losing all rights. In the past, this was known as outlawry or attainder, terms which fed into the Forfeiture Act 1870. Defining either of these is not an easy task, however, to summarise Blackstone *outlawry* and *attainder* were clearly related:

'When sentence of death, the most terrible and highest judgment in the laws of England, is pronounced, the immediate inseparable consequence by the common law is attainder. For when it is now clear beyond all dispute, that the criminal is no longer fit to live upon the earth, but is to be exterminated as a monster and a bane to human society... He is then called attaint, stained, or blackened. He is no longer of any credit or reputation; he is dead in law.'[56]

The Forfeiture Act 1870 is regularly cited as the source of prisoner disenfranchisement in English law.[57] However ironically, the 1870 Act was enacted to liberalise the ancient system of the *attainder*, intended 'to give a simple remedy for an oppressive injustice.'[58] The Act retained several restrictions on the civic participation of convicted felons serving more than 12 months' imprisonment, including preventing them from voting or standing as candidates in any election for the duration of their imprisonment. It is important to note here, that due to the temporal clause (sentences over 12 months) that although the Act is commonly cited by Parliament as justification of a continued ban, that if the Act itself were to be enacted in present day that it would pass the requirements of the ECtHR in abolishing a blanket ban allowing some class of prisoners to vote.

Notwithstanding the intentions of the Act, the realities were very different, as in practice even those who qualified to vote under the limited statutory restrictions meant that all classes of convicted prisoner, including those held on remand, continued to suffer 'administrative disenfranchisement' where prisoners were often prevented from attending the polls by way of their incarceration. However, the fact that the act was not followed in practice does

---

55 Sumption L at para. 164. *R (on the application of Chester) (Appellant) v. Secretary of State for Justice (Respondent) McGeoch (AP) (Appellant) v. The Lord President of the Council and another (Respondents) (Scotland)* [2013] UKSC 63 On appeal from: [2010] EWCA Civ 1439; [2011] CSIH 67.

56 Quote from Blackstone's Commentaries on the Laws of England (1765–1769).

57 See C.R.G. Murray, 'Playing for Time: Prisoner Disenfranchisement under the ECHR after *Hirst v. United Kingdom*' (2012) 22 *Kings Law Journal* 309–334, and C.R.G. Murray, 'A Perfect Storm: Parliament and Prisoner Disenfranchisement' (2012) *Parliamentary Affairs* 1–29, 4–12.

58 C. Forster, MP (1980) 30 *HC Deb* 200, 932.

not take away from the fact that in theory the Act is much more accommodating to prisoners than the current RPA.

The idea of the blanket ban being intrinsic to British democratic process becomes more illogical when one considers the upheaval of voting rules surrounding World War II, particularly those pertaining to prisoners, whereby all prisoners were allowed to vote.[59] The first important alteration of the UK's electoral arrangements occurred when the post-war Labour Government introduced postal ballots under the RPA 1948, making them available even to individuals 'no longer resident at their qualifying addresses.' This simple amendment meant that that, 'prisoners confined in prisons outside their constituencies would be accepted by Returning Officers as eligible to vote by post.'[60] Following the enactment of the Criminal Law Act 1967, prisoners across the UK, regardless of the length of their sentence, could participate by postal ballot in the parliamentary by-elections and local government elections held between January 1968 and April 1969. However, progress in this area was turned on its head with little debate in Parliament,[61] in a remarkable move when all convicted prisoners throughout the UK were again disenfranchised under the RPA 1969.[62]

What is clear from a brief overview of the idea of civic death, and the attached history of the term, is that it clearly cannot be said that the blanket ban has long been a strong and steadfast part of British history. Even this perfunctory account has proved that the law has been subject to toing and froing on the subject and that the current blanket ban is still only a relatively recent phenomenon.

In terms of progression, it is also noteworthy here that as the remainder of the penal system has evolved, the blanket ban is a key provision that has not, holding on steadfastly to a tradition inherent more to Victorian than modern times. Executions, and the widespread tortuous acts which formed a part of the penological system in place when the civic death argument was created, are long forgotten, deemed archaic, unnecessary and not in keeping with modern penological change. Why, therefore, should the blanket ban be the only exception allowed to continue in use?

---

59 RPA 1948, s. 8(1)(e) and see RPA 1948, s. 8(4)(b) for the requirement that a new address must be outside the constituency if a postal vote was sought on the basis of not being resident at a qualifying address.

60 In the years following this amendment no serious objection was raised in relation to the enfranchisement of prisoners in Britain, on the contrary the success of those in Scottish prisons being afforded the vote with no negligible effect felt on the democratic process served as justification for this to continue.

61 Ibid.

62 RPA 1969, s. 4.

3.2. THE CIVIC VIRTUE ARGUMENT

The civic virtue and civic death arguments, although predominantly intertwined and spawned from the same ideology, differ on the actual reason or main aim of their use. The civic virtue argument on the contrary stems from the actual abstract and objective committing of a crime as a member of a democratic process. This strand of this argument asserts that when one violates the laws one participated in creating, that one defaults on the agreement to respect the law and hence forfeits any right to assist further in creating it.[63]

However, in order to say that prisoners lack civic virtue, certain generalisations must be inferred about their character and although it is true that people who break the law seemingly do not respect the law, the justification on this premise for taking away their vote appears to create or infer a second punishment. Traditionally in most jurisdictions, most sentences for crimes appear in the form of incarceration, thereby invoking the issue that if there has already been a punishment given, then what is the second crime then that prisoners are being punished for by forfeiting their vote?[64] Under the Criminal Justice Act 2003 five different rationales for sentencing offenders are set out, the first being punishment that is proportionate to the seriousness of the crime committed.[65] It is clear here then that the blanket ban could affect this section of the criminal justice act. John Hirst, for instance, the prisoner who brought the issue to the European Court of Human Rights in 2005, was given a 14-year sentence but was detained longer by the parole board because he was considered to be of potential danger to the public. By this point, he had served the supposedly punitive part of his sentence, but continued to be punished by not being allowed to vote.

Clearly, Hirst unnecessarily received greater punishment than his trial judge felt was proportionate because of this. Essentially disenfranchisement is fundamentally an additional punishment and as such requires an additional justification, particularly when one takes this provision of the Criminal Justice Act into account, yet none has as far as this author can gage, ever been supplied. Consequentially this idea of civic death or a second punishment appears jurisprudentially to be morally unjustifiable. Thomas Hammarberg, former

---

63 In other words, if you refuse to follow the law, you clearly do not respect it and should lose the ability to partake in its development.

64 Incarceration as a punishment is particularly noteworthy, as recent developments have indicated alternatives to imprisonment, what would occur in these situations, if say, someone is under house arrest or serving an alternative means of sentencing can they still vote if they are remaining at their own address? It is evident that disenfranchisement only operates when you are imprisoned. Why is that? Because it is seen that only the most serious offences result in imprisonment, but that is clearly not always the case. In addition, how does this work re remand prisoners who have not been convicted?

65 Criminal Justice Act 2005, Part 12, Chapter 1, Section 142, General Provisions About Sentencing: <www.legislation.gov.uk/United Kingdompga/2003/44/contents>.

Commissioner for Human Rights at the Council of Europe, has articulated his opinion on this matter stating that:

> 'Prisoners though deprived of physical liberty, have human rights … Measures should be taken to ensure that imprisonment does not undermine rights, which are unconnected to the intention of the punishment.'[66]

It is clear therefore the civic virtue argument is decidedly weak and standing as it does on feeble and unpersuasive evidence. The term civic virtue is used as haphazardly as civic death in support of prisoner disenfranchisement, with little evidence that its proponents can even define the essential term of the premise nor explain how it justifies the ban.

3.3. THE SOCIAL CONTRACT

The idea of a social contract as advocated for by Jacques Rousseau and Thomas Hobbes can be simply summarised in this context as the following: that people who misbehave have broken a social contract, and must be punished by the stripping of the rights supplied by the said contract. The social contract presents two main forms of argument; the first is that rights have corresponding duties, and secondly with respect to the right to vote, the duty of the citizen is to uphold the social contract (in practice, not to break the law). Therefore, by respecting the law and acting upon the duties prescribed by the social contract the citizen receives certain benefits.

The social contract theory has been used to justify the current stance taken in Australasia by the Australian and New Zealand legislators respectively. In Australia, prisoners serving sentences of more than three years are denied the right to vote, and the Australian Human Rights Commission recognised that this is in breach of the state's obligations under Article 25 ICCPR. In New Zealand, the position is much more severe, mirroring the UK's stance with the effect that no person incarcerated after the amendment could register on the electoral roll.[67] Sam Bookman, writing for the New Zealand Human Rights Blog discusses the basis and consequences of this amendment:

> 'To the untrained eye this flies in the face of section 12(a) of our Bill of Rights Act 1990 and section 25 of the International Covenant on Civil and Political Rights 1966 (ICCPR). But to the apparently learned eye of politicians, we can justify any measure

66 Quote by Thomas Hammarberg taken from, T. Whitehead, 'Denying prisoners the vote makes them "non people" says human rights chief' 2011 *Home Affairs* <www.telegraph.co.uk/news/UnitedKingdomnews/law-and-order/8419767/Denying-prisoners-the-vote-makes-them-non-people-says-human-rights-chief.html>.

67 In late 2010, New Zealand amended section 80(1)(d) of the Electoral Act 1993 to reflect this ban.

> that causes prisoners ill on the basis that they have already committed a wrong, and hence deserve to suffer the consequences of that wrong.'[68]

The use of the social contract argument places a great deal of trust and onus onto the effectiveness of the criminal justice system in the UK, as in order for the social contract theory to stick as a justification, we would need to ensure that all criminals are incarcerated or there would need to be an insured and complete consistency in sentencing process and a clear delineation of such. Pursuant to this, the social contract theory gives no guidance as to how we should do this or how we should create this degree of seriousness and minimal threshold. Furthermore, this argument neglects the comparative and complementary question of whether society has upheld its duties to the criminal, the person given obligations under the social contract. In short, we must not forget that the contract is bilateral. A further issue with this argument is how or why exactly the punishment for breaking or forsaking obligations under the contract is disenfranchisement. On this point, it is evident that merely showing criminals have clearly disregarded criminal law, does not make clear which of those rules they should lose the protection of:

> 'The Government have submitted that the measure pursues the aim of preventing crime by sanctioning the conduct of convicted prisoners and also the aim of enhancing civic responsibility and respect for the rule of law ... the Government stated that the aim of the bar on convicted prisoners was to confer an additional punishment ... it may nevertheless be considered as implied in the references to the forfeiting of rights that the measure is meant to give an incentive to citizen-like conduct.'[69]

The second strand of the social contract argument can perhaps be offered as an indicator of why the punishment manifests itself in such a way. The social contract theory asserts that when one violates the laws one participated in creating that the criminal defaults on the agreement to respect the law and

---

68 Currently in Australia, people who have been sentenced for more than three years in prison do not have the right to vote in federal elections while they are serving their sentence. Some argue that it may be reasonable to punish prisoners who have committed serious crimes by depriving them of the right to vote. However, the United Nations Human Rights Committee considers that depriving persons who have been convicted of a felony of the right to vote does not meet the obligations in Article 25 of the ICCPR nor does it serve the rehabilitation goals of Article 10(3) of the Covenant. (Human Rights Committee 18 December 2006). The Australian Human Rights Commission does not support the view that prisoners should have their right to vote suspended during their period of imprisonment. For an excellent analysis of this see: S. Bookman, 'Denying voting rights to prisoners in New Zealand: What was Parliament thinking?' 14 March 2013 <http://nzhumanrightsblog.com/newzealand/denying-voting-rights-to-prisoners-in-new-zealand-what-was-parliament-thinking/>.

69 *Hirst v. the United Kingdom*, no. 74025/01, ECHR 2005-II, §74.

hence abdicates any right to assist further in creating it.[70] In short, while the first argument is based on the fact of the law breaking, the latter part of the argument claims that society can deny the vote to citizens based on an inference about their attitude to the law, given their law-breaking. In summary, both the civic death and social contract argument appear to follow the rather arbitrary approach that if you refuse to follow the law you clearly do not respect it and should lose the ability to partake in its development.

3.4. ACHIEVING SENTENCING AIMS

A further justification often presented in favour of a continuing ban on prisoner enfranchisement is the premise that the blanket ban serves certain sentencing aims. During a recent statement providing evidence before the Joint Committee on the Draft Voting Eligibility (Prisoner) Bill, the Right Honourable Jack Straw MP (former Home Secretary and Justice Secretary) and David Davies MP (former Shadow Home Secretary and Minister for Europe) both advocated this approach.[71] Notwithstanding this opinion, the use of sentencing aims as a justification for denying the vote is in the author's opinion the weakest of the three. This weakness stems exclusively from the fact that whenever this point is given, that no actual evidence or reasoning is provided, it is merely stated that a blanket ban aids sentencing aims and the prisoner's rehabilitation.

Consequently, despite the over-generalisation of politicians contrary to this, research proves that maintaining a life as close to normality as possible will make re-integration an easier process, aide rehabilitation and diminish recidivism rates upon the prisoner's release.[72] This point was recognised by Judge Caflisch in *Hirst (No. 2)* at para. 5 of his concurring judgment where he stated that:

> 'The UK Government further contended that disenfranchisement in the present case was in harmony with the objectives of preventing crime and punishing offenders,

---

70 For more on this point or for a contrasting view of democracy as an exclusionary system see P. Ramsay, 'Faking Democracy with Prisoners' Voting Rights', *LSE Law Society and Economy Working Papers* 7/2013 London School of Economics and Political Science & Law Department.

71 The Right Honourable Jack Straw MP and David Davies MP appearing as witnesses before the Joint Committee on the Draft Voting Eligibility (Prisoners) Bill on: Wednesday 17 July at 9.36am. Ended at 10.41am.

72 For more on prisoner disenfranchisement and rehabilitation see: S. Easton, 'Electing the Electorate: The Problem of Prisoner Disenfranchisement' (2006) 69(3) *The Modern Law Review* 443–452. For the value of education on rehabilitating prisoners see: J.S. Vacca, 'Educated Prisoners Are Less Likely to Return to Prison' (2004) 55(4) *Journal of Correctional Education* 297–305; for more general writings on the merits of rehabilitation see: M. Monash and E.A. Anderson, 'Liberal Thinking on Rehabilitation: A Work-Able Solution to Crime' (1978) 25(5) *Social Problems* 556–563; P. Lutz, 'Probation and Rehabilitation' (1935) 25(6) *Journal of Criminal Law and Criminology* 914–917; C.R. Tittle, 'Institutional Living and

thereby enhancing civic responsibility (judgment, §50). I doubt that very much. I believe, on the contrary, that participation in the democratic process may serve as a first step toward re-socialisation.'[73]

Also reiterating this point was Dr Peter Selby, former Bishop to Her Majesty's Prisons and now President of the National Council for Independent Monitoring Boards for Prisons who has stated that:

> 'Denying convicted prisoners the right to vote serves no purpose of deterrence or reform. What it does is to state in the clearest terms society's belief that once convicted you are a non-person, one who should have no say in how our society is to develop ... It is making someone an "outlaw" ... it has no place in expressing a civilised attitude towards those in prison.'[74]

The justification itself however follows several trains of thought, the first of those being denunciation. The supporting claim here is that the loss of the vote sends a clear message to the wrongdoer about the evil of their conduct: are we telling them that because they are a bad person they will not only be incarcerated but also further excluded as they committed a crime and their opinion is no longer valued? The second aim offered under the title of sentencing aims is deterrence. Much like its predecessor, this is also deeply flawed yet is unfortunately frequently offered by governments such as the UK and Australia as a reason for denying the vote.[75] The government defended deterrence as the main purpose behind the blanket ban in *Hirst*:

> 'The Government argued that the disqualification in this case pursued the intertwined legitimate aims of punishing offenders, enhancing civic responsibility and respect for the rule of law by depriving those who had breached the basic rules of society of the right to have a say in the way such rules were made for the duration of their sentence. Convicted prisoners had breached the social contract and so could be regarded as (temporarily) forfeiting the right to take part in the government of the country.'[76]

Rehabilitation' (1972) 13(3) *Journal of Health and Social Behaviour* 263–275; C.A. Visher and J. Travis, 'Transitions from Prison to Community: Understanding Individual Pathways' (2003) 29 *Annual Review of Sociology* 89–113.

73 *Hirst v. the United Kingdom*, no. 74025/01, ECHR 2005-II, Concurring Opinion of Judge Caflisch, §5.

74 'People in prison are citizens, says Archbishop ahead of prisoners voting debate' 2011 *Prison Reform Trust* <www.prisonreformtrust.org.uk/PressPolicy/News/vw/1/ItemID/114> accessed 11.08.2011.

75 The Australasian governments have been particularly adamant about the merits of prisoner disenfranchisement and sentencing aims. For a more detailed and subjective, account of this see S. Bookmann, 'Denying voting rights to prisoners in New Zealand: What was Parliament thinking?' 2013 *NZ Human Rights Blog* <http://nzhumanrightsblog.com/newzealand/denying-voting-rights-to-prisoners-in-new-zealand-what-was-parliament-thinking/>.

76 *Hirst v. the United Kingdom, no.* 74025/01, ECHR 2005-II, §51.

However, there is little evidence to support this stance and therefore this justification fails for two reasons. Firstly, policy makers are assuming that people know about disenfranchisement laws. However, upon commencing research on prisoner disenfranchisement, it became quickly apparent that not many people actually know about prison disenfranchisement. While this may be a generalisation, it is one supported by many working and writing on this topic.[77] As evidence suggests however the majority of those incarcerated are more concerned with maintaining their personal and familial relationships and losing their freedom than with their suffrage.[78] Thus, the deterrence value of the deprivation of a right to vote is slim to none. Acknowledging that there are of course exceptions to each rule it appears that if a person has chosen to forsake their civil liberties that deprivation of their electoral rights may not provide effective deterrence. On the contrary, greater civic involvement actually contributes to an easier transition into life post-incarceration.

4. POLITICS, POLITICAL DENIALISM AND THE PRISONER DISENFRANCHISEMENT DEBATE: A MORAL PANIC?

This section of the paper will address the *'why'* element, namely why the UK has chosen to deny prisoners their voting rights and to deny its international obligations and in doing so, the Court's legitimacy to enforce both Convention norms. The drive behind the UK's act of political denialism is clearly framed against the backdrop of the changing attitudes to the ECtHR within the UK. This section will highlight that within acts of political denialism, there is often an element on which the perpetrator can fasten their argument. In the case of the UK, this would initially be the aforementioned justifications based on 'democratic traditions', but also those based upon the creation of a 'moral panic', with two parallel and interconnected aims. The meaning of this in the context of the prisoner voting debate will be discussed shortly.

As a founder of the ECHR, one could be forgiven for thinking that the UK would be a staunch supporter of the Convention system and associated Court. More recently however, the UK's relationship to the ECtHR has become tinged with controversy. Leading politicians advocate an enhanced approach to domestic protection of ECHR rights, as evidenced during the UK's chairmanship

---

77 S. Bookmann, 'Denying voting rights to prisoners in New Zealand: What was Parliament thinking?' 2013 *NZ Human Rights Blog* <http://nzhumanrightsblog.com/newzealand/denying-voting-rights-to-prisoners-in-new-zealand-what-was-parliament-thinking/>.

78 The Right Honourable Jack Straw MP and David Davies MP appearing as witnesses before the Joint Committee on the Draft Voting Eligibility (Prisoners) Bill on: Wednesday 17 July at 9.36am. Ended at 10.41am and see: S. Easton, 'Electing the Electorate: The Problem of Prisoner Disenfranchisement' (2006) 69(3) *The Modern Law Review* 443–452.

of the Council or Europe and there is renewed interest in the age of subsidiarity present at the Brighton Conference.[79] As these issues fall beyond the constraints and remit of this paper, they will not be considered, however what is important here is the general attitude present within the current UK government towards the ECtHR and prisoner voting rights.

> 'It is frustrating and disappointing to see that, largely because of a single judgment concerning the right to vote of some categories of convicted prisoners, the court has become a sort of *hate figure*, not just in the popular press, but also in the soundbites of politicians.'[80]

As articulated in the opening part of this paper, the UK is a knowing and complicit perpetrator of political denialism. In denying prisoners the vote for political motivations, the UK is blatantly disregarding the judgments of the ECtHR on prisoner disenfranchisement. It is suggested, that in exploring why the UK is denying to recognise and fulfil its Convention obligations, that there is an element of moral panic at play. That the prisoner voting debate is not only an example of political denialism but also of an 'overreaction', or creation of a moral panic.[81]

---

79 Steering Committee for Human Rights (CDDH), Final Report on measures requiring amendment of the European Convention on Human Rights (CDDH/2012/R74 Addendum I), 15 February 2012 <www.coe.int/t/dgi/brightonconference/Documents/CDDH-amendment-measures-report_en.pdf>. The PM, speaking at the Parliamentary Assembly of the Council of Europe, lamented the current interventionist approach of the Court and touted enhanced subsidiarity as key to building a more understanding relationship between states and the Court. In doing so he referenced both terrorism and prisoner disenfranchisement as prime examples of the Court's flaws. He went on to propose that where a state had democratically debated the issue and once the judgment had passed the scrutiny of the domestic judiciary that the Court should not be able to intervene in the matter. The members of the assembly, which Cameron addressed, agreed and voted in a total majority that the Court should become subsidiary to national courts and bodies, acting in an enhanced advisory role.

80 N. Bratza quoted in E. Bjorge, 'Prisoners' Voting Rights: The Gift That Keeps on Giving' 2012 *Oxford Human Rights Hub* <http://ohrh.law.ox.ac.uk/prisoners-voting-rights-the-gift-that-keeps-on-giving/> accessed 16.04.2015.

81 It is interesting to note here the work of those such as A. Von Hirsch, and M. Wasik, 'Civil Disqualifications Attending Conviction: A Suggested Conceptual Framework' (1997) 56 *Cambridge Law Journal* 599, supported by C.R.G. Murray, 'A Perfect Storm: Parliament and Prisoner Disenfranchisement' (2012) *Parliamentary Affairs* 1–29, who maintain that the fact that prisoners were invited and urged to vote during and post WWII in order to maintain a proper electorate completely undermines the main justification for the blanket ban; that it is a traditional and historic feature of the United Kingdom's electoral tradition: 'Universal disenfranchisement of prisoners has not been an ever-present feature of the United Kingdom's electoral system over the last century. Indeed, the restrictions on the franchise have often rested on very limited legal authority and, by the middle of the twentieth century, were subject to extensive exceptions. Nonetheless, in an attempt to persuade the electorate that prisoner disenfranchisement is hardwired into the United Kingdom's system of representative democracy, the opponents of prisoner enfranchisement continue to insist that it was 'never an issue in the British prison system until the lawyers got hold of it through the European Convention on Human Rights.' (B. Jenkin, MP (2011) 523 *HC Deb.* 494).

Cohen suggested in his book *Folk Devils and Moral Panics*, that a moral panic occurs when a 'condition, episode, person or group of persons emerges to become defined as a threat to societal values and interests.'[82] Cohen saw moral panic and denialism as connected ideas, and this is certainly true within political acts of denialism.[83] 'Cohen's understanding of the overreaction to putative social problems, most evident in moral panic, is balanced by his keen observation on the underreaction in which knowledge of human rights violations is concealed and denied.'[84]

If moral panic is the 'overreaction', the denialism is representative of an underreaction, the turning of 'a blind eye to human rights abuses perpetuated by the state.'[85] Indeed prisoner disenfranchisement fulfils many of the characteristics that Goode and Ben-Yehuda developed from Cohen's principles, characteristics which determine whether an event is a moral panic, they list these as concern, hostility, consensus and disproportionality.

Firstly, there is clearly concern that enfranchising prisoners will have a negative effect on society.[86] Secondly, there is hostility towards prisoners due to their having committed a crime to become incarcerated; this is supported by a consensus among both the public and polity that the incarcerated provide a risk to society. Finally, it can be argued that the support behind a continued ban on prisoner enfranchisement is rooted in disproportionality especially as evidenced above, that enfranchising prisoners is linked to better rehabilitation post-incarceration and the majority of European countries have no means of restrictions on the voting rights of those incarcerated.

It is thus suggested, that where the act of denying prisoners their voting rights is an act of political denialism, that the reasoning behind this denial rests upon the creation of two elements of 'moral panic' and that intrinsically for a political power to rely upon denialism that an element of moral panic is key.[87] The first of

82 S. Cohen, *Folk Devils And Moral Panics*, MacGibbon & Kee, London 1972.

83 S. Cohen, 'Human rights and crimes of the state: the culture of denial' (1993) 26 *Australian and New Zealand Journal of Criminology 2*, 97–115.

84 M. Welsh, 'Moral panic, denial, and human rights: scanning the spectrum from overreaction to underreaction' in: D. Downes, P. Rock, C. Chinkin and C. Gearty, *Crime Social Control and Human Rights From Moral Panics to States of Denial: Essays in Honour of Stanley Cohen*, Willen Publishing, London 2007.

85 Ibid.

86 This is clearly represented by the traction which the current prisoner voting debate has created in the UK, as articulated in this section it is due to the moral panic created by the idea that 'criminals, rapists and paedophiles' be allowed to vote which has created the impetus for the Government to challenge the Court's decision on this matter.

87 Clearly in order to garner the public support necessary to be elected or to create popular and lasting political legacy, politicians need to draw their manifestos based on what will encourage the electorate to support them and vote for them. In appealing to issues of morality and particularly on the issue of prisoner disenfranchisement, clearly a reason why the debate is so fraught and contentious is that it appeals to people's morality and incites a reaction.

these is based upon the public's views on criminals, whereby the majority view the enfranchisement of prisoners to be distasteful or morally reprehensible:

> 'When a person commits a crime which is sufficiently serious to put him in prison, he sacrifices his liberty, his freedom of association, and his vote. When we vote in a government, we choose a group of men and women to make laws on our behalf. Convicted prisoners should have no say in this; those who break the law cannot make the law.'[88]

Speaking on this issue David Cameron, Prime Minister, stated that allowing those incarcerated to partake in the democratic process made him 'physically ill.' This position is strongly represented within public opinion on the matter[89] and excluding criminals from the democratic process has therefore garnered easy support for politicians.

The other element to the moral panic surrounding prisoner disenfranchisement rests upon the Court's role. Criticism of the ECHR and the Court is constant both among politicians and the public, and the constant vilifying of the Court has gained much traction both in politics and through the media:[90]

> 'The media, then – in a sense – can create social problems, they can present them dramatically and overwhelmingly, and, most important, they can do it suddenly. The media can very quickly and effectively fan public indignation and engineer what one might call "a moral panic".'[91]

Opposition to human rights has become an apparent favoured policy for politicians across the political spectrum especially regarding prisoner voting rights. It is clear from the refusal of consecutive governments, since the *Hirst* judgment in 2005, to implement the ECtHR judgments and amending the RPA 1998, that prisoner voting rights is not an issue behind which the public can align themselves. Rather, it is clear that upholding the ban and connecting this to British traditions and values, as many politicians have, is the more popular position:

> 'In attempting to overrule British law on prisoner voting rights, Strasbourg judges have exceeded the limits of their proper authority. If the Court does not reflect the

---

88 Talk given to University College London By the Rt Hon Dominic Grieve, QC, MP, 'Why Human Rights should matter to Conservatives', 3 December 2014.

89 Above note 40.

90 One of the reasons politicians find it so easy to criticise human rights is that the popular press have laid the groundwork for them to do so. For some of the myths perpetuated by the British Press regarding human rights see the excellent rightsinfo.org: 'The 14 Worst Human Rights Myths' <http://rightsinfo.org/infographics/the-14-worst-human-rights-myths/>.

91 J. Young in S. Cohen, *Images of Deviance*, MacGibbon & Kee, London 1971, p. 71.

views of member states of the Council of Europe, there will be conflict. Where the court infringes our constitutional rights, we will not back down.'[92]

It also appears that prisoner voting rights was the ideal issue behind which politicians could drive public support, as Professor Helen Fenwick details, the prisoner voting rights debate has 'proved convenient' for the UK in challenging the ECtHR system.

However, it is not just prisoner voting rights that is causing tension between Strasbourg and the UK. While the prisoner voting debate highlights most of the issues considered to be at stake by the UK Government, there are deeper issues at play in how the UK views and interacts with the ECtHR and Convention system. It now appears that anti-ECtHR sentiment is so prevalent within politics that the Conservative Party has promised to repeal the HRA 1998 if it obtains a majority at the 2015 election. Further, the Party has even threatened withdrawal from the ECHR and Council of Europe system.[93] Speaking on his Party's plan's to create a British Bill of Rights, Former Attorney General, Dominic Grieve, has summed up the current issue between the Government and Strasbourg rather succinctly:

> '[T]he real problem for [the Conservatives] is not so much the interpretation of the Convention by the Strasbourg Court or indeed our own domestic courts but the frustration that an international legal obligation prevents the UK Government from being able to ignore judgments when it considers that they are adverse to its view of what is in the public interest.'[94]

Clearly, the second element of moral panic is tied to this representation of the Strasbourg Court as an 'interfering' or 'meddling' Court. A Court which oversteps its' ambit in seeking to enforce 'un-British values' upon the UK,[95] 'the Strasbourg Court has taken upon itself an extraordinary and unnecessary power to micromanage the legal systems of the Member States of the Council of Europe (or at any rate, those who pay attention to its decisions.'[96]

This position is proliferated all too willingly by the British press, who regularly misrepresent the Strasbourg Court and its judgments, representing

---

92 D. Davis and J. Straw, 'We must defy Strasbourg on prisoner votes' 2012 *The Telegraph* <www.telegraph.co.uk/news/uknews/law-and-order/9287633/We-must-defy-Strasbourg-on-prisoner-votes.html accessed 13.04.2015.

93 'A Great Day for British Justice: Theresa May Vows UK to leave ECtHR' *Daily Mail* <www.dailymail.co.uk/news/article-2287183/A-great-day-British-justice-Theresa-May-vows-UKEuropean-Court-Human-Rights.html> accessed 13.04.2015. Specifically over prisoner votes: D. Davis and J. Straw, 'We must defy Strasbourg on prisoner votes'.

94 Talk to University College London By the Rt. Hon. Dominic Grieve QC MP, Why Human Rights should matter to Conservatives, 3rd December 2014.

95 D. Davies and J. Straw, 'We Must Defy Strasbourg on Prisoner Votes' 2012 *The Telegraph* <www.telegraph.co.uk/news/UnitedKingdomnews/law-and-order/9287633/We-must-defy-Strasbourg-on-prisoner-votes.html>.

96 L. Hoffmann, *Forward to Policy Exchange*, Pamphlet 2011.

the Court as a body in which criminals, terrorists etc. use human rights to surpass and trample the rights of UK citizens. Most notable for doing so are the *Daily Mail*, the *Daily Express* and the *Sun*, which consistently refer to the HRA as the 'Hated Human Rights Act'.[97] The *Daily Mail* is renowned for calling the ECHR a 'charter for criminals and parasites'. It is easy to see consequently, where the support for a ban on prisoner disenfranchisement comes from when one considers media portrayals of human rights and the political manifesto on human rights issues. In what becomes a vicious circle, the misrepresentations peddled by both politicians and media are enthusiastically deployed by further politicians and other media outlets, resulting in the situation currently unfolding in the UK, where regard for human rights under the Convention system is at an all-time low.[98]

Therefore, it can be argued that in answering 'why' the UK has chosen to deny both its obligations under the ECHR system and to deny prisoners the vote that the answer clearly lies in the proliferation of the negative attitude towards the Court and prisoner enfranchisement. Adam Wagner, QC credits this as 'monstering of human rights…where the Human Rights Act and the European Court of Human Rights have become monsters in the eyes of the public, and

97 'May: Scrap the Human Rights Act. Home Secretary Calls for hated laws to be axed' *The Sun* <www.thesun.co.uk/sol/homepage/news/3848868/May-Scrap-the-Human-Rights-Act.html>; 'Tories pledge to scrap "dangerous" Human Rights Act' *Express* <www.express.co.uk/news/uk/381630/Tories-pledge-to-scrap-dangerous-Human-Rights-Act>; 'Human rights is a charter for criminals and parasites our anger is no longer enough' 2012 *Mail on Sunday*; 'Human rights laws are a charter for criminals, say 75% of Britons' 2012 *Daily Mail* <www.dailymail.co.uk/news/article-2130224/Human-rights-laws-charter-criminals-say-75 Britons.html> accessed 13.03.2015; 'Migrant facing deportation wins right to stay in Britain… because he's got a cat' 2009 *Daily Mail* <www.dailymail.co.uk/news/article-1221353/Youve-got-cat-OK-stay-Britain-officials-tell-Bolivianimmigrant.html> accessed 13.04.2015; 'Immigrant allowed to stay because of pet' 2009 *Daily Telegraph* <www.telegraph.co.uk/news/newstopics/howaboutthat/6360116/Immigrant-allowed-to-stay-becauseof-pet-cat.html> accessed 13.04.2015; D. Barrett, '102 foreign criminals and illegal immigrants we can't deport' 2011 *Sunday Telegraph* <www.telegraph.co.uk/news/uknews/law-and-order/8570639/102-foreign-criminals-and-illegalimmigrants-we-cant-deport.html> accessed 13.04.2015.

98 Arguably leaving the ECHR and CoE system will not resolve all issues that the UK has with human rights and external influence. Devolution must be considered. The Conservative Party's the Bill of Rights Commission eventually figured out that devolution is an integral part of plans to withdraw from the ECHR system. As a result, Parliament's options may be limited whilst issues surrounding Scotland, Northern Ireland and Wales and their say in the matter remain under-appraised. Consequently, the UK would be sending a significant signal to other states also not implementing ECtHR judgments. Any justification for leaving must be balanced against the very significant signal which the UK would be sending that it has lost confidence in the European Convention on Human Rights. Moreover, the British Bill of Rights would have to mitigate all the factors that leaving Strasbourg would arguably create. If the British Bill of Rights is not up to par with Convention protections, this would leave individuals in the UK in a weaker position against the state if their rights are breached. The key question is therefore whether the current plans to withdraw from the European Court of Human Rights will solve the problems which the Conservative Party and press are so fond of highlighting.

those who claim using human rights law have themselves been monstered.'[99] In short, it appears that this monstering or increasingly poor public and political attitude towards the ECtHR has been utilised by the Government to drive public support. Consequently, the monstering of human rights is key to the prisoner enfranchisement debate, as it is the impetus or driving force behind support for the UK's committing such a blatant act of denialism.[100]

5. CONCLUSION

In conclusion, the aim of this paper has been to examine the reasoning and justifications behind support for the continued blanket ban on prisoner disenfranchisement in the UK. The example of denialism represented by prisoner disenfranchisement in the UK has been addressed from two angles. Firstly the '*how*' was explored – how the UK can justify such a blatant denial of both the rights of prisoners to vote and as a result deny both the legitimacy of the ECtHR and its human rights obligations. The main justifications – civic death, civic virtue, the social contract and the ambiguous achieving of sentencing aims – were all explored as valid justifications for continuation of the ban. It is apparent from an exploration of these that each of the justifications is easily refuted, undermining any value to the argument proposed in support of the ban.

Secondly, the '*why*' element was explored, namely why the UK has chosen to deny prisoners their voting rights and to acknowledge its international obligations, consequently denying the Court's legitimacy to enforce the Convention. The main reason why this concrete case of denialism is playing

99 A. Wagner, 'The Monstering of Human Rights,' conference paper delivered at Human Rights in the UK Media: Representation and Reality, University of Liverpool, 19 September 2014 <http://ukhumanrightsblog.com/2014/09/22/the-monstering-of-human-rights> accessed 16.04.2015.

100 On this point, academics have suggested many reasons why the Conservative Coalition Government has chosen to challenge the Court's authority. It is argued that this is predominantly rooted, as Grieve (referenced in main text) articulates it appears that ultimately the ECHR system is viewed as an inconvenient as it gets in the government's way, or hampers certain societal policies. On this point see A. Hirsch, 'The MPs voting against prisoners, and 21st century civic death' 2011 *The Guardian*; M. Elliott, 'Repealing the Human Rights Act, withdrawing from the ECHR: be careful what you wish for' 2013 *Public Law For Everyone* <http://publiclawforeveryone.wordpress.com/2013/03/04/repealing-the-human-rights-act-withdrawing-from-the-echr-be-careful-what-you-wish-for/>; C. Murray 'Prisoner Voting: The Human Rights Issue that Keeps on Giving' 2013 *Bloglovin* <www.bloglovin.com/frame?post=1278443997&group=0&frame_type=a&blog=6976793&link=aHR0cDovL2ZlZWRwcm94eS5nb29nbGUuY29tL35yL2h1bWFucmlnaHRzL2t4THUvfjMvNE9oUXpEZnU0SHMv&frame=1&click=0&user=0>; J. Duffy, 'Apocalypse soon? The UK without the European Convention on Human Rights' 2013 *UK Human Rights Blog* <http://ukhumanrightsblog.com/2013/05/17/apocalypse-soon-the-uk-without-the-european-convention-on-human-rights/>; H. Fenwick 'An appeasement approach in the European Court of Human Rights?' 2012 *UK Constitutional Law Association* <http://ukconstitutionallaw.org/2012/04/05/helen-fenwick-an-appeasement-approach-in-the-european-court-of-human-rights/>.

out was addressed against the backdrop of the changing attitudes to the ECtHR within the UK. It was highlighted that within acts of political denialism, there is often an element on which the perpetrator can fasten their argument. In the case of the UK, this was held to be the aforementioned justifications based on 'democratic traditions', but also those based upon the creation of a 'moral panic', with two parallel and interconnected aims. One side of which is fuelled by public distaste for those incarcerated and the other driven by an undermining of the ECtHR system through vilifying of the Court.

Thus, while it is clear that being devoid of strong justifications will not cause the UK to depart suddenly from its current position, it does amount to a certain lack of credibility regarding its adopted position on the rights of prisoners to vote in the face of clear decisions to the contrary by the ECtHR. This lack of credibility when coupled with the continuing threat of not only being still in breach of treaty obligations holds to seriously undermine the UK's stance as a key figure within European human rights, especially as the UK continues to flout the Court's rulings in refusing to implement the judgments, lifting the blanket ban.

The validity of these justifications is evidently not of concern to the UK as proponents of this concrete case of denialism. Rather, this is grounds within which to utilise public policy arguments to justify a political stance against an international legal body (the ECtHR). This paper has addressed these public policy insights and justifications to gain insight into concrete situations where a human rights abuse is supported by and committed by a state itself. In highlighting both how the UK has attempted to justify its current position and why it is committing such a blatant denial of human rights and its international obligations, this paper seeks to contribute to research within political motivated instances of denialism against human rights provisions. The prisoner voting rights debate thus provides an excellent example within which to address why and how denialism is committed, and consequently how a leading state within the European human rights system can justify continued human rights violations.

PART V

SOCIAL, ECONOMIC AND CULTURAL RIGHTS

CHAPTER XVIII

POVERTY, JUST WORLD THINKING AND HUMAN RIGHTS LAW

A Study of the Relevance of Denial for Normative Legal Research

Gustavo AROSEMENA

1. INTRODUCTION

Why is poverty continuously sidelined as a human rights concern? Can it be the case that we are collectively in denial about the true extent of this global social problem? And if denial is taking place, what should the law do about it? If we identify a form of self-deception as the 'root cause' of the sidelining of poverty as a human rights concern, what follows from a legal perspective? In addressing these questions, this contribution defends two theses:

(1) It is *prima facie* plausible that a systematic and pervasive form of denial known as just world thinking or belief in a just world (BJW) lies behind the constant sidelining of poverty as a human rights concern.
(2) The identification of denial is necessary, but not sufficient to derive normative conclusions in the field of law. The finding of BJW in operation in the sidelining of poverty as a human rights concern does not, by itself, provide guidance as to what changes (if any) need to be made to the law.

The goals of this contribution are methodological.[1] It aims to show both the importance and the limits of certain 'unmasking' research programmes that claim to reveal hidden biases and motivations in human action (of which

1 Hopefully in the tradition of serious methodological reflection about the theory and practice of human rights law exemplified by F. COOMANS, F. GRUNFELD and M. KAMMINGA, *Methods of Human Rights Research*, Intersentia, Antwerp 2009.

theories of denial and BJW form part)[2] for normative legal research. Poverty and BJW are used as a springboard to derive more general conclusions about the relevance of this sort of social-scientific research for law.

The paper is organised as follows. Section 2 introduces the concept of denial. Then sections 3, 4 and 5 argue for thesis (1). Section 3 describes the problem of global poverty and the deficient response it has received from human rights law. Section 4 lists various forms of bad arguments that have been used to justify the relative exclusion of poverty as a human rights concern. Section 5 shows how these bad arguments can be explained as arising out of a form of denial. BJW is introduced as an overarching explanation of the pervasiveness and influence of bad arguments for the exclusion and downgrading of poverty as a human rights concern. Finally, sections 6 and 7 argue for thesis (2). Section 6 argues that, even if denial is taking place, diagnosing it is by itself insufficient for grounding normative conclusions in the field of law. Independent normative theorising is still called for. In counterpoint, section 7 shows that even if BJW is not sufficient for deriving normative legal conclusions, it still provides necessary input for carrying out this task, including some powerful objections against certain sorts of normative theories which assume that human beings always know what is valuable, just and fair.

2. CHARACTERISING DENIAL

Denial is characterised as a state of self-deception, a paradoxical form of 'knowing and not knowing' that aims to shut out uncomfortable or unbearable information.[3]

As a state of self-deception denial is different from a mere lie as the liar knows that he is hiding the truth, but a person in denial, *at some level*, is unaware of the facts. Likewise, denial is different from a mere error, as the person who commits an error truly does not know the truth, while a person in denial *at some level*, knows what is really the case but prefers to reject reality. Denial, strictly speaking, is to be found in the middle ground between lies and error.[4] To make sense of how one could at the same time know and not know, both lie and be in error about some fact, the theory of denial suggests a complex psyche where some parts of the mind can censor other parts in a way that the conscious self cannot always fully grasp or understand.[5] This is well in line with

2 On the vitality of 'unmasking' research programmes today, see B. Leiter, 'The hermeneutics of suspicion: recovering Marx, Nietzsche, and Freud' in: B. Leiter (ed.), *The Future for Philosophy*, Oxford University Press, Oxford 2006, pp. 74–105.

3 This apt phrase is from Cohen. See S. Cohen, *States of Denial: Knowing About Atrocities and Suffering*, Polity Press, London 2001, p. 21.

4 Ibid., p. 6.

5 On the contradictory, paradoxical nature of self-deception see J. Elster, *Ulysses and the sirens: Studies in rationality and irrationality*, Cambridge University Press, Cambridge 1979, pp. 157–158.

Freudian psychology, from which the idea of denial originates,[6] but the idea of a complex and opaque mind and the psychology of denial have a large degree of independence from their questionable Freudian origins.[7]

Denial aims to shut out uncomfortable information. As such, the self-deception perpetrated in cases of denial is self-interested. It aims to protect the self against uncomfortable truths.[8] It is important to know that in this context self-interest does not mean anything like selfishness. Denial can both protect the perpetrator against realising the suffering of his victims and the victim against realising the injustice of his victimisation.[9] It is enough to say that denial is protective of the self, its projects and its worldview, and these can be moral or immoral, laudable or shameful.

On the face of it, the phenomenon of denial is of tremendous importance for the practice of human rights. It has been argued that the path towards a society that upholds human rights is structured around practices of bearing witness to the crimes that have been perpetrated, preventing future crimes, providing aid for victims and creating a culture of solidarity.[10] By obscuring the crimes that have been committed, as well as the nature of the crimes as illegitimate and unjust, in order to preserve a false but comfortable status quo, denial is almost, by definition, opposed to all these processes.

It is important to realise that denial is just one of the various 'self-deceptive' mechanisms that social scientific research claims to have uncovered. In fact, a significant branch of social science sees itself as essentially 'emancipatory', unmasking our hidden biases and liberating us from them.[11] What is said here about the relevance of denial for legal analysis applies *mutatis mutandi* to other forms of self-deception revealed by the 'emancipatory' social scientific project. Hence the methodological importance of understanding the implications of denial; it sets the stage for the interface between (large swaths of) social science and law. To exemplify this point, what this article argues about the relevance of denial for law would also apply to 'ideology in the pejorative

6 S. Cohen, *States of Denial: Knowing About Atrocities and Suffering*, Polity Press, London 2001, p. 25 et seq.

7 See for example S. Cohen, *States of Denial: Knowing About Atrocities and Suffering*, Polity Press, London 2001, pp. 47–48.

8 See J. Elster, *Ulysses and the sirens: Studies in rationality and irrationality*, Cambridge University Press, Cambridge 1979, p. 174.

9 S. Cohen, *States of Denial: Knowing About Atrocities and Suffering*, Polity Press, London 2001, pp. 14–15.

10 On these practices among others, see F. Kurasawa, *The work of global justice: Human rights as practices*, Cambridge University Press, Cambridge 2007, p. 16 et passim.

11 See, for instance, R. Bhaskar, *Scientific realism and human emancipation*. Routledge, London 2009, pp. xxvii, xxviii. See also G.A. Cohen, *Karl Marx's theory of history: a defence*. Oxford University Press, Oxford 2000, Appendix 1, 'On the Withering Away of Social Science.'

sense',[12] a phenomenon that can be taken to be the sociological counterpart of denial.

'Ideology in the pejorative sense' refers to a social construct that legitimises an unjust social order by making it appear as necessary, natural or beneficial to *both*, the oppressed and those doing the oppression. A paradigm case of ideology appears in the Marxian denunciation of capitalism. According to Marx, capitalism's formal concepts of freedom of contract and equality under the law obscure the real relations of domination between the capitalist class and the proletariat. On the surface, fundamental rights declare every citizen to be free and equal, and protect the property rights of everyone. This is the overt role of fundamental rights which makes them appear to be desirable for everyone. But, given basic inequalities of access to and ownership of the means of production, fundamental rights covertly protect the capitalist class from redistributive action from the proletariat, while preserving the appearance of freedom and equality. This is the real role of fundamental rights, which has a function in maintaining the integrity of the capitalist socio-economic system. This covert role is diametrically opposed to its stated role. In fact, for fundamental rights to carry out their real, covert role, they have to convince the proletariat of the reality of their false overt role. Hence rights constitute themselves as an 'objective illusion'. A falsehood the social order is invested in maintaining, which has real and important consequences.[13] The intellectual worth of Marxism is questionable. Yet, rather than discuss the merits of Marxism, the main point of this contribution is to show that if it turns out that we really live in a world plagued by an obscurantist ideology, unmasking the illusion is necessary, but not sufficient, to fulfil the demands of normative legal research.

3. THE SIDELINING OF POVERTY IN INTERNATIONAL HUMAN RIGHTS LAW

Concern for poverty has somehow failed to achieve the attention that it is warranted to provide to it if one takes into consideration the immense impact it has on human dignity. At the moment of writing approximately 1 billion people live below the absolute poverty line.[14] There is a clear correlation between poverty and life expectancy, with the poorest countries of the world having a life expectancy below fifty years of age.[15] That is not to say anything about how

12 On the pejorative concept of ideology, see R. Geuss, *The idea of a critical theory. Habermas and the Frankfurt School*, Cambridge University Press, Cambridge 1981.

13 Ibid., pp. 70–72.

14 See UNDP, *The Millennium Development Goals Report 2014*, pp. 8–9.

15 This correlation is known as the Preston Curve. Discussing this correlation (amongst others) see D.M. Cutler, A.S. Deaton and A. Lleras-Muney, 'The determinants of mortality' (2006) 20 *Journal of Economic Perspectives* 97–120.

poverty curtails actual human fulfilment, the development of the talents and abilities that seem to constitute a truly fortunate human life.[16]

Despite the tremendous extent and impact of poverty as a persistent evil in the life of millions, the response of international human rights law is characteristically weak. Although literally there is no human right not to be poor, the so-called 'economic, social and cultural rights' (ESC rights) enshrined in the International Covenant on Economic, Social and Cultural Rights (ICESCR) can be seen as the countermeasure to widespread poverty and want. By looking at the status of these rights one can measure the degree to which poverty has been downgraded as a human rights issue.

The 'stepchild' status of ESC rights is easy to see. The ICESCR is preceded by an umbrella clause that severely limits the strength of the rights that are stipulated in said treaty.[17] Even more, the ICESCR, understood literally, demands no provision of judicial remedies for ESC rights, either at the international level or at the domestic level. If one takes seriously the maxim 'where there is a right there is a remedy', this lack of remedies for ESC rights proves troubling. It suggests that despite being called 'rights' these provisions tend to function in practice more as 'guiding principles' or solemn political commitments than real rights.[18] Only with the advent of the Optional Protocol to the ICESCR have some of these limitations been removed by the introduction of an international complaints mechanism, from which a demand to provide domestic remedies can be inferred.[19] That said, (counting from the date of adoption of the ICESCR)[20] it took 42 years for the Optional Protocol to be formally adopted and opened for signature and five additional years for it to enter into force, and at the moment of writing only twenty countries have ratified this instrument. It is hard to

---

16 On abilities to do and achieve as vital components of a desirable human life, see MC. Nussbaum, *Creating capabilities*, Harvard University Press, Cambridge, MA 2011.

17 The relevant provision reads: 'Each State Party to the present Covenant undertakes to take steps, individually and through international assistance and co-operation, especially economic and technical, to the maximum of its available resources, with a view to achieving progressively the full realization of the rights recognized in the present Covenant by all appropriate means, including particularly the adoption of legislative measures.'

18 It is also notable that the language of 'violation' is absent from the ICESCR. See F. Coomans, 'The International Covenant on Economic, Social and Cultural Rights. From Stepchild to Full Member of the Human Rights Family' in: F. Gomez Isa and K. De Feyter, *International Human Rights Law in a Global Context*, University of Deusto, Bilbao 2009, p. 296.

19 This due to the fact that the Optional Protocol, in its Article 3(1) requires claimants to exhaust all domestic remedies. This suggests that domestic remedies must be provided. As stated by Coomans, 'the mere possibility that complaints may be brought before an international forum should stimulate governments to ensure that effective remedies are available at the domestic level'. See F. Coomans, 'The International Covenant on Economic, Social and Cultural Rights. From Stepchild to Full Member of the Human Rights Family' in: F. Gomez Isa and K. De Feyter, *International Human Rights Law in a Global Context*, University of Deusto, Bilbao 2009, pp. 315–316.

20 This is rather generous considering that ESC rights where already present in the Universal Declaration on Human Rights of 1948.

understand how this could have taken so long given the urgency of the problem of poverty. Taking all of this together it is very easy to conclude that the position of ESC rights at the international level has always been severely underprivileged and is likely to remain so for the near future.

Things look slightly better at the domestic level. Countries such as South Africa and Colombia have developed a mature jurisprudence of protection of ESC rights.[21] Still, these advances can only provide a limited degree of satisfaction. It is open to question: why did it take at least 34 years for the world to see a case like *Grootboom*, which is in many ways still a lukewarm response to the evils of deprivation?[22] And why have these developments taken place almost exclusively in the third world, whereas it would be much easier to use legal means to tackle severe deprivation in first world countries?[23]

4. FLIMSY EXCUSES

This persistent sidelining of poverty demands explanation. And this demand is only further strengthened by the fact that the most common academic and political justifications for the exclusion of ESC rights from legal protection are flimsy and unpersuasive.

The most frequent justification concentrates on supposed attributes that ESC rights have that civil and political rights (CP rights) do not have: costliness, vagueness, positive character and inapplicability in some situations (for instance when resources are lacking). The problem is that all the attributes invoked appear also in CP rights, albeit often to a lesser degree.[24] This is something that was already known by the time of drafting of the ICESCR, although it took some time for this point to receive sophisticated theoretical articulation.[25] During

21 For an overview of these developments, see M. Langford, 'The Justiciability of Social Rights: From Practice to Theory' in: M. Langford (ed.), *Social rights jurisprudence: emerging trends in international and comparative law*, Cambridge University Press, Cambridge 2008. The arguments presented in this section are developed at greater length in G. Arosemena, *Rights, scarcity and justice. An analytical inquiry into the adjudication of the welfare aspects of human rights*, Intersentia, Antwerp 2014.

22 Again, we are counting from the date of adoption of the ICESCR. Here we are referring to the *Grootboom* decision of the South African Constitutional Court due to its global salience and for being the first official formulation of reasonableness review at the level of the South African Constitutional Court. See *Government of the Republic of South Africa and Others v. Grootboom and Others* (CCT11/00) [2000] ZACC 19; 2001 (1) SA 46; 2000 (11) BCLR 1169 (4 October 2000).

23 Although slightly dated, the leading comparative analysis of ESC rights jurisprudence illustrate that social rights litigation is a third world phenomenon. See F. Coomans (ed.), *Justiciability of economic and social rights: experiences from domestic systems*, Intersentia, Antwerp 2006 and M. Langford (ed.), *Social rights jurisprudence: emerging trends in international and comparative law*, Cambridge University Press, Cambridge 2008.

24 An influential formulation of this point can be found in S. Holmes and C. Sunstein, *The Cost of Liberty. Why Freedom Depends on Taxes*, Norton, New York 1999.

25 During the debates on the drafting of the two international covenants on human rights Israel expressed the idea that no right can be immediately applied, all rights need the setting up of

the debates on the drafting of the two international covenants on human rights Israel expressed the idea that no right can be immediately applied, all rights need the setting up of domestic implementation mechanisms, and it argued that certain rights have components of both CP and ESC rights, giving the example of trade union freedoms.[26] Similarly, Chile argued that it might be extremely difficult to reform an immigration law or to change people's fixed ideas and Iraq argued that poverty limits the factual exercise of CP rights.[27] Yet the fact that the differences between CP rights and ESC rights are not really drastic has been consistently ignored and a difference of degree has been treated, in practice, as a radical difference in kind. So instead of providing less powerful mechanisms of judicial review, in proportion to the extent to which ESC rights are costlier, positive, vague and generally more difficult to adjudicate, the answer has been simply to provide them with *no* mechanism of judicial protection at all.

It has also been claimed that while for CP rights (*qua* negative rights) the identification of correlative duties is straightforward, such identification is problematic for ESC (*qua* positive rights). It has been claimed that it is plain that everyone has a duty to refrain from infringing the negative rights of everyone, while for positive rights, it is unclear who has to bear the duty to aid and to what extent.[28] This point is correct philosophically, but irrelevant legally. First of all, it is clear that the state is the duty bearer for ESC rights so the distributive question of who has to pay for what does not arise, the state has to pay for everything.[29] Second, if the extent of the duties is unclear, then they should be clarified. Law gives ample instruments for this task, for instance, the creation of domestic legislation that specifies nature and content of ESC rights.[30]

Sometimes the idea that negative rights are ready to use without further steps of identification of correlative duties while positive rights need this further

domestic implementation mechanisms, and it argued that certain rights have components of both CP and ESC rights, giving the example of trade union freedoms. See UN Doc. A/C.3/SR.360 General Assembly, Third Committee, Sixth Session, Official Records, 5 December 1951, paragraphs 52–58. Similarly, Chile argued that it might be extremely difficult to reform an immigration law or to change people's fixed ideas and Iraq argued that poverty limits the factual exercise of CP rights See UN Doc A/C.3/SR.362 General Assembly, Third Committee, Sixth Session, Official Records, 12 December 1951, paragraphs 47 and 57.

26 See UN Doc. A/C.3/SR.360 General Assembly, Third Committee, Sixth Session, Official Records, 5 December 1951, paragraphs 52–58.

27 See UN Doc. A/C.3/SR.362 General Assembly, Third Committee, Sixth Session, Official Records, 12 December 1951, paragraphs 47 and 57.

28 The well-argued work of Onora O'Neill can be taken to be a good elaboration of this point, even if she ultimately does recognise obligations to address demands of need using the non-standard terminology of virtue. See O. O'Neill, *Towards Justice and Virtue*, Cambridge University Press, Cambridge 1996, pp. 128–136. It is open to question whether her accommodation of demands of need under the heading of virtue is satisfactory given the fact that in doing so she excludes need from the sphere of justice, p. 136.

29 See H. Shue, 'Mediating duties' (1988) 98 *Ethics* 687–704.

30 See F. Coomans, and K. Yakpo, 'A framework law on the right to food – an international and South African perspective' (2004) 4 *African Human Rights Law Journal* 17–33.

step, and the idea that negative rights are context invariant while positive rights are heavily context dependent are used to suggest that only negative rights are natural rights.[31] These assumptions can be contested (as they are in this section), but even if this is granted, a huge gap remains. Why should the natural be privileged over the artificial? The importance of rights might be more sensibly thought to arise from the urgency of the needs they serve, and if it happens to be the case that in some contexts positive rights are more urgent, then they are more important irrespective of their artificiality.[32]

Another line of critique is based on the alleged asymmetry between negative and positive action. Charles Fried writes 'we can fail to assault infinity of people every hour of the day' and this is taken to show that negative rights are inherently more practicable that positive ones.[33] In this light the demand 'never violate rights' makes sense as an absolute demand that trumps our limited ability to reach goals, which represents our capacity to comply with positive rights.[34]

Nevertheless, such sharp distinction is not persuasive. The asymmetry between negative and positive action is grossly overstated. It is not axiomatic that negative action is always possible. Quite trivially, real opportunities to do wrong can tempt agents and may at some point defeat their psychological commitment to do what is right. There is no *a priori* guarantee that one will have enough motivation to resist every temptation to act wrongly. Furthermore, when one is concerned with personal responsibility it only makes sense to speak of an omission when one has the power to do otherwise.[35] It makes no sense to say that in writing this paper in Maastricht I forbear from breaking the traffic laws of Aachen, for the obvious reason that being in Maastricht it is not in my physical power to do things in Aachen. There is nothing absolutely special about negative action as opposed to positive action. All things considered, negative demands are easier to deal with, than positive demands. But once more, this is a mere difference of degree, that hardly justifies the almost complete exclusion to which ESC rights have been traditionally subject.

Finally, there is a frequent assumption that violations of negative rights simply are more severe than violations of positive rights,[36] or that CP rights simply are

---

31 Using a form of this argument see M. Cranston, 'Are there any human rights?' (1983) 112 *Daedalus* 1–17.

32 Here one might usefully be referred to Mill's denunciation of the naturalness of something as a special term of praise. See J.S. Mill, 'Nature' in: J.S. Mill, *Three Essays on Religion*, many editions. What is said here of natural can be said of any other attribute that does not appeal to value. For instance, some rights might be universal in the sense that they can be applied everywhere, but why does this make them more important and urgent than rights related to some local and contexualised need?

33 See C. Fried, *Right and wrong*, Harvard University Press, Cambridge 1978, p. 112.

34 Ibid., p. 111.

35 See G.H. Von Wright, *Norm and Action. A Logical Inquiry*, Routledge and Kegan Paul, London 1969, p. 45.

36 F.M. Kamm, 'Harming, not aiding, and positive rights' (1986) 15 *Philosophy & Public Affairs* 3–32.

more important than poverty relief. Pereira-Menaut argues 'the common man, if asked, would probably feel that having a free pair of spectacles given by the National Health Service ... is less indispensable and more matter-of-choice than having one's home free from undue intrusions. The same man would not probably find having the right to a clean environment suppressed equally dangerous and anti-constitutional as having free speech suppressed ...'[37] And Cranston writes that ESC rights are merely 'vague wishes' as opposed to CP rights, which are 'sharp imperatives'.[38] There is nothing wrong with claims of self-evidence of this sort. All chains of justification must come to an end somewhere, but these sorts of claims to self-evidence seem very weak if they arise from the point of view of the wealthy and privileged. The argument fully collapses if one takes into consideration the fact that much of present status quo derives from past violations of negative rights (cases of colonialism for instance) which have been later legitimated through mechanisms such as inheritance, but never redressed.

Without aspirations of being comprehensive, one can catalogue at least the following argumentative failings that appear repeatedly in the sidelining of ESC rights:

(a) categorical reasoning when gradual reasoning is called for;
(b) ungrounded appeals to self-evidence; and
(c) unjustified preference in favour of the natural or the status quo.

In response to these fallacies it must be countered that differences of degree in the difficulty of implementing certain rights warrant differences of degree in the extent of judicial protection of rights, not differences in kind; that appeals to self-evidence must be defensible also from the standpoint of the person who loses out with the proposed rule of policy; and that the fact that some duties are easier to understand as natural or pre-institutional does nothing to prove their relative importance in relation to duties that depend on artificial human arrangements.

5. EXPLAINING THE FLIMSY EXCUSES: BELIEF IN JUST A WORLD

The preceding facts and bad arguments by themselves do not allow us to speak of denial. For that it is necessary to present a theory that shows how these facts and arguments can be explained as being something more than mere mistakes, as deliberate falsifications and as forms of self-deception aimed at shutting out uncomfortable truths.

---

37 A.C. Pereira-Menaut, 'Against Positive Rights' (1987) 22 *Valparaiso University Law Review* 368–369.

38 See M. Cranston, 'Are there any human rights?' (1983) 112 *Daedalus* 1–17, 12.

A plausible explanation is provided by the mental mechanism of 'belief in a just world' (BJW): the unfounded assumption that for the most part the world is fair, that people receive their just desserts, with good being rewarded and evil punished[39] which is characterised as a form of denial.[40]

According to its proponents, BJW is a self-protective mental device that reduces the uncomfortable feeling of guilt that we experience when we realise that there is much that we should do to help the downtrodden and that we are not doing it, and the anxiety that we experience in cognising that our own success is wholly fortuitous.[41] As MJ Lerner points out: '[BJW] creates a rather chilling image of humanity. It begins by describing how we live in a society that tolerates the widespread suffering and deprivation of innocent victims. [] We want to-have to-believe that our world is so constructed that terrible things happen to people who deserve them because they were "terrible" to others.'[42] Otherwise, claims Lerner, we would have to feel 'degraded' by the amount of suffering we tolerate, and the petty excuses we make that allow it to continue unabated.[43]

BJW provides an explanation for the ease with which bad arguments have been accepted for sidelining poverty as a human rights concern and the difficulties faced by scholars and activists in countering these bad arguments. It must be true that these rights just are different, that the status quo is in an important way natural, and that negative duties are privileged. Otherwise we would not be innocent. The mere fact that we do not kill, torture or steal would not be enough to discharge our duties towards each other. We would stand accused of maintaining a world in which 805 million people do not have enough to eat even though we could do a lot to aid these people with little difficulty for ourselves. And it would seemingly put to shame a legal system that allows this to happen. In essence, the sidelining of poverty as a human rights concern is a way of maintaining the positive self-image of the affluent west amidst its gross sins of omission. There is no reason to think that academics, practitioners and officials are immune to the effects of BJW. The mechanisms of BJW make no exceptions for such persons. As a matter of fact, the pressure to think of oneself as just must appear even greater if one's profession is thinking and writing about law and justice.

---

39 See M.J. Lerner, *The belief in a just world. A fundamental delusion*, Springer, New York 1980, pp. 9–10, 12. Given that the purposes of this article are juridical and methodological and not psychological, the extensive literature on BJW will not be elaborated upon. What is presented here is enough to satisfy the demand for a *prima facie* case. For a relatively recent overview of the development of this idea, see A. Furnham, 'Belief in a just world: Research progress over the past decade' (2003) 34 *Personality and Individual Differences* 795–817.

40 S. Cohen, *States of Denial: Knowing About Atrocities and Suffering*, Polity Press, London 2001, pp. 71–72.

41 See M.J. Lerner, *The belief in a just world. A fundamental delusion*, Springer, New York 1980, pp. 14–15.

42 Ibid., p. 73.

43 Ibid.

Certainly, one should be wary of assuming that BJW or some other form of denial provides the complete explanation of the neglect of poverty in international law. Other factors may be in play. Nevertheless, that does nothing to discount denial as being an important factor amongst others which should be counteracted. It might even be a form of denial to pretend that because a full explanation of the causes of poverty is not available one cannot or should not aim to correct one of the factors that most probably feed into this phenomenon. The same can be said for excessive scepticism about the truth of the findings of researchers about BJW. There are certainly other theories that 'fit the data', and one may want to argue that BJW theory has not disproven alternative hypotheses. But one should be wary of setting the bar too high. The problem of poverty is big enough, and the evidence of denial is good enough, that we should not wait until certainty is achieved in order to take action. Evidence of denial needs to be taken seriously.

Nevertheless, for translating the findings of BJW researchers into guides to action, even more, to action in the field of law, there is much work to be done. A theory of denial, as an explanation, cannot take us all the way into judgments about what should be done in legal reform and judicial decision making. The next section bears out that, while accounts about denial are useful and even necessary, they are by no means sufficient for guiding work in the world of law.

6. THE INCOMPLETENESS OF BJW AND THE NEED FOR NORMATIVE STANDARDS

The previous sections hypothesise that denial, in the form of BJW, does play a significant role in the sidelining of poverty as a human rights concern. This paper is not psychological and as such it does not aim to go further in developing this hypothesis. What interests us mainly is how legal analysis should react to this possibility. The point of this section is to show that even if denial is real, legal conclusions do not automatically follow. This is grounded in the following considerations:

6.1. THE EXPLANATION-JUSTIFICATION GAP

First it is important to note that the presence or absence of denial does not prove anything about what legal measures should be taken in response to it. In particular, it would be question begging to assume that because poverty is displaced from the human rights agenda thought denial, it follows that the one should have a right not to be poor or some other legal remedy. A further argument would always need to be made. The main reason for this is that theories of denial do not have the right logical form for giving us answers to what should be done. They provide explanations of human behaviour, but what is called for is a justification of what the right behaviour should be, and this is something that cannot be provided by psychological theorising alone. Normative theorising is called for.[44]

This is point can be best elaborated upon with an example. Let's assume, reasonably, that what ought to be done in general is what leads us to human fulfilment. It may be the case that, for reasons different than the bad reasons described above (section 3) ESC rights backfire and do not really lead to this goal. Although there is no conclusive evidence to this effect, this is certainly a possible outcome.[45] If this were the case, the fact that something like BJW was present in the mental operations of academic detractors to ESC rights is logically irrelevant to settling the issue as to whether these rights should be protected and to what extent. We would say of the academic detractors of ESC rights, with the benefit of hindsight, their thinking was faulty, their reasoning was bad, but after all their conclusions were the right ones.

In any case, we will not be able to find out whether ESC rights are truly worthwhile by researching the organisation of our own minds. It is necessary to engage with the values that ESC rights embody, with the different possible distributions that may be achieved, and with the social context in which rights need to be applied. And it is necessary to find to choose between a variety of different policies with different strengths and weaknesses. In this way, normative research in law overshoots psychological theorising. When psychological theorising is done, and denial is uncovered, the work of normative legal research is just beginning.

6.2. THE INESCAPABLE NEED FOR NORMATIVE STANDARDS

A second problem is that denial discourse tacitly assumes the existence of normative standards, but often no explicit standard is provided. And the implicit standards used are relatively weak and unrefined by comparison to what would be desirable.[46]

---

44 Recognising this for BJW, see J. Maes, C. Tarnai and J. Schuster, 'About Is and Ought in Research on Belief in a Just World: The Janus-Faced Just-World Motivation' in: E. Kals and J. Maes, *Justice and Conflicts, Theoretical and Empirical Contributions*, Springer, Heidelberg 2012.

45 Evidence against social rights has been provided in C. Bjørnskov and J. Mchangama, 'Do Social Rights Affect Social Outcomes?', Economics Working Papers, Aarhus University <ftp://ftp.econ.au.dk/afn/wp/13/wp13_18.pdf>. The methodology of Bjørnskov and Mchangama is questionable, and from a juridical point of view simplistic, nevertheless, they raise a troubling possibility that scholars in the field of human rights should not ignore.

46 In my view, Cohen recognises this opaquely. He states: 'we can condemn passivity, indifference and bad faith only within the meta-psychology of the targeted and desirable Amnesty/Oxfam self'. See S. Cohen, *States of Denial: Knowing About Atrocities and Suffering,*

To show convincingly that one is in denial about X, one first needs to have made a good case about X, otherwise one is just begging the question. If I don't feel bad about the people I could help by simply donating €50 tonight to Oxfam, to argue seriously about denial it needs to be shown that I *ought* to feel bad about this and that my mental functioning is somehow improper if it shuts out this fact. Otherwise my ignorance would be as harmless as trying to ignore the noisiness of my neighbours by turning on a source of white noise (is this not a project of wilful self-deception? Am I not both aware and unaware that my neighbours are playing carnival music?). Maybe because matters of value are often considered unscientific, there seems to be a significant degree of reticence at setting up clear standards in academic work on denial. This reticence is cashed out in two ways.

One alternative is to assume that 'sympathy' or 'empathy', just by itself, will provide the right measure of human rights and so one can avoid setting up normative standards after all. Human rights is just the 'practice of empathy', but its work is obstructed by denial, and therefore there is nothing further to be done besides identifying denial and criticising it.[47] This outlook unwarranted. Sympathy, however valuable, can be misplaced. One is a worse person by feeling sympathy for a criminal whose plans have been foiled. And clearly there are circumstances in which unrestrained sympathy can cause injustice or regrettable consequences.

One might be suspicious that the project of getting things right by simply uncovering self-deception is a covert appeal to the myth of the noble savage. The working assumption seems to be that underneath human self-deception there is one right way of looking at the world, and that consequently the unmasking project can only makes us better. In reality, there is no reason to think that this is true. Human self-deception may be better than all the available alternatives. For instance, instead of moving from a state of denial to one of charity, people might move to a state of selfishness. How this could happen is easy to see: people enjoy living somewhere in between selfishness and charity, if this mix is attacked as illegitimate and unauthentic, still people may find that complete charity is not fulfilling or even viable for them, and prefer to move to complete selfishness in order to cope. Once the truth is shown, hypocrisy may be replaced by indifference or hostility.

The other alternative is to use very crude pragmatic standards. Recent work on BJW has argued that BJW can be 'adaptive' in the minimally hedonistic way of helping people get through the day, but clearly there are individual and social goals that are more important than getting people to feel good about

Polity Press, London 2001, p. 278. This suggest that some ideals about proper functioning are needed in order to identify and reveal malfunctions such as denial.

47 This is the approach most often taken by Lerner. See M.J. Lerner, *The belief in a just world. A fundamental delusion*, Springer, New York 1980.

themselves,[48] for instance the creation of a just social order oriented towards human fulfilment that was discussed in the preceding subsection. This just social order might not be the paradise of sympathy of the noble savage, but just as well it might require us to do more than what gets us through the day.

6.3. THE PARTICULAR AIMS OF LAW

Not only are normative standards needed in order to derive normative conclusions and to characterise something as denial, but the law has a need for standards of a certain sort. Utopian aspirations and plain moralising often make for bad legal theory. The standards of law are not the standards of the morally best person. Certainly only a fraction of the things that we can demand of people morally can we demand of people legally. This is a price to be paid for a having a free society where people can pursue their own projects and disagree about the best way to live one's life.[49]

If law makes it possible for one to sit in a warm room enjoying a nice cup of coffee, while ignoring thousands of others who suffer in the cold, this should not necessarily be taken to mean that law is radically defective (even though our morals might be). Law needs to calibrate its apportionments of guilt and blame in such a way to achieve social order and in doing so it may need to tolerate some of our defects in order to control our worst vices. It may be argued persuasively that law still lets us get away with too much, but this needs to be shown.

One commentator discussing the relationship between denial and human rights worries 'that the dominance of legalism within human rights discourses places a limitation upon their capacity to express ordinary human and moral sensitivity to the suffering of others – particularly among non-lawyers'.[50] This worry is misplaced. Precisely the point about human rights is to create a rigid legal baseline of protection. The rigidity of rights is as useful and necessary as the rigidity of bones, and, if it is working properly, it does nothing to detract from other sorts of discourses, such as those of shame, guilt or denial. It creates a framework of order in which they can safely operate. These other discourses can and should complete what legal doctrine necessarily leaves incomplete.

---

48 Discussing this tendency, see J. Maes, C. Tarnai and J. Schuster, 'About Is and Ought in Research on Belief in a Just World: The Janus-Faced Just-World Motivation' in: E. Kals and J. Maes, *Justice and Conflicts, Theoretical and Empirical Contributions*, Springer, Heidelberg 2012, p. 93. Cohen also makes reference to the usefulness of denial. See S. Cohen, *States of Denial: Knowing About Atrocities and Suffering*, Polity Press, London 2001, p. 15.

49 J.S. Mill famously differentiated what ought to be done morally, from what ought to be required legally. See J.S. Mill, *Utilitarianism*, various editions, Chapter V.

50 R. Jamieson and K. McEvoy, 'Conflict, suffering and the promise of human rights' in: D. Downes, P. Rock, C. Chinkin and C. Gearty (eds.), *Crime, Social Control Human Rights: From Moral Panics to States of Denial, Essays in Honour of Stanley Cohen*, Routledge, London 2013.

6.4. THE DANGERS OF UNDERMINING ACADEMIC COMMUNICATION

Reading the work of authors like Cohen and Lerner, one might get the impression that denial and self-deception are at work everywhere. No mistake is just a mistake; there is always a self-serving story that shows the mistake to be perpetrated in the protection of the self. And one can wonder whether any sort of contestation of the work of these authors is going to be well received. Resistance to the theory of denial may be easily seen as further evidence of denial that needs to be unmasked.

It is easy to see how this can undermine academic communication. The game of unmasking can be played by all ideological teams. In response to the defence of social rights provided in sections 3 and 4, a convinced neoliberal might argue that experience has shown that the capitalism is the only effective mechanism to ensure development, and that human rights scholars are defending their own interests in championing human rights as a universal solution to all social problems. How can human rights scholars defend themselves against these accusations? Maybe with more far-reaching counter-accusations of intellectual dishonesty? A real slippery slope emerges.

Would it not be more profitable, most of the time, to leave talk of denial out of the room, and to focus on presenting the best possible arguments for what measures the law should take to improve social order? The idea that one's academic opponents must really be moved by hidden, irrational agendas are a sure-fire way to make it impossible to learn from them.

7. THE CONTINUING RELEVANCE OF DENIAL

All that being said, there is still good reason to believe that denial exists and that it has a significant impact on the development of human rights. All the concerns set forth in Section 6 of this paper should not be taken to signify something else. Evidence for the phenomenon of denial must not be set aside, it must be taken into consideration as one relevant factor – albeit not the only relevant factor – in developing the right legal standards for a just society.

If we have scientific evidence about the existence of a tendency for bias in our judgments, we have to be wary of it. The fact that a theory of denial such as BJW cannot point out the forms of justice we must be striving for, does not mean that it cannot tell us what pitfalls we are bound to fall into when trying to achieve what justice demands, and arm us against them. In other words, the fact that a theory of denial by itself is insufficient for normative theorising does not deny that it provides a valuable, even necessary component for this enterprise. Although normative theorising is logically different from the identification of psychological biases –matters of social justice overshoot psychology – we have to use our minds in order to find out what the right standards are, and therefore we must aim to make sure that this instrument is working properly. Without desire to be exhaustive, the present article concludes by singling out some essential contributions that uncovering denial makes and aims to show how they impact the feasibility of other research projects: those of law and economics and political liberalism.

7.1. THE IDENTIFICATION OF VALUE

In one way value is subjective because it is value for us. In another it is objective because it aims to connect with the world. We desire to 'win the race' not only to have the elation of having won through other means (say through the use of drugs). This requirement of connectedness with the world[51] suggests that we can be radically mistaken about value. Our self-delusions may prevent us from really seeing things as they are. For instance, the enjoyment a person has in a relationship may be a sham that covers up the fact that the relationship is one-sided and abusive. We need to have the right mental disposition to perceive what is truly valuable. And here, denial plays a vital role in covering up what really matters, as there will be a natural tendency to accept a subjectively pleasing lie over the reality that what is sought for remains unachieved.

This insight poses significant problems for normative legal research that takes preferences or hedonic experiences as given. This is emphatically the case for most forms of law and economics. People's given preferences may not represent their real interests, what is best for them.[52] Forms of psychological self-deception, such as denial, may obscure individual access to what is really worthwhile. This point should not be overstated. Revealed preferences are often a good proxy to value, in many contexts they are the best way to analyse a particular social problem; but it should be kept in mind that the approach has limitations.

---

51 For the purposes of this essay it is not necessary to elucubrate on the robustness of the world-connectness in question. Many models are available, ranging from the 'quasi-realist' to the full blown realist. Arguing that these models will not differ on this point, see S. Blackburn, 'Truth Beauty and Goodness' in: S. Blackburn *Practical Tortoise Raising*, Oxford University Press, Oxford 2010.

52 On the concept of real interests see R. Geuss, *The idea of a critical theory. Habermas and the Frankfurt School*, Cambridge University Press, Cambridge 1981, p. 45.

7.2. UNDERMINING SOME FORMS OF POLITICAL LIBERALISM

The existence and possibility of denial creates significant difficulties for 'constructivist' theories of social justice of a certain sort: those that have an *a priori* filter that shuts out certain types of arguments that are deemed unacceptable because they question the authority of citizens' individual conceptions of what is right.

In the second phase of his academic career, John Rawls argued that a just society is a regime that diverse citizens can agree to while addressing themselves exclusively on 'public reasons', that is, reasons that all can appreciate and accept to while seeing themselves as 'free and equal' fully capable of exercising their powers to form their own conception of justice and the good life. This would be the basis for a truly 'political liberalism', a liberalism that brackets questions about what is really good for human beings, what is really just, etc., and stays on the surface of what everyone, as motivated by the demands of good citizenship, can agree to.[53] The work of Rawls has been followed by many authors such as Christiano, Macedo and Gaus, and can be considered today one of the dominant branches of liberal political theory.[54] More significantly for our purposes, it has influenced the theory of human rights in the work of authors such as Charles Beitz.[55]

Rawlsian 'political liberalism' imposes strict demands on what may be taken into consideration in defining what is right and just. All arguments which are not defensible on public reason, which do not presuppose from the start that all citizens are free and equal must be are excluded from consideration. For instance, arguments on divine revelation against homosexuality are ruled out by political liberalism. They cannot be proven to secular homosexuals and they offend their own self-respect.[56] But the possibility of denial puts into question the viability of political liberalism's bracketing strategy.

If denial is a real, pervasive phenomenon with significant social impact – and we have reason to believe it is – then the free equality of all citizens is often (in one specific sense) a myth. A person in denial is not equal in the ability to exercise moral judgment. His access to reality is strongly compromised and this impacts his ability to sympathise with the plight of his fellow men. He is in this

---

53 See J. Rawls, *Political Liberalism. Expanded Edition*, Columbia University Press, New York 2005.

54 See T. Christiano, *The constitution of equality: Democratic authority and its limits*, Oxford University Press, Oxford 2008; S. Macedo, 'In defense of liberal public reason: are slavery and abortion hard cases' (1997) 42 *American Journal of Jurisprudence* 1; and, especially, G. Gaus, *The order of public reason: A theory of freedom and morality in a diverse and bounded world*, Cambridge University Press, Cambridge 2010.

55 See C.R. Beitz, *The idea of human rights*, Oxford University Press, Oxford 2011.

56 See J. Rawls, *Political Liberalism. Expanded Edition*, Columbia University Press, New York 2005, Lecture VI.

respect in an inferior position, unfree, and unequal in access to the truth.[57] Yet under political liberalism it might be unacceptable to take measures against such denial, or to accuse someone of denial in the public forum. Accusations of denial will normally offend the self-respect of those being accused and they inevitably claim that the person suffering from denial is in some sense not his own master. Yet by limiting accusations of denial, political liberalism would be *shielding* instead of uncovering self-deception. Under political liberalism, the points of view of those suffering from denial would be considered to be politically valid and would be allowed to have an impact on the public construction of the social order. In fact, the deceived perspectives would not only be shielded, but even validated as part of the social definition of justice. Rawls is a constructivist about justice. That is, for Rawls, justice *simply and fundamentally is nothing but* what people agree to on the basis of public reason. If this includes beliefs fuelled by denial, then this is plainly hard to accept.

Rawls developed some relatively strict rules about the distribution of wealth. But there is nothing in the methodology of public reason that guarantees this result. Gaus seems to come to very different conclusions.[58] Moreover, despite the endorsement of relatively strict redistributive rules, it is arguable that in subtle ways Rawls nevertheless does sideline poverty. In the first phase of his work, compliance with the famous 'difference principle' turned out to be so hard to verify that both very conservative and very radical conclusions could be derived from it. Rawls himself was very serious about the need for redistribution and securing basic welfare for all, but the methodology employed in his work often forced this concern into an ambiguous place in the background.[59]

In light of the preceding arguments, it is an open question as to what extent a theory of public reason can accommodate the reality of various forms of self-deception. Maybe constructivism ought to be rejected, and public reason should be kept as a fallible guide as to what is good and just so that at some times it can be claimed that public reason has led us to the wrong conclusion. Rawls himself sometimes seems to interpret his own theory accordingly.[60] Alternatively, constructivism may be kept, but the idea of public reason as a filter must be left out. There should be no *a priori*, dogmatic filter.

---

57 This is especially true if one gives credence to the link between knowledge and truth established by emancipatory social science. See again R. Bhaskar, *Scientific realism and human emancipation*, Routledge, London 2009.

58 See G. Gaus, *The order of public reason: A theory of freedom and morality in a diverse and bounded world*, Cambridge University Press, Cambridge 2010, pp. 367–368.

59 See R. Geuss 'Neither History nor Praxis' in: R. Geuss (ed.), *Outside Ethics*, Princeton University Press, Princeton 2005.

60 See J. Rawls, *Political Liberalism. Expanded Edition*, Columbia University Press, New York 2005, p. 128.

8. CONCLUSIONS

Theories of denial must be handled with care; they are not sufficient for determining what ought to be done in the field of social justice, but they are certainly necessary. We need to be aware of the potential pitfalls of our thinking and be armed against them, but still what is decisive will not lie anywhere else than in the best theories of social justice that we can come up with. Our theories about justice and rights are surely full of hidden biases and distortions. But that does not make them in any way dispensable. Any account of human irrationality presupposes an account of rationality and is question begging otherwise. A full theory of what needs to be done in the field of law must take into account both our strengths, as rational thinking animals, and our weaknesses as fragile, limited creatures.

CHAPTER XIX
GENOCIDE DENIAL AND REFUGEES
A Lack of Protection in International Law?

Regina MENACHERY PAULOSE*

1. INTRODUCTION

Raphael Lemkin, the legal scholar who coined the word 'genocide', was a refugee from Poland. 'Lemkin understood that people deemed him biased because he himself was a refugee.'[1] In *Axis Rule*, Lemkin wrote: 'information and reports which slip out from behind the frontiers of occupied countries are very often labeled as untrustworthy atrocity stories because they are so gruesome that people simply refuse to believe them.'[2] Despite these hurdles, Lemkin led the fight for the international community to recognise genocide and adopt a legal regime to prevent the crime of genocide. It may not be apparent, but the voices of refugees have played a critical role in how the international community understands genocide.

There are two prominent Conventions which can impact a person who flees genocide: the Convention on the Prevention and Punishment of Genocide and the 1951 Refugee Convention. These two Conventions, which are the focus of this paper, are not intertwined and appear to have little to offer the refugee that flees genocide. As Professor Jonassohn astutely observed, '[s]cholarly attempts to understand the causes of genocide, the appearance of famines, and the generating of flows of refugees have been seriously hampered by overspecialization.'[3] The study of refugee movements during genocide normally would be considered an anthropological study. Anthropologists generally discuss the impact of genocide on people, their collective memory, and the 'representations of a violent

* Special thanks to Jennifer Carmen, JD and Tina Thomas, JD.

1 S. POWER, 'Introduction' in: R. LEMKIN, *Axis Rule in Occupied Europe*, 2nd ed., The Law Book Exchange, New Jersey 2008, p. xix.

2 R. LEMKIN, *Axis Rule in Occupied Europe*, 2nd ed., The Law Book Exchange, New Jersey 2008, p. 94.

3 K. JONASSHOHN, 'Famine, Genocide, and Refugees' (1993) 30(6) *Society* 72–76.

past structured by one's positioning as a survivor, perpetrator, journalist, or ethnographer.'[4] Unfortunately, given the rule of law's bumbling presence with regard to refugees and the empty political promises made by national leaders, the international legal community needs to revisit what further protections a refugee who flees genocide ought to be given, and needs to address this in a holistic manner.

This, of course, is no easy task and juxtaposing the two Conventions presents challenges. Adding to these challenges is genocide denial, simply defined as an attempt to minimise or deny statements of the scale and severity of genocide, which is a subtle and sometimes overt problem when there is a discussion on any aspect of genocide. I argue that the current framework in the status quo allows for genocide denial to manifest itself in many ways, some of which may not be obvious to those engaged in refugee protection. If the international community is serious about addressing genocide, then revisiting how these Conventions interact with each other will be a very important step to take.

I attempt to create a starting point for these discussions. This article begins with a brief discussion of the particularities of the Convention on the Prevention and Punishment of Genocide (hereinafter Genocide Convention) followed by a discussion of certain particularities[5] of the 1951 Refugee Convention (hereinafter Refugee Convention). I will then discuss how these Conventions essentially neglect or deny refugees protection when faced with genocide. This neglect causes a second cycle of genocide denial to take place. One case study discussed in this article analyses the interaction between the two frameworks during the Bangladesh genocide. I will then finalise with a discussion on options the international community could consider to rectify the inadequate protections that exist as a result of the gaps in both Conventions.

2. GENOCIDE CONVENTION

In 1933, with the work of Raphael Lemkin on genocide already underway, coupled with the tough lessons the international community had gleaned from World War II, the groundwork for the adoption of the 1948 Genocide Convention was laid. The Genocide Convention encouraged states to: (i) criminalise genocide and punish the perpetrators within a domestic legal setting, and (ii) provide

4 K. Lewis O'Neill, 'Anthropology and Genocide' in: D. Bloxham and A.D. Moses, *The Oxford Handbook of Genocide Studies*, Oxford University Press, Oxford 2013, p. 183.

5 It is important to remind the reader that the conversation surrounding the Conventions is brief and only focuses on certain aspects of the Convention. There are many articles that go into great detail about the entirety of these Conventions, which due to space is not done in this article.

for judicial cooperation of parties to the Convention for the 'suppression of the crime'.[6] The final contours of the definition of genocide became:

Genocide means any of the following acts committed with intent to destroy, in whole or in part, a national, ethnical, racial or religious group, such as:

(a) killing members of the group;
(b) causing serious bodily or mental harm to members of the group;
(c) deliberately inflicting on the group conditions of life calculated to bring about its physical destruction in whole or in part;
(d) imposing measures intended to prevent births within the group; or
(c) forcibly transferring children of the group to another group.[7]

There are two distinguishing features between the Genocide Convention and the Refugee Convention, which is itself discussed in more detail later in this article. First, the Genocide Convention's application is limited to a narrow range of groups, as opposed to the broad category of groups covered in the Refugee Convention. Second, the language of the Genocide Convention imbues a particular focus on the intent of the perpetrator, as opposed to protection from the perpetrator. On its face, the language of the Refugee Convention bars a person from gaining asylum if they have been found *guilty* of perpetrating genocide. Of course, proponents of the Genocide Convention would argue that pursuing prosecution does lead to protection for survivors and witnesses. Unfortunately, the opposite in many cases is true because political gridlock (genocide denial) prevents many from being tried in court, let alone, being found guilty of the 'crime of all crimes'.

2.1. GROUPS

The groups enumerated in Article 2 of the Genocide Convention are ethnic, racial, or religious groups. These groups are not defined in the Convention and 'there is no universal understanding of what constitutes a national, ethnic, racial, or religious group'.[8] Since the birth of the Convention, there have been attempts to broaden the current categories. The Whitaker Report to the United Nations Economic and Social Council recommended that sexual minorities ought to be included within the definition of 'national' or 'ethnic' groups.[9] In the legal

---

6 A. Cassese, *International Criminal Law*, Oxford University Press, Oxford 2013, p. 111.

7 Convention on the Prevention and Punishment of the Crime of Genocide, adopted by Resolution 260 III, 1948.

8 D. Lisson, 'Defining National Groups in the Genocide Convention: A Case Study of Timor Leste' (2008) 60 *Stan. L. Rev.* 1459, 1464.

9 B. Whitaker, 'Revised and updated Report on the question of the prevention and punishment of the crime of genocide', United Nations Economic and Social Council, E/CN.4/Sub.2/1985/6, paragraph 30.

realm, *ad hoc* tribunals such as the International Criminal Tribunal for the former Yugoslavia (notably in *Jelisic*) and the International Criminal Tribunal for Rwanda (notably in *Akayesu*), have added subjective tests in defining the groups enumerated in the Genocide Convention.[10] Unfortunately, 'the Akayesu Trial Chamber's approach was never affirmed by the Appeals Chamber of the International Criminal Tribunal for Rwanda, and has been ignored by other Trial Chambers.'[11]

This probably closely conforms to Lemkin's vision of the protections he wanted to afford various groups. In his view, genocide could be interpreted broadly enough as targeting the personal security of the group. Therefore, '[u]nder Lemkin's broad protections, nearly any step taken with the aim of destroying a protected group would amount to genocide.'[12] Unfortunately, Lemkin's vision for broad protections was narrowed for the Genocide Convention and no international court has deviated from the four 'stable' and 'permanent' groups listed within the Convention.[13]

It is important to note here that the debate over groups is relatively absent under the Refugee Convention where the groups are interpreted to 'consider cultural changes'.[14] However, the openness of the groups cannot be interpreted in a manner 'to render the other Convention grounds superfluous or to function as a "catch all" that applies to anyone fearing persecution.'[15]

2.2. INTENT

Genocide is a crime of special intent. It requires that the perpetrator target a specified group 'with a deliberate desire to inflict destruction upon the group itself'.[16] What distinguishes genocide from other international crimes is 'the need for proof of intention' which is the 'distinguishing evidentiary element for

10 A. Cassese, *International Criminal Law*, Oxford University Press, Oxford 2013, pp. 120–121.

11 W. Schabas, 'Symposium 2008: The United Nations Genocide Convention: a 60th Anniversary Commemoration: Genocide Law in a Time of Transition: Recent Developments in the Law of Genocide' (2008) 61 *Rutgers L. Rev.* 161,171.

12 K. Mundorff, 'Other People's Children: A Textual and Contextual Interpretation of the Genocide Convention, Article 2(e)' (2009) 50 *Harv Int'l L.J* 61, 75.

13 D. Lisson, 'Defining National Groups in the Genocide Convention: A Case Study of Timor Leste' (2008) 60 *Stan. L. Rev.* 1459, 1465.

14 W. Worster, 'The Evolving Definition of Refugee in International Law' (2012) 30 *Berkeley J. Int'l L.* 94, 98.

15 E. Nilson, 'The "refugee" and the "nexus" requirement. The relation between subject and persecution the United Nations Refugee Convention' (2014) *Women's Studies International Forum* 123–131, 126.

16 A. Grenawalt, 'Note: Rethinking Genocidal Intent: The Case for a Knowledge Based Interpretation' (2009) 99 *Colum L. Rev.* 2259, 2265. Grenawalt states 'although nothing in the statute explicitly provides for a distinct genocidal intent standard, one might argue that the origins and development of the prohibition against genocide provide an external source of interpretive authority that trumps the Rome Statute's default *mens rea* provision.'

proving genocide crimes'.[17] Therefore, genocide cannot 'exist in the abstract'.[18] The Convention specifically refers to the *intent of the perpetrator*, which needs to take into account that, under international law, 'genocide is not the crime of a lone deviant but *the act of a state*'.[19] The special intent, or *dolus specialis*, means that 'it is only necessary that the perpetrator harbour the specific intent to destroy the group while carrying out one of those acts' regardless of whether it is achieved.[20] 'The requirement of special intent, therefore, has a preventative function.'[21]

What makes this element particularly difficult is described by Whitaker in his report: '[n]ot all genocidal regimes are likely to be as thoroughly documented as the Nazi one was.' Therefore, the court should be able to 'infer the necessary intent from sufficient evidence, and that in certain cases this would include actions or omissions'.[22] However, in practice this 'preventative function' fails for many political reasons, as was evident during and after the Bangladesh genocide.

In a recent decision by the International Court of Justice, the Court discussed the special intent requirement. The Court held 'it is difficult to establish intent on the basis of isolated acts' and in the absence of direct evidence there must be evidence of: (i) acts on a scale that establishes an intent not only to target certain individuals because of their membership of a particular group, but (ii) also destroy the group itself whole or in part.[23] The Court went on to hold that while genocidal intent may be 'established indirectly by inference', it must also be 'reasonably drawn from the acts in question'.[24]

It is clear from the most recent decision by the International Criminal Court of Justice in *Croatia v. Serbia* that a high bar exists for finding *dolus specialis* once the *actus* element is satisfied.

2.3. GENOCIDE DENIAL

One of the most significant aspects of genocide is genocide denial. Genocide denial is not an element of genocide, nor discussed in the Genocide

---

17 M. Findlay, 'Enunciating Genocide: Crime, Rights and the Impact of Judicial Intervention' (2013) 13 *International Criminal Law* 297–317, 305.

18 Ibid., p. 305.

19 W. Schabas, 'The Law and Genocide' in: D. Bloxham and A.D. Moses, *The Oxford Handbook of Genocide Studies*, Oxford University Press, Oxford 2013, p. 138.

20 A. Cassese, *International Criminal Law*, Oxford University Press, Oxford 2013, p. 119.

21 Ibid., p. 119.

22 B. Whitaker, 'Revised and updated Report on the question of the prevention and punishment of the crime of genocide', United Nations Economic and Social Council, E/CN.4/Sub.2/1985/6, paragraph 39.

23 *Croatia v. Serbia*, Application of the Convention on the Prevention and Punishment of the Crime of Genocide, 03.02.2015, Judgment, paragraph 139.

24 Ibid., paragraph 148.

Convention.[25] Gregory Stanton discusses the 8 Stages of Genocide. Those stages are classification, symbolisation, dehumanisation, organisation, polarisation, preparation, extermination, and denial. Stanton posits that genocide denial occurs after genocide has taken place.

However, I contend, based on the Genocide Convention, that denial is a dynamic ingredient in genocide. Genocide denial can be seen in some cases as the continuation of the acts of genocide by perpetrators. It is 'full consonant with the original methods of the perpetrators'. As Lawrence Douglas explains in the context of Nazi Germany, 'the tactics of denial used by the perpetrators were not simply designed to cover their tracks from the Allies or to hide their actions from the German population. Rather, *denial was a means of performing genocide*'.[26]

After genocide, denial manifests in different ways and harms survivors/victims further. 'Instead of a benign, harmonious extension of genocide recognition from one case to another, one group's victimisation experience is often traded against another's in a competitive political struggle. This leads at best to contentious searches for the right historical analogy and at worst to the denial of the "other's" genocide.'[27]

Another perspective offered by Johannes Houwink ten Cate is 'perhaps the true problem of genocide denial is not that individuals deny a particular genocide. The problem more generally, as many victims know from first-hand experience, is that perpetrators are frequently in denial.' He continues, 'the continuity of political regimes makes it difficult to concede that genocide has taken place.'[28]

During the Bangladesh genocide, denial manifested in many different ways before and after genocide. 'Pakistan has never accepted responsibility for what happened. Moreover, historians and journalists have come perilously close to genocide denial, or have seemed motivated by desire to minimize the numbers involved.'[29]

It is now pertinent to examine the Refugee Convention and different aspects of the Refugee Convention which can contribute to genocide denialism.

---

25 C. Fournet, *The Crime of Destruction and the Law of Genocide: Their Impact on Collective Memory*, 2007, p. 83.

26 L. Douglas, *Genocide Denials and the Law. 'From Trying the Perpetrator to Trying the Denier and Back Again'*, Oxford University Press, Oxford, p. 54.

27 M. Shaw, *Genocide and International Relations*, Cambridge University Press, Cambridge 2013, p. 22.

28 J. Houwink Ten Cate, 'On Outlawing Genocide Denial' in: H.G. Van Der Wilt (ed.), *The Genocide Convention: The Legacy of 60 Years*, Martinus Nijhoff Publishers, Leiden 2012, p. 156.

29 P. Hensher, 'The War Bangladesh Can Never Forget' 2013 *The Independent* <www.independent.co.uk/news/world/asia/the-war-bangladesh-can-never-forget-8501636.html>.

3. REFUGEE CONVENTION

Against the backdrop of the refugee flows in World War I, the League of Nations created the 1951 UN Convention on Refugees, which was subsequently strengthened after the influx of refugee issues which surfaced throughout and after World War II.[30] The Convention was later amended through the 1967 Protocol to lift the temporal and geographic restrictions.[31] The Convention on Refugees represents the 'most comprehensive codification' as well as 'endorses a single definition of the term refugee'.[32]

Article 1(a)(2) labels a 'refugee' as those persons who:

> 'as a result of events occurring before 1 January 1951 and owing to well-founded fear of persecution for reasons of race, religion, nationality, membership of a particular social group or political opinion, is outside the country of his nationality and is unable or, owing to such fear, is unwilling to avail himself of the protection of that country; or who, not having a nationality and being outside the country of his former habitual residence as a result of such events, is unable or, owing to such fear, is unwilling to return to it.'

The definition of a 'refugee' has been interpreted in an 'expansive fashion'[33] and that expansive definition is 'well accepted' in the international community.[34] However, there is a balance struck in states using 'additional rules' to determine who may be a refugee.[35] This balance is struck through various interpretations of the Refugee Convention memorialised in national legislation. I now turn to two requirements that have arisen from those interpretations, the well-founded fear of persecution and the nexus requirement.

3.1. WELL-FOUNDED FEAR – PERSECUTION

A refugee who seeks asylum (temporary refuge) in a country must prove certain elements in order to be granted asylum. One of the first elements is to show that they have a well-founded fear of persecution. In practice, in order to prove a 'well-founded' fear exists, the UNHCR Handbook advises that 'both the

---

30 S. OGATA, *The Refugee Convention 1951, The Travaux Preparatoires Analyzed with Commentary by Dr. Paul Weis*, Foreword <www.unhcr.org/4ca34be29.html> accessed 01.01.2015.

31 UNHCR, Convention and Protocol Relating to the Status of Refugees, p. 2.

32 Ibid., p. 3.

33 W. WORSTER, 'The Evolving Definition of Refugee in International Law' (2012) 30 *Berkeley J. Int'l L.* 94, 106.

34 Ibid., p. 128.

35 Ibid., p. 16.

subjective element, the fear is genuine, and the objective element, supported by an objective situation, must be met.'[36]

The term 'persecution' is not defined in the Refugee Convention.[37] However, the persecution must be 'relatively recent'.[38] This fear of persecution 'looks to the future' and can result when a person is absent from their country as a result of 'intervening political change'.[39] While fear of persecution and the lack of protection are interrelated concepts, there is no 'necessary linkage between persecution and Government authority'. The refugee in this situation must prove that they are 'unable or unwilling to avail themselves to the State for protection'.[40]

This is distinguishable from the Genocide Convention, where there *must* be a link between the group the individual belongs to and the actions (*actus reus*) by the government in order for it to even raise to the level of genocide.

3.2. NEXUS

Scholars have begun to pinpoint another area of concern for refugees known as the 'nexus' requirement. In many countries, refugees are asked to show a causal link between the 'well-founded' fear of persecution because (on account of) they belong to one of the following groups listed in the Convention. One scholar pointedly mentions, '[t]he Convention gave no guidance as to how to interpret or implement the nexus requirement. Indeed, it appears the drafters of the Convention were relatively unconcerned with the substantive elements of the refugee definition.'[41]

The nexus requirement proves troublesome in practice as it shifts the burden to the refugee to prove the intent of the person who persecutes. As illustrated above, the requirements to prove genocide are particularly challenging. For a refugee to have to bear this burden of proof would be unimaginable. As the Michigan Guidelines suggest, '[t]he standard of causation must also take account of the practical realities of refugee status determination, in particular the complex combinations of circumstances which may give rise to the risk of being

36 UNHCR Handbook on Procedures and Criteria for Determining Refugee Status under the 1951 Convention and the 1967 Protocol relating to the Status of Refugees, paragraph 38 (reedited 1992).

37 G.S. Gill, 'Introductory Note: Convention Relating to the Status of Refugees' 1967 *Audiovisual Library of International Law* <http://legal.un.org/avl/ha/prsr/prsr.html> accessed 01.12.2014.

38 C. Bohmer and A. Shuman, *Rejecting Refugees*, Routledge Press, London 2008, p. 181.

39 G.S. Gill, 'Introductory Note: Convention Relating to the Status of Refugees' 1967 *Audiovisual Library of International Law* <http://legal.un.org/avl/ha/prsr/prsr.html> accessed 01.12.2014.

40 Ibid.

41 A. Gupta, 'The New Nexus' (2014) 85 *U. Colo. L. Rev.* 377, 387.

persecuted, the prevalence of evidentiary gaps, and the difficulty of eliciting evidence across linguistic and cultural divides.'[42]

There are two other factors that should be mentioned, which contribute to further genocide and genocide denialism. The first is the lack of provisions for prevention in the Convention. This lack can lead to further human rights violations, which can in turn accomplish genocide. The second is the asylum process itself, which can bring about genocide denial. Both are discussed below.

3.3. CAUSES OF FLIGHTS OR PROVISION FOR PREVENTION

The Convention on Refugees 'does not address the question of "causes" of flight or make provision for prevention.'[43] Refugees who flee from persecution, particularly those who flee from genocide, end up in a situation where they face more strenuous human rights problems once they reach a 'safe' place. These problems are factors which can accomplish the intent of the genocidaire:

> 'The large numbers of persons who are forced to live in refugee camps, where inadequate nutrition, poor sanitation, and scarce medical supplies are endemic, pose a threat to international security and international health. Such conditions also ensure high mortality rates among the refugees ... The most commonly reported causes of death among refugees and internally displaced persons are diarrheal diseases, acute respiratory infections, measles, malaria, and cholera. These are contagious diseases which are costly to treat, imposing a public health threat and financial obligations upon surrounding countries.'[44]

Further, refugee movements 'often threaten inter-communal harmony and undermine major societal values by altering the ethnic, cultural, religious, and linguistic composition of host populations.' While this may sound more like xenophobic propaganda, in countries where tensions exist, a 'refugee influx can create a great strain on the system.'[45] On the flip side, 'life in refugee camps has become increasingly dangerous.'[46] This is not mere academic speculation. In

---

42 J.C. Hathaway, 'The Causal Nexus In International Refugee Law' (2002) *Michigan Journal of International Law* <https://www.law.umich.edu/centersandprograms/refugeeandasylumlaw/Documents/2001_Michigan_Guidelines_on_Nexus_to_Convention_Ground.pdf>.

43 G.S. Gill, 'Introductory Note: Convention Relating to the Status of Refugees' 1967 *Audiovisual Library of International Law* <http://legal.un.org/avl/ha/prsr/prsr.html> accessed 01.12.2014.

44 K. Gabraith, 'Note: Moving People: Forced Migration and International Law' (1999) 13 *Geo. Immigr. L.J.* 597 referring to B. Gessner, 'Mortality Rates, Causes of Death and Health Status among Displaced and Resident Populations of Kabul, Afghanistan' (1994) 272 *JAMA* 382, 385.

45 G. Loescher, 'Refugees as a ground for international action' in: E. Newman and J. Van Selm (eds.), *Refugees and Forced Displacement: International Security, Human Vulnerability, and the State*, United Nations University Press, Tokyo 2003, p. 34.

46 Ibid., p. 36.

one instance, humanitarian protection was given to Rwandan genocidaires who overran refugee camps in Zaire and the Democratic Republic of Congo.[47] Few refugee camps provide effective security to prevent crime, armed combat, and robbery. Therefore, refugees are subjected to 'chronic violence'.[48]

The Bangladesh genocide, and now in Syrian refugee camps throughout the Middle East, the limitations of the Convention on Refugees are apparent.[49] However, from a genocide perpetrator's perspective, the act of killing the targeted group can be completed simply by forcing the group to flee the country into these kinds of conditions. This simple act or intention may never equate to genocide within the parameters of the Genocide Convention.

3.4. ASYLUM PROCESS AND DENIALISM

While most governments believe that their asylum laws are clear, in reality refugees face many obstacles in the process of seeking asylum. Given the political nature of the asylum process, the system becomes a breeding ground for genocide denialism to be furthered. In North America, as well as throughout Europe, countries seek documentation from applicants to verify the refugee narrative. This is 'rare' because most of the countries from which people flee persecution 'don't have the kind of press that reports details of political activism. It is only in those unusual cases where someone is well known that there is likely to be a written record.'[50] There is also another practice using 'country reports' to determine the goings-on in specific countries.[51] This practice can enable genocide denial. In the United States and similarly in the United Kingdom, the reports produced on countries contain selective information. Those reports are 'sometimes unduly kind to friendly or allied regimes, which means that they don't report the human rights abuses that are claimed by the applicant.'[52] While NGOs may also submit and prepare reports on behalf of refugees, it is up to the officer to determine whether they find this kind of evidence corroborates the asylum seeker's story. However this exchange between asylum officers and refugees is crucial. '[I]f practitioners and scholars are interested in identifying

---

47 E. Hozer, 'What happens to Law in a Refugee Camp?' (2013) 47 *Law and Soc'y Rev.* 837, 843.

48 Ibid., p. 844.

49 S. Tisdall, 'Inside a refugee camp in Jordan three years after the Syrian uprising began' 2014 *The Guardian* <www.theguardian.com/world/2014/mar/11/inside-zaatari-refugee-camp-jordan-syria-uprising-three-years> accessed 01.01.2015.

50 C. Bohmer and A. Shuman, *Rejecting Refugees*, Routledge Press, London 2008, p. 117.

51 There are different processes which occur for asylum; I only investigate some in this paper. However for an interesting study on the current decision making regimes in asylum, see R. Hamlin, 'International Law and Administrative Insulation: A Comparison of Refugee Status Determination Regimes in the United States, Canada, and Australia' (2012) 37 *Law & Soc Inquiry* 933.

52 C. Bohmer and A. Shuman, *Rejecting Refugees*, Routledge Press, London 2008, p. 133.

accurate sources of information they need not look farther than refugee populations.'[53] In many cases where evidence is missing to bring genocidaires to Court, these documented narratives could make a difference.

3.5. EXCLUSION

While the Convention is victim-centred and lacks certain burden shifting, there are provisions under which a perpetrator can be excluded from the asylum process. Under Article 1 F of the Convention on Refugees, persons can be excluded from refugee protection if they commit certain acts, including those acts which are *contrary to the purposes and principles of the United Nations.* Article 1 includes those who are found guilty under the Convention on Genocide.[54]

The phrase found in Article 1 F(c), *contrary to the purposes and principles of the United Nations* is considered vague, and there is very little guidance in the preparatory documents or the Convention itself to determine what it means.[55] However, the UNHCR handbook provides that while Article 1 F(c) does not introduce a 'new element', it is intended to 'cover in such a general way' such acts that may not be covered in the two preceding exclusion clauses.[56] It also seems that the United Nations may define those principles in accordance with worldwide events. For example, in UN General Assembly Resolution 51/210, those who apply for asylum must not have 'participated in terrorist acts', which should incorporate a determination whether the person is being investigated for such acts or has been 'convicted' of offences connected to terrorism. Further, the person cannot use refugee status to shield themselves from prosecution of terrorism related crimes.[57]

Despite the language of Article 1 F, many perpetrators have circumvented this to find haven in countries such as the United States.[58] William Aceves and Paul Hoffman state:

---

53 D. Bleacher, *The Genocide Debate*, Palgrave Macmillan, New York 2011, p. 32.

54 UNHCR Handbook on Procedures and Criteria for Determining Refugee Status under the 1951 Convention and the 1967 Protocol relating to the Status of Refugees, Annex VI, paragraph 4 (re-edited 1992).

55 S. Sivakumaran, 'Exclusion from Refugee Status: The Purposes and Principles of the United Nations and Article 1F(c) of the Refugee Convention' (2014) 26 *International Journal of Refugee Law* 350–381, 351.

56 UNHCR Handbook on Procedures and Criteria for Determining Refugee Status under the 1951 Convention and the 1967 Protocol relating to the Status of Refugees, Annex VI, paragraph 4 (re-edited 1992), paragraph 162.

57 UN General Assembly Resolution 51/210 17 December 1996 <www.un.org/documents/ga/res/51/a51r210.htm>.

58 See W. Aceves and P. Hoffman, 'Article: Using Immigration Law to Protect Human Rights: A Critique of Recent Legislative Proposals' (2002) 23 *Mich J. Int'l L.* 733.

'For example, genocide applies only to actions committed against a national, ethnic, racial or religious group. To constitute genocide, those actions also have to be committed with the specific intent of destroying a protected group in whole or in part. Further, the genocide bar applies only to those "engaged" in genocide, which arguably does not include those who may have incited, assisted, conspired or attempted to engage in genocide. Similarly, to be barred for particularly severe violations of religious freedom, the individual must be a foreign official who has engaged in those violations in the last twenty-four months. Those who have "ordered, incited, assisted or otherwise participated in" persecution are statutorily barred from admission as a refugee and from obtaining asylum status or withholding of removal, but they are eligible to enter the United States, to adjust their status to lawful permanent residence, and to obtain United States citizenship.'[59]

There is a delicate balance that is kept here despite the tough language and interpretation that is used under Article 1 F. The Genocide Convention does not offer any other support on this matter. However, Article 7 does bar genocide as a political crime for extradition.

4. TYING IN THE CONVENTIONS – BANGLADESH

Given the central theme of this article, the 1971 Bangladesh genocide serves as an illustrative example to highlight the tensions between the two Conventions and the role denialism can play, since Pakistan continues to deny its role in the genocide.[60]

4.1. GENOCIDE

In 1971, West Pakistan began targeted military crackdowns in East Pakistan because of alleged political uprisings by the Bengali people. The West Pakistani army, supported by allied militia groups, went on a murderous campaign targeting specific groups within East Pakistan (now known as Bangladesh). 'Operation Searchlight' was aimed at crushing Bengali resistance, destroying members of the 'intelligentsia', and 'able-bodied Bengali males'. Included in this specific group were students at Dhaka University.[61] The atrocities

59 Ibid., p. 744, citing Adopted Orphans Citizenship Act and Anti-Atrocity Alien Deportation Act: Hearing on H.R. 2833 and H.R. 3058 Before the Subcomm. on Immigration and Claims of the Comm. on the Judiciary, 106th Cong. 22 (2000) (statement of James Castello, Associate Deputy Attorney General, US Department of Justice).

60 T. Anam, 'Pakistan's State of Denial' 2013 *New York Times* <www.nytimes.com/2013/12/27/opinion/anam-pakistans-overdue-apology.html> accessed 21.06.2015.

61 A. Ahmed, 'Bangladesh 1971: War Crimes, Genocide, and Crimes Against Humanity, Operation Searchlight: The Targets' 2009 Kean University Conference

committed by the military and militia groups were reported through several channels. The World Bank described how 'in all cities visited there are areas that have been razed; and in all districts visited there are villages which have simply ceased to exist.'[62] Journalists were quick to expose the horrid details of the events through the eyes of refugees and survivors who managed to flee the orchestrated persecution. During the Bangladesh genocide a notable journalist was Sydney Schanberg of the New York Times. Schanberg wrote in 1971: '[o]f the more than six million Bengalis who are believed to have fled to India to escape the army's terror, at least four million are Hindus. The troops are still killing Hindus and burning and looting their villages.'[63] He later reported, '[t]he Pakistani Army has painted big yellow "H's" on the Hindu shops still standing in this town to identify the property of the minority eighth of the population that it has made special targets.'[64] Schanberg concluded: 'it was a genocide – perhaps even a more clear case than Cambodia.'[65] Schanberg was subsequently expelled from Pakistan.[66]

There are two points worth mentioning at this juncture. First, although the killing of the Hindus during the Bangladesh genocide would fall neatly into one of groups in the Genocide Convention, it could be argued that students and political opponents who were targeted would not fall under the protected groups of the Genocide Convention. However, 'the vast majority of victims of this violence were Bengalis, the majority ethnic group in East Pakistan.'[67] Second, some could challenge whether officials from West Pakistan had the requisite intent to destroy ethnic groups since there was also violence which came from groups in East Pakistan.[68] However, 'it is clear that particular groups were deliberately targeted by the Army, on the grounds that they constituted enemies of the state', and this is further supported by official Pakistani accounts which 'concurred that resulting atrocities were partly the result of a failure by officers to constrain or limit the unlawful actions of the soldiers – and indeed of their encouragement of such actions.'[69]

<www.kean.edu/~bgsg/Conference09/Papers_and_Presentations/Anis%20Ahmed_Paper_OperationSearchlight.pdf>.

62 G. Bass, *The Blood Telegram*, Vintage Books, New York 2013, p. 132 citing World Bank Report 8 July 1971.

63 M. Rahman, 'The demons of 1971' 2007 *Rediff India Abroad* <www.rediff.com/news/2007/jan/04spec.htm> accessed 05.03.2015.

64 Ibid.

65 G. Bass, *The Blood Telegram*, Vintage Books, New York 2013, p. 203.

66 M. Rahman, 'The demons of 1971' 2007 *Rediff India Abroad* <www.rediff.com/news/2007/jan/04spec.htm> accessed 05.03.2015.

67 G. Robinson, 'State-Sponsored Violence and Secessionist Rebellions in Asia' in: D. Bloxham and A.D. Moses, *The Oxford Handbook of Genocide Studies*, Oxford University Press, Oxford 2013, p. 468.

68 Ibid.

69 Ibid., p. 470.

4.2. REFUGEES

Approximately ten million refugees fled into India as a result of the ongoing genocide.[70] India 'frantically built refugee camps, each holding some forty thousand people' to avoid a national health disaster, given the impoverished conditions and climate conditions the refugees would face.[71] The Indian government determined that 90% of the refugees that had fled into India were Hindu, even though the population of East Pakistan was only 16–17% Hindu.[72] During this tumultuous time, India adhered to the principles of *non-refoulment* that are enshrined within the Refugee Convention. India was not at that time, nor is presently, a signatory to the 1951 Convention on Refugees. In a most unusual act for a foreign leader, Prime Minister Indira Gandhi went to visit the refugee camps herself. During the visits, Gandhi's 'moral sensibilities' were 'assaulted' given the 'face-to-face' stories of terror she heard from real people, as opposed to the 'abstract statistics of refugees and rupees.'[73] Ghandi 'went around the world saying this was genocide.'[74] No country was moved by the speeches, the statistics, or the reality the refugees faced. While many countries donated aid to help the refugees, the international community labeled the actions of the Pakistani regime an internal matter.

Based on refugee narratives and the potential hazards the millions of refugees created,[75] India was seriously forced to consider, and later decided upon, military intervention against West Pakistan. India justified its actions with the Genocide Convention, which was a 'concern of the international community'.[76] After the birth of Bangladesh, the largest repatriation of refugees occurred.[77] This brief depiction of events in Bangladesh illustrates how important refugees can become in conflict, and how, if they are not properly taken care of, further humanitarian disasters can result.

Subsequently, the 'preventative' function of the Genocide Convention has proven to be a false safety net. Bangladesh has started prosecution of people who supported Pakistan during the genocide. These trials do not meet any international standards and have been heavily criticised. Pakistan continues to deny the genocide and others who aided Pakistan remain silent with respect to their complicity.

---

70 UNHCR, 'The State of The World's Refugees 2000: Fifty Years of Humanitarian Action', Geneva, 2000.

71 G. Bass, *The Blood Telegram*, Vintage Books, New York 2013, p. 120, 132.

72 Ibid., p. 121.

73 Ibid., p. 125.

74 Ibid., p. 243, quoting Admiral Mihir Roy.

75 Among these problems included foreign fighters, possible subversive groups among the refugees, social and religious tensions. Ibid., pp. 120–121, 129, 133.

76 Ibid., p. 284.,

77 P. Grbac, 'India and its 1971 Refugee 'Problem' *McGill Blogs*, 2014, citing UNHCR, 'The State of The World's Refugees 2000: Fifty Years of Humanitarian Action', Geneva, 2000 <http://oppenheimer.mcgill.ca/India-and-its-1971-Refugee-Problem>.

5. CONCLUSION: POTENTIAL SOLUTIONS

I propose the following considerations to address the problems that I have raised above. I hope of course that it will be the subject of more debate and consideration.

First, states should use every opportunity at their disposal to engage refugees and record their narratives so that there is a more complete historical record, even if that record is never used in a court room.

Second, regardless of the political leaning of countries with recognising genocide, immigration officers should be well informed of the dynamics that refugees in conflict may be facing and be trained to be sensitive to those situations. This may help avoid a situation where a refugee has to face continued denial and prevents the refugee from being placed in a position to prove genocide is or has taken place.

Third, countries should create a complete bar to alleged perpetrators of genocide so that they may not benefit from protection. This includes those perpetrators who may be complicit, take part in a conspiracy, and/or are accessories to genocide. While this broad interpretation is not currently supported, it is important that all countries stop impunity for crimes such as genocide.

Fourth, the international community should reconsider the current state of the Genocide Convention and incorporate survivor/victim centred amendments to the Convention so that targeted groups are offered protection when seeking safety. These amendments should be consistent with the Convention on Refugees.

Finally, while the international community must do more than pay lip service to the phrase 'never again' and uphold their obligations under both Conventions.

In legal scholarship each convention is analysed separately because they deal with two different legal areas. It makes sense that these two conventions are not discussed together in most cases because the elements are different and both are meant to accomplish different objectives. However, as illustrated in this article, how the world comes to learn about the most intimate details of genocide is by refugees who have fled violence.

CHAPTER XX

CLIMATE JUSTICE: CLIMATE CHANGE AND HUMAN RIGHTS

Zoi ALIOZI

The inadequate commitment of academia to climate change research, and the neglected, under-developed state of climate justice, must be addressed and counter-acted. The following paper aspires to pay a small contribution to that specific cause. This essay is based on the fact that climate change is undermining the fulfillment of internationally protected human rights, like the rights to health and life; the right to food, water, shelter, property; rights associated with livelihood and culture; with migration and resettlement; and with personal security in the event of conflict. The worst effects of climate change are principally felt by those whose rights protections are already insufficient. In this essay, I highlight these risks and advocate their consideration. Additionally I ask questions such as: what are the human rights repercussions of climate change, and how does the extensive organisation of international human rights law and knowledge, convey that phenomenon? Where does international human rights law overlap with or provoke duties under the embryonic climate justice regime? Where should climate change strategies challenge human rights essentials? My ambition is to clarify the confusion covering this area of study, and by examining the relationship between climate change and human rights, an attempt is made to discover, examine, and analyse their most essential links.

1. INTRODUCTION

It seems to me that any discourse on climate justice would be incomplete without a reflection on climate change denial. However, allow me to start by stressing the need to draw clear distinguishing lines between, denialism, denialist, and denial. Scholars tend to use them interchangeably, as if these terms refer to the same thing, but from the perspective of the author of this paper on the issues at stake, they do not signify the same idea.

So, the first realisation on the topic at hand is that we need to construct a comprehensive theory that will explain denialism's essence. In an Aristotelian sense, discovering the essence of the subject of our concern, requires breaking it down into its most essential elements. In the same line of reasoning, any epistemological discourse, implies a quest for Truth, while approaching on occasions at the 'unconcealedness'[1] of the '*aletheia*'[2] in language. This is not the purpose of this paper, but by staying with that train of thought, I will just touch upon a necessary philosophically driven clarification. Any reasonable woman would agree, that to talk about denial is not the same thing as to talk about denialism. Thus, an etymological examination could offer us preliminary fruitful results, in the sense of a Derridian[3] genealogical deconstructive exercise. For example, the term denialism is a synthetic term, which is constructed by two synthetics: firstly, the word 'denial', and secondly, the suffix –ism. If we assume that we know what denial refers to, namely the refusal to accept a certain proposal as being true, then a look at the suffix –ism is necessary, since the suffix –ism, is usually shared by terms describing political theories, such as commun-ism, liberal-ism, capital-ism, anarch-ism, and so on and so forth. Accordingly, the suffix –ism, which originates in Greek (–ισμός), refers to a system of ideas and is destined to form abstract nouns of action. A preliminary observation, is to point out that the suffix –ism gives us the first hint, since one could easily argue that it serves to categorise denialism as an organised political theory, with means, ends, and narratives. Although we still need much stronger justifications to argue in that line of reasoning, it seems to me that this observation is offering us a raw glimpse of the truth.

So, to clarify what is at stake, lets see the working definitions of the three terms:

(1) *denialist* is a person who refuses to admit the truth of a concept or proposition that is supported by the majority of scientific or historical evidence;[4]
(2) *denialism* is denial writ large – when an entire segment of society, often struggling with the trauma of change, turns away from reality in favour of a more comfortable lie;[5] and
(3) *denial* is understood as an unconscious defense mechanism for coping with guilt, anxiety and other upsetting emotions aroused by reality. The psyche blocks off information that is literally unthinkable or unbearable. The

1 M. Heidegger, *Being and Time*, J. Stambaugh, trans., Harper Torchbooks 1972, p. 79.

2 The Greek word for 'truth', aletheia (αλήθεια), meaning 'un-forgetfulness' or 'un-concealment'. See: Z. Aliozi, 'A Critique of State-terrorism' (2012) 6(1) *The Crit, A Critical Legal Studies Journal*.

3 As Derrida has said: 'So we have to go back to the origin, not in order to cultivate the origin or in order to protect the etymology, the etymon, the philological purity of the origin, but in order first of all to understand where it comes from'. See: <http://hydra.humanities.uci.edu/derrida/vill2.html> accessed 07.2015.

4 See: <www.oxforddictionaries.com/definition/english/Denialist> accessed 06.2015.

5 M. Specter, *Denialism: How Irrational Thinking Hinders Scientific Progress, Harms the Planet, and Threatens Our Lives*, Penguin Press HC, Hudson 2009.

> unconscious sets up a barrier, which prevents the thought from reaching conscious knowledge. Information and memories slip into an inaccessible region of the mind.[6]

So, these examples could offer the basic canvas for grasping the essential differences between these terms. However, the underlining concern of this paper, is fuelled by the climate change denialism, and the inability of denialists to date to accept the harmful impact of human-made climate change to fundamental human rights. Hence, climate change denialism is a denial or dismissal of the scientific consensus on the anthropogenic climate change, the degree of global warming, its consequences, and its connection to human action, mainly in support of the western capitalist business interests, so basically for commercial or neoliberal ideological reasons. It is not a secret anymore, that this special category of denialism has been associated with the fossil fuels lobby, the Koch brothers, industry advocates and capitalist or free market interests.

It is interesting that an increasing number of scholars are labelling *climate change denial* as a special and different form of denialism. It seems to me that this labelling trend is based on strong and valid epistemological justifications. Since, this particular kind of denialism has been adopted by a great number of people and groups, that argue against the acceptance of the anthropogenic climate change, and its harmful effects both on the planet, and to human rights. Today, there is an undisputed scientific consensus, that human activities – such as the burning of fossil fuels releasing carbon dioxide gas in the atmosphere, the conversion of land for agriculture, or fracking to name the most famous ones – have a negative effect on the climate, meaning that human-made harm is being inflicted on the planet, since for example these anthropogenic harms are dangerously warming the earth. Nevertheless, we are still witnessing the political and business worlds joined by the media, shamelessly forming what we call the 'denial machine'.[7] The denial machine which has hindered global struggles to prevent future climate change and guarantee a sustainable future for humankind and future generations. It is an undeniable truth, however, and easily observable, that much of the climate change denialist's debate focuses on the finances of global warming[8] and one could argue that it is in a way, a self-defence mechanism generated by the multi-billion carbon-based economy, its beneficiaries and its supporters, that are as powerful in business as unfortunately in politics. In simple terms, climate justice for these groups is just another obstacle in making money, and these short-sighted capitalist driven but

6 S. Cohen, *States of Denial: Knowing About Atrocities and Suffering*, Polity Press, London 2001.

7 P. Jacques, R. Dunlap and M. Freeman, 'The organization of denial: Conservative think tanks and environmental scepticism' (2008) 17(3) *Environmental Politics* 349–385.

8 N. Oreskes, 'The Scientific Consensus on Climate Change: How Do We Know We're Not Wrong?' in: J.F.C. Di Mento and P.M. Dougman, *Climate Change: What It Means for Us, Our Children, and Our Grandchildren*, The MIT Press, Cambridge 2007, pp. 65–66.

powerful groups, will obviously do everything in their power to minimise the legal-binding reach of climate agreements like the UNFCCC and recently the COP21, and any duty bearing rules stemming from climate change policies, that could eventually mean less profits for their industry. We don't need to be rocket scientists to realise which are the ultimate intentions of the *denial machine*.

It seems to me that in order to grasp the necessity and urgency involved in the terrain of climate justice, we need to put a face to the victims of climate change. That can be achieved partly by considering that climate change endangers the existence of many island states in the Pacific, since the sea level is expected to rise more than one metre before the next century. For example, the coast of Nauru, which is the only habitable area of the state, is gradually corroding, while populations in Papua New Guinea and the Solomon Islands have already had to involuntarily flee their homes to avoid the floods and tides. The nations of Tuvalu, Kiribati and the Marshall Islands may vanish entirely under the sea, in the near future. These are scientifically predicted facts that require the United Nations and global community's attention urgently. For example, the suggested plans of action in the case of small island states and their special urgent circumstances are undeniably not well designed, and consequently not fully satisfactory to all parties involved. Proposed solutions to the threat of their homelands disappearance, include strategies such as the absorption of the homeless nation into another country, exercising its own sovereignty to pay for the transfer. For instance, in exchange for power and Kiribati's sovereign territory, India could receive Kiribati's populace and offer relocation aid, such as professional training and economic support. This proposal advocates for the relocation of an island nation in exchange for the sovereignty and management of its assets and maritime zone, which could be proven to be beneficial in the long term for all nations involved. This is not a hypothetical science-fiction film scenario, it is an official proposal currently examined by governments around the world.

According to scientific findings, our planet will have to deal with the rise in the sea level, the submersion of islands, loss of land, and the consequence of climate refugees due to climate change and global warming. The law of the seas or for refugees, and other relevant international legislation, has not been proven sufficient for dealing with these unprecedented cases. There is an urgent necessity to draw the attention of the international community to these pressing matters, since the risk of harm involved has reached the highest point. The need to prepare for confronting the problems that will rise together with the rise of the seas has never been so urgent and threatening, which means that the UN has an incomparable duty to implement toward a legal framework that would cover the tackling of the catastrophes and the protection of nations and peoples. What should be underlined is that this new legal framework should be in accordance with the established human rights regime and respect its principles and legal rules. While the directly threatened nations have every right in the world to keep on seeking alternative ways to protect their nations, citizens, and homelands in the best possible way.

That been said, I will proceed in a descriptive analysis of the connecting links between climate change and human rights, in an attempt to understand the urgent necessity to work for the development of climate justice.

2. CONNECTING HUMAN RIGHTS TO CLIMATE CHANGE

Climate change's links to the human rights regime, arise from the simple fact that human-made climate change affects the human rights of all. The language used in human rights discourse is different from the vocabulary employed in climate change negotiations; each has a unique referential background and connotations. In the present essay, 'human rights', indicate an organised set of claims about the entitlements of all human beings, regardless of any possible differentiation. The United Nations International Bill of Human Rights, originally laid out these claims, and they are understood to carry both an extensive universalist moral authority and a legal weight. Since the Universal Declaraion of human rights is not legally binding, the principal source writings under international law are: the 1966 International Covenants on Civil and Political Rights (ICCPR), and the Economic, Social and Cultural Rights (ICESCR). The two Treaties are legally binding to the majority of the world's countries, or in legal terms, to all states that have ratified them, and are complemented by additional human rights binding agreements, in the national, regional and international arena. All these texts are supported by the legal precedent and established case law of international, regional and national tribunals, by a body of 'soft law', referring to non-binding resolutions and other texts from transnational organisations such as the UN General Assembly.

For instance, the statement in the first Article of both laws clearly says that: '[i]n no case may a people be deprived of its own means of subsistence.' This is noticeably applicable where a changing climate has exactly this result. One could argue that basic subsistence needs are: water, food, healthcare, shelter and so on and so forth. It should be noted that the terminology of rights does not require to assume a legal language in place of an altruistic one. However it implies and commands the application of an umbrella of intercontinentally established rules that have elevated those basic needs for survival to the level of claims for all. While the United Nations Framework Convention on Climate Change (UNFCCC), includes in its mandate the 'protection of the climate system for the benefit of present and future generations of humankind', it is not designed to offer human rights protection, humanitarian aid or redress to individuals or communities who have experienced environmental harm. This is the greatest shortfall of the law in question. However, while this law has great difficulties in practice due to its nonbinding nature, it has generated a number of concepts, including: intergenerational equity, sustainable development, and the Precautionary Principle.

The UNFCCC is an agreement amongst states to: 'anticipate, prevent or minimize the causes of climate change and mitigate its adverse effects.'[9] The violations of human rights due to human-made harmful impacts on climate change fall easily into the category of obligations imposed on states as stated in the UNFCCC. This is not a broad misinterpretation but a matter of fact, arising from many current legal cases like the *Inuit*, and the *Small Islands States* cases. It is useful to point out that the increasing interest in the human rights dimensions of climate change has been ignited mainly by the *Inuit*[10] and the *Small Island States* cases. In their 2005 petition before the Inter-American Commission on human rights the Inuit argued that the effects of climate change could be credited to actions and omissions of the US and violated their fundamental human rights, namely rights such as: the benefits of culture; property; the preservation of health; life; physical integrity; security; means of subsistence; residence; movement; and inviolability of the home.[11] These rights, it was argued, were protected under several international human rights instruments, including the American Declaration of the Rights and Duties of Man.[12] The Commission declined to review the merits of the petition, stating that the 'information provided does not enable us to determine whether the alleged facts would tend to characterize a violation of rights protected by the American Declaration.'[13]

Although the Inuit petition did not proceed any further, it drew attention to the links between climate change and human rights and led to a 'Hearing of a General Nature' on human rights and global warming.[14] The hearing was held on 1 March 2007, and included statements from the Chair of the Inuit Circumpolar Conference (ICC) and its lawyers, but not representatives of the

---

9 UNFCCC Articles 3(1) and (3). A range of preventive measures, including technology transfer, emissions reduction measures, education and scientific studies, are set forth in Articles 4–6 and 9.

10 See: S. Watt-Cloutier, 'Climate Change and Human Rights' in: Human Rights Dialogues, *Environmental Rights*, 22.04.2004.

11 Organisation of American States, Inter-American Commission on Human Rights, Petition Seeking Relief from Violations Resulting from Global Warming Caused by Acts and Omissions of the United States 2005. See: <www.inuitcircumpolar.com/files/up-loads/icc-files/FINALPetitionICC.pdf> accessed 05.2015.

12 American Declaration on the Rights and Duties of Man, April 1948, OAS Resolution XXX, OEA/Ser.L.V/II.82 doc.6 rev.1.

13 J. George, 'ICC Climate Change Petition Rejected' 2006 *Nunatsiaq News* <www.nunatsiaq.com/archives/61215/news/nunavut/61215_02.html> accessed 04.2015.

14 'Inter-American Commission on Human Rights, IACHR Announces Webcast of Public Hearings of the 127th Regular Period of Sessions' No. 8/07 Press Release <www.cidh.org/Comunicados/English/2007/8.07eng.htm.> accessed 03.2015.

US.[15] The Commission unfortunately has not taken any further action, but the ICC petition generated considerable debate in the academic literature.[16]

Meanwhile, the small island states, and the Maldives in particular, launched a campaign to link climate change and human rights. Representatives of small island developing states met in November 2007 to adopt the Malé Declaration on the Human Dimension of Global Climate Change, requesting *inter alia* that the United Nations Human Rights Council organise a discussion on climate change and human rights.[17] The Council adopted a Resolution tabled by Maldives entitled Human Rights and Climate Change in March 2008 that requested that the Office of the High Commissioner for Human Rights (OHCHR) conduct a detailed analytical study on the relationship between climate change and human rights.[18]

Following these developments, the OHCHR published its study on the relationship between climate change and human rights on January 2009.[19] The study argued that climate change threatens the enjoyment of a wide spectrum of human rights, including rights to life, health, food, water, housing, and self-determination. It fell short of finding that climate change necessarily or categorically *violates* human rights,[20] but it did accept that States have duties under human rights law to address climate change. The Human Rights Council decided in March 2009 to hear a panel debate on the topic and encouraged its Special Procedures mandate-holders to consider the implications of climate change for human rights within their mandates.[21]

In a similar vein, in the Americas, Argentina drafted and tabled a resolution on human rights and climate change that was adopted by the General Assembly

---

15 J. Harrington, 'Climate Change, Human Rights and the Right to be Cold' (2007) 18 *Fordham Envt'l L. Rev.* 513.

16 Many articles have been inspired by the Inuit Case. See: A. Sinden, 'Climate Change and Human Rights' (2007) 27 *J. Land Resources & Envt'l L.* 255; H.M. Osofsky, 'The Inuit Petition as a Bridge? Beyond the Dialectics of Climate Change and Indigenous Peoples' Rights' (2007) 31(2) *Am. Indian L. Rev.* 675; R.S. Abate, 'Climate Change, the United States and the Impacts of Arctic Melting: A Case Study in the Need for Enforceable International Environmental Human Rights' (2007) 26 *Stan. Envt'l. L.J.* 3; T. Koivurova, 'International Legal Avenues to Address the Plight of Victims of Climate Change: Problems and Prospects' (2007) 22 *Envt'l L. & Litig.* 267; S.C. Aminzdeh, 'A Moral Imperative: The Human Rights Implications of Climate Change' (2007) 30(2) *Hastings Int'l Comp. I. L. Rev.* 231; and M.E. Middaugh, 'Linking Global Warming to Inuit Human Rights' (2006) 8 *San Diego Int'l L.J.* 179.

17 Malé Declaration on the Human Dimension of Global Climate Change (14.11.2007) <www.meew.gov.mv/downloads/download.php?f=32> accessed 01.2015.

18 United Nations Office of the High Commissioner for Human Rights, Human Rights and Climate Change, Resolution 7/23 (28.03.2008) <http://ap.ohchr.org/documents/E/HRC/resolutions/A_HRC_RES_7_23.pdf.> accessed 03.2015.

19 United Nations Office of the High Commissioner for Human Rights, Report on the Relationship Between Climate Change and Human Rights, UN Doc. A/HRC/10/61 (15.01.2009).

20 Ibid.

21 United Nations Human Rights Council Resolution 10/4 para. 3, in United Nations Human Rights Council, Draft Report of the Human Rights Council on its Tenth Session, UN Doc. A/HRC/10/L.11 (31.03.2009).

of the Organisation of American States in June 2008. The Resolution instructed the Inter-American Commission on Human Rights to 'determine the possible existence of a link between adverse effects of climate change and the full enjoyment of human rights'.[22] Argentina expressed concern that the inequitable impacts of climate change will place an undue strain on vulnerable States that will need to introduce climate policies and measures to ensure that they meet their human rights obligations.[23]

The emerging interest in human rights in the climate change terrain can possibly be credited to a certain point, to a growing international condemnation of the pace and directions of multilateral diplomacy.[24] Yet the slow advancement of international negotiations are not in line to the urgent necessity that streams from the sufficient, while worrying, scientific knowledge and undeniable consensus of the scientific community, about the role of human activities in causing climate change.

A review of the politics of human rights in the international negotiations on climate change does not yield straightforward answers. Yet a consideration of certain political issues is deemed necessary. For example, a total of 88 UN Member States supported the Human Rights Council's Consensus Resolution 10/4 (2009), encouraging greater involvement by human rights expert bodies in the UNFCCC process.[25] Co-sponsoring States, particularly those most immediately threatened by climate change, typically highlight the importance of human rights in stressing the human face and impacts of climate change, as part of a legal or moral claim for strengthened international mitigation commitments and adaptation support from wealthier countries and major emitters. It is important to note the role of Mohamed Nasheed the former president of the Maldives, who has been instrumental in raising international awareness on climate change and pushing the international community and the UN towards direct political and legal action.

Explicit human rights arguments have yet to gain traction to any visible extent within the climate change negotiations under the UNFCCC framework. Although a number of States have presented strong human rights arguments, still, a revised negotiating text for the outcome document for the 15th Conference of the Parties (COP15) released following the Bonn climate change talks in June 2009, contained only two relatively modest explicit human rights references.[26]

---

22 Organization of American States, Human Rights and Climate Change in the Americas, Resolution 2429, AG/RES. 2429 (XXXVIII-O/08) (03.06.2008).

23 Press Release, Centre for Human Rights and Environment, OAS Approves Human Rights and Climate Change Resolution (04.06.2008).

24 M. Limon, 'Human Eights and Climate Change: Constructing a Case for Political Action' (2009) 33(2) *Harvard Environmental Law Review* 439–476.

25 Res. 10/4 (March 2009).

26 At the Fifth Session (29 March–8 April, Bonn) of the Ad-Hoc Working Group on Long-Term Cooperative Action under the Convention (a supplementary group of the UNFCCC tasked under the Bali Action Plan to pursue the full, effective, and sustained implementation of the

Certain states conceive differently the potential effect of human rights inclusion in the climate change setting and the result of such a legal symbiosis. Some critical voices argue that human rights might jeopardise an already overburdened and unstable climate change agenda, however it seems to me that this is not a sufficient reason to overlook the commands of justice and fairness. human rights have also been described as a source of mistrust between governments, with certain developing countries expressing the concern that human rights could be used as a way of either preventing their development, or human rights may be operating as conditionalities on climate change adaptation funds.[27] On the same debate, some developed countries, argue that an official recognition of human rights and climate change linkages, could be used as a 'political weapon against them'.[28] These evolving political dynamics form an important part of the context in which the international legal analysis and policy needs to be addressed.

Yet, as is the case with the majority of international treaties, under the UNFCCC the primary obligations of the signatory States are held towards one another. However in human rights treaties, their duties are principally held in respect of citizens, and in some cases other residents or applicants, and so are generally reserved, violated, or challenged firstly at national level, up to the level of the international human rights courts. Irrefutably, it is not possible to moderate and tackle the human-made effects of climate change without ensuring

Convention), the Maldives delegation initiated the course of trying to integrate human rights language into the draft negotiating text being arranged by the Chair of the AWG LCA. See: Maldives Delegation to the Fifth Session of the Ad-Hoc Working Group on Long-Term Cooperative Action, Proposed Draft Wording to Be Sent as National Submission to Be Included in the Negotiating Text Under Shared Vision (April 2009) <www.maldivesmission.ch/fileadmin/Pdf/Environment/Maldives_wording_AWG-LCA_April_09.pdf> accessed 22.10.2014. A text dated 22 June 2009 (FCCC/ AWGLCA/2009/INF.1) which was prepared by the chair of the AWG-LCA and designed to offer a departing point for the negotiations towards an Agreed Outcome at COP15 in Copenhagen, echoing viewpoints and suggestions suggested by Parties to the UNFCCC. The two draft provisions were: paragraph 2, reflecting proposals made by Small Island States, stating that adverse effects of climate change 'have a range of direct and indirect implications for the full and effective enjoyment of human rights including the right to self determination, statehood, life, food and health and the right to a people not to be deprived of its own means of subsistence, particularly in developing countries'; and paragraph 22(a)(iii) adding a new condition or regulatory norm for adaptation measures: 'The respect for, protection and promotion of fundamental human rights and basic rights as outlined in the Universal Declaration of Human Rights, International Covenant on Economic, Social and Cultural Rights, International Covenant on Civil and Political Rights and other relevant conventions and treaties.' The text also explicitly incorporated the recognition reflected in the UN Human Rights Council's Resolution 10/1 (March 2009) that the adverse 'effects of climate change will be felt most acutely by those segments of the population who are already in vulnerable situations owing to such factors as geography, poverty, gender, age, indigenous or minority status and disability', facilitating the turn of standpoint and attention, from authorities and markets to individuals and societies affected by climate change.

27 M. Limon, 'Human Eights and Climate Change: Constructing a Case for Political Action' (2009) 33(2) *Harvard Environmental Law Review* 439–476, 461.

28 Ibid., pp. 460–461.

climate justice, and we cannot ensure climate justice without the inclusion of human rights into the UNFCCC process.

What human rights application to the climate change regime can positively bring, is an expansion of the mandate and legal reach of the laws in question. For instance, by the principle that wants the States obligations to not stop at their own borders, meaning that States have a distinctive obligation to screen and regulate the conduct of private bodies within their reach, even if these entities are operating abroad. This is exceptionally essential in the paradigm of climate change, where the direct roots of harm commonly originate in private business undertakings. Before proceeding to the next section of this paper, it is fair to mention the latest developments deriving from the Paris Climate Conference, the 21st Session of the Conference of the Parties (COP21), which took place in December 2015. The legally-binding agreement that was produced from COP21 fell short to the expectations of activists, human rights scholars, and other interested groups. In the agreement the terms human rights can be found only twice. Once in the first page, in the proposal by the President, in the draft decision –/CP.21, and a second time where the same statement is being adopted, namely it is stated that:

> 'Acknowledging that climate change is a common concern of humankind, Parties should, when taking action to address climate change, respect, promote and consider their respective obligations on human rights, the right to health, the rights of indigenous peoples, local communities, migrants, children, persons with disabilities and people in vulnerable situations and the right to development, as well as gender equality, empowerment of women and intergenerational equity'.[29]

Unfortunately this is the only time human rights are mentioned in the 2015 Paris Agreement. Some argue that 'something is better than nothing'; however it does not seem to be very convincing as an argument especially when one considers the issues at stake. Nonetheless, it is a step towards the right direction, and this needs to be acknowledged.

3. CLIMATE CHANGE AND HUMAN RIGHTS: REASONS OF SILENCE

It is no secret that the human rights at stake are very difficult to enforce in practice. climate change disturbs categories of human rights that have already problematic enjoyment, since in practice weak application systems exist under international law – for instance, social and economic rights; the rights of

29 United Nations Framework Convention on Climate Change (12.12.2015). Paris Agreement: FCCC/CP/2015/L.9/Rev.1 <http://unfccc.int/resource/docs/2015/cop21/eng/l09r01.pdf> accessed 12.2015.

migrants; and rights protections during conflicts.[30] With the abstract idea of the rights of future generations being on the top of the ladder, which it might make sense in theory, but in practice is a whole different utopic proposition. In practice even rights with solid safeguards, such as rights to life and to property, cannot be claimed through their customary application and enforcement methods, since the damages caused by climate change cannot be attributed directly in our existing legal systems, which are build upon an allocation of blame framework.

On the same train of thought, to constitute extraterritorial responsibility is another challenging task, since human rights law traditionally places the primary duty to act, in a case that rights are infringed, on the claimant's government. However in the case of climate change, responsibility for harming effects in the most weak and vulnerable states, the restoration of justice and the protection of rights, becomes a rather complicated issue, and regularly this function is assumed by another government, or an international institution. The universality of human rights law is not as powerful in practice as it is in theory, in other words, it cannot easily extend accountability across international borders.[31] Likewise, local culpability is very hard to be established. Although poor countries are not major emitters of greenhouse gases, is anticipated that they are likely to suffer more from the harmful effects of climate change, and also the severity and consequences of these effects will be more detrimental given their inability to adapt.

It seems to me important to highlight that 'undeveloped' countries have fewer resources, and therefore their inadequacies in protecting the basic human rights of their citizens have engendered the principle of 'progressive realisation' of those rights under international law. However, it is possible that climate change will lead to a progressive weakening of those equivalent rights. So instead of moving forward and making progress as far as rights protection is concerned, we are basically losing ground. According to a very interesting approach,

---

30 Some human rights bodies, notably the European Court of Human Rights, have found rights violations due to environmental impacts, including of the right to health. In a recent case, *Öneryıldız v. Turkey*, no. 48939/99, ECHR 2004, the Court found against Turkey for failing to act on an environmental impact assessment, and for contributing to deaths caused by a methane explosion.

31 Legal precedent suggests that states have responsibility for: (i) state actions taken in other countries; (ii) human rights protections in countries where they exercise 'effective control'; and (iii) some violations committed abroad by private actors who fall under their jurisdiction. See, for example, *Lopez Burgos v. Uruguay*, HRC Comm. No. R12/52 (1979), Views of 29 July 1981; *Legal Consequences of the Construction of a Wall in the Occupied Palestinian Territory*, ICJ Advisory Opinion of 9 July 2004; *Coard et al. v. United States*, IACHR Case No. 10.951, Reports No. 109/99, 29 September 1999; *Banković v. Belgium*, no. 52207/99, ECHR 2001. However, the case law is sparse and its applicability to climate-related harms is unclear. Alternative mechanisms involving 'long-arm' domestic jurisdiction – such as the US Alien Tort Claims Act – may be of limited value. Although state responsibility for extraterritorial violations of social and economic rights has not been widely discussed, the particular harms caused by global warming may generate plausible claims of this kind.

human rights is a project for centuries, and requires strategic steps in order to progressively realise the proposition of 'human rights for all, everywhere and forever', part of this process as Manfred Nowak wisely expressed it, is the prevention of human rights violations, which can be an important human rights instrument in the future: 'Prevention that also means to address the root causes of systematic human rights violations.'[32] It is common sense that if a government is genuinely not able to ensure and provide basic human rights for its people, any form of accountability for this shortage would be in vain and in a way even unfair, consequently it will certainly be impossible to hold this government liable for conditions it did not generate.[33]

There is also the context of emergency conditions, which are associated with rules generated by sovereignty and national security, and are cases that constrain and limit the function of human rights law. One could argue that climate change could fall within the purposes of emergency conditions. In such an argument it is important to clarify that international human rights law, just as national constitutional law, customarily permits the interruption of human rights, and 'puts them on ice'.[34] The conflict of rights, conversely, between different parties is also an expected problem, however, the conflict and struggles in legal cases of that nature, does not come as a surprise to international legal practitioners.

The legal reasoning above is not insignificant. A necessity exists to recognise the dichotomy between formal and substantive justice. The firm canon of human rights law *versus* the soft-law, policy-orientated, political agreement with weaker legal enforceability of the UNFCCC, and the climate justice regime. 'Equity' in the UNFCCC, is not as strong as the 'equality' in human rights law, similarly the distinctions in the UNFCCC between 'Annex I' and 'non-Annex I' countries, as a method, contradict the universal human rights legal approach which is imposing obligations to all countries irrespective of their special conditions. Climate change law and policy develops at a very slow pace, and it is observable that the philosophy guiding its path is characterised by compromise, political double standards and economic interests. In the same breath I need to note that: 'it is a common practice of the law-makers in international law, to use broad language, in order to achieve consensus and "signatures" by States; while the most common side effect of this broad language, is that the law becomes unclear as to what it actually commands.'[35]

32 M. Nowak, *Introduction to the Human Rights Regime*, The Raoul Wallenberg Institute For Human Rights Library, Martinus Nijhoff Publishers, Leiden-Boston 2003, p. 341.

33 Certain vulnerable countries are developing into bigger GHG emitters, for example China, India and Brazil. Hence, the importance and relevance of human rights law will depend on the domestic legal texts and safeguarding capabilities of human rights rules in the States in question. Variables that change significantly from country to country.

34 For accounts of the applicability of human rights during emergencies see IASC (2006) and OHCHR (2003), chapter 16.

35 Z. Aliozi, 'Human Rights Law Review: Article 4 of the UNFCC 1992' *Climate Emergency Institute* (November 2013) <www.climateemergencyinstitute.com/uploads/ZoiUNFCCCArt4 – HumanRights-Nov2013.pdf> accessed 08.2015.

Human rights law is applicable and appropriate to climate change since the latter affects the former, and also for predictive reasons. Harm caused by climate change will eventually result in more people that are negatively affected turning to human rights language, and enforcement mechanisms for protection, just like in the *Inuit* case. This is a new legal paradox, and there is not sufficient legal precedent to guide the evolution of the unification of these two regimes. Thus, it seems to me, that this is why a great and urgent duty is imposed on academia, to work on these questions, produce research and knowledge, and assist in the development of the climate justice regime.

4. CONCLUSIVE REMARKS

Climate change must be addressed in earnest urgency, and this requires measures that go beyond the existing Kyoto Protocol. It is critical to ensure that climate change is conceived in a broader manner that goes beyond the environmental and economic dimensions that have been central to the existing regime. Giving a central place to human vulnerability and incorporating human rights language in climate change law is crucial. This must be achieved alongside a broader rethinking of the place of differential treatment in the climate justice's regime, to ensure that it better reflects countries' and peoples' vulnerabilities in the future.

As discussed in the introduction, we need to use the terms denial, denialism and denialist responsibly, and acknowledge their different nature. In that sense, denialism is the refusal to accept well-established theory, law, fact or evidence, while denial refers to the action of denying. Denialism, refers to a system of ideas, systematic in nature, and requires by definition a collective action. The denialist, however, which is a derivative of denialism, fully dismisses factual truths – truth that from a philosophical perspective has epistemological concerns, but from a scientific viewpoint offers the only truth.

Nevertheless, these three terms are different and cannot be treated as referring to the same concept. Denialism as a terminological construction, is a synthetic term, comprised of two synthetics, while as said above, the suffix –ism, which comes from the Greek [ισμός], is indicating belief, theory, or principle; and denial refers to a negative reply to another's request or to the action of denying something.

There is a plethora of issues that my paper is just touching upon, or due to the lack of space are not even mentioned. But the need I stressed in my introduction for further research in the humanities, my call for clarifications regarding the terms and language we use in this field, and consequently the theoretical foundations on which we are basing our discourses, is backed up by strong justifications of the most urgent type. Denialism seems to have grown into a virus based on pseudo-science, questionable political motives fuelled by neoliberal ideas, whose sole purpose, it seems, in placing obstacles in the progress of climate justice, is the perpetuation of their carbon-based economies and their financial benefits.

No reasonable legal mind can deny, that the human rights enforcement and complaint procedures can only be beneficial as utensils, in restoring inadequate environmental rights safeguarding: 'as compared to efforts to incorporate a right to environment in human rights treaties'.[36] This is a way to escape the obstacles rising from abstract questions such as: 'what is meant by a healthy environment'. As it has been stressed numerous times in this paper, we have in our disposal a better structured body of supporting institutions for the implementation of these rules; and, at the end of the day, there is a more efficient way to administer justice, since there is the possibility for victims to file a complaint, be heard, and seek redress.

Some legal scholars advocate for the need to re-focus on the procedural and substantive rights and the paramount role they play in linking human rights and the environment. In doing so, one needs to look no further than, the freedom of information provisions enshrined in Principle 10 of the Rio Declaration and in other human rights instruments, such as Article 10 of the European Convention on Human Rights and Fundamental Freedoms.[37] Substantive rights also provide a legal basis for litigation based on environmental concerns as illustrated by the use of Article 8 (right to privacy) of the European Human Rights Convention.[38] Even these scholars, however, admit that to speak of 'a human right to the environment' is a rather problematic argument, especially when we take into account the 'balancing it with other human rights'.[39]

In conclusion, the area of climate change has an inherent crucial urgency that justifies the calls for necessary further research through a multidisciplinary methodology, as well as for deeper examination of the links between climate change and human rights claims, equity for future generations, of the problem arising from the questions on sustainable development, and the vulnerability principle in legal terms. There are questions relating to the dominance of climate change in environmental law, and the debates on Climate and international justice. It should also be highlighted that human rights appear to have a more evident role in each succeeding rights-sensitive suggestion on climate change. The relevant negotiations of the law-making global organs have developed discussion agendas based predominantly on a utilitarian philosophical basis,

---

36 R. Picolotti and D. Taillant, *Linking Human Rights and Environment*, University of Arizona Press, Arizona University 2003, p. 1.

37 This formed the ground for bringing a complaint before the European Court of Human Rights in the famous case: *Guerra v. Italy*, no. 14967/89, ECHR 1998.

38 *López Ostra v. Spain*, no. 16798/90, ECHR 1994.

39 R. Picolotti and D. Taillant, *Linking Human Rights and Environment*, University of Arizona Press, Arizona University 2003, p. 22.

and with a consensus built upon a seemingly mutual understanding of the issues in question, which it seems to me are dependent on cost–benefit and other welfare hypothesising paths. To date it is observable that the negotiating States have utilised human rights language principally for its normative value, to boost paradigms of distributional justice, but without admitting its status as applicable positive international law.

Ideally, the current attitudes should employ human rights vocabulary to support a fairer international climate justice system. However, to date there has been a failure to undertake an examination of the in-depth specific human rights damages arising from climate change, or to guarantee the inclusion of human rights rules into the relevant climate change law. At the end of the day, they call for human rights in order to move uncertain action on climate change policies, instead of supporting climate justice action in order to prevent human rights costs.[40]

Scanning for human rights language is, undeniably not the strongest tool for analysis and examination, since it is rather a poor diagnostic tool. However, the preliminary findings of such an analytical exercise are indicative of the unjustified absence of human rights language, which is a well-established legal structure that as all the evidence suggests, ought to be part of the climate justice regime with a more active role. All the requirements for justifying such an inclusion are present in the climate change phenomenon, for example, the harm to human beings' rights enjoyment by acts that could otherwise been avoided. climate change has a human source, since it is partly anthropogenic, and this contributory connection makes climate change an area of study uniquely suitable for human rights assessment.

My main argument is that human rights law is applicable, because the human-made impacts of climate change cause human rights violations, and hence, a human rights approach can be beneficial when dealing with climate change. The human rights context redirects the analysis of the phenomenon in its essential effects on humankind, and since climate change is about suffering, is connected with the harm humans are doing to nature. Numerous populations experience the adverse effects of warming temperatures, yet few solutions have been available to them to date. The human rights regime can offer a solution to these injustices, by providing the raw materials for constructing an interconnected climate justice legal structure.

In summary, the future of climate justice depends on the inclusion of human rights. We need immediate action in order to prevent disaster scenarios. The human rights regime can offer to climate justice the best possible framework

40 The adaptation funding calls, as 'compensation' for harms inflicted by the actions of the Annex I countries. In this line of reasoning, they call for human rights as an ethical rather than legal imperative. See, for example, Oxfam International, 'Adapting to Climate Change: What's Needed in Poor Countries and Who Should Pay' (2007) 104 *Oxfam, Briefing Paper.*

for accountability, law-enforcing tools, individual and collective justice claims, and the real and actual implementation of environmental law. climate change discourses, should not be guided solely by environmental law, politics and in the worst-case scenario by economic interests. As a human-inflicted harm to other human beings, it must be addressed as bearing responsibility.

If we bring human rights standards into our climate justice's future development, then it will be easier to identify those that are under threat and how to protect them. climate change texts, show up a myriad failings in our existing established design, including the lack of human rights mechanisms. Tackling these drawbacks will involve reform of the global policies, from information gathering and collective decision making, and from law making to practice and enforcement, to resource distribution.

According to the Universal Declaration of human rights, 'everyone is entitled to a social and international order in which [their] rights and freedoms … can be fully realized'. climate change interrupts this process and the realisation and enjoyment of fundamental human rights.

human rights by essence and definition place limits and barriers to what governments and powerful corporations can do. This is what human rights can bring to the climate justice arena and accordingly contribute to tackling, preventing and minimising climate change's harmful effects on humankind. Things should be called by their name, and the fact is that today we are witnessing the ultimate violation of the human rights of the most vulnerable people. It has been scientifically proven that the area of climate change has an inherent crucial urgency; that climate change and human rights claims are strongly connected; that equity for future generations is a defining legal principle; as well as the necessity to acknowledge clearly, firmly, and decisively, that the ultimate human rights violation of mankind's known history will be the only thing 'flourishing' due to anthropogenic climate change.

The science has been clear about the threats we are collectively facing, there is no other option than to work together in preventing the catastrophic consequences that human-made climate change brings. In the words of Mary Robinson: 'We have to do it, together with work on sustainable development goals, and we have to do it in 2015.' We all share responsibility for our home's well being, sustainable management, our planet's survival, and for the right to life of future generations.

It is true that: 'We are the first generation to feel the impact of climate change, and the last generation that can do something about it.'[41]

[41] Jay Inslee, the 63-year-old governor of Washington State, USA (since January 2013) in the nine-part documentary 'Years of Living Dangerously' on climate change that premiered on 13 April 2014 on the premium TV network Showtime.

CHAPTER XXI

A STATE IN DENIAL

The 'Intentional' Sexual Transmission of HIV in South Africa

Annelize NIENABER

The call for papers for the Maastricht conference on 'Denialism and Human Rights' referred to Thabo Mbeki, former South African President: 'After having rejected the scientific wisdom about AIDS, former South African President Thabo Mbeki and his government were directly responsible for many avoidable deaths according to research by Harvard University' (*The Guardian*, 2008).

On the face of it, present-day South Africa has moved beyond this kind of AIDS denialism, with the present government embracing scientific approaches to HIV prevention and treatment. However, I argue that AIDS denialism is still very present in South Africa, especially in our courts' approach to the 'intentional' transmission of HIV to sexual partners. This paper, therefore, examines the implications of the recent North Gauteng High Court decision in *Phiri v. S.* for potential charges regarding the wrongful transmission of HIV, and questions the appropriateness of the court's decision in the context of public health efforts to curb the HIV epidemic.

I employ Stanley Cohen's analysis of the elementary forms of denial as a basis of my argument that *Phiri v. S.* is an instance where the South African courts, when they should have affirmed human rights, instead provided for denialist defence mechanisms, so facilitating the denial of the human rights of those infected and affected by HIV and AIDS in South Africa.

1. INTRODUCTION

On the face of it, present-day South Africa has moved beyond the kind of AIDS denialism that was espoused by former President Thabo Mbeki. The current South African government embraces scientific approaches to HIV prevention and treatment and South Africa presently has the largest HIV antiretroviral programme in the world, despite isolated concerns regarding delivery.

Nevertheless, notwithstanding these advances, a form of AIDS denialism is still very present in South Africa, especially in our courts' approach to the 'intentional' transmission of HIV to sexual partners. This paper, therefore, examines the implications of the recent North Gauteng High Court decision in *Phiri v. S.* for potential charges regarding the wrongful transmission of HIV, and questions the appropriateness of the court's decision in the context of public health efforts to curb the HIV epidemic. I begin the discussion by outlining Stanley Cohen's theory of denial, highlighting the different kinds of denialism he describes. Next, I provide a short outline of the different forms and definitions of fault in South African criminal law in the context of HIV transmission, as these are pertinent to the issues raised in the case. Then follows an outline of the facts and the North Gauteng High Court's decision in *Phiri v. S.*, after which the wisdom of the court's decision on the facts is questioned. I argue that the court's decision in *Phiri v. S.* exemplifies Cohen's notion of implicatory denial, as it is evidence of a disjuncture between cognition and action. I conclude the discussion by arguing that the judgment in the case has disastrous consequences for public health efforts regarding HIV prevention in South Africa, and that, although intended to protect human rights, it instead violates human rights.

2. STANLEY COHEN'S STATES OF DENIAL

In his treatise on the denial of human rights entitled *States of Denial: Knowing About Atrocities and Suffering*, Stanley Cohen sketches three possibilities as regards what exactly is being 'denied' – these are literal, interpretive and implicatory.[1] Literal denial is the 'assertion that something did not happen or is not true'.[2] Former President Thabo Mbeki's denial that HIV causes AIDS fits this form of denial – Mbeki simply rejected the scientific wisdom about AIDS as untrue.[3] The second form of denial – interpretive denial – is when the 'raw facts' are 'given a different meaning from what seems apparent to others'.[4] Cohen provides the example of the killing of civilians that is called 'collateral damage',

---

1 S. Cohen, *States of Denial Knowing about Atrocities and Suffering*, Polity Press, Cambridge 2001, p. 7.

2 Ibid.

3 For an enlightening account of former South African President Thabo Mbeki's stance of HIV, see P. Fouri, *The political management of HIV and AIDS in South Africa: One burden too many?*, Palgrave Macmillan, New York 2006.

4 S. Cohen, *States of Denial Knowing about Atrocities and Suffering*, Polity Press, Cambridge 2001, p. 7.

or torture which is called 'moderate physical pressure'.[5] Words are changed or technical jargon is used to disguise or deny the true state of affairs.[6]

A third form of denial is implicatory denial. In this form of denial, there is 'no attempt to deny either the facts or their conventional interpretation'.[7] Rather, what are denied are the implications of the facts – whether they be psychological, political or moral.[8] Cohen explains implicatory denial further: 'Unlike literal or interpretive denial, knowledge itself is not at issue, but doing the "right" thing with this knowledge. These are matters of mobilization, commitment and involvement'.[9] It is this third form of denial that is relevant in the context of the discussion of the case below – as we shall see, in South Africa it is no longer being denied that HIV causes AIDS (literal denial), but it is doing the 'right' thing with this knowledge that is at issue. Below I turn to a discussion of the intentional sexual transmission of HIV, outlining the different criminal law elements of fault.

3. THE CRIMINAL LAW ELEMENT OF FAULT IN RELATION TO HIV TRANSMISSION TO SEXUAL PARTNERS

Most legal practitioners and laypersons agree, if someone deliberately or intentionally transmits the Human Immunodeficiency Virus (HIV) to a sexual partner, that person deserves legal sanction.[10] South Africa has opted not to establish a separate set of criminal offences to criminalise HIV transmission in this context,[11] unlike several other African countries that have established separate crimes for the intentional or negligent transmission of HIV.[12] In South

5 Ibid., p. 8.
6 Ibid.
7 Ibid.
8 Ibid.
9 Ibid., p. 9.
10 Cases where HIV was deliberately transmitted are rare. See R. Bunnell et al., 'Changes in sexual risk behaviour and risk of HIV transmission after antiretroviral therapy and prevention interventions in rural Uganda' (2006) 20 *AIDS* 85–92 and G. Marks, N. Crepaz and R.S. Janssen, 'Meta-analysis of high-risk sexual behavior in persons aware and unaware they are infected with HIV in the United States: implications for HIV prevention programs' (2005) 10 *Journal of Acquired Immune Deficiency Syndromes* 446–453.
11 'Project 85 Fifth interim report on aspects of the law relating to AIDS: The need for a statutory offence aimed at harmful HIV-related behaviour' 2001 *South Africa Law Commission* <www.justice.gov.za/salrc/reports/r_prj85_harmb_2001apr.pdf> accessed on 19.01.2015.
12 For example, in Benin, Botswana, Lesotho, Malawi, Mali, Niger, Sierra Leone, Uganda, Tanzania, Togo, Zambia and Zimbabwe; in this regard, see P.M. Eba, 'Pandora's box: The criminalisation of HIV transmission or exposure in SADC countries' in: F. Viljoen and S. Precious (eds.), *Human rights under threat: Four perspectives on HIV, AIDS, and the law in Southern Africa*, PULP, Pretoria 2007, pp. 29–34; M. Pieterse, 'Disentangling illness, crime and morality: Towards a rights-based approach to HIV prevention in Africa' (2011)

Africa, policy considerations have prompted the application of existing criminal law principles in cases of the intentional or negligent transmission of HIV to sexual partners.[13]

Up to now, surprisingly few civil or criminal cases that relate to the wrongful or unlawful transmission of HIV during sexual intercourse have reached our courts. As I have pointed out elsewhere[14] this is due to a variety of factors, most importantly, however, in the context of the transmission of communicable diseases such as HIV, that it is difficult to prove the element of causation – specifically factual causation – required for criminal and delictual liability.[15] The best-known case concerning the intentional or negligent transmission of HIV to a sexual partner that has been reported is a delictual action for damages, namely, *Venter v. Nel*.[16] Regrettably, *Venter v. Nel* is considered 'bad' law because the claimant's action was unopposed and judgement by default was granted.[17]

South African criminal law distinguishes between two forms of fault: intention and negligence.[18] As a form of fault, negligence is an attitude or conduct by a person which reflects 'carelessness, thoughtlessness or imprudence because, by giving insufficient attention to his actions he failed to adhere to the standard of care legally required of him'.[19] As the accused in the case under discussion was charged with attempted murder, for which intention and not negligence is required, I here leave the discussion of negligence and below focus on intention.

The elements of the crime attempted murder as outlined by our courts are unlawfulness, intention (to kill) and an attempt.[20] Attempted murder, then, may

---

1 *African Human Rights Law Journal* 57; and R. Pearshouse, 'A Human Rights Analysis of the N'djamena model legislation on AIDS and HIV specific legislation in Benin, Guinea, Guinea Bissau, Mali, Niger, Sierra Leone and Togo' 2007 *Canadian HIV/AIDS Legal Network* <www.aidslaw.ca/site/wp-content/uploads/2013/03/LN_HumanRtLegislnRvw_en.pdf> accessed 19.01.2015.

13 Regarding the academic debate in South Africa about the possible criminalisation of sexual HIV transmission, see e.g. C. Van Wyk, 'The need for a new statutory offence aimed at harmful HIV related behaviour: The general public interest perspective' (2000) *Codicillus* 2; F. Viljoen, 'Stigmatising HIV/AIDS, stigmatising Sex? A reply to Professor Van Wyk' (2000) *Codicillus* 11.

14 A. Nienaber, 'Liability for the wrongful transmission of communicable diseases in South African prisons: What about HIV?' (2013) 28 *Southern African Public Law* 163, 164.

15 Ibid., pp. 163–164.

16 *Venter v. Nel* [1997] 4 SA 1014 (D).

17 The plaintiff sought damages from a previous sexual partner who had infected her with HIV during consensual sexual intercourse. This case does not provide a good precedent on the difficulties when establishing the element of causation (or even fault) in the case of wrongful HIV infection as the action was unopposed and default judgment was granted.

18 J.M. Burchell, *Principles of Criminal Law*, 3rd ed., Juta, Kenwyn 2006, p. 545; C.R. Snyman, *Criminal Law*, 5th ed., LexisNexis Butterworths, Durban 2008, p. 159.

19 J. Neethling, J.M. Potgieter and P.J. Visser, *Law of delict*, LexisNexis Butterworths, Durban 2006, p. 116.

20 *S. v. Ndlovu* [1984] ZASCA 84; 1984 (3) SA 23(A). At 26 I: '*Die bestanddele van poging tot moord wat per se ŉ misdaad is, is wederregtelikheid, opset en ŉ pogingshandeling. Die*

be defined as the unlawful intentional attempted killing or causing the death of another human being.[21] Causality is not an element of attempted murder:[22]

> 'It is now generally accepted that a conviction for attempt will lie even when the act constituting the attempt is frustrated or rendered impossible by circumstances not within the contemplation of the perpetrator. ... This view rests on the premise that criminal law has as its aim the protection [of] public and social interests. Therefore, the question of the criminality of an attempt will depend in part on the actor's intent and in part on the degree of actual danger to social or public interest arising from such acts.'

Fault, in the form of intention, needs to be proved beyond reasonable doubt for an accused to be guilty of attempted murder.[23] Intention, or *dolus*, is present when a person commits an act 'while his will is directed towards the commission of the act or the causing of the result; in the knowledge of the existence of the circumstances mentioned in the definitional elements of the relevant crime; and in the knowledge of the unlawfulness of the act'.[24] Intention consists of two elements: a cognitive (or intellectual) element and a conative (volitional or voluntative) element.[25] Three forms of intention exist: direct intention; indirect intention; and *dolus eventualis*.[26] To prove a charge of attempted murder, the state needs to prove the presence of any one of the three forms of intention in the actions of the accused.

In the case of direct intention, or *dolus directus*, the person is directing his will towards achieving a result (the result or act is her goal).[27] In the context of the transmission of HIV to a sexual partner, *dolus directus* is present in instances where the HIV-positive partner has sexual intercourse with someone with the direct intention of transmitting the virus. In other words, his aim is expressly to infect the other person and he is directing his will towards achieving that result;

---

strafbedreiging is gerig teen die wederregtelike opsetlike bedreiging van die lewe van ŉ mens. Die beskermde regsbelang is die lewe van ŉ mens. ŉ Geykte voorbeeld van voltooide poging tot moord is waar A sy vuurwapen op B rig met die bedoeling om hom te dood, en die skoot afvuur wat B mis of verwond sodat B die wederregtelike aanslag op sy lewe oorleef. A het alles van sy kant gedoen om B te vermoor maar die moord is onvoltooid. Die opset om die slagoffer te vermoor kan afgelei word uit die pogingshandeling asook ander aanvaarbare bewysmateriaal. Die wederrregtelikheid van die pogingshandeling is geleë in die bedreiging van ŉ regsbelang, naamlik die lewe van ŉ mens'.

21 J.M. Burchell, *Principles of Criminal Law*, 3rd ed., Juta, Kenwyn 2006, p. 159; C.R. Snyman, *Criminal Law*, 5th ed., LexisNexis Butterworths, Durban 2008, p. 423.

22 *S. v. Ndlovu* [1984] ZASCA 84; 1984 (3) SA 23(A), para. 28 A–C.

23 J.M. Burchell, *Principles of Criminal Law*, 3rd ed., Juta, Kenwyn 2006, p. 157; C.R. Snyman, *Criminal Law*, 5th ed., LexisNexis Butterworths, Durban 2008, p. 425.

24 C.R. Snyman, *Criminal Law*, 5th ed., LexisNexis Butterworths, Durban 2008, p. 181.

25 Ibid., p. 182.

26 J.M. Burchell, *Principles of Criminal Law*, 3rd ed., Juta, Kenwyn 2006, p. 157; C.R. Snyman, *Criminal Law*, 5th ed., LexisNexis Butterworths, Durban 2008, p. 425.

27 C.R. Snyman, *Criminal Law*, 5th ed., LexisNexis Butterworths, Durban 2008, p. 183.

towards infecting his partner. Thankfully, instances of the transmission of HIV in which direct intention is present, are rare.[28]

In the case of indirect intention, or *dolus indirectus*, the prohibited act or result is not the person's goal, but he realises, if he wants to achieve his goal, the prohibited act or result will of necessity materialise.[29] In the context of HIV transmission, the transmission of the virus is not the HIV-positive sexual partner's goal but he realises, if he wants to achieve his goal, the transmission of the virus will of necessity materialise. Put differently, this form of intention requires that the HIV-positive sexual partner must foresee, as a certainty, the transmission of the virus to his sexual partner and he must have reconciled himself to that certainty. Indirect intention differs from direct intention with regard to the sexual transmission of HIV in that, in the case of indirect intention, the HIV-positive partner does not specifically will the infection of the other partner as his aim, but foresees it (as a certainty) and reconciles himself to it. Of course, indirect intention in the context of the transmission of HIV during sexual intercourse will be almost impossible to establish: it is scientifically impossible to be sure that one will transmit the HIV virus during sexual intercourse. In fact, one's chances of transmitting the virus are as low as 0.04% per sexual encounter.[30] The certainty required for indirect intention to be present, then, is unlikely, if ever, to be established in the case of the sexual transmission of HIV.

The third form of intention, *dolus eventualis*, is most relevant to the sexual transmission of HIV in the case under discussion. *Dolus eventualis*, as a form of intention, may be defined as follows: the doer 'actively foresees'[31] the possibility that, in striving to attain his main aim, the unlawful act may be committed or the unlawful result may be caused, and reconciles himself to that possibility.[32] This form of intention requires that the HIV-positive sexual partner foresees the possibility of the infection of the other partner and reconciles himself to that possibility.[33] Although not directly willing his sexual partner's infection with HIV, he will have *reconciled* himself to the *possibility* that sexual intercourse may bring about his sexual partner's HIV infection.

---

28 See above note 1.

29 C.R. Snyman, *Criminal Law*, 5th ed., LexisNexis Butterworths, Durban 2008, p. 183.

30 This is for vaginal intercourse. Expressed as an estimated per-act probability of acquiring HIV from an infected source, by exposure act, the probability of acquiring HIV is as follows: For receptive anal intercourse: 138 per 10,000 exposures; for insertive anal intercourse: 11 per 10,000 exposures; for receptive penile-vaginal intercourse: 8 per 10,000 exposures; and for insertive penile-vaginal intercourse: 4 per 10,000 exposures. See 'HIV/AIDS Statistics overview: Transmission risk', Centers for Disease Control and Prevention, 2011 <www.cdc.gov/hiv/policies/law/risk.html> accessed 01.08.2014.

31 C.R. Snyman, *Criminal Law*, 5th ed., LexisNexis Butterworths, Durban 2008, p. 184.

32 Ibid.

33 Ibid.

It is important to distinguish *dolus eventualis* from negligence. In respect of negligence, the HIV-positive sexual partner does not foresee the eventuality of infecting the HIV-negative sexual partner, though he reasonably should have foreseen it, and, therefore, does not take the steps reasonably required of him to prevent the infection of his sexual partner. In the case of *dolus eventualis*, the HIV-positive sexual partner foresees the risk of infection and reconciles himself with that risk.

Whether the intentional transmission of HIV to a sexual partner during intercourse constitutes a criminal offence was considered by our courts in *S. v. Nyalungu.*[34] In *Nyalungu* it was established that conduct by a HIV-positive sexual partner who does not take measures to prevent transmission during sexual intercourse constitutes the necessary *mens rea* and amounts to attempted murder.[35] Below, the facts of *Phiri v. S.*[36] as well as the North Gauteng High Court's judgement in the matter are outlined, followed by conclusions regarding the potential impact of the Court's judgment upon a charge of the intentional transmission of HIV during sexual intercourse. Note that it is not the aim of this discussion to analyse the High Court's treatment of the element of fault in detail, but rather to examine the implications of the Court's judgment in respect of future litigation regarding the sexual transmission of HIV.

4. NORTH GAUTENG HIGH COURT'S JUDGMENT IN *PHIRI v. S.*

The case concerns an appeal to the North Gauteng High Court from the Piet Retief Regional Court, in which the appellant, Mphikeleli Lovers Phiri, was convicted of attempted murder and given a six-year prison sentence. The appellant was employed as a HIV counsellor at the complainant's local clinic.[37] They met when the complainant underwent a HIV test.[38] The complainant tested HIV-negative.[39] At that stage Phiri had been living with HIV for about three years and he was aware of his HIV-positive status.[40]

Subsequently, a relationship developed between the complainant and Phiri during which they had sexual intercourse on two occasions.[41] On neither occasion did Phiri use a condom, despite being requested to do so by the

34 *S. v. Nyalungu* [2013] 2 SACR 99 (T) 1. The case was reported only in 2013.
35 Ibid.
36 *Phiri v. S* [2013] ZAGPPHC 279 (08.08.2013).
37 Ibid., para. 2.
38 Ibid.
39 Ibid.
40 Ibid.
41 Ibid., para. 3.

complainant.[42] The complainant subsequently tested HIV-positive.[43] As she had had sex with no one but Phiri the complainant confronted him, whereupon Phiri apologised and asked for her 'forgiveness'.[44]

The only issue in dispute before the trial court was whether Phiri had used a condom during sexual intercourse.[45] After initially stating that he did not tell the complainant that he was HIV-positive, he changed his version during cross-examination and then stated that he had told the complainant that he was HIV-positive before they had intercourse for the first time and that he had used a condom on both occasions.[46] The trial court rejected Phiri's version of events and found him guilty of attempted murder.[47]

Before the North Gauteng High Court, the appellant alleged that the Regional Court had erred in its evaluation of the evidence and its application of the law, as he did not have the necessary *mens rea* to sustain a conviction of attempted murder.[48] No proof was tendered either in the trial court or the appeal court that the appellant in fact infected the claimant with HIV.

The North Gauteng High Court, per Makgoka J and Baloyi AJ, stressed that they cannot interfere with the trial court's finding on the facts (rejecting Phiri's version that he had used a condom on both occasions during sexual intercourse) as lacking in credibility and not being supported by the evidence.[49] In its judgment, the court did not specify why, in its mind, fault in the form of *dolus eventualis* was present in the appellant's behaviour. Instead, relying on *S. v. Nyalungu*, the court found that the appellant acted with intention, and merely stated:[50]

> 'It is to be borne in mind that the appellant was not convicted of having in fact transmitted HIV to the complainant. The State did not have to go that far. It was sufficient for a conviction on the count of attempted murder, to establish that the appellant, knowing that he was HIV positive, engaged in sexual intercourse with the complainant, whom she knew to be HIV negative, without any preventative measures. This entails the presence of *mens rea* in the form of *dolus eventualis*.'

The learned judges equally rejected the appellant's argument that he should have been found guilty not of attempted murder but of assault or assault with the intent to cause grievous bodily harm.[51] In this regard the court stressed

42 Ibid.
43 Ibid.
44 Ibid., para. 2.
45 Ibid., para. 4.
46 Ibid.
47 Ibid.
48 Ibid., para. 5.
49 Ibid., para. 9.
50 Ibid.
51 Ibid.

that there is still no cure for AIDS and infection with HIV is likely to result in a reduced lifespan.[52] The court further stated that it was established in *S. v. Nyalungu*[53] that conduct of this kind (sexual intercourse without a condom) constitutes attempted murder and not assault, and that the appellant was thus properly convicted of attempted murder in the trial court.[54]

As regards the appeal against the appellant's six-year prison sentence, the court rejected the appellant's argument that a six-year prison term is 'disturbingly inappropriate' for a first offender who is HIV-positive.[55] It was also contended that the trial court did not take sufficiently into account that the appellant and the complainant were in a relationship and, therefore, that there was no forced sexual intercourse[56] The judges rejected these arguments as well. They stated that this could rather be an aggravating factor, as was the fact that the appellant was a HIV and AIDS counsellor.[57] The North Gauteng High Court dismissed the appeal, and the appellant's conviction and sentence were confirmed.[58]

5. A STATE IN DENIAL: IMPLICATIONS OF CULPABILITY FOR THE UNLAWFUL TRANSMISSION OF HIV DURING SEXUAL INTERCOURSE

As said above, the discussion does not concern itself with the soundness of the Gauteng North High Court's finding or, specifically, the soundness of its approach regarding fault as a criminal element in cases concerning the sexual transmission of HIV, but rather with the possible consequences of the court's judgment for public health efforts to combat the HIV and AIDS epidemics, and how the judgement resonates with Stanley Cohen's exposition on the states of human rights denial.

Below I highlight the implications of the court's judgment for public health efforts to curb the HIV and AIDS epidemics in South Africa. I then indicate why, in my opinion, the court's judgment typifies Cohen's notion of implicatory denial, and I point to the consequences this holds for South Africa in its fight against HIV and AIDS.

---

52 Ibid.
53 *S. v. Nyalungu* [2013] 2 SACR 99 (T) 1.
54 *Phiri v. S.* [2013] ZAGPPHC 279 (08.08.2013), para. 9.
55 Ibid., para. 14.
56 Ibid., para. 15.
57 Ibid.
58 Ibid., paras. 10, 18–19.

A finding that fault in the form of *dolus eventualis* is present and also is sufficient for a conviction of attempted murder in cases concerning the sexual transmission of HIV if the HIV-positive sexual partner fails to wear a condom, on the face of it, sends a necessary warning to sexual partners to take preventive measures and so curb the spread of the HIV epidemic. Such a finding may be seen by many as a laudable attempt to curb the spread of the HIV epidemic. But let us consider whether the court's finding really advances public health efforts in the context of the HIV epidemic in South Africa.

As evidence was never presented either in the trial court or in the Gauteng High Court that the appellant actually infected the complainant (it was merely deduced that he infected her with HIV on her evidence that he was the only person she had had sexual intercourse with) and as, after all, causation is not an element to be proved for a conviction on a charge of attempted murder, the court's finding, in fact, is punishing mere *exposure* to HIV in the form of unprotected sex as attempted murder, rather than unprotected sex resulting in actual transmission. The appellant was found guilty and sentenced because he, on the evidence of the complainant, had unprotected sexual intercourse with her while being HIV-positive. In other words, it was not necessary to be proved that the appellant had in fact infected the complainant.

From the High Court's judgment, therefore, it is clear that for a conviction on a charge of attempted murder in cases of the alleged sexual transmission of HIV, it must be established beyond reasonable doubt: (a) the HIV-positive sexual partner knew that he was HIV-positive; and (b) that he had unprotected sex with the complainant knowing that he put that complainant at risk of infection. Such an approach has several limitations from a public health perspective. I discuss these in the following paragraphs.

First, HIV and AIDS are again stigmatised[59] or treated as 'exceptional' diseases:[60] there have been no cases reported where the intentional exposure of another person to other potentially deadly infectious diseases such as multi-drug-resistant tuberculosis, smallpox, cholera or Ebola has resulted

59 'Through stigmatisation social distinctions are enhanced. Stigma thus becomes part of the social struggle for power. Difference is transformed into inequality. Moreover, it is used to produce, legitimise and reproduce social inequalities by establishing difference and using difference thus constituted to ascertain where groups of people fit into the structures of power' (P.M. Eba, 'Stigma[ta]' (2008) *Aids Review 2007*, p. 12).

60 'AIDS exceptionalism' is the notion that the epidemic requires a response above and beyond 'normal' health interventions. Recently, AIDS exceptionalism came to refer to the disease-specific global response and the resources dedicated to addressing the epidemic. There has been a backlash against this exceptionalism, with critics claiming that HIV and AIDS receive a disproportionate amount of international aid and health funding. For more on so-called 'AIDS exceptionalism', see J.H. Smith and A. Whiteside, 'The history of AIDS exceptionalism' (2010) 13 *Journal of the International AIDS Society* 47, and P. Piot, 'AIDS: Exceptionalism revisited', lecture given at the London School of Economics and Political Science, 15.05.2008.

in successful convictions of attempted murder. HIV and AIDS are singled out for special legal sanction.

Much has been written about the motivations behind the stigmatisation of diseases, most notably the stigmatisation of HIV and AIDS. The stigmatisation of HIV and AIDS is viewed as aiming at conceptually separating those who are ill from the unaffected population, so externalising the threat of the disease and appeasing public fears of contagion.[61] Consequently, society is divided into a healthy 'us' and an infected 'them':[62] blame for infection is apportioned to those who are ill; 'healthy members of society can reassure themselves that they are safe against infection and justify their lack of compassion with those who have fallen ill'.[63] By employing criminal sanction, not only is HIV and AIDS stigmatised by the court but those who are ill may be blamed for spreading the disease. I return to this point below.

Second, the North Gauteng High Court's approach is unscientific as it fails to distinguish between different levels of risk per exposure to HIV – the Court found that mere exposure is enough for a conviction and ignored the fact that various factors, not just the use of a condom, can increase or decrease the transmission risk of HIV per exposure. For example, taking antiretroviral therapy can reduce the risk of an HIV-infected person transmitting the infection to another by as much as 96%.[64] Conversely, having a sexually transmitted infection or a high level of HI virus in the blood (which happens in early and late stages of HIV infection) may increase the transmission risk.[65] The High Court did not consider whether the appellant, in fact, was on antiretroviral therapy at the time of exposing the complainant to determine the risk of HIV transmission, only whether he wore a condom. In other jurisdictions, the question whether the accused is on antiretroviral therapy is an important consideration in determining guilt.[66]

Third, as indicated before, the motivation behind the court's judgment may well be to encourage safe sex practices amongst sexual partners and to encourage HIV-positive partners to disclose their status. The court is, in Cohen's words, attempting to do the 'right' thing. In South Africa, however, the disclosure of

61 M. Pieterse, 'Disentangling illness, crime and morality: Towards a rights-based approach to HIV prevention in Africa' (2011) 1 *African Human Rights Law Journal* 57, 60.

62 Ibid.

63 Ibid.

64 M.S. Cohen et al., 'HPTN 052 Study Team. Prevention of HIV-1 Infection with early antiretroviral therapy' (2011) 365(6) *New England Journal of Medicine* 493–505.

65 See 'HIV/AIDS Statistics overview: Transmission risk', Centers for Disease Control and Prevention, 2011 <www.cdc.gov/hiv/policies/law/risk.html> accessed 01.08.2014.

66 Such as Switzerland; see R. Gasquez, 'Pour la dépénalisation de l'exposition au VIH (For the Decriminalization of HIV Exposure)' (2009) *Plaidoyer* 4 <www.aidslex.org/site_documents/CR-0095F.pdf> accessed 01.08.2014. See, generally, 'Antiretroviral therapy and sexual transmission of HIV' 2008 *UNAIDS/WHO* <http://data.unaids.org/pub/PressStatement/2008/080201_hivtransmission_en.pdf> accessed 01.08.2014.

one's HIV status is not a simple matter. In South Africa, it may well be that sexual partners do not disclose their HIV-positive status because of the fear of violence or other serious negative consequences. On occasions, women living with HIV and AIDS are killed when they reveal their status, as in the well-publicised case of Gugu Dlamini, who was stoned to death by her neighbours.

South African women are worse hit by the epidemic than men, as a result of socio-economic factors, as well as biological factors.[67] Thus, it is likely that women, rather than men, will be charged with attempted murder for exposing their sexual partners to HIV infection. In some cases it may well be that they neglect to reveal their status, either because of economic dependency on their male partner, or because of their fear of violence and stigmatisation. Women who live with HIV and AIDS are stigmatised (sometimes they are even blamed for spreading HIV):[68]

> 'Moreover, HIV-positive women in these communities [Hammanskraal and Temba] are stigmatised as being prostitutes, or "loose women", or as having "invited" HIV infection to claim access to social grants.'

Stigmatisation leads to discrimination and a violation of equality:[69]

> 'The rights of people living with HIV/AIDS are often violated because of their presumed or known HIV status, causing them to suffer both the burden of the disease and the burden of discrimination. Stigmatisation and discrimination may affect the uptake of [antiretroviral] treatment, and may also affect employment, housing and other rights.'

Linked to the negative consequences of revealing one's status outlined above, is my fourth point of criticism against the North Gauteng High Court's judgment. In order to avoid being charged with attempted murder, many will refuse to be tested for HIV (as it is required for *dolus evenualis* that the HIV-positive sexual partner *foresees* the possibility of the infection of the other partner and

67 'Several anatomical and physiological characteristics of women and girls play a role in the transmission and acquisition of HIV. Since the female genital tract has a greater exposed area than the male genital tract, women may be prone to greater per exposure risk of HIV-infection. Coercive or forced sex can lead to microlesions (very small tears in the vagina) that facilitate entry of the virus. Young women, in particular, who have less mature tissue, are more susceptible to infection, as well as more susceptible to coercive sex' (IAVI, *Gender in HIV vaccine trials: Addressing challenges in developing countries*, IAVI, New York 2004, p. 2.

68 A. Alexander and M. Mbali, 'Beyond "bitches and prostitutes": Folding the materiality of gender and sexuality into rights-based HIV/AIDS interventions' in: F. Viljoen (ed.), *Righting stigma: Exploring a rights-based approach to addressing stigma*, AIDS and Human Rights Research Unit, Centre for Human Rights, Pretoria 2005, p. 51.

69 F. Zuberi, '"If you (be)come HIV-positive, you will lose your human rights" – HIV/AIDS stigma and human rights: A localised investigation of Hammanskraal communities' in: F. Viljoen (ed.), *Righting stigma: Exploring a rights-based approach to addressing stigma*, AIDS and Human Rights Research Unit, Centre for Human Rights, Pretoria 2005, p. 13.

reconciles himself to that possibility): if one is unaware of one's status, one is unable to foresee the infection of another during sexual intercourse. The North Gauteng High Court's judgment may actually be counter-productive and increase the spread of HIV: because of the fear of being charged with attempted murder many may not get tested for HIV, persist in unsafe sexual practices, and the epidemic will continue. Together with the stigmatisation of HIV, it contributes to the vulnerability of others to infection. A fear of the negative consequences of knowing one's status, criminal sanction and HIV-related stigma and discrimination discourage individuals infected with and affected by HIV from contacting health and social services.[70] It is in this context that we should see the High Court's judgment.

Finally, the North Gauteng High Court's judgment is contrary to public health studies which show that criminal law, because it assumes, incorrectly, that people engage in sexual intercourse as if reasoned, rational and informed behaviour, it entirely fails to deter high-risk conduct and, consequently, exposure to HIV.[71] In addition, punishing HIV transmission puts the blame for spreading the epidemic once again on HIV-positive people, absolving the rest of the population from taking measures to limit their exposure to the virus and, consequently, accelerating the spread of the epidemic.[72]

Stanley Cohen explains the cognitive 'process' of implicatory denial as follows: 'This is not a refusal to acknowledge reality, but a denial of its significance or implications'.[73] According to Cohen, denial includes cognition (where the facts are not acknowledged; typical in literal denial); morality (not recognising wrongness or responsibility; typical of interpretive denial); and action (not taking active steps in response to knowledge; typical of implicatory denial).[74] In the case of implicatory denial, then, there is a disjunction between cognition (which does take place in the case of implicatory denial) and the action that is called for by that cognition: in Cohen's words, '[u]nlike literal

70 Ibid.

71 UNAIDS, *Criminal law, public health and HIV transmission: A policy options paper*, 2002, p. 21; UNAIDS, *Policy brief on criminalisation of HIV transmission*, 2008, p. 4; P.M. Eba, 'Pandora's box: The criminalisation of HIV transmission or exposure in SADC countries' in: F. Viljoen and S. Precious (eds.), *Human rights under threat: Four perspectives on HIV, AIDS, and the law in Southern Africa*, PULP, Pretoria 2007, pp. 38–39; B.D. Adam et al., 'Effects of the criminalisation of HIV transmission in *Cuerrier* in men reporting unprotected sex with men' (2008) 23 *Canadian Journal of Law and Society* 157; R. Bunnell et al., 'Changes in sexual risk behaviour and risk of HIV transmission after antiretroviral therapy and prevention interventions in rural Uganda' (2006) 20 *AIDS* 85–92; and G. Marks, N. Crepaz and R.S. Janssen, 'Meta-analysis of high-risk sexual behavior in persons aware and unaware they are infected with HIV in the United States: implications for HIV prevention programs' (2005) 10 *Journal of Acquired Immune Deficiency Syndromes* 446–453.

72 F. Viljoen, 'Stigmatising HIV/AIDS, stigmatising Sex? A reply to Professor Van Wyk' (2000) *Codicillus* 11, 14.

73 S. Cohen, *States of Denial Knowing about Atrocities and Suffering*, Polity Press, Cambridge 2001, p. 9.

74 Ibid.

or interpretive denial, knowledge itself is not at issue, but doing the "right" thing with this knowledge. These are matters of mobilization, commitment and involvement'.[75] The South African government, here acting through the judiciary, realises (cognition) that it is facing a devastating HIV epidemic that requires drastic and effective public health efforts, but fails to do the 'right' thing with that knowledge (take the correct action), as pointed out in my discussion above of the potentially devastating implications and consequences of the court's judgment in *Phiri v. S.*

What, then, is the motivation behind the South African government's AIDS denial (or failure to take appropriate action)?

AIDS denial in the context of the case discussed above may very well be an ill-reasoned and desperate response to the sheer extent of the HIV crisis in South Africa. By criminalising the (intentional) sexual transmission of HIV, the court is being seen as doing something concrete – taking action – in the battle against HIV. Unfortunately, the criminalisation of HIV transmission may also be a way for the government to avoid addressing the challenges posed by the massive scale of the HIV epidemic in South Africa. Instead of dealing with the daunting political and socio-economic challenges posed by HIV and AIDS, the court in *Phiri v. S.* sought and found an easy way out – we should apportion blame to, and incarcerate those responsible for spreading the virus. In this manner, AIDS denial provides a potential 'solution' for the South African government faced with a devastating crisis. The reasoning behind the court's judgment in *Phiri v. S.* may well be as follows: Everyone who intentionally spreads HIV will be removed from society and the spread of the virus will be curbed in this way. This absolves the government from other – more costly and time-consuming – public health-orientated HIV-prevention campaigns: it is not necessary to spend money on costly campaigns, expensive antiretrovirals or other treatment modalities, there is a much easier solution to the problem – we send everybody who spreads the virus to gaol, with the added benefit of sending a message to other members of society that this may happen to them too, should they transgress.

As pointed out above, Cohen's categories of denial all are based on refusal: A refusal to do something, whether it is to know, recognise, or to act. Because the scientific evidence that HIV causes AIDS is not disputable, the court in *Phiri v. S.* disavows the moral or legal implications that flow from it, as well as its (or the South African government's) responsibility to act in a certain way to curb the epidemic. With its judgment, the court inserts a shield of easy solutions between the facts (the transmission of HIV during sexual intercourse) and the actions that are required of the state to stop this (an effective and costly public health campaign).

Of course, the court's judgment in *Phiri v. S.* is but one form of AIDS denial – since the beginning of the HIV and AIDS epidemics in South Africa

75 Ibid.

we have seen other examples of HIV or AIDS denial that are implicatory in nature: For example, in South Africa the spread of HIV is sometimes presented as a socio-economic problem, embodied in former President Thabo Mbeki's words that 'poverty causes AIDS'. In this case, the government has a cover for not dealing with the spread of HIV as an urgent or immediate issue. The government's obligation is reduced to slowly or progressively improving the material conditions of South Africans, within its available resources (as enshrined in the Constitution of the Republic of South Africa, 1996). It is true that social conditions are contributing factors to the spread of HIV, but again they are used to absolve government of its responsibility to take urgent action.[76]

I pointed out above in my discussion of the implications of the court's judgment in *Phiri v. S.*, that by employing criminal sanction, not only are HIV and AIDS stigmatised by the court, but those who are ill may be blamed for spreading the disease. This is one of Cohen's most obvious forms of denial: he calls this the 'denial of the victim'.[77] He writes: 'In political atrocities, denial of the victim is more ideologically rooted in historically indeterminate narratives of blaming the other. ... They deserve to be punished; justice is on our side'.[78] In the context of the court's judgment, this form of denial is along the lines of 'everybody should know that that they can get infected with HIV through unprotected sexual intercourse. If they have unprotected sexual intercourse it is their fault'.

As remarked above, the court's judgment in *Phiri v. S.* substitutes well-founded and effective public health campaigns with a strategy that relies on the criminalisation of unprotected sexual intercourse. By finding the appellant guilty of attempted murder for infecting the complainant with HIV during unprotected sexual intercourse, the court hopes to reduce the spread of HIV (which, of course, is impossible to achieve in this way, as pointed out above).

To my mind, of Cohen's three forms of denial, implicatory denial probably is the most difficult form of denial to resist, especially when perpetrated by structures of the state – the courts – as is seen in the case under discussion. Instead of relying on punishing the perpetrator, the court in *Phiri v. S.* could have done better by 'doing the "right" thing' – by calling on the South African government to appropriate action.

---

76 See M. Mbali, 'AIDS discourses and the South African state: Government denialism and post-apartheid policy-making' (2004) 54 *Critical Perspectives on Southern Africa* 104–122, who argues a similar point.

77 S. Cohen, *States of Denial Knowing about Atrocities and Suffering*, Polity Press, Cambridge 2001, p. 96.

78 Ibid.

6. CONCLUSION

South African academic and author Marius Pieterse states:[79]

> 'It is probably fair to say that HIV and AIDS have challenged the way in which we think about the relationship between public health, morality and law, more so than any other disease.'

This verdict is indeed true for the challenges posed by the criminalisation of the transmission of HIV – criminalisation remains a controversial issue. On the one hand it is argued that criminal sanction will prevent or lessen the intentional transmission of HIV; on the other, public health experts warn that the criminalisation of HIV transmission will hamper efforts to mount an effective public health effort to curb the spread of HIV.

There are no data indicating that the application of criminal law to HIV transmission, in the form of criminal sanction in the form of convictions for attempted murder, will achieve either criminal justice or prevent HIV transmission.[80] Instead, as shown above, criminal sanction, in many instances, actually hampers public health efforts to curb the spread of HIV by prompting people to avoid HIV testing and so avoid contacting the public health service.

It is in this context that the judgment on *Phiri v. S.* should be seen. Not only does it appear that *Phiri v. S.* confirms the criminalisation of mere exposure to HIV during unprotected sex, ignoring the fact that by undergoing antiretroviral treatment the risk of HIV transmission is substantially lowered, but, also, it is likely to prompt a decrease in the voluntary uptake of HIV testing.

The court's judgment in *Phiri v. S.*, therefore, is an instance where South African courts, when they should have affirmed human rights, instead provided for denialist defence mechanisms, so facilitating the denial of the human rights of those infected and affected by HIV and AIDS in South Africa. Further, the court's judgment shows that AIDS denial is able to facilitate human rights violations, as the judgment denies the true nature of the problems involved in curbing the spread of the epidemic, reaching for a convenient solution, while appropriate action, in the form of well-thought-out public health measures, remains absent.

South Africa indeed has come a long way from former President Thabo Mbeki's literal denialist stance that HIV does not cause AIDS. 'Knowledge itself' is no longer an issue – again in Stanley Cohen's words – 'but doing the "right" thing with this knowledge. These are matters of mobilization, commitment and

79 M. Pieterse, 'Disentangling illness, crime and morality: Towards a rights-based approach to HIV prevention in Africa' (2011) 1 *African Human Rights Law Journal* 57, 57.

80 'Antiretroviral therapy and sexual transmission of HIV' 2008 *UNAIDS/WHO*, p. 1 <http://data.unaids.org/pub/PressStatement/2008/080201_hivtransmission_en.pdf> accessed 01.08.2014.

involvement'.[81] In future, South African courts should take heed of the warning of UNAIDS that urges governments to limit the criminalisation of the sexual HIV transmission to cases of intentional transmission, i.e. in which a person knows his HIV-positive status and acts with the deliberate and calculated intention to transmit the virus.[82] Courts should, instead, find an accused guilty of attempted murder only in circumstances where direct intention in the form of a wilful and calculated intent to transmit the virus – instead of mere *dolus eventualis* – is proved. As well, the South African government should expand programmes which have been demonstrated to reduce HIV transmission and protect the human rights both of people living with HIV and those who are HIV-negative.[83]

I conclude with a dire warning regarding the consequences of denialism in the context of climate change:[84]

> 'Denialism has already killed. AIDS denial has killed an estimated 330,000 South Africans. Tobacco denial delayed action to prevent smoking-related deaths. Vaccine denial has given a new lease of life to killer diseases like measles and polio. Meanwhile, climate change denial delays action to prevent warming.'

And the words of Stanley Cohen:[85]

> 'Between those who actively refuse to see anything wrong and those who see everything as wrong, the vast majority in between can be nudged into acknowledging that something was wrong – *yet at the same time* sustain their denials. Cultures of denial encourage turning a collective blind eye, leaving horrors unexplained or normalized as being part of the rhythms of everyday life.'

May the horrors of the HIV and AIDS epidemics in South Africa never be 'normalised' in this way.

---

81 S. Cohen, *States of Denial Knowing about Atrocities and Suffering*, Polity Press, Cambridge 2001, p. 9.

82 Ibid.

83 Ibid., p. 2.

84 D. Mackenzie, 'Living in denial: Why sensible people reject the truth' (2010) 2760 *New Scientist* 41.

85 S. Cohen, *States of Denial Knowing about Atrocities and Suffering*, Polity Press, Cambridge 2001, p. 101; italics in the original.

CHAPTER XXII

OLYMPIC IDEALISM AND HUMAN RIGHTS INFRINGEMENTS

How Athletes Cope with an Uncomfortable Reality

Radka BABJAKOVÁ, Sharon DETEN, Jennifer ETORÉ, Kim GEURTJENS, Roland MOERLAND and Hans NELEN*

1. INTRODUCTION

Every two years, in the world of sport athletes aim at achieving the most prestigious reward in their careers, an Olympic gold medal. However, the Olympic (winter and summer) Games are not only associated with exciting matches and outstanding sports performances, but some of them have a rather dark side as well. History has shown that if the political or socio-economic situation in a hosting country is entwined with human rights violations, this may cast a shadow on the glamorous side of the event. The most striking example of such an entwinement was the abuse by the Nazi regime of the Olympic Games of 1936 in Berlin. More recently, the Summer Games in 2008 in Beijing raised huge concerns with regard to the limitation of free speech and the infringement of self-determination of the people of Tibet. The last Winter Games of 2014 in Sochi triggered a debate on discrimination on grounds of sexual orientation. Moreover, due to the commercialisation of sport in general, and the Olympics in particular, the Games are also increasingly linked with serious forms of crime. Like the *Fédération Internationale de Football Association* (FIFA) in professional football, members of the board of the International Olympic Committee (IOC) have been accused of participating in serious fraud and corruption schemes, in particular concerning host venues for important competitions, allocation of rights, nomination for positions and commissioning construction works

* The first four authors conducted this explorative research as part of a PREMIUM research project at Maastricht University. They were supervised by the latter two authors. Hans Nelen edited the research paper for this volume.

for sports arenas and other venues.[1] These forms of corruption not only have a negative impact on the integrity of the Olympic movement, but may have detrimental effects on the socio-economic conditions under which the Games are organised as well. Many horrifying stories can be presented on casualties on construction sites as a result of poor working conditions, and forced evictions of inhabitants who have to leave their neighborhoods because of the construction of new stadiums or other Olympic facilities.[2]

The protection of human rights is universally agreed upon and ratified in various Conventions.[3] Recently, the Human Rights Council Advisory Committee published a report on the possibilities of using sport and the Olympic ideal to promote human rights for all and to strengthen universal respect for them.[4] In section 8 of this report it is acknowledged that 'sport is important in promoting human rights worldwide through the interactions it generates between people from different backgrounds and cultures. Sport and the Olympic ideal can also be a means to advance the cause of peace, promote development and combat all forms of discrimination.' Section 9 emphasises that sport and all those involved in sporting events are key to promoting, educating and sensitising people about the importance of human rights. Moreover, the Human Rights Council Advisory Committee advises to use sport as a channel to promote equal opportunities for education, health, gender and ethnic equality, and to protect the rights of persons with disabilities and the environment. It is also clear from the general principles of the IOC Charter and the subsequent articles that it seeks to improve '*universal, fundamental ethical principles*'.

So far, concerns on human rights infringements in relation to the Games have mainly been expressed by government officials, celebrities and non-governmental organisations (NGOs), like Human Rights Watch and Amnesty International. When the media extensively report on human rights violations before the beginning of the Games, this may trigger a serious public debate.[5] However, as soon as the opening ceremony starts, the Olympic torch is lit and

---

1 W. Maennig, 'Corruption in international sports and sport management; Forms, tendencies, extent and countermeasures' (2005) 5(2) *European Sport Management Quarterly* 187–225.

2 J. Yardley, 'Beijing Confirms Deaths of 6 Workers at Olympic Construction Sites' 2008 *The New York Times* <http.//www.nytimes.com/2008/01/29/world/asia/29beijing.html> accessed 18.11.2015; A. Johal, 'Rights: Millions Displaced By Olympic Games' 2007 *Inter Press Service* <www.ipsnews.net/2007/06/rights-millions-displaced-by-olympic-games/> accessed 18.11.2015. Interestingly, the concerns not only relate to the conditions when the events are organised in non-Western or non-democratic countries. Also when the events were organised in Western and democratic countries human rights were often at stake.

3 Such as the International Covenant on Civil and Political Rights (ICCPR), the International Covenant on Economic, Social and Cultural Rights (ICESCR) and other UN human rights treaties.

4 The report of Human Rights Council Advisory Committee (A/HRC/30/50) was presented to the General Assembly of the United Nations on 17 August 2015.

5 'Winter Olympics 2014' 2006–2014 *The Guardian*, pp. 12–18 <www.theguardian.com/sport/winter-olympics-2014> accessed 18.11.2015.

the athletes take their starting positions, the discussion on the protection of human rights fades into the background. The athletes now become the centre of attention: they try to make their dreams come true, win medals, break records, and the whole world is watching them. Occasionally, sports officials and athletes have raised their voices to denounce serious violations during the Games. For instance, during the Olympic Games in Mexico in 1968, athletes Tommie Smith and John Carlos raised their black-gloved hands as the American National Anthem played during the victory ceremony.[6] These athletes expressed their disgust regarding racial discrimination, but their gestures were immediately associated with the symbols of the Black Panther movement. Both athletes were suspended from the US Olympic team and were asked to leave the host country.[7]

The main question of this chapter is whether athletes are aware of the human rights violations surrounding the Olympic Games in which they compete, and, if so, how these violations have an impact on them and, last but not least, how they deal with them. In cultural criminological terms the paper explores what the prospect of being confronted with serious human rights violations actually means to athletes. The design of the study consisted of a literature review and a limited number of interviews with athletes themselves. 186 athletes were approached by email for participation in an interview, of which thirty responded. A total of 12 athletes from numerous Olympic sports participated in a face-to-face interview, a Skype interview or answered questions by email.[8] All athletes were participants of the Olympic Games in Beijing 2008, Vancouver 2010, London 2012, and/or Sochi 2014. Additionally, interviews were conducted with representatives of Amnesty International and Human Rights Watch.

Due to the low number of respondents, the results of the interviews cannot be considered to be representative of the group of athletes as a whole. It is not our ambition to give an extensive overview of perceptions in the world of sport on human rights violations. Rather, the goal is to focus on a number of dilemmas that athletes might face in relation to human rights violations and how they overcome these dilemmas. Excerpts from the 14 interviews are used as forms of illustration throughout the text.

The fact that only a minority of the athletes responded to our request indicates that the topic at hand is considered to be either irrelevant or sensitive to them (or both). This low response rate is not surprising. After all, also during the Winter Games in Sochi 2014 only a small group of athletes took the stage to openly raise their voices against human rights violations. On the opening

6 'Black athletes make silent protest' 2015 *BBC* <http://news.bbc.co.uk/onthisday/hi/dates/stories/october/17/newsid_3535000/3535348.stm> accessed 18.11.2015.

7 S. Burnton, '50 Stunning Olympic moments No13: Tommie Smith and John Carlos salute' 2012 *The Guardian* <www.theguardian.com/sport/blog/2012/feb/08/olympic-moments-tommie-smith-john-carlos> accessed 18.11.2015.

8 The respondents participated in either the Olympics or Paralympics.

evening of these Olympics, approximately fifty former and current Olympians, including 12 out of the 3,000 athletes participating in the 2014 Games (that is, less than 0.5%!), called on the Russian authorities to reconsider new laws that banned the current anti-gay legislation and approach.[9] Of course, there are various reasons for athletes to remain silent, but, as our interview data indicates, many of these reasons can be related to mechanisms of denial. Most athletes seem to be able to distance themselves (as professional sportsmen – and women) from the human rights violations. This does not mean that they are completely unaware of and unaffected by these infringements. They tend to get involved in a process of *desensitisation*,[10] or, to use Cohen's concept, in a process of *implicatory denial*.[11]

Before we show what denial at work looks like in the context of athletes participating in the Olympic Games the main principles of Olympic idealism are introduced. After the presentation of the main results of the research project, the theoretical implications thereof will be discussed.

2. OLYMPIC IDEALISM AND HUMAN RIGHTS

One of the main goals of the Olympic Games is the use of sports to unite people and uphold human rights, human dignity and fight discrimination, and thereby to promote a peaceful society concerned with the preservation of human dignity.[12] According to the Olympic Charter, there should not be discrimination on any ground during the Games, such as race, colour, sex, sexual orientation, language, religion, political or other opinions.[13]

It has often been emphasised that the Games are an international sports event and not a political arena. In the aforementioned report of the Human Rights Council Advisory Committee on the possibilities of using sport and the Olympic ideal to promote human rights it is stressed that: 'the cohesion and neutrality of the sporting movement are important factors for achieving the Olympic ideal and values. Sporting events should not be used to demonstrate

9 'Following global outcry, IOC adds anti-discrimination clause to Olympic host city contract' 2014 *Athlete Ally* <https://www.athleteally.org/news/following-global-outcry-ioc-adds-anti-discrimination-clause-olympic-host-city-contract/> accessed 18.11.2015.

10 I. Bruna Seu, 'Your stomach makes you feel that you don't want to know anything about it: Desensitization, defence mechanisms and rhetoric in response to human rights abuses' (2003) 2(2) *Journal of Human Rights* 183–196.

11 S. Cohen, *States of Denial: Knowing about Atrocities and Suffering*, 2nd ed., Polity Press, Cambridge 2010.

12 IOC, 'Olympic Charter. In force as from 9 September 2013' 2013 *International Olympic Committee*, pp. 11–12 <www.olympic.org/Documents/Olympic%20Charter/Olympic_Charter_through_time/2013-Olympic_Charter.pdf> accessed 18.11.2015; for the updated version of 2 August 2015 see <www.olympic.org/Documents/olympic_charter_en.pdf> accessed 18.11.2015.

13 Ibid.

political protests or boycotts as measures of political pressure.'[14] The claim of neutrality is problematic when faced with human rights violations. There is ample research which shows that 'standing by' or 'being neutral' actually strengthens the dynamic of victimisation, because perpetrators are facilitated in their actions by the willful ignorance and passivity of other actors. By not taking constructive action they signal to the perpetrators that they can continue with what they are doing. It has even been argued that by staying neutral in the face of human rights violations, you actually end up corroborating with the perpetrators, because you fail to come to the rescue of the victims.[15] Moreover, it can very well be argued that standing up for people who are victims of human rights violations is in line with the Olympic ideal to promote a peaceful society and preserve human dignity.

Despite the efforts to separate sports and politics, many examples exist that the Games and politics are intrinsically interwoven. Until 1984, it was quite common that countries boycotted the Olympic Games for political reasons. In 1956, for instance, several countries, including the Netherlands, Spain and Sweden, boycotted the Melbourne Summer Games as a protest against the invasion of Hungary by the former Soviet Union.[16] In 1974, New Zealand's national rugby team, the All Blacks, toured apartheid South Africa but was allowed to compete in the Montreal Games. This incensed the people of several African, Middle Eastern, and Caribbean countries, spurring Tanzania to lead a boycott. Eventually, 26 countries abstained from participating in the Games, which pulled 300 athletes out of competition.[17] And in 1980, 62 countries, led by the United States, staged a boycott of the games in Moscow, following the Soviet Union's intervention in Afghanistan in 1979.[18] During recent decades, the boycotting of the Games has become less popular, but politicians are still inclined to openly take a firm stance in relation to human rights issues in a host country. For instance, before the 2014 Winter Games in Sochi, public debates in several countries arose on whether to send political representatives or royals to the opening ceremony.[19] Belgium, Germany, France and Great Britain refused to send their heads of state, while the Netherlands decided to

---

14 Report of Human Rights Council Advisory Committee on the possibilities of using sport and the Olympic ideal to promote human rights (A/HRC/30/50), no. 12.

15 S. Cohen, *States of Denial: Knowing about Atrocities and Suffering*, 2nd ed., Polity Press, Cambridge 2010; F. Grünfeld, 'The role of bystanders in human rights violations' in: F. Coomans (ed.), *Rendering justice to the vulnerable: Liber amoricum in honour of Theo van Boven*, Kluwer Law International, The Hague 2000.

16 M. Garcia 'The long history of Olympic boycotts, protests and demonstrations' 2014 *advocate.com* <www.advocate.com/sports/2014/01/27/long-history-olympic-boycotts-protests-and-demonstrations> accessed 18.11.2015.

17 Ibid.

18 Ibid.

19 G. Mirzayan, 'Sochi boycott would have been counterproductive' 2014 *The Telegraph* <https://www.telegraph.co.uk/sponsored/rbth/opinion/10611084/sochi-2014-boycott-failure.html> accessed 18.11.2015.

send the King, Queen, Prime Minister and the Minister of Sports to Sochi, because, according to the Dutch government, 'it was preferable to engage in a dialogue'.[20] The United States, on the contrary, refused to send a political representative but instead named two openly gay (former) athletes as delegates, sending a very clear message about the United States' opinion on the treatment of the LGBT community in Russia.[21] Despite the various responses, these examples reveal that the Olympic Games are, and always will be, inherently entwined with politics.

In Article 50(3) of the Charter is stated that 'no kind of demonstration or political, religious or racial propaganda is permitted in any Olympic sites, venues or other areas'.[22] Before the 2008 Games in Beijing, the IOC issued guidelines on the interpretation of this provision, emphasising that: 'The Games are about sport. They are not a stage for different kinds of political statements about issues such as armed conflicts, regional differences, religious disputes and many others'.[23] On the other hand, it is stated in the guidelines that athletes do not violate the Charter by expressing their opinions in interviews or statements, however, it is not allowed in the areas 'for which an official Olympic accreditation is required'.[24]

It is necessary to highlight that the Charter contains the explicit prohibition of 'speeches of any kind' only with regard to 'representatives of any government or other public authority'.[25] It is obvious that a clear-cut distinction between political statements and expressions against violations of

---

20 'Dutch King, Queen and Prime Minister will go to Sochi Winter Olympics' 2014 *Dutch News.com* <www.dutchnews.nl/news/archives/2014/01/dutch_king_queen_and_prime_min/> accessed 18.11.2015.

21 'Obama names Billie Jean King as one of two gay Sochi Olympic delegates' 2013 *The Guardian* <www.theguardian.com/sport/2013/dec/18/obama-names-gay-delegates-sochi-olympics> accessed 18.11.2015.

22 Any violation of the provisions may result in disqualification or withdrawal of the accreditation of the person concerned. The decisions of the IOC Executive Board regarding this matter shall be final (By-law to rule 50), see: 'Olympic Charter. In force as from 9 September 2013' 2013 *International Olympic Committee*, p. 94 <www.olympic.org/Documents/Olympic%20Charter/Olympic_Charter_through_time/2013-Olympic_Charter.pdf> accessed 18.11.2015.

23 P. Miró, 'Guidelines on the Interpretation of Rule 51.3 of the Olympic Charter' 2008 *International Olympic Committee* <www.teamusa.org/~/media/TeamUSA/Documents/Athlete%20Ombudsman/Eligibility/IOC_Letter_on_Rule_51.pdf> accessed 18.11.2015.

24 Ibid. The guidelines were probably drafted with the idea in mind that athletes would use the Olympic event to make political statements concerning events in their home countries or other conflicts abroad, so human rights issues *external* to the Olympic event itself. What complicates the matter is that many of the issues raised in this article actually concern human rights issues that are not external to the event, but are intrinsic to the organisation of the event or the situation in the host country. It is the event itself or the situation in the host country that is the cause of concern and not some situation abroad.

25 IOC Charter Article 55(3), see: 'Olympic Charter. In force as from 9 September 2013' 2013 *International Olympic Committee*, p. 98 <www.olympic.org/Documents/Olympic%20Charter/Olympic_Charter_through_time/2013-Olympic_Charter.pdf> accessed 18.11.2015.

human rights is not possible. Potentially each statement made with the aim to protect human rights may be seen as politically motivated. The interpretation of a specific statement is in the eye of the beholder. For example, statements expressing support for the LGBT community in the Russian Federation made in 2014 by Australian snowboarder Belle Brockhoff also included criticism of the current Russian legislation.[26]

Another issue is whether statements (or other expressions) in favour of the protection of human rights can be subsumed under the term 'propaganda' in the Charter. No clear definition on propaganda exists and opinions may vary. A representative of a human rights organisation explained that they interpreted this rule as a mechanism for preventing the exchange of political statements between countries which have ongoing conflicts.

One of the roles of the IOC is to act against any form of discrimination affecting the Olympic Movement.[27] The most far-reaching decision by the IOC in this respect was taken in 1964, when South Africa was officially barred from involvement in the Games due to the country's apartheid policies. This ban lasted until 1992. But are individual athletes allowed to pursue this objective as well? Already in 1968, the Charter included the fundamental principle that no discrimination is allowed against any person on grounds of race, religion and political affiliation.[28] Can the actions of Tommie Smith and John Carlos really be seen as 'advertising their domestic political views', which amounted to a so-called 'deliberate and violent breach of the fundamental principles of the Olympic spirit'?[29]

According to the Guidelines, compliance with the Article 50(3) implies avoiding the display of any sign, banner, piece of equipment, or clothing which could be perceived as any kind of demonstration or propaganda.[30] But what is the basis for the decision that something could be perceived as any kind of demonstration or propaganda? It seems that participating in the Games wearing

26 M. Brown, 'Sochi 2014: Gay Australian snowboarder Belle Brockhoff joins LGBT cause at Winter Olympics' 2014 *ABC News* <www.abc.net.au/news/2014-02-06/gay-sochi-matt-brown/5241380> accessed 18.11.2015.

27 IOC Charter Article 2(6), see: 'Olympic Charter. In force as from 9 September 2013' 2013 *International Olympic Committee*, p. 16 <www.olympic.org/Documents/Olympic%20Charter/Olympic_Charter_through_time/2013-Olympic_Charter.pdf> accessed 18.11.2015.

28 'The Olympic Games' 1967 *International Olympic Committee*, p. 11 <www.olympic.org/Documents/Olympic%20Charter/Olympic_Charter_through_time/1967-Olympic_Charter.pdf> accessed 18.11.2015.

29 S. Burnton, '50 Stunning Olympic moments No 13: Tommie Smith and John Carlos salute' 2012 *The Guardian* <www.theguardian.com/sport/blog/2012/feb/08/olympic-moments-tommie-smith-john-carlos> accessed 18.11.2015.

30 P. Miró, 'Guidelines on the Interpretation of Rule 51.3 of the Olympic Charter' 2008 *International Olympic Committee* <www.teamusa.org/~/media/TeamUSA/Documents/Athlete%20Ombudsman/Eligibility/IOC_Letter_on_Rule_51.pdf> accessed 18.11.2015.

a hijab,[31] showing religious symbols,[32] or protesting against violation of rights of the LGBT community by wearing a small symbol are all permitted.[33] The IOC did not object to these possible violations of the Charter, but it is not clear where the Committee exactly draws the line.

So, not only does the provision of Article 50(3) lack clarity, but an unambiguous interpretation of the particular terms is missing as well. Moreover, it may well be that the official interpretation of the IOC contradicts the fundamental principles of Olympism, which include prohibition of discrimination of any kind. It could very well be argued that athletes should not be punished for their statements or other form of expressions in favour of the protection of human rights, due to the fact that these statements cannot be considered as propaganda in the true nature of the term. In addition, these statements or gestures are in compliance with the fundamental principles of Olympism and the objectives expressed in the Charter. A remaining question is whether this provision has influence on the athletes and whether they are inclined to openly denounce human rights violations in the host country of the Olympic Games.

3. DENIAL AT WORK

As previously mentioned, most athletes want to be focused on their performance and try to avoid any distraction. The interviews confirm that athletes aim at withdrawing into their shells to achieve an outstanding result. Next to their own personal goals, they are mainly preoccupied with the fact that they can represent their country at a unique event and that they are part of the Olympic community. As one of the respondents put it:

> 'The Olympics were my dream. I'd been training for years to get there. And once I had access to the Games and the opportunity to participate, I had the feeling that I was part of something bigger. I immediately knew I had to cherish these moments. The Olympic village, the atmosphere, the other athletes, it's hard to describe what happens to you when you belong to this community. It's sad that all these bad things

---

31 A. Shergold, 'The Muslim women who overcame the odds and the prejudice to make history today on the Olympic stage' 2012 *Daily Mail* <www.dailymail.co.uk/news/article-2183262/Olympics-2012-The-Muslim-women-overcame-odds-make-London.html> accessed 18.11.2015.

32 During the Games in London 2012 the Ethiopian athlete Meseret Defar pulled a picture of the Virgin Mary out from under her jersey, showed it to the cameras and held it up to her face in deep prayer, when she crossed the finish line in the 5000 meter race to win the gold medal, see: 'Virgin Mary crosses the finish line with gold runner' 2012 *Catholic News Agency* <www.catholicnewsagency.com/news/virgin-mary-crosses-the-finish-line-with-olympic-gold-runner> accessed 18.11.2015.

33 During the Games in Sochi 2014 athletes showed their support to the LGBT rights and their disagreement with discrimination of the LGBT community in Russia by wearing symbols of the campaign, see: Principle 6, 'What is Principle 6?' 2015 <www.principle6.org/> accessed 18.11.2015.

happen around it, but I did not want to think about it because I was there for one reason only'.

On top of the personal goals of the athletes, many of them share the official principle of the IOC that sports and politics should be separated. The following quote reflects that premise:

> 'The Games are about sports. I know that the Games have become big business and are sometimes organized in dubious countries, but they are still the meeting place for the best athletes of the planet. That should stay the focus of the event.'

Another athlete made very clear that 'the games and politics should be separated.'[34]

A third argument to keep silent on human rights issues that can be derived from the interview material is that many athletes are convinced that it is not up to them to speak out. 'We have no role to play in this matter', as one of the respondents put it.

Opinions on making statements regarding human rights violations varied amongst the respondents. Some athletes stipulated that no one should make political statements surrounding the Games, not even politicians. One person completely distanced himself from any athlete making a statement:

> 'Of course what's happening there is bad and you have freedom of speech and a personal choice to demonstrate. But as an athlete, you should not do it during the Games because it's a sports event and there's no place for politics there'.

Yet, another group of athletes stipulated that although they are not inclined to make a statement themselves, they would approve if other athletes or politicians were to do so. Some of them explicitly mentioned that they have respect for 'role models who take the floor'. Reference was made, in this respect, both to contemporary role models, such as the aforementioned Australian snowboarder Belle Brockhoff, Dutch snowboarder Cheryl Maas,[35] and cyclist Lizzie Armitstead,[36] but also to

---

34 The claim that sports and politics should be separated is interesting due to the fact that the Games are also political events. Athletes carry the flag of their countries, anthems are played, and it is hard to see, for instance, the grand opening of the Games at Sochi not as politically significant move.

35 Cheryl Maas wore a unicorn rainbow glove during her performance in Sochi (2014) as a silent protest against discrimination of the LGBT community, see: J.M. Nichols, 'Cheryl Maas, Lesbian snowboarder in Russia, raises rainbow glove in Sochi' 2014 *The Huffington Post* <www.huffingtonpost.com/2014/02/07/olympics-rainbow-glove_n_4745548.html> accessed 18.11.2015.

36 When Lizzie Armitstead won silver in the London 2012 Olympic cycling road race she used the opportunity to courageously speak up about sexism in her sport. See M. Moore, 'Inclusion, Diversity and the Power of Sporting Role Models' 2015 *Women's Sport Trust* <www.womenssporttrust.com/inclusion-diversity-and-the-power-of-sporting-role-models> accessed 18.11.2015.

former super stars, like professional tennis player Billy Jean King. Besides her exceptional talents as a tennis player which led her to become the world number one in her sport in the 1970s, King was, and still is, recognised as a strong advocate for sexual equality. On various occasions she openly denounced serious human rights violations in her home country, the USA, and beyond.

The athletes who support the idea that during the Games statements are made on serious infringements put their faith in the role of politicians. They are the ones who should explicitly use the event to discuss human rights, because without the Olympics taking place in certain countries with a bad reputation on human rights violations, the general public would be insufficiently aware of these violations. From the latter perspective, the Olympic Games are perceived as an opportunity to draw attention to poor human rights conditions and improve these circumstances. This is also the main argument of human rights organisations, such as Amnesty International and Human Rights Watch. According to representatives of these organisations, the Olympic Games can be used as a means to achieve improvement in human rights. If countries apply to become the host country of the Games, they will be in the IOC's spotlight and will have to convince the world that they are fit in all respects to organise the Games. Thus, by becoming a candidate, a country inevitably has to improve the standards in compliance with human rights Conventions. According to the representatives of human rights organisations, if the Games were never held in countries with bad human rights reputations, there is a great chance that there would be no additional incentive to improve the human rights situations.[37] On the other hand, the same representatives acknowledge the negative side-effect that by being in the spotlight, the pressure on a country to create a perfect image of itself as a human rights-abiding nation will increase. As a result, journalists and critics may be silenced, and censorship may be enhanced.

The interview material suggests that human rights issues are hardly discussed amongst athletes and officials. In the Netherlands, the national sports association NOC/NSF tends to organise meetings for athletes before the start of each Olympic Games. This is done in cooperation with Amnesty International. According to the athletes who attended one of these meetings, the goal is to inform them on all relevant aspects in relation to the Olympics, including the human rights situation in the host country. A meeting was also organised in Sochi about sports and human rights by the Dutch Olympic Committee.[38] The Director of Amnesty was present at this meeting and delivered a speech about the relationship between

[37] It was also noted that the absence of 'sanctions' by the IOC was a problem. Due to the lack of negative repercussions there was no real or hard incentive to change the situation.

[38] Amnesty International, 'IOC moet mensenrechtenstandaard invoeren' 2014 <www.amnesty.nl/nieuwsportaal/nieuws/ioc-moet-mensenrechtenstandaard-invoeren> accessed 18.11.2015.

sports and human rights.[39] According to the athletes present, his speech was mostly taken for granted and did not trigger an extensive debate amongst them.[40]

4. THEORETICAL REFLECTION

The aforementioned results show that from a theoretical perspective, most athletes do not deny the notion of human dignity or rights as such. Instead, they tend to justify their inaction citing reasons why it is not their responsibility to act, leading to *implicatory denial mechanisms*.[41] These mechanisms deny the (moral) consequences that would normally follow from certain actions. Many athletes personally disapprove of human rights violations, but in their role as athletes, they do not feel the responsibility to address these issues. In other words, speaking out against human rights violations is perceived a noble endeavour, but athletes do not think that they and other competitors in the Olympic Games have a specific responsibility in this respect. Their appeal to *higher loyalties* – to use a term form the classic work of Matza and Sykes[42] – consists of both the pressure to perform on behalf of their nation and to avoid embarrassment for the team of which they are a member. The latter reflects the strong sense of community among the athletes. In addition, and most importantly, the desire to win a gold medal also resembles their personal goal to achieve ever-better results in their field of sports. Hence, *self-fulfillment*, as described by Scott and Lyman as *'self-development and discovery of competences'*,[43] is also a widely used neutralisation of athletes.

Bruna Seu uses the term *desensitisation* to explain one of the many possible responses of the public to human rights appeals. In desensitisation, there are two distinctive ways to deal with unpleasant information. One can be seen as a defence mechanism whereas the other results from overexposure. Either people shut themselves off in order to defend themselves against injustice or appalling information – they do not want to know about it – or the information does not impress people anymore because they have been confronted with it

39 E. Nazarski (Director of Amnesty International) speech during a meeting with the Dutch minister of Health, Welfare and Sports, the Dutch Sports Federation NOC*NSF and participating Dutch athletes on 18 February 2014 to create awareness about human rights violations during the preparations for the Sochi Winter Games and the objectives of Amnesty International to improve the situation <https://www.amnesty.nl/sotsji-eduard-nazarski-1822014> accessed 18.11.2015.

40 Interestingly, the rules concerning what is permitted to be stated at Olympic events and what not do also seem to have a self-censoring effect. During the interviews some athletes not only noted that certain statements were not allowed, but also that certain statements were 'at least not wanted'.

41 S. Cohen, *States of Denial: Knowing About Atrocities and Suffering*, Polity Press, Cambridge 2001.

42 G. Sykes and D. Matza, 'Techniques of Neutralization: A Theory of Delinquency' (1957) 22 *American Sociological Review* 664–670.

43 M. Scott and S. Lyman, 'Accounts' (1968) 33 *American Sociological Review* 52.

so many times that they have gotten used to it.[44] The interviews indicate that in the world of sports desensitisation primarily takes the form of a defence mechanism. For instance, some of the athletes said they could imagine the pitifully bad working conditions of the construction workers – some had even witnessed these circumstances themselves – but they all tried to forget about it and distance themselves from the situation. In relation to forced evictions of inhabitants one respondent argued 'that these also take place if a government plans to build a new highway or dam, so "what's the big deal"?' These responses reinstate that (implicatory) denial is sophisticated and reflexive: even though people acknowledge the morale behind addressing human rights violations, they seem to use their own knowledge to justify their passive attitude or actions towards it.[45] The reluctance to act reflects a *bystander effect* that seems to cast a shadow on all persons involved in the Olympic Games. Athletes emphasise that it is not their responsibility, politicians and human rights organisations prefer to talk to officials rather than taking firm action themselves, and the IOC does not have the will to fundamentally change the situation. The founding fathers of the concept of the *bystander effect*, Darley and Latané, argue that in the course of making a decision on whether to act or not, 'an individual bystander will be considerably influenced by the decisions he perceives other bystanders to be taking. If everyone else in a group of onlookers seems to regard an event as non-serious and the proper course of action to be non-intervention, this consensus may strongly affect the perceptions of any single individual and inhibit his potential intervention'.[46] In addition, some of the athletes mentioned that they were never asked for their opinion on human rights violations. Since the *bystander effect* is an interpersonal phenomenon, it is not limited to sportsmen but also includes journalists who avoid asking human rights violations related questions, coaches or officials who do not speak with athletes about these problems, sport organisations which do not provide athletes with information on the issues, the media which does not cover cases of violations of human rights during the Games, or organisers of the Games who fail to prevent violations.

In sum, the Olympic Games, as a large gathering of athletes and numerous other actors, provide an opportunity structure for the *bystander effect* to flourish and for a subsequent '*conspiracy of silence*'. Zerubavel referred to the latter concept in relation to situations in which 'a group of people tacitly agree

44 I. Bruna Seu, 'Your stomach makes you feel that you don't want to know anything about it: Desensitization, defence mechanisms and rhetoric in response to human rights abuses' (2003) 2(2) *Journal of Human Rights* 189.

45 I. Bruna Seu, 'Doing denial: audience reaction to human rights appeals' (2010) 21(4) *Discourse & Society* 452.

46 B. Latané and J.M. Darley, 'Group Inhibition of Bystander Intervention in Emergencies' (1968) 10 *Journal of Personality and Social Psychology* 216.

to outwardly ignore something of which they are personally aware'.[47] Thus, an individual can be aware of a problem but publicly unaware in the sense that he or she does not address it. Zerubavel argues that conspiracies of silence therefore 'presuppose mutual denial, whereby at least two people collaborate to jointly avoid acknowledging something'.[48] Furthermore, he remarks that this conspiracy is also exemplified by a 'don't ask, don't tell mentality'.[49] Therefore it may be concluded that the topic of violations of human rights in connection to the Games belongs to the category 'generally known but cannot be spoken of'.[50] Being silent involves more than absence of action, because things about which people are silent, are in fact actively avoided.[51] The concept of things which should be ignored is created by members of particular social communities with particular social conventions of attention and communication, in this case teams of sportsmen or the sports community as a whole. The members of the community are socialised to act in a certain way, but also to notice and to ignore other things.[52]

5. EPILOGUE

In the summer of 2016 the next Olympic Games will be held in Rio de Janeiro. Without doubt, the world will gape once again at the spectacular event and the dazzling performances of the athletes, excelling in their sports disciplines. Of course, these athletes deserve our full attention and admiration. However, history shows that the organisation of the Olympics always comes at a price, both literally and figuratively. And we do not always want to know who exactly has to pay this price. In the case of Rio concerns exist on a variety of human rights violations. The Brazilian government had promised that any urban construction projects involving, for instance, resettlement of communities and improvements in urban mobility would be conducted with citizen participation in the decision-making process and transparency. It was claimed that the projects would benefit the most marginalised groups. However, it seems that the reality has been somewhat different. In recent months and years, several reports have been published and submitted to local and international authorities containing allegations of human rights abuses, such as forced displacements and evictions, forced labour, discrimination, lack of consultation of affected communities,

47 E. Zerubavel, *The Elephant in the Room: Silence and Denial in Everyday Life*, Oxford University Press, Oxford 2008, p. 2.
48 Ibid., p. 4.
49 Ibid., p. 4.
50 Ibid., p. 3.
51 Ibid., p. 9.
52 Ibid., p. 20; for example, one athlete stated that: 'as a guest, you wouldn't want to offend the host', and another noted that: 'we discussed it in the team so that we would avoid such political questions during interviews'.

child labour, and violent repression of protesters. On top of that, several NGOs have raised the alarm on child prostitution and sexual exploitation. With regard to the latter, one year ahead of the Games, *Terre des hommes* launched the report 'Children Rights and Mega Sporting Events' in 2014 and called for an increase in media coverage and scrutiny on mega sporting events, including the 2016 Rio Games. In this report reference is made to the general pattern that media attention of human rights (and children's rights issues in particular) increases and peaks directly before mega sporting events, drops during the events and vanishes afterwards. But even before the start of the Olympics, the media coverage hardly culminates into public outrage on a large scale. Human rights violations are almost taken for granted and the process of denial can be observed within all sections of society, including the world of sports itself.

In this chapter, some of the main underlying mechanisms of denialism in the world of sport were explored with a special focus on the athletes competing in the Olympic Games. The main goal was to find out whether athletes are aware of the human rights violations surrounding the Olympic Games, and, if so, how they cope with the uncomfortable reality that they are expected to turn in a record performance while at the same time other human beings suffer, due to the same event.

Of course, it did not come as a surprise that our interviews showed that athletes completely focus on their performances, since an Olympic gold medal is the highest attainable prize in the field of sport. Moreover, they have trained for the Games for years, needing to be at their physical and mental best. Therefore it is not difficult to imagine that issues like human rights violations might distract athletes from their ultimate goals. On the other hand, athletes increasingly serve as role models to their fans and spectators around the world. Their statements might have a huge impact, but most of the athletes deny the possible role they could play in expressing concerns about human rights violations (denial of agency). As such, they contribute to the conspiracy of silence that exists in relation to human rights violations surrounding the Olympic Games.

To a certain extent, the athletes are right in arguing that it is not up to them to take the lead in the human rights debate. Politicians, academic scholars and other human rights experts bear a greater responsibility in this aspect. Nobody expects athletes to take the floor and start protesting collectively. On the other hand, the athletes themselves tend to underestimate the significance of their contributions. Just imagine if Usain Bolt, Daphne Schippers or Michael Phelps made a firm statement on the human rights situation in Rio de Janeiro. Without doubt, such a statement would have more impact than a formal gesture made by, for instance, the Dutch Secretary of Foreign Affairs. One could argue that with such great power comes great responsibility. In order to break down the 'walls of silence' it is of added value if influential people in sports publicly address a sensitive human rights issue. Most likely this example will be followed by many others and the issue might stay on the agenda even after the Games are over. The Winter Games in Sochi 2014 showed that some progress can be made and the rules can change because of external pressure on the IOC. After a coalition of human rights organisations and a group of athletes had started a campaign against the discriminatory character of the legislation of the Russian Federation in relation to the rights of the LGBT community, the IOC changed Article 6 of the Olympic Charter. This Srticle entails a fundamental principle of the Olympic spirit and now reads that: 'the enjoyment of the rights and freedoms set forth in this Olympic Charter shall be secured without discrimination of any kind, such as race, colour, sex, *sexual orientation*, language, religion, political or other opinion, national or social origin, property, birth or other status.' The element of sexual orientation was added after the Sochi Games.[53]

Although it may be argued that this amendment is just a tiny step forward, countries that are interested in organising the Games in the future will have to take this new Article of the Charter into account. A relevant precondition for further progress is that the IOC is willing to enforce its rules and regulations more rigorously than it has done in the past. Countries in which elementary human rights are seriously violated should not be allowed to become candidates for the organisation of the event in the first place. Of course, a decision to exclude countries from organising the Games runs the risk of becoming highly politically influenced. That's why such a decision has to be fully transparent and sufficiently substantiated. Although it is emphasised by many – including the IOC itself and the Human Rights Council of the United Nations – that the Olympic Games are primarily about sports, and that politics should be kept out of them, our analysis shows that this premise is untenable. The claim that the Games and politics should be separated is maybe the most brazen form of denial that was discussed in this article. If we actually embrace the idea that the Olympic Games are sports events to bring people from all over the world together to celebrate and enhance human rights and human dignity, we cannot look the other way if human rights in the organising country are seriously violated. This problem is also ignored by academics. With this paper, we hope to 'break' the current academic silence on this particular issue and facilitate a fruitful discussion on how to effectively address human rights violations inherent to mega sports events, such as the Olympic Games.

53 'Olympic Charter. In force as from 2 August 2015' 2015 *International Olympic Committee*, p. 15 <www.olympic.org/Documents/olympic_charter_en.pdf> accessed 18.11.2015.

CHAPTER XXIII

DENIALISM AND HUMAN RIGHTS: AN AFTERWORD

David NELKEN

'[S]ince wars begin in the minds of men, it is in the minds of men that the defenses of peace must be constructed and that peace must be founded, if it is not to fail, upon the intellectual and moral solidarity of mankind.'[1]

In the late 1970s while teaching philosophy of law in Edinburgh I was invited to dinner where another guest was an upcoming MP.[2] Making (heavy) conversation I asked how we could justify not helping desperate people in the world who were so much less fortunate than we were. Was it just a question of geography? If they were actually at the door starving would we not give up our superfluous goods so as to ensure their basic survival – and how could geography make a difference to our obligations? My fellow guest did not see that we had any such obligations, and my questions were no doubt put clumsily. And yet, now with the arrival of so many often desperate people from poorer countries trying to cross borders despite heavy-handed efforts to stop them, even the argument from geography falls away. Some of the same unease arises when we worry about our obligations to those who live elsewhere but on whose work in intolerable conditions we rely to supply our food, our raw materials, our clothes and even the manufacture of the computers on which we assemble our arguments. There may be some plausible arguments – other than the facts of geography – that set limits to our responsibilities to others.[3] But until we formulate these properly we risk remaining 'in denial' about the possible obligations that we may have.

The organisers of the workshop whose proceedings are collected in this volume are professors at a leading centre for the study of human rights. They therefore seek to examine the role of human rights in all this. Why is it, they

1 Taken from the UNESCO Declaration of Principles of International Cultural Co-operation (4 November 1966).

2 This MP, who later served as foreign secretary, was prominent in fighting for the human rights of those who wanted to do so to be allowed to emigrate from communist countries. It is interesting that his political party is now strongly invested in resisting the rights of people who want to immigrate.

3 See e.g. K.A. APPIAH, *Cosmopolitanism*, Penguin, London 2006.

ask, that despite efforts to secure human rights 'violations do still occur and injustice remains rampant'. They reply that 'central to this problem appears to be that social, economic, cultural and political structures in societies provide for denialist defence mechanisms'. 'Such deeply embedded denialism causes and/or facilitates human rights violations, because the true nature of the problems involved remains fully or partly unacknowledged and as a result appropriate action remains absent. In order 'to safeguard the effectuation of human rights it is thus pertinent to acknowledge and address this problem of denialism and develop strategies to move beyond it'.[4] Those invited to the workshop were encouraged 'to unearth and address denialism in the context of their own particular areas of research'[5] and I was assigned the not so simple task of trying to bring out some of the common ideas that have emerged as a result of these efforts.

In issuing their invitation the editors proposed the following roadmap of what they hoped would come out of their workshop:

(1) A clear conception and definition of denialism should be developed. What does denialism exactly entail? On what social, economic, cultural and political structures and mechanisms in societies does it operate and how? What ideologies and prejudices are involved?
(2) Denialism operating in practice should be investigated and its relation to and particular relevance for human rights issues should be clarified. In which concrete cases do we see denialism 'at work'? What are the implications in terms of human rights? How is the effectuation of these rights blocked or obstructed? Is denialism only destructive or can it also be constructive? Can human rights discourse itself be in denial?
(3) How should we deal with denialism and move to a situation of human rights consistent behaviour and change? Is it always possible to move from denial to compliance? What are suitable strategies or policies? Is legislation required? Which factors obstruct human rights change in denialist situations?[6]

I have taken these questions, understood broadly, as the framework for organising this afterword.[7] The first section is concerned with defining denialism. It begins by linking this workshop to Cohen's pioneering book *States*

4 R. Moerland, H. Nelen and J. Willems, 'Introduction', in this volume, p. 2.

5 This MP, who later served as foreign secretary, was prominent in fighting for the human rights of those who wanted to do so to be allowed to emigrate from communist countries. It is interesting that his political party is now strongly invested in resisting the rights of people who want to immigrate.

6 Ibid.

7 These issues are of course overlapping and/or interrelated. Any response to denialism will depend on how the problems it creates are defined and understood.

of Denial.[8] Have the authors succeeded in resolving the ambiguities in Cohen's arguments about social censures? In doing so have they perhaps gone too far? The second section goes on to deal with the key questions of how to connect denialism to human rights. What are the different ways it can produce such violations? What more do we need to know about the way it operates? Finally, building on the previous discussions, the last section discusses the role human rights can and should play in responding to denialism. How do they relate to other responses? Can their use even be counterproductive?

As will be seen, the contributions to the workshop raise more issues then they resolve. The meaning and utility of the concept of denialism remains highly controversial, as does the role of human rights in dealing with it. But this collection does mark some progress, not least in showing the range of possible reactions when scholars are invited to identify examples of well-entrenched structures of denialism and suggest ways to overcome them.

1. DEFINING DENIALISM: GOING BEYOND 'COHEN'S STATES OF DENIAL'

The project bristles with definitional difficulties. What is meant by 'denialism' (and how does it relate to denial?)[9] Can adding 'ism' as a suffix change the significance of a central aspect of human communication?[10] How are we to distinguish denialism from scepticism, revisionism or healthy disagreement? Is denialism a description or an evaluation of behaviour?[11] Is the discussion of denialism part of the same process or can it stand above it? What if anything puts certain claims beyond argument? According to the Oxford Dictionary, 'denialist' is used to refer to a person who refuses to admit the truth of a concept or proposition that is supported by the majority of scientific or historical evidence.[12] Wikipedia goes a little further. Denialism is taken to mean 'an ideological position whereby one systematically reacts by refusing reality

8 S. COHEN, *States of Denial: Knowing About Atrocities and Suffering*, Polity Press, Cambridge 2001.

9 All denialism necessarily involves denial but not all denial constitutes denialism. J. WILLEMS, 'Too Close to Home? The Denial of Prejudice and Discrimination against Children', in this volume, p. 83, suggests that denialism is an aggravated form of denial, that is, a form with one or more negative elements added'.

10 Ibid., p. 74. Willems goes further and links denialism to the concepts of 'childism, parentiarchy, transism (short for transgenerational discrimination), and adultism'.

11 G. AROSEMENA, 'Poverty, Just World Thinking and Human Rights Law: A study of the Relevance of Denial for Normative Legal Research', in this volume, p. 367. The editors note that while some contributors 'maintain a certain 'distance' from the object under study ... other authors are more engaging in their approach and identify themselves more closely with the issues being addressed. See R. MOERLAND, H. NELEN and J. WILLEMS, 'Introduction', in this volume, p. 3.

12 See <www.oxforddictionaries.com/definition/english/Denialist> accessed June 2015.

and truth, for ideological purposes, of facts that, by and large, are accepted by almost all experts and lay persons as having been established on the basis of overwhelming evidence'.[13]

Amongst legal scholars, the term is most well known as a way of denying historical truths, as in the case of Holocaust denial, or genocide denial more generally. (In Italian this is actually called 'negazion*ismo*'). In popular science writing, it has been applied to widespread resistance to the truth claims of science and medicine. According to Michael Specter, 'Denialism, is Denial writ large – when an entire segment of society, often struggling with the trauma of change, turns away from reality in favour of a more comfortable lie'.[14] What is distinctive about the papers brought together here, however, is the attempt:

(1) to include as examples of denialism matters as different as 'covering up' social problems, and being 'in denial' about them; and
(2) to use as a common denominator of denial all situations where human rights are thereby put at risk.

This volume seeks to work towards an expanded definition of denialism. But is this helpful? To get some purchase on the protean use of the concept it can be helpful to trace back the different definitions of denialism used by the contributors in this workshop to Cohen's original ideas in his book, as well as his later, all too brief, reconsiderations of his argument. Cohen's concern with denial arose from his first-hand experience, in both South Africa and, later, Israel/Palestine, of how some people manage to turn a blind eye to inhumane behaviour even when information about it begins to be circulated. He examined this and similar behaviour in terms of denial of the facts, their reinterpretation, or the rejection of the need to do anything about them. The relevance of Cohen's work is noted by many of the contributors.

The most sustained discussions can be found in the two plenaries. Irene Bruna Seu, in her well-crafted study, is concerned with Cohen's question 'what do we do with our knowledge about the suffering of others, and what does this knowledge do to us?'[15] She seeks to understand the phenomenon of being 'in denial' when people are asked to recognise episodes of mass suffering and the need to make some contribution to helping reduce it. She adopts a psychosocial approach so as to develop the psychological aspects of Cohen's work. Seu advises us to study 'conflict and ambivalence, and be attentive to factors originating from "out there" and "inside" of people', if we want to arrive at 'a thicker and more complex understanding of the conflictual, dynamic and fluid nature of

---

13 <https://en.wikipedia.org/wiki/Denialism> accessed May 2016.

14 M. Specter, *Denialism: How Irrational Thinking Hinders Scientific Progress, Harms the Planet, and Threatens Our Lives*, Penguin Press HC, Hudson 2009, p. 3.

15 I.B. Seu, 'Denial and Acknowledgment in Public Responses to Information about Human Rights Violations', in this volume, p. 25.

public (un)responsiveness' to appeals for aid.'[16] Individual and social denialism are closely related. For Seu, quoting Cohen, '[i]nstead of a personal and private state that might last a lifetime, denialism is expressed in a learned, shared public language; the activities of claim makers and moral entrepreneurs are organised, planned, intentional'.[17]

Seu is able to avoid the question of what behaviour it is correct to describe as denialism (and who should decide) because her approach is premised on the assumption that people do (half) know that they are 'in denial'. By contrast, most of the other contributors to this workshop go well beyond cases of people being 'in denial' and choose to characterise as denialism a large variety of situations in which people participate in denying or covering up (alleged) social harms. In the other plenary, Willem De Haan issues an eloquent warning against extending Cohen's project beyond situations where people are 'in denial'. Cohen, he says, uses the term 'denial' to refer to situations 'when persons, who, as audiences, bystanders, observers, onlookers, spectators or witnesses, have come to see, hear or know what happened or is going on – either at the time or later, for whatever reason – in good or bad faith – claim not to know'.[18] 'As a coping mechanism, denialism seems similar to denial to the extent that both are based on unintentional and – in many circumstances – understandable, if not entirely forgivable, human shortcomings'.[19] But, he complains, 'the "ism" of "denialism" would suggest a philosophical, political or moral system of mutually supportive beliefs' whereas in actual fact, according to him, 'denialism is more a form of newspeak. It is used as a polemical term.'[20] 'Denialism', for De Haan, entails rhetorical arguments to discredit and undermine well-established but unwelcome positions in scientific debates … the aim of denialism is not to engage in legitimate scientific debate, but merely to create the appearance of a scientific debate'.[21]

De Haan also draws a sharp (perhaps over-sharp?) distinction between historical and scientific facts. He cautions us against looking for equivalence between debates about the Holocaust and, for example, climate change, because 'the Holocaust refers to a well-documented set of events that happened in recorded history, while climate change is a scientific prediction of what is likely to happen in the future'.[22] In the case of climate change, there is and ought to be room for *respectable* (my italics) scientific scepticism, whereas with regard to the

16 Ibid., p. 47.
17 Ibid., p.29.
18 Ibid., p. 13.
19 W. De Haan, 'Denialism and the Problem of Indifference', in this volume, p. 14.
20 Ibid.
21 Ibid. But Cohen, like most of the contributors to this collection, was relatively uninterested in using the term denialism to describe those who subscribe to outlandish theories about scientific matters.
22 Ibid., p. 15.

Holocaust there is not and ought not to be room for 'reasonable doubt'.[23] It is in this vein, that – at least in some jurisdictions – Holocaust denial is a criminal offense whereas denial of climate change is, at least legally, legitimate under the principle of freedom of expression.[24]

De Haan's (somewhat paradoxical) conclusion is that we need to avoid speaking about denial*ism* even or perhaps above all in relation to matters such as Holocaust denial. '[I]n relation to gross human rights violations, we should have serious doubts about the analytical usefulness and political implications of denialism as a concept ... By applying denialism the way the term is currently used, we run the risk that gross human rights violations and crimes against humanity become an object of pseudo-scientific debate about facts and their interpretation, while – if only as an unintended consequence – the moral dimensions of denial are overlooked, i.e. the moral responsibility of acknowledging the facts and the moral obligation to intervene in order to protect.'[25] In other words, for De Haan, by talking about extreme human rights violations in terms of denialism we implicitly concede that there is something to debate. But whilst it may indeed be unjustified to deny certain 'self-evident' (historical or other) facts, it could be argued that we still need a term such as denialism to describe those who persist in doing so.[26]

Nonetheless, De Haan's plenary poses the central dilemma that runs through this volume. Are those calling others denialists any less prescriptive than those they wish to condemn? What grounds the claim that 'you are exaggerating, but I am uncovering denialism'? It was Cohen himself, who, as one of the leading sociologists in the 1970s and 1980s, sought to show how societies' response to problems (largely) constituted them as such.[27] Social problems require claims makers to place and keep them on the public agenda, also in terms of their relative importance compared to other problems. Importantly, for our purposes, Cohen spoke of many societal reactions as being disproportionate *over*-reactions,[28] coining (along with Jock Young) the term 'moral panic' so

---

23 Ibid.

24 Ibid.

25 Ibid.

26 For some writers, denialism as a term refers precisely to denying that which cannot or should not be denied. Moerland argues that the reason to use the term is that 'In the context of genocide the notion of an 'alternative perspective' is highly problematic. ... [because] by presenting another side to the story deniers reduce an indisputable historical event to a conflict between two opposing opinions'. See R. Moerland, 'The BBC Documentary "Rwanda's Untold Story": Acknowledging Genocide or Denying It?', in this volume, p. 170.

27 We are concerned here with the influence of Cohen's writings on discussions of denialism. But there are of course other approaches such as the social disorganisation approach, value conflict, or Marxist approach, which place less emphasis on social construction of social problems. There are also important points of disagreement between so-called 'radical' and 'moderate' versions of social constructionism.

28 M. Welsh, 'Moral panic, denial, and human rights: scanning the spectrum from overreaction to underreaction' in: D. Downes, P. Rock, C. Chinkin and C. Gearty (eds.), *Crime Social*

as to capture the way such responses often focused on convenient 'folk devils' such as young offenders, students and drug takers (now, of course, they are more likely to be unwelcome migrants).[29] Our contributors claim that the importance of the social problems they highlight are being improperly denied. They therefore appear to be making the opposite, but equally contestable, claim that there is *under*-reaction to a given problems.[30] But is there any objective way to distinguish what is an unfounded moral panic from cases where denialism prevents the recognition of a well-founded problem? Or is this just an evaluation – part of the debate over a given social problem? There is surprisingly little discussion of this issue in the case studies presented by the contributors to this collection.

One of Cohen's later writings, on climate change, does suggest that some social problems are more worthy of the name than others. But it is important to note that the focus of that paper, as his book itself, is on those 'in denial'.[31] When it comes to deciding which social problems matter, Cohen came to think that the difference between moral panic and denialism was largely a matter of political choice (which does not mean that is arbitrary). In his most relevant recent piece, appropriately entitled 'Whose side were we on?',[32] he described the emergence in the 1980s of a new set of social problems concerned that were linked to progressive causes such as feminism or the control of corporate misbehaviour. The difference between the 'old' and 'new' social problems is that 'we' are more likely to agree with the new 'moral entrepreneurs' that the problems they raise are not being taken seriously enough, and more willing to identify with the

Control and Human Rights: From Moral Panics to States of Denial: Essays in Honour of Stanley Cohen, Willan Publishing, Milton 2007, p. 92.

29 The use of the term 'panic' presupposes that the worrying is not objectively justified. Whether the term is a description or an evaluation and what makes something a moral panic is itself debated and debatable. What some call uncovering denial, others might call a witch hunt. Interestingly, sociologists writing about moral panics and denialism link them both to periods of rapid social change. There is an extensive secondary literature about the term: see e.g. K. Thompson, *Moral Panics*, Routledge, London 1998.

30 Alternatively, in some cases denialism and moral panics may overlap rather than be opposites. 'Moral entrepreneurs' create a moral panic about a group so that its rights are denied. See S. Morgan-Williams, 'Justifying Acts of Denialism: The Case of Prisoner Disenfranchisement in the UK', in this volume, p. 358, who tells us that 'the act of denying prisoners their voting rights is an act of political denialism, that the reasoning behind this denial rests upon the creation of two elements of "moral panic" and that intrinsically for a political power to rely upon denialism that an element of moral panic is key.' But there is also a possible asymmetry between the notions of moral panic and denialism. Moral panic is usually produced at second hand (with the media playing a major role) whereas the chapters here have little to say about this (with the exception of R. Moerland, 'The BBC Documentary "Rwanda's Untold Story": Acknowledging Genocide or Denying It?', in this volume)).

31 S. Cohen, 'Climate change in a perverse culture' in: S. Weintrobe (ed.), *Engaging with Climate Change: Psychoanalytic and Interdisciplinary Perspectives*, Routledge, London 2012, pp. 26–27.

32 S. Cohen, 'Whose side were we on? The undeclared politics of moral panic theory' (2011) 7(3) *Crime, Media, Culture* 237–243.

victims of such problems who often come from weaker groups, or poorer parts of the world.[33] If the social problems are ones we take sufficiently seriously then it may be legitimate to describe as denialists those who take a different view, though we should not assume that Cohen would necessarily endorse as genuine all claims of denialism made by the contributors to this volume.

For Cohen then it is not so much a matter of distinguishing self-evident facts from those that are debatable, but rather of the need to take a stand. He pointed to a triple loyalty: 'first, an overriding obligation to honest intellectual enquiry itself (however sceptical, provisional, irrelevant and unrealistic), second, a political commitment to social justice, but also (and potentially conflicting with both) the pressing and immediate demands for short term humanitarian help. We have to appease these three voracious gods'.[34] But exactly the 'overriding 'obligation to honest enquiry requires the admission (which Cohen makes) that the choice of which problems to privilege is a political one. The problem with drawing the line on political grounds, however, is that it can make it too easy for those described as denialists to reject the label – or throw it back at those who condemn them. Could there be a more 'objective' basis?

For many contributors what is crucial are the social and economic interests that they allege lie behind their opponents' arguments. As Willems puts it, 'denial serves particular (well described) economic, political and/or ideological interests or sentiments'.[35] Certainly some such connection between ideas and social forces is implied by the term 'structures of denialism' that the editors wish to dismantle. A straightforward illustration is provided by the anti-climate change lobby funded by oil companies and others. But there is a risk that this would stretch the concept of denialism too far given that many (most?) organisations often deny matters for economic advantage or self-preservation. Interests can shape arguments on both sides of any debate.

Perhaps we should look for intrinsic evidence of what makes something count as denialism? For dictionary definitions the tell-tale signs can be detected in the rhetorical techniques that denialists employ to persuade others of the justice of their cause. 'These include distortions, half-truths, misrepresentation of their opponents' positions and expedient shifts of premises and logic'.[36] 'They make

---

33 Ibid., p. 240. In general, Cohen devoted much of his influential writing to producing a critical criminology that challenged state definitions of harmful behaviour. Although this theme is relatively absent amongst our contributors (most of who are not criminologists), the struggle to defeat denialism could be linked to the view that society should spend less effort on low level delinquency by individuals when much more harm is produced by states and corporations.

34 S. Cohen, 'Intellectual Scepticism and Political Commitment: The Case of Radical Criminology' in: P. Walton and J. Young, *The New Criminology Revisited*, Macmillan, London 1998, p. 222.

35 J. Willems, 'Too Close to Home? The Denial of Prejudice and Discrimination against Children', in this volume, p. 84.

36 <https://en.wikipedia.org/wiki/Denialism> accessed May 2016.

great play of the inescapable indeterminacy of figures and statistics', as scientific studies of many areas rely on probability analysis of sets of data, and in historical studies the precise numbers of victims and other facts may not be available in the primary source. Their arguments involve cherry picking, false experts, moving the goalposts, relying on fallacies filling the void left after attacking them, and – not least – a strong endorsement of conspiracy thinking.[37] Both Cohen and De Haan see denial as sometimes involving manipulative techniques – indeed one of the main sources of Cohen's ideas about denial is Sykes and Matza's brilliant short discussion of the 'techniques of neutralisation' used by juvenile delinquents to help justify their behaviour.[38]

It is a pity that our contributors do not tell us more about the kind of techniques used by the denialists they are contesting. (This might also have helped us understand how they vary from topic to topic.) But there are some interesting exceptions. The discussion of the Colombian army assassinations by Hurtado describes the techniques used as part of the cover up even if they are not exactly examples of efforts to deny social problems as such.[39] In her contribution, Seu describes the techniques of those 'in denial' who 'resolve the dilemma of not wanting to know about human rights violations and at the same time not wanting to be seen to be doing by resorting to psychological explanations of being desensitised and experiencing compassion fatigue.' She focuses on two types of vocabularies of denial: 'in countries like that' and 'switching off', representing two ways in which people 'do denial'. The first, 'in countries like that', exemplifies a vocabulary of implicatory denial which is particularly potent in the UK at the moment. The second, 'switching off', is discussed as functioning both as a socio-cultural script and an intra-psychic defence mechanism.[40]

Perhaps of most relevance, however, the chapter that criticises a BBC report questioning the received views about Rwanda genocide, describes this as denialism (or more precisely, secondary denialism), precisely because it reproduced the tropes and arguments used in mainstream 'official' denial discourse.[41] As Moerland puts it, 'a reversal of the victim rates not only contradicts virtually all expert research on the death toll of the genocide, it moreover confirms what the official denial discourse has been promoting, namely that the real victims are the Hutu and not the Tutsi.'[42] He concludes, 'the violence, the victim rate, the downing of the plane, etc. are thus not simply

---

37 Ibid.

38 G. Sykes and D. Matza, 'Techniques of Neutralization: A Theory of Delinquency' (1957) 22 *American Sociological Review* 664–670.

39 M.R. Hurtado, 'Killing Through the State in the Colombian War and Getting Away with Murder: An Exploration of Organisational Crime and Its Denial', in this volume, p. 285.

40 I.B. Seu, 'Denial and Acknowledgment in Public Responses to Information about Human Rights Violations', in this volume, p. 25.

41 R. Moerland, 'The BBC Documentary "Rwanda's Untold Story": Acknowledging Genocide or Denying It?', in this volume, p. 170.

42 Ibid., p. 167.

"alternative perspectives" with regard to what happened. Instead, they make up key discursive elements of a political and criminal discourse that aims to deny'.[43]

For most of the contributors, however, it is not so much the *techniques* of discourse that matter but rather the strength of the cases they make about the harm caused to rights bearers as opposed to the poverty of the arguments used by denialists. They therefore spend most of their chapters setting out their better reasons. But using weak arguments cannot in itself constitute denialism. Often bad or at least questionable arguments can be pressed into the service of a good cause. And some of the claims made by our anti-denialist contributors are far from self-evident. In arguing for more recognition of children's rights, for example, Dwyer strongly asserts the rights of the state to override parental claims and shows little patience for the claims of communal ties, arguing that 'the native culture cannot be of such importance as to override every other consideration, as evidenced by the millions of autonomous adults who choose to leave their place of origin to find a better life in a different culture, with full awareness of what they leave behind. And there is no sense to the idea of "maintaining one's culture" when one is a newborn or infant'.[44] His approach is an interesting one, but, as De Haan would put it, surely there could also be 'respectable' arguments on the other side. More, bad arguments need to be defeated with better arguments, whereas it is easy to assume that those 'in denial' are less in need of good arguments than of being woken up to face the truth.[45] Not surprisingly, Cohen tells us that he is uninterested in the quality of what he calls their 'first order' arguments in support of the seriousness of given social problems when he seeks to show what (if anything) distinguishes recent moral entrepreneurs from past ones.[46]

Is there any other way to define what we should take to be an unacceptable argument? Dictionary or encyclopaedia definitions of denialism tell us that the arguments that are not 'respectable' are those that go against 'the majority of scientific or historical evidence'[47], or, even more stringently, that they deny positions that 'almost all experts and lay persons (see) as having been established on the basis of overwhelming evidence'.[48] Such denial may even be considered a sign of irrationality or being influenced by conspiracy theories. The claim

---

43 Ibid., p. 170.

44 J.G. Dwyer, 'Diagnosing and Dispelling Denialism Regarding Children', in this volume, p. 61.

45 C.J. Hunt, 'Jim Crow 3.0: Denial, Human Rights, and American Racialised Mass Incarceration', in this volume, p. 324.

46 S. Cohen, 'Intellectual Scepticism and Political Commitment: The Case of Radical Criminology' in: P. Walton and J. Young, *The New Criminology Revisited*, Macmillan, London 1998, p. 222.

47 Ibid., p. 12. As Specter notes, those who defy the scientific consensus may not be only a fanatical or conspiratorial minority but a large part of the general population who are worried about losing control whilst attempting to cope with social change in a globalising world.

48 Ibid., p. 13.

that a scientific consensus is being irrationally rejected is frequently made by authorities defending official positions, for example when government scientific officers criticise those who insist on the dangers of genetically modified crops. On the other hand, sometimes it is the authorities, relying on tame experts, who are accused of engaging in denialism of supposed consensual values. This is the case for example for the chapters that show governments pursuing strategies of (racialised) mass incarceration, denying prisoners the vote, or the exploitation of workers in building sports stadiums or the clearing of favelas that Olympic athletes ought to be denouncing.[49] In other chapters, authorities are accused of trying to manipulate the consensus, for example over the Armenian genocide,[50] climate change,[51] or international adoptions.[52]

Consensus is of limited help in guiding us to true cases of denialism given that both those engaged in denialism and those denouncing are in a battle to try to create such consensus whilst at the same insisting that the truth does not depend on existing consensus. State authorities are the ones most likely to succeed in creating consensus in the population. But this does not mean it should be accepted. Writing about children's rights, Dwyer tells us. '[P]arentage based on nothing other than procreation is so universal and matches what occurred millennia ago in human groupings lacking any form of state apparatus, it appears natural and inevitable. But it is not "natural" in the sense of being written in the stars or mountain tops and effected without human action; it is today a state-created legal practice that each society collectively chooses'.[53] 'Today' he argues, 'it would be obvious to us that the state is implicated if the law conferred on husbands the power to decide whether and where wives would receive education or privileged husbands to hit their wives, and we would treat this state action as presumptively and egregiously wrong. Likewise, if the state changed the legal rules governing guardianship to permit corporal punishment of adult wards with diminished mental capacity – for example, an elderly parent suffering from dementia. That the state itself had deprived the dependent adults of something important would be evident. But somehow there is widespread denial that what parents do to children they do because the state has enabled and empowered them to do it'.[54]

---

49 R. Babjakov, S. Deten, J. Etor, K. Geurtjens, R. Moerland and H. Nelen, 'Olympic Idealism and Human Rights Infringements: How Athletes, Cope with an Uncomfortable Reality', in this volume, p. 437.

50 S. Garibian, 'On the Breaking of Consensus: The Perinçek Case, the Armenian Genocide and International Criminal Law', in this volume, p. 235.

51 Z. Aliozi, 'Climate Justice: Climate Change and Human Rights', in this volume, p. 403.

52 E. Loibl, Crime in the Intercountry Adoption Industry – Towards a Broader Definition of Child Trafficking', in this volume, p. 119.

53 J.G. Dwyer, 'Diagnosing and Dispelling Denialism Regarding Children', in this volume, p. 57.

54 Ibid., p. 59.

But the most plausible ground for distinguishing over from under reactions that Cohen offers is also the one that which is most relevant for present purposes. As Morgan-Williams tells us, 'Cohen's understanding of the overreaction to putative social problems, most evident in moral panic, is balanced by his keen observation on the under reaction in which knowledge of human rights violations is concealed and denied'.[55] In the years before writing his *States of Denial*, Cohen sought to ground ethics in opposition to cultural relativism in the bedrock in human rights, arguing that 'the idea (and ideal) of core and universal human rights is the last meta-narrative still alive – and that it deserves defending against the excesses of post modernism'.[56]

2. CONNECTING DENIALISM AND HUMAN RIGHTS: THE HARM OF DENIAL AND HARM BY DENIAL

The editors and most of the contributors to this collection can thus claim to be building on Cohen's approach when they describe as denialism a wide variety of actions that help perpetuate social problems that involve violations of human rights.[57] Or as Willems puts it succinctly (and more narrowly), 'denial is related to (past, present and/or future/to be expected) gross human rights violations.'[58] Using human rights as a common denominator is the answer to De Haan's challenge that it can be misleading or even dangerous to group case studies of such different forms of denial together.[59] The editors of this collection are aware of the contrasting uses of the term denialism.[60] But they explain that their interest in the concept lies only in its implications for human rights.

55 S. Morgan-Williams, 'Justifying Acts of Denialism: The Case of Prisoner Disenfranchisement in the UK', in this volume, p. 358.

56 S. Cohen, 'Preface' in: C. Banks, *Developing cultural criminology: Theory and practice in Papua New Guinea,* Institute of Criminology, Sydney 2000, p. 2. See also S. Cohen, 'Crime and Politics: Spot the difference' (1996) 47 *British Journal of Sociology* 1, 13.

57 But not all the contributors would necessarily accept that they talking about 'social problems'. The term fits awkwardly to the case studies, at one end, of extreme human rights violations such as Genocide, or the forced disappearances in Colombia, and – at the opposite end – the issue of denying UK prisoners the right to vote.

58 J. Willems, 'Too Close to Home? The Denial of Prejudice and Discrimination against Children', in this volume, p. 84.

59 Of course this presupposes agreement on the existence of human rights. If we were to follow Bentham in his celebrated put down that 'Human Rights is nonsense on stilts', it would be perverse expect them put to rest doubts about scientific and historical debates.

60 This is seen in the disparate categories (Children's Rights, Genocide, (Inter)national organisations, New Penology, and Social, Economic and Cultural Rights) into which they have divided the book. On the other hand, many of the contributions to this workshop do succeed in showing that there are unexpected connections between different kinds of denialism. Denying both historical and scientific facts can have social consequences for given social groups – and be intended to have them.

'[D]enialism', they say 'does not denominate one specific form or variety of denial, but it refers to an overarching concept elaborated or explored from a human rights perspective.'[61]

The problem of course is to be able to show without using circular arguments that human rights are being violated where this is being denied. Denialism and breaches of human rights may overlap, but they do not have to do so. Not all cases when human rights are denied are necessarily relevant to the study of the role of denialism. Those who violate social and economic rights may do so without engaging in denialism (except in the banal sense that breaking human rights presupposes that they have been denied). On the other hand, some denialists, such as those who believe in scientific conspiracies, may be making claims that do not actually challenge human rights or involve (human) victims (as in the case of animal rights in factory farming). The contributors to this collection go to great lengths to explain why and how the different examples of denialism they examine are linked to breaches of human rights. But where the problem for some contributors may be more that of establishing evidence of indisputable facts, at other times the effort seems mainly designed to show that human rights have been breached.

At one end of the continuum, the breach of human rights may indeed be beyond question but the question may be whether it adds much to call it denialism. The chapter about the denial of votes to prisoners in the UK tells us that successive governments (both Labour and Conservative) have refused to allow prisoners to vote.[62] The current government is accused of engaging in denialism because it refuses to recognise that a binding decision on this has already been made by the European Court of Human rights. There is (or at least, it is argued, there should be) no place for further argument once something has been legally defined in terms of human rights by a superior court. On one reading, the denialism being engaged in here, which involves challenging the authority of the ECHR over this issue (or more generally), has little in common psychologically with other common uses of the term. It would seem better to say that the government is openly contesting a decision it rejects politically, and seeking to circumscribe or postpone compliance. But it could be replied that this case could be compared to those where a government seeks to gain popular support by denying the rights of (other) unpopular minorities, such as gypsies or economic migrants in Europe. In this case it would seem to be very much to the point in discussions of denialism.

In other cases the charge of denialism is persuasive but the evidence of human rights less clear. We could take as examples the discussions of athletes

61 R. Moerland, H. Nelen and J. Willems, 'Introduction', in this volume, p. 3.

62 S. Cohen, 'Whose side were we on? The undeclared politics of moral panic theory' (2011) 7(3) *Crime, Media, Culture* 237–243.

criticised for failing to criticise their hosts at meetings of the Olympics,[63] or the analysis of why people sometimes refuse to respond to appeals for help from activist organisations.[64] Their involvement of these denialists in breaches of human rights is at most at one remove from those actually perpetrating them. But it could certainly be argued that they engage in denialism so as to minimise even that degree of involvement.

Where is the harm in denial? Or, put differently, how does denial produce harm? A previous conference organised by the same Maastricht centre[65] (in which I also participated)[66] set out to show the links between corruption and human rights. Not all were in favour of making such connections.[67] But, for the majority who were, this meant finding ways to show how corruption – and its consequences – could be translated into the language of violations of a variety of human rights conventions to which the states concerned were signatories. Corrupt behaviour typically involved, for example, the misuse of power, lack of accountability and the institutionalisation of various forms of unjust discrimination.[68] In the case of denialism we again can consider denialism as such as a violation, or examine its role in producing harm. Looking at it from the point of view of victims we need to consider both suffering from denial and the denial of suffering.

What makes the denial toxic in the first case is the (supposed) obviousness of the (historical or scientific) facts being rejected, in the second case it is the consequences – the unnecessary suffering being inflicted by the failure to take action that denialism has produced. The main example of the first kind of case is Holocaust denial[69] (though, where victims are dead, it can be more difficult to say whose rights are being denied and how they are being harmed). Violations

---

63 Z. Aliozi, 'Climate Justice: Climate Change and Human Rights', in this volume, p. 403.

64 I.B. Seu, 'Denial and Acknowledgment in Public Responses to Information about Human Rights Violations', in this volume, p. 25.

65 See M. Boersma and H. Nelen (eds.), *Corruption & Human Rights: Interdisciplinary Perspectives,* Intersentia, Antwerp 2010.

66 D. Nelken, 'Corruption and Human Rights: An Afterword' in: M. Boersma and H. Nelen (eds.), *Corruption & Human Rights: Interdisciplinary Perspectives,* Intersentia, Antwerp 2010, p. 241.

67 M. Goodwin and K. Rose-Sender, 'Linking corruption and human rights: an unwelcome addition to the development discourse' in: M. Boersma and H. Nelen (eds.), *Corruption & Human Rights: Interdisciplinary Perspectives,* Intersentia, Antwerp 2010, p. 221, where it was argued that making such connections was not just a technical question but meant breathing new life into a particular story of how economic development is to be achieved.

68 See in M. Boersma and H. Nelen (eds.), *Corruption & Human Rights: Interdisciplinary Perspectives,* Intersentia, Antwerp 2010, the chapters M.S Carmona, M. Sepúlveda and J.B. Terracino, 'Corruption and human rights: Making the connection', p. 25, and M. Boersma, 'Corruption as a violation of economic, social and cultural rights: reflections on the right to education', p. 51.

69 Though there were also speakers at the workshop who took the threat of climate change so seriously that they argued for its denial to be prohibited as much as Holocaust denial, without any need to link it to specific harmful consequences.

may also have symbolic and not merely instrumental significance; Holocaust denial is taken by some of our contributors to be a way of condemning those who refuse to commit to the new European order of human rights established after the Second World War.

But, whilst it may be important for some purposes to bear in mind the dichotomy between denial *as* harm and harm *through* denial, there is no hard and fast line between them. 'Structures of denialism' may involve either or both of these – in ways that reinforce each other. In the case of denial of the Holocaust, or of genocide more generally, there is at least some concern that allowing this to happen may facilitate the commission of other genocides in the future (as when Hitler remarked 'who ever speaks about the Armenians?'). It can also be difficult to separate the 'hate speech' aspects of genocide denial from the 'historical revisionism' aspects of it. For better or worse, as Kahn tells us, some acts of genocide denial are both statements about history as well as speech acts that (sometimes intentionally) harm members of victim groups.[70] In one of the most provocative chapters, focusing on BBC attempts to challenge the consensus view about what happened in Rwanda, Moerland tells us that 'genocide encompasses both the killing of life' (when it helps cover up what is going on) and ' the killing of death' (when there is denial afterwards that it has taken place).[71]

The large majority of the case studies in this collection, however, focus on alleged causal connections between denialism and human rights rather than the harm of denialism in itself. Denial is problematic in the case of climate change, the UN General Assembly Special Rapporteur explains, because 'climate change is undermining the fulfilment of internationally protected Human Rights, like the rights to health and life; right to food, water, shelter, property; rights associated with livelihood and culture; with migration and resettlement; and with personal security in the event of conflict. The worst effects of climate change are principally felt by those whose rights protections are already insufficient'.[72] Likewise, Dwyer, writing about cases of violations of children's rights, points to the 'mischief' caused by denying what to him is the self-evident fact that parents have no intrinsic rights to other than those conceded to them by the state. For him, '[t]he denial of this reality does great mischief because it absolves the state – and, again, that means us, adult society, whom the state represents – from having to justify conferring these powers and privileges'.[73]

---

70 See R. Kahn, 'Can the Law Understand the Harm of Genocide Denial?', in this volume, p. 222.

71 R. Moerland, 'The BBC Documentary "Rwanda's Untold Story": Acknowledging Genocide or Denying It?', in this volume, p. 153.

72 Report of the Special Rapporteur on the issue of human rights obligations relating to the enjoyment of a safe, clean, healthy and sustainable environment, United Nations 2016, p. 8. See Z. Aliozi, 'Climate Justice: Climate Change and Human Rights', in this volume, p. 403.

73 J.G. Dwyer, 'Diagnosing and Dispelling Denialism Regarding Children', in this volume, p.58.

The case studies in this volume spell out some of the mechanisms by which constructed lack of knowledge can cause harm. The account of the cover up of disappearances in Colombia by Hurtado is particularly graphic. 'The language used is revealing of repetition and imitation in the organisation, as it is also classic evidence of dehumanisation of the victims. Weapons, ammunition and explosives were popularly referred to as "toys" or "decorations." Whenever the operation implied the use of an informant to single out the victims, that person would be referred to as the "lamp" or the "flashlight".'[74] Denialism produces its effects here by 'creating organisational goals and not asking how they are achieved. Powerful agents (both public and private) intervened in the organisational process, enabling or tolerating the horrific, but organisationally useful practice. Most were not engaged in the commission of atrocity, just in its knowledge.'[75]

Hurtado tells us that '[c]ommon sense dictates that pressure to produce results cannot be equated with an order to kill in cold blood. But there is nothing common about military sense, especially in war. When killing-the-enemy is expressed as an organisational goal of a total institution officially mandated to kill in war, and the enemy is not around to be killed, innovation is an easy ride to obtaining organisational goals'.[76] For Hurtado, '[t]he specification of the tangible results expected does, however, unmistakably explain why battalion commanders were always pressing for 50 kills or why twisted competitions took place at the end of a year between units nearing the 150 mark.'[77] But the precise role of denial (and what is meant by it) in this, and other cases, needs careful specification. In explaining the Colombian atrocities, other commentators write, 'the rhetoric of social cleansing, security and self-defence cannot be reduced to mechanisms of denial by combatants.' '[I]nstead', they suggest, 'it reveals how the dirty work of neo-conservatism social control becomes a banal reality. The conflict in Colombia offered career opportunities in the work of securitisation for the poor in a transitional period with high unemployment. For lower level operatives involved the important thing was to try to do a "good job"'.[78]

Another case study in this volume traces the way denialism plays a part in the use of formal social control against poor inner city people of colour following the white loss of state sponsored racial domination due to the civil rights advances of the 1950s, 1960s, and 1970s.[79] It tells us that 'the overwhelming majority of men

74 M.R. Hurtado, 'Killing Through the State in the Colombian War and Getting Away with Murder: An Exploration of Organisational Crime and Its Denial', in this volume, p. 299.

75 Ibid., p. 314.

76 Ibid., p. 312.

77 Ibid., p. 308.

78 G.M. Rueda and S. Tanner, 'To prevent the existence of people causing trouble. Dirty work, social control and paramilitaries in Colombia' (2016) 56 *British Journal of Criminology*, 87, 102.

79 C.J. Hunt, 'Jim Crow 3.0: Denial, Human Rights, and American Racialised Mass Incarceration', in this volume, p. 324.

of color that have been caught up in America's obsession with mass incarceration, have been imprisoned for minor and non-violent low level drug offences as part of this nation's so-called "War on Drugs"'.[80] This is seen not as a deliberate conspiracy but rather as 'an evolving social and political response, resistance, and resentment to judicially imposed racial equality in America.'[81] The author is surprised at the lack of public reaction and argues that being 'in denial' makes it easier to take no action. Similarly, in the case of Olympic athletes, we are told that '[t]hey tend to get involved in a process of desensitisation, or, to use Cohen's concept, in a process of implicatory denial.'[82] 'From a theoretical perspective, most athletes do not deny the notion of human dignity or rights as such. Instead, they tend to justify their inaction with reasons why it is not their responsibility to act, leading to implicatory denial mechanisms. These mechanisms deny the (moral) consequences that would normally follow from certain actions. Many athletes personally disapprove of human rights violations, but in their role as athletes, they do not feel the responsibility'.[83]

The most clear-cut case of denialism (and the only one where the term is already used legally) is that of Holocaust denial and genocide denial more generally. So it is surprising that the collection does not begin with those chapters but rather with the pieces on children's rights, cases where most of the effort of the writers has to be devoted to proving, as against conventional wisdom, that the supposed rights exist (and not only that they are being trampled on). But the editors may see the arguments of children's rights advocates as particularly interesting because they show how denialism can lead to refusal even to acknowledge the existence of a given set of rights. On the other hand, by the same token, what makes these chapters controversial is that they sometimes seem to beg the question whether the specific rights they are arguing for do actually exist. Whatever the reason for the order of the chapters, however, it is important to remember the implications for distinguishing 'moral panics' from unacknowledged social problems. When the consequences of denial for human rights in any given case study are not self-evident, because these rights are not – yet – widely accepted, it becomes more difficult to say that this can be the criterion that clearly shows the example not to be a case of moral panic.

If we are to make further progress in showing how denialism may lead to violations of human rights it is important to distinguish the circumstances in which this may occur. We have already noticed that types of denialism come in variety of forms, including refusing rights to specific groups, denial that something happened, denying that something is true and denying that

80 Ibid., p. 328.
81 Ibid., p. 326.
82 R. Babjakov, S. Deten, J. Etor, K. Geurtjens, R. Moerland and H. Nelen, 'Olympic Idealism and Human Rights Infringements: How Athletes, Cope with an Uncomfortable Reality', in this volume, p. 440.
83 Ibid., p. 447.

something does harm. What is being denied? Who is doing so? Where, when, how and why is denial being attempted? Different kinds of denial (such as that being done by marginal groups, as compared to that involving the state or hegemonic groups, can have different implications for human rights. In any given episode of denialism there may be different types of denial going on at different levels, involving different actors, in different groups and organisations.

What is being denied can and does vary. There can be denial that human rights exist, or argument about the status of specific rights. As Cohen explained, denial can concern the facts, interpretations or their implications. His categories are referenced by many of the contributors.[84] In the case study of disappearances in Colombia, for instance, we learn that '[l]iteral denial hovers over a large, still undetermined, portion of the killings by COLAR; interpretative denial is embedded in the social understanding of the sham-KIAs; and implicatory denial thrives as only "bad apples" are called to bear the responsibility, this was population exchange, not ethnic cleansing'; 'this was not torture, but robust and legitimate interrogation'.[85] Likewise we are told that, in discussions about USA mass imprisonment, the facts are acknowledged even as their implications denied.[86]

Some of the contributors seek to introduce other categories, such as normative denialism, justifiable denialism, political and functional denialism. We are told that political denialism, for example is where denialism is seen as necessary by a political power or intrinsic to its values.[87] But it is questionable whether it is helpful to conflate types of denial with reasons for denial.

As far as *who does the denying* is concerned our contributors attribute denialism to states and governments, and politicians or civil servants, but also to larger political unions – such as the African Union[88] – the army, corporations, the media, courts, professionals, such as social workers,[89] and academics, such as historians. Ordinary people, both in groups and as

---

84 Such shared reference is importance if denialism is to become a more widely used term. Another contributor, Fred Grünfeld, in analysing the denial of genocide by bystanders usefully adopts the categories used by Seu in this volume, as his main point of reference, when analysing the dynamics of bystander denial in the cases of Srebrenica – when discussing how international actors such as states and the UN fail to intervene. See F. Grünfeld, 'Denial of Genocide by Bystanders in International Politics', in this volume, p. 253.

85 M.R. Hurtado, 'Killing Through the State in the Colombian War and Getting Away with Murder: An Exploration of Organisational Crime and Its Denial', in this volume, p. 28.

86 C.J. Hunt, 'Jim Crow 3.0: Denial, Human Rights, and American Racialised Mass Incarceration', in this volume, p. 324.

87 S. Morgan-Williams, 'Justifying Acts of Denialism: The Case of Prisoner Disenfranchisement in the UK', in this volume, p. 358.

88 K.D. Magliveras, 'International Organisations and Denialism: The Case of the African Union', in this volume, p. 267.

89 See A.M. Weterings (in collaboration with Jan C.M. Willems), 'Denial of Developmental Needs of Foster Children by Dutch Youth Care Services', in this volume, p. 97.

individuals are also seen as playing a part. Different issues are posed depending on whether we are talking about those involved in cover ups or those who could do something to help. Victims will usually face difficulties in being heard, but a few of them may be 'in denial' about the abuse they are suffering. At the extreme, some denialists may even believe that it is they who are fighting denial!

Significant questions arise about the way individual action is conditioned by the larger context. Cohen treats denial as shaped collectively; people learn from one another what they are socially expected to ignore – that is, not look at, not listen to, not speak about. Collective denial is based on a 'shared reconstruction' of events. De Haan too suggests that there can be different forms of denial: individual, personal or shared, collective, social or cultural. It is all too true that there can be a thin line between those committing atrocities and those supporting them.[90] But sometimes the agents of denialism are characterised so broadly that it is hard to imagine useful steps could be taken to deal with them, as when we are told that 'America' is guilty of overwhelming incarceration of black offenders,[91] or that 'proponents of inter-country adoption' underestimate the violations of rights this entails.

Where denial is carried out is also important, as explained both by Keiler and by Kahn in their chapters on Holocaust denial. For Kahn, the attempt to answer the question whether it can ever be right to ban opinions operates at too high a level of generality. What is missing is an appreciation of how a given speech act, in this case genocide denial, can change its meaning depending on its precise content and the context in which it arise. Holocaust denial may be a special problem in Germany or Austria – where official denial was common during the immediate the post-war period and there are particular fears about the risk of recrudescence.[92] On the other hand, given the global spread of social media it is increasingly difficult to police communications as if they are rooted in one place.[93] Both denial and the response to it involve timing.

---

90 See H. Verbitsky and J.P. Bohoslavsky, *The Economic Accomplices to the Argentine Dictatorship*, Cambridge University Press, Cambridge 2015.

91 C.J. Hunt, 'Jim Crow 3.0: Denial, Human Rights, and American Racialised Mass Incarceration', in this volume, p. 322, tells us that 'America is either wilfully ignorant, wilfully callous, or in deep and "collective denial" regarding the systemic, stunning, and deeply distressing human rights abuses that are inflicted on whole communities of racial minorities all over the country ... little doubt that "the phenomenon of mass incarceration has filtered into the public consciousness through cycles of media coverage and political debates".'

92 J. Keiler, 'Fighting NS Ideology and Holocaust Denial in Austria: Past and Present Perspectives', in this volume, p. 175; R. Kahn, 'Can the Law Understand the Harm of Genocide Denial?', in this volume, p. 215. Context is not only a matter of geography. It is suggested that even if 'unsuppressed falsity' can cause harm to the general public such dangers are diminished in academic settings.

93 I have personal experience of being one of number of people targeted by neo-Nazis from web sites based in Italy (taken sufficiently seriously for the Ministry of the Interior to have closed down me to receive unwelcome regular visits from the police to check if they have

Denial can help facilitate atrocities beforehand, by stigmatising those who are to be attacked, at the time of attack by engaging in 'cover up' what is going on, and afterwards by concealing or belittling what has already been done.[94] In the immediate aftermath of mass atrocities involving interethnic or group rivalries, denial might prevent concrete acts of justice such as punishing perpetrators or compensating victims. As the killings recede into the deeper past these types of practical concerns fade away.

Finally, it is always useful to consider *why* denial is taking place. Are we dealing, as is so often alleged, with political or economic interests, reflections of underlying social conflicts? Is the key (also) religious beliefs, difficulties in identification with certain victims, or self-deception to avoid psychological unease? Denial is often also the result an aspect of our sociable tendencies, as shown by the classic social psychology studies on conformity by Solomon Asch,[95] or on 'destructive obedience' by Stanley Milgram.[96] The founding myths of many nation states conceal – or even celebrate – the bloodshed that accompanied their creation.[97] Remembering, not just forgetting, can be a form of denialism.

We also need to remember that connections are construed differently by different disciplines and that this can have implications for how we make them. Law, sociology and psychology are the main approaches represented here. But many other disciplines could also be relevant. Willems tell us that he looks forward to 'a more in-depth comparison and combination of all these concepts, which have been developed from various disciplines – prejudice studies, philosophy of law, human rights law, history, psychology and sociology'.[98] But perspectives may also compete. For example, some sociologists think the way the law prioritises rights can obscure the social structural causes that enable and shape such violations. For psychiatrists, denialism comes about because the unconscious sets up a barrier, which prevents the thought from reaching conscious knowledge. Information and memories slip into an inaccessible region of the mind and this needs to be 'recovered', not stigmatised or sanctioned.

---

been further developments). But nothing can be done against the recycling of such material on sites based outside Italy and even that placed on Italian sites continues to lead a fugitive existence on the net.

94 As with the 'techniques of neutralisation' by juvenile offenders, whose description by Sykes and Matza influenced Cohen's approach to denialism.

95 S.E. Asch, *Readings about the social animal,* Worth Publishers, New York 1955.

96 S. Milgram, 'Behavioral Study of obedience' (1963) 67 *The Journal of Abnormal and Social Psychology* 371–378.

97 M.A. Milburn and S.D. Conrad, *The Politics of Denial,* MIT Press, London 1996.

98 J. Willems, 'Too Close to Home? The Denial of Prejudice and Discrimination against Children', in this volume, p. 75.

3. RESPONDING TO DENIALISM: PUTTING THE WORLD TO RIGHTS

The final set of questions to be discussed here have to do with what can be done about denialism once its implications for human rights have been teased out. How could we put into practice the editors' call to dismantle the structures through which denialism flourishes? What does it take to deny denialism? How and when should we condemn those who do not condemn?[99] To sort these difficult and possibly even irresolvable questions (when framed in such broad terms) we first need to decide what it is that we are trying to achieve. For example, are we more interested in bringing about acknowledgement of the (potential) harm caused by denialism or is our aim to impose compliance even if offenders persist in their wrong beliefs?

Given that this workshop was organised by a centre on human rights it is understandable that the contributors were asked not only to examine the link between denialism and human rights violations but also to assess how the apparatus of human rights could play a role in taking action to deal with denial. Those who campaign against climate change denialism, in fact, assure us that, 'If we assemble human rights standards into our climate justice's future development, then it will be easier to identify the ones under threat and how to protect them … Tackling these drawbacks will involve a makeover of the global policies, from information-gathering and collective decision, and from law-making to practice and enforcement.'[100] Yet most of the authors – with the exception of those writing about Holocaust or genocide denial – spend surprisingly little time on explaining exactly how exposing denialism would make it possible to improve human rights and the problems doing this this might face.

Nonetheless, even if the other discussions lack the same detail, a review of their arguments may still give us some idea of the range of possible choices in deciding what is to be done. Much will again depend on the what, who, where, when and why of denial (as described in the last section). *What* is being denied is of course crucial as is the difference between denial seen as intrinsically harmful to human rights or more as a means to that end. The *who* also matters, not only because we need to know who is involved in causing harm but also because we need to identify who should have been doing something about it, as well as who (and what) is being affected and how they could be better protected. It

99 I.B. Seu, 'Denial and Acknowledgment in Public Responses to Information about Human Rights Violations', in this volume, p. 37, advises us that a direct attack on those 'in denial' will fail: 'the data suggest that shock tactics and overly traumatic communications, particularly when de-contextualised or in sound bites, are counterproductive in general. Often these evoke helplessness and result in disconnection'.

100 Z. Aliozi, 'Climate Justice: Climate Change and Human Rights', in this volume, p. 403.

is not just a matter of holding nation states to their human rights obligations (to which in theory many have already signed up). Many other public and private actors are also involved. We need different responses in the case of perpetrators, participants, and bystanders. Different issues arise in responding to denialism produced by individuals and groups or within organisations such as governments, legislatures, courts, armies, corporations, and institutions. Who should be the ones to intervene? Should it be public actors and agencies, non-governmental or intergovernmental organisations, businesses, or professional bodies?[101] As in the example of climate change, the denialist structures that lie behind some problems may include many or even all of these groups.

The appropriate timing of any response depends on a variety of factors. The social problems covered up by denialists may often have a 'natural history',[102] one that evolves through cycles of increasing and then declining concern (relative to other competing problems. Some types of cover ups may also have a limited time span. Hurtado explains that '[a]n illegal practice in an organisation that tends to overregulate to achieve calculated disorder … does not survive on the books, it survives and thrives based on a cycle of execution-acceptance, repetition-tolerance, and binge-connivance. The cycle eventually breaks as a result of the practice being exposed'.[103] But is can often be difficult to know, except with hindsight, when is the best time to expose such cover ups. In the recent efforts to deal with so called historical cases of (concealed) sex abuse by people in high places in the UK, nothing was done until social mores changed. But campaigns against denialism can themselves play a part in changing the acceptability of given practices.[104]

Human rights instruments take their place alongside, or in combination with, a variety of other possible responses. The case studies canvass a wide range of these, from the use of criminal sanctions to better education. Whilst the possibility of resorting to law is at least hinted at by most contributors, the most thorough analyses of its strengths and weaknesses are, understandably, found in the papers dealing with Holocaust and genocide denial – where denialism as such has already been criminalised But it is interesting that the chapters discussing this extreme type of violation of human rights are also those which seem most sceptical about the value of this way acting against denialists. If there

101 *Mein Kampf* has just been reissued in Germany this year in a critical edition that relies on the accompanying comments of historians to draw its sting. At the same time pseudo-historical institutions, such as the Institute of Historical Review, dedicate themselves to questioning the official narrative and undermining sympathy for Holocaust victims.

102 R. Fuller and R. Myers, 'The Natural History of a Social Problem' (1941) 6 *American Sociological Review* 320–329.

103 M.R. Hurtado, 'Killing Through the State in the Colombian War and Getting Away with Murder: An Exploration of Organisational Crime and Its Denial', in this volume, p. 309.

104 From a sociological point of view a limit of many of the contributions is the failure to describe the different groups, and, most importantly, social movements, who are engaged in fighting over given causes and the part played by rights claims in such struggles.

are doubts about the efficacy of using human rights law in response to extreme human rights violations does this mean that we can have even less confidence about using the law to deal with less clear-cut social problems?

Here again it may be helpful to distinguish between denialism *as* harm and denialism as a *means* to harm. Many would argue that even the most objectionable and misguided opinions should be allowed to circulate, trusting that the truth will and can only emerge from free competition of ideas. Trying to forbid the expression of opinions carries the whiff of heresy hunting (though others worry that ideas and actions are not so easily separable). In his analysis of the problem Kahn tells us that it is not easy to treat Holocaust denial as a hate crime 'as this would turn on questioning good faith engagement of the sources demonstrating the existence of the genocidal act in question. Since this can be difficult to demonstrate, an easier solution is to limit punishment to genocide denial to those acts that threaten an identifiable victim or are used to spread coded messages of hate.'[105] For him, 'the only way forward in deciding when denial should be punished (or removed from social media) 'is a context-laden approach in which legislators, judges, and scholars in the field evaluate speech acts on a case by case method'. Who sent the message? What type of language was used? Who was the intended audience? Only by asking these questions can we begin to sort out when genocide denial is hateful or racist.'[106]

In dealing with the more common cases of denialism as a cause of social harm one problem is how early we want to authorise state prevention.[107] A further challenge of denialism for criminal law is establishing the required mental element where the level of knowledge involved can range from 'open secrets', 'virtual blindness', 'not needing to know', 'not wanting to know', 'refusing to know', 'compartmentalisation' or 'moral ambivalence'. Knowledge and acknowledgement have a complicated relationship.[108] For some authors, law's way of dealing with cover ups can even be a way of entrenching denialism. The chapter about military killings in Colombia explains that denialism thrived also because of the way the criminal law response individualised blame. 'The law helped provide impunity by allowing higher level officials to deny that

---

105 See R. Kahn, 'Can the Law Understand the Harm of Genocide Denial?', in this volume, p. 233.

106 Ibid., p. 234.

107 Theorists of criminal law are already worried about the growth of what they call 'pre-crime' (see L. Zedner, 'Pre-crime and post-criminology?' (2007) 11 *Theoretical Criminology* 261–281). It is a characteristic of authoritarian governments and dictatorships that they seek to stop even the potential for harm.

108 'Only last year Andrew Haldane, chief economist at the Bank of England, told the German magazine Der Spiegel that the balances of the big banks are "the blackest of black holes". Haldane is responsible for the stability of the financial sector as a whole. He knowingly told a journalist that he couldn't possibly have an idea of what the banks have on their books. And? Nothing happened.' See <www.theguardian.com/business/2015/sep/30/how-the-banks-ignored-lessons-of-crash>.

it could have happened because it wasn't explicitly ordered. The answer for Hurtado is that, 'all officers and civilian authorities engaged in the promotion or cover-up of the sham-KIAs need to be purged from duty, and those having individual criminal responsibility need to be prosecuted'.[109] 'This result was that the 'implications of the practice have not been publicly acknowledged; and hierarchical and organisational responsibility resulting from the official stimulus and facilitation of the kills is emphatically disavowed. Each murder has been addressed as an isolated incident, and existing convictions give credence to the official story pointing to soldiers and a few officers as bad apples in a tidy barrel.'[110]

At the other end of the continuum the answer is seen as spreading knowledge about the causes of the social harm that are being covered up (as well as educating people about the not always obvious links between local action and the consequences elsewhere). For Dwyer, for instance, '[d]enialism is a useful lens through which to think about children's legal and social situation. Diagnosing it might also be a relatively effective way of producing progress. By pinpointing explicit or implicit premises in the reasoning of those who would justify unjust treatment of a group and showing the premises entail denial of something demonstrably true, one might make greater headway in converting those others than one might by presenting the case in favor of just treatment. Many people cannot open their minds to others' views until forced to see problems with their own views.'[111]

But the discussions of Holocaust denial in this volume put even the achievement of even this goal into question. As Verbeeck points out, it is far from obvious that our knowing more about atrocities stops others from occurring. 'Notorious examples are the Killing Fields in Cambodia, precisely at a time when the Western world was experiencing its first wave in Holocaust awareness, or Rwanda's mass murders in 1994, only a few weeks after Schindler's List was in the middle of a whirlwind of international media publicity.'[112] For him, '[t]he conventional wisdom, that those who refuse to learn from history are bound to repeat it, is unconvincing. Debatable, however, is the degree to which this increased awareness of literally the worst crime of our age is necessarily desirable. Serious criticism has been raised concerning (1) the political and

---

109 M.R. Hurtado, 'Killing Through the State in the Colombian War and Getting Away with Murder: An Exploration of Organisational Crime and Its Denial', in this volume, p. 314.

110 Ibid.

111 This was the purpose, for example, of the 2012 film *The Act of Killing* by Joshua Oppenheimer. Indonesia's National Commission on Human Rights said of the film: 'If we are to transform Indonesia into the democracy it claims to be, citizens must recognise the terror and repression on which our contemporary history has been built. No film, or any other work of art for that matter, has done this more effectively than The Act of Killing. [It] is essential viewing for us all.'

112 See R. Kahn, 'Can the Law Understand the Harm of Genocide Denial?', in this volume, p. 211.

ideological use of the Holocaust; (2) the inappropriate expectations regarding the lessons that can be learned; and (3) the often unintended moral and pedagogical consequences of an over-representation of the Holocaust.'[113] Verbeeck is especially worried by the use of false analogies.[114]

In between the extremes of criminalisation and of education the contributors mention a wide range of other methods for dealing with denialism.[115] For some what is needed is more and better legislation (and the political lobbying this may require), so as to confront climate change, or meet the needs of refugees, where, we are told, 'inadequate protections reflect "gaps" in conventions'.[116] But there is also an important role for courts in dealing with cases of denial. Garibian, for example, argues that the courts should have reacted differently in dealing with Turkish genocide denial.[117] Nienaber examines the recycling of stereotypes about Aids in a trial of someone accused of knowingly spreading the disease.[118]

The papers on children's rights tell us that what is needed are both social policy changes and drastic rethinking by relevant professionals. As Dwyer puts it, '[t]he way forward, then, is either to transform the thinking of directors at well-funded child-advocacy organisations, to get them to recognise the forms of denialism outlined above and the illicit ways laws and policies harm children, or to secure sufficient funding for the individuals and organisations who have already broken free of the denialism and are intellectually prepared and motivated to advance serious reform efforts'.[119] Others, like Seu, see a larger role for psychological techniques as an alternative to legal instruments. De Haan

---

113 G. Verbeeck, 'The Holocaust and its Denial: A Paradigm in our Historical Culture', in this volume, p. 208.

114 Ibid., p. 209, Verbeeck tells us that the Holocaust 'has come to be instrumentalised in a vast number of political and ethical causes. Best-known examples are the radical opponents of abortion who refer to abortion as "Baby-caust"; animal rights activists who describe the treatment of animals in the agricultural and food industry in terms of an "Animal-caust", an "Auschwitz for animals"; and the radical pacifists and environmentalists who predict the horrors of a looming "nuclear Holocaust". It is highly questionable whether these labels and comparisons actually help gathering support for these (just) causes. It remains to be seen whether the equating the fate of animals, unborn babies with the victims of the Nazi extermination camps has any positive effect in these campaigns. Could a deeply troublesome consequence of this "abuse" of the Holocaust paradigm not be a form of trivialization, ultimately leading to indifference? If everything is linked to the Holocaust, it loses its warning capacity'.

115 But it is curious to find no mention of strengthening legal and political protections for whistle-blowers who so often courageously (if controversially) uncover what organisations seek to conceal.

116 P. Regina Menachery, 'Genocide Denial and Refugees: A Lack of Protection in International Law?', in this volume, p. 388.

117 S. Garibian, 'On the Breaking of Consensus: The Perinçek Case, the Armenian Genocide and International Criminal Law', in this volume, p. 235.

118 A. Nienaber, 'A State in Denial: The "Intentional" Sexual Transmission of HIV in South Africa', in this volume, p. 419.

119 J.G. Dwyer, 'Diagnosing and Dispelling Denialism Regarding Children', in this volume, p. 68.

(quoting Cohen) also suggests that a possible remedy is to try make people feel ashamed rather than guilty about being uninformed about the suffering of distant others. Using these other methods can also bring collateral educational benefits. 'Even if not always successful', Dwyer tells us, in the context of children's rights, 'such efforts spark public discussions; they lift the curtain to some degree from taken-for-granted practices, exposing the ways in which they reflect a denial of children's personhood, distinct interests, and experience and of the state's role in creating children's suffering and thwarted lives.'[120]

But the problem is not just that human rights remedies cannot do the job alone and need to be implemented or supplemented by other modalities. They also have their limits and downsides. It is hard to get more demanding social and economic standards respected in places where even rights with solid safeguards, such as rights to life and to property, often cannot be claimed. Is it fair to ask poor countries to protect the environment which was despoiled by countries that industrialised earlier? Even in the domestic contexts of richer societies, human rights face well-documented dilemmas, such as how to square freedom with equality, as well as the tensions between different kinds of rights, such as individual and group rights or between potentially competing values such as freedom of speech and people's desire not to be offended. Sometimes some rights are given up in the name of higher ideals – as in projects for Truth and Reconciliation. But at least this was done as a way of uncovering what happened (a competition between fighting denialism and safeguarding human rights?). This is not always so – we could think of the way the Allies tried to hide the full extent of Nazi horrors[121] in order to further German reconstruction and the fight against Russia exported Communism.

As the editors acknowledge, human rights can also be more part of the problem than the solution.[122] Human rights, as usually promoted, reflect a liberal individualistic philosophy (even if they have a broader genealogy)

120 Ibid.

121 This included censoring Alfred Hitchcock's eye witness film about the liberation of Bergen Belsen. The film, which drew on footage shot by the British Army Film Unit in Nazi concentration camps in 1945, was only released in the mid-1980s.

122 As David Kennedy, a leading Harvard based 'progressive' international lawyer, puts it, 'arguments from human rights have been used to strengthen, defend, and legitimate a variety of repressive initiatives – to legitimate war, defend the death penalty, the entitlements of majorities, religious repression, access to (or restriction of) abortion, and so forth. In some places, human rights implementation can make a repressive State more efficient … rights discourse is used to deflect attention from the reality of Western implication in this suffering, by presenting the problem in a manner which disguises that implication. However, in both cases it is also true that the needs and demands of these marginalised populations can be expressed through – and given significant additional support by – universal rights discourse. Thus human rights function, through their indeterminacy and their restricted but alterable focus, as both cause and solution to the problem; as both critique and justification. Human rights discourse facilitates the perpetuation of the problem.' See D. Kennedy, 'The International Human Rights Movement: Part of the Problem?' (2001) 3 *European Human Rights Law Review* 245–267.

but insist on their universalistic pretensions.[123] As with world views such as Christianity, Islam or Marxism, with human rights too it can be difficult to put those universalistic aspirations in question. And it is a standard ploy, for those denialists challenging the establishment rather than representing it, to say they are telling the truth that others do not want to hear. But we cannot assume that denialists are always in the wrong or that there is nothing to learn from them.[124] Progress towards, and by, modern science frequently took place through challenging religious consensus. Even nowadays some of those resisting authority, including scientific expertise, may be the bearers of truth. Of course these are not the sort of denialists being discussed here. But can we be sure that they would not lose out in any organised attempt to curb the others? The BBC is criticised by Moerland for recycling denialist discourse on Rwanda in its effort to challenge the consensus.[125] But some historical revisionists – for instance the Israeli 'new historians' – have sometimes played a crucial role in uncovering denialism. There may even be space for what De Haan excluded as a possibility, namely 'respectable' arguments about events that some observers characterise as genocide.[126]

There may be other occasions where we should be more concerned about what is done in the name of fighting denialism. The use of the term, as we have seen, presupposes that we are speaking about (social) problems where there is, by definition, too little reaction. But this does not tell us how much, or what kind, of reaction would be the ideal and when reaction becomes counter-productive. After all, most of the research into moral panics purported to show that reacting to problems can sometimes make them worse. There is no reason to assume that this could not be true also when responding to denialism. So even if it may be right to do more, it may not always be expedient to do so.

Most obviously this may be seen in the way some UK politicians are currently trying to curb the denialism of those justifying the atrocities committed by ('so-called') Islamic State. For many in the Muslim communities this campaign is seen as damaging because of the way it seeks ever stronger signs of adhesion

123 C. Douzinas, *The End of Human Rights*, Hart, Oxford 2000.

124 Cohen, as we have seen, takes inspiration for his ideas about the neutralisation of guilt through denial from the criminological theory put forward by Sykes and Matza. These justifications included (importantly) 'denial of the victim', as well as 'condemning of the condemners', 'denial of responsibility or harm', and 'appeal to higher loyalties'. But Sykes and Matza's larger concern was less to condemn this underdog group for their denials and more to show us how they could be seen as extensions of more or less acceptable excuses used by the often hypocritical adults world. See also D. Matza and G. Sykes 'Juvenile Delinquency and Subterranean Values' (1961) 26 *American Sociological Review* 712–719.

125 R. Moerland, 'The BBC Documentary "Rwanda's Untold Story": Acknowledging Genocide or Denying It?', in this volume, p. 170.

126 There is a genuine debate about whether what happened in Darfur is rightly termed genocide. Compare J. Hagan and W. Rymond-Richmond, *Darfur and the Crime of Genocide*, Cambridge University Press, Cambridge 2008 with A. de Waal (ed.), *War in Darfur and the Search for Peace*, Harvard University Press, Cambridge Mass 2007.

to mainstream consensus on what remain controversial geo-political issues.[127] But even the best calibrated human right interventions may have unintended consequences. Even where better targeted, overreaction may only provide oxygen to those peddling views that are far from the mainstream. For the people who really believe in them, when we start seriously trying to debunk conspiracy theories this can be exactly the confirmation they are looking for to prove that the conspiracy is real. Could the wrong sort of response lead some denialists to move on from the first type of Cohen's three kinds of denial to ones more difficult to dislodge (from questioning facts to arguing about interpretations to questioning the need for action?) There is also the danger of making martyrs of some offenders (even including Holocaust deniers) – although this is a risk that may sometimes have to be run. Clearly there is need for much more discussion (and empirical testing) of these and other claims.

To conclude. I agree with De Haan that great caution is needed before seeking to operationalise an expansive definition of denialism (though my reasons for this are somewhat different from his). Simply put, setting out to destroy all the psychological, social, economic, cultural and political structures that make denialism possible is both an impossible and dangerous project. Every way of seeing is also way of not seeing.[128] A tendency to denial and forgetting is a characteristic both of the individual psyche and of social life. At the level of the individual the availability of too much information means one has to be selective. To remember it is also necessary to forget. But, at the societal level too, forgetting can be a valuable process.[129] And procedures in institutions such as courts are sometimes deliberately constructed so as to conceal (prejudicial) information.

But history does not stand still. Human rights organisations play a crucial role in uncovering facts and bringing perspectives to bear which countries, social groups, and organisations might prefer to hide. Their actions bring about what many would see as progressive social change – even if the chances of success are mainly dependent on larger social economic and cultural developments. For example, claims of ethnic or racial superiority, once advanced even by those fighting against fascism, have become completely unacceptable, at least in some places.[130] We are at an earlier stage in other struggles, such as those involving

---

127 See <www.bbc.co.uk/news/uk-33590305>.

128 Attitudes to social problems (and estimates of their relative seriousness) correlate with differences in more right or left political sympathies. Going beyond this, M. Douglas and A. Wildavsky, *Risk and Culture,* University of California Press, Berkeley 1992, apply 'cultural theory (with its distinction between world views associated with bureaucrats, businessmen, egalitarians and fatalists) to show how views of social problems, such as climate change, are shaped by the way such groups are bounded by loyalties and rules'.

129 M. Auge (trans. M.D. Jager), *Oblivion,* University of Minnesota Press, Minneapolis 2004.

130 As recently as 1937, for example, Winston Churchill told the Palestine Royal Commission 'I do not admit for instance, that a great wrong has been done to the Red Indians of America or the black people of Australia. I do not admit that a wrong has been done to these people by

the exposure of supply chains connecting consumers with the brutal conditions of production of 'blood diamonds', 'blood oil', etc. But the power – though also the vulnerability – of such anti-denialism is shown by the way activist non-governmental organisations are increasingly under attack in many countries round the world. This includes the latest efforts in Israel to treat as traitors the non-governmental group Breaking the Silence, who believe they are fighting what Cohen might well accept to call denialism, as they seek to uncover what he (and most contributors to this volume) would describe rather as 'denial by the State'.[131]

the fact that a stronger race, a higher-grade race, a more worldly wise race to put it that way, has come in and taken their place.'

131 <www.jpost.com/Israel-News/Politics-And-Diplomacy/PM-says-insufferable-Breaking-the-Silence-is-being-dealt-with-448630> accessed May 2016.

ABOUT THE AUTHORS

Zoi Aliozi is a human rights scholar and activist. She lectures human rights law and philosophy in the Irish Centre for Human Rights of the Faculty of Law of NUIG. Her research and teaching interests include: philosophy, international law, human rights, state-terrorism, climate justice, transitional justice, feminist legal scholarship, aesthetics, art, and cinematography.

Gustavo Arosemena is a lecturer at Maastricht University. He completed his PhD at Maastricht in 2014. He also carried out graduate studies in law at Utrecht University and at the University of Texas at Austin, the latter under a Fulbright Scholarship. He has published various articles and books in the intersection between human rights and legal theory.

Radka Babjaková participated in the Premium Honours programme on Sports and Crime as part of the Master's programme on Forensics, Criminology and Law at the Faculty of Law of Maastricht University.

Irene Bruna Seu is Reader in Psychosocial Studies at Birkbeck, University of London and a practicing psychoanalytic psychotherapist. For the last fifteen years she has researched public responses to mediated communications of human rights violations and humanitarian crises, both in the UK and Spain.

Sharon Deten participated in the Premium Honours programme on Sports and Crime as part of the Master's programme on Forensics, Criminology and Law at the Faculty of Law of Maastricht University.

James Dwyer is Professor of Law at the College of William & Mary in Virginia, USA, where he teaches courses in youth law, family law, and law and social justice. He has authored several books and dozens of articles on the rights of children in various family law contexts.

Jennifer Etoré participated in the Premium Honours programme on Sports and Crime as part of the master program on Forensics, Criminology and Law at the Faculty of Law of Maastricht University.

Sévane Garibian is Assistant Professor of Law at the University of Geneva (Swiss National Science Foundation Professorship) and Associate Professor of Law at the University of Neuchâtel. Her work focuses on issues related to the role of law in addressing state-sponsored crimes.

Kim Geurtjens participated in the Premium Honours programme on Sports and Crime as part of the Master's programme on Forensics, Criminology and Law at the Faculty of Law of Maastricht University. She is currently conducting her PhD research at Maastricht University on outlaw motorcycle gangs.

Fred Grünfeld was an Associate Professor of International Relations at Maastricht University and Professor in Causes of Gross Human Rights Violations at the University of Utrecht.

Willem de Haan is Professor of Criminology emeritus and senior research fellow in the Department of Criminal Law and Criminology at the Vrije Universiteit Amsterdam. His publications are on theory and research of violence in the public domain. His current research concerns corporate involvement in international crimes.

Cecil Hunt is a Full Professor at the John Marshall Law School, Chicago, Illinois. He does research, teaches courses, publishes articles, and delivers papers all over the US and abroad on such diverse areas as property law, secured transactions, human rights, race and mass incarceration, race and the law, and legal theory.

Michael J. Reed Hurtado is a Colombian/US lawyer and journalist with twenty years of experience in the human rights and humanitarian fields. His work has focused, amongst others, on effective criminal prosecution of system crimes, prison conditions and reform, and forced displacement of persons. He is currently a faculty fellow and senior lecturer at Yale University.

Rob Kahn is an Associate Professor at St. Thomas University Law School in Minnesota. He has written extensively on Holocaust denial and the law, the Danish Cartoon controversy, the debate in the United States over cross-burning bans, and the permissibility of restrictions on Muslim clothing in Europe and the United States.

Johannes Keiler is Assistant Professor in Criminal Law at the Faculty of Law of Maastricht University. His research focuses on European and comparative criminal law as well as on criminal sanctions and European cooperation in criminal matters.

Elvira Loibl is a PhD candidate at the Department of Private Law in the Faculty of Law of Maastricht University. She is conducting criminological research into the trafficking of children for purposes of adoption.

Konstantinos D. Magliveras is Professor of Public International Law and the Law of International Organisations at the Department of Mediterranean Studies, University of the Aegean. He has conducted research and published extensively in related areas and has a special interest in African legal affairs.

Roland Moerland is Assistant Professor of Criminology at the Department of Criminal Law and Criminology of the Faculty of Law of Maastricht University. His interests lie in the fields of supranational and organisational criminology. Recently he published the results of an elaborate study of the ways denial operates in the context of the genocide in Rwanda against the Tutsi.

Hans Nelen is Professor of Criminology at the Department of Criminal Law and Criminology of the Faculty of Law of Maastricht University. He has conducted research and published extensively on a variety of criminological subjects, including police, drugs, corruption, fraud, organised crime, corporate and occupational crime.

David Nelken PhD, LLD (Cambridge) is Professor of Comparative and Transnational Law and Head of Research at the Dickson Poon School of Law, King's College London. His work, covering both theoretical enquiry and empirical investigation, is in the areas of comparative sociology of law, criminology, and legal and social theory.

Annelize Nienaber is Professor of International Law and Bioethics in the Department of Public Law at the Faculty of Law, University of Pretoria, South Africa. She has published extensively on the law related to clinical research, bioethics, and legal aspects of HIV and AIDS.

Regina Menachery Paulose is an international criminal law/international human rights attorney based in the United States. She has published articles on transnational organised crime and genocide.

Georgi Verbeeck is Professor of German History at the University of Leuven and Associate Professor of Modern History and Political History at Maastricht University. His research field includes modern political history of Germany, the politics of history, the history of the Holocaust and its denial.

Tonny Weterings is an expert at the Dutch Expert Centre 'Child in Foster Care' and advises courts on foster cases. She has conducted research on children in youth care, especially in foster care, at Utrecht University and the University of Leiden.

Jan Willems is a researcher on children's rights, early childhood and structural prevention of child maltreatment at Maastricht University, the Netherlands.

Samantha (Morgan-)Williams is a PhD candidate and assistant lecturer (criminal law) at University College Cork. Her doctoral research is entitled 'The European Convention on Human Rights in times of Economic Crisis: the Effect of Austerity Measures upon Convention Usage and Implementation'.

MAASTRICHT SERIES IN HUMAN RIGHTS

The *Maastricht Centre for Human Rights* facilitates and supports research in the field of human rights at Maastricht University's Faculty of Law. Research conducted at the Centre is interdisciplinary, with a focus on public international law, criminal law and social sciences. Titles appearing in the Maastricht Series in Human Rights have been peer reviewed under the responsibility of the Board of the Centre.

Published titles within the Series:

1. Ineke Boerefijn, Fons Coomans, Jenny Goldschmidt, Rikki Holtmaat and Ria Wolleswinkel (eds.), *Temporary Special Measures. Accelerating de facto Equality of Women under Article 4(1) UN Convention on the Elimination of All Forms of Discrimination against Women* (2003)
   ISBN 90-5095-359-X
2. Fons Coomans and Menno T. Kamminga (eds.), *Extraterritorial Application of Human Rights Treaties* (2004)
   ISBN 90-5095-394-8
3. Koen De Feyter and Felipe Gómez Isa (eds.), *Privatisation and Human Rights in the Age of Globalisation* (2005)
   ISBN 90-5095-422-7
4. Ingrid Westendorp and Ria Wolleswinkel (eds.), *Violence in the domestic sphere* (2005)
   ISBN 90-5095-526-6
5. Fons Coomans (ed.), *Justiciability of Economic and Social Rights* (2006)
   ISBN 978-90-5095-582-9
6. Jan C.M. Willems (ed.), *Developmental and Autonomy Rights of Children: Empowering Children, Caregivers and Communities. 2nd revised edition* (2007)
   ISBN 978-90-5095-726-7
7. Alette Smeulers and Roelof Haveman (eds.), *Supranational Criminology: Towards a Criminology of International Crimes* (2008)
   ISBN 978-90-5095-791-5
8. Hans van Crombrugge, Wouter Vandenhole and Jan C.M. Willems (eds.), *Shared Pedagogical Responsibility* (2008)
   ISBN 978-90-5095-813-4
9. Hildegard Schneider and Peter Van den Bossche (eds.), *Protection of Cultural Diversity from a European and International Perspective* (2008)
   ISBN 978-90-5095-864-6

10. Fons Coomans, Fred Grünfeld and Menno T. Kamminga (eds.), *Methods of Human Rights Research* (2009)
ISBN 978-90-5095-879-0
11. Jan C.M. Willems (ed.), *Children's Rights and Human Development. A Multidisciplinary Reader* (2010)
ISBN 978-94-000-0032-2
12. Martine Boersma and Hans Nelen (eds.), *Corruption & Human Rights: Interdisciplinary Perspectives* (2010)
ISBN 978-94-000-0085-8
13. Hans Nelen and Jacques Claessen (eds.), *Beyond the Death Penalty* (2012)
ISBN 978-1-78068-060-6
14. Fons Coomans and Rolf Künneman (eds.), *Cases and Concepts on Extraterritorial Obligations in the Area of Economic, Social and Cultural Rights* (2012)
ISBN 978-94-000-0046-9
15. Chen Weidong and Taru Spronken (eds.), *Three Approaches to Combating Torture in China* (2012)
ISBN 978-1-78068-088-0
16. Michele Panzavolta, Dorris de Vocht, Marc Van Oosterhout and Miet Vanderhallen (eds.), *Interrogating Young Suspects. Procedural Safeguards from a Legal Perspective* (2015)
ISBN 978-1-78068-299-0
17. Miet Vanderhallen, Marc van Oosterhout, Michele Panzavolta and Dorris de Vocht (eds.), *Interrogating Young Suspects. Procedural Safeguards from an Empirical Perspective* (2016)
ISBN 978-1-78068-301-0

www.ingramcontent.com/pod-product-compliance
Ingram Content Group UK Ltd.
Pitfield, Milton Keynes, MK11 3LW, UK
UKHW051925100926
8556IPUK00022B/1368